E 6

DEVELOPMENT
FROM BELOW

DEVELOPMENT FROM BELOW

*Local Government and
Finance in Developing Countries
of the Commonwealth*

BY

URSULA K. HICKS

OXFORD
AT THE CLARENDON PRESS

Oxford University Press, Ely House, London W. 1

GLASGOW NEW YORK TORONTO MELBOURNE WELLINGTON
CAPE TOWN SALISBURY IBÀDAN NAIROBI DAR ES SALAAM LUSAKA ADDIS ABABA
BOMBAY CALCUTTA MADRAS KARACHI LAHORE DACCA
KUALA LUMPUR SINGAPORE HONG KONG TOKYO

FIRST PUBLISHED 1961

REPRINTED LITHOGRAPHICALLY IN GREAT BRITAIN
AT THE UNIVERSITY PRESS, OXFORD
BY VIVIAN RIDLER
PRINTER TO THE UNIVERSITY
1971

PREFACE

MY interest in the development of local government overseas was first aroused in the summer of 1950, when I toured Nigeria with a Commission appointed by the Nigerian Government to allocate revenue between the Regions, as a preliminary to the introduction of a Federal Constitution. At this time I was able to see the system of Indirect Rule in full working order in the Northern Region, while in the Eastern Region the experiment in representative and responsible local government was already beginning. Earlier in the same year I had been shown some very lively panchayats in the neighbourhood of Delhi; in retrospect this confirmed the impression I was forming of the potentialities of Development from Below. Then in 1954, when my husband and I were on a financial mission to Jamaica, the reform of local government finance fell directly within our terms of reference. We were especially impressed by the way in which neglect and frustration at the hands of the Island Government had failed to destroy the individual life of the traditional Parochial Boards.

It was at about this time that my duties at Oxford began to include the training of overseas officers in local government finance, in order that they should pass on what they had learned to the people themselves. Thus I found myself personally drawn into the net of the experiment which I am to describe. This experiment, the building-up of local government as a preparation for Independence, in the formerly colonial territories of the Commonwealth, is the true hero of this book.

These officers were drawn from many areas, predominantly but by no means wholly from the African territories; but they also came from the West Indies, Malaya, and Singapore. Others came from India, Pakistan, and Ceylon on somewhat different assignments, but with a very similar general approach. It thus turned out that in a very real sense the book became a co-operative exercise. These officers were true collaborators, without the benefit of whose field experience most freely given to me, the book could hardly have come to life. I have listed below those who especially helped me, but there were many others who played a part in the gradual build up.

Since the work was thus so co-operative the use of the comparative method was inevitable, but I am confident that it is in any case the right approach. Local government investigation needs to be comparative if it is to get beneath the surface. In every country local authorities develop individual characters of their own, depending on such factors as the economic and physical environment and the traditions of the local population. All of this is irretrievably submerged if one works with aggregates and averages. This is true within a single country; it is manifestly even more true when comparing one country with another. Comparison is of first importance in the countries I have studied, from many points of view. Happily it can be meaningful and suggestive because in all of them there is essentially the same basis, of British experience, both in respect of ideology and of administrative institutions. It is for this reason (and certainly not from any desire to suggest either that the British system is perfect in itself or suitable for export without considerable adjustment) that I have found it necessary to describe British institutions in some detail from time to time. *Mutatis mutandis*, this also explains why I have felt it necessary to sketch in something both of the historical background of local government in the various territories and also (in Africa) their tribal structure.

Although the comparative method is (I am sure) the right one, and although the necessary basis for it exists, it is not very easy to apply. Only in those territories where some central authority insists on collected editions of local Estimates, is it possible to get an adequate sample of local budgets from which to choose. Worse than this, a little experience of working with the Estimates convinced me first, that there is no substitute to going right down to the accounts of the individual authority, but secondly and more seriously, that without first-hand knowledge of the country and even the locality it was easy to fall into gross errors of interpretation. As it is I may well have done this on occasion as I could not visit everywhere. Besides the visits to Nigeria, Jamaica, and parts of India that have been mentioned, I have been able to see something of the other West African Territories (Ghana and Sierra Leone, but not the Gambia) and of all the East African Territories, Kenya, Tanganyika, and Uganda (and for that matter Zanzibar), as well as Ceylon.

It was my intention to spread my net wider than eventually

proved possible, so as to include Northern Rhodesia and Nyasaland, Malaya, and perhaps Pakistan and Mauritius, as well as to make a more thorough study of India. It seemed, however, that most of these countries were followers rather than pioneers in the development of local government; and as it was, the book was already long enough. Further time was lacking for additional field studies. If the book was to be of any practical use it was desirable to get it out as quickly as possible.

Since finishing writing I have, however, visited parts of Malaya and also Hong Kong, and am all the more sorry that I could not have included something from South-East Asia. At Penang in Malaya I saw the working of an almost model multiracial council: Malayan, Chinese, and Indian. There was much evidence not only of the good relations between councillors of different race, but also between councillors and their constituents. The new town of Petaling Jaya on the outskirts of Kuala Lumpur was also a model of careful planning and rapid construction. Most impressive of all was the refugee housing in Kowloon, Hong Kong. In less than three years 250,000 family units had been provided in large blocks of flats (for which alone there was room). They presented a minimum but adequate provision for living, with shops, playgrounds, schools and clinics right at hand, the whole estate placed next door to the factory quarter. Moreover they were let at astonishingly low rents—10 to 20 Hong Kong dollars a month (the Hong Kong dollar = 1s. 3d.)—which involved hardly any subsidy. Of these South-East Asian examples only Penang was true local government, but the other activities were clearly within the range of things that larger local authorities could do elsewhere, and would hardly be beyond the powers of smaller towns given appropriate government assistance.

Finally I must express my thanks. The first debt is to the Oppenheimer Foundation which provided funds for two research assistants in the early stages of the investigation. These two: William Demas of Trinidad and Emmanuel College, Cambridge, and Ann Husband of Somerville College, Oxford, saved me much time and trouble in reducing the mass of available material to manageable proportions. Mr. Demas's knowledge of parts of the West Indies which I had not visited was also of considerable assistance. My best thanks are due to officers of the Colonial Office and of overseas governments who smoothed my way for visits to remote local authorities, and were always ready to discuss problems and answer questions.

My greatest debt (as already mentioned) is to District and Local Government officers overseas who were themselves actively engaged in development from below. A number of them were my own students and it was particularly delightful to meet them again in their proper background. Of these many gentlemen Sri Barfivala of Bombay, who has devoted the whole of his life to the cause of local self-government in India stands in a special place. I was also much helped with the mass of Indian material by Dr. H. K. Paranjape, now of the Institute of Public Administration, Delhi. I am grateful also to the Municipal Commissioners of Bombay, Poona, and Madras, as well as to those of Colombo and Nuwara Eliya in Ceylon. In Nigeria the officers of the Regional Ministries of Local Government (Mr. I. Duncan, Mr. P. Dyson, and Mr. G. R. I. Dees from the Eastern, Western, and Northern Regions respectively) were particularly helpful, so also was Mr. P. Grant whose knowledge of Community Development in the Eastern Region is unrivalled. In Ghana Messrs. Dobbs and Anakwa, then in charge respectively of urban and rural local government, helped me to make the very most of an all too short visit; Mr. J. Watson did the same in Sierra Leone.

In the East African Territories I received much help from the research workers at the East African Institute of Social Research (especially from C. J. Pratt and W. Elkan), and also from the Statistical Office of the High Commission. In Kenya I learned a great deal from Mr. A. Altorfer and his unique team of Financial Advisers. I would also specially mention Mr. R. Winser, now District Commissioner in Elgon Nyanza. In Uganda Messrs. N. Oram and T. Gee have been extremely helpful in answering questions, while Mr. Hull Lewis, then District Commissioner at Fort Portal, first introduced me to his system of assessment of graduated personal tax which has since spread through the Territory. In Tanganyika my discussions with Mr. B. Duddridge in Dar es Salaam made evident to me the great amount of thought which is going into the development of local government in that Territory. In Bukoba I was able to visit Mr. I. Woodruffe, one of my most helpful and thoughtful students on the Devonshire Course.

In the West Indies, besides Mr. Demas, Mr. E. Kentish of the

Ministry of Local Government in Kingston, Jamaica, helped me with a most useful survey of the situation in the other islands. His combination of first-class cricket (which took him on frequent inter-island tours) and local government knowledge gave him unique opportunities for investigation. I should also like to mention the help given to me by Mr. H. Mosley of St. Kitts, Mr. S. Meade of Montserrat, Mr. A. Seignoret of Dominica, and Mr. C. H. P. da Silva of British Guiana.

Something must be said of the part which Mr. Nehru played (although quite unconsciously) by coining the phrase Development from Below, which was just what I was looking for as a title to the book. Mr. Nehru is himself an example of the benefits of local government training for national politics, and is an unshakeable believer in the potentialities of local government, particularly in the rural setting.

Finally it would be wrong not to mention the very special part which my husband, Professor J. R. Hicks, has played in my researches. Our first (English) investigations into local government finance were a joint operation; we were together on the Nigerian expedition of 1950 and on the Jamaican investigation of 1954. He accompanied me on many of my expeditions in East Africa, India, and Ceylon in 1957. Had it not been for his encouragement and physical assistance in the later stages the book would have taken very much longer to emerge.

URSULA K. HICKS

Oxford, August 1960

CONTENTS

List of Tables   xiv

List of Sketch Maps   xv

PART I
LOCAL GOVERNMENT AND ECONOMIC DEVELOPMENT
1. The New Policy   3
2. The Instruments of Policy   10
3. The British View of Local Government   19

PART II
BACKGROUNDS AND BEGINNINGS
(THE COLONIAL SYSTEM UP TO 1940)
4. Beginnings in the West Indies   29
   Barbados, 29; Jamaica, 32; Trinidad, 34; British Guiana, 36
5. Beginnings in India and Ceylon   42
   India, 42; Ceylon, 58
6. The African Background: Tribal Authority and Indirect Rule   67
7. Beginnings in West Africa   82
   Gold Coast (Ghana), 82; the Regions of Nigeria, 91; Sierra Leone, 106
8. Beginnings in East Africa   113
   Uganda, 113; Kenya, 122; Tanganyika, 131

PART III
THE TRANSITION TO MODERN INSTITUTIONS
9. Transition in the West Indies   139
   Jamaica, 139; Barbados, 142; Trinidad, 143; British Guiana, 145; Dominica, 148
10. Transition in India and Ceylon   150
    India, 150; Ceylon, 160

11. Transition in West Africa   167

Nigeria, 167; Eastern Region, 169; Western Region, 176; Northern Region, 180; Ghana, 183; Sierra Leone, 195

12. Transition in East Africa   206

Uganda, 206; Kenya, 212; Tanganyika, 221

PART IV

THE LOCAL BUDGET

13. Budgetary Accounts 1. Current Expenditure   233

Effects of adult suffrage and growing political consciousness, 233; size of local budgets and functional breakdown, 237; expenditure on administration, 242; on health and medical services, 250; on education, 255; on communications, 263; on natural resources, 266; on trading services 268

14. Budgetary Accounts 2. Current Revenue   277

Influence of British thinking on practice overseas, 277; income from provision of goods and services, 283; from rents and interest, 287; revenue from licences, 290; from miscellaneous taxes, 291; from taxes on land and buildings, 295; from taxes on persons, 298; from grants, 304

15. The Taxation of Farmers and Rural Communities   321

Importance of taxation of farm incomes for development, 321; tax payments in kind, 324; Indian land revenue, 326; lump sum assessment in Northern Nigeria, 330; valuation problems, 332; produce taxes, 335; taxation of potential income, 339

16. The Taxation of Urban Land and Buildings   347

Advantages of a tax on urban realty, 347; types of such a tax in use, 349; the choice of tax base, 355; valuation problems, 359

17. Budgetary Accounts, 3. The Capital Account   368

Importance of local investment for development, 368; form of capital account, 370; functional breakdown and relative importance in different areas, 375; problems of resource allocation and maintenance of works, 385; finance of capital formation, 396

18. Grants   409

Influence of British experience, 409; types of grant according to objective, block grants 415, specific grants 424, grants to assist capital formation 428

PART V

FINANCE AND POLITICS

19. Relations with the Central Government   433
Allocation of powers and duties, 438; budgetary control 1, estimates and ways and means, 443; budgetary control 2, accounting 449; form of accounts showing functional breakdown, 452; auditing and disciplinary measures, 454; need for continuing advice from the central administration, 457

20. Urban Problems   464
The problem of urban immigration, 467; constructional needs, 470; low income housing, 472; new towns, 478; finance of urban development, 482; special problems of urban administration, 483

21. Problems of Rural Local Government   495
Questions of tiering: in Africa, 496; in India and Ceylon, 500; optimum population for local government areas, 506; optimum size of councils, 513; relations of local government with other organizations: missions, co-operatives, local representatives of central departments, 516; relations with the Community Development Movement: in India, 522; in Nigeria, 524; local government in small islands, 528

22. A Postscript on Training   532
Index   541

LIST OF TABLES

1. Main Heads of Current Expenditure, Ghana   271
2. Main Heads of Current Expenditure, Nigeria, Northern Region   272
3. Main Heads of Current Expenditure, Nigeria, Eastern Region   273
4. Main Heads of Current Expenditure, Nigeria, Western Region   274
5. Main Heads of Current Expenditure, Uganda, African Local Councils   275
6. Main Heads of Current Expenditure, Kenya, African District Councils   276
7. Main Heads of Current Revenue, Ghana   315
8. Main Heads of Current Revenue, Nigeria, Northern Region   316
9. Main Heads of Current Revenue, Nigeria, Eastern Region   317
10. Main Heads of Current Revenue, Nigeria, Western Region   318
11. Main Heads of Current Revenue, Uganda, African Local Councils   319
12. Main Heads of Current Revenue, Kenya, African District Councils   320
13. Kenya: Functional Distribution of Main Types of Capital Outlay   377
14. Nigeria: Functional Distribution of Main Types of Capital Outlay, by Regions   382
15. Nigeria: Functional Distribution of Main Capital Grants, Northern and Eastern Regions   401
16. Kenya: Functional Distribution of Loans sanctioned for Local Capital Formation   405
17. West Africa: Comparative Populations of Districts: 507
    (a) Ghana,
    (b) Eastern Nigeria,
    (c) Sierra Leone.

LIST OF SKETCH MAPS

1. The West Indies   30
2. Jamaica   33
3. India   43
4. Ceylon   59
5. Ghana   83
6. Nigeria   92
7. Nigeria: Northern Region   97
8. Nigeria: Eastern and Western Regions   101
9. Sierra Leone   107
10. Uganda   114
11. Kenya   123
12. Tanganyika   132

PART I

LOCAL GOVERNMENT AND
ECONOMIC DEVELOPMENT

1

THE NEW POLICY

THIS is a study of experiments in local government that have
been deliberately undertaken, in a number of British territories, as stages on the road to self-government or independence. Though most of the story relates to very recent years,
its beginnings stretch much farther back. There is indeed one sense
in which they go back to the very beginnings of British expansion.
As soon as British people began to settle overseas, they set to work
creating local institutions on the model of those to which they
were accustomed; from these origins the democracy of the United
States and of the older Dominions has grown up. That part of the
expansion, and transplantation, of British local government will,
however, lie, for the most part, outside our subject. Local democracy of that sort was a natural growth; no deliberate policy lay
behind it. The case was different when dependent territories,
inhabited by non-British peoples, began to be assimilated, in the
minds of their rulers, to the *colonies* of British stock; when the
idea was conceived, as it already was by some enlightened statesmen by the middle of the nineteenth century, that these also should
be expected, and encouraged, to proceed upon similar lines.[1] These
were days when representative local government, of a modern type,
was quite a novelty in England; but there was little delay before the
idea was born that what was good for England herself should also
be good for the territories for which she had assumed responsibility. It was chiefly in India (recognized as the greatest of these
overseas responsibilities) that these ideas, at that time, received
some practical embodiment. We shall find, as we go on, that there
is a significant link between the things that have been done (in
Africa and elsewhere) in our time and the Indian experience in
local government that goes back to the nineteenth century.

There is nevertheless something that is quite novel about the
recent experience: what is it? It is not merely that a policy which
had been pursued, with varying degrees of ardour, in a few

---

[1] See the Dispatch of Earl Grey (1848) quoted below, p. 39.

particular places, has become generalized; that is important, but it is also of importance that the motivation of the policy has changed. Since the last war local government has been regarded as a means, not only to political, but also to economic development. This is clearly stated in the Dispatch to African Governors, which was circulated by the then Secretary of State for the Colonies on 25 February 1947. Though we should be careful not to exaggerate the extent to which this document embodies a new policy (nor the extent to which the response to the dispatch represented anything like a new policy in the territories concerned), it does state the objectives in a way in which they could hardly have been stated at an earlier date.

Since I took office in October [wrote Mr. Creech Jones] I have been considering some of the basic problems of African administration; I think it right that I should now address you on this subject, since our success in handling these problems, and the extent to which we can secure the active co-operation of the Africans themselves, may well determine the measure of our achievement in the programmes of political, social and economic advancement on which we have now embarked. I believe that the key to success lies in the development of an efficient and democratic system of local government. I wish to emphasize the words efficient, democratic and local. I do so, not because they import any new conception into African administration; indeed these have been the aims of our policy over many years. I use these words because they seem to me to contain the kernel of the whole matter: *local* because the system of government must be close to the common people and their problems; *efficient* because it must be capable of managing the local services in a way which will help to raise the standard of living; and *democratic* because it must not only find a place for the growing class of educated men, but at the same time command the respect and support of the mass of the people.

On the political side (as Mr. Creech Jones evidently realized) there was nothing that was particularly new about this. It had long been recognized that local government has a value as an 'education' for democracy. It is educative for the electors, who are called upon to do their voting in relation to issues that are readily comprehensible to them; and for the councillors, who can gain experience in the art of responsible leadership, without being confronted (before they have gained experience) with issues that at that stage may be beyond their grasp. The representative can maintain a direct contact with his constituents in human terms, without having to rely upon those rather synthetic imitations of contact, which (if we are honest) we must admit to be characteristic of party politics upon the national scale. It is easier for local government than for national government to be 'close to the common people'.

Things like this had been said before; but what had things like this to do with the 'standard of living'? There was indeed one quasi-economic argument which would have fitted well with these political arguments; it might have been emphasized that one of the responsibilities which local government can teach is financial responsibility. The connexion between the payment of local taxes and the enjoyment of local services is direct and obvious—so much more convincing to the taxpayer, and so much more stimulating to his interest, than the remoter connexion, which is often so difficult to see, in the national budget. (It is of course essential, if this connexion is to have its effect, that the Local Authority should be a taxing authority; it must not be wholly dependent upon grants from the central government.) Valid as this argument is, and important as it is (we shall often have occasion to return to it), it was hardly a point that was likely to receive particular attention in the conditions of 1947. The economic strand in the 1947 policy was of a different character. *Efficient* local government was to be a means to economic development.

What is the relation between local government and economic development? Not much more is apparent from the document quoted than that local government is a good thing and economic development is a good thing, and their common virtues draw them together. No one since will have denied that economic development, in these territories, is a very good thing; it has even become a more important thing than it was, for as time has gone on, the grievances of political tutelage and of economic underdevelopment have become ever more closely intertwined. The association between the two sorts of development is now accepted by persons of all political persuasions; but historically it is of socialist origin, and it looks somewhat different according as it is placed in a socialist or in a non-socialist setting. This affects one's attitude towards the economic problems of local government; it will therefore be useful for us to look at the issues which come up at this point in both ways.

To a socialist, the economic development (even, for instance, of an African territory) would be assumed to be a socialist development; the impulse, the driving force, of the things that were to be done would come from the State. A British socialist, however, though he accepts that principle, has normally had some reservations about its execution; he is afraid of authoritarianism, he wishes to leave scope for individual initiative in some form or other, he is reluctant to approve of the whole direction of the economy coming from the top. That he feels such reservations is not without importance even in England; but when he turns his mind to the problems of the territories which will be our concern, the need for some reservation becomes even more apparent. Simple State socialism, applied by a government which is not yet democratic, or not wholly democratic, can obviously be tyrannical, or at best paternalistic; it must be dangerous to rely upon it to an undue extent. The case for local government, as an instrument of economic activity, emerges very clearly from this standpoint; it is an attempt to give the people their own socialism, not to rely upon a central government socialism, which must seem to be (and would no doubt for some time have to be) imposed from outside.

This, I think we may recognize, was one strand in the new policy; in the mind of a Labour Secretary of State, in 1947, it may well have been the main strand. Suppose, however, that we do not accept the socialist premise; suppose that it is granted (as it has later come to be fairly generally granted) that a considerable share in economic development is to be left to private enterprise, encouraged (perhaps) but not directed by the State. If it should come about that a considerable part of this enterprise was indigenous, some of the socialist case for local government enterprise would fall to the ground. Is there anything left?

It must surely be reckoned that there is. Even if the main responsibility for the expansion of production and for the development of new industries is to rest upon private enterprise, such expansion remains dependent upon the provision of essential services, such as in almost every country are provided by public bodies. These may be classified into two kinds: the 'economic overheads'—roads, ports, power, water, and so on, on the one side; the 'social overheads'—education and public health, on the other. Under each of these heads some useful economic functions for local government are to be found.

It is of course inevitable that the larger items under each heading (major power projects, irrigation schemes, higher education, general hospitals, to take some examples) should be matters for central, or possibly regional, responsibility. But there is no reason why the smaller should not be within the capacity of local bodies. If a substantial part of the whole programme consists of small works that can be done at the local level, some of the advantage persists which we have just seen when we considered the matter in a socialist setting.

Even though the government is prepared to leave a large part of the responsibility for development to private enterprise, the share of government must remain important; there is still the danger that a disproportionate share in the whole undertaking will be centrally (and therefore in many cases externally) directed. It may not be easy to ensure that indigenous enterprise gets its full opportunity for expression within the 'private sector'. Especially in its origins, such enterprise is a frail craft; it easily comes to grief in the rough and tumble of the market. Economic activity by local government may well be the best way in which the 'people' can play a part in the organization of their own development.

Beyond any question, such participation has its dangers. Mr. Creech Jones was entirely right in the emphasis that he laid upon efficiency. It is easier for public enterprise than for private enterprise, when judged by an economic test, to be a complete and a continuing failure. Unsuccessful local enterprise will not contribute to development, but rather the reverse.

Nevertheless, if the thing can be done, it has its advantages; it even has some technical economic advantages, which are not to be despised. A goodly proportion of small works, the kinds of projects that are suitable for undertaking by local government, is an economic advantage in a development plan.

One of these is a direct consequence of the smallness. It is a normal characteristic of big projects that they take years—sometimes many years—to complete. The period of waiting before they are completed is a period of strain; for a poor country it can be a great strain. Incomes go on being distributed, all this time, to the workers engaged on the construction; as these incomes are spent, new incomes are generated; but nothing has yet been done to enlarge the flow of goods on which these incomes can be spent. Little local projects have a much quicker reaction. Better local roads or a better market can stimulate the output of cash crops within a single season. This is one way in which a fair proportion of local projects can be expected to make a development programme economically easier.

Again, it is a common trouble with the big projects that, even when they are completed, further time must elapse before they can be effectively used. 'Dry' farmers have to be taught how to make the best use of irrigation water; the results of agricultural research have to be disseminated by patient persuasion. The corresponding stages of local projects are relatively easy. Much of the 'extension' work which is required for the national projects can, however, be carried out at the local level; local government organizations are a convenient way of organizing it.[1] But of course it is not possible for this to be done except by co-operation between central and local authorities; this has fiscal and other implications which we shall be considering later.[2]

On the revenue side the economic function of local government can be even more striking. Because of the strain which attempted rapid development imposes on a poor economy, there is a need for diversion of some part of the additional incomes, before they can exercise an inflationary pressure on prices, or cause embarrassment to the balance of payments; without this diversion, all that will happen is a succession of booms and bursts. But in most underdeveloped countries the execution of a fiscal policy of this kind is decidedly difficult. All that the central government has at its disposal, in most cases, is some sort of an income tax (with an exemption limit set on European precedents, so that many of what on native standards are high incomes are exempted from it); together with the ordinary indirect taxes (customs and excise) which fall upon all classes, rich, moderately well off, and very poor alike. The taxation of the moderately well off among the indigenous population by such means is singularly difficult. One way round the difficulty is by taxation at the local level, where a tax that can reasonably be paid by the relatively wealthier classes in particular localities can more easily be devised. The remarkable experiments in this direction which have been made in several African territories will be described in later chapters of this book.

On such grounds as these it is entirely proper that the development of local government in these countries should now be

---

[1] This will be discussed in detail in Chap. 17 below.
[2] See Chap. 18 below.

regarded as in part an economic problem; it is because it is in part an economic problem that the present writer (an economist) has been drawn to its study. Political aspects will not, I hope, be found to have been neglected. It may, however, be claimed to be an advantage of the economic approach that it encourages us to give full weight to the finances of local activity. I would maintain that one gets nearer to the heart of local government in these countries by studying its finances, than one would do in the United Kingdom. In the United Kingdom the Local Authorities are statutory bodies, whose powers and duties are laid down by legislation with great precision. If they stray outside those limits (*ultra vires*) they get into trouble. In most of our countries powers and duties are defined much more broadly; but the services that are actually performed are normally confined to quite a narrow list. Thus it is impossible to tell what is really happening by studying the Ordinances, or by making personal visits, on the scale that is possible for an outsider—though neither of these is to be despised. Exploration in each of these directions always leaves one a good way short of an answer. But there is another source of information which does much to fill the deficiency—the records of local finance.

2

THE INSTRUMENTS OF POLICY

OF the three words which Mr. Creech Jones emphasized, efficiency has already been discussed in the preceding chapter. Something must now be said about the others. What was the prospect of a local government that was 'close to the people' and 'democratic'? Many a theorist has been called upon to draw up a democratic constitution, but institutions which are 'close to the people' cannot so easily be imposed from outside. If they are to satisfy that requirement, they must usually be built upon foundations which are already there. What was already there, in the form of local institutions (democratic or not), at the time the dispatch was written? Some preliminary description of the institutions which were to be found will make later chapters easier to follow.

There are, in the first place, some of our territories where the position can be regarded (as least for present purposes) as fairly straightforward. The local bodies which were to be found in the West Indies were of ancient origin; but it was nevertheless a British origin—they were nothing else but adaptations of English institutions of earlier times. In India, again, so far as the municipalities are concerned, they are simply a transplantation of English town councils; subject to many important, and even fundamental, differences in their practical working, but in principle direct copies of the kind of thing with which the English reader will be familiar. But already in India, when we go outside the towns, there is a decidedly different story. In the countryside of British India, government was for the most part direct government; but the history of British India is by no means devoid of attempts to build with traditional local institutions, such as we shall find to be of major importance in Africa, and which will be of great importance everywhere in the rest of our work.

The idea of using indigenous local institutions as instruments of modern government is perhaps to be ascribed to the great administrator C. T. Metcalfe (British Resident at Delhi, 1811–19).

It was Metcalfe who drew attention to the Village Councils of Elders (*panchayats*),[1] which were to be found in the surrounding territory, and which have subsequently, in our own period, acquired so great a fame.[2] What Metcalfe suggested was actually carried out by his contemporary Sir Thomas Munro (Governor of Madras, 1819–27), who made use of the traditional village officials for the maintenance of law and order, and encouraged the Village Councils to settle simple court cases.[3] Such experiments as these were, however, no more than forerunners; it was not until democracy had developed in other ways that the panchayats were to have a chance of coming into their own.

There is in fact a clearer pedigree to the institutions which will concern us in our other territories from a totally different aspect of Indian government. The indigenous institutions which the (British) government of India did very widely 'use' were those of the princely states. Here the practice was for the native government to be left in being, so far as internal affairs were concerned; it was merely influenced by the presence of a British Resident. In the days before the Mutiny, when the government of India had no compunction about the dispossession of a ruler who had shown himself to be tyrannical or inefficient, the power of the Resident could be considerable; afterwards it was much less. In the light of subsequent events, the government of India can be criticized for the exaggerated respect which it paid to the princely administrations—native institutions, indeed, but such as by its own actions it was causing to become outmoded.

But from this we pass to Africa. The precedent of the Residents at the Indian princely courts gained a new importance when it was used by Lugard in Nigeria as the basis of his great edifice of Indirect Rule. He expressly called his senior administrators in Northern Nigeria Residents, in order to emphasize the intention that there should be continuity of local institutions. The functions of his Residents were nevertheless far wider than those which had been associated in India with this title. The Emirs, with whom

[1] See below, especially pp. 44 ff.

[2] It is interesting to notice that the training college for the Civil Service of independent India is still known as Metcalfe House.

[2] Munro is mainly famous for his defence of the *ryotwari* (free peasant) system of land tenure, and resistance to the introduction of the *zamindari* (landlord) system. This sprang, of course, from the same framework of ideas. See Eric Stokes, *The English Utilitarians and India*, 1959.

they were associated, had been feudal rulers of the normal Moslem type; under Lugard's system their substantive position was greatly changed. In a sense they were turned into civil servants; they were given a fixed salary,[1] and were compelled to tour their Emirates, learning to know their people directly, not as previously at second hand from officials reporting to the palace. The whole administration was supported by a reformed tax system, which was essentially new, though it had a traditional Moslem tax as a foundation, and also owed something to Indian land revenue.[2] Most important of all, the British share in the administration was not confined to the installation of a Resident at the top; there was a whole hierarchy of British officials (District Commissioners and District Officers) working right down to the village level. In Northern Nigeria, as elsewhere in Africa, the heart of British administration has been the District Office with its staff, both of expatriates and of Africans; as we shall see, it is the District Office which has been the jumping-off place for the experiment in responsible local government.

In its original form Lugard's system of Indirect Rule depended upon the existence of local rulers. It was the Emir himself who was constituted a (sole) Native Authority. But there was often another element to be considered: the Emir's Council. In the strictly Moslem areas this was usually of secondary importance (though it was recognized as having a place in the traditional arrangement). But in the southern (Yoruba) parts of Northern Nigeria the council was much more important; attention had to be paid to it by associating its members (drawn from the local aristocracy—the chiefly families) with the ruler, so constituting a Native Authority of ruler in council. When Indirect Rule was extended into Yorubaland proper (what is now the Western Region), this tendency was found to go even farther. The Oba was no longer an effective ruler; his function was 'spiritual' or ceremonial; real power resided with the Council of Chiefs. Here then it was very significant that the council was constituted the Native Authority. And a Native Authority which was a council was clearly capable of further development; without any break in continuity an elective element could be introduced.

But it must next be observed that by no means all the peoples of

[1] According to their grades; see below, p. 96, for further details.
[2] See below, p. 96.

Africa had recognizable rulers, with or without a conciliar element. (This was made plain as soon as it was attempted to extend Indirect Rule to Eastern Nigeria.) As will later be explained in more detail,[1] African peoples can be classified (very broadly and roughly) into two groups: centralized and non-centralized. To the centralized peoples something like the system above described, was applicable, but to the non-centralized peoples it was not applicable, in anything like its classical form. In their cases there seemed to be three alternatives: (1) to rule directly, appointing a hierarchy of chiefs or headmen, to work as subordinates of expatriate officers;[2] (2) to set up chiefs, selected by the British administration, thus imposing something similar to what was elsewhere the traditional arrangement, in order that the British might rule 'indirectly' through it;[3] (3) to search out such small-scale organization as the anthropologists could discover at the clan or village level, and to attempt to build upwards from this. It sometimes happened that nothing relevant to local government could be discovered, and it was necessary to wait until the people themselves were prepared to take the initiative in adjusting to new forms of organization.

What came to be known indifferently as 'Native Authorities' in a system of Indirect Rule thus had many different roots, and the key elements, *chiefs* and *councils*, denoted different things from one territory to another. It is always necessary to bear this in mind, and further, to remember that situations have been changing very rapidly, especially over the last fifteen years.

We can distinguish at least four different connotations of the word 'chief', although they tend to shade into one another and not all of them have any political significance. First, there is the chief (of the type of the Northern Nigerian Emir) who is a real monarch, much more powerful than his nobles in council, and probably more or less in control of the succession. Over the course of decades and the conditioning process of Indirect Rule, he has lost something, but he still retains a great deal, and it is a serious question how far his council will be able to maintain its position once the driving force of the British administration is removed.

This type shades gradually through a situation in which the

---

[1] Chap. 6 below. [2] This was the original plan in Kenya.
[3] This was unsuccessfully tried in Eastern Nigeria.

chief (or Paramount) is elected from a narrow circle of families and is less powerful relatively to the council, to the position of the Yoruba Obas and other chiefs. Here the clan heads of chiefly families are known as chiefs (and the right to the title is very widely interpreted). The Oba or head of each sub-people (Egba, Ibadan, and so on) is elected but strictly from a circle of chiefly families, and more and more simply as a ritual and spiritual head. Any civil power he may now have depends primarily on his personality and this is true also of the jealously exclusive hierarchy of lesser chiefs.

The opposite of these hereditary chiefs is the pure civil servant chief, typical of Kenya and parts of Uganda and Tanganyika, especially among decentralized peoples. Although he has definite functions in connexion with local government, similar to those exercised by real chiefs under Indirect Rule, he is not the same sort of thing at all. Nevertheless, where the people are encouraged to take a hand in electing their own chiefs he sometimes comes to acquire a sort of pseudo-hereditary prestige. One reason for this is no doubt the indirect influence of the presence of real chiefs among neighbouring centralized societies.

Finally, we come to the odd phenomenon of the self-appointed chief who forces or buys his way into a position of importance (social, rather than political or administrative). 'Charismatic' chiefs of this sort (as they have been called[1]) are found among the Ibo of Eastern Nigeria, and also among the Kikuyu of Kenya—both of these being decentralized peoples, which are undergoing a process of rapid change. They have nothing to do with traditional arrangements, but should be regarded as a reaction to the opportunities for leadership (and perhaps of class distinction) that are presented by the modern world.

The various meanings of the word 'council' are closely related to those of 'chief'. We can again distinguish four main types. (1) Those which operate in a strongly centralized system, where the chief has real power. The members of the council are much under the control of the chief, and may mainly be his relatives. (2) The Yoruba councils, with their hierarchies of civil and military chiefs, formerly exercising most of the power over the people, and indeed to a considerable extent over the Oba. (3) The non-traditional councils, normally beginning as wholly appointed bodies—

[1] G. I. Jones, *Report on Chieftainship in the Eastern Region of Nigeria*, 1957.

but whose members might nevertheless be carefully chosen both for their personal qualities and to represent their localities.

All of these first three types are to be thought of as important bodies, with substantial jurisdictions. Over the course of time all could be 'modernized'. Into the traditional councils were first introduced 'representatives' chosen by the government; later all three types had elected members added to them. Thus a council which had initially been wholly appointed might come to have an elected majority. In fact an appointed council is likely to acquire an elected majority rather sooner than a traditional council. But the word 'election' can also have a number of different connotations. It may simply imply a show of hands in open *baraza*[1] (in fact, at the hustings), or again the voters may whisper their choice into the District Officer's ear, after the manner of 'Oranges and Lemons'. In either case the choice of candidates would probably be fairly closely limited by the administration. Nowadays voting by secret ballot is also creeping into local elections, but it is as yet something of a rarity.

The fourth type of council, which we have not yet discussed, consists of the little councils, developing out of traditional clan or elders' councils, more or less at the village level, similar in many respects to Indian panchayats. These are particularly strong among the non-centralized peoples, but they are also now to be found in such a highly centralized social organization as the Northern Nigerian Emirates. In some places these little councils have been formalized as a regular part of the local government structure;[2] in others, an opposite tendency is at work. Whatever their present position, these little councils seem to have two things in common: they are wholly elective (thus close to the people in every sense) and they are nearly always lively. Thus although their range of possible activity is inevitably limited, they have the right characteristics for a sub-structure of responsible local government.

Any one of the types of council we have been discussing would qualify for inclusion in the general term 'Native Authority'. The broad distinguishing characteristic of the Native Authority is that the chairman comes from the District Office, he is part of the administration. This common feature of Native Authorities may of course vary in practice. There is the situation in which the

[1] A Swahili word used throughout East Africa.
[2] Especially the Kenya Location Councils.

chairman has trained his council so well (and the members have co-operated so intelligently), that the council in effect frame their own estimates and take all important decisions, the chairman riding with the lightest of reins. Then there is that in which the District Officer does almost all the work himself, either because he is not good at standing back or because the councillors are irresponsible or factious, or merely very primitive. Within the single territory of Kenya are to be found all shades between these poles.

The essential difference between a Native Authority and a Local Authority[1] turns, then, not so much on the elective principle, as on the transfer of responsibility: from the responsibility of the District Officer to the central government, to the responsibility of the local council on the one side to the local electors and on the other to the central government. Indeed, in some areas (for instance, in Western Nigeria) there may never be wholly elected councils, since seats are being reserved for traditional chiefs. Yet it can hardly be questioned that since 1952 the Western Nigerian councils have been fully responsible. Similarly it is not really relevant whether the central government is wholly independent; or is in the pre-independence stage when its central authority is a 'Council of Ministers' (some of whom are popularly elected); or in the less advanced stage of an 'Ex. Co.',[2] with or without a complete set of definite portfolios headed by a 'Member for . . .'. It might, however, be argued that full responsibility cannot be exercised by a Local Authority until the central government has made at least some progress on the road to self-government. It is evident that within this fundamental distinction of definitive responsibility a great many shades are possible.

These, in broad outline, were the institutions that lay at hand in 1947; but there was another instrument of policy, again primarily (but by no means entirely) of African relevance, which must be noticed before we go on.

The primary responsibility for erecting the new structure of

[1] When discussing features common both to Native Authorities and Local Authorities I have used the more general phrase 'local body'.

[2] Ex. Co. (the common abbreviation will be generally employed in this book) is the Executive Council, which in colonial conditions is the policy-making body, controlled by official members. Leg. Co. the Legislative Council, is a deliberative but not a ruling assembly, sooner or later given an unofficial majority.

responsible local government has fallen on the hierarchy of administrative officers: District Commissioners and District Officers. It must be asked how far they were either adequate or appropriate for the task. In one way the officers in the field were ideal: they were close to the people. It is true that the increasing range of government activities and the rapid accumulation of paper work inseparable from it, were tending to make the District Officer a little less accessible than he used to be. In another way also he was slightly losing contact, in that formerly he toured the District slowly on bicycle or horseback, while now he could cover many miles in his land rover and seldom need spend a night out of station. But if he had ceased to be the 'father of his people', in most territories he still commanded their entire confidence.

The new task to which the District Officer was asked to devote himself was a difficult one. Quite apart from the fact that he was called upon to arrange for his own disappearance from a part of his work which he probably found especially interesting, many field officers were not by nature particularly suited to the task. A surprisingly large proportion had not grown up in an atmosphere of English local government, for overseas service tends to run in families. Many had joined the Service largely for the outdoor life, and had no natural inclination, nor perhaps ability, to think in terms of figures or of budgetary niceties.

The difficulties of this situation were recognized in advance. A committee was set up in 1944 under the Duke of Devonshire to consider the whole question of postwar training for the Colonial Service. This was part of a general concern to raise the standard of administration in the Colonies. For so long the Indian Civil Service had drawn all the best men; but this drain would no longer impede the recruitment of first-rate men for the Colonies. As a result of the deliberations of the Devonshire Committee two training courses were set up,[1] one at the outset of a man's career, the other after he had gained some insight into problems on the spot; both included training in local government. These courses were of quite general reference, but to meet the special needs of Africa an Advisory Panel on local government was set up at the Colonial Office, and a new journal—the *Journal of African Administration*[2] started.

[1] At the Universities of Oxford, Cambridge, and London.
[2] Referred to throughout this book as the *J.A.A.*

There is no doubt that these measures greatly helped the District Officers in their task. Fortunately many of them turned out to be educationalists at heart, and when they grasped the significance of what they were being asked to do they entered on the task with enthusiasm. But it must be emphasized that in preparing for a new system of local government from which they themselves would be excluded, a heavy burden of psychological readjustment was being placed on serving officers. In the next chapter we must briefly examine just what the system was that they were being asked to introduce.

3

THE BRITISH VIEW OF
LOCAL GOVERNMENT

FROM the earliest times it has seemed to the English part of the natural order of things that local communities should have a substantial responsibility for order and for the good conduct of their affairs, under the general eye of the central government. The laws of the Anglo-Saxon kings expressly laid on towns and villages the duties of watch and ward and hue and cry. These local responsibilities developed in three directions: first, the Church Vestry of the citizens, meeting under the chairmanship of the priest or parson to look after charities, and such leading works as roads, bridges, and church repairs; to cover the costs of these activities they levied a rate on occupiers of land and buildings in the parish. Secondly, there came the system of unpaid justices, who not merely looked after law and order, but gradually accumulated a number of responsibilities belonging to the field of local government. Thirdly, there were the town corporations, organized on a very narrow and rigid franchise, but often exercising a high degree of local autonomy. With the Elizabethan Poor Law, local bodies first had statutory duties for social welfare thrust upon them, and as a consequence the local rate became compulsory and permanent. Local bodies of these types were set up overseas as a natural consequence of settlement: in North America, in the West Indies, and in the towns of India, and they endured for decades, even centuries (the Barbadian Vestries were superseded so recently that their successors have hardly begun operations).

Local government institutions such as these sufficed for pre-industrial England, but with the coming of the big manufacturing towns of the North and Midlands, more extended services than they could administer were called for. Cities need such things as water, drainage, street cleaning, and regulation of markets and of traffic. For a time such needs were met through the promotion by individual towns of private Bills in Parliament to secure the establishment of Improvement Commissioners. Some of these

commissoners (for instance, in Liverpool) were very active and
can definitely be accounted as prototypes of modern urban government. General legislation establishing responsible local government
authorities in towns, with councils elected on a (relatively) wide
franchise, came hard on the heels of the first Parliamentary
Reform Act. Although the network of elective Local Authorities
in all areas was only completed in the last quarter of the nineteenth
century, the stamp of the English Local Authority was essentially
fixed by the Municipal Corporations Act of 1835.

It was in that reforming age that the doctrine of the political
and educational value of representative local institutions emerged.
The logical consequence that it would be a good thing to establish
them in the Colonies was already drawn in Earl Grey's Dispatch
to the Governor of British Guiana in 1848.[1] The idea was put into
operation with definite intent in Indian towns by the Ripon
reforms of the 1880's and more deliberately still by the Montagu-
Chelmsford programme of the 1920's.[2] It continued to gain ground;
Colonel Oliver Stanley's Dispatch of 1945 to the West Indian
Governors was a precursor of the Creech Jones Dispatch of 1947
to the African Governors. This last mainly differed from earlier
pronouncements in that it was followed by a more persistent
determination to secure the implementation of the policy. The
explanation of this was very largely the realization that time was
running out and that independence would have to be conceded
to the African territories in a relatively short time.

From 1894 the whole of England and Wales had been covered with
a network of elected councils: in the large towns all-purpose
County Boroughs; in the counties a tiered system of Municipal
Boroughs, Urban District Councils, and Rural District Councils,
below these Parish Councils. In the County Districts (urban and
rural) there were minor variations in powers and duties, depending partly on rank, and partly on population (a chartered borough
having more independence than an Urban District Council even
if the latter was larger). In addition there survived a few *ad hoc*
bodies dating from before the general legislation: Poor Law
Guardians, Highway Boards, and School Boards. Between 1902
(the School Boards) and ending in 1929 (the Poor Law Guardians),
these *ad hoc* bodies were gradually integrated into the regular
structure of local government. Two other changes also emerged,

[1] See below, p. 39.   [2] See below, pp. 54 ff.

which together have considerably altered the position of local government institutions in more recent years: the great increase in grants[1] as a source of local revenue, and the increased concentration of duties in the hands of the top (County Council) tier (outside the County Boroughs), although substantial services still remained to the Municipal Boroughs and County Districts. Moreover, responsibility for levying and collecting the rate remained with the County Districts, the higher (County) and lower (Parish) councils *precepting* upon them according to the stated needs of particular services. From the Rating and Valuation Act of 1925, valuation became more concentrated and was finally 'nationalized' in 1948 when responsibility was transferred to the Inland Revenue. These changes were very largely of the nature of adjustments to the wider responsibilities assumed by governments and the greater degree of co-ordination and centralization implicit in the new national social and economic policy that was demanded by a population growing in wealth and public needs. With the concentration of authority in the larger councils went an expansion of central co-ordination and influence, partly exercised through the grants system, partly by developing other means of bringing pressure on Local Authorities in an indirect way.[2]

These modern developments in English local government naturally bulked very large in the minds of those whose lot it was to supervise the implementation of the post-war policy of establishing responsible local institutions overseas. But on the whole they were modifications due to the emergence of particular conditions in the United Kingdom and did not alter the fundamental character of the system. Indeed, the concentration of power did not even kill the little Parish Councils; after a period of perhaps relative eclipse, they seem now to be on the upgrade in interest and activity. Further, there is no implication that the modifications introduced to meet particular conditions in the United Kingdom would necessarily be suitable for application in Africa or other places where these conditions are certainly not all realized. We must therefore attempt to distinguish the fundamentals of the British view of local government, in their most general form.

Fundamentally, the British idea of local government at the present time implies a system of councils, elected on universal

[1] See Chap. 18.
[2] Cf. D. N. Chester, *Central and Local Government*, 1951.

adult suffrage, responsible to the local community for the conduct of services in the basic fields of law and order, for social services in the widest sense, and for works for the general improvement of the locality. On the other side, and with equal importance, the Local Authorities are responsible to the central government for carrying out their statutory duties in accordance with the broad lines of national policy. In addition to their statutory duties there are a small number of permissive activities, in which the Local Authorities, if they choose to undertake them, can normally do as they like. They have, further, a wide power of making by-laws (subject to ministerial confirmation) to take account of particular local needs in respect of law, orderliness, and it may be of amenities.

The central point of all this is concerned with the statutory powers and duties which (as we have seen[1]) are defined with great precision for each of the grades of local authority. Councils have to watch their step very carefully not to stray outside these. Any step *ultra vires* makes the members liable to personal surcharge. Starting from this basis, the unique character of British local government lies in two directions: in the relation between the council and its executive officers, and in the relation of Parliament to Local Authorities in general, exercised through the central Ministries (particularly the Ministry of Local Government and Housing, the Ministry of Health, and the Ministry of Education). We must examine these two relations in turn.

The usual practice is for councils to appoint their own officers from among those qualified; there is no local government Service Commission, but the different grades of officers are closely organized in professional associations conducting their own qualifying examinations. The appropriate qualifications would normally be insisted upon, together with (for the higher posts) experience in local government service (central approval may be required for some of the top appointments[2]). In all matters of policy the executive officers are unequivocally subordinate to the council. There is thus no officer corresponding to an American City Manager or continental Burgomaster. But the Town Clerk,[3]

---

[1] See Chap. 1. Borough Councils, by reason of their charters, have more freedom in this respect than other types of authority.
[2] Mainly exercised through a grant towards the salaries of approved officers.
[3] Or Clerk to the Council outside a borough.

as chief officer, has a very great responsibility and wields considerable powers. He is invariably a lawyer, in order that he may warn the council in good time when a proposed course of action might be *ultra vires*.

Next in standing (but definitely subordinate) is the chief finance officer (Treasurer), who has full executive responsibility on the budgetary side. Other principal officers are the Director of Education, Medical Officer of Health, Chief Constable (if the authority manages its own police[1]), Borough Engineer, Surveyor, and so on. The full council meets at fairly frequent intervals, once a month would be fairly typical; but the work of the council is very largely conducted by its functional committees (the nucleus of which are statutory) and which normally meet much more often than the full council. In the committees much power is exercised by the chairmen; and the advice of the relevant technical officer (who attends all meetings) is vital. With a lazy committee, an active chairman, and a technical officer who has ideas he wants to try out, the work of the committee may very largely be conducted by these two.

The keystone of the committee system is the Finance Committee, which acts as a kind of cabinet, especially in respect of the Estimates. With the help of the Treasurer, it prunes the Estimates of the functional committees and co-ordinates them into a balanced whole.[2] The chairman of the Finance Committee is consequently a very important person.

The ways in which a Local Authority organizes its committee work vary in detail from council to council,[3] but two considerations are fundamental: first, that all committee decisions are subject to the approval of the whole council. This is no mere rubber stamping, so that it cannot be equated with the system which we shall find operating in some places overseas—for instance, in a number of Indian towns and Uganda districts,[4] where a small Standing Committee really does the work in the place of the council. Secondly, in spite of the close connexion between a committee (especially the chairman) and its technical officer, executive work is wholly the business of the officer and his staff, working according

[1] The Chief Constable also owes a direct responsibility to the Home Office.
[2] This at least is the rationale of the system, but actual practice naturally differs from place to place.
[3] Cf. E. D. Simon, *A City Council from Within*, 1926.
[4] See below, p. 50 and p. 207.

to the decisions of the council, which is unequivocally the policy-making body. This arrangement in no way precludes individual officers from formulating and pushing plans of their own, and a wise council will let a good man have his head over a considerable range. But he can only go forward when he has won his way first with his committee and then with the council.

The framework of the relation between the central government and the Local Authorities is set by the statutory duties and by the doctrine of *ultra vires*. But there are other means, both administrative and financial, whereby the central government can ensure both that Local Authorities do not act illegally nor sink below a tolerable standard of efficiency and that their policy broadly conforms to that of the government.[1] From the central departments, especially the Ministries of Education and of Local Government, there issues a ceaseless stream of Memoranda, Letters of Advice, and so on. Personal contacts between the officers of the central departments and the local committee chairmen and technical officers (especially the Town Clerk) are also very close.

The degree of central control varies from service to service, those over education and housing being especially tight. Much of this control is now exercised through a complicated grants system, which is at once promotional, regulatory, and redistributive in favour of the poorer authorities. (We shall be discussing this in detail in Chapter 18, so that we need not say more about it here.) Almost all the accounts of Local Authorities are subject to central audit, officers from the central department visiting the council offices at regular intervals to examine the books. They have powers of surcharge on individual councillors (which are freely used in case of minor misappropiation of funds). It is, however, always open to a local council to challenge an auditor's decision in the courts. Finally, the central government exercises a basic control over the volume of Local Authority borrowing, although the details of this vary from time to time in accordance with central politics, monetary policy, and so on.

It will be apparent that most of these positive controls are of a fairly flexible nature; in addition, however, there exists a powerful

[1] This does not preclude that there may be prolonged difficulties where the local majority is of the opposite political party to the national government. But central authority must eventually prevail, except in so far as a local council can finance its own policy entirely out of its own resources. In the nature of things this is not very far.

negative control through the fact that local government has only one source of autonomous revenue of any substance: the local rate.[1] It is, however, a real solid source, bringing in a revenue exceeding that of any of the central taxes on outlay save only tobacco.[2] There is no central control whatever over the poundage at which Local Authorities choose to levy their rate; nor is there any control over the size of local budgets or the manner in which councils allocate their resources between services.[3] Full responsibility within flexible limits is a unique characteristic of the British system of local government, reinforcing the ultimate responsibility of councils both for their policy to the electorate and for the good conduct and efficiency of their technical officers.

The British system of local government is thus a combination of local responsibility and central control, poised with considerable subtlety. It would be absurd to pretend that it always works to perfection; but if it conspicuously fails democratic ways can usually be found of putting things straight. It would be still more absurd to claim that it always produces efficient local government. Since the political and social aspects of local government have always ranked high in public estimation, efficiency is only part of its purpose. It is inevitable that there should be some conflict between democracy and efficiency, but, by and large, British local government has solved the conflict tolerably well.

---

[1] A tight control can also be exercised over the quantity and quality of investment, e.g. in housing or school building, by withholding loan sanction for a particular project.

[2] Rate revenue (1958), £635 m.; tobacco revenue, £737 m.

[3] Some indirect control is implicit in statutory obligations, and the grant system unquestionably exercises some 'steering' but these do not seriously interfere with the principle that local budgeting is independent.

PART II

BACKGROUNDS AND BEGINNINGS

(THE COLONIAL SYSTEM UP TO 1940)

4

BEGINNINGS IN THE WEST INDIES

I. BARBADOS

THE roots of local government institutions in the West Indies stretch back to the arrival of the first British settlers in Barbados and Jamaica; Barbados came into British possession in 1625. These early settlers brought with them ideas founded on contemporary institutions, just as the settlers in North America had done. At the centre there was an elected House, called in Barbados the House of Assembly, and in Jamaica the House of Representatives. Similarly, at the local level, organs of self-government were set up, modelled very closely on the Elizabethan Vestries. These local bodies have had a more or less continuous history until the most recent period. In Jamaica, although the local bodies have gone through a number of vicissitudes, they remain virtually intact. In Barbados the Vestries (as we shall see) were finally modernized only by legislation in 1954, and their successors have hardly yet started operations.[1]

Since the course of local government history in these two islands has not been strictly parallel, it will be easier to follow their stories in turn; the Barbadian Vestries claim a chronological priority. The eleven Vestries which emerged were not originally created by the Legislature, but in course of time their activities came to be regulated by a series of Ordinances passed in the seventeenth and eighteenth centuries. Presumably the Vestries were initially, like those in England, a species of town or parish meeting (parallel to the town meetings of New England); but in time they became elected bodies although voting and membership qualifications were so high that only a handful of the inhabitants qualified.[2] The chairman of the Vestry was (right up to 1954) the rector of the parish, and its two main functions were to provide on the one hand for the rector's stipend and on the other for the relief of the poor.

---

[1] See below, p. 143.

[2] In 1950, just before the introduction of adult suffrage, there were in the parish of St. Michael (which contains Bridgetown) 76,000 inhabitants; of these only 20,000 were ratepayers and only 1,119 voters. In fact elections were seldom contested.

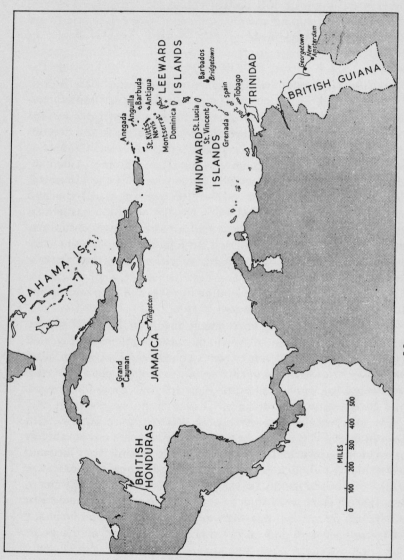

MAP 1. British West Indies.

At one time or another the Vestries were reinforced by *ad hoc* Boards for Poor Relief, Health, and Highways. All of these bodies were more or less closely connected with the Vestries, with much overlapping membership. Up to the late 1930's no serious criticism was made of the Vestries, due no doubt to the absence of change in the structure of the island government. In 1875, it is true, a Commission appointed to consider the administration of poor relief reported in favour of the transfer of poor law functions to a Central Committee of three commissioners; but there was no essential change in the organization of the various local bodies either then, or at the time of the passing of the Vestries Act in 1911. The Boards of Guardians and the Commissioners of Health operated with 100% grants from the Vestries. In Bridgetown, the capital, the Vestry organization was unable to administer the necessary urban services, so that in course of time the island government took over a number of functions normally the responsibility of Local Authorities, such as public health, highways, water supply, markets, and so on, as well as education. As a result of this no change was made in the status of Bridgetown, which retained its primitive Vestry organization.

The West Indian Royal Commission (1938–45) passed severe strictures on the local government of Barbados. There were too many Vestries and far too little central control. As a result there was no co-ordination and much wastage and inefficiency, especially with regard to the control of epidemics. The commissioners also found that the Vestries were too unrepresentative and too bound up with the established Church to form a satisfactory basis for modern local government services.

The tax confusion in the island reflects the general lack of co-ordination. There were three principal taxes, levied respectively on occupancy, ownership, and trade, and three earmarked levies on ownership, for highways, police, and (in Bridgetown) for fire brigades. The occupancy tax was levied on tenants on the basis of their rents.[1] The base of the ownership tax was either annual value or acreage, whichever was the higher. Valuation was nominally carried out annually but was always far below market values. In 1948 there had been no change in values over the previous twenty years; no distinction was made between good and bad land. The

---

[1] It was apparently simple to avoid this by staying away from home during the period when the statutory assessments were made.

base of the trade tax was 'net annual clearance of the business averaged over five years'. The trader was required to make an annual return, and this was the basis of assessment by the Parochial Assessor. If no return was made, the Assessor did the best he could, normally by rule of thumb methods. As reported in 1947–8, the trade and ownership taxes were each responsible for some 44% of revenue (the former was, however, considerably more important in St. Michael, owing to the presence of Bridgetown). The occupancy tax brought in some 10% of the revenue. By some strange idea of equity it was apparently the invariable custom to assess all the taxes at the same rate over an entire parish.

As a result of the adverse Report of the Royal Commission, Sir John Maude, of the British Ministry of Health, was appointed in 1947 to make recommendations for the reform of the structure and finances of Barbadian local government. The details of his report belong to a later stage of our inquiry, but it is worth noting here that among the tax reforms suggested was the abolition of the occupancy tax and of the acreage base for the ownership tax. Further, assessments for the trade tax were to be transferred to the Inland Revenue Department.

II. JAMAICA

The earliest local government Ordinance in Jamaica was that of 1677 establishing (or, more strictly, confirming) fifteen parishes.[1] The early history of local government in Jamaica closely followed that of Barbados. Due to the high qualifications required to exercise a vote, control remained in the hands of a small white (and up to 1834) slave-owning oligarchy. Even after the abolition of slavery the continued domination of this group, both at the centre and in the parishes, made it impossible for reforming Governors to carry out any general scheme of progress or to improve the lot of the ex-slaves. As a result of the attitude of the plantation owners and merchants, the old House of Representatives was abolished in 1865;[2] at the same time the parishes lost their elected boards, which were superseded by appointed bodies. The Colonial Office, acting through the Governor, henceforward exercised more or less Crown

[1] With changing needs the number was increased until it reached twenty-two; from 1867, however, it was again reduced: there are now thirteen parishes.

[2] The constitution had already been within an inch of suspension in 1839 when the House of Representatives virtually went on strike against a Colonial Office instruction to reform the prisons.

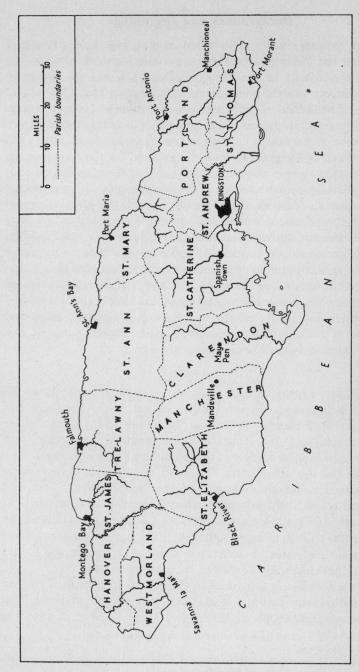

MAP 2. Jamaica.

D

Colony powers—until 1886 when as the result of prolonged agitation the elective principle was partially re-established at the centre and wholly in the Parochial Boards. The final change to adult suffrage in local government took place in 1947.[1]

One of the economic effects of emancipation had been to create a black peasant proprietary, independent of the sugar estates. Over the course of years these yeoman farmers prospered, and after 1886 members of this group increasingly qualified for the franchise. In this way the system of representative government took firm root among a much broader section of the population than was the case in Barbados. Thus among the ordinary folk of Jamaica representative government was already an established institution long before universal suffrage was introduced. Moreover the Parochial Boards developed very much in the British tradition in the sense that the executive officers and the councillors were completely distinct, the former being the servants of the council, and the elected representatives understanding more or less clearly that they must keep their fingers out of the executive pie. Further, there had grown up a viable local tax assessed on the capital value of real estate: on this we shall have more to say later.[2]

III. TRINIDAD

The early history of local government is rather different in the case of Trinidad and British Guiana. Bermuda, the Bahamas, and the Leeward Islands, as well as Barbados and Jamaica, were 'settled colonies', and began with the political rights that were common to English settlers in the seventeenth and eighteenth centuries.[3] On the other hand, Trinidad and British Guiana were 'conquered colonies', captured by the British from Spain and Holland respectively. Government in these two colonies was consequently of Crown Colony type, with power in the hands of the Governor and nominated officials. Any development of local government in these circumstances was not automatic and would have to be specifically conferred by the central executive.

Of the four major territories of the British Carribean, Trinidad has traditionally had the least developed system of rural local government. Although the island had been acquired in 1797 the

[1] Adult suffrage had been introduced at the centre in 1944.
[2] See below, pp. 352–3.
[3] Only in a few of the larger islands did there develop anything remotely like local government outside the principal towns.

first elected member of the Legislature was admitted only in 1925. The counterpart to this direct rule at the centre was a complete absence of local government institutions outside the three urban areas. In 1846 an abortive attempt had been made by the then Governor, Lord Harris, acting on the instructions of the Secretary of State, Earl Grey,[1] to institute something resembling local government in the countryside. Wardens and ward officers were appointed in administrative divisions of the island, known as counties and wards, to collect local taxes to be spent on roads, education, and police, with the advice of nominated boards. But the system soon broke down due to apathy and refusal to pay taxes. By the early 1850's education and police had reverted to central control, and the wardens and ward officers were acting as agents for the central government. In course of time there were established local Health Authorities, local Road Boards, and Public Assistance Boards. The last two bodies were entirely nominated by the Governor, while the local Health Authorities were partly nominated and partly elected on a narrow franchise. These boards were purely advisory and had no legislative nor executive powers. When the Royal Commission visited Trinidad they remarked unfavourably on this position in relation to the other major units, and put it as a matter of urgency that a beginning should be made in developing an adequate system of rural authorities. How, after a rather disappointing start, this was eventually achieved, we shall see in Chapter 9.

Trinidad and British Guiana were unlike the settled islands in that town government had been established at an early stage, and consequently was, and still is, completely outside any system of rural local government, whereas Kingston in Jamaica and Bridgetown in Barbados grew up as part of their respective parish organizations.[2] When the British took over Trinidad the remains of the Spanish town authority, the *Cabildo*, was still functioning; this was reconstituted as a partly elected Town Board in 1840. In 1846, as part of the move to extend local government institutions in the island, a similar board was set up for San Fernando, the second town. Arima, the third town, received its charter in 1888. There is a long history of bad relations between Port of Spain munici-

[1] See below, p. 39 fn.
[2] Under the 1954 Ordinance Bridgetown will be separately organized as a municipal authority.

pality and the island government. The board was caught between increasing duties devolved on it by the island government, and its own inability to evolve an effective system of local revenue. Finally in 1899 the Secretary of State (Joseph Chamberlain) abolished the council because it could not balance its budget. It was not until 1914, after more than a decade of popular agitation, that the elected council was restored. As a condition of restoration it was decreed that the Estimates must be approved by the Governor, although this was not demanded of the other two towns.

IV. BRITISH GUIANA

In Trinidad there was never a compelling reason why local government institutions outside the towns should be established, and so none developed. In British Guiana, on the other hand, circumstances arose which created an imperative need for some form of rural local government as the result of the emancipation of the slaves, and the bankruptcy of many sugar estates which followed on it. In order to understand the connexion between these things, a word must be said on the highly peculiar geography of the territory. About 89% of the population live in the narrow coastal strip, only ten miles wide. Here are to be found the two principal towns of Georgetown (the former Dutch Starbroek) and New Amsterdam.[1] Outside these the population is strung in scattered settlements, alternating with sugar estates, along a coastal road which is the backbone of the whole territory. The houses are on the road, the cultivated lands stretch southward from this into the interior. The coastal strip is three feet below sea-level and the rainfall reaches a hundred inches. Thus for the very existence of the populated area there is a vital double problem of keeping the sea out of the land and of getting the land water safely out into the sea. Inland of the coastal belt population is very sparse (not more than 0·5 per square mile today). A great deal of the country is covered with dense forest leading up to high grasslands on the Brazilian border. The important factor from the point of view of economic and local government development is the highly peculiar coastal situation. Quite unpredictable periods of erosion and accretion succeed one another. During the former, the major problem is to prevent the sea encroaching on the coastal road; so long as population was small, a simple way out was just to move the road farther

[1] The capital of the Dutch colony of Berbice.

inland, but as time went on this became no longer feasible. During the periods of accretion the main problem is to keep the drains open; this is made more difficult by the fact that the exposed mud-banks quickly become riddled and aerated by millions of living organisms, so that the whole coastal mass is rendered highly un-stable. It was only very gradually that the true nature of the problem became apparent.

When the British took over from the Dutch they found a system whereby the frontagers were responsible for sea defence and drain-age. This presumed that there would be sufficient frontagers able and willing to carry out their duties. The history of local govern-ment institutions is largely the history of attempts to secure that local bodies would see that this was done. In the end the task for which Local Authorities had first been created proved too difficult for local government and had to be transferred to the Public Works Department for execution. Later other local services were wanted as well; but the fact that local government proved unequal to its primary task largely explains why the Colony even now possesses no general network of Local Authorities.[1] But the attempts made to solve this basic physical and economic problem at the local level gave rise to a great number of interesting organizational experiments.[2]

The history of local government in British Guiana has been complicated by two factors not present in Barbados or Jamaica. First, the farmers and labourers, discontented with their rents or taxes, early formed the habit of disappearing into the forest, thus threatening the breakdown of any local organization which had been established. Secondly, and partly as a consequence of this instability of the labour force, the sugar and cotton estates found themselves unable to carry on after emancipation without in-dentured labour from India. In 1953 the population included 215,000 of Indian origin as compared with 165,000 of African origin. Thus—quite apart from 18,000 aboriginal Amerindians in the interior—British Guiana has a multi-racial problem to contend with. The chief impact of this, however, appears to be at the national party level; the main body of the East Indians are rice-growing farmers who co-operate reasonably well at the local level.

[1] Such a network was recommended by the Marshall Report of 1955, but as we shall see later (below, pp. 146–7) no action has yet been taken to implement it.
[2] Cf. Allan Young, *Approach to Local Self-Government in British Guiana*, 1958.

The Dutch had left behind them some organization in the two towns, and at the central level two courts,[1] one legislative, but with only a very limited elected element, the other policy-making. In the latter the Governor always commanded a majority, so that right up to the constitutional reforms of the twentieth century the personality of the Governor has been a much more important element in policy than in other colonies. About 80% of the population consisted of ex-slaves and their dependants, and owing to the high qualifications for the franchise these were entirely unrepresented in the legislature up to the late nineteenth century.

Soon after the British took over (1812) the position of the slaves was somewhat ameliorated by an Act of 1825 which allowed them to contract legal marriages and to hold property, but, as in Jamaica, the decisive social and economic change followed emancipation. The sequence of events was, however, very different. In British Guiana emancipation caused an economic crisis; large numbers of the ex-slaves disappeared into the forest, many estates were bankrupted, and the owners left the Colony. This had two results. On the one hand some of the remaining estates started new 'Proprietary' villages of free tenants, in an effort to stabilize the labour force. On the other, groups of peasants clubbed together to buy up abandoned estates on a share basis. With some of the estates continuing to carry on as before, there were thus three types of rural economy; but only in the established estates were sea defence works still carried out effectively. In the free villages not only was it unclear on whom the responsibility really rested; but also the 'shareholding' villagers, having tied up their savings in the purchase of the estate, could not command the necessary resources. Moreover, within a very short time fragmentation of holdings set in. In one village there had been 128 original shareholders; before long they had become 2,000, with consequent deterioration in their ability to perform their obligations.

Successive Governors, always with an eye on sea defence, attempted to deal with the situation piecemeal, by parish or by class of village. In the late 1830's Lord John Russell (who became Secretary of State in 1839) and Sir James Stephen[2] strongly supported local attempts to develop local government institutions by means of a type of voluntary village association with a committee

---

[1] Seeming to correspond broadly with the Leg. Co. and Ex. Co. which succeeded them.   [2] Under Secretary at the Colonial Office.

consisting of a president and seven members. These bodies had the right, on pain of fine by the magistrate, to collect 'subscriptions' for road and bridge works. They had no legal status, but they did serve to keep alive the sense of community, and some survived as late as 1864.

Voluntary subscription quickly proved inadequate, so the next idea was for local Commissions of Roads and Bridges, with the local Justice in the chair and an elective element. (These were thus very similar to the early Boards of Guardians in the United Kingdom.) The then Governor (Walker) suggested that these bodies could appropriately be extended into a general system of District Councils which would also have educational powers. In each District there would be a hospital, dispensary, and workhouse, the whole would be supported by a house tax, based on the number of inmates. Earl Grey at the Colonial Office in 1848[1] was enthusiastic for this plan. His views deserve to be quoted verbatim since they are an excellent statement of the British colonial objective:

I conceive that gradually to prepare them [the Guianese] for a more popular system of government ought to be one of the principal objects of the policy adopted towards them, and it is one of which I never lost sight. It was more particularly with this view that I endeavoured whenever practicable, to create a system of municipal organisation, entertaining a strong conviction that the exercise of the power usually entrusted to municipal bodies is the best training that a population can have for the right usage of a larger measure of political power.

Before the new plan could be implemented, however, Free Trade had caused a disastrous fall in sugar prices. Estate owners attempted to reduce wages, and once again the labour force disappeared into the woods. Although the importation of Indian labour had been sanctioned in 1841, there were not yet enough Indians to replace the Africans; once more estates were abandoned and bought up by Africans. By 1854 the Colony being again prosperous, the Governor (Wodehouse) renewed the attempt to establish a wholly elective system of local councils. They were to prepare their own Estimates and submit them to the District Registrar, a government official. This plan cannot be written down as a failure, but the new system spread only slowly. However, in the 1860's real progress was registered. Under Governor Hinckes, a Central Board of Health was set

---

[1] Secretary of State 1846–52, son of Grey of the Reform Bill.

up, and all the different forms of village organization brought within a system of Sanitary Districts. Hinckes's great achievement was to make villagers willing to pay taxes by offering them health and education services rather than making local government appear to comprise merely onerous tasks. By and large, since Hinckes's time, health services have remained a local responsibility, but increasingly it became necessary to transfer the sea defence services to the Public Works Department. Hinckes's system was so successful that the Colonial Office seriously considered extending it to Jamaica. By a consolidated Ordinance of 1892, the Local Authorities had their powers extended in line with British local institutions, with formal power to levy rates.

Finally, a comprehensive Ordinance in 1907 introduced a Local Government Board of eight appointed members. Four kinds of Local Authority were recognized: the Urban Sanitary Districts of Georgetown and New Amsterdam; Village Districts; Country Districts; Rural Sanitary Districts. The urban authorities were of course elected, the Village Councils might be either elected or appointed, as determined by the Local Government Board, the other Local Authorities were administered: the Country Districts by local staff,[1] the Rural Sanitary Districts directly by the Local Government Board. In spite of this consolidating legislation, considerable survivals of the piecemeal approach remained, and it should be noted that there was no devolution of powers or tiering between any of the authorities. A committee appointed in 1931 to consider how central control over local government institutions could be increased, suggested a two-tier system of County and District Councils, but this was not accepted. In the next year, however, a system of District Commissioners on the African model was introduced. Their chief duties were envisaged as supervising the rural Local Authorities and co-ordinating central departmental activities at the local level. There is no doubt that they have proved their worth, and in the most recent period it is planned to make use of their services to extend local government institutions into the interior.[2]

Thus when the Royal Commission came round the officials could look with pride on the 'sound system of local government

[1] There was provision for a Country District to rise in status, but there was little desire to take on the additional responsibilities which this implied.
[2] In the Marshall Report; see below, pp. 146–7.

which the Colony possesses'. Growth, born of necessity, had indeed been precocious; but three weaknesses remained (and indeed still remain). First, the heterogeneity of the provision for social services; outside the jurisdiction of the Local Authorities estates still provided services very much as they liked, entirely outside government control. Secondly, inland, and even in some coastal districts, there were still large tracts completely without organized services. Thirdly, and most important of all, finances were very weak. This was partly due to diseconomies of small scale. In 1953, of the ninety-two rural Local Authorities, eighty-one had under 3,000 inhabitants; only one (an outer suburb of Georgetown) had over 6,000. Outside the towns little or no money was available for development. In 1954 total local government expenditure amounted to only £622,000, or about 1·7% of the national income. Nearly 70% of this was financed out of rates, and on the whole grants were confined to *ad hoc* aid for specific services or projects.

As in other parts of the West Indies, the administration of the local rate in British Guiana has always left much to be desired. Georgetown rates on annual rental value of land and houses; the government concerns itself neither with valuation nor poundages. This is also true in New Amsterdam, which, however, rates on capital values.[1] In the rural areas valuation is carried out by carpenters, builders, or farmers, appointed by the village committee. In all cases valuations remain well below market prices; in one area there had (in 1955) been no revaluation since 1846. In spite of the interesting and on the whole encouraging history of democratic local government, British Guiana still clearly has an important work of modernization and consolidation to carry through before Local Authorities can pull their weight in development. In Chapter 9 we shall see what changes are proposed to that end.

[1] On the significance of these distinctions, see below, pp. 355 ff.

5

BEGINNINGS IN INDIA AND CEYLON

I. INDIA

LOCAL government in British India, as in the West Indies, began its career in the seventeenth century. The first East India Company was incorporated in 1600; by 1612, in the teeth of Portuguese opposition, it succeeded in establishing a 'factory' (depot) at Surat, on the Gujerat coast. This later developed into the Presidency of Bombay, but not until after a second Presidency had been established at Madras, in the late 1620's.[1] The east coast proved a better trading centre for oriental goods, and the first grant of land in India to the Company was that on which Fort St. George (Madras) stands.[2] The island of Bombay was ceded to Charles II in 1661 as part of Catherine of Braganza's dowry; but Charles failed to observe its strategic importance and within a few years sold it to the Company for £10. The real founder of the city was Governor Aungier, dating from 1669, but it was not until the end of the Mahratta wars opened up the Western Ghat route that its real importance began. Fort William (Calcutta), the third Presidency town, was founded in 1696. Finally in 1708 the rivalries of various British companies trading to India were resolved, and the great East India Company was started on its career. It gradually acquired and ruled over large areas of the sub-continent, up to the Mutiny in 1856.

Nine years before the establishment of Calcutta it had already been decided to set up the first local town council, on British lines, in Madras. This was formally inaugurated in 1688, with a charter similar to that of Portsmouth, from the accident that the Governor of the Company was the Mayor of Portsmouth at the time.[3] It was hoped that the establishment of self-government would increase the propensity of the 'burgesses' to raise taxes for the establishment

[1] For the earlier period, especially, see V. A. Smith, *Oxford History of India*, 3rd ed. 1958; up to 1955 H. Tinker, *The Foundations of Local Self-Government in India, Pakistan and Burma*, 1954, to which I am greatly indebted throughout this chapter. [2] And still houses the local government offices.
[3] Sir Josiah Childs.

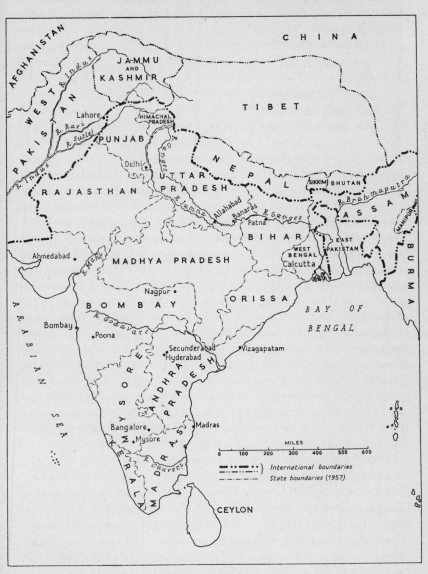

MAP 3. India.

of municipal works and services, a hope that was not fulfilled (merchants are seldom good taxpayers). The council was to be fully elective, with an English Mayor and Recorder,[1] but it was apparently contemplated that there might be an Indian majority on the Court of Aldermen. In 1726 Municipal Councils were established in Bombay and Calcutta, and at the same time a new constitution was given to Madras; but this time there was definitely to be an English majority among the Aldermen.

Thus began the long history of what the Indians like to call 'local self-government'. By 1850 four towns in addition to the Presidencies had received popular institutions; by 1870 the number had increased to 543.[2] Thus the leading towns of India have nearly a century of (more or less) representative local government behind them. Their institutions have been through many experiments and many tribulations, more especially in the 1930's when the combined effect of the Depression and of *swaraj* reduced local government to near chaos even in such important centres as Madras and Calcutta. Over the decades, however, there has grown up in a number of Indian cities a genuine feeling of civic consciousness and responsibility, similar to that of leading British towns.

Outside the towns local government has been less successful. India cannot yet be said to have solved the problem of a general organization of representative bodies covering the whole country, though it may now be just on the threshold of doing so. We have seen that local government in the West Indies inevitably suffers from the difficulties and diseconomies of small scale. In India it has all along suffered from the opposite malady. Time after time a good policy, started with enthusiasm, failed to touch more than a quarter, or even a tenth, of the areas it was planned to cover, before political or economic disaster caused it to be abandoned.

Indian experience in the development of local government institutions is highly relevant for later comers, partly because of its long period of experimentation; but also for the fact that there was very little in the way of indigenous local government institutions from which to start building. Consequently, as in the West Indies, British administrators had to fall back on the home model. For most of the development of Indian local government institutions

[1] As in British towns at that period the corporation was, in addition to its local government duties, a judicial body. See also pp. 46, 47.

[2] Tinker, op. cit., pp. 30–31.

the area that is relevant is that of the former British India. The political officers maintained at the princes' courts for advice and what would now be called public relations, did not wield the power later exercised by Residents in Nigeria or Malaya. Enlightened princely states, such as Mysore and Hyderabad, did however foster a growth of local government institutions parallel to those growing up in British India.

The development of local government institutions in India has suffered all along from the fact that, owing to the vast size of the country, the central government has only been able to encourage local government at second hand, through the provincial governments. This was true even in the days of highly centralized administration, long before a federal constitution was contemplated. This delegation of authority was due not merely to the large size of the country, and consequent difficulty of communications, but also to the chronic shortage of personnel, a shortage that was all the more disastrous because of the rapid turnover of administrators at all levels. Further difficulties have been language, and other ethnic and cultural differences. In combination these eventually made a federal constitution inevitable.

The fact that provincial—now State—governments have been responsible for local affairs has resulted in the first place in programmes and policies being applied irregularly and piecemeal; and secondly in a situation in which it is extremely difficult for the central government or for any state (or for that matter for the investigator), to know what was happening elsewhere, or to achieve a general picture of the whole. Although since Partition there has been no true racial problem in India, the long drawn out struggle between Indians and Moslems, and the effects of the rigid caste system, still exert an influence such as is exercised by multi-racial pressures in Ceylon, Malaya, and parts of Africa.

The only true indigenous local government institution which the British found in India was the village council or panchayat.[1] It is difficult to get a balanced view of this pre-Moghul institution, since clearly panchayats differed greatly in size and vitality from one part of the subcontinent to another. Generally speaking panchayats in the north were much damaged by the centralizing tendencies first of the Moghul and later of the British administration.

---

[1] Literally Council of Five, the Sanskrit *panch* being equivalent to the Greek *pente*, as in pentagon.

In the south there had been less interference and it could still be said that 'the panchayat is God'. As has often happened in the course of history, enthusiastic British administrators coming on an indigenous organization with some vitality, tended not only to equate it with institutions with which they were already familiar,[1] but also to assume its generality over areas which had not yet been investigated.

Thus Metcalfe wrote hopefully of the 'little republics' which he had found flourishing in the country between Agra and Delhi, in the twilight between the Moghul and the British administrations, assuming them to be a general phenomenon. In fact in that region they had been born (or reborn) of the necessity for a defence organization against raiders from the neighbouring desert. They were confined to quite a small area. In the north especially, panchayats tended to be based on caste and religion and rarely covered the whole community. Nevertheless since all their deliberations were held in the open *panchayagarh*,[2] public opinion did count for something. Whatever strength these surviving panchayats may have had, they gradually decayed in the face of the government's centralizing policy, first of 'John Company', and later of the India Office. This was a system which deliberately sought contact with the individual directly rather than through his representatives.

The panchayat organization probably touched rock bottom in the 1850's and 1860's; but by that time, as we have seen, urban self-government was getting firmly established. From a very early stage the larger towns had a substantial resident alien population of traders and so on; they thus differed fundamentally in character from the smaller towns in rural areas. (In some respects the situation was thus somewhat similar to that now existing in East and Central Africa and in Malaya.) This accounts for the different course which the development of local government institutions has taken in the larger towns and the rest of the country respectively.

The first attempt to generalize the institutions already set up in the Presidency towns was an enabling Act of 1850 under which Provinces were encouraged to establish Municipal Boards. By 1858

[1] Another illustration would be their equation of the Buganda Lukiko with some form of parliament; see below, p. 115.
[2] Assembly place, sometimes open, sometimes partly roofed, now often housing the village radio set.

Bombay state had established about fourteen of these and was far ahead of other areas. Outside Bombay the most successful promotion at this stage was at Vizagapatam in Madras Province (now in Andhra state). Later, under the stimulus of provincial Municipal Acts,[1] progress became more rapid.

It should be noted, however, that the Municipal Boards contained no elective element; they were in fact the body of local Justices. In the large towns this system produced a quite unwieldy body: Calcutta corporation numbered 129, Bombay 400. The actual business of local government was organized by a new office: that of Municipal Commissioner, which, from that time has (as we shall see) played a key role in urban government. This office (extended also to Ceylon and Malaya) is without parallel in the West Indies or in Africa, although naturally it has many affinities with the more familiar office of Town Clerk. In form the Indian town organization was not much behind that of contemporary Britain. Even after the passing of the Municipal Corporations Act in 1835 the Justices still played a substantial role in urban affairs.

Local financial institutions developed *pari passu* with political organization. Under the Act of 1850 the towns were given a fairly wide range of tax powers.[2] Some were modifications of previous Mahratta, Moghul, or Sikh indirect taxes. In addition, and especially where there were few such accustomed levies, a tax on house and land vaguely modelled on the British local rate, was introduced (usually in the face of great opposition). Only in the Presidency towns was there any attempt at professional valuation. The indirect tax in Mahratta and Moghul areas (especially Bombay, United Provinces, Punjab, and Central Provinces) was a descendant of the Moghul/Mahratta *Muhtarafa*, a tax on trade and transit. It developed into the powerful but objectionable *octroi* which even today dominates municipal finances in these parts.

Outside the organized towns land revenue had become firmly established by the 1830's.[3] It was assessed and collected in Districts set up primarily for this purpose. In some areas the District Office was assisted by local committees, but these can hardly be regarded as local government organs. The land revenue was for long the pillar of central government finances and for even longer remained the chief support of provincial governments. From 1840, however,

[1] See below, pp. 49–50.   [2] See below, Chap. 14.
[3] See below, Chap. 15.

permission was given to levy a *cess*[1] or additional poundage on it for local purposes, so that from the middle of the century it became effectively a shared tax.

Owing very largely to administrative problems due to size, the history of the development of local government institutions in India from the time of the Mutiny unfolds itself very broadly as a seesaw struggle between the forces of centralization on grounds of efficiency and economy, and repeated attempts at decentralization or devolution[2] on grounds partly of still further economy (by transferring more financial responsibility on to lower layer governments), partly of a genuine belief in the benefits of local control. There has thus been a succession of periods of the strengthening of local institutions, followed by periods of stagnation and even reversal of this policy. The story can only be sketched here in the briefest outline.

Although it is instructive in a number of ways, it makes rather depressing reading at a superficial view. This is not really the right judgement; at each round the receding tide of decentralization left behind it rather firmer and more extensive ground. It must always be borne in mind that India with her long tradition of submissive philosophy, her ideal of contemplation rather than activity (quite apart from her difficult sociological and economic problems), has presented a much greater challenge in political education for democracy and development than that posed in some other Commonwealth countries. A great many West Africans passionately want the twentieth century; on the whole relatively few Indians do so.

Counting the tremendous effort after Independence (which we shall examine in Chapter 10), there have been five separate drives to strengthen local institutions and to awaken a sense of active local interest. The first occurred as a result of the reorientation of policy towards India which succeeded the Mutiny and transfer of power from the East India Company to the British government. The Mutiny had left Indian finances very depleted, and the inelasticity of land revenue (as organized) was already being discovered. James Wilson was sent out by Whitehall to pull Indian finances back into order. Provincial legislatures were established with Legislative and Executive Councils. Wilson proposed (in the

---

[1] On the use of the word cess see p. 292 below.
[2] Defining *decentralization* as control by localized branches of central departments and *devolution* as the transfer of control to lower level governments.

budget speech of 1861) to transfer responsibility for roads and public works to these, leaving the provincial legislatures to make their own arrangements in detail. This established a most important precedent.

There was an immediate response to these proposals from the Punjab, where the Governor, Sir Robert Montgomery, started (without legal warrant) creating Municipal Committees of members chosen for their personal qualities or selected by trade panchayats (and thus including no British officials), in order to carry out municipal improvements. Before 1864 forty-nine of such committees had been constituted. There was considerable enthusiasm, and some were notably successful. Thus Lahore municipality raised a local loan[1] to shift back the course of the river Ravi closer to the town, so as to provide a much needed water supply.

The new policy had the support, both in its financial and in its local government aspects, not only of the home government but also of the Government of India. A dispatch of the Secretary of State had proposed the development of education[2] and of local government institutions. The cost of the Mutiny had convinced British politicians that India must pay her way to a greater extent than hitherto, and in turn the Government of India felt it necessary for its own viability that a greater share of taxes should be collected provincially or locally, and correspondingly greater duties assumed by the Provinces and towns.

This was a perfectly reasonable policy, especially given the difficulties which central officers still had in reaching remote parts; but it was of course liable to abuse, especially at the provincial level where the real responsibility for making the arrangements lay. Thus local bodies were created in Bengal for the sole purpose of collecting funds to support the local police (*chaukudari*). Under Governor Lord Lawrence's Resolution of 1864 municipal institutions with substantial tax rights were offered to any town that would pay for its police. A little later, under Lord Mayo, the provinces were required to take over responsibility for education, roads, and certain medical services. Following on these moves from the centre a number of provincial Municipal Acts were passed, often including

[1] Tinker, op. cit., p. 35.
[2] Universities had been started in the Presidency towns in 1856, as part of the mid-Victorian system of Queens' colleges. They consequently celebrated their centenaries in 1956/7.

the power to introduce an elective element into Municipal Committees.

This policy was in the true tradition of Victorian liberalism, which, even while it had an eye on economy—at home as well as overseas—did firmly believe in the educational and psychological virtues of autonomous local government. The speeches both of Lord Lawrence and of Lord Mayo amply illustrate this element in British policy;[1] and it had its reward. A new class of educated Indians was growing up in some parts, imbued with British liberal ideals, but beginning to demand a share in shaping their own destinies.

The first manifestation of this new spirit was in Bombay city, where the large and wealthy Parsee community was already developing the remarkable civic consciousness for which they have ever since been conspicuous. In 1872 their leader, P. S. Mehta, the first great figure in Indian local government, obtained from the provincial legislature an Act which contained two important innovations. In the first place there was to be a compulsory elective element in the city council. Half was to be directly elected, and one-quarter indirectly by the councillors; consequently only a quarter of the members would be appointed. Secondly, a 'standing committee' of the council was to be set up to undertake the major work of the council and to control the Municipal Commissioner. This committee has become a leading and indispensable feature of Indian urban government. In Bombay its control of the Commissioner has always been very real, distinctly more so than elsewhere. The foundations of autonomous and responsible local government thus firmly laid in Bombay have endured and flourished with only minor emendations right down to the present. Of no other Indian city can this be said.

Apart from Bombay province, the work of Lawrence, Mayo, and their followers did not lead to the hoped for general development of Indian local government. Few towns introduced any elective element. Their finances remained woefully inadequate and were not infrequently strangled by provincial importunities. As a whole

[1] For instance Lord Lawrence: 'The people of this country are perfectly capable of administering their own local affairs. The municipal feeling is deeply rooted in them. The village communities . . . are the most abiding of Indian institutions. . . . Holding the position we do in India, every view of duty and policy should induce us to leave as much as possible of the business of the country to be done by the people.' *Gazette of India*, 14 Sept. 1864, quoted in Tinker, op. cit., p. 36.

the growing Indian middle class had not yet awoken to civic consciousness. Both they and the local British residents were more interested in avoiding taxes than in economic or social development.

The second drive to activate local government in India was launched by Viscount Ripon in May 1882. For a Viceroy Ripon had had an exceptionally advanced background. He had early been associated with F. D. Maurice and the Christian Socialists; he also had close contacts with A. O. Hume, a retired Indian official and grandson of Joseph Hume, the Radical politician. The basic principle of the Ripon proposals was that 'political education is the primary function of local government, of greater importance than administrative efficiency'.[1] Ripon's aim was to establish a general network of Local Authorities throughout the country, getting right away from a system which only touched the larger towns.

Outside the towns India was (as we have seen) divided into 'Collector's Districts'. The areas of these had been drawn up for judicial and fiscal purposes, with no thought that they might ever have a functional place in a system of local government. Even for these specific purposes many of the Districts were on the large side, due to personnel shortages. Ripon's plan was to set up Rural Boards, similar to the Municipal Boards, for manageable units: Tahsils, Taluks, or (where there were in existence no such minor areas) in Districts divided *ad hoc*. The boards were to contain a two-thirds unofficial majority, and it was contemplated that the members would eventually all be elected.

In the more progressive towns the elective principle was to be adopted immediately, and was to spread gradually by informal experimentation. So far as possible chairmen were to be non-officials, and officials were to endeavour to let the boards run themselves, confining their activities to advice and steering from outside, just as Government Agents do in West Africa today.[2] Within these general principles the provinces were left to work out the precise details as best suited to their particular conditions.

The reaction of provincial administrations to these plans was very mixed, much influenced by the outlook of particular Governors. At the District Officers' level the reception was almost entirely hostile; here paternalism was still dominant. Indeed at the rural

[1] Resolution on Local Self-Government, May 1862, para. 5.
[2] See below, p. 447.

level the plan was never really put into effect. The first brave attempt to breathe life into the dying panchayats was an almost complete failure. A certain number of towns tried rather half-heartedly to introduce the elective principle. Where elections were held they were nearly always run on a caste or religious (Hindu/ Moslem) base, not on a territorial ward system. (In this, as in other matters, the city of Bombay was a notable exception.) Further, most board members were lawyers, whose professional outlook was not conducive to a forward policy. Indeed some of the towns after the experience of a few elections abandoned them completely. In 1906 Mr. G. K. Gokhale, then the greatest figure in Indian local government, could assert: 'Local government remains where it was placed by Ripon; in some places it has even been pushed back.'

The causes of the recession of this second tide of reform are complicated. In spite of their progressive outlook, the reformers, and even Ripon himself, lacked drive. Ripon was perfectly correct in seeing clearly that 'an outlet for the ambitions and aspirations created by British civilisation' among the growing Indian middle class was an urgent necessity; but neither he nor his supporters could bring themselves to believe that, once the avenues were properly opened, local government institutions would not evolve of themselves, just as they were considered to have done in nineteenth-century Britain. In the rural areas, again looking back to British experience, they looked ever hopefully for the 'natural leaders of the people'[1] (meaning thereby the landlord class), to come forward and shoulder the burden of making responsible Local Authorities work.

In practice few administrators were prepared to put political education above efficiency, and they were not encouraged in the path of reform by succeeding Viceroys: Elgin, Dufferin, Lansdowne, or Curzon, irrespective of whether they were formerly Liberal or Conservative. Under Curzon's efficient but highly centralized government, officials, especially in branches of the central departments, were finding a new interest in the development of communications and other public works. These were indeed of very great economic importance to the country, but they

---

[1] Just as in the early days (going back to Cornwallis's 'Permanent Settlements' of 1798), it was confidently anticipated that, unless they were too heavily taxed, the landlords would provide the investment and drive for a reformed Indian agriculture; see below, Chap. 15.

did not come in contact with local government. The central government was also, from the middle 1880's, itself in severe financial straits. The Afghan wars emptied the Treasury, while at the same time the continued fall in the value of silver, to which the Indian rupee was tied, also had an adverse effect on the Indian budget.

Nevertheless by the 1890's, in Bombay, Bengal, and Madras at least, elections—although still with a limited franchise—had come to be regarded as the normal method of filling a board. Moreover the Ripon leaven was still working, although somewhat quietly. An increasing number of educated Indians were seeing the light. Gokhale voiced their feelings when he wrote: 'we value local self-government for the fact that it teaches men of different castes and creeds, who have long been kept apart, to work together for a common purpose'.[1] In view of all this it was especially unfortunate that the central government should by then have been sailing on the opposite tack.

The Liberal government which took office in the United Kingdom in 1906 at once tried to do something to reverse the trend of official policy. A Royal Commission on Decentralization was appointed in 1907, and reported in 1909. John Morley, the Secretary of State, took a very great interest in its deliberations. Although nothing much came of it in the end, this episode has the right to be counted as the third drive to instil life into Indian local government institutions.

The Commission diligently collected a mass of evidence concerning the working of local government and made it clear (along the lines sketched above) why things had not worked out as Ripon anticipated. The recommendations of the Commission themselves were not particularly helpful; they have a slightly unreal and doctrinaire flavour, suggesting that in spite of the evidence collected, neither Morley nor the members really understood India as Ripon had done. There is little evidence that they recognized the fundamental change that was taking place in Indian public opinion.

Three matters of some importance, however, did emerge, as an aftermath, if not as a direct result, of the Commission's deliberations. In the first place increased grants from the home government were made available to the government of India, and some of these were filtered through the Provinces to local government. Secondly the Commission devoted much attention to furthering Ripon's policy of revivifying panchayats. These small village units were to

[1] Tinker, op. cit.

be set up wherever possible, and were planned to undertake road construction, to build schools, and so on. Pilot schemes were to be tried out in selected areas, very much on the plan of the post-independence Community Development movement.[1] Nothing much seems to have come of this, and by 1912 little was left of the experiment.

Finally (more at the provincial than at the local level however), following the Commission's inquiries, there emerged a burst of enthusiasm for education. It is significant for the future of local government that the main interest in education was confined to a demand for secondary education. The rising middle class were anxious above all that their sons should qualify for clerical and professional jobs. The poor had as yet no educational ambitions, and by and large there was no demand for mass education. Even today the urge for the extension of primary education comes more from above than from below.[2] Such developments as ensued from the Decentralization Report were rudely cut short by the outbreak of war.

Perhaps the most significant effect of the first world war on India was the way in which it accelerated and precipitated political changes which had gradually been building up for some decades. Before the war ended it was clear both in London and Simla, that the grant of a considerable degree of autonomy would be inevitable. The first official recognition of this was the British government's Declaration of August 1917, promising 'responsible government' to India through 'the gradual development of self-governing institutions'. The Viceroy, Lord Chelmsford, expanded on this in a speech to the Central Legislative Council the following month: 'The domain of urban and rural self government is the great training ground from which political progress and a sense of responsibility have taken their start.'

The Secretary of State, Edwin Montagu, himself came to India and together with the Viceroy worked out the scheme of reform (popularly known as the 'Montford' programme), which in the event has provided the basis for all further schemes of constitutional reform in India, not excluding the Government of India Act, 1935, on which the present Indian Constitution is largely based. The Montford reforms constitute the fourth and greatest

[1] See below, Chap. 21.
[2] Cf. the distribution of local expenditure in Indian budgets, Chap. 13.

drive in pre-independence days to establish a general system of responsible local government, although their primary objective was at the provincial rather than at the local level. The proposed reforms (which were announced in 1920), established something very similar to what would now be called 'internal self-government' (the stage that has since preceded independence in a number of former colonies). 'Provincial autonomy' and 'dyarchy' were expressions used to describe the new—and effectively revolutionary—system.

We are not concerned with the constitutional changes in detail, but only in so far as they affected local government. In principle there was a complete reversal of policy. The whole responsibility for local government, both urban and rural, was transferred to the provinces and taken right out of the hands of officials, whether District Officers or members of central departments. By 1923 all officials had withdrawn and the local branches of central departments had also disappeared. Complete freedom and self-determination was apparently substituted at one blow for an exceptionally tight system of control. At the same time the franchise was substantially widened at all levels.

In reality the change was not so great as appeared. A number of the reforms had already been mooted or attempted under Ripon. In several of the more important provinces there had been a considerable loosening up since the Decentralization Report in 1909. There had been new Municipal Acts and a gradual increase of elected members. Nevertheless the Montford reforms were the beginning of a new era, in local as in central government.

The results of the new freedom differed very much from one part of the country to another. Elections on the new franchise returned Liberal majorities imbued with the 'right' ideas in the United Provinces, Bombay, and the Punjab; in Madras an 'anti-Brahmin' majority followed much the same route. Real advances in urban government were made in some towns, more especially where really first-class leaders emerged, such as Vallabhbhai Patel at Ahmedabad and Jawarharlal Nehru at Allahabad. Again, some District Boards made valiant efforts to get such basic services as elementary education and indigenous medicine into the villages. Further attempts to revive panchayats were fairly general.

On the whole in the 1920's local government struggled manfully and hopefully. Much useful experience was in fact built up, provincial finances also suffered severely from this cause. There was, however, room for energy and experimentation in the panchayats and districts as well as in the towns, but there is no evidence of initiative in this direction.

Nevertheless a real appreciation of the benefits and potentialities of local government was gradually emerging, at least from the time of the Report on Decentralization, and this was much quickened by the Montford reforms. This is perhaps the most cheering aspect of the whole story. In the early 1920's an Institute of Local Self-Government was established in Bombay; by 1927 it had started giving short training courses. Although these were too slight to solve the staffing problem, they were at least a beginning. The greater awareness of local government as a national force was signalized by the foundation of the All India Union of Local Authorities in 1936.

II. CEYLON

Ceylon, like India, is a country with a long tradition of indigenous institutions to which she has clung tenaciously, through many changes in the governing régime. On the whole these traditions were less disrupted by early invaders than were those of India. The Europeans, first Portuguese and later Dutch, attempted little more than coastal forts, while the Tamils who settled in the north and east, and to some extent in the mountainous centre (the last independent King of Kandy was a Tamil), were more akin to the Sinhalese[1] than were the Moghuls to the Hindus. In addition, with an importance quite transcending their numbers there were the 'burghers', a mixed race of Sinhalese/Portuguese and Sinhalese/Dutch, almost exclusively Christian. To these there was no real Indian parallel; the Anglo-Indians being very few in number and of no importance until after independence. The thread of tradition thus held more firmly in Ceylon than in India. On the other hand today Ceylon finds itself with more of a racial problem than post-partition India.

European occupied (coastal) Ceylon was taken from the Dutch by the troops of the East India Company during the French wars. The task was completed by the capture of Colombo in 1796. Apart from trade prospects, which were clearly favourable, the

[1] Anthropologists agree that the Sinhalese were themselves almost certainly immigrants from India.

presence of a magnificent natural harbour at Trincomalee on the
north-east coast made it unlikely that the British would be willing
to give up the island at the end of the war. At first it was subject
to military rule, but after two and a half years of this régime it was
given a civil Governor, responsible to the Governor of Madras. He
was supported by civil servants transferred from Madras.

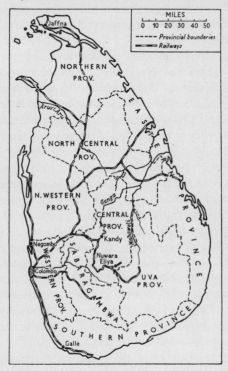

MAP 4. Ceylon.

At the time of the assumption of authority by the British,[1] the
traditional system of local administration by headmen (*mudeliars*)
and assistant headmen had not been disrupted in the low country,
that is the coastal areas in the west and south (subject to the south-
west monsoon) and the 'dry zone' of the north and east (subject
to the variable north-east monsoon). The south-west, outside
of the towns, was almost exclusively Sinhalese, the north-east

[1] For the early period especially I am much indebted to Sir Charles Collins,
Public Administration in Ceylon, 1951.

on the other hand contained substantial settlements of Tamils, and some 'Moors' ultimately of Arabian origin. In all these areas the major headmen at least were recruited from the wealthiest and most respected families. The local government—so far as it can be regarded as such—had a marked feudal tinge, especially as land tenure was on a service basis. It is abundantly evident, however, that the rural Ceylonese regarded the headmen as the proper people both to look after their local interests and to represent their needs to higher authority.

This traditional Ceylon local government did not accord with Madras ideas, where the system of Collectors' Districts was already firmly established. The Madras civil servants consequently decided to abolish the mudeliars and to substitute the Indian system of Districts. To hasten the change Indian Tamils, who knew the ropes, were brought over from Malabar; and *Katcheries* (as the offices were called) were set up throughout the coastal districts. Service tenure was abolished, and in place, taxes on paddy lands (the basic source of food) and on coconut palms were introduced.

This move was doubly unpopular in Ceylon; the presence of the 'foreigners' from India was resented, as were the new taxes, especially on paddy lands, while the abolition of the headmen struck at the roots of one of the firmest and most popular indigenous institutions. The immediate consequence was widespread rioting. Even in the face of this rebuff the Madras government was determined that the new system must be retained; eventually, however, it was forced to give way, the mudeliars and the service tenures were restored (the latter only temporarily). But the Katcheries remained—and still remain.

Enough had by this time occurred to convince the British government that Ceylon traditions were incompatible with Indian administration. In 1802 the island was constituted a Crown Colony, divorced entirely from the East India Company and with a central staff of its own. For the first twelve years or so administration was complicated by the persistence of the independent kingdom of Kandy in the middle of the island, and even after this was transferred to British control (1815) the administration of the high lands remained for many years separate from that of coastal areas, a Board of Commissioners taking the place of Katchery officers. Indeed, but for a Kandyan rebellion in 1817, a system of indirect rule under Kandyan chiefs might well have been established. This might conceivably have leaned more in the (of course much later) African direction than the Indian, as the chiefs were less powerful than most Indian princes and would have more easily been kept under control. As it was, the influence of the chiefs gradually dwindled away, and this would probably have occurred whatever the institutions established in 1815.

In the meantime steps towards social, economic, and political development in the coastal areas had already been made. The Committee of Inquiry set up at the time of the transfer from the East India Company became the foundation of the Governor's (Advisory) Council which lasted until the establishment of Ex. Co. and Leg. Co. in 1833. From the earliest times the administration had shown its anxiety to protect and to help the local inhabitants. The Government Agents and their assistants were bidden to go on circuit in their areas to make themselves familiar with the local people and their needs, and so gradually to reduce the autocratic powers of the mudeliars. The administration early recognized the importance of maintaining irrigation and of opening up the old tanks which were badly decayed. The first step towards the creation of an Education Department had been taken as early as 1803 under the first Governor (Barnes). Education received a great fillip from the coming of the Protestant Missions about 1812. The success of this popular aspect of Christianity, however, alarmed the Buddhist priests, and was partly if not principally responsible for the Kandyan rebellion of 1817. At about the same time as the Missions arrived the country began to be opened up by European plantations which eventually changed the whole face of the island and enormously added to its wealth. Under Governor Barnes a great improvement was made in communications and other aspects of the infra-structure, thus greatly facilitating the marketing of plantation crops. This was achieved at remarkably low cost, by means of 'voluntary' labour (which seems to have been reasonably free will), stiffened by a mobile corps of professional 'pioneers'. By mid-century the days were long past when it was a *promotion* for the Governor (Sir Thomas Maitland, second Governor) to be transferred from Ceylon to Corfu, as it had been in 1815.

A step in constitutional advance which affected both central and local government came with the Report of the Colebrooke (one man) Commission in 1831. Ex. Co. and Leg. Co. were established. The latter contained non-officials, so nominated as to be representative of different groups, which now included European plantation owners as well as Sinhalese, Tamils, and Burghers. At the same time the Kandyan administration was consolidated with the coastal areas, the whole island was divided into Provinces, each subdivided into Districts. Through changes made for administrative convenience there had come by 1889 to be nine Provinces and these have remained unaltered to the present. Indeed the Colebrooke Constitution endured with little alteration of any kind until 1912. A class of educated Ceylonese was rapidly growing up even before the mid-century and local newspapers were already channelling public opinion. An important innovation (from 1870) was the submission to Leg. Co. of a limited part of the Extraordinary (developmental) Estimates. Gradually the range of these were widened, but neither then, nor even much later, was any responsibility transferred; thus Ceylonese leaders had no opportunities of learning gradually the art of government. In spite of this progress and the introduction of many new crops, the middle years of the century were on the whole years of stagnation. The country suffered badly from the British depression in the 1840's. This was accompanied by a serious deterioration in the calibre of the administration, due to economy measures. Further attempts to make the Colony independent of Treasury subsidy led finally to rebellion in 1848.

By the mid-1850's, however, a very great improvement was apparent. The next two decades brought many advances. The disastrous economy experiments in the civil service were abandoned, road communications were improved, Colombo harbour was constructed, and the repair of tanks pushed forward with more vigour. The success of the introduction of new crops was apparent in the fact that the Colony no longer required aid from the British Treasury; revenue was sufficient to cover not only current services but also a substantial amount of development.

These improvements were accompanied by an important development in local government. Under the Irrigation Ordinance of 1856 the old (and very shadowy) village committees (*gam sabhawas*) were revived. By an Ordinance of 1871 their powers were extended. The government guaranteed to find teachers for every school built by a village. More secure in their prospects and finding it easier to get about their districts, the Government Agents were coming truly to represent their people in very much the same way as District Officers have in Africa more recently. Further developments at the local end were the establishment of (nominated) local Boards of Health as a result of a disastrous outbreak of smallpox in Colombo. These were followed by local Road Committees elected on a communal basis. (It must be borne in mind how very limited was the elective element in British local government at this stage.)

These extensions culminated with the Municipal Councils Ordinance of 1865, arranging for the establishment of mixed councils in which the elective element must exceed the nominated. These were given broadly the contemporary powers of British boroughs. Colombo quickly became a municipality, shortly followed by Kandy and Galle. Two further extensions of urban local government were made before the end of the century. A second Local Boards Health Ordinance (1876) made provision for partly elective committees in smaller towns, under chairmanship of the Government Agent or his assistant. Finally (1892) the Sanitary Board Ordinance provided a type of local government for still smaller towns. Education had received further encouragement from the establishment of Directors of Public Instruction in 1871 and although the Great Depression of the 1870's slowed up for a time economic development, the building of schools in the villages went steadily forward. Further, the establishment of a system of village dispensaries (on the Irish model) greatly added to the possibility of improving the health of the rural population.

Alongside these encouraging features there were more disquieting signs. The traditional headman system did not tie up well with local government reforms. Moreover there was a growing class which now resented the feudal element, though many, probably most, villagers still clung tenaciously to old traditions. It was the job of the headmen to act as assistants to the Government Agent; but senior headmen (who were assumed to be wealthy men) received no more than out of pocket expenses, while minor headmen were completely unpaid. This meant on the whole that they neither could nor would do a good job in the new system. But what should be put in their place? The problem of getting local government services properly attended to was eventually solved (but not till near the end of the British régime) by substituting for the headmen Divisional Revenue Officers recruited by competitive examination and subject to posting in any area. This modernization, however, broke the local chain of communication, which the headman system had preserved.

As we shall see, the break with traditional authorities in Ceylon local government exhibited many of the troubles which were much later experienced in several parts of Africa. Although the Ceylonese headman was by no means parallel to the traditional African chief (particularly in that he had no ritual or religious duties, all of which belonged to the Buddhist priesthood), he was in a rather similar way to the African chief, the father of his people.

Ceylon was naturally affected by the wave of anti-colonialism which characterized the British Liberal government in the 1860's. Its immediate effect, however, was somewhat different from that in Africa. It principally showed itself in a demand that Ceylon should pay for all such defence expenditure as was considered to be necessary by the British High Command. This demand led directly to the establishment of a politically minded 'Ceylon League', pressing immediately for the control of the whole (not only of the 'Extraordinary') budget by Leg. Co., and in the longer run for complete self-government. The British government was in a dilemma, since although it was not particularly averse to this in principle it was reluctant to put much responsibility into the hands of what was still a small minority. It was felt that the League was not sufficiently in touch with the mass of the population outside Colombo to represent them adequately. The educated minority, it is true, included as well as the planter element a rapidly expanding group in business and in the professions of 'English educated' Ceylonese, including both Sinhalese and Tamils. This element was recognized as being sufficiently important and homogeneous to be given separate representation in Leg. Co. in the first decade of the twentieth century. This element was more Westernized than any parallel group in India, and throughout the first war the island was exceptionally loyal to the British cause. Nevertheless, the educated intellectuals were by no means behind others in demanding 'complete popular self-government' in 1919.[1] This was obviously an effect of the Congress movement in India.

Since their interest for local government is slight, we need not follow through the successive stages of political progress embodied in the constitutions of 1912 (the first change since 1833), 1920, 1924, 1931 (Donoughmore and 1946 (Soulbury), culminating

[1] From telegram sent to the British government in 1919.

in Dominion status to which the Soulbury Constitution led directly. The repercussions of these political changes on local government were not direct except (as we shall see) in respect of the Donoughmore Constitution. They register a crescendo of power awarded to the unofficial representatives, and especially to the Finance Committee (introduced under Governor McCallum before the first war). Under the Donoughmore Constitution this became (contrary to intention) a kind of cabinet, habitually by-passing the State Council of which it was a subcommittee. Yet (because of the government's apprehension which we have noted above) it continued to be denied any real responsibility, since unofficial members could not hold office. This unhappy arrangement continued to deprive the Ceylonese leaders of the opportunity for training in self-government which their opposite numbers in India were by this time getting in the large towns.

The Donoughmore Constitution has a double interest for the development of local government. It was a unique experiment of applying the essence of the British organization of a Local Authority council at the central level. The State Council was planned to be both executive and legislative. On the executive side it was intended that it would work through committees which would report to the whole council, just as the Standing Committees of the London County Council report to the whole council. (The commission professed, however, that it was basing its ideas on the League of Nations organization rather than on that of the London County Council.) This idea of transplanting that subtle organism of British local government, the committee system,[1] without previous training or experience, was a dismal failure so far as its immediate objective was concerned. As we have seen, the committees, and especially the Finance Committee, by-passed the full council and went straight to the Governor. Further, and in the longer run perhaps more seriously, one may reasonably hazard that this experience has made it specially difficult for Ceylon politicians to grasp the idea of joint cabinet responsibility. The political troubles of 1958 and 1959–60 revealed that this lesson had not yet been learnt.

It is frequently argued that the committee system is a *sine qua non* of the British local government system, and that it cannot be transplanted. Hence it is argued that the attempt to introduce the

[1] See above, p. 23.

British system of local government, for instance in Africa, is fore-doomed to failure. This is a matter on which we shall have a good deal to say later on. It can be argued, however, that the Ceylon experiment is largely irrelevant because of the extreme weakness of indigenous democratic institutions.

So far as local government institutions are concerned the establishment of a Department of Local Government under the Donoughmore Constitution gave a decided stimulus to development in both urban and rural areas. Assistant commissioners under the department were established to take over the supervision of local councils from Government Agents. At the village level the committees were brought nearer to the people and given the right to elect their own chairmen. The Sanitary Board urban grade of Local Authority was abolished, and superseded by urban or (for smaller areas) town councils, with all elective membership. The three municipalities of Colombo, Kandy, and Galle were granted fully elective councils, and an elected Mayor, in place of the previous official chairman. Hence, in principle from this time, the island has been covered with a network of local councils and committees elected on a wide franchise. The structure is, however, an even more artificial creation than in India, where not only were indigenous local institutions stronger in some rural areas, but long familiarity with town government had created a democratic tradition before the arrival of independence.

In fact, local government in Ceylon has never caught fire, and this makes it difficult to collect revenue, which is chronically in arrears. Indeed, finance has all along been the weakest link in a weak chain. The entire autonomous revenue of all Local Authorities in Ceylon in 1954 did not exceed £5 m. At a later stage we shall have to discuss why better results were not achieved and whether energy can yet be breathed into this somewhat inert body.

6

THE AFRICAN BACKGROUND:
TRIBAL AUTHORITY AND INDIRECT RULE

I

THE development of local government in British Africa—
West, East, and Central Africa that is, for South Africa is
another story, with which we are not concerned—hinges, to
a remarkable extent, upon one single episode. When, in 1894, the
Emirs of Northern Nigeria were subdued by Lugard, he devised
for the administration of that territory the system which became
known as Indirect Rule; a system deliberately devised, and
expressly conceived to suit African conditions. In the years which
followed his example was widely followed throughout British
Africa. One by one the other territories followed suit, adapting
Lugard's plan to their own needs and circumstances as best they
could. (The process was not completed until just before the second
world war; Northern Rhodesia and Nyasaland did not adopt the
relevant ordinance until 1936; Sierra Leone until 1937.) In the
process of adaptation the concept of Indirect Rule underwent considerable changes; it did not mean at all precisely the same thing
in one territory as it did in another. But in almost all of the territories with which we shall be concerned, it is a recognizable phase;
and it is the foundation on which all further developments in local
government have been built.

The principal reason for the differences which emerged between
Indirect Rule in one territory and in another is to be found in the
structure of native society, as it was before the European impact.
The labours of historians and anthropologists do not yet enable
us to get an altogether coherent picture of the conditions of
tropical Africa in the days when it was still the Dark Continent.
Some sketch is nevertheless emerging; from it we may borrow a
few points, in order to see what were the kinds of institutions on
which Indirect Rule, in the various territories, was to be imposed. In
contrast to the earlier static picture of Africa before the Europeans
arrived, it is now clear that in all these areas in the seventeenth,

to nineteenth centuries real changes were going on among the peoples themselves. On top of these came the impact of slaving: European (and American) on the west coast, Arab (with close connexions not only with Arabia but also with India) on the east. Occasionally slaving speeded up the process of change. Sometimes it took advantage of indigenous patterns of hostility between various groups, or of movements which were already occurring.

At the slave-trading centres certain tribes, or chiefs, acted as contact men,[1] kidnapping members of peaceful communities and driving them down to the coasts for the raiders to ship overseas. The effect of decades of this trade was to leave, or sometimes just to displace, bits and pieces of tribes, so that any organization they may once have had was completely destroyed.[2] This is particularly noticeable along the coasts of Ghana and Nigeria in the west, and Tanganyika in the east. On the east coast the situation was further complicated by numerous Arab settlements, particularly in the neighbourhood of Mombasa and Zanzibar, both of which were under the control of the Sultan of Zanzibar.

In the long run more important than these were the great folk movements of the nineteenth century. In the west the Fulani,[3] a Sudanic people from the interior, pushed down into Northern Nigeria, in a holy war (*jehad*) which lasted from (roughly) 1805 to 1820, completely overcoming and prosylitizing the Hausa people, and finally stayed only by tougher conditions. East of the Hausa the Kanuri in Bornu and Adamawa eventually proved too much for the conquerors; but fighting continued at least to 1856. In the south, after making some penetration into Yoruba areas to the south of Hausaland, these desert horsemen found themselves defeated by the ravages of the tsetse fly on their horses, once the forest belt had been reached. This Fulani penetration appears to have been the biggest folk movement on the western side of Africa.

On the east side of the continent the impression that emerges is one of ceaseless restless movement, with one very big migration:

---

[1] Such as the Fanti on the Gold Coast and the Yao in Nyasaland. On the east side, however, the Arab slavers themselves penetrated far inland. Ujiji on Lake Tanganyika was a big centre.

[2] For instance I visited a small pocket of Beni-speaking people, to the west of the Volta, near Akuse, very far from their home in Benin.

[3] The Fulani also flowed down farther east (perhaps coming down the east side of Lake Chad), imposing their rule on what afterwards became the French Cameroons. Cf. J. S. Trimingham, *Islam in West Africa*, 1959.

of the Zulus (Ngoni), first from somewhere in the north right down to Natal, and then north again, branching out north-west into Northern Rhodesia, and north-east into Nyasaland, one band of the Ngoni peoples even penetrating as far as Iringa in Southern Tanganyika. Of only slightly less importance were the movements south and east out of what became the Belgian Congo, of which one of the most important was that of the Bemba into the eastern part of Northern Rhodesia. Farther north one gets the impression that most of the tribes of Kenya and Uganda were on the move at one time or another during the seventeenth and eighteenth centuries, for the most part in a southerly direction. (This in addition to the normal wanderings of strictly nomadic peoples such as the Masai.) Even in the absence of slaving these restless shifts tended to leave isolated communities of different background and organization in one place or another.[1]

Thus very broadly we can say that in the nineteenth century the peoples of the countries in which we are interested were subject to four sorts of disturbances: slaving, warlike expeditions of organized warrior bands under unified leadership, chronic raiding, especially by pastoral peoples in search of additional cattle, and lastly innumerable little tribal wars, such as always arise—even between kindred peoples—at a certain stage of development. Among the more important of these last were the repeated wars between the Fanti and Ashanti in Ghana, and between the different branches of Yorubas both within British territory (Ibadans and Abeokutans)[2] and with their kinsmen in French Dahomey. All these disturbances left their mark on the social and political organization of the peoples, although the advent of the Europeans for the most part put an end both to the big migrations and to chronic unprovoked cattle raiding.[3] On the west coast slaving, much reduced after 1807, petered out rapidly after 1861 when an agreement was made with the Americans. In the east and centre it continued to be a heavy scourge until after the middle of the century, in spite of

[1] Such as a little group of Bantus on the Tana river in Kenya, now relatively backward in comparison to those in the Central Province.

[2] See S. O. Biobaku, *The Egba and Their Neighbours, 1842–1872*, 1957.

[3] It will be a long time before an end is put to tribal warfare. A clash between the Okrika and Kalibari in the Niger swamps of Eastern Nigeria (concerning fishing rights) in 1950 reached considerable proportions. There is unfortunately every indication that a sudden withdrawal of colonial powers (e.g. in the Belgian Congo and French Cameroons) may unleash serious pent-up forces of inter-tribal rivalry.

the formal agreement of the Sultan of Zanzibar to a policy of abolition.

Apart from all these influences playing upon them, the peoples themselves certainly differ ethnically, as well as tribally, although just how, and where, is still by no means clear. Broadly, on the west side of Africa, apart from infiltration by strictly Sudanic, not truly negroid peoples, the mass of the population are of negroid races, between different branches of which no clear distinctions can be drawn.[1] While some of their languages are clearly akin, others bear no relation whatever to each other. There is, however, a distinction, which is of considerable administrative importance, between those peoples who speak languages which can fairly easily be put in writing, and those who speak tonal languages which cannot be, and which it is very difficult for outsiders to learn. Where tribes have been broken up the range of the local vernacular may well not be more than ten or fifteen miles.

On the east side of the continent it is possible to be a little more definite. From roughly the middle (from north to south) of Uganda and Kenya, and all the way south to Rhodesia and beyond, the mass of the people speak some sort of Bantu language; this does not necessarily imply ethnic connexion, at least not of any close variety.[2] A number of the languages, however, have distinct affinities (such as those of the Ganda, Haya, Sekuma, Kikuyu, and Kamba); some of these denote a fairly close ethnic connexion, (i.e. between Kikuyu and Kamba). But since languages can jump ethnic fences they are not a sure guide.

Apart from this Bantu-speaking majority, there is to be found in Uganda and Kenya (and to a less extent in Tanganyika) an important element of Nilo-Hamitic peoples[3] (such as the Masai and their relatives and also the Luo, Ankole, and Iteso). There is a very deep cultural distinction between these and their Bantu neighbours, although the social organization of one tribe clearly often influences those around it, even if they are ethnically distinct. Nowadays these cultural differences extend all the way up

---

[1] In Nigeria the Tiv people alone appear to have Bantu affinities.

[2] It does, however, have the great convenience that it has been possible to develop an Arab/Bantu dialect (Swahili) as a lingua franca all over East and Central Africa. As development progresses, however, it is possible that English will take its place.

[3] For characteristics of these peoples see pp. 72 ff.

to national politics;[1] and, what is more relevant to our inquiries, they greatly affect attitudes to local government institutions.

The striking differences in cultural and economic habits which the various peoples now exhibit are no doubt traceable to a substantial degree to these basic ethnic differences, but the terrain in which the peoples find themselves in also important. This is often only very partially of their own choosing, since the weak and peaceable have been pushed about by the strong and fierce. The Bantu are by inclination agriculturalists, the Nilo-Hamites pastoralists. In the west the leading pastoralists are the rural ('cow') Fulani; most of the other peoples are predominantly agriculturalists, apart from fishing peoples along the coasts. Pastoralists live in dry areas, where stock-raising is the obvious occupation. Insufficiency of rainfall makes it in any case impossible for them to grow regular crops unless and until artificial water supplies can be created; the same cause makes these peoples nomadic—of necessity rather than of volition (and thus, as we shall see later, poses special problems in the local tax field). *Mutatis mutandis* dwellers in the fly-infested forest belt cannot keep animals (except for a few goats and a race of tiny and unproductive cattle); they must therefore be tillers of the soil. Only a relatively small number of peoples living on high ground have a choice in principle between different types of farming, and still fewer have the practical knowledge to exercise it. (As we shall see later, education in this respect can be an important function of local government.)[2]

Arising from these ethnic differences and influences playing upon them, the Europeans on arrival found themselves confronted with a number of different patterns of political and social organization. It was many decades before they appreciated these; and much socio-anthropological work remains to be done before their significance can be fully understood. Broadly speaking, social and political organizations within the great majority of these peoples can be classified into two groups: those which, on the arrival of the Europeans, were organized in 'centralized' systems with well-recognized chiefs (often with feudal kingdoms); and those 'non-centralized' societies which had little or no leadership above localized clan levels. These latter were tied together loosely by a diffuse network of kinship relations or age-group responsibilities.

---

[1] Thus the Nilo-Hamites in Kenya were entirely outside and even hostile to Mau Mau. [2] See below, pp. 266 ff.

Within these two broad groups there were almost infinite varieties, especially among the second.

In some cases the chiefs were indistinguishable from the peoples over whom they ruled; if this was so they frequently had the character, more or less, of priest (or divine) kings (unless indeed they were Moslems). More often, where there was a clearly defined head—a Paramount[1] as he came to be called—it was an indication of rule by right of conquest or consent, by an alien people. Clear illustrations of this phenomenon are found among the lacustrine Bantu,[2] and the Hausa of Northern Nigeria with their Fulani rulers. Anthropologists suspect that the one group in Western, and the one in Eastern Nigeria which are peculiar in having hereditary rulers (the Oba of Benin and the Obi of Onitsha[3] respectively) have a similar origin. On the other hand absolute monarchies are a familiar phenomenon in all Moslem lands; the important Ashanti chieftaincies and the original large states of Sierra Leone[4] probably have affinities in this direction.

Descent-group (e.g. clans and lineages) and age-group (e.g. age grade) organizations exist in a great variety of forms, but normally have this in common, that there is a double loyalty: to the descent group and to the age group of physical contemporaries. The relation between these can be illustrated schematically (see diagram);[5] the age grading shown is that of the Masai, where it is particularly clear. Members of a clan trace their origin to a common ancestor but this may apparently vary all the way from a real historical personage (so that the clan is a true extended family), to a mythological person, bird, animal, and so on. In this case loyalty is rather to a symbol than to a family group and 'strangers' can be incorporated into the clan by means of appropriate ceremonies. In this type of organization it is not uncommon for the members

[1] A Paramount is a chief who owes allegiance to no other chief; he probably (but not necessarily) has a hierarchy of subordinate chiefs under him.

[2] Ganda, Haya, and Sekuma round Lake Victoria, but emphatically not among the neighbouring Kikuyu and Kamba.

[3] Who are themselves related.

[4] These big chieftaincies were broken up, on military advice, following the disturbances of the late 1880's. The ephemeral nature of these chiefdoms can be gauged by the extreme difficulty which has since encountered in re-uniting chiefdoms into viable local government bodies; see below, p. 197.

[5] I owe the information on the Masai grading to Alan Jacobs, of Nuffield College, who recently spent two years living with the Tanganyika Masai, Cf. his (unpublished) thesis 'The Political Organization of Tanganyika Masai'.

of a clan to be 'dispersed', living perhaps many miles apart, but immediately recognizing each other as brothers when encountered.

The age-grouping aspect also differs greatly from people to people in clarity, significance, and duties. Entry to the lowest rank is by an initiation ceremony (which may, or may not be, closely related to puberty). Progress up the grades is then determined

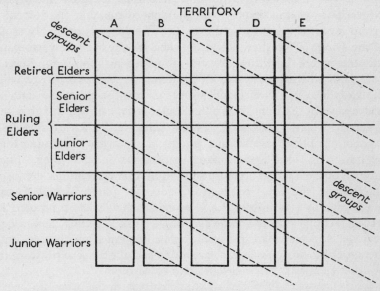

Descent- and Age-Group Organization (Masai)

by time periods, so far as these can be correctly reckoned by primitive peoples. Among those peoples who keep the age grades quite distinct (by holding only intermittent initiations), this aspect of the organization is normally more important than the clan/extended family aspect, and vice versa among those peoples where initiation takes place more or less continuously.[1]

In none of these descent-age-group peoples are there likely to be any real chiefs; their place is filled (so far as it is filled at all),

---

[1] The initiation ceremonies in Sierra Leone are of the more or less continuous type, closely related to puberty. They are of particular interest because they are conducted by two powerful territorywide societies (Porro for the boys and Sande for the girls). From their position these societies could exert a potent political influence, but there is no definite evidence that they have done so as yet. Cf. McCulloch *The Peoples of Sierra Leone Protectorate*, and *Report on the Disturbances in the Provinces*, 1955/6.

by a Council of Elders. These meet in *ad hoc* assemblies to settle disputes and to rebuke misbehaviour. Among the elders one is chosen as the group spokesman (in Masailand he is the *Laigwenai*). He may be accredited with some supernatural powers, but his position is definitely not one of political authority over others. Among some Kenya tribes the age-group aspect of the organization appears to be the more important. Among the peoples of Eastern Nigeria, who mainly belong to this type of organization, the descent-group aspect appears to predominate. The same is probably true of the Tonga of Northern Rhodesia, who are one of the few tribes in this area where the diffuse descent-group organization is dominant.

It cannot be expected that all the different peoples of Africa will fit neatly into this dual classification. Perhaps the most interesting, and certainly the best known deviation, is that of the Yorubas of Western Nigeria. We shall discuss their rather impressive indigenous political organization briefly when we are examining the beginning of local government institutions in that area. The interest of the Yoruba organization is first, that it combines definite chieftaincy (the Oba) with strong conciliar power, which is as much civil as it is military; and secondly that it has promoted a strong feeling of unity among the whole Yoruba people, including very great reverence for the traditional ceremonies which is yet not incompatible with modern occupations and the sincere profession of other religions, whether Christian or Moslem.

The purpose of this brief attempt to interpret the broad findings of the social anthropologists has been to indicate the sort of problems which an alien race, attempting to administer the peoples through their own leaders (as the British certainly did), would be up against. It is evident that the task would be relatively straightforward where there were strong and obvious chiefs. These feudal kingdoms after all had an affinity with what was known both of medieval Europe and of India. On the other hand even if the early administrators had had an inkling of anthropology (which of course was far from being the case), there was little for them to catch hold of in the descent- and age-group organization, and it was not surprising that very great difficulties were experienced before a system that would work was evolved.

It was the chance that Lugard first made contact with the Fulani Emirate organization in Northern Nigeria, admirably

[1] See above p. 72 and for more details see S. Biobaku, op. cit.

suited to his ideas in every way, which enabled Indirect Rule to get off to a flying start, and so caused it to be adopted as the model for all the British African dependencies. Before we examine this foundation of local government institutions there is, however, one more group of complications to be cleared out of the way. The system was to be applied both in West and East Africa, yet the two sides of the continent differed in several vitally important respects, some of which were only very loosely connected with ethnic or social differences.

West Africa, and especially Nigeria, is a country of large peoples; a measure of these can be immediately grasped by the fact that although Northern and Southern Nigeria each contain 16–17 million inhabitants the whole country is dominated by three groups of peoples: Hausa and Fulani in the north, Yorubas in the west, and Ibos in the east. The smallest of these groups is thus about 5 million, two and a half times the total population of Northern Rhodesia or Nyasaland, three times that of Sierra Leone (where there are fourteen different tribes). In Northern and Western Nigeria, no doubt originally for safety reasons, but also for trading convenience, the inhabitants early organized themselves in large towns.[1] Kano, Sokoto, Maiduguri are similar to other Moslem/Arab conurbations, for instance in Egypt or the Sudan. (Kano and its surrounding district has a population of over 3 million.) In Yorubaland Ibadan is over, and Abeokuta just under, 500,000. There are virtually no alien elements in any of these towns.

The existence of such large urban centres of itself necessitates the establishment of some spontaneous sort of local government organization. Generally speaking (and this goes for Southern Ghana and Ashanti[2] also although the towns are not so large) the habit of the population is to live in the towns but to commute to their farms outside, as and when cultivation or harvesting requires their presence. This way of life partly accounts for the fact that each family, or even each individual, carries on a number of occupations at once.[3]

These social habits may well partly account also for the relative

[1] Cf. E. K. Bovill, *The Golden Trade of the Moors*, 1958, and also the great interest taken in market development in Northern Nigeria, Chap. 17.
[2] Cf. P. Hill, *The Gold Coast Cocoa Farmer*, 1956. In Eastern Nigeria the towns are also not so large, and some of the larger (Enugu, Port Harcourt) are artificial creations; but both Ibos and Ibibios (in Calabar) take readily to town life.   [3] Cf. P. T. Bauer, *West African Trade*, 1954.

emancipation of women, who although they do not yet take much part in local government or committee work,[1] often have complete economic and a large degree of social independence. A great deal of both wholesale and retail trade in Southern Nigeria is in the hands of market women; some have incomes running into four figures. They travel ceaselessly in pursuance of their trade, by lorry and even by plane. The tough nature and determination of the Ibo women was demonstrated in the Aba riots of 1928–9;[2] it was re-emphasized in Owerri and other places in January 1958.

In all these respects East and Central Africa present an almost completely different picture. The eastern tribes are much smaller. The Kikuyu, the largest people in Kenya, do not exceed 800,000 and the Ganda of Uganda number little more; many tribes amount to no more than 50,000–100,000.[3] The people, whether Bantu or Nilo-Hamitic, take to town life and trade only with considerable reluctance. As a result, generally speaking African incomes are substantial only in the big export crop (coffee, cotton) areas, and the women are less independent.[4] There are of course exceptions, especially where Africans are in close touch with Europeans, as in the neighbourhood of Nairobi or in Northern Rhodesia, where four-figure incomes are by no means uncommon. Finally there is the all too well known difference of broad racial homogeneity in the west and acute interracial strains in the east and centre. The problem of the dominant, but numerically insignificant, white settlers needs no emphasis; but that of the Asians, although it has received less attention, could become almost as difficult.[5] By and large Uganda and Kenya towns are Asian enclaves, just as in the rural areas there are European enclaves. The racial problem is however more easily discussed in terms of the individual territories, for it differs greatly from one to another.

II

Enough has been said to illustrate the different settings into which something called Indirect Rule was successively introduced,

[1] Cf. I. C. Jackson, *Advance in Africa*, 1956.
[2] See below, p. 105.
[3] Along the coastal fringe of West Africa there are a number of fragmented tribes, much smaller than this, but they are fortuitous exceptions.
[4] Yet a most common sight, especially in Uganda, is a young man with a young woman on his bicycle carrier. This would be unthinkable in India, or even Ceylon.   [5] Cf. the Asian boycott which rent Buganda, 1958–9.

first as a method of general administration, but more recently as an avowed stepping stone to the establishment of responsible and representative local government institutions. Before we start to examine the results of this policy we must endeavour to get some clear idea of what it was its sponsors had in mind.

The idea of administering a conquered country through its own rulers, working within a prescribed range of powers and duties, is very ancient. It was common in the Roman Empire, and, as far as can be judged, could be quite a good arrangement. It was practised by both the Moslem and British invaders of India. What Lugard and his colleagues (especially Sir Donald Cameron)[1] had in mind developed into something at once more elaborate and more constructive than any of these, something in fact that they could refer to when writing to each other as 'the System'.

The broad concept of Indirect Rule had clearly come into Lugard's mind in Uganda. Immediately after the victory of the English forces at Mengo[2] in 1892 he told the assembled chiefs that the English had no intention of destroying their own institutions and traditions, but would rule through them. The terms of his dispatch to his employers, The British East African Company, makes his plan clear:

> With regard to the internal control of Uganda, in my opinion the object to be aimed at . . . is to rule through its own executive government . . . our aim should be to educate and develop the sense of justice. . . . An arbitrary and despotic rule, which takes no account of native customs, traditions and prejudices, is not suited to the successful development of an infant civilisation, nor in my view is it in accordance with the spirit of British colonial rule.[3]

On his way out to take up his position with the Niger Company in 1893[4] Lugard was able to give the matter further thought, so that when in 1894 he achieved a brilliant victory in Northern Nigeria he was able to put a well-balanced system into operation immediately.

Because of the fame which the system of Indirect Rule later attained, a great mass of literature on it has accumulated, explaining

---

[1] Who joined Lugard in Nigeria in 1921 and in 1925 went to Tanganyika.
[2] See below, p. 113.
[3] Quoted in M. Perham, *Life of Lord Lugard*, 1956, pp. 60 ff.
[4] See below, p. 95.

interpreting, reinterpreting, and criticizing.[1] It is clear that in many cases both advocates and critics had in mind something substantially different from that which Lugard launched in the Northern Region in 1894. This is not surprising, nor is it to be regretted, because ultimately what mattered was not what Lugard planned in Nigeria or even in Uganda, but how the principles worked out in different circumstances and places. In this process of reinterpretation Lugard himself took an important part, both in his 'Revision of his Instructions to Political Officers' (intended to apply to the whole of Nigeria) in 1918 and more definitively in 'The Dual Mandate' (1922). Through this medium a much wider public was reached.

One of the great assets of Indirect Rule has in fact been its adaptability. There were, however, some unique and vital aspects in the relation between the British and Native Authorities in Northern Nigeria in 1894 which stamped the main features of the system and influenced the form it took even when they were not, or were not fully, present elsewhere.

In the first place Lugard's victory was decisive enough for him to be able to avoid any sort of a treaty; instead he could dictate terms, not only to the Emirs whom he had actually defeated, but also to those who found it politic to submit although not defeated.[2] Lugard's position in Nigeria was thus very much stronger than it had been in Uganda a few years previously, where the most he could do was to make a treaty with the Kabaka. As we shall see, wherever it has been necessary to make treaties with chiefs, there have been subsequent troubles. Secondly, the Emirs were already ruling in a relatively orderly manner; they were strong enough to be usable as something more than agents. On the other hand there was no question of their being able to interfere with any British interests, in a way which the Ashanti might have done, and which probably made the extradition[3] of the Asantehene two years later unavoidable. By right of conquest in Nigeria suzerainty was transferred to the British (as Lugard insisted) carrying with it the right

---

[1] Some of the more important contributions are B. Hailey, *An African Survey*, revised 1956, 1957; D. C. Cameron, *My Tanganyika Service and Some Nigeria*, 1939; L. P. Mair in *Africa*, 1936; M. Perham, 'A Restatement of Indirect Rule', *Africa*, vol. vii (1939); *Native Administration in Nigeria*, 1937; *Life of Lord Lugard*, vol. i, 1956, vol. ii 1960; N. U. Akpan, *Epitaph to Indirect Rule*, 1955.

[2] See below, p. 96.   [3] See below, p. 86.

to ultimate title in land, to appoint (and dismiss) Emirs and all officers of State, the right of legislation, taxation, and complete control over the armed forces.

In the same breath it was promised that some of the powers lost by defeat 'would through grace be restored by delegation'.[1] It was an important part of the Lugard doctrine that so long as the local rulers behaved themselves they should be supported, and their prestige with their own people enhanced. Lugard expressly desired in the case of the Fulani (with whom he was most impressed) 'to regenerate this capable race and mould them to ideas of justice and mercy, so that in a future generation if not in this, they may become worthy instruments of rule'.

Although Lugard refused to acknowledge it, there were two weaknesses in the concept, even in the propitious circumstances of Northern Nigeria. First, in practice the effort both to control the actions of the ruler and to enhance his prestige was bound to lead to inconsistencies. Secondly, just as happened in India, the mere fact of supporting the ruler strengthened his position, and thus held within it the seeds of stagnation. As we proceed we shall see the effect of these weaknesses.

In the long run it was not so much the political aspect of Indirect Rule which proved important, as its administrative aspect: the foundation of the Native Authority system. It was here that its great merit of adaptability was most clearly shown. Even in the Northern Region the full pattern of native administration only took shape gradually, although it can be claimed that it was implicit from the outset. It was of the essence of the idea that a Native Authority should be established. At first Lugard evidently thought of this as a personal office: the Emir himself as 'sole Native Authority'.[2] In accordance, however, with normal Moslem practice[3] many of the Emirs already had small advisory councils, whose importance, though subordinate, was by no means negligible.[4] Lugard was prepared to recognize this and to constitute a Native Authority as 'The Emir in Council'.[5]

The administrative authority was to be accompanied by a system

[1] Quoted in M. Perham, *Life of Lord Lugard.*
[2] Sole Native Authorities did not vanish completely from the scene until 1952.
[3] For Egyptian practice, see R. Hill, *Egypt in the Sudan,* 1959.
[4] The Council of Six at Sokoto was particularly famous.
[5] Later this was transmuted into 'The Emir and Council', thus giving the council co-ordinate powers; see above p. 12 and below, pp. 99, 182.

of Native Courts. Here again the situation in Northern Nigeria was especially propitious, because a separate system of courts under 'professional' *Alcadi* already existed. It was possible to adapt these courts merely by eliminating practices unacceptable to British or Christian ideals, and no further action was required. Elsewhere it was necessary to create courts dispensing local customary law. Where this had to be done, inevitably it was linked in the minds of the people with the administrative side. One of the great problems of transition to modern institutions has been to separate the judicial from the executive, so as to give representative government a fair start.

The coping stone of the Native Authority system, and the aspect which is our special concern, was the Native Treasury: initially a tax-collecting office (as in India)[1] but soon to become also the local public expenditure department. Without the Native Treasury the Native Authority system was incomplete; but a Treasury could not be established until there were funds to pass through it. As soon as Native Courts were working there would be some fines and fees coming in (and as we shall see later these are still a by no means negligible source of local revenue in West Africa);[2] but these would not be continuous enough to justify the establishment of a Treasury.

Consequently the full development of the Native Authority system could not take place until a regular tax was established. (It was the absence of this in Ghana which so long delayed the completion of the Native Authority system.)[3] Although there could not be Native Treasuries without tax, there could of course be taxes without a Native Treasury—and there certainly were in several African territories, especially wherever Sir Harry Johnston had a hand in shaping institutions.[4] But in such cases revenue was purely for central purposes and was usually very inefficiently assessed and collected.

The factor which established the Native Treasury as something different from the Asian Collector's Office was the early introduction of the practice of sharing the revenue between central and local administrations, by means of commissions on collection, rebates, and so on, thus giving the Native Authorities definite and

[1] See above, p. 47.
[2] See revenue accounts in Chap. 14.
[3] See below, p. 86.
[4] Cf. R. Oliver, *Sir Harry Johnston and the Scramble for Africa*, 1957, and below, pp. 115–16.

regular funds which they could devote to local purposes, determining (within limits) their own priorities. It is this aspect of the
system of Indirect Rule which constitutes its biggest claim to be a
step in the direction of responsible local government.

Thus the mature native administration system had three prongs:
the Native Court, the Native Treasury, and the Native Authority.
To start with the greatest interest often centred round the first,
but ultimately this was the aspect which had the shortest life, as
the process of separating judicial and executive gradually took
place. The position of the Native Treasury was gradually strengthened as more money flowed into it: from grants, property
income, and ultimately from autonomous tax revenue. *Pari passu*
with these changes have come increasing responsibilities. These
are the matters which will be our special concern in sections IV
and V. The Native Authority itself was destined by various
stages, to be transmuted into a fully representative and responsible Local Authority. This process is still proceeding, in some
areas suddenly, at the stroke of a new Ordinance, in others
gradually, by the infiltration of elected members into the council.

Some areas seem able to take the change better than others; but
even in areas where Indirect Rule had a bad start (such as Eastern
Nigeria) it still proved a useful stage in political advancement. I
cannot do better than quote the judgement of a friendly critic
from that Region:[1]

> Our Old Mother Indirect Rule
> Liked, Disliked and Misunderstood;
> Thou Didst Play Thy Part Well,
> Laying Solid Foundations For Days Ahead;
> We Shall Not Forget Thee Whate'er We Do.

[1] N. U. Akpan, op. cit., p. 45. Mr. Akpan has deliberately put his comment
in the manner in which Nigerians universally commemorate in the press the
passing of respected relatives.

7

BEGINNINGS IN WEST AFRICA

I. GHANA

IN spite of the early start of the Creole area of Sierra Leone, it is with Ghana that we must begin our examination of the west coast, both on grounds of chronology and because its experiments in our field form in some sense a bridge between those in India and those in the rest of Africa. Ghana being ahead of the rest of the Coast had initially to forge its own institutions; but finally they came to approximate very closely to the general African pattern of Indirect Rule.[1]

In order to grasp the significance of the relative growth of local government institutions it is necessary to keep clearly in mind the basic geographical divisions of the country. Ghana is divided into three distinct zones, the boundaries running east and west. To the south next to the sea are the Accra plains, rising in the north to the Akwapim hills, and to the east (across the Volta) to the high ground of Togoland. This is the area which in 1874 was annexed as the Gold Coast Colony.[2] North of this lies Ashanti, on fairly high ground, fertile and well-watered in the south, but becoming dry towards the north. North of Ashanti lie the 'Northern Territories' (now Northern Region), very dry and sparsely inhabited, except along the four river basins, the peoples thus tending to be separated into small groups.

The three broad territorial divisions of Ghana are thus extremely distinct; and the type of local government institutions which it was found practicable to establish differed markedly from one area to another. The present administration has a plan for reducing them to homogeneity, but is having great difficulty in putting it into effect.[3] This, however, is to anticipate.

The coastal strip, as we have seen, had been exposed to European contacts from quite an early period. The main coastal towns—

---

[1] In this section I am much indebted to F. M. Bourret, *The Gold Coast*, 1952.
[2] And from which the present personnel of the cabinet exclusively derives.
[3] See below, pp. 191 ff.

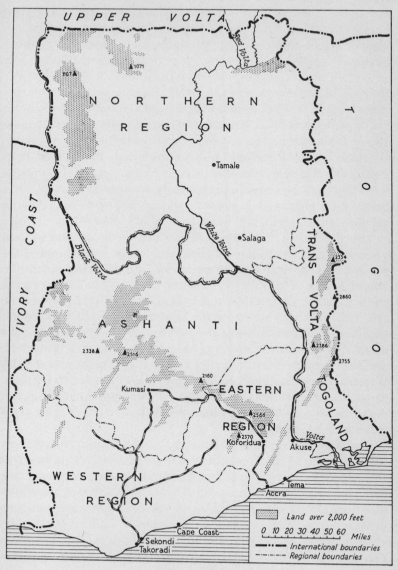

UPPER VOLTA

Red Volta

NORTHERN

REGION

1107▲

▲1071

•Tamale

White Volta

•Salaga

IVORY COAST

Black Volta

ASHANTI

2338▲ ▲2516

2160▲

Kumasi•

EASTERN

TRANS — VOLTA

▲2334

2860•

▲2386•

•2755

TOGOLAND

T O G O

REGION

▲2566

2370▲
Koforidua

Volta

Akuse•

WESTERN

REGION

Tema

Accra

Cape Coast

Sekondi
Takoradi

Land over 2,000 feet

0 10 20 30 40 50 60 Miles

— • • — International boundaries
— • — Regional boundaries

MAP 5. Ghana.

Accra, Sekondi-Takoradi, and Cape Coast—tended to develop outside connexions and a cosmopolitan outlook, as in India, to a much greater extent than in Nigeria. The earliest trade was predominantly in human lives; but after 1807 this was replaced by other products—gold, oil palm products, later cocoa and rubber. This early contact with Europe had a double effect. On the one hand there was a tendency, over considerable parts of the area, for the original organization of the Fanti tribes to break up; on the other there was the emergence of an educated (more or less Christian) middle class of traders and professionals, who tended to look mainly towards the West for their image of the future. But there remained (and still remain today,) even within the Colony area a number of closely knit and powerful chieftaincies. According to the general Ghana pattern these were organized in a hierarchy, each chief with a council: village, division, state would be equivalents in English. The head of the 'state' was dubbed by the British the Paramount. The chiefs were chosen by the councils from the ruling families, and could be deposed (enstooling and destooling as it was called) by the same authority. But while he was in office (on the stool) the chief was in a powerful position, having virtual control over tribal (or 'stool') land and over traditional tribute payments. There was thus from an early stage a diversity of culture, and of institutions, even within the southern area—notwithstanding the fact that some of the more powerful chiefly families early appreciated the advantages of Western education. Though the two elements have drawn together on particular occasions (as at the time of the cocoa boycott against the British buyers' monopoly in 1938), their divergence of interests still bedevils Ghana politics.

North of the coastal zone are the Ashanti tribes, organized in the same way as the Fanti (they also are Akans), but even more elaborately. Their hierarchy of chiefs and states culminated in the Ashanti Confederacy, of which a member of the ruling house of Kumasi (the main Ashanti town) was the supreme Paramount or Asantehene. The wealth of the coastal area (at least of its landward part) in gold, and later in cocoa and rubber, extended through all the southern part of Ashanti. The Ashanti were less exposed to contact with Europe, and a number of them had become Moslems.

North of Ashanti, in the Northern Territories, were more

primitive and less organized tribes, much broken up by conquest and by slave-raiding. They were much attached to their 'animiste' religion, but have nevertheless proved not unreceptive to Christian missions.

In the early period, the British, both Traders and officials, tended to regard the Fanti as natural allies against the raids of the stronger and fiercer Ashanti. Had it not been for British support the Fanti would undoubtedly have been overcome. It was in accordance with this policy, more in the spirit of an alliance than of a truce, that in 1843 the British Government concluded a Bond with the Fanti chiefs. The ambiguity of this arrangement, natural enough under the circumstances, was later to cause a good deal of trouble. The chiefs were able to claim that nothing had been done to curtail their inherent 'rights' (which they interpreted to imply a ban against the levying of direct taxes). As we shall see, the administration repeatedly endeavoured to levy a poll tax, and to establish Native Treasuries, but it never succeeded in doing so.

Among the educated Fanti there was the same reluctance to support collective expenditure as we have observed among a corresponding class in India. They were also reluctant to see any changes which might indirectly increase the power of the chiefs. The chiefs, for their part, were unwilling to submit to any curtailment of court revenues or rights over stool levies. This situation could hardly have endured (once expenditure on economic development was demanded), if it had not been for the steady increase in revenue from cocoa, and from the buoyancy of import duties due to relatively high African incomes. The price paid for this fiscal ease was a failure in the development of local government and fiscal institutions; so that Ghana, in spite of her relatively great wealth and degree of development (substantially exceeding those of other African territories), was a laggard in her fiscal and political education, though not of course in her political consciousness. In order to appreciate the background against which modern local government institutions have finally emerged, it is necessary to go briefly into the key events which determined the way in which the foundations were gradually modified.

Four years after the signing of the Bond an attempt was made to establish a Leg. Co.; and there was the first of many abortive attempts to introduce a direct tax. After that there is nothing that need detain us until the early seventies, when there occurred a series of events which substantially modified the position. The conclusion of the Select Committee of the House of Commons of 1865 (which recommended the ultimate withdrawal of the British)[1] provoked a strong reaction among the educated class. Their constitutional manifesto (the so-called Mankesim Constitution) put the administration into the awkward position of having in the immediate present to go forward or back, whatever they might do in the more remote future. They determined to go forward, and in 1874 the Gold Coast Colony was established, with an Ex. Co. and a Leg. Co. But nothing was said about direct taxation or of any further control of the chiefs.

Up to this point, though the Ashanti chiefs had given recurrent trouble (five wars are enumerated), an uneasy truce had always been re-established. Now a new factor intervened. The Dutch, the last of the other European companies to maintain trading posts on the Coast, sold out to the British in 1872. This put the Ashanti traders in a much worse position than before, since the Fanti-British monopoly was now complete. They reacted strongly, and in 1873–4 (the sixth Ashanti war) strenuous efforts had to be made by the British before they were defeated. The Confederacy was broken up; the Asantehene was deprived of all authority outside his capital city, Kumasi. With their organization destroyed, Ashanti then sank into something like chaos. The chiefs would have welcomed a British consul, but to the British government of that day such extension of responsibility was unthinkable.

Some more precise settlement was nevertheless required in the Colony. Four years after the annexation, a Native Jurisdiction Ordinance was passed, establishing a primitive and rather dangerous type of Indirect Rule. So long as no sort of direct tax was acceptable (and the government was not strong enough to enforce it against resistance), there could be no real place for Native Treasuries. Instead, the chiefs were given a virtually free hand in the courts, with rights over fees and fines—in addition to their customary stool rents and tributes. The British administration had no power to control the proliferation of native tribunals which the Ordinance naturally produced; nor the standards of honesty and equity prevailing in the courts.

[1] Appointed to examine the Report of the Special Commissions sent out to advise whether the Gold Coast should be abandoned or not. Cf. Bourret, op. cit., p. 19.

This Ordinance was followed in 1883 by a Native Authorities Ordinance which attempted to look after the administrative side more adequately. The rights of the Paramount and divisional chiefs were formally recognized; but no mention was made of the traditional rights of the councils to be consulted, nor was there any attempt to regulate enstoolments and destoolments. Nothing was said about a direct tax, nor of any control over stool revenues. Chiefs were encouraged to undertake administrative duties and to issue by-laws, but the task was beyond their capacity; in any case they would have had no means of enforcing them. In practice the result was that the government took over the administration. As one writer has put it[1] 'the position of the chiefs gave the benefits of neither direct nor indirect rule'. This Ordinance endured without major amendment until 1927. During that time there was little decline in the power of the chiefs—at least in those parts of the Colony where they had remained powerful after the Ashanti war. During the governorship of Sir Gordon Guggisberg—when Nana Ofori Atta I, the most powerful Paramount in the Colony, was a member of Leg. Co. (after 1916)—the chiefs would appear to have actually gained ground, much to the annoyance of the detribalized townsmen.

Meanwhile there had been other developments, arising out of the 'scramble for Africa' in the nineties. The French in the Ivory Coast and the Germans in Togoland began to hem in the territories in which the British were interested; Ashanti could not remain as a no man's land. In 1896 the unsatisfactory position there was dealt with—in a manner hardly less unsatisfactory—by exiling the Asantehene to the Seychelles; then, five years later, by annexing the whole territory, and subjecting it to direct rule. Also in 1901 an Ordinance was passed respecting the northern strip (the Northern Territories), the boundaries of which with French and German territories had been delineated a few years earlier.

From this point the administration found itself with three problem children on its hands. The youngest, the Northern Territories, turned out to be much the most docile—but on the other hand there has been little progress with the development of the Africans in that region, even to this day. Such organization as they possessed was associated with the worship of an earth-goddess (Tengam), whose 'attendants' (Tendana) appeared to be

[1] Bourret, op. cit.

a kind of priest-kings. The 1901 Ordinance took them to be chiefs, and merely bade them exercise their customary powers. But in fact this backing put a good deal more power into their hands than had ever been customary, and their exercise of it led to popular discontent. Then the government wisely decided to send an anthropologist (Sir R. Rattray) to try to find out where the real source of control lay. He reported that the tendana were much more priests than kings, and that the traditional functions of the tribal elders should also not be overlooked. As a result of his conclusions there was introduced in the Northern Territories (in 1932) a simple type of Indirect Rule—by that time a tried and accepted system—with traditional chiefs and elders acting together as Native Authority. Two years later a local tax, known as 'tribute tax' (it was regarded as a successor to the chiefs' levies), was introduced into the Northern Territories without difficulty or opposition. But the Northern Territories are always likely to remain a poor and simple area, if only because of their (generally) unpropitious climate. Since 1946 they have received regular grants from government; administration remains largely in the hands of outsiders, either British or southern Ghanaians.

In Ashanti the sequence of events was as follows. After some years of confusion and of great difficulty for the Chief Commissioner and his administration in Kumasi, it was realized that some machinery for keeping administration and people in touch was a necessity. Accordingly, in 1905, the eighteen chiefs of the state were formed into an advisory council. This not only fulfilled its immediate purpose but proved a useful invention from the point of view of the political education of chiefs. Under the long administration of Sir Francis Fuller (1902–20), cocoa cultivation expanded, and revenue was buoyant. Though there was now a demand for educational development, the unwillingness to pay a direct tax persisted; but the buoyancy of revenue from indirect taxation made it just possible (though not very satisfactory) to get on without one.

There was a steady improvement in the relations between the administration and the Ashanti chiefs, until (after the first world war) a rift of the familiar type, between the younger and better educated among the chiefs and the older and more conservative elements, began to appear. It was in this area the administration first called upon Sir R. Rattray for an anthropological survey,[1]

[1] The Gold Coast Department of Anthropology had been established in 1921.

which would guide them in the establishment of a more up-to-date régime. The beginning of the return to a less direct rule may be dated from 1921; in 1925 a Native Jurisdiction Ordinance was passed, with definite rules for election and destoolment. Two years later there was a permissive Ordinance for the establishment of Native Treasuries; but it was more than a decade before much use was made of it, and before any regular system of accounting was introduced. The last Asantehene, Prempeh, had been allowed to return from the Seychelles in 1924; two years later he was restored to his estates and to all his offices save only that of Asantehene. In the meantime a Public Health Board, consisting of appointed Europeans and Africans, had been established at Kumasi; from 1928 it was levying a house tax for local purposes. In 1935 Prempeh's nephew was re-established as Asantehene—supreme Paramount over a confederacy of chiefs. In the same year a Native Authority Ordinance on the Nigeria-Tanganyika model was brought in; but there was no direct tax under it until the forties. Finally, in 1946, there was a union (formally at least) between Ashanti and the Colony.

In the Colony there had been several experiments of constitutional and fiscal character during the 1920's; but in those days of cocoa prosperity there was not much pressure behind them, and not much that was substantial was achieved. There was a new (Guggisberg) constitution in 1925, with a Leg. Co. of fifteen official and fourteen unofficial members. The latter included nine elected Africans, one for each of the three towns and six chiefs, elected by a new organization of provincial councils, on the advice of the chiefs' councils. This arrangement did not satisfy the townsmen, who considered themselves to be underrepresented, and feared that the chiefs would be tools of the British. Contemporaneously the 'State' councils were encouraged to take on new responsibilities. But all this made little difference to the power of the chiefs, and there was still no regular direct tax.

During the depression the finances of the Colony were strained, with falling cocoa prices and an increased real burden of the debt which had been raised for development during the preceding period. Improvements in the revenue system were consequently sought. In 1931 permission was given for the establishment of Native Treasuries, into which stool rents would have been paid. This would have regularized the system of local taxation, but the powers that were given were not used. There were abortive attempts to introduce an income tax; a town water rate and a type of poll tax were tried successively, but failed. But from about 1935 officials were making more strenuous efforts to get Native Treasuries established; and in 1939 there was an Ordinance which made it possible to insist on their establishment. (The provincial and joint-provincial councils, though only consultative, were by now proving increasingly useful.) But it was not until 1944 that the Native Authority position was completely regularized as the result of a Committee of Inquiry into Abuse of Tribunals. It was then laid down that only those appointed by government were entitled to levy a rate; these were rewarded by a grant proportional to the revenue collected.

A separate word is necessary about local government in towns. The three larger colony towns—Accra, Cape Coast, and Sekondi-Takoradi—were early distinguished from the surrounding country; partly because they contained foreign (European) elements, and partly because the educated and politically conscious Africans were concentrated in them. It might at first sight have been expected that these conditions would have led to an earlier emergence of modern local government institutions and to the development of local works and amenities; but a reference to similar conditions in India shows that this was not really likely to be the case. The new business classes were too fully occupied with their own affairs to take much interest in communal services, and too anxious to plough back their profits to enjoy paying taxes. Even today town government can hardly be said to have developed successfully in Ghana.

A form of municipal government had been attempted in Accra and in Cape Coast as early as 1854, but it was a failure. In 1894 a Municipal Ordinance set up regular councils (half elected, half appointed, under an official chairman) in Accra, in Cape Coast, and in Sekondi. Little or no interest was taken in these bodies. In 1929 the majority became elected, but still no interest was aroused. Further attempts to vitalize town government (1943) were scarcely more successful, so that the question of the towns must be regarded as one which was handed over to the government of Ghana in a still unsettled state.[1]

[1] The suspension of the Kumasi and Accra councils in 1957 will be dealt with later, see below, pp. 194–5.

II. NIGERIA

The large area of modern Nigeria is inhabited by a number of peoples, of whom, however, three groups are dominant; the Hausa/Fulani in the north, the Yoruba (including the Egba) in the south-west, and the Ibo, with the closely related Ibibio, in the south-east.

The first contact of the British, working inland from Lagos, was with the Yoruba people, especially with the Egba subdivision of that people whose capital, Abeokuta, had welcomed the Missions, and was for a time in the second half of the nineteenth century the most advanced area of Nigeria. The northern part of Yorubaland, the modern province of Ilorin and Kabba, had been overrun by the Fulani, so that it was, and still is, separated from the rest. When this part of the country was lost many groups of Yorubas trekked south; Abeokuta was a foundation of four different clans, coming together for security; it is still possible to trace their four separate clusters quite clearly. More important for the Yoruba people as a whole, their religious centre at (old) Oyo had been overrun, and the head of their religion (the Alafin) had had to be moved down to (new) Oyo, a little north of Ibadan.

The indigenous religion of the Yorubas was *animiste*, with a strong ceremonial tradition, especially in relation to the needs of agriculture. Although the Alafin of Oyo was formally the spiritual head, he always had a strong rival in the oracle at Ife under the charge of the Oni; as time went on this tended to gain in prestige at the expense of Oyo. The importance of Ife as a centre of the Yoruba people has not seriously been disturbed by the fact that the majority of Yorubas now profess either the Moslem or the Christian faith (rather more of the former than of the latter).

The old traditions and ceremonies, though robbed of their religious significance, are still valued by all Yorubas as symbols of unity—to each other and to their forebears. This attitude has, as we shall see, enabled the Yorubas to adapt themselves to modern ideas and forms of government without the necessity of the jolt caused by a clean break with the past, which has faced other peoples. The other important Yoruba centre has been from an early date Ibadan, inhabited by another sub-group. Although much troubled by the King of Dahomey's Yorubas (supported by the French) in the second half of the nineteenth century, the

Ibadans ultimately won out, both against him, and against the
Abeokutans, largely owing to their better organization. Hence
Ibadan has emerged as the modern capital of Yorubaland.

It is of great interest that the Yorubas had an indigenous political
organization which combined a chiefly head with a strong con-

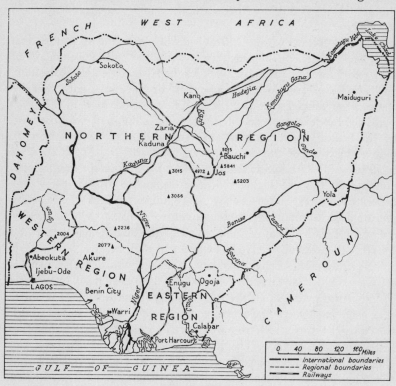

MAP 6. Nigeria.

ciliar organization. This had been developed in the large towns,
for as we have seen, the Yorubas are the town dwellers *par excellence* of West Africa. From far back in history these towns had
been organized on the same model: in quarters, or wards, often
no doubt (certainly in the case of Abeokuta) representing the
settlements of different immigrating clans. The government of
a town had two sides: a military and a civil, each with a hierarchy
of chiefs, whose status depended rigidly on seniority.[1] There

[1] Cf. the description of the organization of Ibadan in M. Perham, *Native
Administration in Nigeria*, cit.

was also traditionally a Council of Elders, the *Ogboni*, who had judicial duties (which they still perform in Abeokuta), and whose business it was to elect the Oba,[1] the official head, from the circle of eligible families. Once elected the Oba had very limited powers, and was rigidly restricted as to his way of life.

It is not surprising that this elaborate organization was stronger on the side of checks and balances, and the maintenance of the power of the elders, than of getting things done. In the first place the range of possible candidates was in practice very wide (the father of the present Oni of Ife had 105 sons), so that whenever a new Oba had to be elected there was a chance of faction fights which might plunge a town into civil war for years. Secondly the rigid hierarchy of chiefs made it extremely difficult for a progressive young man to jump a rung of the ladder of seniority.[2] Yet it was only on the rare occasions when a real leader did break through, that a town could really steal a march over its neighbours.

Although the Yoruba people dominate what is now the West, that Region also contains one other important people: the Beni, with their capital at Benin; as well as a number of smaller tribes, and fragments along the coast. The Beni as we have seen are unique in having an hereditary Oba;[3] they are also unique in having had very early contact with Europeans (the Portuguese), long before the arrival of the British. This area now contains a substantially larger proportion of Christians than the rest of the Western Region. As a whole the Western Region is considerably richer than either the north or east, but this is especially marked in the cocoa-growing areas of the true Yoruba country.

Contacts with the eastern coastal peoples were also made at an early date, well before the middle of the nineteenth century. Apart from establishment of the Mission stations of the Scots Church at Calabar, and of the C.M.S. at Onitsha in the 1850's, no settlements were made for some time. The brisk trade in palm oil (the first important Nigerian export) took place from boats moored off the coast or up the rivers. One reason for this delay was that the shores throughout the area were covered with impenetrable mangrove swamp and tropical forest.

[1] The specific title is taken from the place: the Alafin of Oyo, Alobadan of Ibadan, Alake of Abeokuta, &c.
[2] Cf. Report on the Disturbances in Ibadan, 1953.
[3] See above, p. 72.

An additional difficulty was the character of the people, whose ways were brutal and repulsive, involving human sacrifice, cannibalism, murder of twins, and various forms of torture and poisoning. Moreover both the Ibibio people (in Calabar and the east) and Ibos farther west were organized on a pure clan/age-grade system (with the single exception of the people of Onitsha, who had their hereditary Obi, related to the Oba of Benin). The normal organization was that of a group of about four hamlets, consisting of extended families, joining together in a market situated somewhere in the middle of the group. Within this organization each age grade had its own duties, so that not only every man, but also every woman, was conscious of being part of an organism; loyalty to the village became almost a ruling passion. In spite of the sharp impact of Western civilization on the Ibos (and no people desires the twentieth century more ardently), this intense, but essentially highly localized, loyalty remains as strong as ever.

The only organization allowed for above the village level, was for the calling of an *ad hoc* meeting of elders from different villages, to deal with a particular emergency. There was thus no chief or authority with whom Europeans, either traders, missionaries, or governors could negotiate. Finally the languages of all these peoples were tonal in character, thus placing an additional barrier in making close contact with them; this difficulty did not exist in Yorubaland.

The first official British connexion with Nigeria was the establishment of a consulate for the Bights of Benin and Biafra[1] in 1849, operating under the Governor at Freetown. All this time the British navy, based on Freetown, was patrolling the coast for slavers. Consequently it was also available to go to the help of harassed consuls, or conversely to report to the Governor complaints of traders or missionaries against consuls. The next date of importance is 1861, which was a decisive year for British relations with Nigeria. In the first place an agreement was signed with the United States to put an end to the slave trade on the Atlantic. Secondly, Lagos was annexed and a definite administration established. In the anti-colonial atmosphere of the time it was impossible for the administration to advance farther, except by way of making treaties. Nevertheless an eventual further advance was more or less implicit in this arrangement.

---

[1] These two coastal indentations are separated by the protuberance of the Niger delta, and together comprise the entire coastline of Nigeria.

The signing of the Treaty of Berlin in 1884–5 was the signal for this, and in the following years three important developments took place. First, in 1885 the Niger Company, which under Sir George Goldie had already penetrated far up country along the course of the great rivers, was given the green light to go ahead, being granted a Royal Commission; secondly in 1886 administration independent of Freetown was set up at Lagos, thus initiating the western colony; and thirdly in 1889 Sir Claude Macdonald was dispatched to Calabar, and the Oil Rivers Protectorate declared. At this point the centre of interest shifts abruptly to the north, and in doing so enters a different world.

In 1885 Sir George Goldie and the Niger Company were in a very strong position. They had a practical monopoly of trade on the rivers (they were operating some forty stations on the Niger and Benue) and the Company was bringing in the shareholders a steady 6%;[1] there was consequently no serious shortage of funds to support a forward movement. Goldie had full permission to develop and consolidate in the north; but he soon realized that only a really strong effort would succeed against the fierce horsemen of the warlike Emirs, who were, in addition, receiving more than a little support from France. Goldie therefore engaged the services of Lugard (after much hesitation on the latter's part, because he had hoped to be chosen as the first Governor of Uganda).

Goldie himself had long been convinced that trade could not permanently exist without administration. He was in favour of ruling as far as possible through the native 'princes' whom he found in the north. He thus has a right to rank with Lugard and Johnston as one of the founders of Indirect Rule. For Goldie Indirect Rule was far from being merely a convenient expedient, although his ideas were much less developed than Lugard's. He felt especially that in the circumstances there was no alternative to making use of the medium of traditional rulers, because he was convinced that Englishmen would never be able to understand the minds of the people. Goldie and Lugard were therefore just the men for each other.

[1] This implied that support at home, both from the government or from investors, could be relied on, in sharp contrast to the position in Uganda where the Company was always in trouble. Cf. M. Perham, *Lugard*, especially pp. 167 168, and 387.

As we have seen, in a brilliant campaign Lugard had before the end of 1894 conquered the more important Fulani Emirs in Hausaland, and had reduced the Kanuri Emirates farther east to a position in which they were prepared to submit quietly. Thus came about the opportunity for launching the full experiment of Indirect Rule, which had been maturing in Lugard's mind since his experiences in Buganda a few years previously.

Lugard's plan, as we have seen, was to regenerate the Fulani, retaining their traditional authority, but endeavouring to develop them as agents of modernization. The senior British officials were to be known as Residents, thus emphasizing their advisory capacity. They were to be supreme in the last resort, but were to keep in the background, so as to maintain the prestige of the Emirs in the eyes of their own people. Five grades of Emirs were established, each receiving letters of appointment which exactly defined their rights and duties (thus following an Indian precedent). From the first all received salaries from the government but continued, under control, to levy and collect traditional taxes. On the administrative side the Residents were to be assisted by a hierarchy of officials: Provincial Commissioners, District Commissioners, and District Officers. In spite of the relative affluence of the northern administration, in practice there never were more than a handful of officers. In fact it is evident that originally the system can only have covered a small part of the Northern Region. The Emirates specifically mentioned by Lugard in his first dispatch were Bida, Kano, Sokoto, Katsina, and Zaria, all in the heart of the Hausa–Fulani area.

It was a singular advantage in the north that, although many of the people were miserably poor, the area as a whole was accustomed to paying regular taxes. These consisted first, of the Zakka, or a tithe of certain produce, common in all Moslem states and recognized by the Koran as appropriate for charity. Secondly there was a plantation tax on crops not included in the Zakka, thirdly a capitation tax on cattle (*jangali*), and finally a tax on trades and professions. Although the methods of assessment and collection of these taxes were inefficient and confused, here to hand was obviously a foundation on which a rational and efficient tax system could be based. Already it contained elements of taxation in accordance with ability to pay, and this was strengthened when the two taxes on produce were united in what became

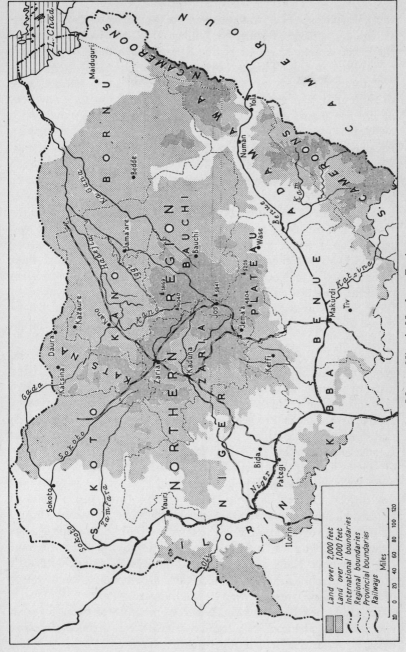

MAP 7. Nigeria Northern Region.

the 'direct tax'. This was assessed on the value of gross output, village by village. Within the village the headman determined the relative assessment of each taxpayer, according to his share of product in this. This is, however, to anticipate.

Although the Emirs were continued and even strengthened in their dignities, the new régime meant a compulsory new way of life for them. They had been accustomed to keep their subordinates, even village headmen, for long periods at the court. As a result of this practice the Emir himself, by perpetually staying at home, tended to lose touch with his people. Lugard changed all this. Instead of staying at home the Emir henceforth was to be occupied in continually touring his jurisdiction, accompanied by the Resident and subordinate officials; this also brought the British officers into touch with the people. This contact was strengthened when the time came (at the turn of the century) for the District Officers to go out into the villages and make their valuations of gross output for the direct tax. This preference for peaceful penetration by the District Officers, over any type of formal order or control, set the tone for the whole system of Indirect Rule, and has been an important influence in increasing its flexibility.

Northern Nigeria was also (as we have seen) a propitious trial ground for the System in that in the Emirates there already existed a strong system of courts, administering a firm corpus of Moslem law and custom. This was fortunate from several points of view. In the first place, there was no danger of the sort of proliferation and confusion of native tribunals which befell Ghana and Sierra Leone. Secondly, there was from the start a fair degree of separation of the executive and judicial, a position which other territories have achieved only after much time and trouble. (It is even now not quite complete in Tanganyika, and in India the process of fission, though now part of official policy, is only beginning.) Thirdly, it proved possible in the north to build round the Native Courts an economical and effective body of native police, who have on the whole been a singular and unique blessing; although obviously such a force could in certain circumstances be a source of political embarrassment and even danger.

In 1900 the charter of the Niger Company was brought to an end, and Lugard and his administrative officers henceforth came directly under the British government; this freed Lugard's hands from commercial preoccupations. By 1903 Northern Nigeria had been organized in fourteen Provinces; the Emirs were established as Native Authorities. From 1904 they were required to pay 25% of the traditional taxes to the government. Two years later it was decided that half the remainder might be applied to local development purposes, and, if desired, some of this might be passed on to the villages for their own development. Gradually the new system of direct tax was introduced with 'lump sum assessment' on the village, to be broken down to the personal level within the village. The retention of part of the revenue for local purposes *ipso facto* necessitated the creation of Native Treasuries, and by 1911 these had been formally established in all the Emirates, although they did not become statutory until 1948. By this time also the Emirs had all formally been turned into salaried officials. This steady progress, however, mainly refers to the Moslem north. In the non-Moslem Middle Belt there was no such tradition on which to build. The Fulani had relied on appointed village headmen to collect whatever they could. District Officers consequently found it impossible to get across the idea of the lump sum assessment, and for practical purposes had to be content with a low rate, flat sum, poll tax, the proceeds of which only sufficed to cover minimum government services and chiefs' salaries.

Lugard himself left Nigeria in 1906, but by that time the system had been firmly established, and was making steady progress. It was a highly centralized and self-contained system, and (except for the Middle Belt) extremely homogeneous. Lugard insisted (and the home government quietly acquiesced) that the Native Authority Accounts should be audited in Kano, rather than be submitted to the more complicated, and probably less understanding, system of colonial audit. In spite of the tendency to centralization, as time went on more and more funds were made available in the Emirates for district and village purposes. In 1915 (after his return) Lugard reported that the Native Authority share of revenue had risen from £70,000 in 1906 to £324,000. As we shall see this tendency has greatly accelerated in the post-war years. In the north, in accordance with the objective of restoring the prestige of the Fulani, the Native Authority was normally the Emir himself: in the Middle Belt, however, it was necessary to take account of Yoruba predilection for councils; Kabba indeed remained without an Emir at all. Even in the north the conciliar element began to gain ground from a fairly early date. Although there was as yet no elective element in it the whole system was in a very real sense popular, and was playing an important part in development from below.

There is no doubt that the smooth tenor of Native Authority administration in the north owed much to the long service which the relatively dry and healthy climate made possible. In the first thirty-five years of British administration in the north there were only six Governors. In the south things were very different, especially in Lagos, and although there were many able administrators their careers were sadly interrupted by illness and mortality was high.[1]

At the time of the annexation of Lagos a treaty had been made with Docemo, 'King' of Lagos, which recognized the British Administration and confined the King to tribal duties. This settlement was later disputed by the Lagosians, and there has been a long history of trouble both between the government and the 'white cap' chiefs (as connexions of the House of Docemo were called), and among the chiefs themselves, whenever a new election had to be made. Both in the 1920's and 1930's there were faction fights in the city, and as late as 1950 a leading local paper could say that 'chieftaincy disputes are one of the greatest troubles of the modern world'. A solution of the relation between the King and the government was finally reached by appointing the King 'President' of the Municipal Council.

Outside Lagos in the early days such rule as existed was frankly direct, with the administration endeavouring to steer a middle course between the missionaries (who felt that they alone understood the Africans) and the traders, who though an enterprising lot, were tough and sometimes brutal. Which of these two interests was regarded with a more kindly eye by the government depended very much on the outlook of the Governor. Glover, who succeeded to the office in 1863, was more favourable to African advance than most of his contemporaries and at one time this almost got him into trouble with the home government. Up country his main efforts (which were still confined to treaty making) were directed to keeping on good terms with Abeokuta, in order to keep

---

[1] The traveller Burton had earlier described Government House, Lagos, as a sort of 'corrugated iron coffin or plank lined morgue, containing a dead consul once a year'. For many years a supply of ready-made coffins was kept at hand.

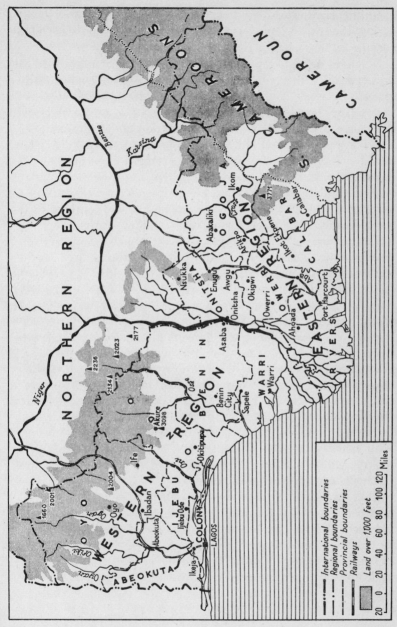

MAP 8. Nigeria, Eastern and Western Regions.

open the trade routes to Ibadan and beyond. During Glover's régime the material progress of Lagos was such that the Colony became self-supporting on indirect taxes.

When in 1886 a separate administration was established for Lagos, the British acquired a considerable degree of control farther inland. Governor McGregor (who was in office, off and on, from 1893 to 1904) could write: 'There is no reason to believe that there is a single disloyal chief. . . . The position and authority of the hereditary and elected chiefs has as far as possible been maintained.' Under the influence of the northern experiment in Indirect Rule McGregor established native councils, which in the eyes of the administration represented a regularizing of Yoruba traditions, parallel to the regularizing of Fulani traditions in the north, through the establishment of Native Authorities.

The position in the south was, however, much less satisfactory. The separate treaties made it difficult to establish anything like uniform institutions, especially on the judicial side. Moreover the varieties of chiefly appointment and conciliar power between different groups of Yorubas was extremely confusing for the administration. District Officers were appointed to look after McGregor's councils, but as they were given no advice or supervision, they could only rely on mother wit to make the best of the situation as they found it. When Governor Egerton came out in 1904 to unite the Lagos Colony with the Oil Rivers Protectorate (a task that was accomplished two years later), it was evident that a considerable encroachment on chiefly affairs by the government was inevitable. New services were being demanded, new works were being constructed (the Lagos–Ibadan railway was opened at the beginning of the century). All these innovations passed the comprehension of the traditional authorities.

Thus in Yorubaland much less progress in producing a tidy foundation for local government had been made by 1904 than in the north. In the east, among the Ibos and Ibibios, still less had been accomplished. Working from an island off the coast (for safety and salubriousness) Sir Harry Johnston had in the early 1880's made a small beginning, concluding a few treaties where there was anyone to negotiate them with, and performing a considerable service by tracing a suitable ethnic boundary between the Protectorate and the German Cameroons.

No real beginning of an administration in the east can, however, be said to have started until the arrival of Sir Claude Macdonald at Calabar in 1889. He persuaded the riverine peoples to agree to a customs duty, which by 1893 was bringing in £136,000. Thus fortified, the administration could begin to contemplate a more active policy. Four years later, however, the massacre of Consul General Phillips and six companions at Benin (which at that time formed part of the Protectorate) was an indication of the sort of costs that might have to be incurred before any kind of stable administration could be set up in the east. In fact, year by year, well into the present century, the annual reports from the area tend to be little more than an account of the year's military operations—operations undertaken much more to maintain law and order in the areas already under control, than with any desire to extend control.

Egerton's amalgamation of the Protectorate with the west in 1906 had called for an attempt at some general form of administration in the area. Since, broadly speaking, there were no authoritative chiefs, the government adopted the device of appointing such leaders as it could find, as Government Agents, mainly for court duties. At a later and more sophisticated stage of administration this device was used with success in East Africa, especially in Tanganyika. In Eastern Nigeria the 'Warrant Chiefs', as they were called, were on the whole a sad failure. In some cases the wrong men (noisy ruffians) were chosen; everywhere they were completely alien to indigenous traditions, which as we have seen, were very strong. The Districts, moreover, were set up with regard only to the convenience of the administration of justice, not to local government. Nevertheless the Warrant Chiefs were not wholly bad, and unquestionably the system did something to introduce the peoples of the east to the idea of local administration at a level above the clan. Appointments of Warrant Chiefs were made up to 1929, and as late as 1958 a few still survived. The spread of the idea of chieftaincy in the Eastern Region since 1953 has contributed to making them more acceptable than they were in the first decade of the century.

In 1914 Lugard returned to Nigeria with a mandate to amalgamate north and south and to extend the northern system of Indirect Rule over the whole country. In Yorubaland enough had already been accomplished to make this seem a relatively simple process, and in some ways it was. The legal confusion due to treaty differences was formally swept away when the new District boundaries were drawn up. But, underneath, the differences persisted, and have continued to cause sporadic trouble ever since: for instance Abeokuta has not forgotten that its treaty gave it considerably more independence than those of other places.

The administration's worst mistake was probably in respect of Ibadan. For seventeen years (up to 1934) this growing, wealthy, and aggressive city was kept under the Native Authority rule of traditionalist Oyo. Finally Ibadan was granted a District of its own, but the Resident remained at Oyo. The error was perhaps due to mistaking the religious and ceremonial priority of the Alafin for some sort of political authority; or it may have been merely the result of a general desire to rearrange Yorubaland in large units similar to the northern Emirates. It was, however, indicative of the difficulties which were likely to arise in extending Indirect Rule to other forms of social organization, even to one where it was relatively appropriate.

By and large, however, Yorubaland was safely steered into the fold of Indirect Rule. No more trouble was experienced in raising a direct tax (poll tax) than had been met with in the Yoruba areas in the north.

Things did not go at all so well in the east. The difficulties that would be encountered there were hardly apprehended, but it was very soon apparent that a poll tax of the Yoruba variety would be an impossibility, and Lugard was forced to give up the idea. Soon after he arrived (in 1919) Governor Clifford decided to have a detailed survey of the area made by an officer who had experience of this sort of work in other parts of the country. The report was presented in 1922, and gave a useful account of the experiences of the administration, although it did not attempt to dive below the surface into the anthropological structure. It was made clear that nothing worth the name of Indirect Rule existed in the area. Court Districts were very large and bore no relation either to tribal grouping nor to anything the people had been accustomed to. As a result of this report a process of slow and patient reform was started. The need for accepting some form of taxation was carefully explained to the people. As a result it was possible by 1928 to make the first collections of poll tax without apparently too much opposition. Native Treasuries were created (they had of course no basis in tradition), and into these half the revenue was paid for local purposes.

In the following year, however, there broke out serious rioting at Aba in Owerri Province. To everyone's surprise this was organized entirely by the women; but there was no withstanding them. It was clear that misunderstanding of the intentions of the administration had by no means yet been eliminated. A new start had to be made. This time District Officers were asked to find out for their own Districts as much as they could about the indigenous social and political organization of the people, with the object of discovering a firm basis for the establishment of a system of Indirect Rule. They took up the task with enthusiasm, and by 1934 199 reports had been sent in. A number of these were very valuable; that of Meek for Nsukka was a document of real anthropological importance.

The reports revealed to the government for the first time the basic clan/age grade organization of the eastern peoples. It was also demonstrated, however, that when they came in contact with other forms of social organization, the Ibo people were adaptable enough to absorb some of this into their own organization. Thus (as we have seen), Onitsha had its Obi in Beni style, Awka had priest chiefs, and Nsukka showed influence of Idda and Atta across the northern border. The area was thus far from homogeneous, although the distinctions were much less deep than, for instance, that between Hausaland and the Middle Belt.

It so happened that at the time the reports were coming in the Governor in Lagos was Sir Donald Cameron, Lugard's most earnest and successful disciple. Although a centralizer as regards territorial matters, Cameron was quite prepared to go down to rock bottom to reach a firm indigenous base for Indirect Rule. If there were no organization above the village, then, Cameron argued, Native Authorities should be organized at the village level.

There ensued a wild fragmentation of the Native Authorities in the east. For instance in Warri Province the fifty local court Districts were split into 250; Owerri emerged with 245 Native Authorities. The cost of restoring the clan organization to its former position was the establishment of Native Treasuries whose jurisdictions were too small and finances too meagre to be able to play an effective part in local government organization and development. This episode is especially interesting as being the first swing of the pendulum, which has been on the move ever since, between centralization and fragmentation in the Region.

Thus by the mid-1930's all the area of Nigeria had been formally amalgamated into a single unit, throughout which Indirect
Rule had been established, and direct tax was being paid into a network of Native Treasuries which covered the whole country. The
amalgamation of north and south, however, did not go much below
the surface. Certain common services depended directly on the
Governor, but there was as yet no central secretariat. The Territorial budget was no more than a last stage amalgamation of the
budgets of north and south. Nor was even this degree of unity very
persistent. In 1939, for administrative convenience, the south was
divided into an Eastern and a Western Region, the Benin area
going to the West.

And so it was that, largely as the result of historical accident, the
Federation of Nigeria eventually emerged with three Regions[1] each
dominated by a particular people and their social organization, but
in each case containing also a substantial alien, or at least non-
homogeneous, element. This awkward political outcome might
possibly have been avoided if Lugard's original idea of a strong
provincial organization had taken root; but this it failed to do in
any Region. Even if it had done so, it is unlikely that the fundamental differences in local government and finance with which we
shall be concerned, would not have made their way up to the
surface from their indigenous bases.

III. SIERRA LEONE

Sierra Leone is a small territory (with less than 25% of the
inhabitants of Ghana), lying between latitudes 7° and 10° N.
Its landward boundaries march with Guinea and Liberia. The
fine harbour (or fiord) of Freetown has always given it importance
as a naval base, and it was much used for this purpose in the second
world war. In the nineteenth century it was the centre for naval
operations up and down the coast in the suppression of the slave
trade. Freetown was for long the capital of British administration
on the Coast, to which the Gold Coast and the Nigerian colonies
were subordinate.[2]

British connexions in this area started with the purchase of the
mountainous peninsula on which Freetown stands, as a home for

---

[1] The Trust territory of the Cameroons was attached to the contiguous
Regions (East and North).

[2] See above, p. 94.

liberated slaves, captured on the high seas or brought back from North America and the Caribbean. Those who had only recently been deported and knew where they came from, were given the option of being returned to their people. But the great majority were completely detribalized, English was their only language and

MAP 9. Sierra Leone.

Christianity their religion. Some of these educated Creoles[1] were of great assistance to the Missions and administrators during the early days of the west coast colonies.[2] Their way of life has always been much more like that of the West Indies than of other Africans.

Complete ignorance of tropical ecology made the deeply wooded slopes of the Sierra appear an ideal location for setting the Creoles up as farmers. Too late it was realized that the vegetation was a once for all growth; once the bush was cleared the steep contours and perpetual rain made it inevitable that the hills would soon be eroded beyond reclamation. Today about 17,000 Creoles,

[1] Who still class themselves as 'African non-natives'.
[2] For example, in Lagos and Abeokuta; cf. Beobaku, op. cit.

descendants of the emancipated slaves, eke out a scanty farming existence in the peninsula and in the neighbouring island of Sherbro (which together formed the Colony area). The remainder of the total of 60,000 Creoles live in Freetown. The presence of these Creoles, although they are now a minority even in the peninsula, cause the social organization of the Colony area to diverge from that of the hinterland to a much greater extent than has ever been the case in Ghana or Nigeria.

The peninsula was transferred to the Crown from the originating Sierra Leonian Company in 1807, and was early given a measure of influence over its affairs, in that a Creole was put on the Governor's Advisory Council in 1811. In 1843 Sierra Leone was declared a 'settled colony' in the West Indian sense,[1] implying the intention to develop internal governmental institutions. In 1888 the Governor's Council was transformed into a Legislative Council of the usual pattern, and in 1893 Freetown was declared a municipality, with an elected majority on the council. (Unfortunately the council did not work well and had later to be replaced by a nominated board with an official president.)[2]

Up to the 1880's only the most shadowy connexions had been maintained with the hinterland; but in the late 1880's several events occurred that made it inevitable that more definite responsibility for the wild tribes be assumed. On the one hand Freetown and the flat lands between it and the isthmus were subject to repeated harrying and infiltration from the tribesmen. (Today 75% of the inhabitants of the Colony are non-Creole, and the proportion is steadily increasing.) On the other hand, by the Treaties of Berlin and Brussels, the European powers had undertaken to maintain order and to inaugurate development in their respective 'spheres of influence'. Not only was it necessary for the government to control the forays of the up-country tribes into the Colony; they had also now some responsibility for their actions on the frontier of French Guinea. Accordingly in 1896 a Protectorate was declared over the whole sphere of influence, corresponding to the present territory.

Insufficient anthropological research has been made into the indigenous organization of the peoples of Sierra Leone to give a

[1] See above, p. 34.
[2] The elective council was restored at the end of the second world war and seems to work reasonably well; see below, Chaps. 13, 14, 17.

satisfactory picture. What seems to emerge from the early reports[1] is a juxtaposition of two relatively large peoples, the Mende near Freetown and the Temne farther north and east, with smaller tribes tucked into various corners. Of these the Sherbro, not far from Freetown, were the most sophisticated. Several of the up-country tribes were not really small,[2] but had their centre across the border, in French Guinea or Liberia. All were organized as independent chiefdoms, the chiefs being elected in the normal West African manner from a narrow circle of eligible families. It would appear that once elected a chief could rule his people autocratically with much less need to consult a council than would for instance have been the case in Yorubaland or even in Hausaland, and without the constant threat of destoolment which might have hung over him in the Fanti or Ashanti country. How far the autocratic power of the chiefs was really indigenous and how far it crystallized as a result of British support (in the usual manner) is not easy to say; but the Moslem[3] influence, which was fairly strong, would favour autocratic rule.

The serious disturbances, which led to the British assumption of authority over the hinterland, had led (on the advice of the military) to a breaking up of some of the larger chiefdoms at the time of the declaration of the Protectorate; this process resulted in the administration being faced with a disorganized and somewhat atomistic tribal structure. The framers of the first comprehensive Ordinance for the Protectorate took the easy way out, by allowing any independent chief to call himself a Paramount, even if he had no junior chiefs under him.

This decision gave the country a start with 216 Paramounts. No doubt the constitution makers felt that this debasement of the coinage could do no great harm, and no doubt would have argued that it was forced on them by the break-up of the larger chiefdoms. Unfortunately the title 'Paramount' carried with it a certain aura, prompted by comparisons with other territories. It also implied the right to certain free services, such as the provision of a house, porterage, and transport, which was to give trouble when these

[1] Cf. also McCulloch, *Peoples of the Sierra Leone Protectorate*, op. cit.

[2] Much less attention to tribal boundaries seems to have been made than for instance in drawing the boundary between Eastern Nigeria and the Cameroons (later the British mandated S. Cameroons). Cf. R. Oliver, *Sir Harry Johnston*, op. cit.

[3] Today 50–75% of the population over most of the territory are reported as being Moslems, cf. Trimingham, op. cit.

came to be defined in modern terms. By and large this situation has endured, in spite of such amalgamations as the government has felt able to bring about. The country (with certainly not more than 2 million inhabitants) is still supporting over 140 separate Chiefdom Authorities under Paramounts.

From this brief account it emerges that in Sierra Leone we have to take account of three separate varieties of local government institutions: (1) the municipality of Freetown, (2) the councils of the rural area of the Colony, and (3) that of the Provinces (as the Protectorate is now called). It is in the Provinces that by far the most interesting and crucial developments have taken place.

Immediately on the proclamation of the Protectorate the introduction of taxation was announced, in the form of an annual payment of 5s. for a small house and 10s. for a larger one; this was to start in 1898. This was accompanied by other innovations, such as measures to suppress the universal domestic slavery. As we have seen, the hinterland was very disturbed at the time of the establishment of the Protectorate. It is therefore not surprising that these sudden actions caused trouble, almost amounting to rebellion, before the Ordinance of 1901 introduced some sort of order.

Under this, informal Tribal Authorities were set up, and given certain powers and duties, to be financed out of government grant, for independent tax powers were not included. The chiefs and headmen were made personally responsible for the collection of house tax, so that it had no connexion with the Tribal Authorities. Each chief was given a quota of revenue which he was required to produce. In practice this gave them no trouble since their powers were such that they could easily enforce full—or overfull—compliance with this very modest requirement. Powers of control, and later of taxation, within the city were also given to the headmen of the fourteen tribes of the Protectorate which had filtered into Freetown.

It is probable that the measures against domestic slavery were a more important cause of the ensuing unrest, but the government took fright and abandoned the higher (10s.) tax rate. This was a pity as it helped to fix in the minds of the people the belief that the proper rate of house tax always was, and always would be, 5s. In 1901 it was perhaps not unduly low, but in 1954 when the system was finally changed, it was derisory in relation to what was being cheerfully paid in other parts of the Coast.

Over the succeeding decades the governmental changes introduced were few and far between. A joint Legislative Council for the Colony and Protectorate was set up in 1924; it included three elected members from the Colony and three Paramounts from the Protectorate. In 1925 the courageous step was taken of announcing that domestic slavery must come to an end by 1927. Although this was formally achieved, as a social reform it was only partially successful. On the one hand freed slaves were in danger of losing their houses and such economic security as they had; on the other chiefs who really wished to continue their domestic amenities could easily do so by marrying some more 'wives'.

Sierra Leone was, however, moving slowly towards more sophisticated institutions. In 1932 a Native Courts Ordinance was passed, similar to those already in force in other parts of the Coast. Since, however, it was felt necessary to recognize all existing headman's courts, the country was soon overrun with courts, just as had happened in Ghana. About this time the separate jurisdiction of tribal headmen in Freetown came to an end, making it possible in principle to treat all citizens alike.

It was not, however, until 1937 that a decisive step forward in local government organization was taken. By the Tribal Authorities Chiefdom Tax and Treasuries Ordinance of that year, provision for the familiar pattern of organized Native Authorities was at last made in Sierra Leone. Formal councils were set up, without however any elective element, and mainly consisting of chiefs, their relatives and dependants. Reformed 'Chiefdom Authorities' gradually took the place of the unorganized Tribal Authorities, although some unreformed councils were still in existence in 1958, and some of the reformed authorities were so only in name.

Provision was made for a chiefdom tax, at a uniform rate of 4s. a year, throughout the territory, which was supposed to take the place of the dues and tributes formerly paid to the chiefs. Experience was to show that the attempted abolition of tribute was only very partially effective.[1] About one-third of the Chiefdom Treasury revenue was to remain as a perquisite of the chief. The rest was under the Ordinance to be paid into the Chiefdom Treasury under the strict supervision of an administrative officer, for the general purposes of the area. Later, this provision for payment was allowed to slide, or in some places was actually abrogated on the plea that it was inconvenient.

[1] See below, p. 201.

The new tax was in name on houses; it was in reality based on family units; but as the demand was issued at the same time and by the same people as were responsible for the government house tax, it was widely regarded as just an increase in the house tax. In fact the basis of the latter was also switched on to family units, but this was never made clear. The old form of Returns continued to be used, so that not only fathers of families, but also young men 'of marriageable age' living alone were classed as 'houses'. Chiefs continued to be responsible for collection in their chiefdoms, the actual work being carried out by headmen appointed by the chiefs.

Receipts continued to be given only to the chiefs when they handed in their quotas. Thus the ordinary man continued to have no direct contact with the local body; nor could there be any check on the amount paid by an individual. The chiefs were prompt and regular in handing over their quotas, no doubt for the reasons suggested above. Again there was no check on the persons assessed to tax. It was obvious that 'marriageable age' could be very variously interpreted; later events were to show that this had indeed been done.

The 'reformed' Chiefdom Authorities were instructed to prepare their Estimates with the advice of the District Officer; he was not, however, given any power of veto. They were then approved by the Provincial Commissioner. Thus, perhaps with more zeal than discretion, Sierra Leone attempted at one stroke a degree of emancipation from the administration as great as that achieved in other territories after long experience and experimentation.

By 1939, in spite of a latter-day effort of catching up, Sierra Leone had no more than laid the foundations of an effective local government system, much less a representative or responsible one. The country was still, by and large, completely undeveloped. Two railways did indeed crawl into the interior; the course from Freetown to Bo was eighteen hours (it can now be done in two hours by plane, but the traffic is small). Population remained low, centres small and isolated. Even among the chiefs the rate of literacy was low. Outside the Colony the Christian Missions had no more than touched the fringes. Nor in Freetown or the Colony is there much to record, other than the retrograde, but no doubt salutary, suspension of the Municipal Council.[1]

[1] See above, p. 108.

8

BEGINNINGS IN EAST AFRICA

I. UGANDA

THERE are comprised, within the modern Protectorate of Uganda, four 'agreement states'—Buganda, Toro, Ankole, and Bunyoro—as well as a large block of territory, mostly on the east and north, including no less than half the area, and containing (1948) more than half of the population of the whole country. The other agreement states (in the west along the Ruwenzori) are much smaller than Buganda, which, from its central position and historical importance, has given its name (with characteristic Bantu change of prefix) to the whole. The history of Uganda during the last seventy years is largely a matter of the relations between the British government and the Baganda people; but it must never be forgotten that Buganda is only a quarter of Uganda, and that the Baganda people are less than a quarter of the whole population.

The state of Buganda was formed long before the coming of the British; though it is not to be compared with Moslem states, like the Nigerian Emirates, it was distinctly more 'advanced' than most of what was to be found in Bantu Africa. The first Europeans to report on it (the explorers Speke and Grant in 1863) were decidedly impressed. These were the days of the Kabaka Mutesa I, who (though supported by a chiefly organization of a recognizable type) was the unquestioned master of his kingdom, and ruled it with ability. Then the discovery of this patch of settled government (or so it seemed) aroused the interest, not so much of traders (at least at the first round) as of missionaries. But for Uganda the arrival of the missionaries was a disaster.

Mutesa died in 1884; and within a few years, under the reign of his weak and dissolute son Mwanga, the country was in a state of civil war, with Catholic (French) and Protestant (English) missionaries supporting rival factions. Order was restored by the first British intervention, the expedition of Captain Lugard (as he then was), acting not yet on behalf of the British government, but

on behalf of the Imperial British East Africa Company, which for
a brief period (1887–93) was used as a means of pressing British
interests in that part of the world. The agreements which were made
by Lugard in 1889 were accordingly somewhat provisional in

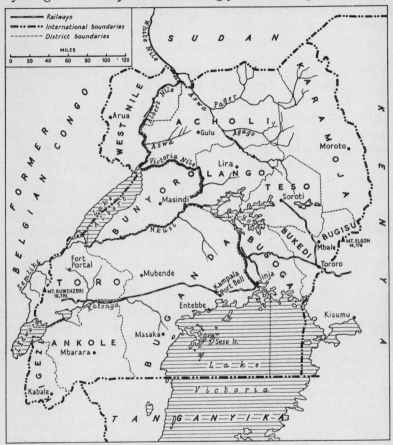

MAP 10. Uganda.

character; they antedate the Protectorate, which was only set up
after the Company had been dissolved in 1893. (They also antedate
Lugard's work in Northern Nigeria, in 1894 and later.) They
did nevertheless set the pattern on which British rule in Uganda
was to develop, just as they mark the origin of the ideas which
Lugard was to develop into a 'system' elsewhere.

Lugard's idea was to build up a monarchy, limited by a landed aristocracy, and advised by British officials. It was thus already in principle more constitutional than the Indian princely states, where the ruler, apart from his British Resident, was an autocrat. The makings of the 'aristocracy' were already there; there was a hierarchy of officials, major chiefs and clan elders, with (it appears) some territorial rights; below these there were lesser chiefs without territorial attachments. All together composed the Kabaka's 'audience', the *Lukiko*, a loose advisory council of unwieldly dimensions, which it was easy to take to be a body of real authority. Though there were no cash taxes, chiefs were entitled to customary tributes, of which *luwalo* (labour for public works), *busulu* (tribute labour to the chief), and *envujo* (a percentage on crops) were the most important. At an early stage of the British administration *saza* (or county) chiefs were turned into a landed aristocracy, their land being known as *mailo* land from the measurement used, the hierarchy of lesser chiefs was somewhat straightened out, and the Lukiko was strengthened, in the hope that it might develop into something like a parliament. Formerly the Kabaka had had no fixed residence; it was now settled at Kampala—or rather at Mengo, for Kampala is the name of the European and Asian city that has grown up beside the Buganda capital. These things were a beginning; but in Lugard's day the reforms could not go far—Uganda was too isolated. Further developments had to await, not so much the declaration of the Protectorate (1893) as the coming of the railway. The name with which they are to be associated is that of Sir Harry Johnston.

When Johnston came out, as Special Commissioner, in 1899, he was able to travel as far as Naivasha (in Kenya) by the new railway. Two years later the railway reached Kisumu (on Lake Victoria); since the telephone had come to Kampala in 1900, the extreme physical isolation of Uganda was now over. His previous work in Nyasaland and Nigeria[1] revealed that Johnston had very definite ideas about starting an administration. Like Lugard, he was essentially a centralizer—partly because he was acutely conscious of the need to draw jurisdictions so that they could be fiscally viable. As in Nyasaland, he insisted that a hut tax should be established at the earliest possible moment, even if initially it was impossible to collect anything like the correct amounts.[2] Thus the

[1] Cf. A. J. Hanna, *The Beginnings of Nyasaland*, 1956 and R. Oliver, op. cit.
[2] He was not unwilling to accept payment in kind, even in hippos.

mistake made in many colonies, of failing to make people tax-conscious from the first, was avoided in Uganda.

No less than Lugard, Johnston was a believer in Indirect Rule, but in a much less precise way than that which Lugard was working out in Northern Nigeria. He was anxious to make as little disturbance as possible to existing systems and customary rights. He had no faith in the future of white colonization in tropical Africa, and no great love for white settlers. He looked forward (no doubt in the far distant future) to the emergence of an African government.[1] Even to regard this as a distant possibility showed a rare openness of mind in 1900.

Johnston's first task was to make a more precise settlement in Buganda. He established the administration at Entebbe ('the seat'), away from Kampala, in delightful surroundings by the lake shore.[2] Already, by Lugard's Agreement, the Kabaka had been shorn, at least in principle, of his absolute authority; but the constitution under which Buganda has been governed since 1900, and according to which it is in some measure integrated with the rest of the Protectorate, dates from Johnston. What this integration meant in practice, at least to begin with, was that the British took over the day-to-day administration, leaving the Lukiko with a rather indeterminate kind of veto. (Though this worked fairly well for some decades, its weaknesses have become only too apparent in recent years.) But in order to get so far, considerable concessions had to be made. Most of these were concerned with land; the African's perpetual dread that the European is scheming to deprive him of his land showed up at an early stage of negotiations.[3] Before the Agreement was signed (in 1901) some 784 private estates had been granted in Buganda. There was also a condition which is of particular relevance for our purposes: that no direct taxation should be imposed in Buganda without the consent of the Lukiko. This did not apply to the hut tax (already in existence), but it did

[1] He was, perhaps as a consequence, in favour of individual land tenure (as the quickest way to the development of a cash economy)—the view that was taken by the East African Commission of 1955.

[2] For many years the advantages of this separation more than counterbalanced its inconvenience; it was only in 1959 that the decision was taken to move back to Kampala, it has not yet been implemented.

[3] This was not mainly a question of European colonization, though this was not excluded as it subsequently became, when the superior attractiveness of Kenya had been revealed. The main issue arose out of differing views about the requirements of, and even the need for, shifting cultivation.

block the way—how completely has of course been the object of much subsequent argument—to other forms of local taxation.

The Buganda agreement signed, Johnston hastened to make agreements with the other states. The intention was to follow the Buganda precedent, but conditions were by no means perfectly similar, so that to follow identically the same course was not easy. In Bunyoro there was a strong ruler who was induced, with some difficulty, to submit to much the same terms. In Toro the main authority rested with the saza chiefs, who had to be induced to 'federate', under a leader (the Mukama); hut tax was here to be collected by the saza chiefs, who could retain 10% as commission. Greater difficulty was found in Ankole, where the chiefs (of more Hamitic traditions) would not readily submit to a Paramount. Nevertheless, by 1901 all the western states had been brought in, with agreements which gave the Protectorate government substantially more power than it had been able to secure in Buganda.[1]

In the east things were different. Among the Bantu population of Busoga it was impossible to find a suitable leader; the District Commissioner had virtually to act as Paramount. This solution could not be adopted in the north; but in fact these parts were being opened up (with the encouragement of the government) by Buganda levies, and the Baganda were allowed to impose an administration upon these Nilo-Hamitic peoples. Those of Teso, in particular, proved adaptable to this arrangement; they adopted Baganda words into their language, and Baganda customs into their ways of life. (This is the District which in later days became the centre of cotton cultivation.)[2]

We now come to the period of Sir Hesketh Bell, who was appointed Commissioner in 1905, and became the first Governor in 1907. This was a time of economic development; Port Bell, the port of Kampala, was connected by steamer with the railhead at Kisumu; it then became apparent that the peasant cultivation of cotton was an economic possibility. Hitherto Uganda had been without substantial exports, and the government was at its wits' end to find some taxable capacity; for some years it was anxious to attract white settlers, merely in order to have something to tax.

[1] The District of Kigezi in the south-west is not an agreement state. It was added after a frontier settlement with the Belgian Congo in 1924.
[2] A considerable area of what is now Kenya was originally included in Uganda. These eastern Provinces were transferred to Kenya in 1901.

With the growth of cotton, and with the demonstration of the superior attractiveness of Kenya as a country for settlement, ideas of this kind were (fortunately) dropped. In fact, from at least the early 1920's, Uganda has been developed in the interests of its African inhabitants; though the part which they have played in the initiation and even in the execution of that policy has remained quite remarkably small.

It was at this time that the structure of local administration was formalized (Native Courts Ordinance, 1908) in a system which has remained in its broad lines even up to the present. The Protectorate was divided into Districts (ultimately fourteen in number), which were on the whole determined by tribal boundaries; but there were three Districts in Buganda, and those tribes which were too small to form a District on their own were put into a District along with other tribes. At the head of each District was a (European) District Commissioner; the European administration was nevertheless very small, and below this level was almost entirely in the hands of Africans.

Within a District there were four to eight sazas (translated counties); in Buganda the saza chiefs were the clan elders of the old régime, who themselves constituted a major element in the Lukiko.[1] Since the saza chiefs had been empowered to collect the government hut tax they had implicitly become government servants. Below the sazas were sub-county areas (*gombololas*), six or seven to a saza; but their function was legal and judicial, rather than administrative or financial; though there is some trace of gombololas before the British came, they seem largely to have been a British creation. The same is still more true of such organization as there was, at *muruka* or village level.

This local organization long remained distinctly sketchy; substantial power rested with the Protectorate administration, exercised through the District Commissioners and the (four) Provincial Commissioners set over them. Though the Buganda Provincial Commissioner may be reckoned to correspond to a British Resident with a Nigerian Emir, his rule was in fact much more direct. The Lukiko was playing a very passive role; the funds it controlled were minute, and neither the Baganda nor the administration paid much attention to it.

[1] In Johnston's time the Lukiko consisted of the twenty saza chiefs (of Buganda) and sixty-six other notables.

The twenties were a period of economic boom in Uganda; cotton was flourishing and coffee was beginning to develop. Revenue was in consequence flowing more freely, and with the improved credit status of the Uganda government, capital could be invested in the expansion of public services. But this expansion involved a re-inforcement of the hitherto exiguous outfit of British adminis-strators and technicians; though the efficiency of the Uganda government was improving, the gap between it and the native institutions was widening. (An Ex. Co. and Leg. Co., on the normal colonial pattern, had been set up in 1920.) But the position in the different Provinces was distinctly different.

Outside Buganda the chiefs were mere government appointees; they were approximating to a lower grade of the Civil Service. (This process had gone farthest in the Nilo-Hamitic areas of the north, but in the western Agreement states, though the position of the chiefs was formally stronger, the tendency was in the same direction.) It was now (since 1919) everywhere the position that unsatisfactory chiefs could be set aside by the administration; but in Buganda there was a conflict between these administration claims and those of the Kabaka, who still succeeded in keeping the appointment and dismissal of saza chiefs under his own con-trol. Such control was, however, in its turn becoming a formality; for in fact even the Baganda chiefs were realizing that they held of the British, in so far as their position was not held by hereditary right (even today half of the saza chiefs and not much short of 40% of gombolola chiefs are the sons of chiefs). The boom in-creased the value of the mailo land; the Baganda chiefs were fast becoming a territorial aristocracy. This, it may be, would not have been a source of distress to Lugard, or even to Johnston; but by the 1920's the interest of the peasants was the major pre-occupation of government, so that a clash between their interests and the need to maintain the authority of the chiefs, as a link in the administrative chain, was a source of concern.

Economic advance was meanwhile facilitating a number of im-provements on the fiscal side. The direct taxation on the African had previously consisted of (1) the hut tax instituted by Johnston— it was now becoming a poll tax; (2) the customary tributes of the chiefs, largely payable in kind; and (3) a tribute of labour services (luwalo), also in its origin customary, but which had been regu-larized in its application to public improvements (roads and so on) by an Ordinance of 1919. The spread of the money economy made it possible to replace these by something less archaic. In 1923 the personal tributes were converted into a local government tax—a tax which was to be paid into the Native Court Fund (as the Provincial Commissioners very properly insisted) to be used for local purposes. Already in the early twenties the *luwalo* was being commuted for a cash payment, in one place after another; in 1928 this change was made universal. Meanwhile it has been decreed that a portion of the poll tax (which was of course a central tax), varying from 10 to 30%, could be retained in the Districts. In all of these ways local revenues were increasing, and the duties of local administrations were expanding; but the administration was still carried on through the chiefs, who must now (at least outside Buganda) to be thought of as parts of the regular administrative machine.

Thus by 1930 the paternalist government (for such it must clearly be described) had many achievements to its credit. But it had failed to establish a *modus vivendi* with the traditional authorities (the Kabaka and his magnates), and it was failing to find a sufficient place for the energies of the new generation of more educated Africans, who, as a result of the development that had occurred, were naturally appearing upon the scene. At first, indeed, the latter was not so serious a question as it was in other territories; for District Commissioners were only too pleased to find the opportunity of making appointments which, from their point of view, were of higher grade; so long as the new kind of applicant was not aiming too high, there were ample opportunities in the public service. Strains nevertheless arose between the new-comers and the older type of chief; and in Buganda itself there were similar strains between the Kabaka and his court and the administration. This was the state of Uganda when she encountered the depression of 1930, which, for about five years, seriously hindered economic development.

The retrenchment of the depression years left little scope for political and administrative development either; revenue had been largely relying on the cotton export duty, and with the fall in the price of cotton,[1] the government suffered great financial loss. Nevertheless, during these years, the social changes which had been set

[1] The value of cotton exports fell from £3·3 m. in 1929 to £1·5 m. in 1930 and 1931.

in motion by the prosperity of the twenties were bound to continue. The proportion of the population whose outlook had been formed by their experience of the new Uganda steadily rose. That there were three points of view in Uganda—that of the administration, that of the traditional authorities, and that of the new Africans —became steadily more apparent. It was also apparent that the Kabaka and the Lukiko, who had accepted the earlier stages of British rule with remarkable passivity, would not be—perhaps we should say they would not be able to be—so passive at the next round.[1]

Between the depression and the second world war there comes an important episode—the governorship of Sir Philip Mitchell (as he became) that began in 1935. He came from Tanganyika, where he had worked with Sir Donald Cameron; thus he had an experience of a form of Indirect Rule at least as sophisticated as the Nigerian; far more sophisticated than that which had come of it in Uganda. Like Cameron he was much concerned with the understanding of tribal custom; it was there that he sought for an explanation of the resistance to chiefly authority, which, at the relatively advanced stage which Uganda had then reached, was more probably to be understood in other ways. Mitchell's anthropological interest did nevertheless have one most important result. It was perhaps his realization that the council (rather than the chief) was, as often as not, an integral part of the indigenous institutions of Africa, that led him to encourage the setting up of councils even at the village level (as well as District Councils). There were parts of Uganda where this development appeared to have a remarkable success. In the east (which, as we have seen, had formerly failed to develop any native 'state'), the Busoga set up 238 Parish Councils, as well as 52 Sub-county and 8 County Councils at higher 'tiers'. The main business of the lower councils was to act as an informal means of electing representatives for the next level; their existence did nevertheless mean that a wider circle was drawn in to take some interest in local government. The councils were formalized by the Native Authority Incorporation Order of 1938. As yet, they were no more than advisory (though by 1940 estimates began to be laid before the District Councils);

[1] The administration would have liked to develop the Lukiko in a more representative direction, with the idea that it might serve as a place of contact between the older and newer classes, as indeed it would have to do if it were to play a part in a future constitutional self-government. But all that could be achieved was the admission of one elected member!

but their existence made it possible to look forward to the day when the chief as Native Authority would be superseded by the council as Native Administration.

The war years were another period of standstill, in which (on the whole) things rather slipped back. There was at first a remarkable demonstration of loyalty, indicated (in the field with which we are concerned) by a ready acceptance of tax increases that had formerly been resisted—an income tax on expatriate Europeans and on Asians, and a sharp increase in the poll tax on Africans. But as the war went on, and the European administrators were thinned out, more and more power fell into the hands of the chiefs who (as we have seen) had effectively become a lower order of the administration. Though the councils (excepting the Lukiko) now contained a substantial number of elected members, they had not been allowed to develop executive powers. On the whole the chiefs were backward looking; they tended, especially in Buganda, to relapse into quarrelling and incompetence. The educated class, still denied what they considered their rightful place, now for the first time took to nationalist politics. In January 1945 there were some rather serious riots at Kampala.

We shall be considering the subsequent developments in another place.

II. KENYA

As we have seen, the peoples of modern Kenya belong to more or less the same ethnic groups as those of Uganda. So far as the Africans are concerned, however, a much greater proportion of the area is inhabited by the Nilo-Hamitic groups, largely still nomadic. To a great extent this is dictated by the low rainfall and scant vegetation. Without extensive development of water supplies (even if this were possible) little cultivation could be undertaken over vast areas of the territory. Two other fundamental ethnic differences as compared with Uganda are the obvious one of European settlement, and the greater thickness of the 'wedge of India' driven in from the time of the building of the railway at the beginning of the century.

When the British arrived they found the tribes less well organized, and on the whole less advanced, than in Uganda, certainly much less advanced than the Baganda. Only among the Luhia of Elgon and the Luo of the Kavirondo (who are not Bantu) was

there anything approaching the chiefly organization of most parts
of Uganda. Among both the Kikuyu, however, and their neighbours the Kamba, opportunities were already available for enterprising natural leaders to push or buy their way into leading
positions in the councils of 'elders' (owing to the use of a peculiar

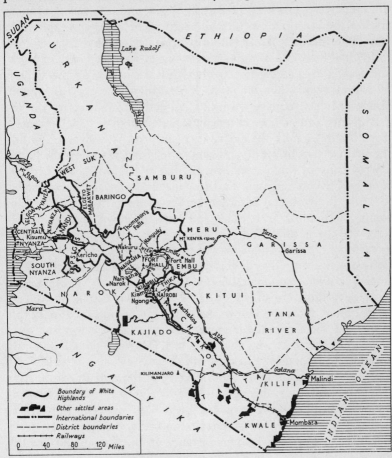

MAP 11. Kenya.

circular system of age grading it often occurred that comparatively
young men could attain the highest grades).

Alien settlement—of Arabs—along the coastal belt had taken
place at a very early stage, and Arab elements are still important
there, especially in Mombasa; for long they owed allegiance to the

Sultan of Zanzibar. The process of the alienation of land for white settlement began early in the present century. Largely as an aftermath of the Boer war, considerable numbers of Boer farmers were taking refuge in Kenya from what promised to be an uncomfortable situation for them in the Union. The bulk of the European immigrants were, however, of British origin, and this was even more true of the second wave of white settlement, after the first world war. The 'Settled' Areas (the distinction being that they contain individual land rights) today cover an area about the size of Yorkshire, inhabited (according to the 1948 census) by 62,700 whites, of whom 15,000 live on farms. In addition these areas contain about 500,000 Africans, working, directly or indirectly, for the Europeans, and so more or less detached from their tribal organizations. As in Uganda, the Asians are mainly town dwellers, providing the greater part of retail, and some wholesale, trade. In the larger towns many of them have professional and middle class occupations and live in a manner indistinguishable from the Europeans.

These fundamental differences—between the two forms of land tenure, individual and tribal, and between town and country— have led to a double dichotomy in the development of local government organization: between town and country and between Settled Area and African Reserves. Given these awkward conditions it would seem inevitable that the development of responsible local government institutions for Kenya as a whole must have been a much more difficult process than in Uganda. In a sense this is so and consequently in some respects Kenya has certainly lagged. The first African chairman of a District Council was only appointed in 1959 (in Elgon Nyanza), and the same year saw the first African appointed by the Secretary of State to an administrative post. Moreover, throughout, the development of local government institutions in Kenya has been very uneven; but this is partly due to difficulties of terrain, and to the consequent backwardness of certain tribes, for instance on the Somaliland border. On the other hand, from quite an early stage some executive responsibility was given to Africans, through the organization of African District Councils,[1] an experiment which was not without influence on the development of democratic institutions in other parts of Africa. It will thus be apparent that in tracing the history of local government and finance in Kenya (the task in which we

[1] See p. 127.

must now turn), we have to concern ourselves (as in Sierra Leone) with the diverse fortunes of separate streams of local government institutions, which though their jurisdictions may be physically contiguous, even interlocked, have no connexion with each other. This is almost as true today as it was when the African District Councils were first established. But this is to anticipate.

Due to its more accessible position the Kenya area had earlier contact with Europeans than Uganda. Krapf, the German explorer, reached the Tana river in 1848, and made friends with some of the Kamba tribe. Teleki and Höhnel, two other continental explorers who were in the country in 1887, left an invaluable account of the people and their organization. This was on the eve of the granting of the charter of the British East Africa Company. For the protection of its transport the Company had early to establish a line of forts along the route to Uganda. Lugard himself built the first of these, near Nairobi; Machakos was also developed as a centre at an early stage. The Foreign Office took over from the Company in 1895, and the following year the construction of the railway started. In 1899 Nairobi was founded as its headquarters, and shortly afterwards was chosen as the capital of the East African Protectorate as it had now become. The railway wound its slow and painful way westwards to Kisumu (which was reached in 1900), with a branch to the north, taking off at Nakuru, traversing the main white settlement area, and eventually the Uganda border. On its way it had to contend with severe opposition, at first from wild beasts, and later from equally wild tribes; the Nandi north of Kisumu were particularly savage.

Formal administration of the country can hardly be said to have started before 1897. In that year the jurisdiction of traditional courts was recognized, at least as a temporary measure. As late as 1903 there were no more than eighty-seven officers in the whole territory concerned with African matters. In 1905 the Colonial Office took over from the Foreign Office. This soon led to a decided step forward. The next year an African Affairs Department was established. Since there were, generally speaking, no traditional chiefs, the system had early been adopted of appointing 'chiefs' and 'headmen' who were of course purely civil servants, to look after administration locally; as yet there was no thought of anything but direct rule. Under the Native Courts Ordinance of 1908 an attempt was made to carry on the administration of justice through the joint efforts of these chiefs and the traditional members of elders' councils—a step perhaps in the direction of Indirect Rule. A large number of additional chiefs were appointed for the purpose. But the experiment was not a success, and it was decided, even at this early stage, effectively to separate the executive and the judicial. The position of the Native Courts was regularized by rules put into effect between 1911 and 1913.

On the executive side the development of local government received an important stimulus on the appointment of Sir Percy Girouard, who had had experience in Nigeria, as Governor in 1909. Under his guidance the first Native Authority Ordinance was promulgated in 1912. Although this established no new system it strengthened the hands of the traditional councils, and—important for the future—it transferred to them some minor executive functions, with provision for consultation on a wider range of subjects. Although willing, for want of any previous experience in such matters the councils were unable to contribute very much at first. Consequently most of the work continued to be done by the chiefs and headmen. At this point further developments were held up by the war.

Before we proceed with the interwar developments of African local government it will be convenient to see what progress had been made with the other streams up to this point; there is very little to relate. The year after the railway had established its headquarters at Nairobi the town was given a Municipal Committee of five members, with some unofficials, but chaired by an official. From the first the Asian community was represented among the unofficial members. Two years later a first Townships Ordinance was passed (1903). Nairobi and Mombasa were the first towns to come under it. Mombasa, because of its strategic position at the head of the railway, had already started on the rapid expansion which was to increase its population 200% between 1911 and 1926. These two were followed by three smaller towns, Nakuru, Naivasha, and Eldoret, and shortly afterwards by Kiambu and Machakos, (both of these within a short distance of Nairobi). These smaller towns were managed by the local District Commissioner, presently supported by advisory committees. Their executive responsibilities were small; for finance they depended wholly on the government. Among the white settlers on the farms there was as yet no demand for any form of local government, and then and much later, considerable opposition to any suggestion of local taxation.

The beginnings of local government in the African areas had, as we have seen, been built on the foundation of the traditional councils, which even at their most definite (for instance in Kikuyu and Kamba areas), were confined to the strictly neighbourhood unit (what would now be called the 'location' or 'sublocation' level). Some larger unit for consultation immediately, and eventually for executive powers, would clearly be needed. On the other hand the interest taken by Africans in local government projects was encouraging. For instance the Nandi, who had so recently harried the workers on the railway, by 1918 had got to the point of building themselves a general Assembly Hall. It even proved possible to organize a rudimentary council among the nomadic Masai. In relatively advanced Central Nyanza the chiefs had begun to meet for quarterly consultations. In Kisumu in the same area, the establishment of more formal councils was already under discussion before the war. At Fort Hall in the northern Kikuyu country an advisory committee of seventeen Africans was working successfully from the early 1920's. In view of all this advance among Africans it is not surprising that the beginning of political consciousness among the Africans of the Central Province (the Kikuyu and their relatives) can be traced from the same period.

All of these movements had reference to larger areas than the locations, and, it will be observed, they were not confined to any one part of the country. At the centre too, more interest was being taken in African development, notwithstanding the impact of the second large wave of white settlement. In 1920 Kenya was promoted from a protectorate to a colony. Two years later the first Member for African Affairs was appointed to Ex. Co.

The fruits of this greater interest in local government were seen in the important Native Councils Ordinance of 1924. This definitely broke with the attempts to build solely on the traditional elders' councils. Members of the new councils were appointed (by the Governor on the recommendation of the District Commissioner), so as to represent as large a range of relevant interests as possible. They held office for three years. The new councils were empowered to raise a 'rate' (in fact the usual flat sum poll tax), and were encouraged to make by-laws on such diverse subjects as water supply, food quality, latrines, agriculture and soil conservation, markets and slaughter houses. Although subject to confirmation by the Governor, these by-laws were normally given the force of law immediately.

All councils were of course under the presidency of the District Commissioner (and, as we have seen, by and large this is still the case). Their first duty was unquestionably that of consultation, and of providing the administration with information concerning the feelings of Africans in the Reserves. Their second duty was to act as agents for carrying out government policy, especially in respect of social and economic services. In this they were working alongside of the government-appointed chiefs. In all of this there was much in common with the system being worked out in Uganda, but with two important differences. In Kenya there was nothing of the element of hereditary chiefs which had resulted from the social organization of some of the tribes and from the agreements negotiated at the beginning of the century. Secondly, from a very early stage, the deliberations of Kenya councils were given a genuine meaning, mainly because they had definite executive functions, and hence decisions had to be taken by them.

By the end of 1925 African District Councils, as they came to be called, had been set up in almost all areas of the Colony. Their performance, however, varied considerably. To some extent this was due to the immense differences in their financial resources. Central Nyanza had a budget of over £10,000; Baringo could dispose of no more than £172. Initiative, however, was by no means correlated with wealth and size. The Baringo council took an active share in stock culling. The Kajiado Masai imposed a special tax (in 1929) for the improvement of water supplies. In 1935 the Embu council introduced a by-law to reduce the extent of the operation of female circumcision at the initiation ceremony.

A Native Authority Ordinance and a Chiefs' Ordinance of 1937 looked forward to the further development of the District Councils, including the introduction of the elective principle. A good foundation had already been laid. Moreover it was one which could be adjusted to transition to responsible representative institutions without fundamental alteration. In contrast to the position in Uganda, conciliar development in Kenya did not imply that the services of chiefs were any less necessary than before. Instead of a fifth wheel in the system, they were becoming a sort of subordinate cadre of District Officers, or more strictly Government Agents. By the Chiefs' Ordinance of 1937 their pay was provided by the government and they became formally responsible to the District Commissioner for their Locations. They have an important duty to keep themselves familiar with every part and every aspect of their territory, by frequent journeys throughout the area. The chiefs (and the headmen under them) thus serve as true liaison officers in a three way sense, between the administration, the council, and the elders.

In the meantime the sluggish stream of local government in the European areas was beginning to show some sign of movement; there is some progress to report in the rural, and much more in the urban areas. From 1919 advisory 'District' committees were being established outside the urban areas, and the following year local Road Boards were set up, frequently with identical membership. The settlers were beginning to take an interest at least in local roads (which they required for the evacuation of their crops), although not to the extent of paying for them themselves, other than through the general tax system of the Colony.

Meantime in Nairobi the official majority on the council had been abolished (1918), all officials except the District Officer being withdrawn. The next year the town was declared a municipality with self-accounting powers. This implied that its budget was free of government control save in respect of those services which were grant aided. Asians, however, refused to sit on the new council until (in 1925) its constitution was revised so as to provide for twelve members (five elected Europeans, five nominated Asians (including one Goan), one official, and one other nominated member). No African members were appointed until 1946. From 1923 the council had been thrown on its own resources to a considerable extent, since the government ceased to finance the important services of roads, drainage, public health, as well as staff salaries. These costs were met by the council out of a property rate (of which more below). Outside Nairobi a 1918 amendment to the Townships Ordinance enabled the government to declare a group of houses a 'trading centre', thus putting its foot on the first rung of what was to become a regular ladder of progressive local autonomy. At this stage it would however still be administered by the District Commissioner.

Government interest in the development of local institutions was demonstrated by the appointment in 1926 of a Commission under Mr. Feetham who had been responsible for the organization of local government in South Africa, to examine the whole question of local government institutions in Kenya. As a result of the report of this Commission a coherent and forward-looking system (albeit still running in separate streams) emerged in a series of Ordinances promulgated during the next few years. In the first place in the rural parts of the Settled Areas District Councils were set up. They were planned to consist of not less than ten elected Europeans and two appointed Africans. The new councils were empowered to levy a rate on unimproved land values, to impose either a flat or a graduated rate on land area in agricultural neighbourhoods, or an industrial rate on land not used for agriculture. European farmers were still very uninterested in local government (although some of them thought that an ambulance might be a good idea); so that it was not until much later, in the 1950's, that much use was made of these powers.

Much more progress was made in urban government. Under the Municipal Ordinance of 1928 and the Townships Ordinance of 1930 the government developed further the idea of a regular ladder of urban emancipation; this idea was later adopted by Tanganyika, and quite recently (by the Urban Ordinance of 1958) by Uganda. The lowest rung in the ladder was, as we have seen, the 'trading centre'; at this stage the council worked wholly under the direction of the District Commissioner, but was not entirely without responsibility, since it was forced to direct its attention to the particular problems of its own little multiracial cluster. Above this came two grades of 'Township', with gradually widening responsibilities. In both of these the District Commissioner remained the executive, but in the upper layer he was assisted by an elected committee. Above this came the grades of Municipal Board and Municipal Council. The fundamental distinction between these two was that Municipal Councils frame their Estimates without reference to any other authority, while Boards require to obtain government approval. The exact powers and duties of a particular body were laid down in its individual instrument, as we have found to be so common in West Africa. In municipalities municipal European and Asian members were and still are elected on a common roll. African members being appointed on the recommendation of the relevant African District Council.

Soon after the Ordinance was adopted Nairobi was given further powers, while Mombasa, Nakuru, Eldoret, Kisumu, and

Kitale were declared municipalities. By and large this system of gradual urban education in the responsibilities of local government has remained. When however the system of Settled Area County Councils was established (in 1952), the smaller towns became urban districts within the county areas. Under the Local Government Rating Ordinance of 1928 Municipal Councils were given power to rate on improvements as well as on the unimproved value of land; but so far little advantage has been taken of this within urban areas. These are matters which we shall be discussing extensively at a later stage, so that they need not detain us now.

III. TANGANYIKA

Tanganyika is that part of the former German East Africa which fell in 1919 under a British mandate; it is, however, worth noticing that there was some British penetration of the territory even before it became a German colony. Zanzibar (which remained a British protectorate) was the base from which this proceeded; its initial object was the control of the (Arab) slave trade, which had a major route from Ujiji (on Lake Tanganyika) to Zanzibar. The effect of the slave trade on tribal organization, all over the future territory, was shattering; it must never be forgotten that the slave trade continued here until a much later date than in West Africa. It is, however, unlikely that even in the absence of slaving the tribes of Tanganyika could have developed, on their own, much cohesion; the nature of the country—an archipelago of habitable patches in a sea of desert—was too unfavourable. They fall, even today, into a number of decidedly separate groups, which may be roughly classified as follows.

First, round the shores of Lake Victoria (the Haya on the south-west, the Sukuma on the south-east) are a group of tribes that, if it were not for political boundaries, would look towards Uganda; they have Hima chiefs, like the Baganda, though their indigenous organization (especially among the Sukuma) is less advanced. Then, on the slopes of Kilimanjaro and in that neighbourhood, there are the Chagga—now important and prosperous with their arabica coffee, but formed, in comparatively recent times, out of Kamba, Teite, and Masai elements. They may thus be regarded as an overflow from what is now Kenya. The Masai extend from Kenya into the centre of Tanganyika, where they abut upon the Gogo, a large but backward tribe in an inhospitable territory. On the other side of this central semi-desert, toward Nyasaland and Mozambique, are tribes (much broken up by slaving) that have affinities over those borders. All the main tribes are accordingly outward-looking, in different directions.

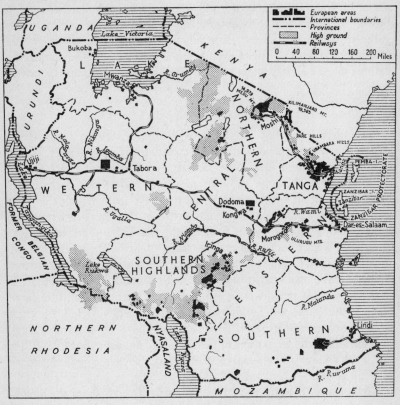

MAP 12. Tanganyika.

An historical sketch must begin with the German period. The territory was recognized as German in 1890, but at that date German penetration had only begun. For some years the German administration was largely military; the territory had to be subdued, and the administrative posts were essentially forts. Such development as occurred at this stage was for the benefit of the settlers, who were encouraged to set up plantations on the slopes of Kilimanjaro and Mount Meru, in the Usumbaras and in the Tanga region. There was large expenditure on administration,[1] but an acute shortage of administrative personnel. Accordingly, though the administration was essentially 'direct', there was a widespread use of native assistants (*akidas* and *jumbes*). Wherever such a system has been used (as it was, for instance, with the 'court clerks' of Eastern Nigeria) it has been a source of abuse. Only in the extreme west (in Bukoba among the Haya, and in Ruanda-Urundi) was there any attempt to make use of indigenous authorities with German Residents. On the whole this was an unhappy period. It culminated in the Maji-Maji rebellion of 1905; this was rapidly suppressed, but after it was over there was an improvement.

Under the rule of Governor Dernberg (1905–10) the interests of the Africans were more considered. African agriculture was encouraged; there were restrictions on the use of forced labour and upon the alienation of land to Europeans. Some provision was made for African education and public health services were set up. After 1910 there was a reaction, with renewed emphasis on economic development in the interest of the Europeans (by 1914 the trade of German East Africa exceeded the total of Kenya's and Uganda's). But some of the better feeling of the Dernberg years was retained; most of the Tanganyika Africans remained faithful to the Germans during the war that followed.

British administration in Tanganyika (the first British Governor arrived in 1920) began with a phase that was rather experimental. The former German estates were auctioned to other Europeans; but apart from these all land was vested in the Crown, which could grant 'rights of occupancy' to existing holders—by this device native land was effectively protected. Almost at once the *akida* system was abolished; in its place there was to be introduced a system of Native Authorities and Native Courts (with British District Officers) more or less on the Uganda model.[2] But at this point the British were expecting to find that the Tanganyika tribes had traditional chiefs (admittedly they would have been submerged by the Germans); when once the chief had been discovered, he would be set up as Native Authority, in accordance with the principles of 'early' Indirect Rule. As time went on, it became

[1] Already in 1900 the budget of German East Africa was equivalent to £618,000—to be compared with £193,000 for the whole of British East Africa.
[2] Native Courts Ordinance 1920; Native Administration Ordinances 1921 and 1923.

apparent that (excepting among the lacustrine tribes of the north-west, with their Hima chiefs) such chiefs did not exist. Thus the new system of Native Authorities got off to rather a slow start.[1]

Nevertheless, even before the governorship of Sir Donald Cameron (which began in 1925) things were beginning to move. Economically the Territory was prosperous; it had already ceased by 1925 to be a charge on the British Treasury. The new adminis-trators were finding their feet; ideas of building native administra-tions, to which the British official would be no more than an adviser (and even the idea of 'federation', which was later to be so important a means to that end) were already being canvassed. But it was Cameron who brought these ideas together into a policy.

He came to Tanganyika from Northern Nigeria, where he had worked with Lugard, and may indeed be regarded as Lugard's chief disciple.[2] By this time, it will be remembered, the Lugard ideas were very well developed; the *Dual Mandate* had appeared in 1922. Thus the notions of Indirect Rule which Cameron brought with him to Tanganyika were no longer of the older type, centred upon the chief or other potentate as native authority; they had already attained a new flexibility. It was a part of his philosophy that 'the function of Indirect Rule is in the field of local govern-ment; it is a progressive, not a static system'.

The search for indigenous institutions, on which a new system could be based, was now taken up with vigour. (The use of anthropological assistance, in a matter of this sort, was an innova-tion in which Tanganyika led the way in East Africa.)[3] The success, or at least the immediate success that was achieved was of course various; there were the lake tribes, with their well-known institu-tions, which presented no problem; there were possibilities of developing contact with traditional institutions among the Chagga, in the Usambaras and in Iringa; elsewhere there were greater difficulties. Everywhere, however, some sort of native administra-tion was set up, under a new Ordinance (1926), which gave powers for several sorts of adaptation to local conditions. Cameron was prepared to recognize four main types: (1) a federation of chiefs, (2) individual chiefs, (3) tribal councils, (4) individual headmen;

[1] Cf. M. L. Bates, *Tanganyika, The Development of a Trust Territory.* To be published by O.U.P.

[2] See above, p. 77.

[3] The Gold Coast Department of Anthropology had been established in 1921. See above, p. 88.

any of these arrangements was acceptable so long as it fitted in with the things the people would do for themselves. In fact, by the beginning of 1927, there were 184 superior authorities and 495 inferior authorities, over the thirty-three Districts of Tanganyika.

In his search for institutions which would mean something to the people themselves, Cameron was prepared to go right down to the village level (to something which may almost be compared with the Indian panchayat). Nevertheless, at this level, fiscal autonomy was an impossibility; for administrative and fiscal purposes some sort of grouping was essential. But even this grouping Cameron was reluctant to impose from on top; if the initiative could be taken from below it was much preferred. In Sukumaland, for instance, there were at first no less than twenty-six superior and 156 inferior authorities; but as early as 1929 there was joint action, for such purposes as fly control. (Formal federation did not come until 1942.) The amalgamation of Native Treasuries proceeded more actively than the grouping of native administrations themselves.

In Tanganyika, as in many other territories, the side of government in which popular interest could most easily be aroused was the Native Courts. Cameron desired to take advantage of this, and encouraged his British officials to go deeply into this part of their responsibilities. Lack of specialization between administrative and judicial functions has been rather a characteristic of Tanganyika. At the earliest stage of development it had its point; but its defects, in distracting the attention of officials, and in directing the minds of the Africans towards this, rather than towards more constructive aspects of local government, have become more apparent as time has gone on.

It was always a weakness of the Cameron system that the financial resources available to the authorities which were being set up, were so extremely slender. The normal rate of hut (or poll) tax, in the years after 1925, was 10s. (with minor variations from year to year and from place to place). But the major part of the proceeds of this tax accrued to the Territorial government; as such, it amounted to something of the order of 40% of Territorial revenues. The share which could be left for local purposes was therefore extremely small; and out of this the chiefs' salaries had to be paid (the old customary tributes had been abolished). It was not until after 1940 that the local share of the direct tax reached 25%. It is true that from 1928 the native administrations had the power to levy a 'rate' (poll tax) on a graduated scale; but no use seems to have been made of this until 1944.

It is indeed apparent that during the thirties (Cameron left in 1930) much of the drive for which he had been responsible was lost. This is largely, of course, to be explained by the depression; at this time a reaction was general; it may nevertheless be said to have been more marked in Tanganyika than in some other places. With a succession of short governorships the administration lost its coherence; the Secretariat for African Affairs (the instrument of Cameron's policy) was abolished; the development of local institutions was no longer a matter with which the Territorial government was much concerned. It may nevertheless be maintained that there are some points of view from which a period of *laisser-aller* was not useless; if the new institutions were to develop they must develop on their own—though it is indeed probable that they were left to develop on their own too soon. In some areas, at least, such progress did occur. 1932 is the date of the passage of the Chagga Co-operative Societies Ordinance. The Kilimanjaro Native Coffee Union (K.N.C.U.), which has since been the organ of much social development in Chaggaland (even in the field of education) was founded in 1935. It may well be said that among the Chagga conditions were exceptionally favourable; even greater credit may therefore be given for the developments, which occurred at the same time, in the coastal areas, especially in the neighbourhood of Dar-es-Salaam itself. This was a district where tribal organization had been destroyed; but under the guidance of locally chosen Liwalis (a brilliant contrast to the Warrant Chiefs of Eastern Nigeria) a local consciousness was gradually built up. A key to success seems to have been found in the removal of the rural organization outside the town; emphasizing that town and country problems were sharply distinct.

These, however, were special cases; on the whole, in the years after Cameron, things slipped back. There were some rather spectacular failures. Cameron had even attempted to establish a form of Indirect Rule among the Gogo—a wholly pastoral tribe, some half-million strong, in a drought-stricken region. Repeated efforts to establish a tribal council always broke down, and in the end the search for an acceptable form of organization, at anything above the clan level, had to be abandoned.

PART III

THE TRANSITION TO MODERN INSTITUTIONS

9

TRANSITION IN THE WEST INDIES

THE immediate pre-war years were marked by depression and unrest in the West Indies, with serious rioting in some places, and a sharp upswing of political consciousness. The British government was much concerned with these occurrences; a Comptroller of Development and Welfare was appointed, and in 1938 a Royal Commission was set up to make a thorough economic social and political investigation into the whole area.[1] Although its report was not published until the end of the war, its inquiries and suggestions had begun to stimulate interest in the Islands in advance of publication. Following the recommendations of the Commission, the Secretary of State (Colonel Oliver Stanley) sent a Dispatch to the West Indian Governors (March 1945), very much on the lines of the subsequent Creech Jones Dispatch to the African Governors in 1947.

The Commission (as we have already seen in relation to Barbados)[2] took the view that a reform and extension of the local government institutions in the Islands was urgently needed, both as a steadying influence and to improve the standard of services. Colonel Stanley, in announcing that it was the policy of the United Kingdom government to lead the Islands to self-government, emphasized the importance of promoting the growth of citizenship and of a sense of responsibility. This he felt could best be achieved by the development of local government, which would give valuable experience, especially in committee work. He also attached great importance to the development of community services, on lines already suggested by the Comptroller of Development and Welfare.

I. JAMAICA

Already before the war a body of opinion in Jamaica was forming in favour of modernizing the traditional Parochial Boards, although (as we have seen) these were functioning more successfully

[1] See above, p. 31.   [2] Ibid.

as local government authorities than any others in the West Indies. In 1942 Mr. L. C. Hill, from the United Kingdom local government service, was asked to report on the organization and finance of Local Authorities in Jamaica. His report,[1] published the following year, dealt in turn with basic organization, local taxation, and the financial relation between the Island government and the Parochial Boards. In respect of organization Hill suggested scrapping the existing boards and substituting on the one hand larger rural units, on the other a rather odd sort of town council built up from District Committees. None of this part of the report was accepted. This need not surprise us, not merely because the Parochial Boards were an integral part of Jamaican life which would not have been set aside without very good cause, but because there was little evidence that they were unsuited to the rather limited functions which alone would fall to local bodies in a small island.

In the later parts of the Hill Report there were two interesting and forward-looking points. Hill was especially anxious that his proposed District Committees should be fully democratic, elected by universal suffrage. When adult suffrage was adopted for the Island government (actually in the following year), it naturally followed in the Parochial Boards. In respect of local taxation Hill felt strongly that all should contribute; without this it would be impossible to develop a consciousness of responsible citizenship. If this were to have been really carried out it would presumably have implied some sort of poll or personal tax, since certainly at that time by no means the whole community was making a contribution through the parish rate. Although there is a case for a personal tax (and as we shall see a small and modified form is now being introduced in Jamaica), the case is much less strong than in a country where the responsibilities of local bodies are likely to be greater. Further, since all land is held in individual right, there is no insurmountable problem such as faces the assessment of a property rate in tribal areas.

Whatever the exact form of local tax to be used, Mr. Hill's emphasis on the need for a wider base of tax incidence was very much to the point. One of the enduring difficulties in the West Indies is that so much reliance has been placed on taxes on outlay (especially customs duties) that the feeling of individual respon-

[1] L. C. Hill, *Local Government in Jamaica*, 1943.

sibility has never been developed. Hill was also anxious to see further financial opportunities available to the Local Authorities through grants from the Island government. In particular he wished to see specific grants for poor relief and roads. There was indeed a very good case for more specific grants, especially as they would have given the government a means of equalizing opportunities between the parishes, which are very differently placed in respect of economic opportunity. As we shall see, extensive road grants have since developed, although on lines that have more of a political than an economic orientation. Grants for poor relief would probably have been an expense beyond the resources of the Island government.

The basic trouble with local government in Jamaica was—and unfortunately still is—the weakness of its autonomous revenue. As we have seen, the traditional base of the local rate was full capital value: there was, however, a strong party in the Island which wished to change over to the unimproved value base, in order to encourage development, and (in the eyes of some) to relieve the small farmer of a charge that was felt to be beyond his means.

There was, however, no agreement whether the change should be made. In the meantime valuation was getting more and more out of date. From about 1952 Parochial Boards, in desperate straits for revenue, began to work on what was somewhat oddly called a 'sliding scale'. This implied the introduction of progressively higher poundages as the unit of property holding increased. In Jamaican conditions the higher poundages fell with particular intensity on the sugar plantations and on the new bauxite firms, both industries especially dependent on large acreages. This form of tax also encouraged the artificial fragmentation of properties in order to escape the high poundages at the top of the scale. All this could have been avoided if a revaluation had been promptly carried through, whatever the basis of assessment subsequently imposed. Within a few years the sliding scale had got quite out of hand in some parishes, with a single large landowner paying more than half the total rate revenue, quite irrespective of the level of his taxable profits. In order to stop this flagrant inequity the Island government felt bound to freeze the scale of parish rates, making good the deficit in parish finances by the not very satisfactory method of a block grant based on the previous year's revenue collection. After further advice and assistance the government finally decided to adopt the unimproved value base (the first idea was to use full capital value assessment for service charges, but this was subsequently abandoned). By the end of 1958 two of the thirteen parishes had been revalued on the new base, with results which we shall discuss at a later stage.[1]

The depressing feature of the whole episode has been not so much the failure to reach agreement concerning the base of the tax; on this there might reasonably be two views. Nor was it even the delay in completing the revaluation, however regrettable. Rather it was the deprivation for so many vital years of the responsibility of Parochial Boards to fix their own poundages, and to use the local rate as the balancing factor in their budgets. Up to the war and even beyond, local government in Jamaica had displayed a surprisingly persistent virility (if we except those parishes overwhelmed by natural disaster). Only time, and the restoration of budgetary freedom (whenever that occurs), will show whether it has been able to survive the years of enforced dependence.

II. BARBADOS

As we have seen, the Royal Commission was extremely critical of the working of the Barbadian Vestries. The franchise was extremely narrow, yet the system of annual election made for instability and inhibited any sort of planning. The whole system was still tied closely to the established Church. The authorities suffered chronically from the diseconomies of small scale, while at the same time neither they nor the *ad hoc* boards received any help or guidance from the Island government. The Reports of the Chief Medical Officer for the Island[2] described the chaotic conditions existing and concluded that 'while the island continues to be serviced by nine practically independent medical departments, six miscellaneous medical services, twelve separate public health boards or bodies and eleven District Poor Law boards, no fundamental progress can be expected'.

In June 1948 the Barbados government, driven on by growing expressions of dissatisfaction, requested the Secretary of State to send Sir John Maude to review the whole system. In his report the following year he recommended a complete scrapping of the existing structure, substituting one Municipal Council for Bridge-

[1] See below pp. 353 ff.   [2] In 1939–41.

town and two Rural Districts to cover the rest of the Island, all elected on universal suffrage. It was suggested that the range of local government services might be expanded, for instance by the inclusion of housing.[1] There should also be much closer control of local activities by a Ministry of Local Government, to be established. Somewhat tardily a Local Government Ordinance of 1954 proceeded to implement these recommendations in full. Further, a Public Assistance Ordinance established an Assistance Board including delegates from the councils, whose business it would be to inspect public assistance work carried out at District level. The executive bodies for this purpose were to be Public Assistance Committees of the councils, reinforced by co-opted members. Finally a Public Health Ordinance was passed, the purpose of which was to co-ordinate public health work throughout the Island. By 1959 the work of reorganization had been completed: but there has as yet been insufficient time to judge of its working.

III. TRINIDAD

The post-war developments of local government in Trinidad have undoubtedly been the most interesting in the whole of the West Indies. As we have seen,[2] owing to the fact that Trinidad had not been acquired by settlement, there was no traditional local government outside the three towns of Port of Spain, San Fernando, and Arima. The Royal Commission regretted this situation and recommended that early steps should be taken to amend it. They were in favour of a gradual approach, through advisory District Councils, being apprehensive that councils with executive powers would be dominated by the few locally powerful citizens. No action was taken on this, but there was a growing feeling that purely advisory councils would be ineffective. In 1945 a Commission was in the Island examining the situation with a view to the introduction of a more advanced constitution, based on universal suffrage. The question of the establishment of rural authorities (to be called County Councils) was included in their terms of reference; this was recommended, but it was assumed that these would be (to start with at least) purely advisory.

Following this advice seven County Councils (including Tobago) were set up in 1946 on an advisory basis; it was soon recognized that on this basis they were going to be useless. The following

---

[1] Hitherto an Island matter.   [2] See above, p. 34.

year Governor Shaw, who was an enthusiast for local government, took things into his own hands, appointing a local committee under the chairmanship of the Solicitor General to recommend ways in which the councils could be made more effective; the possibility of some sort of tiering was also envisaged. At this point it proved possible to call in Sir John Maude on his way to Barbados, and also to enlist the services of two other experts (Sir Charles des Forges and Sir John Imrie, City Chamberlain of Edinburgh) whose primary business was to advise on town finances. These experts reported that the existence of Parish Wardens, several Local Health Authorities, two Local Roads Boards, seven Public Assistance Boards, and the seven new County Councils did not add up to an effective system of local government. Only the last were fully elective and they (as we have seen) were without executive powers. The main recommendations of the experts were first, that the County Councils should be granted executive powers, and secondly that they should collect and allocate at least a part of the funds required to carry out their duties. The experts also thought that it would be better if members of Leg. Co. were not *ex officio* members of the County Councils. Contact with the central legislature should instead be maintained by a Local Government Department in the Secretariat. It was also suggested that the County Councils should be empowered to set up village committees, delegating some of their powers to these latter.

After the not very promising start of the County Councils no very great hopes were placed in the new arrangements; but these expectations have been belied. Sir John Imrie visited the Island again in 1957, to report (*inter alia*) on the progress of the County and Village Councils. He was able to affirm that in the four years of their existence the counties had made 'marked advances on the various fronts in which they find themselves engaged. . . . The attitude of mind and general approach of the council members and officials to their problems augur well for their future.' The populations of the councils range from 186,000 to 21,000, so that they need not suffer from diseconomies of small scale in respect of any of the functions they are likely to be called on to perform. These lie in the fields of communications and public health in the broad sense; but the provisions of the Ordinance are very flexible, so that any other duties can be added to any council by order of the Governor.

The councils are very closely controlled in the sense that their budgets are checked by the Commissioner for Local Government, and then go before Leg. Co. No extra-budgetary expenditure whatever is allowed. On the other hand there appears to be no interference with the actual construction of their budgets. Sir John Imrie was so impressed with the responsible attitude of the councils that he suggested that the time had come for them to draw up five-year development plans. Under the Ordinance the councils have a duty to encourage the formation of Community, District, and Village Councils, whose finances they would control, and indeed largely supply. In the first four years nearly 200 Village Councils had been established, and were working well. It is especially interesting that 60% of the county councillors had received their first training in local government at the village level.

This good start had largely been financed by increasing grants from the Island budget, whose contribution had expanded 46% over the four years, against a rise in autonomous revenue of only 10%. As usual it would appear that finance is the weak side of the whole structure; but this need not necessarily be so, and indeed finance need not be a closely limiting factor in any sense since the Island income is expanding satisfactorily. The sources of County Council revenue (apart from grants from the Island government) are the usual land and buildings tax (assessed on annual value). The revenue from this had failed to expand *pari passu* with needs, first because of continued rent control, secondly because a pre-war ceiling of poundage ($7\frac{1}{2}$%) had not been raised. A revaluation was also overdue. A committee had been appointed to set this in order. At a later stage we shall be discussing the Trinidad local government structure in relation to that of other small islands. It would seem to be an admirable example of the way in which interest can be aroused and maintained, even at a very restricted level.

IV. BRITISH GUIANA

As we saw in Chapter 4 the early history of local government in British Guiana was of exceptional interest. From the beginning the government had been faced with an inescapable need to have certain public works[1] (essential for the very existence of the country), adequately looked after. These appeared to be within the

[1] See above, pp. 36 ff.

competence of local communities; only gradually and reluctantly
was it realized that this was far from being the case. At least the
resources of the central Public Works Department would be required. In the meantime the demand had arisen for social services,
and some of these, especially health and medical, appeared to be
appropriate for local responsibility. There ensued a period when
responsibility for these and similar matters was shuttled to and fro
between the central government and such local bodies as had been
established. This history had left the country with an odd and
patchy assortment of councils: two town councils (in Georgetown
and New Amsterdam), and in rural coastal areas little clusters of
councils interspersed with stretches in which virtually no services
were organized, outside of those which might happen to have been
established by estate owners. For most of the inland areas there
was very little in the way of organized services, except again on
estate (or mining) company property.

No immediate change was made in the local government structure at the end of the war. A Local Government Ordinance of 1945
merely confirmed that of 1907. In the meantime, however, political consciousness had made its appearance with some violence,
exacerbated by the multiracialism which the era of Indian
indentured labour had left in its wake. As we have seen, adult
suffrage was being introduced in the Islands, at both central and
local government levels, during the 1940's. It was impossible that
this change should by-pass British Guiana, and in 1953 a new constitution was introduced based on adult suffrage. Unfortunately
this proved almost immediately to be unworkable, and had to
be withdrawn. It was decided to start again at the bottom, by
reforming and extending the system of local councils on a fully
elective basis. Dr. A. H. Marshall, a United Kingdom expert with
wide experience of local government not only at home but also in
developing countries, was asked to visit the country and to prepare
a scheme with this intention.

The Marshall recommendations can be summarized under three
aspects: (i) organizational, (ii) Local Authority powers and duties,
(iii) financial. In respect of the first the establishment of a Ministry
of Local Government at the centre was recommended in place of
the Local Government Board;[1] this was entirely in line with experience of what had been found useful in other countries. A

¹ See above, p. 40.

single-tier form of local council was recommended for the whole of the coastland areas, including those parts where no services had yet been organized, except possibly by neighbouring estates. In the interior local government institutions were to be introduced gradually, in the first place by the District Commissioner in an informal manner. (It will be recalled that British Guiana had been given a system of District Commissioners in 1907 very much on African lines.) A separation between the deliberative and executive function in councils was to be clearly made, and to be backed up by the engagement of more qualified officers, such as Treasurers, Chief Clerks, Works Officers, and Social Welfare Officers. The last-named would be necessary because it was also recommended that the powers and duties of Local Authorities should be extended to include social welfare and certain aspects of agricultural education. Both of these were designed to stimulate local interest in development.

The success of the Marshall recommendations would clearly depend very much on the finance available; here again the Report was eminently sensible. There was to be a rate based on full capital values of land and buildings, subject to a decennial valuation by professional valuers, employed by the central government. In British Guiana conditions it is also essential to have a drainage rate on poldered areas, both for maintenance purposes and to re-cover some of the 'unearned increment' on value on improved farms. Secondly it was recommended that a well-conceived grant system, which would be equalizing as well as promotional, should be introduced. The Marshall plan was little more than a blueprint; it was intended that a further team of experts should go out to plan the system in detail, particularly in respect of boun-daries, and of future agricultural progress. There was, however, difficulty and delay over this, so that although the blueprint was accepted *in toto* nothing has yet been done to make its operation possible.

Excellent as the Marshall Report is, there are two points on which reasonable doubts might be expressed. First, there is the purely technical point as to whether decennial revaluation would be sufficiently frequent in view of the fundamental changes in values (both absolute and relative), which must be expected with an accelerated degree of development, especially the poldering of additional areas. More fundamentally, in conditions as peculiar as those of British Guiana, it may be questionable whether a full panoply of councils covering even the entire coastal areas would not be an unnecessary expense at the present stage of development. The central government would in any case be administering roads and drainage works in the sparsely inhabited areas, and it might reasonably make a start with other services as population expanded, up to the point where a sufficient local community had developed to justify the establishment of a local authority. This sort of policy would be very similar to that of Kenya, Tanganyika, and other territories which have to administer vast uninhabited tracts.

V. DOMINICA

In view of our later discussions concerning local government in small islands (below, Chapter 21), the post-war experiences of Dominica deserve some mention. Dominica is, relatively speaking, one of the larger islands, but owing to its extremely difficult terrain (such that the few relatively level areas are separated from each other by damp and almost impenetrable mountains) it is extremely underdeveloped. The population is less than 60,000. A town council in the capital (Roseau, 13,000 inhabitants) is of long standing; it was reorganized in 1937. As so often happens, its relations with the Island government have never been happy. Portsmouth, the second town (population 3,000), had a town board for some years, which was turned into a council in 1954. Both of these urban areas are obviously too small to be accorded responsibility for the conduct of many services. The more interesting developments have been in the field of rural government.

One or two Village Councils had been started in the middle 1930's through the energy of individual Englishmen, but interest had tended to lapse when they went away. In 1954 a Local Government Ordinance gave formal recognition to such bodies, and the following year they became elective; they were also given power to levy a rate up to 12 cents a room. In 1956 the Ministerial system was introduced into the island, and local government was put under the portfolio of Social Welfare. It cannot be said that the Village Councils have been an unbounded success; from time to time some have been suppressed, others have just lapsed. Nevertheless a tradition of real interest in the local community does seem to be developing, and this has been particularly marked since 1956. With a little tactful encouragement villagers built by voluntary effort a most important road in very difficult country, only accessible to man and donkey power. Without this help the project would probably have been beyond the Island's financial competence.

It can now be said that six councils are functioning satisfactorily, more on a community development than on a true local government basis; but this is probably the right note to strike. One of the initial mistakes was probably trying to make too formal a set-up. On these lines there does seem to be a definite future for the Village Councils. It would obviously be a great advantage if more help, by way of advice and encouragement, if not of finance, could be given by the Island government. In 1958 the staff of the Ministry available for this purpose was only two. Dominican experience suggests that there may well be scope for similar development in other islands, which although smaller are many of them richer and more developed.

Thus, although from a superficial point of view it might well be concluded that local government in the West Indies has little future, if we look deeper it appears that in fact it has reached an interesting stage of transition. The idea of responsible elective bodies is taking firm root in many different and perhaps unexpected places. The main problems now seem to be to work out a range of powers and duties, which though necessarily limited, would still impart a desire for local development and welfare, and would promote a local civic consciousness. For success this implies the introduction of a form of tax in which all can learn to share according to their capacity. These problems must, however, await further discussion as we proceed.

10

TRANSITION IN INDIA AND CEYLON

I. INDIA

IN Chapter 5 we saw that the development of local government institutions in India has proceeded in a series of drives, alternating with periods of consolidation, and indeed often of relative stagnation (though this was mainly due to economic causes). In the off-periods, however, development did not wholly stop. Local councils, at least in the more progressive areas, were learning their jobs; the principle of responsible government through elected representatives was becoming more and more firmly established. The last of these drives under British administration had been in connexion with the 'Montford' reforms of the 1920's. During the depression local government, like most other things, had ceased to move forward, and during the years of Swaraj 'non-co-operation' local government services had suffered a serious setback. The country was therefore more than ready for a renewed drive. The story that we now have to follow is that of the latest and largest of the drives to improve local government institutions, carried through with all the enthusiasm of the new independent government.

In the 1930's Congress had been very suspicious that the British were fobbing them off with 'local self-government' in order to postpone the day when self-determination would have to be granted. In fact, however, as we have already seen, leading members of the Congress Party had found for themselves that local government was very much worth having. It could play an important part in development; and it was an excellent training ground for politicians. They consequently needed it for their own policy. The Gandhian exaltation of the simple peasant and his handicrafts, no less than the psychological need to stress traditional culture as part of a self-conscious nationalism, all directed attention to the rural areas and an even greater emphasis on the 'panchayat raj' than had been attempted before. Article 40 of the constitution laid it down that 'States shall take steps to organize village panchayats, and to endow them with such powers and duties as may be necessary to enable them to function as units of self-government.'

The government of the Indian Union is unique among federal governments in the great interest it takes in local government institutions. A Local Government Department was set up in the Ministry of Health, and through this Delhi has increasingly taken a part in development. There was much to be done. Independence brought with it the absorption of the former princely states into the Union. In only a few of these (notably in the south) was there any system of urban or rural local government, at all comparable to that well established in the former Provinces of British India. Independence also brought with it universal suffrage. In some areas this made hardly any difference at all; in the majority of towns, however, it considerably increased instability, and has led to some changes in the internal organization of urban government.

For its own purposes, if for nothing else, the government of India needed to find out as much as it could about the working of local government. It therefore appointed a Local Finance Inquiry Committee, which reported in 1951, and is one of the chief sources of information on the subject. Another inquiry, the Tax Inquiry Commission, also touched on matters of local finance from the state end. In 1954 the Union government sponsored the formation of a Central Council of Local Self-Government, with the Minister of Health as chairman and the State Ministers for Local Self-Government and Panchayats as members. The functions of the Council were primarily 'to consider and recommend broad lines of policy in local self-government matters; to draw up a common programme of action; and to coordinate and supply information on Local Self-Government to State Governments'. In 1956 the council published a most valuable conspectus of the whole range of local self-government administration, state by state. We shall be discussing the findings of these various inquiries in due course in the relevant chapters.

It will be clear from all this that in spite of India being a federation, and local government a state matter, information is much more readily available than might be expected. Unfortunately, however, this is much more true of the administrative than of the financial field. For a comprehensive budget study it would still be necessary to visit separately all the states and large cities, and this would clearly be a gigantic undertaking.

Having furnished itself with what information it could gather, the Union government set about getting the states to plan the development of their institutions. Some of them have already reported. Indeed in some cases (for instance Madras) the state government had already taken the initiative and had obtained the views of all relevant parties. These reports form an excellent basis for the discussion of the many problems with which Indian local government is confronted; we shall refer to them below.

There is one further aspect of post-independence policy in respect of local government, which is of special relevance to rural authorities, namely the Community Development movement. This arose from the First Five-Year Plan (starting in 1951), which itself had a rural or agricultural bias. The idea behind Community Development was specifically development from below, 'a people's programme with government participation'. A pilot scheme was first launched with fifty-five projects, in three 'blocks' of roughly 100 villages each. (Villages in India tend to be nucleated, not to say congested, but some of them are very small, containing not more than forty to sixty families; populations of less than 500 are common.)

The pilot project was so promising that it was decided to extend Community Development to the whole country, but clearly this would take a matter of years. In the meantime it was determined to try out a thinner spread of pre-Community Development (the National Extension Scheme) as an interim measure. In terms of money outlay this was about half as intense as Community Development proper. The key workers in the whole programme are the Village Level Officers, who, in keeping with the idea of a people's project are repeatedly enjoined not to think of themselves as leaders imposed from outside, but as members of the community. This is a difficult position, and by no means all of them have the capacity to strike the right note; but when they do so the effect is very impressive. The tasks entrusted to Community Development are very wide: first, agricultural development, including better methods of cultivation, seed and stock improvement, growing of fruit and vegetables, and the encouragement of inland fisheries. The Village Level Officer is to proceed as far as possible by demonstration, making not less than five demonstrations in any one village. Secondly, Community Development is to concern itself with environmental health, including housing, village replanning, pure water supply and latrines, roads and drains. Its third field is recreative and cultural, including the purchase of village radio sets, and the holding of classes, especially for women.

The importance which the government attaches to the Community Development movement is shown by the fact that a special Ministry was established at Delhi to look after it; it is also a very particular interest of the Plan Organization. Since 1952 the movement has spread widely through the country, but it is now agreed that it cannot cover the whole until at least half-way through the Third Five-Year Plan. A great number of progress reports and criticisms of the movement have been issued from time to time. Of these by far the most important is the Mehta Report of 1957,[1] which we shall be examining in due course. This is of special relevance to our inquiries, because, with the Community Development organization in sight of covering the whole country, the question of its integration with the panchayats and with the rest of the rural local government set-up (however it may develop) becomes urgent.

Before we turn to such problems, however, it will be useful to recapitulate briefly where the local government structure which we watched developing in Chapter 5 had got to by the early 1950's. Although the precise details differ from state to state the broad pattern runs right through. There are four types of local government in India, but it is important to notice that there is no tiering, or devolution between them, as there is in the United Kingdom and as has been established in most of the African territories. First come the large cities (and they are very large; Bombay has over 4 mn. inhabitants, Calcutta over 2 mn.); nine others in addition to the three original Presidency towns had been established by 1950. All of these cities are completely independent of their states. Generally speaking the council is strong, and the Municipal Commissioner finds himself more or less in the position of the Town Clerk of a large British city. Below these come some 1,425 smaller towns and urban areas. These are not completely independent, either of the state in which they are situated or of the Collector's District. In progressive states the state influence is very decidedly on the upgrade. The characteristic institution of this group is the chief executive, who as Municipal Commissioner is more and more

[1] Report of the Committee to study Community Development and National Extension Service led by Balavantary G. Mehta.

tending to become an appointee from a state cadre. It is on this grade that the impact of universal suffrage has had its greatest effect, leading in some cases to so much instability that it has been necessary very considerably to increase the powers of the Municipal Commissioner, notwithstanding the decline in responsible democracy which this implies. In a large number of towns today the Commissioner not merely prepares the budget (which is his statutory duty), but does most of the work of local government.

On the rural side there are upwards of 300 Regional Boards; in some cases these are *ad hoc* creations to look after (for instance) education; a majority, however, are the old Collectors' Districts, whose areas were determined very long ago with no thought of local government functions. The *ad hoc* boards are all appointed, and are now quite anomalous. The District Boards may contain some elected members, but their functions are almost wholly advisory. The areas are very large and carry no community feeling whatever. Below these are the panchayats, which at the time of the Report of the Local Finance Inquiry Commission numbered about 100,000 but have since been rapidly increasing, as a result of state action under article 40 of the constitution, steadily prodded by the Plan Organization. Panchayats are of very varying sizes, largely it would seem, according to the individual ideology of the different states; this is a point we shall come back to in Chapter 21. Each panchayat has a village headman as chairman; he is normally elected. There is also a paid secretary, and a small committee, which is becoming of increasing importance. It is normally composed of the elders of the village.

Each of these local government sectors has its own difficulties. In the urban sector progressive state governments are steadily encroaching on the field of local government. Even a powerful city like Bombay feels itself cramped by the activities of state boards and commercial enterprises. Both the smaller towns and District Boards that have attempted local government activity are losing ground to the states, who are tending to take over functions, especially education, because they are not being efficiently conducted. These local authorities have no protection, since they are the creatures of the state; those who like to rule in their own house tend to suffer with those who lack interest. In India, as in Africa, it has proved relatively easy to breathe life into local government at the village level, where the results of effort are immediately apparent.

The small authorities have been steadily encouraged, both by the states and by the Plan Organization; but it is clear that they are too weak to carry through any but the very smallest development projects, and there is really more desperate need of larger schemes.

The backbone of local, as of state, revenue has always been land revenue. This tax has an extremely interesting history which we shall have to examine in Chapter 15. It figures in the budgets of state and local government (of various types) in different ways, sometimes as a pure shared tax, sometimes by means of a surcharge or cess allowed to the local authorities. Formerly it accounted for 50% or more of local revenue; this declined to one-third, but is now tending to rise slightly. Owing to archaic valuations (and the staggering cost of attempting to make new ones on any large scale), not much hope can be put in it as an expanding source of revenue.

Next in importance in principle (although not by any means always in practice) is the property rate assessed on annual value (although there is very little renting). The use of this extends right down to the panchayat level, where, however, there is clearly very little to assess. (Perhaps in compensation for this, panchayats are allowed to substitute a capital value for an annual value base if they so desire.)[1] The valuations for this tax are also in almost all areas extremely out of date, so that it is only in a few progressive cities like Bombay that it really pulls the weight it could and should do. This is a general problem which we shall be discussing in Chapter 16.

In a number of towns, especially in the Mahratta areas, the most important tax is *octroi*, levied on goods and persons entering the jurisdiction. Although apparently remunerative (the revenue *net* of costs of collection is seldom computed), the tax is a most objectionable obstacle to a proper flow of inter-local trade. Beyond this there are a number of minor taxes, including one on trades and professions, which is presumably intended as a crude income tax. With proper accounting it would probably be found that the *net* yield of many of these taxes is negative.

It is thus apparent that Indian local government is not short of opportunities for raising autonomous revenue. What appears to be wrong is a general lack of responsibility, unwillingness to raise tax rates, graft and inefficiency in collection. As we have seen, Indian townsmen have not a good tradition of taxpaying, particularly the local rich, who are important in local government matters.

[1] On the significance of this difference, see below, pp. 355 ff.

In addition to autonomous revenue, grants are available from state governments, the extent and regularity of these depending very much on the current position of state finances, which may themselves be very weak. The greater part of the grants are specific, either in aid of the salaries of local officers, or of a capital nature, for specific projects. It is significant that the Tax Inquiry Commission reported: 'No state has a grant-in-aid code that embodies simple and defined principles.' An exception must now be made in respect of grants to panchayats which are of a promotional, matching type, with definite signs of a policy behind them. This suggests that when states are interested they can act much more efficiently. The relative percentages of grants to autonomous revenue in local budgets at one time differed fantastically from one state to another, but more regularity is being introduced into this, if only because the Union government has shown increasing willingness to come to the aid of financially weak states.

From all this it will be seen that in spite of its long tradition, all is not yet well with Indian local government and particularly with its finances; hence the current heart-searching at both central and state levels which we noted earlier. Before ending our review of transition it will be instructive to take a brief look at what are considered to be the most urgent local government problems. They can be grouped under the headings of: (i) control and direction, (ii) jurisdictions, and (iii) finance.

In respect of organization and control there is room for improvement, even at the central level. In the post-war period three Ministries have had a finger in the local government pie: the Ministry of Health, the Ministry of Community Development, and the Plan Organization. Communication between them is by no means perfect. With the increasing tendency to concentrate on building a structure of local government from the bottom upwards it is essential either that responsibility should become more concentrated or at least that the respective spheres of the three Ministries should be much more carefully defined.

At the state level even more needs to be done. Changes in state boundaries, such as have recently occurred, do not make for good planning, either on the part of the state or of the transferred councils. More generally, states have to make up their minds what local services they really need to take over. In the interest of efficiency a number of states are tending to absorb such services as primary education, housing, and public utilities. These are some of the things that make local government most interesting, and it is at least arguable, on the one side that as it is local authorities do not have enough to do, on the other that if efforts were concentrated on raising the general level of administration many of these services could be performed as well at the local as at the state level. Local government is always a compromise between democracy and efficiency. In India it is easy to sympathize with those who rank efficiency high; but there are many ways in which it can be improved without sacrificing democracy.

States have also to make up their minds on the source and nature of their control over local authorities. The Tax Inquiry Commission found that both external audit and the internal control of expenditure were very weak. Help, and even discipline, in this direction is clearly a matter for the state, and need not in any way impinge on local budgetary freedom. Some states, however, interfere directly with local budgeting, dictating the proportion of outlay to be allocated to different services, or earmarking taxes for particular purposes. This should not be necessary, although on the other hand there may be a case for fixing minimum tax rates to be levied in order to assist local bodies to stand up to unwilling taxpayers.

Again who is to exercise actual control? Should a state establish a Commissioner for local government, with a field staff under his control, or should control over the towns and urban areas continue to be the responsibility of the chairman of the District Board? Apparently opinion is divided on this point;[1] but whichever method is chosen it is evident that much more advice and steering is necessary than exist at present. Finally there is the question of organization within the towns and urban areas; for this the states are also largely responsible. Is the Municipal Commissioner to be subordinate to the council, as he is in the large cities? Is he to be effectively chairman or is his job to be abolished altogether as some of the Madras towns suggested? According to present tendencies his position approaches that of an American City Manager or continental Burgomaster. Is this really what is wanted?

The question of the basic unit of local government outside the cities and large towns is clearly still in the melting pot. According

[1] See for instance White Paper on Local Administration in Madras, published in the *Quarterly Journal of the Local Self-Government Institute*, January 1957.

to present tendencies a small unit is gaining favour. It is generally agreed that the old Districts are too large to command local interest. It does not follow that they are too large for the efficient administration of certain joint services: major (as distinct from government trunk) roads, secondary education, hospitals, all technically call for a fairly large unit. With improving transport facilities many Districts would be quite suitable for these. In fact the independent Madras Committee put in a strong plea for *adding* to the powers of District Councils in the interests of efficiency. In any case until the network of panchayats is complete it will be necessary to retain the Districts.

If the panchayat emerges as the basic local government unit panchayats will have to be combined in some way. Madras envisages uniting them in population groups of 10,000 to 25,000; but this is still too small to provide sufficient resources for real development. It would consequently be necessary to have some means of federating them into some larger units. The Mehta Report puts forward the idea of *Samiti panchayats* which would then be the basic local government unit. One or two of the states have very recently introduced legislation in this direction (Rajasthan, 1959, for instance). The place of the individual village panchayat inside such a union would have to be worked out carefully. This problem is very similar to that faced in many African territories, such for instance as the relation between Kenya District Councils, Location and Sublocation Councils.

If there were one (or perhaps two) layers of panchayat local government, would it also be desirable to have a middle layer, between the Samiti panchayats and the Districts? Several states, including Madras, tried working with Taluk boards within Districts, but they never seemed quite to come to life and have mostly been abandoned. The Union government's view (supporting the Mehta Committee) turns towards a unit of the size of Community Development block for the basic unit; this would give areas of 75,000 to 100,000 inhabitants (for which there would be many African parallels). The alternative to this (favoured by Madras) is while keeping the basic unit small, to establish joint committees for the conduct of services which call for a larger unit on technical grounds. This also is a possibility. A more fundamental question is whether India should change over from layers to tiers, that is to say whether, and how, there should be devolution of duties from larger to smaller units within them. At present, as we have seen there is none. These questions are of vital importance to all countries endeavouring to set up new local government structures, and we shall be discussing them at length in Chapter 21.

As we have seen, finance is the crux of Indian local government at all levels. At the upper levels the problem that is most in need of attention is tax administration; at the lower levels there is urgent need of additional sources of revenue also. Perhaps the weakest aspect of all is the poor use at present being made of the tax on land and buildings. Madras is keenly aware of this and recommends a valuation at state level of property in all local authority areas, to be carried out at regular intervals. This would be invaluable, and from experience elsewhere would not only double or treble the tax yield, but would also greatly increase equity by bringing in the many properties which at present escape assessment. The question of the optimum base for the tax also requires consideration; by giving panchayats the right to use capital values some beginning has been made towards a change over to what would almost certainly be a more appropriate base than the annual value derived from British practice. This is a matter which we shall be discussing in Chapter 16. If once the property tax were rehabilitated it should be possible to get rid of both octroi and other vexatious taxes.

At the village level, however, not much can be expected from the property rate, and, as we have seen, not much expansion can be looked for from land revenue. In so far as Community Development is financed at the local level this is done by personal contributions, either in real resources (labour or gifts of property) or in cash. The essence of Community Development is that these payments should be voluntary; as time goes on, however, increasing pressure is certainly put by the community on those who do not provide the share they could afford. In some areas the contributions already approximate to a self-assessed tax. When the present phase of Community Development is complete and the units in which it is organized are merged in a permanent structure of Local Authorities, there would seem to be a strong argument for regularizing such personal payments into a graduated personal tax. As we shall see there are excellent precedents for this in Africa. If, then, state grant systems can be extended and regularized (with the help of Union funds where necessary), there would seem to be no reason why revenue at least as adequate should not be found for Indian local government as in other developing countries with similar income structures. Our investigations should reveal how far this is a practicable proposition.

A recital of the problems still facing local government in India should not divert attention from the really impressive way in which development from below has been tackled since independence. In many areas there is an entirely new spirit of determination on the part of the authorities and of keenness on the part of the people. But to quote the Mehta Report, progress is 'impressive relative to the previous stagnation, but not relative to the needs of the people'.

II. CEYLON

Ceylon, like India, had in principle already taken the essential steps towards the establishment of a representative, responsible system of Local Authorities before the second world war. The Donoughmore Constitution of 1931 envisaged a large extension of the elective element; a Committee on Local Administration considered this in 1938 and a series of measures passed in the early post-war years filled in the details. The Town Councils Ordinance of 1946 and the Municipal Ordinance of 1947 abolished the non-representative Sanitary Boards,[1] and established fully elective councils in every area which could possibly be regarded as urban: in addition there were village committees (later renamed councils). No time was lost in implementing these plans. To the three long-standing municipalities of Colombo, Kandy, and Galle were rapidly added Jaffna, Kunegala, Nuwara Eliya, and Negombo. In addition there were thirty-six urban councils in the larger towns, thirty-eight town councils in the smaller ones (the normal nomenclature is reversed), and 403 village committees. The whole island was thus covered with a network of elective councils. They were certainly local enough; some of the 'town' councils had populations of less than 2,000. It would be hard to maintain, however, that by and large they have been either responsible or efficient. On the whole the most persistent liveliness seems to reside at the village committee level; but there the powers and duties are inevitably very restricted. Hence in a sense the true transition has yet to come.

It is evident in all this that the Island government was at considerable pains to provide the conditions for development from

[1] See above, p. 63.

below. For this the late Mr. S. R. D. Bandaranaike, as Minister for Local Government (before he was Prime Minister), was largely responsible. A Rural Development service was established in 1947, thus anticipating the Indian Community Development programme. Yet it was soon clear that the system had not got off to a good start. Accordingly in 1953 a strong Commission of Inquiry, under the chairmanship of N. K. Choksy, Q.C., was set up to examine the whole field of local government and finance. It numbered only four, but they were leading citizens of great experience, and included a Tamil as well as the three Sinhalese. The Choksy Report (of 1955) is a document of first-rate importance concerning the way in which local government worked (or did not work) in Ceylon. Unfortunately the absence of good local government statistics (which still persists) makes it difficult to determine what weight should be given to the many criticisms which were made.

In reviewing transition in Ceylon there is thus no steady rate of progress to record, as there certainly is in some parts of the Indian system, and even more definitely in a number of the African territories. Ceylon's particular problems and growing pains (as some of them surely are) will be discussed in detail in the relevant chapters. Many of them are of quite general relevance, and may hence be as instructive as a catalogue of success. The aim of the present section is merely to give a background picture of Ceylonese local government institutions as they have appeared in the post-war world.

Ceylon is not a very small island, and it has a population of about $8\frac{1}{2}$ mn., comparable with one of the Southern Regions of Nigeria and larger than most of the other African territories. From the details given above it will be apparent that the island has been very well endowed with local jurisdictions. Not merely are the village committee jurisdictions very small, but only two of the upper-grade urban areas exceed 50,000 inhabitants (and these two are almost outer suburbs of Colombo). There is, therefore, a good case for thinking that a great many of the jurisdictions are too small to be efficient; this is borne out by high administrative costs. Not only are the jurisdictions over-small, but a case can be made out for saying that the councils themselves (at least below the municipal level) are too small also. Urban council membership ranges between five and seven, town councils have no more than three to five members. There are two disadvantages of this very small membership. On the one hand, if they really try to perform their duties conscientiously, the councillors are overwhelmed with work. On the other, there are so few of them that they are not easily accessible to the public. It is hard for the ordinary citizen to take any pride, or even interest, in a council of these dimensions.

The size of the Municipal Councils which is not excessive as it is in some other countries, is such that they should be fully large enough to cope with the necessary business. It would rather seem that it is in the internal organization of the Ceylon municipalities that trouble arises. On the one hand the internal organization seems to be unnecessarily complicated; on the other the relations between the Mayor, the Council, and the Municipal Commissioner seem unhappy, not only in Colombo but in Galle and Jaffna also. By statute the councils must have two Standing Committees of which Finance is one. Colombo has a complicated system of seven, of which Finance is not clearly top dog; it is thus difficult to implement a coherent policy. (The parallelism between this and some experiences of the central government is worth noting.)

Under Ceylon statute, as contrasted with Indian, the chief executive is the Mayor, not the Municipal Commissioner. The other officers, however, are directly responsible to the Commissioner, and hence only indirectly responsible through him to the Mayor and council. This should lead to better democratic control than the Indian system, where, as we have seen, the council needs to be both active and alert if it is going to keep its end up *vis-à-vis* the Commissioner. The nominal term of office of the Mayor is three years, but by a comparatively recent amendment he can be unseated at any time by a simple majority. The result of this change has been disastrous, more particularly in a country where party feeling runs as high as it does in Ceylon. The Mayor naturally attempts to get the most out of the office while he is in the chair and has no interest in long-term plans. The only force of stability and continuity is the Commissioner; but here again there is a difficulty. Commissioners are appointed by the Local Government Service Commission from a central cadre. Since the numbers on this are inevitably small it may well be that there is no candidate agreeable to a town (or the politics of a town may change after the Commissioner has been appointed); so that the Commissioner and the council too easily tend to be at loggerheads.[1]

[1] This was the situation in Galle when I attempted to do some field work there.

These organizational difficulties should not be sufficient to cause serious trouble to councils which were interested in the jobs to be done, but it is clear that this is not so. One possible weakness could be that they do not have a sufficient range of powers and duties to make council work worthwhile. There are two possibilities here. Before the establishment of the present democratic system of local government such local services as were provided were the business of the Katcheries,[1] local tax-collecting offices corresponding to the Indian Collectors' Districts. Over the course of time these tax offices had absorbed a number of local government responsibilities, very much in the way in which the Justices in England did before the establishment of democratic Local Authorities. It would certainly have been more sensible to have removed their local government duties from the Katcheries when establishing the new councils, even if their tax-collecting responsibilities could not immediately be spared. But this again would not appear to be a very important consideration.

In all the African territories the service which above all has aroused the interest of local councils has been primary education. In Ceylon education has always been a highly centralized service, so that no local bodies have any say whatever in its organization in their own areas, and no responsibility for its finance. It may be, of course, that even if some responsibility for primary education were transferred to councils it would not arouse local enthusiasm in at all the same way as it does in Africa. Asians, with a long tradition of indigenous culture behind them, are not so interested in the twentieth century as are Africans. But the transfer of some share of educational responsibility as a booster is a possibility that might be tried.

It is evident that the government was of the opinion that a major weakness of Ceylon local government was that its powers were insufficient, for in 1952 a Local Government Enlargement of Powers Statute was passed. It is difficult to trace that it affected any improvement. The range of actual services undertaken by most Ceylon local authorities is indeed very limited, often little more than elementary sanitary services and minor roads; but what would seem to be wrong is not so much paucity of opportunities as paucity of finances.

In Ceylon the basic local tax is one on land and buildings

[1] See above, p 60.

assessed on annual value, exactly parallel to the British local rate. The range of this is very wide, including all authorities except the purely rural areas of Village Council jurisdictions. It is extremely unpopular, and local authorities undoubtedly have great difficulty in wringing payment out of the people; this may of course merely reflect a general lack of interest in local government. There is no doubt, however, that the tax is badly handled. Valuations are very out of date. Although the central government has an efficient Valuation Department, whose services are available to Local Authorities in principle, in practice there are not enough staff to go round, and the cost of hiring them is prohibitive to most Local Authorities. If the central government is in earnest about local government it could certainly help a great deal here. Taxpayers cannot be expected to contribute willingly to what is patently an unfair system. Moreover, since very few properties in Ceylon are rented (less than one-third even in Colombo), the annual value base is far less appropriate than a capital base would be.[1]

The autonomous finance of the village councils is even weaker. As we have seen the Indian panchayats rely very largely on a surcharge on land revenue for their finance. Although this leaves much to be desired, it is at least a steady, and not by any means negligible, source of revenue. In Ceylon there is no such opportunity; village councils have to rely wholly on a flat acreage tax, and due to the tradition against taxing paddy lands (the source of the nation's food), an exemption limit of 5 acres has been set on this. The great bulk of the farmers thus make no contribution to local government at all, although they are by no means destitute, and in any case much better off than most Indian farmers. It would often be open to a village council to declare part of its area to be sufficiently urbanized to qualify for the local rate on land and buildings; but anticipating the storm of abuse that would fall upon its head if it did so, it prefers to stay as they are.

From the point of view of getting things done, poverty of local revenue would not matter so much if the government were to come forward with a well thought out grant system. This is not the case either; total grants paid to local government authorities do not exceed 4% of central government revenue, and although they bulk quite largely in local budgets (30 or 40% of local revenue), this is only because the local budgets are themselves so small. Few urban

[1] See Chap. 16.

councils have more than £50,000 at their disposal; a substantial number of town councils have no more than £5,000. Clearly this forms no adequate basis for development. Moreover the grants, such as they are, are not of a nature to facilitate long-term planning. Some are based on population figures long out of date; others depend on the Minister's fiat from year to year.[1] This points to an essential weakness of Ceylon finances, indeed of the whole Ceylonese economy. Far more than most countries, Ceylon's national income depends on world prices for her three basic export products: tea, rubber, and coconut; the greater part of central tax revenue is derived from export taxes on these three. The revenue is thus inherently unstable. This instability communicates itself to local finances both through the instability of grants, and more directly through fluctuations in local tax collections. As Ceylon develops, and also as she improves her tax structure, these difficulties should decline. In the meantime it should be by no means impossible for the central government to guarantee some regularity in grants for local authorities, so that they can plan at least a few years ahead.

The final weakness of Ceylon local government appears to be in the relation between central and local government. We have already noticed several ways in which the central government could help more than it does at present. Other illustrations are easy to come by. For instance, the Rural Development service, instead of working alongside of, and even through, the local government set-up (as on the whole the Indian Community Development programme works with the panchayats), in Ceylon keeps itself apart. It is well endowed with funds, while the village councils who feel they have real work to do, are without a cent. Again, there is a Local Loans Fund which in principle is ready to make loans freely for eligible projects. One of the most eligible of these is urban water supplies. Even Colombo has not yet achieved an adequate pure water supply (80% of the patients in the Colombo hospitals are reported to be suffering from waterborne diseases). Yet Ceylon is by no means a dry country, even the so-called dry zone expects a rainfall of from 40 to 60 inches. The difficulty appears to lie in the reluctance of the government and the monetary authorities to sanction loans when they feel that the island finances are themselves in a parlous condition. It is clearly important that something should be done to break this deadlock.

[1] See below, p. 421.

Given the basic weaknesses of Ceylon Local Authorities it would seem to be especially desirable that the central Ministry should do its best to give them all the advice and help it can. Here too there seems to be a lacuna. It is not the practice of Ministry officials to visit councils; consequently their advice must inevitably seem remote, and often irrelevant. It may well be that the Ministry has an impossibly large number of separate authorities to look after. Contemplating the experience of other countries, however, there are two possible ways round this difficulty. The Ministry might establish a cadre of Government Agents, working in the field, but closely under its own supervision and not that of the Katcheries (whose so-called Government Agents appear to be merely tax collectors). Alternatively it might be appropriate to set up a higher tier unit of local government. Since the existing councils are so very small there would seem to be a good case for this. It was a favourite plan of Mr. Bandaranaike's to set up about twenty superior councils, working on lines very close to British County Councils. By this means he hoped also to afford a somewhat greater degree of local autonomy to racially different areas. The number twenty corresponds to the present Katchery areas, but there would seem to be nothing sacred about that. Such County Councils would presumably be responsible for between 300,000 and 400,000 population, not very different from the District Council of Uganda or Kenya; but it might be better if they were rather more numerous and smaller.[1]

In reviewing the history of Ceylon local government in the post-war years it is thus only too easy to find things that are unfortunate, or things that look all right but somehow fail to work. In most cases all that would really seem to be necessary to put things right is a little more drive and initiative, with some real confidence in future stability. Once the central government can put its own house in order in these respects, local government should have as good a chance as in other countries to make its proper contribution to development.

[1] See below, pp. 507 ff.

11

TRANSITION IN WEST AFRICA

I. NIGERIA

THE new interest in the development of local government institutions in dependent territories which had been gathering momentum during the later years of the war, was (as we have seen) especially directed towards Africa. Mr. Creech Jones had toured the British dependencies on that continent soon after his appointment in the autumn of 1946; he had addressed his Dispatch to the Governors in February of the following year. The series of conferences at Cambridge which started in the summer of 1947, were concerned with problems of African administration, although not in any narrow sense. The African Studies Branch in the Colonial Office was set up before the end of 1947 and began the publication of the *Journal of African Administration* in 1949, with the express purposes of increasing interest and disseminating information among field officers. Finally an Advisory Panel on Local Government in Africa was set up at the Colonial Office, in order to mobilize experience in the British local government service in the interests of those countries experimenting for the first time in representative institutions.

In Nigeria the reaction to all this stimulus was rapid and apparently highly responsive. In fact, however, the political set-up had continued to evolve throughout the war. Since these constitutional changes affected both the relation of the central government to local government and the composition of local authorities themselves, it is necessary to make brief mention of them.

As we have seen, up to the middle 1930's the process of closer integration of the north and south had been proceeding steadily. The separation of the southern Provinces into East and West in 1939 made little difference to this; the strength of the centre and the size of its secretariat were steadily expanding. A re-enactment of the Native Authority Ordinance for the whole country in 1940 emphasized this unification. Nevertheless the process by which Nigeria had by 1960 reached the position of a loose federation with strong state and weak central powers, had already started during the war. From 1945 there were active discussions proceeding on all sides. These matured in a new constitution in 1947 (the Richards Constitution), which although by no means federal in form, did clearly foreshadow the emergence of some such arrangement. In the first place Regional Councils were set up in the three Regions which had now clearly emerged. These were purely deliberative and advisory, with no legislative powers and with no rights of appropriation. It was recognized that this could only be an interim position, and it was intended to set up a committee to discuss what, or when, further action should be taken. In the event things moved too fast for such a procedure.

The Regions were encouraged to set up their own secretariats, under deputies paralleling the central Directors. Certain revenues were allocated to the Regions, to be spent as determined by the centre. (They were thus earmarked taxes rather than assigned revenues.)[1] Some part, however, was retained centrally to be distributed to the Regions as grants according to a code, for education, health, and agriculture. Of particular interest was the system of education grants, designed by Sir Sidney Phillipson (then Financial Secretary to the central government), together with the Director of Education, Eastern Region. The grants were made as a percentage of specific services, mainly for the salaries of approved teachers in primary schools. The important point was that the amount going to any Native Authority area was determined on the basis not only of the number of approved teachers, but also of an amount of a so called 'Assumed Local Contribution' which would be raised locally. How much each locality would have to raise depended essentially on its wealth or poverty, as certified by the Education Officer. Although the actual outlay of the grant money was mainly carried out by the Missions, local bodies were thus for the first time directly drawn into the finance of development.

Education had specifically been declared a Regional subject. Under the Richards Constitution it was tacitly assumed that this would also be true in future of the whole of local government. A further logical step in constitutional development was taken under the first Macpherson Constitution in 1950. This was definitely the beginning of federalism. Legislative power over a certain range of subjects was transferred to the Regions, although the

[1] For this distinction, see below, p. 282.

central government retained, in form at least, concurrent powers. The unofficial (and hence ultimately elective) elements were increased in both central and Regional legislatures. Executive Councils with a majority of non-official members were established at both central and Regional levels, and a beginning was made with a Ministerial system. Regional secretariats were heavily increased and the size of central departments curtailed *pari passu*. Since local government had already effectively been regionalized, this constitutional change made little direct difference *within* Regions. Indirectly, however, the greater general responsibility which regional governments now had, and the increase in the unofficial element, encouraged them to think out their own local government problems more fundamentally.

As a result, in the Eastern and Western Regions entirely new systems of local government were substituted for the Native Authorities; in the Northern Region this drastic step was not taken, so that local government still centres round the Emirates, exactly as it had been established by Lugard, except for the fact that the councils are more important, and contain a larger elective element. In both East and West there have been three distinct phases. First, in the early fifties, elective councils were substituted for the mainly appointed Native Authorities. The District Officers and traditional authorities (chiefs or elders) both found themselves largely shut out of the new system. After a few years' working it became apparent that the change had been too sudden. Legislation or a process of adjustment in the middle fifties permitted the co-option of traditional authorities in strictly limited quotas, and at the same time restored some of the influence of the District Officers, by means of advice and inspection, although not of control. Finally at the end of the decade, in contemplation of independence, there is taking place a new alignment of local jurisdictions; this does not, however, imply any fundamental change in the system already established.[1]

The Eastern Region was first in the field; this was only natural since it was plain to all that the Northern system of Indirect Rule could not appropriately be fitted to the social organization of the eastern peoples. It was determined both to give Local Authorities more powers and at the same time to make the system entirely

[1] As we shall see, the story in Ghana is closely parallel to that in southern Nigeria.

elective. Already in 1948 a beginning was made by setting up a Town Council in Port Harcourt containing a majority of African members, elected by ward on a wide franchise. A somewhat similar experiment was made with a District Council in Onitsha. For the generalization of the elective system, however, a decision had to be taken concerning the structure to be set up. A certain amount of progress had gradually been made in amalgamating the smaller Native Authorities left by the Cameron fragmentation,[1] but it was strongly felt that some considerably larger unit was needed, both for efficient administration, and also to satisfy the ambitions of the progressive and literate men whom it was hoped to attract to the local government service. At the same time it was unthinkable in eastern conditions that there should not be one, or perhaps two, layers of smaller councils which would bring local government close to the people. The problem was which way to start: at the top or at the bottom.

In order to get some light on this problem Brigadier Gibbons[2] was sent in 1948 to investigate the African local councils which had been established in Uganda and Kenya. It was thought that they might provide some precedent, notwithstanding the fact that they contained no elective element and were fully controlled by the administration. Since these two territories had been organized in a few large Districts, which seemed to work well, Gibbons naturally came back desirous of starting at the top, County, level. These would be the key authorities, with lower-layer councils gradually built up beneath them. These proposals were accepted by a Select Committee of the Eastern Legislature, but, as a result of prolonged discussion with the Native Authorities, when the Ordinance appeared the emphasis had been fundamentally changed. All three layers of local government were to materialize, but instead of the County, the District would be the pivotal level and taxing authority. The Counties would obtain their funds partly by grants from the Region, partly by precepting on the District Councils.

Besides this fundamental organization (which was broadly copied in the Western Region and in Ghana), the Eastern reforms are important in three other respects. First, since the District Officers were excluded from any power in the new councils, it was all the more important to secure effective control over the whole system of local government at the Regional level. The first idea in this

[1] See above, p. 105.
[2] An officer of the Region.

respect had been to set up an advisory Local Government Board comprising six African non-officials and two officials. This was rejected in favour of more direct contact with the Regional executive. Control was vested in a Regional Authority (the Governor acting through an office set up in the Regional Secretariat). This was the beginning of the Ministry of Local Government.

Secondly, local tax powers were increased to include not only a levy on incomes (including if desired a progressive rate on higher incomes), but also a tax on land and buildings of the nature of the local rate. Little use in practice was made of either of these possibilities and it is only in the most recent period that there has been any development of the tax on land and buildings. Thirdly, the powers and duties of Local Authorities were only laid down in a very general way in the Ordinance (they included a positive duty in the prevention of crime and wide permissive powers in the field of public works and social services); but provision was made for the exact powers and duties of each authority to be determined by the instrument establishing it. This method of gradually introducing councils to local government activities has since been very commonly used in a wide range of territories.

The new councils were established only gradually. A start was made at Ikot Ekpene where the Native Authorities were relatively coherent and efficient. Local councillors were chosen by direct election from a group of villages, and these councils then formed electoral colleges for the District and County Councils. By 1952 Ikot Ekpene had its County Council, 3 Rural District Councils, 1 Urban District Council, and 23 local councils. Niger county had 4 Rural District Councils and 139 local councils, Eket county 4 Rural District Councils and 24 local councils; in addition there were Urban District Councils at Enugu and Calabar. In most areas shortage of staff, the difficulties of overcoming clan parochialism and the process of 'educating people in an understanding of the new machinery' slowed down progress. Yet there was no lack of eagerness, either at the Regional or local level. Questions were asked in the House of Assembly by representatives of areas which had not yet been reformed. The Governor in his Address in 1952 reaffirmed that 'efficient and democratic local government councils, accepting ever-increasing responsibility for local services provides one of the surest means of achieving political progress, and guaranteeing the continuance of it'.

It was soon apparent that in this abrupt adoption of an essentially British structure of local government many difficulties had been overlooked. The worst troubles were concerned with, first, the appointment and dismissal of staff, secondly with the attitude and activities of councillors, especially in relation to contracts, and thirdly with stresses and strains between the different layers of councils. Before establishing the new system the advisability of a unified local government service had been discussed, but rejected for fear of encroaching on the autonomy of the Local Authorities. Councils could therefore appoint and dismiss staff at will and regulate their conditions of service as they pleased. Councils tended to insist on having a 'son of the soil' even if there was no one with suitable qualifications. There were constant difficulties between old-fashioned staff taken over from the previous system and young men, who might for instance have been sent for training in the United Kingdom only to find that their jobs had gone while they were away. There was also unquestionably much buying and selling of appointments. Hanging over all was the chronic shortage of suitable staff. Even if it had been decided to establish a unified service from the start it would have been impossible to fill the cadres.

Bad as were the staffing problems, difficulties over councillors were still more serious. The great majority had no idea what they were supposed to do. Many had sought office for the allowances and perquisites involved. Few could be made to realize that they were not themselves in an executive position. An investigator[1] touring the Region in 1955 took an extremely gloomy view of the whole situation. His opinion was to some extent confirmed by inquiries which had to be instituted at Port Harcourt, Aba, Onitsha, and Eastern Ngwa. In all cases councils had to be suspended. The Member for Port Harcourt alleged in the House that in his town 'organised corruption and bribery, organised graft and racketeering, nepotism, favouritism, administrative incompetency, oppression, official victimisation and misuse of council funds' were to be found. There is no doubt that a good deal of this was true, not only in Port Harcourt.

Now that more experience has been gained of setting up representative and responsible local bodies for the first time, it can be stated with confidence that just these difficulties will almost

[1] R. E. Wraith, see articles in *West Africa*, 1955.

certainly appear. To some extent they are merely growing pains and will be relieved as councillors get more used to the job and more and better-trained staff become available. This was by and large the view taken by the Eastern Regional government, and on the whole they were justified. Experience also shows, however, that in the long run definite machinery is likely to be required to guard against certain chronic difficulties such as the appointment and dismissal of staff and the acceptance of contracts. These are matters which we shall be discussing at length later on, so that they need not detain us here. It must be borne in mind that the British relation between councillors and the executive staff which the Eastern Region was asking its Local Authorities to understand and work at one stroke is a unique and somewhat subtle one, highly successful when it goes right, but peculiarly liable to go wrong, as has been discovered in Indian urban government, even after decades of experience. The wonder rather should be that some of the most essential points were in fact grasped in a relatively short space of time in the Eastern Region.

A word must be said concerning the relations between councils, for while this is not of universal relevance in the same way as staffing problems, it has been a vital concern not only in the Eastern Region but also in the West and in Ghana. The County jurisdictions had been planned to coincide closely with the existing Provinces; it was hoped that these had been in existence long enough for the people to have developed a real 'provincial consciousness'. We have seen, however, that even in the North, where people were used to the idea of large jurisdictions, the idea of the Provinces had never taken hold. This was even truer in the East. There was great confusion and some jealousy concerning the functions of the County Councils. The system of establishing each authority with its own unique instrument added to the confusion. In the hopes of straightening things out the Regional Authority for Local Government issued a pamphlet 'What Local Government is and how it Works' in 1953, setting out in general terms the spheres of activity of the different layers. Since, however, many of the services apparently overlapped (for instance education, road works, maintenance of law and order, and 'local projects for the benefit of the community') this effort was only partially successful.

In the meantime some of the District Councils had been showing a tendency to kick over the traces, taking everything into their own hands, and even refusing the County precept. A temporary way was found round this difficulty by awarding certain Districts 'county powers', in other words making them into all-purpose authorities. This worked much better, particularly where the County was large and its headquarters remote, perhaps in another tribal area.

In general, however, in spite of considerable success in working the new system here and there (including the development of committee work and successful co-ordination between the different local government layers in some areas), it was judged that further legislative steps to strengthen control over the whole system were required. The result was the Local Government Ordinance of 1955. The control of the Regional Authority was abrogated, in favour of more direct responsibility for the Minister (local government was at that time still in the Ministry of Home Affairs, and Dr. Azikiwe was the Minister). Ministerial approval for the dismissal of senior staff was required; budgets were to be directly vetted in the Ministry. A Local Government Inspectorate was formally established. This turned out to be the District Officers in disguise, and in a short space of time in very many areas they regained the confidence of the people. Generally speaking after this, things settled down much more happily. The Minister delegated certain powers to the 'Inspectors' (such as authorizing certain expenditure pending the approval of the budget); they were given more responsibilities for advising councils and for inspection of books and records.

Although the power of the District Officers was thus in some measure restored, in the longer run the direct influence of the Ministry of Local Government has tended to increase and that of the field officers (in local government) to decrease. This is partly due to a better understanding and more general acceptance of the new system; partly to the extreme pressure on the time of field officers, as personnel shrank and services expanded.

The 1955 Ordinance also foreshadowed the establishment of a Local Government Service Commission and a network of provincial Tenders Boards to arrange contracts. It is only in the most recent period, however, that what promises to be suitable machinery to deal with these thorny problems has been established. Finally the ill feeling arising from the exclusion of elders from the councils was removed (in 1956) by making provision for a ceremonial

President of a council, and the co-option of up to one-fifth of the numbers of the Council of Chiefs or other notables, if any councils so desired. In this the East, with a new interest in chiefs on political grounds, was following in the steps of the West.[1]

Financial weakness is unfortunately typical of the Eastern Region; as we have seen the eastern peoples only agreed to the introduction of the direct tax in the late 1920's, more than twelve years after it had started in the West, and of course much longer still after the North. During the years when the new local government institutions were being set up the Regional government was itself desperately short of funds. Consequently there was a very wide gap between local ambitions and the possibility of satisfying them. On the other hand by no means full use was made of the various local tax opportunities which had been granted to the councils; their systems of assessing and collecting direct tax were inexpert, and although the people were always willing to make voluntary contributions, the discipline of regular tax payments was unwelcome. There was no tradition of a duty to support Emirs or Obas.

The Regional government had from the first intended to introduce universal free primary education at as early a date as possible. In 1956 it rather suddenly decided to take the plunge, and in order to provide the very large funds that would be required, it decided to kill two birds with the one stone by transferring the unused direct tax powers to itself, where they would be subsumed in a new progressive income tax. The Local Authorities were to be left with rights over personal tax only up to 5s. per taxpayer; nothing however was done to interfere with their right to levy a rate on land and buildings.

It soon appeared that the government had again moved too fast. A small number of urban authorities began to look into the possibilities of taxing land and buildings, a problem they had never before tackled; but this solution offered little help in rural areas. Some Districts were in very dire straits, in spite of large increased grants from the Region (which were supposed to compensate for loss of direct tax previously levied, but did so very imperfectly). The Regional government consequently agreed to raise the ceiling on the local personal tax from 5s. to 15s. and at the same time encouraged Local Authorities to have recourse to the old system

[1] See above, p. 14.

of 'assumed local contributions'[1] (in other words a semi-voluntary tax which the Missions found little difficulty in collecting, so long as it was to be spent on education).

The results of these changes on the relation between the Regional Authorities and local government was drastic. From an area making little use of grants in aid for local purposes, the East has become a high grant area, with consequent implications—or at least possibilities—of tighter central control. Large-scale expansion has for the time being been stopped at the local end. It is significant that local budgets are stationary or even falling, in strong contrast to both the West and the North, where the rise is continuing to accelerate. On the other hand the representative system is by now well established in the Region, and small-scale development from below has by no means stopped. Nor is there any evidence that the Regional government now wishes to increase the degree of centralization; this would be quite out of keeping with Ibo traditions.

Indeed there is some evidence in the opposite direction. A solution has been found for the problem of the stresses between different layers of councils and of the difficulties of the County Councils, although in a somewhat draconian manner. This implies abolishing at one stroke all the County Councils, sacrificing the few good ones for the (admittedly more numerous) unsuccessful experiments. At the same time by reducing the powers of the local councils, the system of tiering will virtually be abolished. At a later stage we shall have to discuss the implications of this in relation to the size of councils and their efficiency.[2] As things stand, however, all attempts at organizing local government in the Eastern Region in large units has been abandoned. There may even be a danger of renewed fragmentation, although this would be contrary to the government's declared policy.

The transition to modern local government institutions in the Western Region need not detain us long, since by and large the changes were similar to those in the East, although throughout there was less haste and consequently a more orderly progress. As in the East, discussion of local government reforms had already started in 1948. These centred in particular round three points: the desirability of increasing the elective element in councils, the need to improve the efficiency of the staff and the possibility of federating

---

[1] See above, p. 168.   [2] See below, pp. 507 ff.

small Native Authorities into more viable units. During the 1940's indeed a substantial amount of regularization of jurisdictions had been taking place. The number of 'superior' Local Authorities had fallen from 137 in 1945 to 53 in 1951, and the five Sole Native Authorities which had existed in 1939 had disappeared. By a Native Authority Amendment Ordinance of 1950 Native Authorities were permitted to establish committees (including if they so desired an Executive Committee which would take over the active work of the authority). Provision had also been made for the extension of non-statutory Village and Clan Councils.

The Ordinance which substituted elective councils for Native Authorities was introduced by Chief Awolowo, leader of the Action Group Party[1] in 1952; it became law the following year. In introducing the Ordinance Chief Awolowo emphasized his faith in representative institutions in terms that are worth quoting: 'The importance of local government cannot be overemphasized. It is the foundation on which the magnificent and massive super-structure of regional, state or central government is erected. It is also the training ground for a larger number of public spirited citizens than can ever have room to cooperate on the regional or national level.'

The Ordinance provided for a wide and flexible organization. The possibilities were carefully explained to each Native Authority and they were asked to select the form most suitable for their area. The most usual choice was for an upper layer (in this Region known as Divisional—not County—Councils) and a layer of District Councils below it, with perhaps some local councils at the village level. The formal structure was consequently practically identical with that adopted in the Eastern Region, and conformed very closely to the British model. A total of 21 Divisional Councils, 100 District (of which 22 were all purpose), and 95 local councils was planned; eventually numbers slightly exceeded this. They took the place of 71 Native Authorities, so that clearly no saving in staff was implied. Provision was made for a majority of elected members, to be chosen directly at the lower levels, and indirectly for the Divisions, by secret ballot if desired (and in fact this was largely used.) In addition to the elected members, in accordance with Yoruba traditions, provision was made for up to one-quarter of the councillors to represent the chiefs. These could either be

---

[1] And Premier of the Region when that office was established.

appointed individually for an indefinite period, be chosen by an
electoral college of chiefs, or be appointed by rotation for a
definite period. One of these was to be chosen as president, the real
work of the council, however, being done by the elected chairman.
In strong contrast to the Eastern Region every council appointed
its quota of traditional members.

As in the Eastern Region, each council was gazetted with its
individual instrument, defining its powers and duties. Virtually
speaking a selection could be made from eighty-two possible
functions. There was thus no clear distinction between Divisional and District Councils, and much overlapping (the effect of
this will become evident when we examine the current budgets of
this Region in Chapter 13). It was possible for either a Divisional
or a District Council to be designated the rating authority, the other
layer precepting upon it. Generally speaking, and rather significantly, the choice fell on the District level. Rating was regarded as
a privilege and carried with it some prestige.

The Western Region has had its share of teething troubles in the
working of local representative institutions; this has been specially
marked in the larger towns, that is in Abeokuta and Ibadan.
Generally speaking the troubles were of the type rapidly becoming
familiar: too much interference on the part of councillors (especially
the chairman) with the work of the executive; corruption, nepotism, and incompetence, accompanied by chronic difficulties in
engaging responsible and trained staff who would be prepared to
stand up to importunate councillors. The worst trouble occurred
in Ibadan where conditions were complicated, on the one hand by
the rigid hierarchy of the local chiefly system[1] and on the other by
the early impact of national politics.

Initially in the Eastern Region it had been hoped to keep national
politics out of local government; but this proved no more possible
than in England. However, in that Region it cannot be said that
politics have impinged very seriously at the local level except in
towns like Enugu and Aba which contain a large 'stranger' element.
This no doubt is principally due to the dominating role which the
N.C.N.C.[2] Party holds in the Region. In the Western Region
where the N.C.N.C. is in a substantial minority to the Action
Group Party, politics have tended to play a more important part
in local government. This is especially true in Ibadan which

---

[1] See above, p. 93.   [2] National Council of Nigeria and the Cameroons.

normally elects an N.C.N.C. majority and where in consequence the council tends to be at chronic loggerheads with the Regional government.

The troubles in Ibadan led to a careful inquiry which is useful in throwing light on conditions in local government in the Western Region in 1955. Ibadan council was suspended and temporarily replaced by an appointed caretaker council. On the other hand two of the biggest mistakes which had been made in the East: the total exclusion of traditional authorities and the total removal of the counsels of the District Officer, had been avoided in the West. It was therefore considered that no fresh legislation was needed at that time[1] to deal with the difficulties that had been experienced; a tightening up of existing methods of control would be sufficient. This view seems to have been quite justified.

In the Western Region local councils were given a choice of methods of raising revenue virtually identical to those available in the Eastern Region. On the whole the West has been considerably more successful in raising revenue by direct tax (due no doubt mainly to the greater wealth of the area, especially in the cocoa-growing districts). On the other hand there has been much more opposition to the development of a local rate on land and buildings.

Local finance and outlay in the Region expanded gradually, on an even keel, until 1955 when the Regional government judged that the time had come to adopt universal free primary education. In spite of increased grants from the Region (which were, how-ever, largely absorbed by salary increases already granted), the effect of this decision on local finances was staggering. Local outlay on education in 1948–9 had amounted to £556,000; in 1956–7 it became £4·2 mn.

As in the East, the Western government decided to support this expansion by a stiff progressive income tax; but unlike the East, Local Authorities were expected to take a full share in assessing and collecting this. They were given exclusive rights over tax on the first £300, with the Regional tax starting above this level. Thus in fact an integrated income tax on the Scandinavian model was introduced (later on we shall have to discuss in detail the interest-ing possibilities suggested by this).[2] Generally speaking the Local Authorities rose magnificently to the occasion, those which did not

---

[1] A new Local Government Ordinance was, however, passed in 1957.
[2] See below, p. 303.

were soon hearing from the Regional government. In some cases taxpayers found their tax liability increased sevenfold in a year. It is not surprising that there was some violent reaction to this in the form of riots, in which one or two tax collectors lost their lives. By and large, however, the objective was attained.

As a result of the effects of this drastic increase in local expenditure (it had trebled between 1951 and 1957), and also as a result of some years' experience in the working of representative bodies, the Regional government decided to appoint a small departmental committee to conduct a general investigation into the working of financial relations between the Western Region and the local authorities, especially in view of the commitments put on local authorities by government policy; it reported in 1957. The recommendations broadly took the line that the Regional government should accept wider administrative and financial responsibilities in a number of fields. In order to simplify the structure of local government (and if possible to cheapen it) it was decided that there should be a concentration at the District level. The top layer of councils would virtually disappear, save in a few places (such as Ibadan) where it would be convenient to have separate authorities for urban and rural areas, even though the rural councils would require substantial help. Village councils would be partly submerged, or in some cases turned into area committees, to satisfy local patriotism.

In spite of its conservatism some progress had been made in the Northern Region towards the institution of representative councils by 1948, but by and large the Native Authorities remained and (still in 1960) remain very much as they had been established by Lugard. In order to appreciate the situation in the North it is necessary to emphasize the fundamental difference between what is understood as local government there and in the south, or indeed in most other places. A great deal more, both of the business of governing and of the provision of services, is carried out by the Emirates than by local authorities, or native administrations, elsewhere. This is done partly on an agency basis (with subsequent reimbursement by the central authority), but quite largely as part of the normal business of the Native Authorities.

The nature of the difference between the two halves of the country might perhaps be put in this way: if for any reason the

Northern Native Authorities were to cease to function the wheels of government in the region would probably grind to a standstill. On the other hand if the Regional government were to pack up (presuming that the same volume of assistance from the federal government continued to be available), the Emirates could carry on without very much trouble. Today, as much as ever (indeed perhaps rather more than formerly because of relative loss of strength by the administration), and in spite of the increase in elected members of councils, a strong and determined Emir can get his own way. In the southern Regions on the contrary, if the Local Authorities were to cease to function something very real and important would be lost, but the Regional government would not be seriously embarrassed; it could quite well cope with their functions. On the other hand, without the Regional government most Local Authorities would be more or less at sea.

From this it will be apparent that the sort of changes since 1948 which have to be recorded in the North are those of gradual modernization rather than of any fundamental transition. One of the most interesting of these changes has been the growth of District and Village Councils within the Emirates. These originated from a recommendation of a Residents' Conference in 1945. Their original purpose was to spread an interest in local improvements on to a wider basis, and to increase the contacts between the native administrations and the people. From 1947 some part of the direct tax was earmarked (on a *per capita*—taxpayers' basis) for their expenses. Many of these little councils have become active and enthusiastic developers from below. In the Middle Belt they have taken a great part in school building.

A parallel, although differently oriented development has been the establishment of so-called 'Outer Councils', expressly to advise the Emir and to keep him in touch with popular opinion and ideas. The members are nominated, with the intention of making them representative of as wide a range of interests as possible. All Members of the House of Assembly in the Emirate are members *ex officio*. The first of the Outer Councils was established at Bornu in 1947 and they have become very generally popular. There is no doubt that as development takes place and services become more complicated, additional links of this nature can play a most valuable part.

In 1950 on a motion by Mallam Tafawa Balewa two experienced

officers were asked to make a general report on the progress of local government in the Region. As might be expected nothing very startling emerged: general progress in breaking down over-large Emirates and in amalgamating smaller ones, and a steady increase in the elective element in councils, and of councils themselves. (Sole Native Authorities had ceased by a decision taken in 1951.) In 1953 the energetic Sardauna of Sokoto became Minister of Local Government, combining it the following year with the premiership of the Region. From 1954 considerably more attention has been paid to the development of town government, via councils with subordinate ward organizations: not very much progress seems to have been made, however. A development of wider than Regional interest was the establishment of the area round the Regional capital at Kaduna as a Capital District, administered by an officer directly responsible to the Regional Governor, somewhat after the manner of Washington, Ottawa, or Delhi. At a later stage we shall have to devote some attention to the merits of this device.

The Native Authorities continue to be financed by a share of the (Regional) direct tax, supplemented by grants from the Region, to the extent that on balance, and on the average, the Native Authorities are substantial net gainers. This is especially true in the Middle Belt where the incidence of the education grant (still distributed on the Phillipson system),[1] is much higher than in the less educationally developed remainder of the Region. The rate of direct tax is not high: on the average equivalent to a flat sum of about 33s.; not much more than half the *lowest* rate in the Western Region. Although there is provision for a graduated tax 'assessed' on higher incomes little use is made of it. In addition in the cattle-rearing Districts the *jangali* capitation tax on cattle is levied, and is also shared with the Region. The revenue, however, does not show the increase that might be expected from the expansion of the cattle population. On the whole, revenue assessment and collection in the Northern Region is, within its limits, reasonably efficient. The special 'ability to pay' character of the original Lugard lump sum method of assessing direct tax has, however, been almost completely submerged by the failure to revalue at post-war prices. Very serious discussion concerning the advisability of imposing a progressive income tax after the manner of the other

[1] See above, p. 168.

Regions has been held; but although it has been agreed in principle an opportune moment for imposing it has not yet been found.

Lest it should appear that local government in the Northern Region is stationary, it must be emphasized that in fact native administration expenditure is expanding very rapidly, particularly in respect of education, where it is stimulated by massive grants from the Regional government. Another interesting feature is the development of capital works at the Native Authority level; these we shall examine in Chapter 17. Each Native Authority has its own ten-year plan, in addition to planning at the Regional level.

Before concluding this review of transition in Nigeria one other way in which Nigeria has been in advance of other territories must be emphasized: namely in training staff for local government (and in some cases not only staff but councillors also). Two training institutions, giving one-year courses, were early established by the Regions, one at Ibadan (which can also draw on the University College) for the southern Regions (each, however, conducts its own course), and one at Zaria for the north. These were later transferred to federal responsibility. Although there are not yet sufficient trained staff, a most gratifying advance in the standard of the executive, both in the Native Authorities and in local councils, is already apparent. This is another matter which we shall have to discuss later on;[1] there are few more vital needs if local government is to continue to develop satisfactorily after independence, than a high standard of locally recruited council officers.

II. GHANA

The transition from Native Authorities to representative local councils in Ghana, followed (as has already been indicated) very much the same course as in Nigeria, and with approximately the same timing. There were, however, three strands, or more accurately three aspects of the same strand, with which the Ghana fabric was shot through, which hardly existed in Nigeria. There was nothing new in any of these; we have already met them, going right back into the history of the nineteenth century: but they have coloured the whole situation in Ghana so strongly throughout the post-war years that they must be re-emphasized here. Although they did not directly affect local government their indirect influence was very great indeed.

[1] See Chap. 22.

In the first place the chiefs in Ghana were much stronger, more closely organized and had a greater power over their people than in the southern Regions of Nigeria. This was largely due to their control of extensive *stool* lands on the one hand and to the organized chiefs' councils on the other. Secondly the growth of political consciousness had been much more rapid than in Nigeria. The educated young men who were forcing the hands of the government were violently anti-chief. Further, they were drawn almost exclusively from the Colony Fanti, and since the most powerful chiefs were in Ashanti, to political and intellectual opposition to the old order, was added the strain of traditional tribal enmity. In answer to this there was a strong undercurrent of demand that more regional autonomy ought to be given—or rather more autonomy for Ashanti, since no influential Ghanaian bothered much about the feelings of the people in the Northern Territories. This demand for regionalism has come to a head on three separate occasions since 1950, and on each occasion it has been defeated by the Fanti element.

In all this tangled skein the dominant motif has been a fight to the death between the educated commoners in the south and the chiefs, whether in the South or in Ashanti. It has not, however, been possible for the politicians to proceed too fast (quite apart from the administration's attempts to hold the ring) both because the chiefs are obviously still very strongly entrenched and because a major showdown with Ashanti was better avoided, since it might have had awkward repercussions. We are not concerned directly with the constitutional proposals and advances which followed one another in rapid succession; but we cannot pass them by completely since questions of the organization and control of local government institutions were closely related to interregional politics.

As we have seen, Indirect Rule was introduced into Ghana at a much later date than into any of the Regions of Nigeria:[1] even then it spread slowly. The weakness of the local will to tax and be taxed hindered the full establishment of Native Treasuries in many areas. In fact it was only by the end of the late war that the network of Native Authorities was complete in the Colony, although it had been working successfully for some time in the Northern Territories. Even when they had been established the

[1] See above, p. 88.

Native Authorities (outside the Northern Territories) differed in a very important way from those in Nigeria, because of the very widespread existence of chiefs' state councils, drawn from the aristocratic families. The state councils were in theory distinct from the Native Authorities, but in practice membership was often identical, so that the introduction of Indirect Rule had hardly changed anything.

Nevertheless some improvements were effected (or attempted) before the war ended. In 1943 a Municipal Ordinance was promulgated giving the four important towns (Accra, Kumasi, Sekondi-Takoradi, and Cape Coast) councils with elected majorities. Unfortunately this aroused very little interest (municipal local government seems only to have come to life with the introduction of national party politics). Few voted at the elections, and there was little enthusiasm for local development if it called for the payment of taxes. More progress was apparent in rural areas. By 1946 practically all the Native Authorities had modernized their Treasuries and accounting systems (under an Ordinance of 1939). After prolonged discussion a new Native Authority Ordinance was passed in 1944. This gave the Governor power both to amalgamate existing chiefdoms into viable units (a very useful provision since in the Colony alone there were sixty-three different states, many with subdivisions), and also to put in a council in any area where, due to an emergency or disputed succession, there was no effective chief, thus ensuring the continuity of local administration.

The effect of this legislation was indeed to strengthen the hands of the leading chiefs; the government was still following the traditional policy of encouraging development through the 'natural leaders of the people'. At the same time the Governor's own powers were still more enhanced, since he could in principle determine local jurisdictions, and in great measure control the actions of the chiefs. In view of this greater control it was judged practical to inaugurate a system of grants for local development from the central government, based on the energy of the Native Authority in question in collecting taxes, and in proceeding with development. Although the changes introduced by the Ordinance were modest, they do seem to have succeeded in breathing more life into local government.

It was apparent to all that a considerable measure of constitutional advance would have to be conceded to the Gold Coast as soon as the war was over. The government's first constitutional proposals were launched in 1944. They provided for a joint Leg. Co. and Ex. Co. for Ashanti and the Colony, but Ex. Co. was to consist entirely of officials, and the five elected members of Leg. Co. were only representative of the towns. This old-fashioned structure overlooked completely the rapid increase in political consciousness which the war had brought about. It also took no account of the restlessness of returned ex-service men on the one hand, and of cocoa farmers, incensed by the policy of the Marketing Board, on the other. As the matter was put by a subsequent Commission of Inquiry (Watson Report): 'The Constitution was outmoded at birth.' This was in 1946; it had not been possible to secure any implementation at an earlier date. It was immediately clear that the constitution of 1946 would not be accepted; a period of intense unrest and disturbance ensued, culminating in serious riots in Accra in 1948.

It was now evident that the government would have to start again. Accepting in principle the criticisms of the Watson Commission, a strong Committee on Constitutional Reform was set up under the chairmanship of Judge (later Sir Henley) Coussey. This consisted of forty Africans, mainly drawn from the older intellectuals, and some of the more educated chiefs, including senior members of the United Gold Coast Convention, up to that time the spearpoint of opposition. We are not concerned with the constitutional reforms recommended (which, however, put the Gold Coast on the high road to independence), nor with the split in the ranks of the U.G.C.C. which led Dr. Nkrumah to break away and form the Convention People's Party, soon to become the major political force in the Gold Coast. But the recommendations of the Coussey Commission on local government reform are vital to our investigations.

The Commission felt strongly that the Native Authority system was no longer adapted to modern requirements. 'The native authorities, through which local government is at present carried out are virtually the old state councils, vested with modern administrative powers' (p. 11). They recommended that the Native Authorities should be replaced by democratically elected councils, which should nevertheless retain a place for the chiefs, who were recognized as having an important role in Gold Coast life. In this the Commission was taking a more conservative view than the

Watson Commission, which had tended to regard the chiefs as anachronistic survivals. The Coussey Commission envisaged four statutory Regional Councils with administrative powers, and beneath these a tiered system of local councils: at the District and at the village (or municipal level). The government quickly responded to these suggestions. Committees were appointed to review local government in the Colony and Ashanti respectively, while a third committee was bidden to make a general report on local government finance. These all reported in 1950–1.

The Local Government Ordinance of 1951 was the result of these investigations; in introducing it the Minister for Local Government summarized his government's views: 'First local government means the administration of local services by local people: secondly there must be a definite separation of the authorities responsible for the ceremonial, ritual, constitutional, and customary functions, from those responsible for the administration of local government.' The Ordinance provided for the establishment of District (upper tier) Councils with local and urban councils beneath them. Two-thirds of the members would be elected, the remaining seats being reserved for traditional authorities. Either District or local councils could be designated rating authorities. Provision was made for a president drawn from the ranks of the chiefs, but the business of the council would be the responsibility of the chairman. Except for the larger part assigned to the chiefs, the structure was thus virtually identical to that established in Yorubaland in the following year. But there was one important difference: in Ghana the chiefs' councils remained in being at all levels, including the higher (provincial) level. Although their functions were confined to ceremonial and customary matters, the mere fact of their continued existence retained the organization of the chiefly interest as a powerful factor in the country.

The democratization of local government was a matter of general agreement, but even while the Ordinance was being prepared it became a plaything of party politics. In particular the C.P.P. saw in it a means of extending its influence throughout the country, and thereby reducing, and eventually removing, the authority of British administrators on the one hand and of the chiefs on the other. In particular, opportunities would arise of removing any anti-C.P.P. chiefs and replacing them by party nominees. Failing this, C.P.P.-controlled councils could reduce

stool revenues (which under the Ordinance were to be shared
between the councils and the stools), to the point where the chiefs
would be rendered powerless.

In spite of strong opposition from the chiefs and the remnants
of the U.G.C.C. during the debates, the final structure of the
Ordinance facilitated the realization of all these aims. The C.P.P.
had one further triumph at the same time. It had been recommended by the Coussey Commission that Regional Councils
should be established, with administrative powers. Following this
Sir Sydney Phillipson[1] was asked to make a report on the organization of these. His report, issued in 1951, recommended something
very much on the lines of the Nigerian Regions as they stood
under the first Macpherson Constitution, which did in fact prove
to be the first step towards federalism. The institution of such
councils would have run contrary to all the plans of the C.P.P. and,
not surprisingly, the scheme was not proceeded with. This was the
first defeat of regionalist interests; they returned to the attack with
renewed vigour in 1955 and again in 1957.

The Ordinance of 1951 also succeeded in dissociating District
Officers from the work of the new councils, which were put
directly under the control of the Ministry of Local Government.
During the early years of the working of the new system considerable friction arose between the councils and the administration,
but eventually a *modus vivendi* was reached, very similar to that in
Nigeria. By 1953 the Regions had been increased to five (by the
hiving off of Trans-Volta Togoland and the division of the Colony
into an Eastern and a Western Region). These areas were in
charge of central government officers, supported by a hierarchy
of Governments Agents, and Assistant Government Agents in the
Districts; these were of course the former District Officers, but
now having no power over local government. However there was
provision in the Ordinance for the Minister to delegate some of his
powers, and this he proceeded to do. Government Agents could
now attend council meetings, including budget sessions (in which
they may be called upon to play a very large part); they can also
demand to see records and accounts. Thus although they have
become wholly the agents of the Ministry of Local Government,
and are through the Regional Officers the channel of communication between the Ministry and the local councils, they perform

[1] Then Commissioner on Special Duties in Nigeria.

many of the duties formerly undertaken by District Officers for the Native Authorities. The Government Agent's office plays an important part in exercising control over local council expenditure. Inspections of Local Authorities by Government Agents take place regularly (they are supposed to call in about once a month, but tend to devote the greater part of their attention to councils in difficulties). On the whole relations appear to be about as happy as in the old days, irrespective of whether the Government Agent is an expatriate or a Ghanaian.

The war against the chiefs proved a more serious business. Under the Ordinance, revenues were to be shared between the local council and the state council, in agreed proportions. No ruling on this was, however, laid down, and some councils proceeded to appropriate an undue share themselves, so that funds for customary ceremonies and the expenses of the chiefs' households were quite inadequate. By 1954 the Minister was finding it necessary to remind councillors that they must make due provision for these matters. In some cases he took the opportunity of a new instrument to write in compulsory proportions for sharing. Where agreement between the two parties could not be reached the Minister himself took action to cut the knot. This difficulty was not wholly due to politics. With the new duties which councils were urged to undertake, and which many were endeavouring to fulfil, funds were insufficient to go round. This difficulty was recognized by making additional grants available in poor areas, particularly in the coastal areas of the Western Region.

The victorious C.P.P. also took advantage of the general feeling against the chiefs to bring about a fantastically large number of destoolments. The new chiefs who replaced those who were destooled tended to be better educated men, but they, whatever their original convictions, found themselves absorbing the atmosphere of royalty. They underwent a process of indoctrination by the elders, learning the traditions of their people and of chiefs. There have been instances of C.P.P.-appointed chiefs resisting C.P.P. measures. The growing independence of the chiefs won them considerable respect, and popular opinion in many of the villages swung back into support of traditional elements as against the politicians. Moreover, since this infusion of new blood, the Joint Provincial Council has been taking a more active and intelligent interest in public affairs. Nevertheless, in the longer run, the tightening control of the C.P.P. at the centre, which can through the Regional Officers and Government Agents be extended to the Districts, implies that the cards are heavily stacked against the chiefs.

This was confirmed by the abortive second attempt to establish more or less Regional authorities. In 1952 the government had begun preparations for a new constitution. It appeared to be generally agreed that this would be unitary, but in the course of consultations with various interests, including the chiefs, the demand for some sort of federalism appeared to be so strong that the government felt obliged to set up a Select Committee to make a report on its feasibility. The opposition, distrusting the intentions of the government on this, refused to co-operate, and an independent constitutional adviser (Sir Frederick Bourne) was appointed. He reported in 1955 in a manner which clearly supported the chiefs. It was suggested that there should be Regional Assemblies, consisting of all members of the House of Assembly in the Region, together with representatives of local councils. They were to be debarred from passing resolutions affecting the position of chiefs without full consultation and a free vote. Where chiefs' councils existed they were empowered to give advice to the Regional Assembly, which would then be bound to discuss the questions raised.

The most important aspect of the Bourne Report, and the one which made it basically unacceptable, was the suggestion that the Regional Assembly should have transferred to it most of the powers of control over Local Authorities vested in the Minister. In addition the Regional bodies would have substantial powers in the siting and implementation of development projects in their areas. They were further to be consulted about the appointment of Regional representatives of statutory boards and committees. A conference of delegations of interested parties was later held at Achimota to discuss the Bourne Report; if anything the general tenor was in favour of even more power for the Regional Assemblies—which were to be supported by Regional Houses of chiefs— than the report had suggested.

The government did not formally reject the Bourne Report. On the contrary in its 'Statement on the Report of the Constitutional Adviser and of the Achimota Conference' it professed general agreement with the recommendations, and went so far as to say: 'Where Government has not accepted any recommendation in full it will be found that any variation proposed by Government is a matter of administrative detail or an alteration of emphasis, neither of which implies any rejection or modification of the principles underlying the Conference's proposals.' By that time, however, the critical stages of negotiations for independence were drawing near. It seemed absurd to hold up negotiations for independence in order to settle the powers and duties of Regional Assemblies, especially as the main principles of the Bourne Report seemed to be agreed. Among these were the recommendation that the assemblies should have executive and administrative powers, although without independent tax rights. Accordingly the Ghana Constitutional Order in Council of February 1957 provided first that Regional Authorities should be established, and second that the Governor General should appoint a Regional Constitutional Commission which would be required not only to make recommendations relating to the Regional Assemblies themselves, but also concerning the 'functions of local authorities and the division of responsibility between central, regional and local government'. To the implications of this we must return in a moment.

In accordance with the constitution the Regional Commission was duly appointed, under the chairmanship of Mr. Justice van Laare; it reported in 1958, reiterating many of the recommendations of the Bourne Report, and in particular stressing the view that the Regional Assemblies should have executive powers and some control over finances. When the Report came before the House it was accepted by the government in its entirety, save for the single, but absolutely vital, exception that the Assemblies should not be executive bodies: they were to be purely advisory. Thus truncated, even their supporters lost interest in them. Thus the government of Ghana, having neatly by-passed this third round of Regional aspirations, remains highly centralized, and retains a tight control of local government.

This does not in any way imply that the government had lost interest in the development of responsible local authorities, which would be able to play their part in the general development of the country; on the contrary, already before the end of 1956 the Permanent Secretary[1] of the Ministry of Local Government had been instructed to make a detailed inquiry into the working of the

[1] Mr. A. F. Greenwood.

local councils established under the 1951 Ordinance. His report appeared in 1957, and gives a most valuable picture of the organization of Local Authorities and their finances, including their relations with traditional authorities. Broadly the picture is a familiar one, although aggravated by the special difficulties of Ghana.

It is recalled that the 1951 Ordinance was implemented with such speed that there was no time to consider the size of effective and viable units of local government. The Local Authority jurisdictions followed those of the Native Authorities, and these in turn had been based on native states. Very little progress had been made in any but the Northern Region in establishing a higher tier of authorities, so that the basic unit remained the very small area. Fragmentation was greatest in Ashanti where thirty-one of the eighty-three councils had less than 10,000 inhabitants, twenty indeed had less than 5,000. Even in those areas where a few higher tier councils had been established their administration was not above suspicion; their demands by way of precept on the local councils were excessive, in some cases exceeding the collection of basic tax in the area. Only in the Northern Region was there a different picture. The indigenous tribal groupings in that area were, as we have seen,[1] too small to be the basis of any local government, consequently viable Native Authority areas had been carved out; to these the councils had succeeded.

The two basic problems facing the further development of local government in Ghana were consequently the organization of more viable units and the provision of more adequate autonomous finance. Clearly the solution of the first problem would greatly simplify the solution of the second. The Commissioner demonstrated effectively the way in which the persistence of small units was wasting scarce resources on salaries, office expenses and allowances to councillors. There were further arguments in favour of larger units. Having a smaller number of units to deal with would greatly facilitate the task of the Government Agents and officers of the Ministry in giving necessary advice and supervision. In some cases the adjustment of interlocal disputes which at present held up development would be facilitated if all the parties were brought together in a bigger unit which could undertake worthwhile works.

As a result of this part of the Greenwood Report a reorganization

[1] See above, p. 88.

of all local government jurisdictions, on the basis of a single-tier all-purpose authority of about District level (to be called, however, *local* councils) was started in the course of 1958. With the long separatist tradition of Ghana local government it will obviously take months, perhaps years, to implement successfully; but if the process can be achieved it should effect a lasting reform in this aspect of local government. As we shall see later the size of the new councils would conform closely to those being adopted in Southern Nigeria, and indeed elsewhere.[1]

Perhaps an even greater weakness in Ghana local government was the absence of provision of adequate finance for the development of local services. The 1951 Ordinance had offered Local Authorities four possibilities: a basic, flat sum poll tax, a graduated personal tax, a tax on land and buildings, and one on movable property. Almost everything was wrong with the administration of these. The last three were hardly used at all (apart from a tax on land and buildings in town areas). The basic tax varied in level very much from area to area, being as low as 4s. a year for men in some places but in others as high as £3 (rates for women were half of those for men). Not only were these rates very low compared with, for instance, even poor areas in Nigeria, but the higher levies could very simply be avoided. Owing to the small local government jurisdictions and the large and scattered possessions of wealthy farmers, it was usually possible for them to pay tax in a low rate area, a certificate of having paid tax in one area providing a discharge for any other area.

This administrative weakness (which could have been remedied without much trouble), was matched by carelessness of clerks and collectors in the administration of the tax; nominal rolls of tax-payers hardly existed in many Districts; it seemed to be nobody's business to supervise the collections. Moreover the question of stool land revenue was continuing to give trouble, and this was of course deeply involved in party politics. Under the Ordinance the local councils were charged with the duty of collecting the revenue, to be subsequently shared (as we have seen) with the stool holders. The stool holders complained that the councils deprived them of funds by failing to make adequate collections. The local authorities complained that the stool holders rendered their task impossible by failing to report concessions and contracts, and reserving

[1] See below, pp. 507 ff.

the rents for themselves. No doubt from place to place both complaints were justified. Where the concessionaires were mining or timber companies (as was often the case in Ashanti and the north of the southern Regions) the sums involved were very considerable.

A small beginning with a graduated rate had been made in the Northern Region and had yielded considerable additional revenue. Since, however, the government had placed a very low ceiling on possibilities in this direction (tax of 1% of income with a maximum of £5 on an income of £500) in order to protect its own income tax which started at this point, it looked as though not very much could be expected in this direction. (It will be recalled that in Western Nigeria the Regional government felt that its own income tax was sufficiently protected if it allowed unlimited local collections to an income level of £300.) As a result of his review of tax possibilities for local government the Commissioner pinned most of his faith on the better administration of existing taxes, including the use of a simple form of tax on land and buildings in urban areas outside the big towns. There is no question that better collection would have been greatly simplified by larger jurisdictions.

In respect of urban local government the Commissioner found less cause for despondency. An Ordinance of 1943 had established fully elective corporations in the four large towns. The populations of all but Cape Coast were large and growing fast, and they were undoubtedly potentially viable units. Their main source of revenue was a local rate, assessed on the annual value of land and buildings, including all the complications of the British local rate, and consequently requiring expert valuation. The tax was nevertheless assessed on owners. The Commissioner found that by no means full use was made of this, largely owing to valuation difficulties. He consequently advised a change over to rating on full capital values, believing, moreover, that these could be more simply assessed by the central government without calling on outside experts. This raises a problem of great importance for urban areas in developing countries, which we shall have to consider carefully at a later stage.[1]

The main difficulty about town local government in Ghana is however the impact of national politics on local councils, thus adding the sting of party favouritism to the usual tendency for corruption, nepotism, and inefficiency. Indeed as a result of

[1] See below, pp. 355 ff.

repeated troubles, in the year after the report was issued, all the town councils except that of Cape Coast were suspended.

The answer to many of the problems with which Ghana local government is struggling, not least the evil ways of town councillors, lies in the direction of providing adequately trained and independent minded staff for local councils. Ghana has made some progress in this direction by establishing a small local government school in Accra. It gives short courses in rather inadequate premises, and occasionally rises to the height of the British N.A.L.G.O. certificate. All this, however, is much less than adequate, and incidentally compares unfavourably with training opportunities in Nigeria. The problems of training for African rural councils need to be thought out on their own basis; for substantial towns professional qualifications are necessary. These are problems which we shall have to discuss at a later stage.[1] The Ministry of Local Government is deeply conscious both of the need for more training facilities and of the general shortcomings of local government in Ghana; it is determined to carry through its reforms. Indeed the good sense and keenness of the Ministry is one of the most hopeful signs in the whole field of local government.

III. SIERRA LEONE

The little colony of Sierra Leone regained something of its mid-nineteenth century importance during the war from its position as an essential part of the defence system of the Western Approaches. Large numbers of tribesmen from up country were drawn into Freetown, and for many of them the change was permanent. This undoubtedly contributed to a general loosening of tribal customs and of the authority of the chiefs. In the middle 1950's the discovery of alluvial diamonds in many of the river beds led to a further movement of peoples and to general upheaval. These changes impinged on a social and economic organization that was still a good deal more primitive than in other west coast dependencies, so that the effects have been particularly disturbing. Before the end of the war two minor constitutional advances can be recorded: in 1943 two African members were added to Leg. Co. More notable, the custom of holding regular conferences of chiefs in the Protectorate at the District level, which had been

[1] See below, Chap. 22.

gradually growing up, was given statutory recognition. This was significant of the pressure for advancement outside the Colony.

The first constitutional changes however took place within the Colony: in Freetown and in the Rural Area (as the rest of the peninsula was described). The elective town council of Freetown (which it will be remembered had in 1925–6 been removed)[1] was restored in 1948, although the franchise was not widened to adult suffrage until 1957. That the town was now able to govern itself may be deduced from the relatively small change that took place when this event occurred. The new town council contains twelve elected members, three nominated councillors, and three aldermen, in addition to the Mayor.

In 1949 an experiment was made of providing a complete new set of local government institutions in the Rural Area, in the hopes of breathing life into that somewhat derelict countryside. The 115 'villages' (hamlets would describe many of them more accurately) were grouped into twenty-eight Village Area Committees (later called Village Group Councils). The main occupation of these was envisaged as carrying out works for higher layer governments; but in addition they were given some minor public health and public works opportunities, in aid of which they were empowered to levy an 'improvement cess'; they also acted as electoral colleges for six Rural District Councils which had considerably wider powers, especially in the provision of water supplies, and in town and country planning. These latter were responsible also for poor relief and for 'any other services approved by the Governor', including the 'purchase, distribution, and sale of any commodity in the public interest'. The Rural District Councils were also the rating authorities for the Rural Area, and in addition elected one member each to a body called the Rural Area Committee, which was designed to co-ordinate public health services and public works throughout the Colony, as well as acting as a link between the Colony and the central government.

Thus a complete three-tier system of local government was set up for a population of some 17,000 people living in fairly compact groups in a well-cleared and accessible area. Unfortunately financial resources were as much in under supply as political institutions were in over supply; the structure never really came alive. In the meantime the expansion of Freetown over the neighbouring rural

[1] See above, p. 108.

districts was creating new problems and opportunities. We must return to consider these later.

The centre of interest now shifts to the Protectorate. It will be remembered that the generosity of the 1901 Ordinance in respect of paramountcy had saddled the little country with 216[1] independent chieftaincies. It was the government's settled policy to reduce the number of these, although it was rather timidly pursued, normally waiting until a death gave the opportunity of suppressing a chieftaincy; by this means the number had been reduced to 148 by 1950. A limited reform had been introduced into the system of chiefdom councils, whereby they were now formally gazetted, and their membership registered: but in many areas membership was still undetermined as late as 1956, and even gazetted councils (for instance Nongowa) might have as many as 423 members, all chief's nominees. They were thus only representative in any sense so long as everyone trusted the chiefs all the way. Tax assessments remained at the 1937 poll tax rate of 4*s.*, plus the government house tax, unaltered since 1901 at 5*s.*

In 1949 the Commissioner for the Protectorate[2] put out a comprehensive economic and social development plan for the whole area. It was clear that the Chiefdom Authorities as constituted would not be capable of taking much part in this. However the spontaneous development of District chiefs' meetings noted above, seemed to provide the answer. The areas covered by these were very much larger than the Chiefdom Authorities; indeed they were so large that it was questionable whether, in Sierra Leonean conditions, they would qualify as local government bodies at all. This, however, was irrelevant at the moment, since it was only planned to use them as government agencies. Accordingly the District Councils Ordinance of 1950 gave the Governor powers to establish District Councils, consisting of two representatives of each chiefdom (of which one was to be the Paramount), and if desired, a maximum of three other members. The District Commissioner was to be the *ex-officio* president. The functions of the council were defined in the broadest possible way 'to promote the development of the District and the welfare of its people with the funds at its disposal'. No formal independent revenue was arranged for, but in fact, in addition to the 100% grant from the government

---

[1] See below, p. 109.
[2] Mr. Herbert Childs.

with which they mainly operated, some of the councils managed to squeeze some extra funds out of Chiefdom Authorities by a kind of informal precept. The central funds made available to the District Councils were partly derived from current territorial revenue, partly from the war-time accumulated reserves of produce marketing boards. It was obvious that the real power in the District Councils would be wielded by the Paramounts; indeed this was intended, since it was confidently believed that that was the way the people wanted it—with what justification the anti-chief riots of 1955 were to show. The educated younger generation of commoners had been late in appearing in Sierra Leone; but war-time conditions had at last produced them.

As regards activities the District Councils got off to a flying start, establishing health centres, dispensaries, sanitary services, maintaining protected forests and seedling nurseries. In some areas they were eager to take over full responsibility for social welfare and community development, as well as for the upkeep of roads, bridges, and ferries. A Commission[1] inspecting them in 1952 recommended not only that these further powers should be conceded, but that the District Councils should be able to raise autonomous revenue by formally 'precepting' on the Chiefdom Authorities. In fact what emerged was not a precept in the sense of a charge limited to the costs of a particular service (as in the United Kingdom), but a general surcharge of unlimited amount on the Chiefdom Authority revenues.

Apart from this obvious cause of friction it was evident that many of the services which the District Councils were now to undertake overlapped with those for which the Chiefdom Authorities had previously had sole responsibility. There was thus every chance of a conflict of jurisdictions. This does not seem to have worried the government; presumably they considered that since the power of the Paramounts was equally strong in the two forms of local body no difficulties could arise. In 1955 still another form of Local Authority started operations: independent Local Education Boards. These consisted very largely of missionaries and teachers, and so were well geared to sponsor a badly needed drive to raise the standard of literacy; but they conflicted directly with a duty hitherto regarded as belonging to the Chiefdom Authorities.

The years 1954–5 were momentous for Sierra Leone in three

[1] Davidson Committee.

other ways: first the diamond rush, to which we have already
alluded and which flooded the country with adventurers from
neighbouring territories, and with an undreamt-of level of cash
incomes. Secondly a new constitution[1] widened the electoral basis
in the Provinces (as they were now to be called) to taxpayers'
suffrage; thus altering substantially the balance of power at Freetown. Thirdly a Local Government Ordinance and a Tax Ordinance carried the new system through to the local level.

The new constitution awarded just under half the seats in the
new House of Assembly to the Paramounts, but up country their
influence was such that they could control most of the remainder.
On a strict population basis the Creoles of the Colony were still
over-represented; but the balance had been shifted definitely
in the direction of the Paramounts. The taxpayers' franchise in the
new constitution made it necessary for the first time to give individual receipts for tax payments, instead of as hitherto one to the
chief in respect of his total collections. At the same time, in conformity with the favourable reports[1] on the activities of District
Councils, statutory recognition was given to their power to 'precept' on the Native Authorities (as they were now to be called). As
we have seen, many of the District Councils were full of ideas, but
up to this point they had been called upon to exercise no real
financial responsibility since they were operating almost entirely
with government money. In fact this situation could not have
endured, since the accumulated war-time reserves on which they
had been drawing had by this time dried up.

It was implicit in these changes first, that there would be a
sudden and sharp rise in the demand for local revenue on the
Native Authorities, and secondly that the uniform tax rates to
which the Territory had always been accustomed would quickly
disappear. In fact although the rise in rates was sharp, incidence
was still very moderate in comparison with other west coast
territories. It was the methods of tax assessment and collection,
rather than the amount of tax liability, which led to the troubles
of 1955.

The changes in local government which were introduced at
this time were in fact greater than these two Ordinances would
suggest. Although the District Councils had only been formally

[1] Resulting from the (Keith-Lucas) *Report of the Electoral Reform Commission.*
[2] In addition to the Davidson Committee, that of Mr. Morriss.

in existence since 1950, and had so far exercised no real financial responsibility, it was planned to make them the starting-point for a very bold experiment. By a Sessional Paper of 1954 control over local government, including approval of the Estimates, conditions of service, election of chiefs, raising of rates and taxes, and all other relevant matters were transferred from the Protectorate administration centrally situated at Bo to a new Ministry of Local Government in Freetown; given the poor communications of the interior this made control very much more remote. At the same time it was planned to withdraw the District Commissioners completely from local government, in two stages. In the first, the Governor would appoint an African president of the District Council, the District Commissioner remaining as an ordinary member of the council; in the second stage he would disappear completely from the scene.

In themselves these changes were very closely in line with those made in the early fifties in other territories. As we have seen it was there soon discovered that the withdrawal of the administration had been too abrupt, and they had had effectively to be brought in again by the back door. In Sierra Leone the situation was considerably more unfortunate, first because the position of the District Commissioners was not so well established (and could not be, since the councils themselves were only a recent creation); secondly, it followed from this that there had been no opportunity for education in responsible budgeting such as had in fact been given in Nigeria over many decades. From his position as an ordinary member of the council the District Commissioner could exercise no control, perhaps even less than if he had been completely outside.[1]

The government evidently took the view at this time that there was nothing much wrong with the Chiefdom Authorities, and no change in their organization was suggested. The Cox Committee[2] which investigated the system after the riots gave a rather different picture. Even the 'reformed' Authorities were of unmanageable size and were filled with chiefs' nominees; they met only twice a year. More serious from the point of view of the ordinary man were the three-member Assessment Committees whose business

[1] Unquestionably much of their expenditure was irresponsible. The idea of African presidents seems to have gone to the heads of councillors, and many elaborate 'coronations' were staged, not uninfluenced by what they had read of contemporary events in London.

[2] Report on *Disturbances in the Provinces*, 1956.

it was to visit each village annually to declare the list of those liable to tax. These also consisted of chiefs' relatives, and clearly in some places at least every sort of abuse was practised.[1]

Frauds on taxpayers and illegal exactions are of course always liable to occur where taxpayers are illiterate. They are difficult for the administration to check because fraudulent tax collectors are normally very prompt in delivering the right revenue. Conditions in Sierra Leone were, however, especially favourable for such practices. In the first place formal tax liability was very low, well below taxable capacity in many places, so that there was plenty of room for illegal extortion. Secondly, tax was not paid into the Native Treasury, but to individual headmen. As many of these were also illiterate they were given receipts signed in advance to distribute, no doubt according to their inclinations; this also could lead to great inequity. There is hence every reason to believe that tax abuses were considerably larger in Sierra Leone than in other territories.

It was in these conditions that the riots of 1955 broke out; even after the reports of two committees[2] it is difficult to assess whether these were primarily anti-chief or anti-tax. In a sense the two causes cannot be separated, since the chiefs were responsible for the tax collection methods. The local government tax, swollen by the District Council precepts, was at that time running at about 25*s*. a head in most Districts. According to the Cox Committee Report, if we allow for additional illegal exactions, the sum the taxpayer would have to meet would be about 75*s*., quite a substantial amount for the family which was still mainly in the subsistence economy (as a fairly large proportion still were), but very moderate for the better off. It seems to have been the opinion of the government that the tax level was the main cause of trouble, and each committee was asked to make recommendations on tax reform as well as on the distribution of powers and duties between Native Authorities and District Councils.

It would take us too far afield to examine the proposals of these committees in detail; but certain points, both of agreement and

[1] Such as 'shake hands', compulsory presents of foods, even if the Assessment Committee was staying only a few hours in a village, 'beg off' fees for removing names fraudulently entered on the register, and 'fines' for such offences as death in childbirth or falling out of a palm-tree.

[2] i.e. Cox Committee, cit., and (Wann) *Local Government Inquiry* Committee, 1957.

divergence, are of interest in view of the experience of other territories. For main revenue sources the Cox Committee recommended first a simple property tax (or rate) on houses based on size and type of construction, and area in which the property was situated. Secondly they proposed that the local government tax should be replaced by a graduated poll tax, based on a roll kept in the Registrar's Office at District headquarters. In order to eliminate the abuses of the Assessment Committees, tax would have to be paid directly into the Chiefdom Treasuries.

The Wann Committee on the other hand recommended first a *graduated* local property rate, based on accommodation and type of construction, but without reference to location. Secondly they recommended a basic local poll tax at a single flat rate throughout the Territory. The system of assessment and collection would be as before, except that all headmen (instead of as hitherto a limited number), would be licensed tax collectors. In the first instance the local property tax was to be introduced cautiously into a very limited number of areas. It is hard to see that any of the causes of the troubles would have been removed by the Wann recommendations; nor would they have provided anything more than a negligible additional revenue. On the other hand the Cox proposals could have laid the foundations of an effective local tax system. The government took the simple way out of leaving the local poll tax at the flat 25s. rate.[1]

Both committees agreed that the District Councils should be given a more limited range of powers, and that certain functions should be transferred back to the Native Authorities. The Cox Committee recommended that both types of council should be given grants in aid by the government, and that their budgets should be more closely checked by the Ministry of Local Government. This would *ipso facto* have given the government much better powers of control. In addition they proposed to put an end to the precepting system, except in so far as it might be kept in reserve as a means of coercing a backward Native Authority when all the rest of the District was in favour of a particular project. This would have left the District Councils mainly as advisory bodies, serving on the one hand as joint committees of Native

---

[1] At that moment the government was in a financial crisis due very largely to the fall in import duty revenue consequent on the expulsion of high-spending alien diamond hunters.

Authorities, and on the other as a means whereby the government could from time to time secure co-operation in implementing particular works or services. Bearing in mind that the District Council areas were on the large size for local government jurisdictions, these were eminently sensible proposals as a basis for a rational reorganization of local government institutions.

The Wann Committee, once again more conservative, proposed to leave the District Councils in the same position as before, although shorn of many of their powers, and to continue the precepting system so long as a precept did not exceed two-fifths of the local revenue collection. Neither committee produced any suggestion for tackling the fundamental difficulty of the fragmented Native Authorities. The shadow of the 1901 Ordinance was still hanging over the country and could only be exorcised by a drastic policy of amalgamation (of Treasuries if not of Native Authorities), such as had been carried through many years previously in most other territories.

Two minor, but by no means unimportant changes were, however, presently introduced. First, by the Electoral Ordinance 1956, the District Councils became wholly elective; even allowing for the continuing influence of the Paramounts, this gave the 'young men' a chance of taking a part in affairs. At the same time it implied that the councils should not again drift so far away from public opinion as they evidently had done in 1955. Secondly, the Local Education Boards were abolished in favour of Education Committees of the District Councils with power to co-opt outside members. It is evidently the government's intention to see what can be made of the present constitution of District Councils, and probably to let the Native Authorities fade into the background. It remains to be seen whether the District jurisdictions will prove a suitable size as a basic local government unit. On the experience of other west coast territories they would seem to be over large.[1]

We must now return to the Colony and Freetown. In the capital, although things have not gone altogether smoothly (there were some nasty riots in 1955, essentially between the Christian Creoles and aggressive Moslem elements from the Provinces), some sort of settled programme does seem to be working. In the Rural Area the Local Government Ordinance of 1955 introduced several minor and one substantial change: the Rural Area Com-

[1] See below, pp. 507 ff.

mittee took over responsibility for rating from the District Councils (these were renamed Divisional Councils to avoid confusion with the District Councils in the Provinces). Nothing, however, was done to change the character of the local tax (basically a tax on house property on a very antique valuation) nor to improve the standard of assessment. Moreover Freetown and the Colony remain without any form of personal tax below £800 (the exemption limit for the central income tax). If it is intended to introduce an effective personal tax in the Provinces there is every reason to extend it to the Colony also, both on grounds of equity and because otherwise the problem of urban drift could easily become unmanageable.

The worst sufferers from this financial stagnation are the Divisional Councils abutting on Freetown, which are fast becoming urbanized, and which consequently urgently need to develop modern standards of sewerage, water supply, street paving, lighting, and so on. Much of their trouble merely arises from the failure to carry out a revaluation which would bring the tax base more into line with current values. A change to a broader base than annual value would also greatly help in these expanding areas.[1] In the absence of any help in this direction it was not surprising to find the wealthiest hankering after a progressive rate.[2] Unfortunately the valuation unit which had been built up in Freetown was allowed to disperse when its work there was done.

In Freetown itself there is considerably more progress to report. The comprehensive revaluation carried out by a team organized by a United Kingdom expert, came into force in November 1957. A 60% increase in rateable value permitted the realization of a substantially higher revenue (£450,000 as against £245,000), at a lower poundage (4s. 9d. as against 6s. 8d.). There is no reason why this poundage should not be increased gradually, since the inter-property assessments are now reasonably equitable. The city now having a satisfactory financial base, the government has embarked on a process of transferring to the corporation responsibility for certain health, highway, and primary education services. Initially grants are available for the setting up costs of these, but although they imply an additional burden on the rates in the long run, they will make the work of the council both more responsible

[1] See below, pp. 352 ff.
[2] Similar to the Jamaican sliding scale, above, p. 141.

and more interesting. Following the adoption of adult suffrage for the new House of Assembly, the city franchise was similarly extended. The immediate result of this was that younger less experienced, and to some extent less responsible, councillors were returned. However, thanks to the continuation of the aldermanic system and to the retention of an experienced Mayor, no great difficulty seems likely to arise on this account. There still remain a number of problems to be tackled in Freetown, in particular those connected with town planning and land use. These are closely related to the question of the extension of the city bounds. These problems, however, appear mild relatively to those still confronting both the Rural Area and the Provinces.

12

TRANSITION IN EAST AFRICA

I. UGANDA

WHEN they contemplated the state of Uganda at the end of the war (in spite of the Kampala riots of January 1945 and the endemic difficulties with the Kabaka), the administration is likely to have felt that there was cause for some satisfaction. The policy of development in the interests of the Africans was firmly established; some very forward-looking plans were indeed in the air. It was accepted[1] that some non-agricultural development would be called for, if the potentialities of the territory were to be at all fully realized. It was remembered that many years ago Winston Churchill had drawn attention to the opportunities for hydro-electricity that existed at Owen Falls. But for the moment there was the back-log of the depression and of the war years to be made good; these bright visions of power and industry would have to wait for the time being.

This being their state of mind, it is understandable that they should have given a somewhat cold reception to the Creech Jones Despatch—especially to that part of it which drew the attention of the colonial governments to the desirability of educating Africans in local self-government, as a step towards the national self-government which (it was now accepted) must lie not so far ahead. The experience which Uganda had had in that direction did not look, to a critical eye, so very promising. The Busoga councils, which had been started with such enthusiasm, had had to be completely reconstituted (in 1940) on account of an inability to maintain law and order. Certainly there was no shortage of candidates for chiefly office; but it was the emoluments that were the attraction, together with the patronage and other plums (secondary education for one's children, nomination of candidates for training courses in the United Kingdom, and so on) that went with them. All who had any hope of attaining a chiefship in the future were ready to

[1] Sir John Hall who became Governor in 1944 was particularly interested in economic development.

support higher pay for the chiefs. As one writer has put it, 'factional disputes for office and influence in the native administration were a major aspect in the political life of every district'.[1] Standards of government still depended on the power of the District Commissioner; it could well be argued that this would long continue to be the case.

In the event, the administration's answer to the Creech Jones Despatch was the Local Government Ordinance of 1949. This was a scheme that had been drawn up by the Provincial Commissioners; it reflected their conservative bias. Though the elective element in the District Councils was increased, their powers remained slender. They had little budgetary independence; their by-laws had to be approved at Entebbe. Though the District Commissioner was not a member of the council, he was chairman of its Standing Committee. And since the councils were often extremely large (that of Busoga had 138 members) its work was in fact performed by the Standing Committee, over which the District Commission tended to retain control. The chief was in the anomalous position of being a full member of the council, though he was appointed by government, and responsible to government. Doubtless this was a step in the direction that Creech Jones had indicated, but it was (and was felt to be) a very little step.

Then a new wind began to blow. From 1952 to December 1956 the Protectorate was subjected to the strong views and dynamic personality of Governor (Sir Andrew) Cohen. Things began to move in several directions. On the side of economic development, there was the building of the dam at Owen Falls, the opening of copper mines in the Ruwenzori, the taking of the railway to the Ruwenzori, further encouragement of cotton and coffee (including cotton ginning by Africans). On the side of higher education, there was the further development of Makerere College, which was transformed into the leading university institution in East Africa. Primary education was still (in the main) a matter for the missions; councils were nevertheless empowered to make grants for such education, and to finance them out of taxation raised for the purpose. But this brings us to the Cohen reforms in local government, which will be the subject of the rest of this chapter.

It was only in 1955 (towards the end of the Cohen régime) that these reforms were embodied in an Ordinance; but they had been

[1] C. J. Pratt in *A History of East Africa*, vol. 2, to be published by O.U.P.

prepared, and were under discussion and negotiation, long before
that. Already in 1952 there had been a Report on Local Government by C. A. G. Wallis of the Colonial Office, in which the failure
of the existing councils to act as local government authorities, in
any real sense, was shown up. The basis of the new plan was the
District Councils, which were almost wholly to consist of members
elected by the lower layers (although chiefs still remained members)
so that the direct influence of the administration upon them
(through District Commissioners and chiefs) was at least in
principle removed. At the same time their powers were to be
enhanced, both on the side of expenditure and of revenue—the
detailed arrangements on this side will be considered later. Though
estimates were to be subject to approval at Entebbe, the degree of
freedom that was to be left to local initiative was very striking
indeed.

It might have been expected (and it would seem that it was
expected by the Governor) that so substantial a measure of self-
government would be welcomed with open arms. That, however,
was by no means the case. Nor was the obstacle the same as that
which has appeared at similar stages in other territories—the unwillingness of nationalist politicians to accept the fulfilment of a
part of their demands, when they hope that by standing off they
may soon get the whole. There was one general difficulty which
applied in all districts: it had been made a condition of the reform
that the size of the councils should be reduced, since the unwieldiness of their former membership made it hard to conceive that
they could transact the business which would now fall upon them.
The loss of patronage, which this would imply, was bitterly felt.
More important, however, was the special difficulty—the threat
to the special institutions of Buganda which the Cohen reforms
would have presented, if they had been carried out in their
original form.

The story of the clash between Governor Cohen and the Kabaka
Mutesa II is well known; it is unnecessary to repeat it here. The
'suspension' of the Kabaka and his subsequent return, in conditions which (to Africans at least) looked like a triumph, led to a
significant change in the character of the Cohen reforms. If
the principle of the original plan had been carried out, the three
Districts of Buganda would have had councils, like those in the
other Districts of Uganda; each, it was hoped, would have been

of a more or less democratic character, ready to act as 'County Councils', arms of the future democratic government of the whole of Uganda. (When it is remembered that the Districts were themselves based upon tribal areas, this was perhaps in any case a shade optimistic.) In fact, though the Kabaka came back as 'constitutional monarch', the restoration of the monarchy of Buganda was the significant thing that occurred. The Buganda Districts were stillborn; Buganda reappeared as a *unitary* 'native state' within the Protectorate. It is true that the Lukiko was reformed, at least on paper, so as to appear to fit in to some extent with the new scheme; it now consists of four members from each saza, the saza chief and three members elected by the saza council—but the substantial result of this arrangement is to give something very similar to the twenty saza chiefs and sixty-six appointed members of former times. The size of the Lukiko was not effectively reduced. The substantial result of the Cohen reforms, as far as Buganda was concerned, was to make the Kabaka's government distinctly more like a government than it was previously. It now enjoys substantial tax powers, as well as a grant from the Protectorate government. It is housed in a new secretariat building, considerably more impressive than the buildings the Protectorate government has had at Entebbe. The relations between this new nucleus and the Uganda government, or with the rest of Uganda, are very much a question for the future.

Outside Buganda, in the outer Provinces (comprising, we must never forget, three-quarters of the area and population of the whole territory), there was no such complication as this, though in some of the other Agreement States (especially in Bunyoro) Buganda separatism has raised an echo. On the whole, in these outer Districts, the Cohen plan appears to have gone through; though since the 1955 legislation was only permissive, and it has taken time for the new arrangements to be accepted in one District after another, formal completion is still recent at the time of writing, and it is early to pronounce upon their practical results. We must nevertheless now turn to a consideration of the content of the 1955 District Councils Ordinance, with special reference to its fiscal aspects.

On the political side, outside Buganda, the original plan has largely been carried out. The size of the councils has been reduced; they have ceased to have official members; their authority has been made quite separate from that of the District Commissioner. The chief is a pure civil servant, a servant of the commissioner on the side of law and order, of the council in respect of other functions. Initiative over the appointment and dismissal of chiefs (and other officials) appears to rest with the councils.

With regard to functions, certain formerly government functions in the fields of agriculture, medical and veterinary services, and public works, have been wholly transferred to the councils. There is also a long list of permissive functions, including the construction of trading centres and housing estates, and the control of drinking and dancing.

Apart from miscellaneous items such as licences and court fees (not in total very considerable) the main revenues, from which this expenditure is financed, consist, in approximately equal measure, of direct tax and of grants from the Uganda government. The direct tax is the successor of the old poll tax (or hut tax), now almost entirely handed over from the central government to the councils. (In 1954, before the introduction of the new system, there had been a poll tax of 15s., all over the country, together with a local tax of 25s., and an education tax of 5s. The government tax was reduced to 6s. under the new Ordinance.) Now, under the new system, while the education tax seems still to be levied on the old basis, the rest of the (local) direct tax has been converted into a graduated tax, levied at varying rates, in some relation at least to the wealth of the taxpayer. In the 1955 Ordinance such graduation was (naturally) only permissive; but the permission has been acted on (even in Buganda); three or four years later some degree of graduation has become the general practice. The details of this most interesting and important development will be discussed in another chapter.

From the purely financial point of view, the expansion of activities, of expenditure and also of the revenue to pay for it, there can be no doubt that the new councils have been, at least so far, a great success. Graduation has made it possible to raise more revenue without imposing an intolerable burden on those least able to pay; already, between 1953 and 1956, the revenue from the local government tax had doubled (while the national income rose by no more than 18%).[1] The introduction of something which is broadly equivalent to a local income tax does indeed raise problems

---

[1] From £139 mn. to £164 mn. Cf. *Statistical Abstract* 1958. An Estimate of subsistence income is included.

of the relation between central and local taxes (though the highest rung of the local progression remains low by central standards); but these are questions for the future. For the moment, the stimulus which has been given to local activity, and the interest that has been aroused in the new local institutions, is distinctly gratifying.

The political consequences of the new arrangements are, however, less reassuring. The exclusion of the District Commissioners from the new councils, and the demotion of the chiefs (for such it must have appeared) will have caused the administration as a whole to 'lose face'. The relation between those local functions that remain to the administration, and those that have been transferred to the councils, has not been fully worked out. There have been the usual troubles over appointments (dismissals of chiefs who appeared to the administration to be thoroughly efficient, and their replacement by others of more dubious qualifications), and over contracts (in this latter field it has already been necessary to do some tightening-up). But these things are by no means peculiar to Uganda. It is of much more importance, in the Uganda setting, that the Districts are tribal units, so that the councils are apt to find their main function in the pressing of tribal interests, and thus to become expressions of those disintegrating tendencies, which threaten to tear Uganda apart. Buganda is itself (as we have seen) the worst case, but it is by no means the only case. Though it seems probable that the new local government institutions have something to their credit in the training of the individual communities for self-government, the greater communal self-consciousness, which this implies, is by no means all gain, since it makes it harder for each of them to live with its neighbours.

Something must be said, in conclusion, on local government in towns. This is rather a separate matter from those which have been discussed, merely because, in Uganda (as in the rest of East Africa) the towns are rather separate from the African community. The population statistics for the two largest towns (1948 figures) tell their own tale. In thousands

	Kampala	*Jinja*
Europeans . .	1·0	0·2
Other non-Africans .	9·1	3·8
Africans . . .	11·9	4·4

Even Kampala, as will be seen, was of very modest size by any but East African standards; further, in each case, nearly half of the population was non-African, chiefly Indian (including Pakistani and Goan). Though the Kabaka's capital (the Kibuga, as it is now called) abuts upon Kampala, what amounts to a frontier is drawn between them. There could be no question of fitting these towns into the rest of the local government system; by their character they had already taken themselves outside.

An Urban Authorities Ordinance was nevertheless prepared alongside the District Councils Ordinance which we have been discussing; but it was not until 1958 that it came into force. It is accordingly too early to describe its working, and even to see at all clearly what is to be the range of urban authorities to which it is to apply. Three grades of town are envisaged—a town in process of formation, to be governed by an appointed town board; a second stage, with a town council, having some elected element; and a full municipality, with a council that would soon become entirely elected. So far, however, Kampala (1949), Jinja (1958), and Mbale (1959) are the only municipalities in Uganda. Masaka, Tororo, and Soroti appear to be regarded as candidates for the second batch.

When a town has reached the stage of municipality, its powers and duties become quite wide. It has duties in the fields of public health and public order, and powers in the fields of education, housing, trading services, and so on. It receives grants from government, but like the English municipality, on which it is clearly modelled, its chief source of revenue is the local rate. (Rates in the smaller townships are limited to 20% of annual value; municipalities, on the other hand, do not appear to be restricted.) In practice, both Kampala and Jinja levy rates on capital value, with a different poundage on the capital value of site and improvement—a compromise between improved value and unimproved value rating.

II. KENYA

Progress in the development of local government institutions in Kenya does not seem to have been seriously held up by the second world war. By 1947 most of the African District Councils included some elected members. In 1947 a Committee on the Financial Relations between the Central Government and the African Councils was appointed; its report led to a new African District Council

Ordinance of 1950. This activity may have been stimulated by the Creech Jones Despatch, but in its absence developments would probably not have been very different. Contrary to a widely held view, the development of local government institutions among Africans in Kenya has owed something to the presence of substantial numbers of Europeans, brought up in a tradition of responsible local government, and so tending to regard its establishment among Africans as a natural aspect of development. Many Europeans have been prepared to give voluntary service to improving the lot of Africans as well as other races.

As a consequence of this background local government institutions in Kenya have been growing up with a much closer approximation to British practices than elsewhere. A sharp distinction must be drawn between the outward form and structure of British local government, which, as we have seen, tend to be far too readily copied in the dependent territories, without sufficient understanding of their significance or appropriateness to the social and political organization of the country in question, and a system based on a real understanding of the spirit of British local government. When this exists, as it does in Kenya, it should, as we have already argued, be possible to establish the essentials of the British system in a number of varying circumstances.

It is this real understanding, which has animated those responsible for organizing local government in Kenya which makes the story of its development especially interesting and suggestive. The story can be followed in great detail in the Annual Reports of the Ministry of Local Government, from 1948 in respect of the Settled Areas and since 1953 in respect of the African District Councils also. The authority of the Ministry was extended to them in that year, but unlike the European councils they are not compelled to furnish annual reports; in fact many of them are obviously pleased to have the opportunity of relating their progress. Here we can only briefly sketch the main lines of development, but points of general interest will find their place in the ensuing chapters.

The big drive for the development of local government institutions in the post-war period may be dated from the arrival from the United Kingdom of two very experienced local government officers (J. E. Hunter and A. Altorfer), as Commissioner and Inspector for Local Government respectively. Both had strong ideas as to how they considered that local institutions should develop in Kenya, and how its finances should be organized. As a result, on the one hand a strong general system of control, unique in colonial circumstances, has been built up; and on the other a force of professional local government financial advisers is at work throughout the territory. As a result, there is now a skilled professionalism about Kenya local government and finance, which makes parallel institutions in other dependent territories look merely amateur. As an illustration of the difference, in Kenya in 1957 there were thirty local government officers (all Europeans) with the full training and diploma of the Institute of Municipal Treasurers and Accountants, in Uganda there were three, and in Tanganyika two. With Kenya numbers, effective on the job training (which for most officers may well be more useful than training in the United Kingdom) becomes an actuality; elsewhere it is not possible. However, professionalism is not the only thing in local government. In Kenya there has unfortunately grown up a certain strain between the Town Clerk-Municipal Treasurer class and the administrative service, the average District Officer neither knowing nor caring much about financial niceties. It is likely, and it is certainly to be hoped, that this trouble is quite temporary; so long as it lasts however full co-operation between the two streams of administration is difficult.

Improved organization at the centre accompanied this new start. For this the Minister, Mr. (now Sir Ernest) Vasey was largely responsible. In 1950 a valuation organization was set up in the Lands Department. It quickly proceeded to prepare a new roll for Nairobi where nominal values had been stationary for some time; as a result within a short period rate revenues were doubled. At the Ministry two Standing Committees were set up to scrutinize the budgets of authorities in the Settled Areas. In 1953 when the African District Councils came within the purview of the Ministry a Standing Committee was set up for them too, including five Africans (mostly members of Leg. Co.). So long as the budgets of African District Councils are carefully scrutinized (and often largely drawn up) by District Officers, the work of this committee rarely takes more than a day; but it is gaining most valuable experience.

The most important organizational change was the establishment of County Councils as an upper tier in Settled Area local government (1952), very much on British lines, the former District Councils and smaller towns becoming County Districts within them. Owing to the peculiar boundaries of the Settled Areas and the African Reserves the administration of these Counties is sometimes very awkward. Nevertheless most of them got off to a good start. This Ordinance seems to have succeeded where everything previously had failed, in arousing an interest in local government services among the European population. There is a real keenness to develop the area, in the interests of all races. The Health Service, stimulated by generous grants from the centre, has received most attention. This is a service in which the larger area afforded by County administration is a particular advantage. The County Councils Ordinance provides that more than two-thirds of the members must be elected; they could include Asians, but so far are almost exclusively Europeans. The remaining third of the members represent the County Districts. The Rural District Councils are fully elective, but the members are all European; in the townships and urban districts there is provision for multi-racialism, with some appointed membership. By 1958 there had been some promotions up the urban ladder; in each case it was made a condition of greater financial freedom that local rates must be introduced (generally speaking the choice falls on unimproved values), and an investigation is conducted by the Commissioner into the readiness of the area for greater financial responsibility. Except for any area granted municipal status (similar to that of a British county borough) all the towns will be absorbed as urban districts of counties sooner or later.

In respect of African District Councils the most important post-war legislation has been the African District Councils Ordinance of 1950; but a stream of by-laws has poured from the councils (in 1953-4 alone there were 155). As things stand the African councils actually have wider powers than the European. In the first place they have a general statutory duty of promoting peaceful progress in the area, in pursuit of which they have wide powers of initiative. Secondly they have special duties assigned to them: in the fields of education, and public health in particular (where their assumption of new duties is stimulated by a 50% grant of approved expenditure). They have also been active in the development of agricultural and forestry services. In view of this increasing activity and interest, the government issued a new White Paper defining the

spheres of central and local activity (1957),[1] and making arrangements for further finance through grants and rates. At a later stage
we shall be discussing the provisions of this, since it is one of the
all too few attempts to think out central-local relations in a comprehensive manner.

An interesting development in the post-war period has been
that of the Location Councils; as we have seen in a number of areas
it was possible to form these on the basis of traditional population
groups. In a District there are normally about six to nine Locations,
and each may contain three to six Sub-Locations (the exact number
naturally varies greatly with population density). In the more
developed areas (Kikuyu, Kamba, and Central Nyanza) Locations
have tended to group themselves into Divisions in order to co-
operate on larger projects. There is no doubt that the Locations
are the growing point of development from below in Kenya. The
Districts are too large to be considered strictly 'local' government,
and judging by West African experience they may prove too large
for efficient management once they come completely under African management. As things are at present they appear to be developing as a top tier in a system of African local government; in
fact some District Commissioners regard a triple-tiered system
as already established.

The Districts are for the most part purely artificial creations;
their size reflects the situation when the administration was very
sparse. The average Kenya District is, however, not so large as
the Uganda average, and in two ways it seems to be a happier
organization. In the first place District boundaries do not narrowly
coincide with tribal boundaries. In some places tribes extend
beyond the District bounds (thus many Kikuyu live outside the
Kikuyu Districts); in others a number of tribes seem to live happily
together in a single District (thus Elgon Nyanza contains a majority
of Abaluyia Bantu, but also includes some Nilo-Hamitic Masai
and Nandi, and Hamitic Iteso near the Uganda border). It is a
relatively new District but has the distinction (as we have seen) of
having the first African chairman. Secondly the Kenya government
seems to be much more flexible than the Uganda government in
respect of District boundaries. At one stage indeed the tendency
was to consolidate and reduce the number of Districts; more
recently this policy has been reversed, usually with the object of

[1] See below, p. 220.

enabling a higher standard of services to be developed in a more compact area.

Before leaving the question of organizational changes mention must be made of the effect of the Mau Mau Emergency on local government institutions. Formally this lasted from December 1952 to January 1960, but many of the restrictive regulations had been removed long before the formal end. It is generally realized that although Mau Mau had an anti-European anti-Christian aspect, it was above all a civil war between different sections of the Kikuyu and their near relatives, the Meru and Embu. These were the areas which were primarily affected. The neighbouring Kamba, although also related, were very little touched by what was going on on their westward flank, while the Nilo-Hamitic tribes remained entirely outside. In the heavily involved areas the immediate effect of the episode (as it can now be regarded) on local development was disastrous. In 1953 African District Councils were obliged to impose a 10% cut in the Estimates. In spite of a large grant from the United Kingdom Treasury, and assistance from the British army, the Territorial coffers were empty, and nothing could be spared for development. In the worst affected areas agricultural output was severely curtailed and it became impossible to collect taxes. The African District Councils in Kikuyuland struggled manfully to keep going, but their work inevitably suffered a severe set-back.

Yet there are some important things to set down on the other side of the account also. In the first place the numbers of the administration were greatly increased all over the Central Province; this paid unexpectedly big dividends. District Officers for the first time were able to get into effective touch with their people, to appreciate far better than ever before the ways and aspirations, both of the sophisticated Bantu of these areas and of the neighbouring Masai. Secondly there was a big increase in road development throughout these areas, and this is greatly accelerating its economic opening up. Thirdly the concentration of scattered Kikuyu farm families into emergency villages, where the houses were cheek by jowl, and neighbours could chat across the fence, introduced them to new ideas and new forms of social organization. Discussions and lectures were organized, centring round improved agricultural methods on the one hand and housewifery on the other. Simultaneously the evacuation of the farms enabled the land to be replanned in consolidated plots and crops to be reorganized, in a much shorter space of time than would otherwise have been possible.

An important way in which the Emergency affected the whole of African life in Kenya, and which had a beneficial effect on the development of local government, was through the reorganization of the educational system. We shall be discussing the significance of this at a later stage, so that it need not detain us here. It is relevant to notice, however, that opportunity was taken of drawing the District and Location Councils more closely into the educational business, by encouraging them to build schools, and more recently by submitting to them the Estimates of the District Education Boards. At a later stage it is planned to substitute for these nominated bodies local Education Committees within the District Councils, which would include some co-opted or appointed members of professional standing. In every District taxpayers have responded enthusiastically to the demands of higher expenditure on education.

These hopeful signs of development of local government institutions in Kenya cannot mature unless adequate finance is available, more particularly in the form of autonomous resources which the councils can themselves control. This is the weakest aspect of local government throughout the Territory. In the towns the use of the unimproved value basis (total derating of buildings) for property rating is universal; we shall have to discuss how far this is adequate after a certain stage of development has been reached; but up to the present it appears to be universally accepted (except perhaps in Mombasa). The County Councils have on paper a choice of seven methods of local taxation, but at present most of these are impracticable. Experiments with a tax on land and buildings have been made in peri-urban areas, as a more remunerative substitute for the established crude acreage tax; but so far satisfactory methods of valuation have not been evolved.

The African District Councils are confined to a flat sum poll tax for general purposes, with a surcharge for education on the same base. A number of them would like to move on to a graduated tax of the Uganda variety. This has recently been introduced by the government, but is reserved for central purposes. In addition to the District Council tax the Location Councils normally collect a small sum (2*s.* or 4*s.*) for their own purposes. This is most willingly paid but the result is so tiny that revenue must be accumulated over several years before it can finance any effective development. In view of what is now being collected from Africans, both in Uganda and in Nigeria, there is little doubt that considerable tax potential in Kenya is at present going untapped. This is clearly not due either to lack of interest in development or to unwillingness to be taxed, such as we have found in some other countries. The Ministry of Local Government, in close conformity with the traditions of British policy, regards taxes on persons and their incomes as properly belonging to the central government sphere, and taxes on land and buildings as the proper field for local finance. It looks forward to the day when African District Councils will be able to get their autonomous revenue from a property rate. This, however, cannot come to pass until individual land holding has advanced very much beyond what it is today.

The result of these rather poor tax possibilities for Kenya Local Authorities is twofold. On the one hand councils of every sort have need to derive additional revenue from the provision of services; on the other the Territorial government has had to come more fully to the aid of Local Authorities through grants, than in most other places. The government has always encouraged Local Authorities to make full use of service charges for such things as conservancy or water, which elsewhere are often supplied (partly at least) out of general revenue. In the same spirit 'self-balancing' services, such as markets and slaughter-houses, really do balance in Kenya; this again is rare. Further, every encouragement is given to local councils to set up commercial undertakings, such as beer halls, timber nurseries, milk supply, and so on. The effect of these on local budgets is not inconsiderable, as we shall see later. It is evident that the social philosophy lying behind this policy is substantially different from what we have found in many other places, for instance Nigeria.

Kenya is an outstanding example of a country which has attempted to evolve a rational grant system which would provide at one and the same time encouragement, control, and some measure of additional help for poor areas. In addition, the European councils receive substantial sums in lieu of rates on Crown land. There is no reason in general why the government should not pay for services provided for its property just like anyone else, but the Kenya circumstances are peculiar in two ways. In the first place most of the land on which the government pays rates is unalienated Crown land, from which it is deriving no return. When the land is remuneratively let, generally speaking it can recoup itself. Secondly, this form of revenue is not available to African areas because there is as yet no property rating within them. On the other hand the African councils make no contribution towards the expense of the very extensive clerical and administrative services provided by the District Offices.

In addition to these forms of assistance extensive specific grants have been available to Settled Area Councils. The terms of these are carefully planned so as to relate assistance to financial ability and local effort. Until the proposals of the White Paper of 1957[1] the African councils were receiving only a block grant of 2s. a head collected by them in poll tax, plus a very limited grant towards salaries of trained staff. In future the latter source will be expanded, and the former substituted by a block grant inversely related to local tax income.

Finally the Territorial government has been anxious to provide means for local councils to borrow in order to finance capital works. A Local Loans Board was established in advance of all other territories, and as we shall see, it has made loans of varying sizes over a large range of works.[2] It is a condition of the award of a loan that not only should the finances of the council concerned be in a sound condition, but that its accounting and financial control should also be adequate. For this reason African councils have only comparatively recently been able to take their share of loans.

This brings us to yet another way in which the Kenya government has been a pioneer in the sphere of local finances. Mention has already been made of the cadre of Financial Advisers established by the Inspector of Local Government. These are fully trained professional treasurers and accountants who are seconded to local councils for a period—perhaps of months, perhaps of two years or more. They are designed in the first place to straighten out the finances of a council which has gone wrong, but secondly, and really more importantly, they are there to give on the job training, for so long as is necessary to ensure that the tangle need not occur again. So far the Financial Advisers have all been drawn from the British local government service, but there is no reason why

[1] See above, p. 216, and Chap. 18.　　　　　　[2] See below, p. 405.

they should not be Africans as soon as there is a supply of officers with the necessary professional qualifications. No council is obliged to receive a Financial Adviser (although if they have got into a muddle they are strongly pressed to do so), and the costs to the Authority are minimal, as the adviser remains on the central pay roll. Experience has shown that after a little initial hesitation demand for the services of advisers has steadily exceeded the supply.

Thus, although Kenya has made some important progress in the field of local government and finance, and has evolved ideas and practices which other areas would do well to ponder, if not to copy, it is obvious that the process of transition to responsible local government has as yet hardly started. The elective principle indeed is well understood at all levels, but even this has not yet been completely adopted. Urban government, even in Nairobi, has not been immune from the troubles which have beset the early steps of local government in other countries. Moreover the two streams of local government institutions—Settled Area and African —continue to run in separate channels (there have however been in the most recent period some promising signs of a willingness to co-operate, at least in projects of mutual benefit). The really weak point about Kenya local government remains its limited capacity, dictated by its financial stringency. The total contribution of even the best organized system of local government to development from below must remain tiny so long as councils are limited to the equivalents of about 2s. a head a year plus a few other grants, a meagre flat rate tax and the by no means princely earnings of commercial undertakings.

III. TANGANYIKA

In the dark days of the depression (which as we have seen hit Tanganyika with particular severity), and of the suppression of the Department for Native Affairs, it was the commissioners of the eight Provinces who kept the flag of local government flying in Tanganyika. Owing to the scattered distribution of the population, with large unusable tracts of land between tribal agglomerations, Provincial Headquarters has had to rely on its own resources much more than in other territories. In Mwanza, still more in Bukoba, Dar-es-Salaam is an immensely long way away. What has to be done must often be done on local responsibility, without there being time to refer back to the centre. In 1939 the Provincial Commissioners took the initiative of calling a meeting to discuss among themselves ways and means of promoting local advance. Throughout the war they were busy thinking out plans whereby a new local democratic structure could be inserted into the Native Authority system, not as a substitute to it, but as an alternative which might develop alongside among those advanced peoples who would be ready to take it.

Various factors stimulated these discussions. First, the new Governor arriving in 1941 (Sir Wilfred Jackson) had come from the West Indies where he had seen democratic local institutions at work in fairly simple conditions. He was anxious to see elected members sitting not only in Leg. Co. but also on local councils. Secondly, already in the later 1930's political consciousness was beginning to appear among the young educated Africans, who found themselves excluded from the Native Authority system as it had developed. (We shall come back to this point a little later.) It was also expected that the return of the ex-servicemen would give rise to political trouble. The case of Ghana showed that this was a real possibility, but in the event they settled quietly back into local life in Tanganyika. Apart from plans for new forms of local government the work of rationalizing and consolidating Native Authority and Native Treasury areas into workable units was proceeding steadily, if not very rapidly. In the more progressive councils the idea of the committee system was taking root. The seal was set on all this by the restoration of the post of Secretary for Native Affairs.

At first the stimulus to progress in local government came entirely from the administration, but by 1947-8 Native Authorities themselves were getting interested; indeed there were encouraging signs from unexpected places. The location of the ill-conceived Ground Nuts Scheme at Kongwa had been chosen partly with a view to opening up a particularly poor and backward area. Even although it never operated at all fully, some improvement was noted among the local Gogo, who previously had been too defeatist to agree to plant government maize in order to save themselves from starvation. They now became much more co-operative, and actually agreed to the establishment of a cattle tax to finance local improvements. Among the Zaramo on the coast near Dar-es-Salaam an experimental transitional type of council was tried out successfully. This area was particularly awkward as the tribe had been decimated by slaving and was now disturbed by the influx of educated young city Africans. A small council was organized, with presently some unofficial members; it chose its own president (significantly not Paramount), and soon developed a real interest in the budget.

In the richer areas more progress was possible. The Chagga of Kilimanjaro (the most literate people in Tanganyika, save only the Haya of Bukoba) had already been given permission to impose a tax for education; they would clearly have been prepared to back it up with a levy for general development, but that the growing revenues of the Coffee Co-operative were soon providing for all they wanted. The Chagga had been working since 1929 under councils composed entirely of chiefs; these no longer met their needs, and in 1946 they were granted a new constitution. This provided for a consolidated council covering the whole area; but the Chagga then demanded that they should have a Paramount. Twenty-five years earlier the government would have welcomed this suggestion; but it had now grown more interested in councils than in para- mounts. Nevertheless since a candidate acceptable both to the government and to the Chagga was available the request was not refused. The experiment was not a success. The new Paramount with a degree from the London School of Economics would have been prepared for close co-operation with the neighbouring European farmers. This was moving too fast for his people, and in 1960 they appear to have reverted to the former conciliar system.

It was in Sukumaland, south and east of Lake Victoria, that the greatest experimentation in new forms of local council took place. It had long been the intention to bring about a federation of the Native Authorities in this essentially homogeneous cotton and cattle-rearing area, where they were particularly fragmented along the bounds of small native states. During the war the Sukuma had prospered greatly, but disease had begun to ravage the cattle and the cotton soil was becoming exhausted; it was clearly desir- able to be able to plan in larger units. A Sukuma Federation was finally achieved in 1946; then came the problem of reorganizing the Native Authorities. Eventually the Federation emerged as a Superior Native Authority, but beneath it 901 new councils had sprouted. This clearly would not do; the total number of the

Sukuma did not exceed 900,000. After further discussions it was decided to deal with the situation by setting up a unifying Provincial Council to be a link between the Territorial government and the Native Authorities. It would be mainly advisory, with no independent revenue; but funds might be transferred to it by the central government, and over the allocation of these it would have some discretion. Nothing really came of this, and the Native Authorities continued to do the work.

The government, however, was not willing to give up experimenting with really large units. The following year it offered a Provincial Council to the Southern Highlands but the Europeans refused to have it unless it was to be given independent revenue. The government took no further steps at the moment. The episode is important however because it was a reflection of a new approach to the problem of local government. For the first time it was being thought of as a *system* which should be territory-wide, instead of a collection of individual councils, more or less going their own way. This train of thought had repercussions in two directions. On the one hand it led to a greater realization of the isolation of the remoter parts of the territory; on the other it stimulated discussion as to how, by stages, rural Native Authorities, urban and peri-urban areas, might all eventually be brought into the fold of a network of elective, responsible, local authorities.

The first fruits of these discussions was a Native Courts Ordinance of 1949, which led the way to the eventual separation of the judicial and executive. About the same time a Native Treasury Board was established to hold the excess reserves of treasuries accumulated during the war, and to lend them out to Native Treasuries wanting to finance development projects. More forward-looking still was the Native Authority Ordinance of 1953 (which essentially belongs to the same line of discussion); to this we shall return in a moment.

The problem of integrating units continued to worry the government. It had two aspects, first to provide a necessary link between the central government and the remoter parts of the country, secondly to co-ordinate the local bodies in each area. A Committee on Constitutional Development reporting in 1951 had recommended dividing up the country into Regions, within which would be a tiered system of Local Authorities, from the Village through the Division, to a County Council. (The influence of Nigerian thought on this was obviously strong.) Professor MacKenzie was appointed as Constitutional Adviser to report on the practicability of such a model. He rejected the Regional idea and came down in favour of organizing the country in about twenty-five County Council areas (which would have been very close to the twenty-two Districts into which the Germans had divided it). When this plan was considered in detail a number of practical difficulties emerged. However the government decided to try something out in Sukumaland, reorganizing the Provincial Council by the addition of three non-Sukuma areas, to give it a wider base, and renaming it the South and East Lake County Council. Thus expanded the area proved unworkable as any sort of a local government unit, while it was not particularly appropriate as a government substation.

The County Council idea was later explored also in Chaggaland, where extensive, but ultimately abortive, discussions were held in an effort to establish a multiracial council including both the Chagga and the Kilimanjaro West (European) Farmers Union. The fact that this could even be considered is in itself of great interest. It was becoming clear that the County Council idea (at least as it was being interpreted in Tanganyika), was impracticable. The government decided to retrace its steps in the direction of a pivotal unit at about the District level, including such smaller councils as seemed appropriate in each case, but viewing them mainly as electoral colleges for the District Council.

The 1953 Local Government Ordinance emerged out of all this experimentation and thinking. It aimed at the eventual supersession of Native Authorities by fully elective local government bodies, which would so far as possible be multiracial, at the District Council level. The chairman was to be elected by a council as soon as it was established. The possibility of tiering within these was allowed for (but in fact seems to have been little used). In order to be appropriate to the ineradicable diversity of Tanganyika conditions, each council's instrument would lay down not only its powers and duties, but also the number of members it was to contain of each race. The Ordinance was thus a part of the government's new policy of multi-racialism, and as such constituted a striking break with the past.

The Ordinance was adoptive and could only be introduced if there was a clear desire in an area for the new sort of council. Thus it was envisaged that the two forms of local government would persist side by side for some time. Since the new councils would have no judicial functions, the remaining link (through the employment of District Officers on court work) between the judicial and the executive would be decisively severed. On the other hand the new councils would be undertaking substantially wider executive duties, including roads, and other development works. Although there were some preliminary difficulties in delineating multiracialism in mainly uniracial areas, on the whole the idea was taken up with enthusiasm. By 1957 a substantial number of the new councils were operating experimentally on an informal basis. Unfortunately, however, the road ahead was not entirely clear. The establishment of the new councils while the old ones were still in being led to a new wave of fragmentation. As might be expected this was at its worst in Sukumaland.

More serious, it soon became apparent that the relation between the new councils and the chiefs would require further clarification. The evolution of chieftainship in Tanganyika under British administration is of exceptional interest. As we have seen, initially there were only a few tribes with strong indigenous chieftaincy traditions. The Native Authority system had consequently been established by means of what was virtually a 'Warrant Chief' system. But, unlike the unhappy precedent of Eastern Nigeria, the civil service chiefs were most carefully chosen for their standing and ability. Once established they and their families had in many areas attained a prestige and authority comparable to fully traditional leaders; in fact they were coming to be elected on a family basis rather than on personal qualities. The new Ordinance ignored this development, treating the chiefs as if they were pure civil servants, as they were in Kenya.

To meet this difficulty an African Chiefs Ordinance was promulgated in 1954. It dealt with such matters as the appointment, recognition, suspension and deposition of chiefs, and the nature of their powers, duties, and functions. A further Ordinance in the same year expressly conserved the power of chiefs to make orders regulating, or even reimposing, native law and custom in respect of certain public purposes enumerated in the Ordinance. In view of the characteristic diversity of Tanganyika it is not possible yet to determine how far these measures will succeed in settling the difficult relations between the new councils, the chiefs, and the administrative officers. It would seem that in a number of areas even where there are traditional chiefs, elections and depositions are at least subject to successful steering by the administration. The Ordinance clearly recognizes that chiefs are still regarded as having an important part to play in local government, in addition to their purely tribal duties. With this in mind, courses for chiefs, as well as for councillors and local government officers, have been introduced at the Local Government School established at Mzumbe to cope with the needs of the new councils.

Unfortunately this was not the only direction in which the 1953 Ordinance ran into initial difficulties. It is sad to relate that when, after a few years of very successful experimentation with informal multiracial councils, the time came (1957–8) to turn them into statutory Local Authorities, the influence of politics (no doubt partly derived from events outside the Territory) intervened. Without notice three or four of the councils suddenly refnsed to accept any form of multiracial co-operation, and even preferred to return to the old paternalism of the Native Authority system. There are very good grounds for hoping however that this was only a temporary aberration.

In the meantime the urban aspect of local government had not been neglected in Tanganyika. As in other parts of East Africa, the Tanganyika towns have large multiracial elements; there are, however, fewer Indians and many more Arabs than in other parts, except for the coastal areas of Kenya. Already in 1946 a Municipalities Ordinance had reorganized the government of Dar-es-Salaam, establishing a multiracial council with racial parity, but including three officials. (From 1954 the African members were being elected by the Wards Councils.) In 1952 there followed a new Ordinance providing for the establishment of all-purpose urban authorities, similar to British county boroughs. At the moment this only affected Dar-es-Salaam (and then only to the extent of changing the base of its local rate); since no other town was judged ripe for promotion.

There was, however, emerging a ladder of promotion for urban authorities, similar to that of Kenya. At the lowest level were the *minor settlements* (corresponding to the Kenya trading centres) judged to be sufficiently urban to require sanitary and other basic town services. These were of two grades, the lower completely subordinate to the Native Authority, and hence administered by a District Officer. The larger town was planned to have a council appointed by the Governor, working more independently, but according to certain rules, for instance in respect of sanitary services and town planning. Above these came the townships, with a council that would be partly at least elected, and which would be authorized to choose its own chairman.

Under the Local Government Ordinance, 1953, the township authorities became Town Councils, with extended powers and duties. All this was however planned to deal with the small town growing up in rural surroundings. There is another and more pressing aspect of town development in Africa, namely the problem of the detribalized African, growing up, very often in slum conditions, in the peri-urban areas. The Tanganyika government was also very conscious of this problem, and appointed a senior Provincial Commissioner (Mr. M. J. B. Molohan) to make a report on this and other aspects of urban growth. We shall be discussing his report among other things in Chapters 16 and 20, so that they need not detain us here.

The Tanganyika government has thus been responsible for a number of constructive ideas and experiments in local government in the post-war years. Not all of these have been wise, but it has been the policy of the Ministry of Local Government (as it now is), always to ride a little ahead of demand, and on the whole this has paid excellent dividends. But the crux of successful development is finance, and here things are not so rosy. In Tanganyika the Territorial government feels itself to be chronically poor. This is partly to be explained by the high cost of administering a very large and scattered area. Further, it must be borne in mind that, owing to its membership of the High Commission, Tanganyika is not able to adjust its rates of indirect taxes as much as it might like. At the same time it is clear that Tanganyika is still a long way from attempting the sort of personal tax rates which are increasingly being accepted in some other similarly placed countries.

The basis of African taxation in Tanganyika, as elsewhere, has been the flat sum (house and poll) tax. Off this Native Authorities have been allowed a rebate of the order of 10s. a taxpayer, varying with the tax collected in the area and with the current needs of the central government. Non-Africans paid a graduated tax to the central government. It is evident that such modest revenue as was implied by this arrangement would go no way at all in satisfying local ambitions for advancement. Consequently District Officers, encouraged by the high prices of cash crops, invented a levy on these as they came to market. This they called a 'cess', presumably to emphasize that the revenue would be reserved for local developments. This idea rapidly caught on, and there was soon an enormous crop of cesses, with no uniformity in their rates or bases. (Thus in 1954 coffee paid 10s. a lb. at Moshi, 5% *ad valorem* in Rungwe, and 2½% in Pare. Maize paid 2s. for 200 lb. in Moshi, and 5% *ad valorem* at Morogoro.) Cess was also levied on a wide range of fruit and vegetables.

It is obvious that this chaotic arrangement could not go on. At a later stage we shall have to discuss the propriety of any such taxes, in relation to other possible methods of taxing farmers. Yet however bad they were as taxes it cannot be denied that the cesses did enable tax potential to be tapped that would otherwise have been missed, and thus provided funds to give the new ideas of local government a start they would otherwise not have had.

The Local Government Ordinance of 1953 also had a financial section. The house and poll tax was abolished, and in its place a graduated personal tax was introduced, to which all races were liable: minimum liability was 10s. on an income of £100. In the income tax ranges half the amount paid in personal tax was allowed as an offset to further liability. As we have seen, long before this a few Native Authorities had started some direct taxation for their own purposes; from 1942 they were permitted to impose a graduated rate, but in fact very little use was made of it. The 1953 Ordinance placed a new responsibility for levying local taxes in accordance with ability to pay, on local bodies, both to replace the previous rebate and to take the place of cesses which are now more closely controlled. A further Ordinance in 1955 put Native Authorities on the same footing as local councils. Available taxes for rural local government thus became (1) a flat sum tax (the old poll tax), (2) a rate assessed on immovable property, and (3) a tax on earnings, livelihood, or movables. For the second alternative to be usable either a certain degree of urban development or else individual land-holding must clearly exist. The third alternative, however, gives the basis for a really well-founded tax, such as that now imposed in Uganda.[1] Up to the present in Tanganyika it seems mainly to have been used to tax cattle and traders, without attempting

[1] See above, p. 210.

any more global estimate of ability to pay; even so it is preferable to a cess in that it does not discriminate against farm products.

In urban areas the traditional tax was the house tax, pertaining to the government. It was based on net annual value, and levied at poundages varying from 3s. to 15s., according to the type of house. Any Africans owning property paid the same rates as other races. Under the new Ordinances the basis of urban rating has been altered to unimproved capital value, in accordance with the practice of Kenya. Town councils are not empowered to levy personal tax but they can determine the poundage of their rates, subject only to government approval. The range of poundages is very low, ranging from 2% to 2·75% of site value. A disadvantage of this system is that urban Africans not owning property tend to escape tax altogether; they are thus encouraged to migrate into the towns. This raises a very general problem which we shall have to discuss later on.

Finally the 1953 Ordinance replaced the Native Treasuries Board by a Local Councils Board; this, however, still seems to be a long way short of the Kenya Local Loans Fund,[1] or even its more recently founded parallel in Uganda. The finances of Tanganyika local government are still weak, although on paper the means of improvement would seem to be available.

[1] See above, p. 220.

PART IV

THE LOCAL BUDGET

13

BUDGETARY ACCOUNTS 1. CURRENT EXPENDITURE

I

So far our task has been to trace the gradual emergence of local government authorities, and the development of their finances up to as near to the contemporary situation as information permits. From now onward we shall be concerned with the analysis and evaluation of the consequences of that development, so far as they can be seen. Before we set out on this road it will be useful to summarize the more important changes in the background against which the process of development is taking place.

In almost every one of our countries there have been widespread population changes, in some areas an unprecedented rate of natural growth; in others substantial migrations of peoples seeking better opportunities (sometimes quite literally pastures new).[1] In particular there has been in a great many places a strong movement into the towns. The special problems raised by this we shall have to discuss below.[2]

In almost all the areas with which we are concerned there have been strong forces of economic expansion at work for the greater part of the period. The beginning of this can be dated from the middle 1930's when the turn of the tide of depression revealed the extent to which ground had been lost in the lean years. Since the end of the second world war this process has accelerated, much assisted by the favourable terms of trade for primary commodities which it left in its wake. Even taking account of price falls since 1957 (e.g. in cotton) there has been no real reversal of this situation.

The disturbances of the war were also largely responsible for a rapid growth of political consciousness, accompanied by the demand for, and very general concession of, adult suffrage. In

[1] Such as the north-easterly migration in Northern Nigeria; this seems to be partly motivated by the desire to move towards better veterinary services.
[2] See Chap. 20.

India and in some of the West Indian islands indeed political consciousness was well advanced before the war, and in the former, as
we have seen, it profoundly influenced the functioning of local
government. In Uganda and Tanganyika at the other extreme,
political parties did not emerge until the early thirties. Adult
suffrage was early established both at the central and local levels
in India and Ceylon; in most of the West Indian islands it was
introduced by the early fifties. In Africa the change did not take
place until the middle or late fifties, and then often on a less wide
basis. Its universal adoption, however, is clearly a matter of only
a comparatively short time.

In spite of all this changing background, and against the emergence, or prospect, of political independence, there is so far little
discernible sign of a desire to arrest or even substantially to alter
the course that had been set for the development of representative,
responsible, local government institutions. On the contrary, a
number of emergent governments (India, Ceylon, Ghana, Nigeria,
to which should be added the Sudan) have given particular thought
and attention to the strengthening of local government finance so
as to enable Local Authorities to play the part in national development which they regard as essential. Hence the change in political
status has so far introduced little if any discontinuity into the story
of local government development. The belief that experience in
local government is the best training for political responsibility at
the national level, enunciated (as we have seen) since the middle of
the last century by British administrators, seems to have taken
firm root. This doctrine had already proved itself in India before
the war; fresh instances of its justification are now occurring in
Africa. The emergence of adult suffrage and political consciousness
has led in several countries indeed to the invasion of local government by national politics. In those countries where there is a
strong opposition to the ruling party, at either the centre or at the
state level, this has had some unfortunate results locally. On the
whole, however, electors, in spite of their inexperience, have voted
sensibly, in local government choosing the best man rather than
the party man.

The establishment of modern local government authorities reporting to central Ministries of Local Government, has inevitably
led to the decay, or serious weakening, of ancient local institutions. In Jamaica the parish *Custodes* still exist, but wield no power;

in Barbados the church element is being removed from local government. In India the rulers have all gone and have been followed by the landlords; but none of these changes have been of much significance for local government. The effect of the changes which are taking place in Africa is much deeper. On the one hand there is the gradual removal of 'Traditional Authorities' from governing functions, on the other the retirement of the District Officer, the pivot of Indirect Rule, from his local government responsibilities. The stage which these changes have reached differs greatly from country to country; in Northern Nigeria feudal authority is still important, but it must now take some account of popular representation. In Uganda and in Sierra Leone the position of the chiefs is as yet far from clear. In Kenya and Tanganyika the changes have as yet hardly made an impact on local government. In Ghana the government appears to be engaged in a war to the death with surviving chiefly elements. In Southern Nigeria on the other hand the transition seems to have been accomplished with remarkable little friction.

The financial consequences of these changes, which are our special concern, are complicated and by no means easy to unravel. On the one hand there is some reduction in local financial liabilities where traditional rulers no longer have to be supported in their old pomp. But this is more than counterbalanced by two factors in the new situation. The first is that councils need expensive offices and an array of paid workers, while councillors although unpaid, have expansive ideas of their rights in respect of allowances. The other is that the cost of the new organization falls wholly on local budgets (except in so far as it may be grant aided by central governments), whereas the District Officer and his much more tenuous staff were the financial responsibility of the central government. Not all of the additional cost of modern local government, however, can be ascribed to this political change. With the enormous expansion of local government activity since the war, a very decided increase in the costs of District administration would in any case have occurred. The District Office was becoming more and more concerned with paper work, with a consequent difficulty in continuing the old and much valued personal relationships.

In this part of the work our first concern is to attempt to make a comparative examination of the accounts of local government authorities. In the present chapter we shall examine local expenditure on current account; in the following chapter current revenue resources and in Chapter 17 investment in fixed assets, together with the sources of finance for capital purposes. Any quantitative attempt is full of pitfalls. Of our countries only Kenya has adopted a thorough going separation between current and capital account in its local budgeting, although several other places have made some progress in this direction (Tanganyika, Ghana, Northern Nigeria). It is rare to be able to distinguish actual expenditure, and reliance must be placed on the very weak reed of Revised Estimates: these too may be blurred by supplementary estimates which do not appear in the ordinary accounts. Control of local expenditure is normally poor and *virement* between services wide, so that the final destination of funds may be substantially different from that stated in the Estimates.

These difficulties are general and beset the examination of the accounts of any single territory. In attempting a comparative study there are two further troubles to contend with. Firstly, classification, even of apparently identical services, differs greatly from place to place; the nature of the data does not allow of making full adjustment for this. Secondly, local government authorities in most territories are not arranged in nice neat layers, homogeneous throughout the country, as they are in the United Kingdom: differences in layers (or tiering), and differences in the powers and duties ascribed to the various layers, are bewildering. The situation is further complicated by the fact that initially in most territories the powers and duties of local government authorities were drawn both wide and vague, presumably to give them ample opportunity to show initiative. In fact, as we shall see, the things they actually undertake are drawn from quite a narrow range. The relation between powers and activities is not yet fully rationalized, either between the different layers of local government or between the central and local government sectors.

The heterogeneity of local government authorities is such a widespread feature in developing countries that it is worth pausing for a moment to look at its causes. In the first place, in such countries it is not possible to establish simultaneously by legal enactment a new form of local organization all over the country, as was done in Britain in the later nineteenth century. Generally speaking before any substantial change can be introduced much patient explanation at village level is required. Secondly, it may easily happen that before the new set-up is fully established a change of policy may be decided on, so that the results of several layers of policy are to be found on the ground together (this happened in Ghana). Again, after some experience of the working of an Ordinance, it may be found desirable to modify its effects in certain areas. Thus in Eastern Nigeria it did not prove easy to organize County Councils everywhere, so the way out was taken of giving certain District Councils county powers (in fact as we have seen, this led to the eventual supersession of counties altogether). Finally, it has become the practice to draft legislation in quite general form, but to detail the powers and duties of each authority by separate instrument, so as to correspond with its stage of development, racial composition and so on. Although this looks like a still further complication it is in fact sometimes a simplification, especially in urban local government, because it does mean that powers and duties are properly defined.

In face of all these difficulties it may justly be questioned whether any quantitative comparisons are worthwhile. I believe that they can be very suggestive, so long as the results are not pressed too far. In the first place the information is good enough to establish relative orders of magnitude pretty firmly. Secondly, sufficient regularities emerge to be significant and to spotlight the divergencies. Finally, as anyone who has dabbled in the accounts of public authorities is well aware, the surest way to start a trail of statistical improvement is to draw attention to the shortcomings of existing information.

II

We start our budget analysis on the expenditure side, since even in fairly primitive conditions the active factor in budgeting is the decision to spend; in the great majority of cases revenue can somehow be made to adapt itself to outlay needs. In national accounting practice it is important to distinguish between expenditure on goods and services on the one hand and on transfers on the other. Fortunately in the local accounts of developing countries transfer expenditure is not large, because it is exceedingly difficult to isolate it properly, save in such obvious cases as expenditure on public assistance in the West Indies. Most transfer outlay is in fact concealed in subsidized employment, such as 'special' road works in Jamaica, or the Indian handloom weavers; but although expenditure of this type can be very large it rarely impinges on local budgets.

Consequently we shall ignore the distinction between real and transfer expenditure, and make use instead of a simple functional breakdown:[1] (i) administration, including the maintenance of law and order and the support of 'traditional authorities' (chiefs) if any; (ii) health and medical, including both environmental and personal services and domestic water supply; (iii) education; (iv) works and communications; (v) the development of natural resources: agriculture, animal husbandry, fisheries, forests, and minerals; (vi) trading services, such as markets which are normally intended to cover their costs, and also commercial undertakings. (In fact the net outlay on these last is normally very small, and it has proved easier to lump them all together as 'other' if they are of any importance. There will be more to say about them in the next chapter.)

In analysing the functional breakdown we shall work with simple percentage outlays in each line, but to anchor the result to actual magnitudes they will be tied to the size of the relevant budget in money terms. Before we discuss functions it is worthwhile giving this last point a little run, for the total size of a budget is of great relevance to the activities which a Local Authority can undertake efficiently.[2] There is unquestionably a minimum below which efficient administration is impossible, but where this occurs depends on a number of factors. In a tiered system the minor Local Authorities have often shown that they can find interesting and important things to do on little more than a shoestring; indeed the whole of the Indian policy for panchayat development depends on this being true. But for very small authorities to be effective they normally need a higher layer to look after them, as well as some means of getting round the difficulty of the high cost of administration when the range of activity is very limited. (This can take the form of a salary grant or of the use of voluntary clerical assistance.) Small but growing urban authorities may initially manage on a very limited budget; unit costs will be relatively low because of compact jurisdiction, and normally speaking the range of activities in a small urban area is narrower than

---

[1] See Tables 1–6 at end of chapter.

[2] Strictly speaking, it is the size of the budget *per head* that matters most, but reliable figures for this cannot usually be obtained. Since expenditure is not correlated directly with population total figures can still be significant.

in a rural district, because it is not concerned with agricultural services. In fact it is not uncommon to find that urban district populations are smaller than rural.

At the other extreme there is certainly a maximum above which it is very difficult to secure effective control of local expenditure. Councillors and even local civil servants seem to lose their sense of magnitude if suddenly called upon to handle sums much larger than those they have been accustomed to think in terms of. There are two points of general significance here. In a number of territories a policy of devolving more and more services on to Local Authorities is being followed. This is in the supposed interests of encouraging local government development by providing more things for local authorities to do. It may be suspected it is also implicitly in the interests of relief for the central budget. The danger of inefficient allocation of resources in such a policy should not be overlooked. Secondly, so long as experienced European administrators are available, it may be possible to manage efficiently large districts with budgets running into hundreds of thousands of pounds. When the expatriates depart, as they are rapidly doing, it is by no means certain that large jurisdictions can be efficiently maintained. In fact in West Africa there seems to be a very decided tendency for jurisdictional fragmentation.

The most interesting comparisons that we can make under this head are in the different territories of West and East Africa. In the Western Region of Nigeria, the wealthiest part of the country, even in 1956–7 District Councils were disposing of reasonably large sums, ranging down from over £800,000, with a concentration at about £100,000. The minimum was £17,000, but this was exceptional, £33,000 being much more typical for small poor councils. In the poorer Eastern Region the current account resources of no District Council exceeded £130,000, a few were as low as £72,000, but there were special reasons in such cases (either a small tribal entity or a growing urban area). In the Northern Region the larger Emirates were disposing of very substantial sums: Kano £989,000, two others had over £600,000, but some of the smaller poorer authorities were very badly off, having no more than £10,000 or £15,000 to operate with. By and large it would not seem that Local Authorities in Nigeria fall seriously short of financial opportunities for developing their services.

Elsewhere on the west coast the position is not so satisfactory.

In the wealthier part of Ghana (Eastern Region) a budget of £74,000 was exceptionally large, £15,000 or £14,000 was by no means exceptional. In the Western Region only two Rural Areas had over £50,000 to dispose of. In the Northern Region the resources of few local bodies rose above £25,000, some disposed of less than £2,000. There are some grounds for supposing that want of resources, reflecting the small size of Local Authorities (as well as of less eager tax collection than in Nigeria), was seriously cramping the development of local government. Although individual figures are not available, the position in Sierra Leone was evidently still worse. The total Chiefdom Authorities in 1957 had between them less than £700,000 at their disposal, making an average of under £5,000 each.

In so far as the accounts can be separated, the rural parts of Tanganyika look like the less fiscally developed parts of the west coast. All rural bodies outside the towns had only £3,514,000 between them; in much smaller Ghana the rural authorities controlled £4,865,000, and as we have seen they were far from wealthy. By contrast the large District Councils of Kenya and Uganda are really well off. In Kenya's prosperous Nyanza Province the smallest African District Council had a budget of £107,000, the wealthiest £240,000. At the other extreme in the poor Coast Province the maximum was £49,000 and the minimum (for a normal District) just under £8,000. The Kenya picture, however, is not complete without the Settled Area authorities; here the position is less encouraging. Of the County Councils only Nairobi had more than £50,000 to spend; the small ones commanded no more than £20,000; but, as we have seen, these authorities are still only on the threshold of an active life.

Uganda Districts are even larger than those of Kenya, but, apart from this, their rights in the graduated personal tax gave them much wider opportunities (in the year with which we are concerned, however, this factor had scarcely appeared above the horizon). The Kabaka's government of Buganda had a total budget of £1,900,000; as might be expected it was more wealthy than any other area, notwithstanding the exclusion of Kampala, and a system of tax collection which was, at the least, open to criticism. On the other hand neighbouring Busoga had a budget of £529,000, Bunyoro, the smallest of the Agreement Districts, one of £189,000, only Madi in the relatively backward (though rapidly catching up) north, had a budget below £50,000, which would compare with the norm in Eastern Nigeria.

Inter-territorial comparisons can be rather more firmly founded in respect of municipal than of rural budgets, since on the whole powers and duties are much more similar. On the other hand there are two difficulties of comparison which are not present in rural areas. First, some governments encourage, or even force, towns to administer very large areas, far beyond anything that is likely to be built over in the near future (examples are Dar-es-Salaam in Tanganyika and Nuwara Eliya in Ceylon). It is quite costly for the council even to maintain law and order and mini-mum sanitation in these areas, and normally speaking no revenue will be derived from them. The other point, which precludes some of the most interesting comparisons, is concerned with the extent to which central governments subsidize (or themselves undertake) services in capital cities. Thus Delhi has to be ex-cluded from any comparison, and the same is true of Lagos: this factor does not, however, seriously affect Nairobi, Accra, or the West Indian capitals.

The major Indian towns dispose of substantial sums. Bombay in 1956 had a budget of £9·75 mn. Calcutta, however, had only £4·7 mn. while Madras did not quite reach £2 mn. Poona in 1956 was spending £894,000; Secunderabad the previous year £147,000. Mysore's budget was of the order of £250,000. The enormous populations of Indian towns must always be borne in mind: Bom-bay has over 4 mn.; in relation to this its expenditure is not large. Compared with these figures the West Indian towns look modest. The Kingston[1], Jamaica, budget indeed reached about £1·2 mn. but next came Trinidad's Port of Spain spending £405,000. British Guiana's Georgetown spent £333,000, but the remaining urban budgets in the Islands are all quite small.

The budgets of the larger African towns are broadly comparable. Nairobi tops the list with £1·7 mn., Kampala spends just over £666,000. On the west coast Ibadan's 1956 budget nearly reached £873,000, but this covers an area wider than the town. Accra had £617,000 to spend, Dar-es-Salaam in Tanganyika just under £500,000, Freetown in Sierra Leone was hoping to bring its outlay up to £202,000 in 1956 as a result of revaluation (see above, p. 206). On leaving the principal towns in the various African territories the

[1] But this included the whole urban area.

standard falls away very rapidly. Kenya's second town, Mombasa, did not reach £500,000, Kisumu the third was below £200,000. Uganda's second town, Jinja, spent no more than £121,000, Mbale only £43,000; Tanganyika's second town, Tanga, could only command £13,000. In Nigeria it is only in the southern Regions that the towns are separately organized. There in the West we find Sapele spending just under £100,000, Benin City just £55,000. In the East, Port Harcourt led with £116,000, Enugu disposed of just under £86,000, but the urban district of Onitsha topped £105,000. These are substantial sums compared with Bo, Sierra Leone's second town, which could muster no more than £20,000.

At the other end of the scale some of the smallest budgets of all local government authorities (apart from limited function lower-tier rural authorities) are those of embryo urban areas. In Tanganyika all towns together (excluding Dar-es-Salaam and Tanga) had no more to dispose of than £8,000; Kenya's two independent townships, Machakos and Malindi, spend one just over, the other just under £4,000. On the west coast small urban budgets normally belong to places which are at present hardly more than trading centres, but are just starting on a career of development. For this purpose a budget of say £10,000 to £12,000 would be considered (e.g. in the Eastern Region of Nigeria) to be not unreasonable. Starting off with a modern local government system their resources should grow *pari passu* with their needs. A much more serious problem is posed by the large number of middle-sized towns with budgets round about the £100,000 mark, which already urgently need urban facilities, such as water supply, main drainage, and street lighting. This is a problem which we shall have to examine at length in Chapter 20. There is hardly a town of any size in any of our countries in which slums of the worst type are not prevalent, and moreover the situation is steadily deteriorating. Thus, except in the very small new towns there is already a double problem, of replanning, and of new development. Few national governments seem yet to have woken up to the seriousness of the situation which is arising.

III

We start our functional breakdown of local expenditure with administration, since this is basic everywhere. Unfortunately comparisons are especially difficult in this field, principally because of the different range of services provided, but also because classificatory practices vary substantially. Salaries, office and travelling expenses naturally figure everywhere; but outside Africa it is by no means universal to pay allowances to councillors attending meetings. Bombay for instance gives nothing except free travel on the municipal transport system. Another cause of divergence occurs because technical officers sometimes work for more than one authority and their salaries are shared. Or again the central government may pay a substantial part of the salaries direct, in order to retain some control over the activities of the officers (Jamaica does this with Parish Medical Officers of Health); rather than giving the Local Authority a grant towards the salary. In the first case only part, in the second the whole of the cost, would appear in the local budget.

We should expect salaries and office expenses to be lower in East and Central Africa than elsewhere because the District Office is still the administrative centre, and its costs are borne on the central budget. On the other hand in some parts of Africa support of 'Traditional Authorities' (chiefs) is an additional administrative expense. Payment of tribute to chiefs outside the local government system is everywhere forbidden, but it is impossible to be sure that it does not occur. In Sierra Leone it was the view of the Cox[1] Commission that taxpayers' effective contributions were three times that of their official tax liability. But this was undoubtedly exceptional. Where such a factor is present the main importance is on the revenue side, as affecting willingness to pay the legal tax.

Another significant difference in administrative expenses lies in the extent to which police, prisons, and courts are within the local jurisdiction. In most places the separation of the executive and judicial has now been carried through, but customary courts are still important. In Africa (as we shall see)[2] in a number of territories local bodies still derive substantial revenue from court fees and fines. Elsewhere there is no entry under this head. Indian town budgets normally show a heading 'public safety' which includes a rather small subhead 'police and the destruction of wild dogs'. In Africa the situation as regards police differs from territory to territory, and even within a territory. In Nigeria the fully trained police force is federal, but in the Northern Region, and to a smaller

[1] Loc. cit.; see above, p. 200. [2] See below, p. 286.

extent in the Western, there are also local police forces with simple
uniforms and varying degrees of training. There is a similar provision in Sierra Leone; indeed a trained central police force was
only introduced in that territory shortly before the 1955 riots.
The 'revenue runners' of Jamaica perform something of the same
type of services as rural police. Such forces can be of great assistance to the administration, acting as its eyes and ears, and, being
easily available, can be on the spot to nip trouble in the bud. They
seldom make much of a dent in local budgets except where they
are organized on a really large scale as in Northern Nigeria; but
outlay may expand rapidly in times of disorder.

Many of these differences of coverage can be allowed for, more
or less, in the budget breakdowns. Unfortunately they are far
from fully explaining the great differences which occur in the
importance of outlay on administration.

In India as we have seen there are 12 municipalities, 1,425
towns, 196 District Boards, and many thousands of minor Local
Authorities. It is out of the question to give even a reasonably
complete breakdown of the expenditure of Indian local government. Such figures as follow are put forward more by way of
illustration than as establishing regularities. For the municipalities,
according to the Statistical Abstract, the average share of administrative expenses would appear to be something over 6%, of which
nearly 4% would be for general expenses and the remainder on
account of public safety. Judging by the experience of certain
individual towns these proportions seem decidedly on the low side.
In 1955 Poona was spending 9% on administration, but Bombay as
much as 28% while the Secunderabad accounts show 37%. For
the smaller towns 9% to 11% seems to be a fair average.

It appears that there are very great differences between the outlay of Indian towns on public safety. Some of the high expenses
may be due to the difficulty of coping with very large populations,
as in Bombay. Some of the low costs may reflect slovenly standards
and underpaid local officers. So far as Ceylon is concerned, we
have to be satisfied with global figures.[1] The percentages of budgets
allocated to administrative expenses were respectively: for municipalities 27%, for urban authorities 19·6%, for town authorities
31·3%, and for village committees 35·6%. These differences seem

[1] Cf. Choksy Report on *Local Government in Ceylon*, 1955, cit.

to reflect on the one hand the greater administrative needs in a large town than in a small one, and on the other the very high administrative costs of very small authorities such as the town and village committees in Ceylon.

In the West Indies there seems to be decidedly more homogeneity in respect of administrative expenditure, and an absence of very high percentages. Trinidad's Port of Spain with 20% was exceptional, but on the other hand her County Councils (rural authorities on a very small scale), managed to keep their average administrative outlay down to 10%. In Jamaica, Kingston St. Andrews devoted 18% of its budget to administration, the average of the other parishes was 13%. In British Guiana the towns managed quite cheaply (Georgetown 9%, New Amsterdam 11%) but the rural authorities had heavier charges (their average was 17%), their difficult physical situation appears, perhaps not unnaturally, to run up their administrative costs.[1] Barbados on the other hand has a simple administrative task, and the average of all authorities comes out at 10%. It must be remembered that none of the West Indian Local Authorities have any educational expenses, so that the low administrative outlays suggest either relatively economical management, or, perhaps more likely, underdevelopment of services.

The African territories offer more interesting comparisons. On the west coast, generally speaking, administration absorbs a decidedly higher percentage of budgets than those we have met hitherto. In Northern Nigeria there is exceptional uniformity of local organization, and this is reflected in a considerable degree of homogeneity of administrative outlay. Taking as a sample the largest and smallest Native Authority in each Emirate, we find that twelve Native Authorities were spending 40–43% on administration, one was spending 30%, and the rest lay in between these figures. Included in this were percentages (of the total budget) varying between 1·7% and zero for the support of traditional authorities. In money terms the maximum under this head was £10,000.[2] Expenditure on police and justice included in administration is variable, perhaps somewhat higher in the larger Emirates. It was high in Benue and on The Plateau, low in Adamawa, Katsina, and the Yoruba areas. Some of the smaller Native Authorities have very little outlay under this head, no doubt due to smaller establishments. On the whole in Northern Nigeria there is little

[1] Pp. 36–41.   [2] This excludes normal salaries.

evidence of any definite relation between size, and outlay on administration.

In the southern Regions of Nigeria analysis is complicated by the co-existence of different sorts of councils. The west for instance in 1956 was running[1] (i) Divisional Councils on their own, (ii) Divisional Councils with District Councils within them, to which certain services were devolved, (iii) these District Councils, and (iv) District Councils on their own. Administration in the first class absorbed about 17% of expenditure; in the second it varied greatly, according to the degree of devolution practised. For instance in the Egba Division administration accounted for 26·5% of expenditure, in Ife Divisional Council to 14·5% and in Asaba Division to 7·7%. In the Districts working within Divisions the share of administration was even more varied, ranging from 90% in poor little Okiti Pupa (Ese Odo), down in the mangrove swamps of the Niger delta, and 32% in Asaba (a clear case of substantial devolution) to about 16–17% in Ife District, Sapele, and Oyo, all areas with a relatively high degree of urbanization, and consequently a fairly compact area to administer, while at the same time not so urbanized as to give rise to very complicated problems. The Districts on their own ranged at about this level also.

In a number of western local government areas the cost of maintaining the establishments of Obas was by no means negligible, especially in Egbaland (Abeokuta) with its Alaki and complicated system of Ogboni; in Ibadan also the cost of the elaborate hierarchy[2] of chiefs was considerable, and was in fact very parallel, both absolutely and relatively, to that of the northern Emirates. On the whole, however, administrative costs formed a smaller percentage of outlay than in the North; but this can largely be accounted for by the small establishment of the local police. In the West there seems to be a more definite (inverse) correlation between size of jurisdiction and cost of administration than in the north. One cause of this was probably the experimental nature, and hence diversity, of devolution, in the West compared with the more uniform system of the North.

In the Eastern Region in 1956[3] there was also a variety of councils in existence: (i) all purpose councils (District Councils with County powers), (ii) County Councils, (iii) District Councils

[1] See above, p. 177.   [2] See above, p. 93.
[3] See above, p. 171.

within Counties. These three corresponded very closely with similar arrangements, although with different names, in the West, but the District Councils were separately designated either urban or rural, and none of the County Councils were all-purpose authorities. In addition Port Harcourt and Enugu were separately organized as municipalities.

In these last administrative costs were relatively high, of the order of 39% to 40%; as we shall see in relation to capital development, these towns were attempting to make a beginning with urban amenities; on Port Harcourt in particular additional responsibilities were falling, due to large expenditure by oil companies in the neighbourhood. In the all-purpose District Councils administrative percentages varied fairly widely, for example 33% in Onitsha and 23% in Awgu. In the County Councils, in spite of the fact that they were not public health authorities, they tended to be higher still: for instance 37% and 38% in Ikot Ekpene and Aba/Ngwa, respectively. In the County Districts administrative costs tended to range distinctly higher, from about 45% in Okigwi North to 18% in West Ahoada. In the Region as a whole there was little difference in the administrative percentages of urban and rural budgets, presumably in a number of small urban areas diseconomies of small scale more or less compensated for the greater compactness of their jurisdictions. Throughout the Region there was a fairly distinct inverse correlation between administrative costs and size. It must also be remembered that in the East the absence of a local police force makes the true cost of administration higher than appears at first sight, relative to the other Regions.

It cannot be denied that representative local government in Nigeria is proving expensive on the administrative side. In particular the upper tier of councils showed rather higher percentages than the others. This depended partly on their narrower range of duties, partly it was the inevitable result of a wide jurisdiction in a situation in which councillors expect to be paid generously for travelling and similar expenses. In view of this it is not surprising that both the southern Regions decided in 1958 to go over to a single-tier system. This, however, will bring new problems in the conduct of services (such as secondary education and hospitals) where the jurisdiction of the single-tier council will be too small for efficient management. This is a question that will claim our attention in Chapter 21.

How does the Ghana situation compare with that of Nigeria? In Ghana we are confronted with an even greater variety of councils than in Nigeria, some areas having tiering and others not. There are also a bewilderingly large number of councils: in the Eastern Region twenty-two local and two District Councils, in the Western thirty-four councils, all local, in Ashanti eighty-five local and ten District and in the North seventy-six local and nine District Councils. Since Ghana is comparable in population to either of the southern Regions of Nigeria it is evident that the councils were considerably smaller; we should therefore not be surprised if administrative costs were relatively high. This is indeed the case: the Regional averages vary from 41% to 27%, and for individual councils the relative outlay is very much higher, particularly in the smaller jurisdictions. The cost of maintaining Traditional Authorities also seems to be higher than in Nigeria, especially in Akim Abuakwa (the home of the Ofori Attas the most powerful chiefly family outside Ashanti), where it reached nearly 10% of total outlay: in neighbouring Koforidua and Yila-Krobo it was also well above Nigerian standards.

On the other hand the administrative percentages of the Ghana towns are low on Nigerian standards: Accra 14%, Cape Coast 25%, Kumasi 20% (unfortunately differences in organization do not allow of a very precise comparison). Apparently, however, Ghana towns get into somewhat worse difficulties than do Nigerian towns. In April 1958 four out of the five Municipal Councils were in a state of suspension: the one that was working (and seemed to have in general considerably the best record, Cape Coast)[1] habitually spent relatively more than the others on administration. Although national politics were generally considered to have played a substantial part in the suspensions it may well be that the staff were not of sufficient calibre for their jobs. A point that emerges even more strongly from this brief summary is that Ghana should benefit even more than Nigeria from the rationalization of jurisdictions, the abolition of tiering and the suppression of very small councils.

Turning from West to East Africa: unfortunately there is no mimeographed or printed edition of the Tanganyika local Estimates, so that the investigator is limited on the one hand to what he can collect individually and on the other to global Estimates. On the average the local councils (Native Authorities) spent 45% on

[1] See above, pp. 194–5.

administration; but the average may well have been pulled up by some in which administrative costs were exceptionally high, due to large jurisdictions and sparse population. Morogoro, a prosperous little District 80 miles from Dar-es-Salaam, certainly devoted less than 40% of its outlay to administration. The ill-fated South and East Lake County Council[1] had an administrative percentage of 35, which was perhaps not too immoderate for an upper tier, but it hardly lived long enough to establish a tradition. On the other hand town administration in Tanganyika seems to be relatively economical: Dar-es-Salaam had a percentage of 12.3, Tanga 20%, and the other towns on the average of 23%.

It might be expected that the big Districts of Uganda, with no effective governmental tiering within them, would be economical to run, the more so as the Protectorate government shoulders most of the financial responsibility for police, law, and order; but this seems not to be the case. Administrative percentages ranged from 41% to 24% with a fairly persistent *direct* correlation between size and the share of administration in outlay. This may suggest that some of the larger councils are above the administrative optimum in size. As we have seen, however, a number of the councils are themselves extremely unwieldy, and this circumstance naturally runs up the cost of councillors' allowances and similar expenses connected with the holding of meetings. On the other hand Uganda's towns seem to be rather cheaper to run than Tanganyika's: Kampala administration took 16% of outlay, Jinja's 17.5%.

Kenya appears to be the most economically run of the East African territories, in the sense of devoting the lowest percentages to administration; but three points must be borne in mind. First, at this period a good deal of financial responsibility for law and order fell on the central government (and a not inconsiderable part on the British taxpayer); secondly, differences in the classification of accounts suggest that more administrative costs were imputed to specific services in Kenya than elsewhere; thirdly, Kenya was still enjoying to the full the benefits of the services of the District Office, the costs of which were wholly upon the central budget; this makes a substantial difference relatively to Uganda.

Only in the European areas could Kenya administrative percentages be called really high; in the County Councils they ranged from 58% to 29%, but these figures are *gross* of administrative

[1] See above, p. 225.

expenses charged on District Councils; excluding these it appears that the percentages would be broadly halved. It must be borne in mind that the new structure of European local government is still feeling its way, and it is difficult to estimate a long-run normal position. On the one hand 'setting up' costs borne by the councils are inevitably high, and some at least must fall on current account; against this must be set the consideration that County Councils were still enjoying the high range of tapering grants for the setting up costs of the take over of health services. On the whole the conclusion that local government in Kenya in all ranges is well and economically conducted seems inescapable; but it may fairly be argued that the testing time is yet to come, when major responsibility in the District Councils is handed over to Africans.

IV

The provision of public health services is a hardly less important function of local government than the adequate maintenance of law and order or general administration. There are several ways in which health services can be classified, and this has some importance for their allocation between central and local responsibility. The most fundamental distinction is that between environmental services whose benefits are not allocable to particular persons, and personal services which provide individual allocable benefits. Many individual services are naturally also of collective benefit, for instance the treatment and cure of disease, especially infectious disease, but equally this collective benefit cannot be allocated.

An alternative classification is between preventive and curative services. In practice this works out very similarly since the curative services are naturally personal and the preventive largely, although not wholly, collective. (Spraying against mosquitoes provides unallocable benefits, but innoculations against disease provide allocable benefits.) This latter distinction is sometimes applied directly as a means of dividing responsibility for health services between central and local government (this is done in Jamaica); but although it supplies a rough and ready answer to the problem it is not really satisfactory. Some preventive services (such as mosquito spraying) required to be carried out on a wider than local basis. On the other hand minor curative services can very appropriately be supplied locally, although the expenses of a general hospital would normally be beyond the means of a Local Authority.

The most fundamental environmental health service in developing countries is 'conservancy' (a euphemism for emptying latrine buckets), and this is clearly most easily organized on a strictly local basis. In fact where the powers and finances of Local Authorities are rudimentary, they are often to be found providing just this service alone, or with the addition of minor road works. This is a pity from two points of view. However necessary conservancy may be, it is not an inspiring service on which to base an active interest in local government, and further, since the authorities which undertake it are often small and weak, there is a real danger that the change over to modern sanitary installations, domestic water supply, and waterborne sewerage, will be delayed beyond a point at which their absence becomes a serious menace to health. Unfortunately the great provision in this respect which in the United Kingdom, has been built up over many decades tends not to be appreciated, because the accounts show no valuation of it, and there is no estimate of replacements required.

At the other extreme from those countries which confine local health services to conservancy are those governments, such as Uganda and Kenya, which are making strenuous efforts to unload the bulk of the health services, personal as well as environmental, on to Local Authorities. Admittedly this policy is at its most plausible in the big Districts of Kenya and still more of Uganda. Further, it has to be admitted that the acquisition of health services seems to have given a great boost to the development of active local government in the Kenya Settled Areas. Elsewhere governments would do well to concentrate (as indeed they normally do) on the encouragement of local installations such as clinics, dispensaries, leprosaria, and maternity homes which can be cheaply built and fairly easily manned, partly by the local communities themselves. One great advantage of the wide development of this type of curative service is that simple treatment for most ills and accidents can be applied speedily, always a factor of great importance in tropical conditions. In this respect the West African territories, especially Southern Nigeria, are far in advance of anything in Asia. This is partly no doubt because in Asia religious scruples about the use of Western medicine have not yet been fully allayed.

In West Indian local government relative outlay on health services looks important partly because there is no local responsibility for education; even allowing for this the health services are among the most important local activities throughout the area. In Trinidad, Port of Spain allocated over 50% of its budget in this direction, San Fernando 55%. In Jamaica and Barbados the percentages are not fully comparable with Trinidad because of heavy local charges for public assistance. The Jamaica parishes on the average devoted 34% to health services, those in Barbados 17%. In British Guiana health services are important. Georgetown allocated 28% of its budget for this purpose, New Amsterdam 37%; but these proportions are overtopped by the heavy burden of environmental health services in the non-urban areas (on the average 41%). These are easily accounted for by the necessity of maintaining drainage and other services connected with sea defence.

Differences in classification make it difficult to say anything very precise concerning the cost of health services in Indian cities. They appear relatively large because educational outlay in the cities is very meagre. Bombay corporation has a very lively appreciation of the necessity for public health expenditure: in 1957 it was devoting 25% of its budget in this direction, divided almost equally between environmental and medical services. This included a strenuous effort to eradicate the sources of typhoid, a major scourge in the city. In addition by far the greater part of the city's heavy debt charges was due to the great expense of providing an ample pure water supply, perhaps the biggest single contribution to public health that could be made.

Of other Indian towns, Mysore, allocating 60% of its budget to health was exceptional, but Bangalore reached nearly 40%. Poona in 1957 was spending 21% on various health services, and in addition was making substantial grants to privately owned institutions. It still had in front of it, however, heavy expenditure to bring the water supply up to a satisfactory standard. It would appear that the allocation to health varies greatly among Indian Local Authorities. Almost everywhere it is severely handicapped by lack of water.

The average of the Ceylon municipalities was rather lower than is suggested by these (somewhat desultory) figures for Indian towns; the average being 22·7%: but in the smaller urban and 'town' jurisdictions the public health allocation was high: 38% of budgets. For the most part however this is no more than a reflection of the extent to which conservancy is the main preoccupation of these authorities. The Ceylon village committees are less exclusively health authorities. Their percentage in this direction was on the average 23. In fact their main responsibilities were in connexion with roads: their high administrative charges must also be borne in mind.

For the African territories we can make a more detailed investigation. In Western Nigeria the higher tier Divisional Councils had no direct health responsibilities, but those which had no subordinate District Councils were naturally under an obligation to provide health services: they apparently did so on a very meagre scale, allocating no more than 5% to 8% of their budgets to this service (i.e. about £5,000 to £8,000, according to the budgets we have already discussed). Where there were Districts within a Division it appears to have been a matter for local agreement at which level the health services were provided. Thus Ife Divisional Council allocated over 6% to health services while Ife District had nothing at all to show; on the other hand Asaba Division spent nothing but Asaba District Council allocated 30% of its outlay to health. It would be natural that this growing bridge-head of the trans-Niger trade should be more interested in health services than the Division as a whole; but then its total budget only amounted to £15,800. Throughout the Region the highest relative allocations for health services occurred in the Districts with urban areas. Thus Sapele, with its many traders and 'stranger' elements, allocated 25% of its budget for these purposes (the greater part, however, went on conservancy); Oyo devoted 17·5%; these two, and also Benin City, actually spent more on health services than they did on administration.

In the Eastern Region outlay on health was not such an important element in budgets on the whole as in the west. Enugu had an allocation of 20%. Some of the smaller Districts, which undertook few 'works', showed up to 24% for health. As in the Western Region the upper-tier authorities (County Councils) were not normally responsible for any health services, except in so far as they were co-ordinating authorities for such inter-District works as hospitals. Of these outlays on the whole the largest item was conservancy, but a number of councils had relatively heavy charges for drugs for clinics and dispensaries.

In the Northern Region of Nigeria the share of health services in budgets was on the whole rather smaller than in the south; Sokoto with an allocation of 14% was exceptionally high. Kano, Zaria, and two Native Authorities in Benue Province (Tiv and Keffi) all ranged about 11%, which is the more remarkable, as although all except Keffi have large absolute resources, *per capita* they are relatively poor. Among the smaller (but not necessarily poorer) authorities health expenditure took up no more than 7% or 8% of outlay. Throughout Nigeria, whereas outlay on environmental health went almost wholly on conservancy, in respect of medical services the big outlay was on account of drugs. This reflects the large development of village dispensaries, clinics, and maternities, especially in the southern Regions. Africans are strong believers in Western medicine, especially in the efficacy of a 'shot', which is to the country African what a 'bottle' is to the British National Health Service patient. In this respect Africans could hardly be more different from Indians.[1] At the same time it must be borne in mind that an efficient control of drugs and other supplies at remote dispensaries is an exceptionally difficult task.

As a whole Ghana would appear to be a substantially higher spender on health services than Nigeria. The percentage of town budgets allocated to this purpose ranged from 54% in Cape Coast (a semi-health resort with an exceptional proportion of older people in the population), to 35% in Accra. For Ghana Regions the averages for all local bodies were: Eastern Region 20%, Western Region 16%, Trans-Volta Togoland 12%, Ashanti 18·4%, and the Northern Region 13%. Individual authorities, especially if they were urban in character, showed substantially higher percentages than these, for instance Tarkwa allocated nearly 40% to health services. On the other hand the showing of many of the smaller bodies was very poor indeed. Osuduku, with a total budget larger than that of Okrika, in the Eastern Region of Nigeria, managed to allocate no more than 1·1%, as against Okrika's 11%. The general impression left on the investigator is that Ghana is more interested in health services than Nigeria (relatively to other forms of expenditure), but that development is much more uneven. To this no doubt a number of causes contribute, one probably being the weaker organization of the larger rural authorities. It must also be remembered that so far as medical services are concerned the whole of Western Nigeria, at least, profits greatly from the superb teaching hospital at Ibadan, which is financed by Federal funds.

---

[1] At the time of the Indian general election I witnessed one old man burst into tears, because when he received the indelible pencil mark on his thumb, registering that he had recorded his vote, he took it to be a compulsory vaccination.

Turning to East Africa, we find that among the Kenya African District Councils the relative economy on administrative outlay permits a substantial outlay on health services; this ranges between 10% and 23% of total budgets. It takes such forms as dispensaries, ambulances, health centres, maternity and child welfare services, and health education (a service that seems to be uniquely developed in Kenya). The provision of health services differed considerably from district to district, according to no very obvious pattern. Backward little Garissa in the dry north, whose whole budget only amounted to £1,300, devoted 23% of it to health services; Nandi Samburu, and Tana River were also high spenders. Elsewhere there seems to have been less interest in the subject.

In Uganda the range was completely different: Lango in the north devoting 8% of its budget to health services, was exceptionally generous. Buganda could find no more than 5% and Bunyoro 2%. The higher administrative costs of the Uganda Districts are not sufficient to account for this great difference from Kenya. One contributory cause may well be the greater activity of the central government with its District teams stationed in each area. The matter is of considerable interest since (as we have seen) both the Kenya and Uganda governments would like to unload general health services on to Local Authorities; it would seem that the Kenya councils would be much better prepared to undertake the job than those of Uganda.

Expenditure on various health services is thus an important item in local budgets in every country. In Africa particularly, it is by no means confined to conservancy and the less inspiring aspects. On the contrary, in West Africa especially it is often the case that not enough attention is devoted to drainage and sewerage. This is a matter to which we shall have to return when discussing capital expenditure. In Asia, and especially in India, there is unfortunately still a tremendous leeway to make up in respect of health services. The problem is made more awkward by the attitude of the people to disease on the one hand, and by the widespread shortage of water for most of the year on the other.

v

Education is the third major type of local government outlay in most of our countries. It is of special interest as it is practically everywhere the service which arouses the greatest local enthusiasm.

It is hardly too much to say that where some responsibility for education is given to local bodies, local government will be a success, and the contrary is also nearly true: without educational responsibility local government is apt to languish. The springs of desire for increasing popular education are several. Certain African peoples, above all perhaps the Ibo of Eastern Nigeria and the Chagga of Tanganyika, seem to have an innate curiosity of mind and an exceptional capacity for application. Naturally they also want to 'get on', and in the case of the Ibo the poverty of their own country is a strong incentive to get educated in order to seek their fortunes elsewhere.

In other areas the desire for education is due to the force of example. The Hausa now realize that they must seek education or else the jobs will go to Ibos. In other circumstances the prospect of independence rouses an interest in education. This appears somewhat tardily to be working in Sierra Leone, although only a few years ago even the prospect of total remission of school fees (in the Bo area) brought forward no additional pupils. In some countries again (above all India) the central government is extremely active in pushing education, and in urging the provision of schools by Community Development. These efforts are crowned with a certain, although so far not spectacular, success.

In the West Indies education is invariably an Island responsibility, hence no local comparison is possible. Nevertheless it is of some interest to observe the importance attached to education in some of the smaller islands which are comparable in size to a small Local Authority elsewhere. Thus Montserrat devotes 19% of its current budget to education, the combined administration of St. Kitts, Nevis, and Anguilla 13%.

Again we cannot make a valid comparison with local educational outlay in India, since the education service has always been highly centralized. Today by far the larger part of educational outlay is made by the states; although progressive towns such as Bombay and Poona are in addition spending 14–15% of their budgets on this service. Elsewhere 10% of a municipal budget would be above the average. Indeed many towns seem content to have the state provide almost the whole service.

This once again leaves us with a comparison between the African territories; but this provides a considerable amount of interest, although local differences sometimes impede a direct comparison.

Differences in the educational outlay of local bodies may be due to different methods of sharing responsibility, either between 'tiers' of Local Authorities or between central and local government. Again total outlay may not be correctly stated in local budgets; that part of the revenue coming from grants may be excluded (a most misleading procedure).[1]

Very great differences in local outlay also arise in respect of the extent to which the educational services of the Missions are made use of. In respect of secondary education in particular this is normally still very large. The Missions generally supply the teachers and cover some of the cost, the remainder coming from central government grant, from fees, from a local tax or from a semi-voluntary contribution collected locally by the churches.[2]

These different methods of finance introduce fortuitous differences into local budgets. The extent to which the educational services of the Missions are used differs substantially from area to area. In Moslem parts little or no use is made of them, and consequently the unit cost of education is much higher (e.g. in Northern Nigeria). In course of time the services of Missions in this direction will probably be less widely used everywhere. Partly because of the bickering of the different sects, some governments would like to be rid of them already; but if educational development is not to be stunted, in most of the African territories their services will be indispensable for the foreseeable future. With these provisos in mind we may proceed to compare the relative importance of educational expenditure in African local government.

On the whole Tanganyika makes the worst showing with an average of no more than 15%; but the dispersion around the average is certainly large. In the Chagga country not only is a very high percentage of school age children at school, but a most impressive technical college has been built out of the profits of the Coffee Co-operative (which is entirely managed by the Chagga themselves). The general impression that education is relatively backward in Tanganyika, however, is supported by a number of budgets; one contributory cause of weakness is no doubt the relatively meagre funds available from government grants.

The Uganda Districts devote very substantial proportions of

[1] This has been common in Tanganyika.
[2] Such as the 'assumed local contribution' in Eastern Nigeria; see above, p. 168.

their budgets to education. Madi (the small but progressive District in the north) and Bukedi make the best showing with 43% and 41% respectively; in Bukedi they are especially interested in secondary and higher education (perhaps they spend rather too large a proportion on scholarships to the United Kingdom). The remaining Uganda Districts devote round about 30% of their funds to education.

In Kenya local expenditure on education is strictly controlled in the sense that it must all conform to the Territorial programme. The District Councils and even the Location and Sub-Location Councils, however, are extremely enthusiastic in raising money to build schools. As might be expected, the largest percentage allocations under this head were to be found in the more sophisticated areas such as Kiambu, Meru, and South Nyanza. Exceptionally, little Garissa in the north devoted 23% of its budget to education, but the total budget is so small that in money terms this did not amount to much. The 17% allocated to education by the Narok Masai is interesting, since they are not usually regarded as being eager for education. It must be remembered, however, that schooling for nomads is relatively expensive, since it is necessary to provide boarding accommodation for all.

In Kenya, however, in respect of education there are two quite separate educational 'streams': one in the African Districts, the other in the Settled Areas. The whole of white education in the latter is paid for by the government—out of the much higher taxes derived from the European population. Apart from questions of the justice—or wisdom—of this policy, it has had the unfortunate result that large numbers of Africans resident in the Settled Areas have been left almost without education. This is in strong contrast to the substantial funds devoted to their welfare in other ways.

Turning to the west coast, Ghana education percentages run near the Uganda level. The average outlay of councils in the Eastern Region is 29%, the highest reached about 40%. The Western Region, although poorer, did better, with an average of 32% and a high of 50%. Elsewhere there appears to be less zeal. In Trans-Volta Togoland the average allocation was 25%, in the Northern Region 24%, and in Ashanti no more than 21%. The towns showed lower percentages: Accra 17%, Kumasi 11%. These low allocations were presumably due to greater reliance on the Missions; this is borne out by the case of Cape Coast, which has an exceptionally high standard of both primary and secondary education, yet allocated only 7% of its budget to the service.

School fees tend to be on the high side in Ghana, even at the primary level, so that schooling mainly comes to the relatives of chiefs and wealthy cocoa farmers. Ghana authorities have recently been showing concern at the small supply of trained labour available for work on development, and great efforts have recently been made to raise the standard of upper forms in secondary schools. In this process a heavy responsibility must rest with the government, especially since the new single-tier councils will not be large enough to look after secondary education. The situation is, however, improving; in 1959 for the first time Nigerians were refused entry to the University College, there being sufficient Ghanaians to fill all the available places.

In Nigeria pride of place in educational pioneering must go to the Eastern Region, although in actual numbers of school attenders it has all along lagged somewhat behind the wealthier West. The Eastern people have shown very great eagerness for education, and have contributed not only through taxes but through voluntary effort. Ibo students are to be found in large numbers not only at Ibadan, Nigeria's University College, but also (until 1959) in Ghana, and at Fourah Bay College, Sierra Leone. The Region plans to establish its own university at Nsukka. In 1958–9 (as we have seen)[1] an attempt was made to establish free primary education for all, but revenue failure made it necessary to reimpose fees temporarily in the higher standards. The policy is to abolish fees gradually, standard by standard, as money can be found for additional school places and trained teachers. The highest local expenditure on education has come from the County Councils, one of which was devoting 60% of its revenue to this service. The abolition of these bodies leaves an awkward problem of co-ordination above the primary level.

In contrast to the East, the Northern Region has in the past been backward in education, and hostile to anything that smacked of Christian influence. The exception to this has been in the Yoruba Districts in the south of the Region (where outlay ranges from 25% to 42% of budgets). They have been greatly aided by a grant system which helped those who helped themselves.[2] The realization that there would not be nearly enough northerners to

[1] See above, p. 175.   [2] See above, p. 182.

cover the necessary jobs when self-government was obtained has led to a tremendous educational drive at the Regional level, with large grants to Native Treasuries. Further, Zaria is being developed as a Regional educational centre, with technical colleges and secondary schools (the former, however, are a Federal responsibility). Some Native Treasuries are responding to this drive well, and substantial percentages of Native Treasury budgets are now going to education (in 1956–7 15%–23% would be typical).[1] The North, however, still has a big educational leeway to make up. With a population of more than 50% of the Nigerian total, less than 10% of school enrolments in 1956 were northern children.

All in all the Western Region has apparently been most successful in its educational policy. Universal primary education (up to middle school level) was achieved in 1958, although possibly at the cost of some lowering of standards. There is no question, however, but that both the Yoruba and Beni people put a very high priority on education. In the past, from the local government point of view, the main financial responsibility for educational outlay has rested on Divisional Councils, which have devoted the major part of their resources (60% or even 80%) to this purpose. As in the East, the suppression of this upper layer of local government may pose an awkward problem of co-ordination above the primary level. In the West, Districts on their own have also contributed manfully to education: Ibadan devoting 44% and Ikeja (a Lagos outer suburb) 62%. In addition to its Divisional expenditure Sapele Urban District has devoted 32% of its own funds to this purpose, and had almost reached the point of complete primary coverage before its general adoption in the Region.

What, we must now ask, is the content of this large educational outlay at the local level? Various services are included: primary (sometimes divided into lower and middle), secondary, technical, and commercial, and in some areas adult education. In addition some local bodies are much interested in scholarships to the United Kingdom. Teacher training may be variously provided. In Kenya it is now strictly a territorial responsibility, but elsewhere (for instance in Nigeria) colleges may be built by local voluntary effort, and maintained by the Local Authority.

Differences in classification, and in the imputation of admini-

[1] See further details in Table 2, p. 272.

strative services to education, make exact comparison difficult. It is clear, however, that the really big outlay everywhere is on primary education. (This is equally true in the United Kingdom.) In some areas there is a growing demand for adult education (mass literacy). This is very marked in India; in Northern Nigeria the larger native treasuries devote about one-fifth of their education expenditure to this purpose. Elsewhere (Uganda, Western Nigeria, West Indies) adult education takes the form of extra-mural classes arranged by the university; there should be increasing scope for this type of work as the standard of education rises, not merely on the usual cultural lines, but also in technical directions (such as accounting and book-keeping).

These variants raise the question of balance in education. The case of India, where not very high grade universities are legion and unemployed Arts graduates a national problem, while the general standard of literacy is no higher than 20–30%, is an abiding example of a deliberate but (with hindsight unfortunate) allocation of resources in the past. At the other extreme there is a not inconsiderable danger of an over-concentration on primary education. It must not be forgotten that universal primary education was not established in the United Kingdom until 1870, when a much higher standard of general development had been reached than in the African territories today. It has been suggested (in relation to Ghana)[1] that a developing country should deliberately refrain from expanding primary education in excess of a certain ratio to the foreseeable intake into the secondary schools.

Such a restrictionist policy may sometimes be necessary to correct an unbalance which has already arisen; but as a general policy it would have several disadvantages. In the first place such a limitation would be inimicable to development where a genuine desire for education is backed by a willingness to contribute towards its cost, even at the lowest level of local government. 'Induced' investment in secondary education can almost certainly be relied on to restore the balance.

Secondly, although at the moment the most pressing need is for trained technicians, as development proceeds the demand for literate youths, without any special training, for relatively unskilled jobs in factories, is likely to expand very rapidly. It is only by this means that a sufficient mobility of labour between occupations can

[1] By W. A. Lewis, when Adviser to the Government.

be brought about. In all our countries the biggest gap in the education system today is in respect of the education of girls. This is least serious in the West Indies, and worst in India and Moslem countries. The problem is not so much to provide the schools, but to persuade parents of the advantages of having their daughters educated. This however is more a problem of central policy than of local finance.

As things have developed Kenya now probably has the best balanced educational programme for African Districts. This is the result of the Report of the Beecher Committee of 1949. Educationalists were quicker than others to perceive the political implications of the 'independent' Kikuyu schools, which were subsequently revealed to be at the root of the Mau Mau movement. As a result of the Beecher Report these schools were turned over to the Missions and an integrated national educational programme established. No development outside this programme (not even the building of new schools), is permitted. Further, teacher training was not only made a wholly government responsibility, but has been concentrated into two large colleges to serve the whole Territory.

In spite of this rigorous control, it is evident that the Kenya Education Authorities have not seriously damped enthusiasm for education at the local end; Location and even Sub-Location Councils will cheerfully raise extra taxation for it, and are sometimes with difficulty prevented from devoting their whole budget to school building. One explanation of this is probably the extent to which control is decentralized: from the Central Education Board through Regional to District Education Boards. The District Councils are being drawn into co-operation with these. The education estimates are first submitted to the District Councils before being forwarded to the Regional Educational Officer. It is planned to set up Local Education Authorities, which would later become Education Committees of the District Councils.[1] In the same spirit secondary schools are encouraged to set up Boards of Governors in order to widen the circle of interest.

Public Health and Education are not the only social services undertaken by Local Authorities, although they are by far the most important. In the West Indies, besides poor relief, local councils undertake work for the care of the elderly and homes for children

[1] See above, p. 218.

without means of support. In India mass poverty is too big a problem for local authorities to tackle in any fundamental way; but individual panchayats make strenuous efforts to educate, and to improve the lot of their *harijans* (scheduled classes). The leading towns also in some cases make heroic efforts to deal with the flood of destitute immigrants continually pouring in on them. (This is a matter which we shall discuss in relation to urban problems.)

In parts of West Africa (for instance Eastern Nigeria) a major welfare service is concerned with rescuing children from up country who have been taken from their homes (probably with the consent of their parents, but certainly without their understanding), to be sold as (virtually) domestic slaves, mainly in neighbouring territories. This work is mainly the responsibility of a central Department of Social Welfare, but Local Authorities play an important co-operating role.

A large number of welfare services are run for Africans in the Settled Areas of Kenya. These combine entertainment, education for citizenship, and practical instruction for women in hygiene, household management, and care of children. In another direction are cultural welfare activities: libraries and lectures, village radio, and mobile cinemas. Local Authorities normally have a part in all of these. Elsewhere similar services are provided through a Community Development programme. At a later stage (Chapter 21) we shall have to discuss the relations of Local Authorities to these various activities.

VI

Having dealt at some length with the major local services we can pass more quickly over their remaining activities: (1) communications, (2) natural resources development, (3) trading services and commercial undertakings. In respect of all of these outlay on capital account is as important, or even more important, than on current account, and this we shall be examining in Chapter 17.

Expenditure on communications normally includes outlay on subsidiary installations such as street lighting and fire brigades. Sometimes street cleansing comes under this heading rather than under health. Normally major (trunk) roads are a central government responsibility, with Local Authorities responsible for secondary roads, and villages (sometimes compulsorily) for minor and feeder roads. Central governments define their own responsibilities very differently from territory to territory; and this is frequently a bone of contention between central and local government. There is a further difficulty in assessing road expenditure. In very many countries road making has traditionally been a form of unemployment relief, to be applied locally in accordance with the employment situation, or more likely, in accordance with political pressure. Where this occurs expenditure on roads tends to be both inflated and inefficient. In contrast, in order to take roads out of politics, Kenya has established an *ad hoc* Roads Authority. This does not necessarily secure its objective (in fact strong pressures are brought to bear on the Kenya Roads Authority by white settlers anxious about the evacuation of their crops). There is also an added problem of integrating road development under an *ad hoc* authority with the general development plan.

In view of all these difficulties we shall not be surprised to find very different allocations to communications in local budgets between one country and another. There are some classes of local bodies which seem to exist almost wholly as Road Authorities. This was formerly true of the Trinidad County Councils, and they still allocate more than half their budgets to this purpose (as contrasted with less than 30% for the Jamaica Parish Councils, notwithstanding the bait of 'special' grants). The smaller local committees in Ceylon seem also to exist very largely as Road Authorities; village committees spending 39% of their budget on this service; a purpose for which they are clearly incompetent.[1]

In Kenya the councils in the Settled Areas also traditionally existed as Road Authorities (the settlers having few other demands on local government services). With the establishment of County Councils, and especially where health services have been transferred to them, the percentage devoted to roads is tending to fall. Thus Aberdare County Council (without Public Health) was spending 78% of its budget on this service; those counties which had extended their range of duties, devoted from 40–55% to roads. The situation in African Districts was in strong contrast to this. Only in very sparsely inhabited areas such as Samburu (33%) and Narok (50%) was the allocation really high. For the rest of our sample the average was 18%. South Nyanza, Kiambu, and Kipsigis Districts got away with low percentages, but this was

[1] See Choksy Report on Local Government in Ceylon, 1955, cit.

largely because their areas are intertwined with the Settled Areas.

Both in Tanganyika and (on the whole) in Uganda local bodies are small spenders on roads. The Tanganyika average is 5%, and this reflects the fact that the Territorial government has not yet felt able to tackle the problem of communications systematically. In many areas the results are deplorable. In Uganda on the other hand local expenditure on roads has no need to be very large since the highly efficient central Public Works Department shoulders a large part of the burden, and communications are continually in the forefront of government policy.

Native Authority road expenditure in Northern Nigeria parallels that of Kenya: it is abnormally important where the population is sparse. Thus Bauchi devoted 22%, Tiv 21%, and Daura 25% to roads. Most other Native Authorities tended to have substantially lower percentages. Ghana is another area where a high degree of responsibility for roads is left to local bodies, especially in out-lying areas. Thus the average budget allocation in Trans-Volta Togoland was 26%, in Ashanti 16%, and in the Northern Region 26%. The towns in Ghana also spend heavily on communications (Accra 30%, Kumasi 20%).

The position in Southern Nigeria is confused because of tiering, and varying allocations between tiers in different Divisions. Thus in Ife we found that education was almost wholly a Divisional responsibility; in respect of roads the opposite was the case, the Division allocates less than 4%, but the District was spending 83% of its budget on this service. Broadly in Southern Nigeria it appears that high allocations to communications occur either in substantial urban areas (Benin 34%, Asaba 32%, Onitsha 45%, Enugu 33%, and Calabar 39%) or poor areas in the creeks, where roads and bridges were both especially needed and especially costly due to the (quite literal) scarcity of *terra firma*.

Improved communications of all sorts are necessary for accelerated development; but it is doubtfully good policy for central governments to lay any substantial burden, technical or financial, on the shoulders of local bodies. Main interest in a road may well be outside the local jurisdiction, and the work is therefore frequently neglected. Over large parts of the tropics road building is expensive and technically difficult, due to the violence of the seasonal rains, a wide shortage of suitable road metal (in Africa) or difficult contours (in the West Indies and Ceylon). Moreover adequate survey and the efficient use of modern machinery call for a large unit of control. These arguments do not apply to village feeder roads which are among the most useful works which can be undertaken at the lowest government level, backed up by voluntary labour.

It is exceptional for local bodies to play much part in the development of natural resources, except perhaps as agents of the central government. Where this occurs their position is in fact rather anomalous, since they are compelled to enforce decisions, which may be unpopular and are, in any case, none of their making. Apart from domestic water supplies natural resources development is a matter for rural rather than for urban bodies. By historical accident a few local bodies have inherited mineral resources (such as salt in the Ruwenzori), which they work as commercial undertakings. Apart from these, local efforts are confined to agriculture, including animal husbandry, forestry, and fishing.

The extent to which local farmers can be interested in resources development differs greatly from place to place; and the expenditure of local bodies varies with this. On the whole interest seems to be greatest in stock improvement, perhaps because in this there is unequivocal private ownership. Thus in Nigeria local expenditure on resources development is only substantial in the Northern Region, where animal husbandry is basic. Several Native Authorities devote from 8 to 13% of their budgets to resources development; not all of this goes to stock improvement, but there is an increasing demand for veterinary services.

Kenya District Councils devote a high percentage of their budget to natural resources development. There is a fairly high direct correlation between wealth and relative outlay on these matters. The highest allocations were in the ex-Mau Mau Districts such as Meru and Kiambu, where farms are being consolidated and replanned and new crops introduced. Machakos, only slightly farther from Nairobi than Kiambu, is also greatly interested in crop improvement. In the pastoral areas of Kenya substantial stock improvements are being brought about through the culling of poor animals and improved breeding, in some areas by artificial insemination. The Nandi have been specially successful in this. Kipsigis is another District where there is enthusiasm both for improved agriculture and better stock. A large number of farms have been consolidated and fenced; the Kipsigis are also beginning to grow tea, a crop that is already established among the Meru. Experience in Kenya shows that once interest has been aroused the Location and Village Councils will also be anxious to co-operate. This is extremely useful, since processes such as stock culling demand gentle persuasion which (at least in the early stages) can more effectively be applied at the strictly local level.

The higher percentages of local budgets devoted to natural resources development in Kenya are of course a reflection of the Territorial government's interest in the matter. They also owe something to the large size of the Districts, making it easier for the more wealthy, at least, to employ the services of experts. These conditions also exist in Uganda, but District Councils there appear to be less interested in agricultural improvement. The percentage allocations to these subjects range from 2% to 7%. This is partly a reflection of the higher allocations to administration and education.

At the other extreme, in Ghana and in Southern Nigeria Local Authorities spend little or nothing on agricultural services; indeed in the Western Region natural resources improvement has been declared a Regional and not a local service. In Sierra Leone on the other hand, the District Councils were first used principally as agents for the central government in implementing various agricultural services. No doubt as a result of this experience, once they were awarded independent executive powers and revenue rights, they plunged enthusiastically but not very wisely into the agricultural business.[1] It was the view of the Wann[2] Committee that the Districts should be deprived of these powers, which should either go back to the Chiefdom Authorities or to the central government.

Agriculture (including allied services) is one of the matters in which want of definition between the respective spheres of different layers of government is most serious, and consequently overlapping and misunderstandings most rife. The Kenya government has been a pioneer in attempting a rational distribution of function in this respect; even so the matter is not completely clear.[3] There are,

[1] See above, p. 198.
[2] Sierra Leone, *Report of a Commission of Inquiry into Local Taxation*, cit. 1956.
[3] See *White Paper, 1957, Distribution of Powers between the Protectorate Government and African District Councils*.

however, a few conclusions which can be drawn with a fair degree
of assurance in the light of the experience of a number of countries.

In the first place, research into such things as better strains of
plants, breeds of stock, and the control of pests and diseases, must
necessarily be a central responsibility. If then local councils wish
to keep nurseries in order to sell seeds or plants (as many of them
clearly do), it is important to have close liaison with the central
department to see that they are distributing the best varieties.
Secondly, responsibility for certain agricultural changes, such as a
contouring project, and certain necessary operations such as root-
ing out diseased trees, should not be left to Local Authorities,
since they are likely to bring the councils into opposition with the
people whose confidence they are trying to win. The task of the
technical officers will be lightened, however, if they first secure
the understanding and co-operation of the local council; indeed
without this the whole scheme may founder.[1] On the other hand,
improvements which call for patient and steady pressure, such as
proper use of fertilizers, and culling of poor quality stock, can
more effectively be carried through at the local level once the
council has been convinced of their desirability. Finally, in general,
there can be no two opinions as to the importance of pressing
ahead by every means with improvements in agricultural productivity, which, as is now generally recognized, is among the highest
priorities for development.

Some of the high allocations to natural resources development
will bear an alternative explanation: they are intended as the basis
of a trading service. This may occur in urban as well as in rural
conditions. Thus Poona started by establishing a pound for stray
cattle, which it is gradually evolving as a municipal milk service.
In Bombay there is a long established public milk service which
is most successful. In other territories (especially Kenya) a number
of towns have municipal milk distribution schemes, but for the
most part the milk is brought wholesale from the private sector.
Northern Nigerian Native Authorities are particularly active in
promoting commercial undertakings with an agricultural base.
Thus Bornu operates market gardening, dairying, and a rice
scheme, Igala has poultry, Katsina sells cassava seeds and Bida has
raffia plantations; Kano has a forest reserve. Forestry plantations

[1] As did the bunding scheme in Morogoro, Tanganyika; see below, p. 379.

with a view to future timber sales are also operated by some Kenya African District Councils, notably Kisimu. Morogoro in Tanganyika also has a poultry farm.

Northern Nigerian Native Authorities are also active in other forms of commercial enterprise: Kano has a printing works, wood and mechanical workshop, handloom weaving, pottery works, and operates the marketing of scrap metal (this appears to be a favourite occupation in the Region).[1] Katsina runs a bookshop and a laundry, Bornu goes in for brickmaking. One of the most ambitious Local Authority processing undertakings for local produce was that of the Machakos (Kenya) sisal scheme. This aimed at utilizing a local supply of sisal, originally planted for soil conservation, to produce the fibre on a commercial scale. So far as the District Council was concerned the plan foundered through the difficulty of ensuring a regular supply of the raw material. Ultimately the Territorial government agreed to take it over.

Eastern Nigeria is another area where Local Authorities have been encouraged to start commercial undertakings, particularly weaving and pottery (Okigwi); Abakalaki has a range of little rice mills. All of these Nigerian enterprises (and the same seems to be true in Tanganyika) are of a small and desultory nature. The enterprises seldom bring in a net profit and frequently result in a not negligible loss. In many cases they are relics of the work of enthusiastic District Officers or even Governors. In Kenya the situation is substantially different, since it is the declared policy of the central government to encourage both the African District Councils and Settled Area Councils to add to their independent financial resources from trading profits. Among the most successful of these enterprises are beer halls and even hotels for Africans. In the towns and Settled Areas the profits are normally devoted to welfare services for Africans.

Trading activities merge into self-balancing services, defining the latter as services provided primarily in the interests of public health, such as domestic water supply, markets and slaughter houses, cemeteries, lorry parks; and also occasionally electricity supply. Such services should normally cover their costs, but there is always a danger of under-usage if it is attempted to make a large net profit. These health services are fundamental and it would be wrong for Local Authorities not to undertake them up to an adequate

[1] It mainly consists of antique railway equipment.

level. There are, however, many ways in which the installations may usefully be embellished, making them more attractive and useful to the community and turning them into semi-trading services. Thus markets can be continually improved, graduating from wooden stalls (or no stalls at all), and thatched roofs, to cement slabs and solid roofs, with possible additions of lock-up shops, public conveniences, and snack bars. A lorry park can be laid out conveniently for the market and provided with repair and vulcanizing shops. The whole set-up can be sited (or re-sited) just off the through road so as to clear communications.[1] For installations such as these substantial charges can be made.

It is not always easy to strike the balance of advantage between encouraging or discouraging local councils in these fields. It would clearly be a mistake to allow them to neglect their fundamental duties for such matters. Further, in respect of many of the services which they would like to undertake their jurisdictions are typically too small for economical working. This is true of electric light undertakings[2] and even of municipal transport. Large towns, like Bombay and Lagos, have made good bargains in taking over running transport concerns from private enterprise, and operate them successfully. Accra also does well on transport; but smaller towns usually have difficulty in covering their losses. A further consideration is that most of these services provide additional opportunities for graft and manipulation of the accounts. One operative consideration in policy consequently should be the extent to which the award of contracts has been brought under control.

On the other hand there are two lines of argument which favour the encouragement of public enterprise at the local level. First, running a sort of business is stimulating and educational for councillors; it can engender an especial local pride, both in the service and in the council.[3] Secondly there is a growing number of semi-trading services which it is important to have properly attended to, mainly on health grounds, and for which spontaneous entrepreneurship is unlikely to be forthcoming, on account of the small prospect of profits. One of these services is municipal milk

[1] An excellent example exists at Cape Coast, Ghana.
[2] One parish in Jamaica operates an electric lighting plant, with regular and substantial losses year after year.
[3] H. Finer, *Municipal Trading*, 1941.

supply. A still more important one is the provision of 'high density' (low income) housing. These are matters, however, that touch on so many aspects of our inquiry that we must postpone full discussion of them to a later stage.

TABLE I

GHANA

Main Heads of Current Expenditure (1956–7) as Percentages of Total Current Expenditure

	Total (£'000s)	Adminis-tration %	Health %	Educa-tion %	Roads and works %	Other (housing) %
Towns						
Accra . .	617	14 (2)	39	17	30	—
Cape Coast .	54	25 (4)	56	7	12	—
Sekondi/Tako-radi . .	286	12 (2)	58	6	23	—
Kumasi. .	439	20 (2)	46	11	20	—
Regions (with-out towns)						
Eastern . .	609	34 (14)	20	29	9	7
Western .	609	32 (14)	16	32	6	9
Trans-Volta Togoland .	458	28 (11)	12	25	26	9
Ashanti. .	909	41 (12)	18	21	16	3
Northern .	773	27 (6)	13	24	26	5

Source: Ghana Local Government Financial Statistics.
Note: Bracketed figures in the Administration column denote Justice and Police.

The Local Budget

TABLE 2

NIGERIA, NORTHERN REGION

Native Authorities

Main Heads of Current Expenditure (1956–7) as Percentages of Total Current Expenditure (Largest and Smallest N. A. Budgets in each Province)

Province	Total (£'000s)	Administration %	Health %	Education %	Roads and works %	Natural resources %
Adamawa						
Adamawa . .	314·6	43 (9)	8	21	14	8
Numan . . .	59·9	35 (17)	7	27	19	11
Bauchi						
Bauchi . . .	217·8	40 (19)	8	19	22	8
Jama'ari . .	9·1	34 (12)	8	25	22	7
Benue						
Tiv . . .	266·6	43 (19)	11	16	21	4
Keffi . . .	30·7	47 (20)	11	21	13	6
Bornu						
Bornu . . .	526·7	38 (18)	8	16	20	9
Bedde . . .	26·9	40 (21)	10	21	14	13
Ilorin						
Ilorin . . .	228·0	33 (11)	10	24	24	4
Pategi . . .	12·4	36 (8)	8	42	6	4
Kabba						
Igala . . .	151·7	32 (13)	9	25	22	3
Bassa Komo . .	13·0	32 (13)	7	42	9	3
Kano						
Kano . . .	989·0	42 (18)	11	11	14	5
Kazaure . .	31·8	42 (16)	10	13	16	12
Katsina						
Katsina . . .	516·6	36 (13)	10	15	17	13
Daura . . .	55·9	35 (12)	10	14	25	11
Niger						
Bida . . .	136·5	30 (11)	8	36	11	11
Kamuku . .	8·8	40 (15)	14	25	10	6
Plateau						
Jos . . .	179·2	43 (25)	13	19	17	6
Wase . . .	13·1	39 (20)	8	20	16	12
Sokoto						
Sokoto . . .	619·1	44 (15)	14	11	13	10
Yauri . . .	36·1	37 (15)	9	16	16	7
Zaria						
Zaria . . .	302·1	41 (19)	11	23	12	9
Jema'a . . .	51·3	41 (18)	9	20	15	8

Source: Northern Region Native Administration Estimates.
Notes: 1. Bracketed figures in the Administration column denote Justice and Police.
2. The capital of Adamawa Emirate is Yola, and of Bornu is Maiduguri.

TABLE 3

NIGERIA, EASTERN REGION

Main Heads of Current Expenditure (1956–7) as Percentages of Total Current Expenditure (Sample Budgets)

	Total (£'000s)	Administration %	Health %	Education %	Roads and works %	Other %
District Councils with County Council powers						
Afikpo . .	69·9	24	6	37	27	neg.
Awgu . .	39·4	33	14	15	30	neg.
Ikom . .	26·5	23	6	37	20	neg.
Onitsha Urban	106·7	33	12	4	33	18
County Councils (no responsibility for health)						
Abakaliki .	83·3	29	—	63	1	neg.
Aba·Ngwa .	91·5	38	—	19	42	neg.
Ikot Ekpene* .	129·9	37	—	45	15	neg.
Nsukka*. .	105·3	33	—	31	33	—
Municipalities						
Enugu . .	86·4	39	20	neg.	33	—
Port Harcourt .	116·3	49	19	3	14	—
District Councils						
Aba U.D.C. .	59·2	32	13	5	38	10
West Ahoada R.D.C. .	76·4	18	10	28	41	neg.
North Annang D.C. .	14·4	44	22	16	12	3
Okrika D.C. .	5·7	40	11	11	15	10
Okigwi North D.C. .	18·0	45	24	2	3	5
Owerri U.D.C.	6·9	28	10	29	30	neg.
Calabar U.D.C.	51·8	29	14	7	39	10

Source: Eastern Region Local Government Estimates.
Notes: 1. 'Other' consists almost wholly of Markets and Precepts. In Onitsha total entry is for Markets, in Okrika and Okigwi the major part is for Precepts.
2. The budgets of these County Councils (marked *) were abnormally high in this year due to preparations for universal primary education.

TABLE 4

NIGERIA, WESTERN REGION

Main Heads of Current Expenditure (1956–7) as Percentages of Total Current Expenditure (Sample Budgets)

	Total (£'000s)	Adminis- tration %	Health %	Educa- tion %	Roads and works %	Other %
Divisional Councils with no District Councils						
W. Ijaw . .	94·7	19	8	68	3	—
Ijebo Remo .	134·2	16	5	64	—	15
Independent District Councils						
Ibadan . .	873·1	17	11	44	27	neg.
Ikeja . . .	41·6	17	10	62	11	neg.
Divisional Councils with District Councils						
Egba . . .	391·4	26	neg.	68	15	—
Asaba . .	195·6	7	—	88	1	—
Ife . . .	187·3	14	6	60	4	12
District Council in Divisions						
Ese Odo . .	32·8	90	4	neg.	6	—
Sapele Urban .	97·8	16	25	32	26	—
Oyo South . .	49·5	17	18	neg.	33	31
Benin City . .	54·7	11	12	—	34	33
Asaba Urban .	15·8	32	30	neg.	32	neg.
Ife . . .	33·1	16	—	neg.	83	neg.

Source: Western Region Local Government Council Estimates.
Note: 1. 'Other' consists wholly of Precepts.

TABLE 5

UGANDA

African Local Councils

Main Heads of Current Expenditure (1956–7) as Percentages of Total Current Expenditure (Largest and Smallest Council Budgets in Each Province)

Province	Total (£'000s)	Adminis- tration %	Health %	Educa- tion %	Roads and works %	Natural resources %	Other %
Buganda	1,900·0	37	5	33	16	4	3
Eastern							
Busoga .	528·9	25	3	32	21	6	10
Bukedi .	320·3	41	4	41	7	5	7
Western							
Ankole .	317·1	29	6	30	13	7	12
Bunyoro	188·9	24	2	36	15	5	14
Northern							
Lango .	265·9	29	8	30	19	4	7
Madi .	40·6	25	5	43	22	2	5

Source: Uganda African Local Government Accounts (unpublished).

Notes: 1. The Uganda Accounts do not allow of a proper separation of current and capital outlay. This affects Works and 'Other', which in this territory mainly represents outlay on housing (for employees) and offices.

2. Administration includes the following headings: General Administration, Judicial, Police and Prisons, Pensions and Gratuities, Audit and Treasury. It is thus considerably more inclusive than in most other territories.

TABLE 6

KENYA

African District Councils

Main Heads of Current Expenditure (1956) as Percentages of Total Current Expenditure (Largest and Smallest Council Budgets in Each Province)

Province	Total (£'000s)	Adminis-tration %	Health %	Educa-tion %	Roads and works %	Natural resources %
Nyanza						
S. Nyanza* .	239·6	29 (20)	10	19	11	22
Kipsigis* . .	107·4	18 (11)	12	18	29	18
Rift Valley						
Nandi . .	46·8	19 (8)	19	16	22	19
Samburu . .	12·7	16 (5)	23	15	33	5
Central						
Kiambu* . .	139·8	22 (12)	11	20	11	28
Meru* . .	141·9	16 (7)	14	18	19	25
Southern						
Machakos* .	147·5	15 (7)	14	17	20	25
Narok . .	48·7	10 (5)	8	17	50	12
Coast						
Kilifi . .	49·3	34 (15)	14	14	30	6
Tana River .	8·3	38 (3)	23	12	16	7
Northern						
Garissa . .	1·3	33 (20)	23	23	7	14

Source: Kenya African District Councils Approved Estimates.

Notes: 1. Bracketed figures in the Administration column denote Law and Order.

2. Other outlays in Kenya are small; they include Markets and Slaughter-houses, and Community Development. In the Districts marked * these together amounted to broadly 6% of outlay.

3. In Kiambu a transfer of £75,000 from the Emergency Fund for Law and Order has been ignored, since this was the last year in which any such payment was required.

14

BUDGETARY ACCOUNTS 2. CURRENT REVENUE

I.

IF local bodies are to play any significant part in economic or social development, they must clearly have access to adequate finance. If they are both to act responsibly and to show initiative, some, not negligible, part of this control over resources must be independent, in the sense that the local councils are free to choose the rates (and to some extent the conditions) of their taxes or service charges. Without this right Local Authorities have within their control only partial budgetary responsibility. They can arrange the priorities between different lines of expenditure at the margin (within the limits set by statutory obligations), but they cannot choose between an increment of expenditure and an increment of revenue. Without this second right a Local Authority cannot be fully responsible to its own citizens; nor can the local taxes be (as they should be) the balancing factor in local budgets at the final stage of the budgetary process, when the total outlay has been decided and revenue from all other sources is known.

Beyond all this, as we saw at the beginning, a special responsibility rests on local revenue in developing countries. Taxes are an essential requirement for smooth development, both for the purpose of providing resources for the public sector and as an instrument of control against the inflationary potential generated by the development process. In underdeveloped conditions taxes can often more easily be assessed and collected locally. Hence this is the point at which tax potential can most readily be tapped, on any but the largest incomes (where there may be assessment difficulties). In the present chapter we shall discuss current budgets from the revenue side, as a basis for a judgement concerning the adequacy and potentialities of different financial resources. In Chapters 15, 16, and 18 we shall examine the most important of these resources in more detail.

On the expenditure side of the budget, as we have seen, the

powers and duties of Local Authorities have been drawn very much more vaguely and widely than they ever were in the U.K. On the revenue side, however, overseas governments have found it necessary to define local powers more closely, if only to minimize conflict with central tax powers. In the U.K., the only local tax of any importance has been from the beginning (somewhere in the thirteenth century) a tax on the *occupation* of land and buildings, each 'hereditament' of building and the land pertaining to it being considered as a unit, irrespective of ownership. Since tax liability was expressed as a rate in the pound on a valuation previously made, this tax came to be known as the local *rate*. Due to the fact of this being the local tax *par excellence*, overseas administrators in recent years, misunderstanding the significance of the term 'rate' have tended to equate it with 'local tax', so that today in very many territories are now to be found taxes mistakenly known as 'income rates' which have no reference whatever to any valuation made in advance.

In the early days of British administration overseas it was a tax of the type of the British local rate which was established for local purposes: for instance in the West Indies, in Freetown (Sierra Leone) in the Indian[1] and in Ceylonese towns. Valuation for the local rate in the U.K. was traditionally a local concern; until 1925 no specific efforts were made either to secure uniformity in assessment levels or regular periodic revaluations. Moreover, the principles on which valuation was to be based were couched in language which admitted of several interpretations. The fact that valuation practice in the U.K. had not by 1925 become more diverse than was the case, was very largely due to the pressure of the Inland Revenue Department which had an interest in property valuation as the basis of income tax schedule A, long known as the property tax.[2]

In view of this casualness at home it is not surprising that valuations for the local tax on land and buildings overseas tended to be carried out with even less efficiency or understanding. The Ordinances establishing a local rate in the West Indies frequently gave no guidance as to how the valuation was to be arrived at; nor even whether it was to take the form of an annual or capital value. Some

[1] In the Rural Areas of India on the contrary tax was based on the relative fertility of land, and collected from landlords. We shall examine the implications of this land revenue in Chap. 15. It was not strictly a local tax, but was shared between central and local purposes.

[2] Cf. J. R. and U.K. Hicks, *The Problem of Valuation for Rating*, 1943.

island governments, in order to protect their own revenues, imposed limitations on the poundages which might be levied; the
towns retaliated by treating the valuation as the variable, thus de-
priving it of any objective reality.[1]

Since, generally speaking, evidence of any genuine rent contracts (as distinct from ephemeral room letting) was scarce, it was
easier for the 'valuers' to proceed via ownership and capital value
to an imputed annual rental value. In Jamaica, sensibly enough,
this last step was omitted and the tax settled down on a capital
value base. Elsewhere, however, in India, Ceylon, and some West
African towns, elaborate efforts were made to turn capital into
annual values, no doubt on the understanding that this was the
correct basis for a local tax. This is a matter the principles of which
we shall have to discuss in Chapter 16; here we are only concerned
with explaining the type of tax that predominates in urban conditions overseas.

More recently, in the post-1945 drive to establish responsible
local government in Africa, it was often found impossible to base a
tax on land and buildings because of the absence of individual
holdings outside the towns, hence the proliferation of 'income
rates' (actually modified poll taxes), mentioned above. It is only
since about 1954 that true rating has begun to spread to the smaller
towns. Indications are at present that it will settle down on a capital
(property) rather than on an annual (rental) basis.

Two effects of other phases of British financial thinking can also
clearly be traced overseas. The first of these is the possibility of
basing a land tax on the *surplus* element in its value, that is to say
the part of the value which is due not to the efforts of the owner to
increase the output, but to the expansion of demand, raising value
above production costs on the better placed land. The analysis of
surplus value (or economic rent) was derived ultimately from
Ricardo, and was explicitly the basis of Indian land revenue.[2] More
recently the possibility of stimulating urban development by confining the local rate to the surplus element, and at the same time
securing the value of the surplus for public purposes, has led to
the advocacy of so called unimproved value as the basis for rates.

This concept was actively canvassed in the U.K. in the first

---

[1] Dominica and British Guiana seem to be two specially bad examples, but
the trouble was endemic throughout the area. See pp. 351 ff.

[2] See pp. 326 ff. below.

decade of the present century, and a measure introducing it actually reached the Statute book; but the difficulty of defining and valuing true unimproved value in fully built up areas (where the value of the building was an integral part of the value of the hereditament), defeated the valuers, and the experiment was abandoned. From the U.K., however, the concept passed to some of the Dominions, including South Africa, whence it passed to Central and East Africa, and was taken up with particular enthusiasm in Kenya. Consequently we shall find throughout this area an urban local tax based on a derating of buildings, rather than on a scientific attempt to isolate surplus value. At the other side of the world this base has also seemed attractive to Jamaica, where the concept was probably derived directly from the U.K.

The other phase of British financial thinking in the nineteenth century which has left its mark overseas is that of 'Municipal Socialism', or the local public ownership of undertakings, especially public utilities, with the double purpose of eliminating private monopoly profits and of relieving the rates out of the proceeds. In the heyday of this policy considerable sums were transferred to the Rate Fund Account. Gradually, however, the argument gained ground that to impose sufficiently high service charges to make a substantial net revenue for local purposes, was equivalent to an additional tax over which the central government needed to have control, and was hence undesirable for local operation, quite apart from the economics of the particular pricing policies adopted.

In the U.K. the necessary relief for the rates came through an extension of the grant system. Overseas, as we saw in the last chapter, although several territories encourage local ventures in commercial undertakings, generally speaking not much emphasis has been put on the policy of using them to contribute to the revenue; indeed it is much more usual for losses rather than profits to be made. The chief exception to this generalization is Kenya, where the desirability of establishing profitable undertakings is strongly urged on local bodies. This is one aspect of a general policy (which we shall come across several times) of restricting local tax powers (basically for the protection of the central revenue), and so forcing Local Authorities to seek revenue in other ways, not excluding the charging of school fees and of economic rents on public enterprise houses.[1]

[1] See above, p. 269. In this direction also the influence on Kenya of thinking in South Africa and Southern Rhodesia is apparent.

Elsewhere overseas (with the possible exception of Ghana) policy is far nearer to the current thinking of the Welfare State than of nineteenth-century Britain. Following the policy of the first post-war Labour government in the U.K. public ownership of the means of production is favoured, and social services tend to be supplied free or below cost, so far as means allow. This is especially true in India, but it is noticeable that the Union government is less enthusiastic about commercial undertakings at the State and municipal level than are the local bodies themselves; basically because it will be under pressure to increase grants to cover losses.

Since the intensive drive for the establishment of responsible local government institutions in Africa dates only from the 1940's, it is not surprising that the revenue side of local budgets in Africa should exhibit particular marks of British policy in this period. This is especially true in respect of the financial relations between different 'tiers' of government. Of this there are two aspects: the growth of the system of 'precepting', and the expansion of grants from higher to lower-layer governing bodies. In recent years British policy (which in this respect is essentially 'bipartisan') has favoured a process of concentrating the more important local services in the hands of the larger authorities: County Boroughs and County Councils. Several factors have contributed to this change, such as the expansion of the optimum technical unit of administration as the services become more developed, and the greater ease of communication, making the larger unit feasible as well as plausible.

As a result of this concentration the typical situation of a British ratepayer today in a county area is that 60% or more of his contribution is not spent by the authority to which he pays it, but is transferred to the County Council by means of a precept, to spend in ways over which he has virtually no control. This vicarious system of tax collection gives rise to little or no trouble in the U.K. A table on the back of the Rate Demand Note, which all may read, makes the proportionate application of his contribution to different services completely clear to the ratepayer.

When in the early 1950's in an effort to make a decisive break with the Native Authority/Indirect Rule tradition, experiments were made in Southern Nigeria and Ghana (and somewhat later in Sierra Leone and Tanganyika) in a form of local government modelled on contemporary British practice, the precept, and the 'tiering' of local bodies came in with it.[1] We shall be discussing at a later stage the propriety of this system in the absence of the conditions which made it acceptable in the U.K. In the present chapter our main interest is with the complications precepting has introduced into the revenue side of local budgets during the period with which we are principally concerned.

Grants from the central government to the local authorities have a long history in the U.K. It is safe to say that no other country has such wide and varied experience of their use, as instruments both of stimulus and of control of local activities. For comparative purposes we need to distinguish at this stage only two sorts of grant: those that are specific to particular services, and those which are unallocated and so serve as a general support of local finance.[2]

The earliest grants in the U.K. (in the first half of the nineteenth century) were specific, but later in the century a type of block grant (Goschen's assigned revenues)[3] was introduced with the explicit[4] purpose of increasing the sense of responsibility of Local Authorities by enabling them to draw up their own budgets unbiased by central pressure. The assigned revenue phase of British policy had a profound effect in India. It is still used for the overall allocation of a share of income tax revenue to the states. More relevant to our purposes in a number of Indian states the system is used in the distribution of land revenue to panchayats and other local bodies. In most African territories a portion of poll tax is assigned, sometimes from local governments to the centre, sometimes the other way round.

In spite of the early importance of the unallocated grant in the U.K., the great expansion in Exchequer grants to Local Authorities was due to the (specific) education grant. The block grant element, introduced in 1929, was strengthened in 1948, but the education

[1] See above, p. 21.

[2] Since the Local Government Act of 1928 generally known as 'block grants'.

[3] Assigned revenue, i.e. the transfer of a part of the revenue of a central tax or taxes to lower-layer governing bodies, comes very near to a shared tax; but in a true shared tax each layer has the right of determining (perhaps within statutory limits) the rate of tax it will fix for itself. In so far as the revenue assigned is distributed according to some purposeful pattern (and not merely in accordance with the derivation of the revenue), it comes very near to a grant, but one in which the total to be distributed is determined not on any principle but according to the revenue which happens to have been collected. For further discussion of these points see Chap. 18.

[4] The implicit purpose of putting a ceiling on demands on the Treasury was no doubt also present.

grant remained dominant until 1958, when it was itself replaced by a type of block grant. The common element in all these recent British grants, whether specific or unallocated, has been a substantial element of interlocal redistribution of resources.

Local finance overseas has been much influenced by these trends in British grant policy. As we shall find, most governments make use of specific grants, especially for education; not a few have also experimented with block grants. The substantial grant element in Jamaica's Parish Council finance is very largely based on a block grant; in Eastern Nigeria the block grant is also dominant, and Kenya has some interesting plans in this direction. In India too, unallocated grants at all levels seem to be expanding relatively. More important than these particular practices is the fact that these overseas governments have been growing up in an atmosphere where a large grant element is regarded as a right and proper feature of a local financial structure.

II

With this general background in mind we can proceed to a statistical examination of the available figures on the revenue side of the current budget.[1] Analogously to the social accounting breakdown on the expenditure side, between outlay on goods and services and on transfers, the fundamental breakdown on the revenue side is between incomings derived from the provision of goods and services, and those derived from transfers. Under the first heading come (1) income from services provided: fees, fines, and profits from the operation of enterprises,[2] and (2) income from property: on the one hand rents, and on the other interest on loans and deposits. In respect of transfers we have to distinguish between (1) tax payments made by persons or firms, or by one governing body to another (such as payments in lieu of rates on government property), and (2) transfers from other governments by way of grants in the widest sense.[3]

This is the breakdown which we shall endeavour to carry through, but the results cannot be expected to be very precise. The local

[1] For sample figures see tables at the end of the chapter.
[2] Strictly speaking these should be net of all costs of running the undertaking, including stock maintenance and the depreciation of fixed equipment, but it is often very difficult to ascertain true net profit from the accounts.
[3] Including reimbursements, but excluding assigned revenues.

accounts are normally kept, according to Colonial Office Regulations, under subjective not functional heads, while the above social accounting classification is functional from an economic point of view, that is to say it is intended as an aid in gauging the economic effects of the various revenue items. From the point of view of the taxpayers however it may well be more informative to adopt a classification which shows the means used to finance each service individually, whether from profits, by revenue from the local tax pool, by an earmarked tax, by grant, or by drawing on capital funds. This is the method consistently followed in Kenya.

Unfortunately when the amounts have been put together in one way information is rarely sufficient to reclassify them in another. The factor which strikes the inquirer most forcibly in examining the revenue side of the budget in almost every country, is the want of continuity in almost every item. There may be very good reasons for fluctuations in receipts, for instance of taxes based on the prices of farm products, but more often, it may be suspected, the variations are due to inefficient tax collection and faulty recording.

Local bodies in most of our countries make fairly substantial (*gross*) incomes from the provision of goods and services. Comparison, however, is made difficult due to different methods of charging. Thus charges for public utilities such as water, sewage (or conservancy), and fire brigades may be made on a rateable value base (or other form of general tax revenue) irrespective of usage, or they may take the form of service charges, designed to cover the costs of each particular service separately. This appears to be the basis of the Jamaican system, but as we have seen, in fact costs, even running costs, are not always covered.[1] In Kenya this method of charging is also followed; where water is laid on it is strictly metered, and charged accordingly. Again, education may be financed partly out of fees, partly out of an earmarked education tax, or from general revenue, including grants. Not all of these sources may appear fully in the accounts.

Urban areas naturally have more opportunities for deriving revenue from their services than rural. The larger Indian towns do well (Bombay 30% of revenue, Poona 17%, Secunderabad 17%);

[1] There has, however, been a substantial improvement in the most recent years, receipts under this heading (including, however, also licences which cannot be separated) rising from 9% to 13% of current revenue between 1956–7 and 1958–9.

in these commercial profits seem to be the main item. Among the town councils in Ceylon the average is 25% of current revenue, 18% in urban areas and 15% in municipalities; this revenue is mainly derived from fees. Nuwara Eliya,[1] however, which has a number of commercial irons in the fire, gets no more than 5% contribution from services and undertakings. In all of these percentages school fees are negligible in India; and in Ceylon education is in any case an Island responsibility.

As we might expect, the Kenya towns derive a substantial revenue from profits, fees, and other charges; Nairobi, Kisumu, and Nakuru all derive over 30% of their revenue from this source, Mombasa with 18% does less well. Only Kisumu, however, appears certainly to make a clear net profit on its commercial undertakings. These Kenya results are in strong contrast to the Uganda situation where Kampala derives no more than 3% from this source. The Kenya County Councils do much less well under this head than the towns, mainly no doubt because they have fewer services to charge for. Enterprising Nakuru County collects 16% of its revenue this way, but for the others the average is around 10%. The Kenya African District Councils also gather substantial revenue under this heading: 34% in Samburu and 30% in Nandi are rather exceptionally high, 12% is nearer the average, while the Narok Masai council gets no more than 8%, due no doubt to the difficulty of running profitable services for nomads. In all of these, both profits from beer halls, and education fees are substantial. The policy behind these receipts is at once apparent when they are compared with the—in most respects similar—Uganda District Councils, where Bunyoro is exceptional in getting 11% of its revenue from this source; the normal range appears to be 5–8%, with Buganda taking no more than 2%.

Ghana is another country where a substantial contribution to local finances comes from this source, mainly by way of education fees and court fines, in rural districts, and, in the towns from various charges and some commercial profits. Accra gets over 25% of its revenue thus, Kumasi over 31%, and Cape Coast 29%. A number of the local councils also do well. In the Eastern Region Yilo-Krobo gets over 50%. In Ashanti Obuasi gets nearly 50%; another high one is Bolga near Fra fra in the Northern Region.

---

[1] This tea-growing hill station has clearly not yet adjusted itself to the change wrought by the withdrawal of British capital.

The total of some of these budgets is, however, extremely small (Bolga's is under £11,000) so what is mainly recorded is more likely to be an inability to collect taxes.

On the whole in Ghana the share of court fees and fines in this total is substantial, although smaller than in Nigeria; education fees on the other hand bulk much larger. The most interesting source of revenue under this heading in Ghana consists of receipts from lorry parks. Obuasi gets £14,300 from this source, Tamale Urban £9,400. It is worth noting that this source of revenue—which has an admirable regulatory effect—is less available to local bodies in Nigeria because the Lorry Drivers' Union normally provides the parks.[1] One or two Nigerian Local Authorities (for instance Calabar) do derive some revenue from this source, and also from private car parks.

In Nigeria, from what we know concerning its encouragement of commercial enterprises, we should expect the Northern Region to derive more revenue under this heading than the rest of the country, and to some extent this is the case: Jos derives 22% of its revenue under this heading, Ilorin 15%, Kabba 14%, and Zaria 11%; but the contribution in Kano is very small indeed in spite of its commercial undertakings. It is noticeable that several of the higher percentages come from the Yoruba areas in the south of the Region (the Middle Belt) where enthusiasm for education is high.

In the Southern Region of Nigeria receipts under this heading are generally moderate (policy in respect of education fees plays a part in this). Where the percentage contribution is abnormally large there are usually particular circumstances present as an explanation. As in other areas the towns normally do better than the rural districts. Thus in the West, Sapele Urban District derives 20% of its revenue from this source, Ibadan 17%, and Asaba Urban District Council (the Niger ferry port) 26% (out of a much smaller budget). In the more rural areas contributions of 9%, 7%, 3%, or even less, are usual.

In the Eastern Region Onitsha, the eastern bridgehead of the Niger ferry, derived no less than 35% of its revenue from this source, due largely no doubt to the presence of a magnificent wholesale market.[2] The little town of Aba which has some relatively

---

[1] Cf. E. K. Hawkins, *Road Transport in Nigeria*, 1958.
[2] Provided mainly from Colonial Development and Welfare Funds, i.e. by the British taxpayer.

prosperous industry also did well with 26%, but Okigwi which has experimented both with textiles and pottery got no more than 3%; Calabar reaped 16% and Port Harcourt 11%. In the Rural Areas 6% and 8% were common contributions, although West Ahoada Rural District Council managed to collect 10%.

In Southern Nigeria there are some interesting small items under this broad heading. In the West, Ife, exceptionally for this Region, made some money from the sale of produce, Ikeja, virtually an outer suburb of Lagos, sells standard building plans to those intending to build their own houses. In the Eastern Region there are very commonly takings from sports stadia, and in a number of areas dispensary fees, mainly from the innoculations beloved of Africans. As has been said, some councils also make a small profit from private motor park fees.

The second heading of true income: rents and interest, is percentagewise always very small indeed. (For this reason it tends to get classified elsewhere and often cannot be disentangled.)[1] Yet both are items of some significance. Up to the present, receipts from rents are almost wholly in respect of houses built for and let to local government employees. In time, however, this item will begin to reflect policy in respect of the erection of 'high density' housing. Already substantial policy differences have appeared, concerning the extent to which such houses should be let at subsidized rents. This is a question which we shall have to discuss in Chapter 20. There are also important policy differences behind the second item, interest on loans and deposits.

By far the largest source of revenue under loans and deposits represents the interest on reserves. Reserves may have arisen in several ways. First they may have been gradually accumulated and held as working balances and renewals funds. This would be specially true of the larger towns and would explain Bombay's 7% of revenue from interest and Poona's 3%. The large incomings under the rent-interest head in Kenya's towns (Nairobi and Nakuru 14%, Mombasa and Kisumu 5%) will also partly be accounted for by the interest factor. Secondly, reserves may have been acquired in the exceptional boom conditions of the war and immediate post-war

[1] Thus in Ceylon rent is entered under fees, &c. Among the Jamaican parishes there are no entries under this heading, nor again among the Kenya African District Councils, although in both cases reserves certainly exist.

period in primary produce prices. They may have come to the Local Authorities either directly, or by transfers from marketing boards and similar government agencies. In so far as such reserves were distributed to local bodies as a capital sum it would be natural if they had not yet been completely spent. On the other hand, in some areas it is reasonable to postulate unintentional delay in disbursing them due to various bottle-necks. Thirdly, the keeping of substantial reserves may be enjoined by the central government, as an insurance against famine or disaster.

Northern Nigeria and Ghana both seem to be areas where the second of the above causes have been operating: local bodies have been hampered in spending grants and other transferred funds, due either to insufficient forward planning, or to shortages particularly of skilled personnel. In Nigeria the second of these seems to be the more important. Planning can hardly be said to be insufficient; every Northern Native Authority is working under a periodic plan. In Ghana, on the other hand, the accumulation has taken place more recently and appears to be unplanned.[1] At any rate every Native Authority in Northern Nigeria has incomings from interest which are sometimes quite substantial (Kano £18,000, Sokoto £8,600, Bornu £7,900). In Ghana the figures are somewhat lower, but Tarkwa Urban Council for instance was receiving £3,500.

It must be borne in mind, however, that the interest entry in current budgets is a very inaccurate reflection of the balance sheet position, either in respect of the strength of reserves or of their liquidity. Due to the drastic fall in capital values since the earlier post-war reserves were invested, funds held in long-term securities can only be realized now at a substantial capital loss. This difficulty confronts the Northern Nigerian Native Authorities, some of whom now find themselves in a seriously illiquid position. In other areas, and more recently in Northern Nigeria, the tendency seems to have been rather to lend at short term, by way of Treasury bills or bank deposits. This, however, while maintaining a liquid position, reduces revenue.

The position in the Northern Region contrasts fairly sharply with that in other parts of Nigeria. In the West, Benin indeed

[1] This was suggested to me by the U.N. official in charge of the Ghana Statistical Office. It was also the opinion of the Secretary of the Ministry of Local Government in charge of urban local government.

received £2,500 in interest (it is centrally placed in the rich mahogany area), but elsewhere incomings were negligible, representing less than 1% of revenue. In the East, Aba had incomings of £1,300, but elsewhere a sum of £500 would have seemed a large budgetary contribution. Even allowing for differences in investment policy, there is no doubt that Local Authorities in the south sail very near the wind (as indeed does the Eastern Regional government itself). It must be observed, however, that in these well-watered areas there is little danger of extensive crop failures; the opposite is true in the North where in some of the drier areas food shortage may be lurking round the corner at any time. Some consideration of this no doubt creeps in to the caution in respect of reserves of the Northern Regional government and its Native Authorities.

Central government policy in respect of Local Authority reserves plays an important part in East Africa, although this is not apparent from the Kenya African District Council budgets. Kenya policy is to lay down for each District what amount (or percentage of its budget) it considers to be a safe level, in view of its susceptibility to drought, stock diseases, its taxable capacity, or the fluctuating nature of the local revenue. With a new District the building up of reserves to the required point must be given a high priority. The conditions, however, seem not to be very onerous; Elgon Nyanza attained its objective within three years of its establishment.[1] Uganda also insists on the building of substantial reserves, the greater part of the incomings under the heading interest and rent in this territory are due to this item. Percentagewise 2% seems to be a normal incoming. This is no doubt sufficient in the climatic conditions of the Territory.

The reserve policy of Tanganyika differs substantially from that of the other two East African territories. Not only must local bodies keep large reserves, but they are paid into a government fund, where they are available for borrowing by other Local Authorities.[2] This is a substitute (although, now that excess reserves are getting used up, not an efficient one) for a Local Loans Fund, such as is

---

[1] The finances of the Mau Mau Districts have not yet recovered from the Emergency and the impossibility of efficient tax collection while it was on. Thus Kiambu was running a deficit of £55,600, although poll tax collection had never completely ceased, as it had in the Meru and Embu Districts. In these areas reserves have naturally been dissipated.

[2] See above p. 230 and discussion in Chap. 17.

used in Kenya and Uganda. The result of this policy is that on the average the heading 'interest and rent' was responsible for 10%[1] of local current incomings. Many parts of Tanganyika, like Northern Nigeria, suffer severely from drought, so that no doubt a cautious policy in respect of reserves is desirable.

Before leaving the heading of interest, there is one small item which is beginning to appear in East African budgets, which may be of some economic importance, although it is at present of negligible financial significance. This consists of interest on account of council loans made to individual farmers[2] or groups of farmers for the purpose of carrying out farm improvements, especially water supply. In mixed farming Districts, where co-operation is difficult to manage, this system could be of great benefit, so long as it is possible to ensure that the loans are made on merit and with good security. This is no doubt possible in Kenya and Tanganyika, where the administration is still powerful in local government; but where independent elective local councils have been established it would clearly be necessary to make careful arrangements to guard against abuse.

III

We must now turn to examine the more important, transfer, sources of local revenue: on the one hand taxes and licences, on the other grants and reimbursements. Since the contribution of licences to revenue is a small one, scarcely anywhere exceeding 2% or 3%, we may conveniently get that out of the way first. Licences are an item which often receive undue prominence in the accounts.[3] Basically the purpose of a licence is regulation and control, for which purposes the charge should be no higher than is necessary to secure the objective; but the step from this to including a tax element in the charge is a very easy one. Sometimes there seems to be no stopping place before the licence becomes frankly

[1] Figures from East African Statistical Office. Such individual figures from Council Estimates as I have been able to get hold of (mostly from Lake Province) show substantially smaller proportions. The discrepancy may arise from the inclusion of reimbursements in the heading.

[2] Cf. *Conference on Land Use and Land Tenure*, Cambridge, 1959, cit.

[3] Perhaps because local bodies enjoy exercising their power of saying yes or no. It is apparent from the Cox and Wann Reports on Sierra Leone that they can give rise to much fraud and discrimination if suitable machinery for controlling this power has not been established.

a tax (and a discriminatory one at that), such as the tax on trades and professions common in Indian towns, and formerly in some parts of Nigeria. In view of these considerations it is not surprising that revenue from licences is tending to rise; but the small contribution which it makes to budgets indicates that the regulatory purpose is still uppermost.

Licences which are almost wholly regulatory often reflect local social customs, such as to wield a Dane gun (in West Africa), to drum (in Southern Nigeria), to play the guitar (in Tanganyika), or to practise as a beggar minstrel (in Northern Nigeria, although it is hard to believe that, for instance, Bida needs to collect £1,000 a year from its minstrels for purely regulatory purposes). Liquor licences are a general source of revenue, so also are game and fishing licences in East Africa.

On the other hand licences which belong to the modern world tend to have a larger tax element. This is especially true of cinema licences which come close to an entertainment tax. (Calabar collects 7% of its revenue from this source, but this is exceptional). Animals and means of transport are a traditional subject for licensing. In India, and even more in Ceylon, elaborate tariffs are laid down for different sorts of beasts (including in one place or another camels and elephants), and also for every sort of vehicle, human or animal drawn. In Africa bicycle licences are a growing source of revenue; but the really lucrative and expanding revenue comes from motor vehicle licences. Local bodies never have full control of motor licences, but they are often collected locally and the local budget sometimes benefits by a substantial assignment. This can be of considerable advantage to urban areas, which have, after all, the most pressing need for revenue for development.

We must now make a brief survey of the main categories of local taxes, as a basis for more detailed discussion later. There are three main types which we have to consider: (1) taxes on persons (which in our countries run all the way from a flat sum poll tax of a few shillings a year to a progressive income tax rising to £20 or more), (2) indirect taxes, which may fall (as regards formal incidence) either on consumption or on production; for convenience we have put them into a single category, and (3) taxes assessed in some way on real estate. In respect of these three categories very marked inter-area differences have grown up, partly as a result of policy in the different territories, but very largely by historical accident.

We can distinguish clearly between an 'old' and a 'new' pattern of colonial local taxation, as well as between broad area differences.

Indian towns, which from the first were given much wider tax powers than have ever been available to British Local Authorities, have, mainly on account of their ease of collection, developed a wide range of taxes on production and consumption. They also use a local rate assessed on annual value but have no tax on persons, other than the semi-licences on trades and professions mentioned above. In the Rural Areas there is land revenue, and sometimes a so-called 'cess'[1] on land revenue (an additional levy for a lower layer of government). In Ceylon local revenue is derived from essentially similar sources: a variety of indirect taxes, a local rate based on annual value and a land tax. In detail, however, the Ceylon local taxes differ substantially from those levied in India. In the West Indies the only local tax of any importance is a levy on land and buildings of a somewhat ambivalent type.[2] This set of taxes may be described as the 'old' colonial pattern of local finance.

In strong contrast, a personal tax is the backbone of all local taxation in the African territories. So far there is only a weak usage of real estate taxes, except for the rates on unimproved value levied in the urban areas of East and Central Africa. If we except the Northern Nigerian cattle tax (*jangali*)[3] West Africa makes no use of taxes on production or consumption at the local level. East Africa on the other hand has, in recent years, taking advantage of the high post-war prices of agricultural products, developed a wide range of produce taxes, known as cesses, or market taxes. This and especially the emphasis on personal taxation may be described as the 'new' colonial pattern of local finance.

It will be recalled that the pioneers of African administration such as Lugard, Johnston, and Cameron were insistent on the need to establish a poll tax of some sort at the earliest possible moment, even if to start with payment had to be made partly or wholly in kind. Later administrators in these areas have much to thank them

[1] In British taxation the term 'cess' is confined to levies essentially earmarked for the benefit of particular groups concerned in revenue: a cess on coal was devoted to research into miners' diseases. The term has been widely used in India, primarily with the same understanding (but not apparently in the case of the cess on land revenue mentioned above). In its recent usage in East Africa this aspect has virtually disappeared.

[2] See above, pp. 278–9. The proposed levy on small holdings in Jamaica looks more like a mild poll tax.

[3] A poll tax on cattle.

for. As things are developing, it seems to be considerably easier to move on to an effective income tax where personal taxation of some sort is accepted as part of the natural order of things, than where there is no such tradition.

Since we shall not be analysing them further, this will be a convenient point to take a look at the indirect taxes of India and Ceylon. Given their wide tax powers, Indian towns have been attracted into this line of least resistance, partly because (basically due to poor administration) the local rate on land and buildings failed to produce an adequately expanding revenue, and partly because of the very meagre grants which were available to them from higher tier governments.[1] Local government became a provincial matter in 1928[2] and under the Constitution of the Union of India it is wholly a state matter. Hence generally speaking the Union government must confine its interest in the development of local government to advice and exhortation, although of recent years it seems to be developing a technique of making grants to local bodies *through* the states.

Indian urban indirect taxes can be subsumed into two categories, on the one hand those levied on the possession of vehicles and animals and on entertainments, and on the other taxes on goods, persons, vehicles, and animals entering the jurisdiction (tolls and *octroi*).[3] There can be no particular objection to the first of these categories, except that the animals and vehicles taxed are principally the poor man's means of transport (although wealthy Ceylonese make considerable use of elephants for heavy work). Hence the tax potential is very small, doubtfully worth the cost of collection, and the net effect tends to be regressive.

Octroi is a very different story. Some towns have over thirty different schedules, covering a wide range of food, textiles, and manufactured goods, including paints and photographic materials. The resulting revenue is often very substantial, notwithstanding poor methods of collection, fraud, and consequent loss of revenue. In 1956 Poona was getting 41% of its revenue from indirect taxes, octroi being responsible for 37%, and this experience was by no means unique. Octroi is wholly bad, and has been roundly condemned by impartial observers for many decades. It is regressive

---

[1] See Chap. 18.   [2] See above, p. 55.
[3] This French term is used everywhere in India; since this form of tax has not been used in the U.K. there is no English word for it.

in incidence, inequitable because of fraud, and highly inconvenient to the taxpayer. From the broader economic point of view octroi hampers inter-local trade, bolstering up the economic isolation which is one of the biggest obstacles to development (especially development from below) in India. It is also a warning of the sort of thing that may happen if unnecessarily wide tax powers are allocated to local governments. The best thing that can be said is that octroi does appear to be declining in importance, although it can hardly yet be said to be on the way out. Bombay now derives no more than 7% of its revenue from indirect taxes; ten years ago the octroi contribution to town revenues frequently exceeded 60%.

It is apparent that without octroi the proceeds of local indirect taxes in India would be very meagre. This is exactly what happens in Ceylon (where it is not used), in spite of concentrated efforts to increase the revenue from taxes on animals and vehicles (where the tax potential is little larger than in India), and on entertainments, which in a limited way are fairly lucrative. The obvious remedy for this state of affairs, both in India and Ceylon, is a proper development of the local rate on land and buildings (the possibilities of which we shall examine in Chapter 16). Bombay is able almost to do without octroi because it can derive a large revenue (46% of the total) from the taxation of land and buildings. In contrast Poona can do no better than 23%.

The East African (and Northern Nigerian) indirect taxes differ from those of India and Ceylon in several ways. Here, however, our concern is merely to put them into their place in the picture, because we shall be examining them more thoroughly in the next chapter. In the first place they are levied directly on produce, and hence accrue to rural and not to urban authorities. Secondly their share in local revenue is much more modest. The contribution to District revenue of cesses in Uganda is rarely as high as 7%; 3% or 4% is more usual. Among Kenya African District Councils (there are no cesses in the Settled Areas), some derive 13% (for instance Meru),[1] or even more, of their revenue from cesses. In Tanganyika the average contribution was 7%, but dispersion round the average was extremely high. Morogoro's budget benefitted by as much as 16% from this source. In the prosperous Lake Province the range was from 32% (due to Bukoba's coffee cess)

---

[1] It will, however, be recalled that in this Mau Mau area the collection of poll tax has been very difficult during the Emergency.

and 25% in Mwanza (cotton cess) to virtually zero in some of the smaller Districts. Obviously Lake Province finances would require a major readjustment if the cesses were to be withdrawn.

We need not do more than indicate the place of the other two major forms of independent local revenue: the rate on land and buildings and personal taxes, since we shall be discussing them later. Taxes on land and buildings have a special part to play in the development process because they are particularly appropriate in urban and peri-urban conditions, which, by all precedent, will be the focal growing points as development proceeds. Such taxes have four great merits from the local point of view: first, the base is unequivocally localized, a condition which is far from being realized in the case of an income tax. Secondly, irrespective of the precise base of valuation used, the revenue is relatively stable, because real estate values are notoriously sticky. Thirdly, these taxes are eminently suitable as the balancing factor in local budgets, since, once the valuation has been made, it is a matter of simple arithmetic to calculate the poundage necessary to produce a given sum. Finally, although in so far as the effective incidence falls on occupiers it tends to be regressive, this is usually less so than in respect of other taxes on outlay.[1]

Taxes on land and buildings are essentially urban taxes, especially in the tropics where there is much less need for substantial houses than in colder countries. That is not to say that they are useless in rural conditions. Some of the West Indies, are exceptional in trying to apply them throughout the islands; it must be borne in mind, however, that scattered throughout the larger islands there are substantial little urban clusters where a tax of this nature is perfectly appropriate. Since in Jamaica the rate is the only local tax of any importance (apart from service charges)[2] the share of local revenue derived from it is naturally substantial. In 1956–7 Kingston's percentage was 53%; the parishes varied from just under 30% (in poor St. Elizabeth) to nearly 40% (in wealthy St. Catherine). A few years previously the rate had financed a much higher percentage of revenue. Latterly parish budgets have been increasingly supported by grants.

[1] Cf. J. R. and U. K. Hicks, *The Incidence of Local Rates in Great Britain*, 1945.
[2] And also a small levy on 'wheels and horse kind', cf. J. R. and U. K. Hicks, *Finance and Taxation in Jamaica*, 1955.

Trinidad's County Councils do even better, especially in view of the fact that they were only inaugurated in 1953. By 1956 the total collected in land and building taxes already substantially exceeded that of the Jamaican parishes (£871,000 as against £556,000)[1] and the contribution to local revenues appears to have been close on 90%. Moreover collections were expected to rise at a much faster rate than in Jamaica. The Jamaican Estimates, however, do not take account of the potentialities of the revaluation which has been in progress since 1956.

Next in precedence, although not in importance, is the rate based on the annual value of land and buildings in the towns of India and Ceylon. Bombay (as we have seen) derived 46% of its revenue from this source; a level of 40% is quite usual, and this is the average figure for the Ceylon municipalities. On the whole, however (for reasons which we shall have to examine in Chapter 16), the tax is not really used to full advantage in Indian and Ceylonese towns.

There is little doubt that the most efficient use of a tax belonging to this category is at present in East and Central Africa, where the existence of a number of European-type towns leads to the erection of more substantial buildings and a more orderly delineation of plot boundaries. All these territories discriminate in favour of buildings; in Kenya and Tanganyika they are wholly derated, elsewhere buildings are rated at a fraction of the land poundage. The importance of the tax in local budgets in Kenya is considerable; Mombasa 61%, Nairobi 41%, Nakuru 39%. (These differences are not the reflection of grant differences, but rather of varying receipts from fees and profits.) Uganda is rather less successful, Kampala deriving only 34% of its revenue from this source, but this is partly the reflection of heavy grants in aid.

Kenya is also trying to develop an appropriate tax on land and buildings both for County Councils and for Urban and Rural County Districts.[2] Nairobi County Council was getting 11% of its revenue from this source. In the peri-urban area of Nairobi Urban District a substantial revenue has been quickly worked up,

---

[1] £692,000 including service charges, in Trinidad only sanitary services are separately charged for. The figures for the two islands are not strictly comparable because part of the Jamaican tax has traditionally been assigned to central government. This is effectively redistributed on a needs basis.
[2] See below, Chap. 20.

amounting to 60% of the council's revenue. In Naivasha Rural District and Kericho Urban District the contributions from this source are respectively 81% and 48%. Although in money terms the revenue is not large (since the range of the councils' duties is still small), these contributions seem to indicate a significant reserve of tax potential which has not hitherto been tapped. The Kenya government (as we have seen) looks forward to the day when some form of local tax on land and buildings can be extended to African District Councils. Although the possibility of this still lies some way in the future, it is not altogether inconceivable in those areas where farms have been consolidated under individual ownership (such as Nyeri and Kipsigis). The valuation of farm land, however, raises significantly different (and more difficult) problems than the valuation of urban land. This is a matter which we shall discuss in Chapter 21.

In view of the small amount of individual land holding in West Africa it is not surprising that outside those urban areas which have substantial non-African populations, little use has so far been made of a local rate on land and buildings. In Sierra Leone, Freetown and the Colony peninsula are appropriate for its application since the way of life of the Creoles corresponds more closely to that of the West Indies than to the rest of the Coast. Freetown has a well-established system of rating on annual value. A new valuation came into force in 1957–8, raising the rateable value from £255,000 to £450,000. With a poundage of 3s. 3d. a revenue of over £70,000 can be raised, which served to cover 87% of the current budget.

The rest of the Colony is badly in need of revaluing, so that it is not surprising to find that the wealthier peri-urban councils would like to change over to a graduated rate which, in default of a revaluation would be an easy (though unsatisfactory) way for them to raise additional revenue which is badly needed to provide modern services. Outside the Colony area Bo, the one other municipality, uses a primitive but not unsuccessful form of rate[1] which provides 57% of its revenue. The extension of this form of rating to other areas in the Provinces has been recommended,[2] and for this there is some incentive since the central government has frozen the rate of personal tax at a flat sum of 25s.[3]

[1] Valuation is not professional and is based simply on size and type, not quality or position.   [2] By the Wann Committee, cit.
[3] See above, p. 202.

In Nigeria Lagos also has a well-established system of rates based on annual value and kept up to date by professional valuers. In the Western Region as a whole, however, the only areas which were using a tax on land and buildings were Benin City (where it met 35% of the current budget), and Sapele Urban District (where it contributed 9%). Both of these are areas with substantial 'stranger' elements and large buildings. With the high and progressive income tax now established in the Region a rapid expansion of a tax on land and buildings is unlikely. In the Eastern Region there is less difficulty in extending a property rate, and there is a strong incentive to do so, since the Regional government put a ceiling (now 15s. a taxpayer) on the personal tax on the introduction of the Regional income tax in 1956. In 1957 there was a property rate in force in six council areas,[1] but the valuation was primitive and the poundages very low—ranging from 10d. to 2s. 6d.

The story is similar in Ghana, with perhaps a little more success in the wealthy cocoa areas, where the disappointing results of the personal tax have led some progressive councils to attempt to tax land and buildings, which cannot disappear into bush when the tax collector comes round. Of the Ghana towns Accra and Sekondi/ Takoradi seem to be the most successful with their property rates, deriving 27% of their revenue from this source. In both Nigeria and Ghana the law permits of the raising of a property rate equally with a personal tax. With the rapid development of these countries the scope for a tax on land and buildings is expanding year by year. In a number of towns there are already substantial areas with big buildings: offices, banks, hotels, and department stores, which are making little or no contribution to the costs of local government. The point need not be laboured here, however, since it will be our main concern in Chapter 16.

African direct taxes on persons, described variously as poll tax, hut tax, direct tax, general tax, personal tax, and 'income rates', are now (as has been said) the backbone of local autonomous revenue in the rural areas of all territories. In Nigeria and Ghana they are also generally important in urban areas, but not in Sierra Leone or the larger towns of East and Central Africa. By and large urban Africans in these territories do not pay the ordinary poll

[1] Enugu, Port Harcourt, Aba, Umahia, Calabar, and Onitsha.

taxes, and normally hold their houses on a tenancy too ephemeral to qualify for the local rate. They are thus undertaxed relatively to rural dwellers, a circumstance the consequences of which we shall have to discuss in Chapter 20.

In East Africa, percentagewise, the strongest use of local personal taxes is in Tanganyika. On the average of all councils the contribution to local budgets is 57%; the dispersion about this average is less than in the case of cesses, but in Lake Province a few councils derive 40% or less, while for others the contribution is over 75%. On the whole the rates of poll tax are not high; Bukoba with its lucrative coffee cess was able to get away with a flat sum of 22s., a very simple matter for those who were not coffee-growers. In wealthy Chaggaland tax rates were somewhat higher and proceeded in three steps. The total collections were not very large. In Lake Province only Bukoba exceeded £100,000, Geita and Mwanza, both good cotton areas, did not collect more than £64,400 and £52,500 respectively.

Percentagewise the next highest use of personal taxes was in Uganda, where contributions of 30% to 46% of revenue were usual. Exceptionally, Madi in the dry north found it difficult to raise revenue and had to be substantially grant-aided. These Uganda percentages represent very considerable sums. Even in 1956–7 for instance Busoga was collecting £276,000; by 1958–9 this had risen to £440,000;[1] Bugisu was getting £405,000 at the later date. (It must be remembered, however, that the Uganda Districts are very large.) These sums were all derived from graduated scales assessed on a method which we shall examine in the next chapter.

In Kenya both percentagewise and in money terms poll tax collections were very much lower, making contributions of about 10% to 31% of local revenue, but representing such small sums as £7,300 (in Samburu) and not more than £56,200, in Machakos, near Nairobi. These lower receipts relative to Uganda are partly explained by the smaller size of Kenya council areas, but mainly by the fact that the Territorial government retains the right to a graduated poll tax. It will be observed that in all three East African territories on the average the contribution of personal tax is very substantially higher than that of cesses; but it is understandable that the governments feel unable to take any immediate steps to abolish the latter.

Turning to the west coast: as we saw when we were following

[1] For the 1958–9 Bugisu scale see below, p. 341.

the history of Indirect Rule in Ghana, poll taxes have never been a strong source of revenue.[1] Nevertheless local bodies today derive some 20% of their revenue from this source. Exceptionally, among urban areas, Kumasi realized a contribution of 10%; and both in the relatively wealthy Eastern Region and in Trans-Volta Togoland (potentially wealthy but little developed), some councils were getting well over 30% of their revenue from this source. On the whole, however, the total budgets were very small, so that the actual sums collected were not large.

In Northern Nigeria the share of the 'general tax' in Native Authority revenues is very high, more especially in the Middle Belt areas, where there are no cattle and consequently no jangali to help out. Thus Basso Komo's budget (in Kabba Province) relied as to 75% on this source, heavily populated Kano had a 77% contribution. Other high percentages were Igala (in Kabba) also 72%, Tiv (Benue) 70%, and Zaria 67%: for a Northern Native Treasury to have relied on this tax for less than 40% (as Jos, 38%, did), was quite exceptional. Because of large populations the sums collected were sometimes substantial (£838,000 in Kano, £505,000 in Sokoto); but the variation was immense (Kamuku in Niger Province was only collecting £6,200). Moreover rates of tax were nowhere high, the Regional average being around 33s.[2]

Unfortunately the 1956–7 figures for Southern Nigeria are now of historical interest only, for both the West and the East were inaugurating entirely new systems of Regional taxation, designed in each case to raise a large amount of additional revenue to finance the establishment of universal free public education (U.P.E.). The situation was further complicated by tiering and precepting. In the Western Region, before the change took place, contributions of direct tax to local budgets were of the order of 25–30%. Benin City's percentage was, however, 46%, while allowing for precepting some District Councils had very high percentages (65% to 81%). In the Eastern Region there were some high percentages, 44% in Okrika, 27% in the towns of Aba and Calabar and 41% in the two municipalities of Enugu and Port Harcourt. On the whole the contribution of poll tax to local revenues was lower in the East than in the West.

[1] See above, pp. 90 ff.
[2] This excludes small collections under the progressive scale (Schedule II). See Report of Revenue Allocation Commission, 1951, cit.

Under the new Regional income tax systems the situation has diverged completely in the two Regions. In the West rights over 'income tax' on the first £300 of income were left to the Local Authorities. An initial rate[1] of 2½% (in some areas 3%) was imposed, on a presumed money income of £50 a year; at the upper limit the contribution could reach £15, thus rivalling Uganda in the successful tapping of tax potential. In the Eastern Region in contrast, a ceiling of 5s. a head (soon raised to 15s.)[2] was placed on the direct tax, thus severely cutting down local autonomous revenue. Budgets were supported at about the old level by additional grants, but the significance of the change was that the right to expanding revenue was transferred to the Regional government, except in so far as the Local Authorities could develop the property rate.

These African personal taxes which we have been regarding as local, began life everywhere as central government levies, established in the pioneering stages of colonization. They reflect the British Treasury's constant and determined policy of requiring the Colonies to finance themselves as far as possible (which usually was not very far). From the first, however, poll tax (or hut tax as it then often was)[3] tended to be collected locally. The custom naturally arose of allowing Native Treasuries to retain some part of it for their own use. This share tended to get larger and larger as Territorial governments developed other sources of revenue, principally import and export duties. As the post-war drive for the development of local government institutions gathered force, the tendency was for the local councils to be given more and more liberty in choosing their tax rates, and some central (or Regional) governments have reduced their share virtually to vanishing point.

In Northern Nigeria, exceptionally, the tax remains very much a government tax, the Region taking on the average 10% of general tax and 10% of jangali, where it exists. In Uganda the Protectorate government deliberately reduced its share to 6s. a head in order to encourage the development of District personal taxes, an objective in which it succeeded almost too well. In Tanganyika on the other hand the Territorial government runs a graduated tax more

[1] The Western Region income tax has the distinction of being quite modern in that it is assessed incrementally, at so much in the pound.
[2] See above, p. 175.
[3] It has been claimed that assessment on huts, rather than on males of taxable age (normally 16 or 18 to 60, in so far as age could be gauged), imparted a slight progression, because wealthy taxpayers would own a number of huts.

or less in competition with the local one. How this may work can be seen in the Chagga District. The top range of the two taxes is the same, but the local tax is tougher at the lower end, to compensate for the coffee cess paid in addition to personal tax by the wealthier farmers.

With the exception of Northern Nigeria where Lugard, building on the Moslem *tithe*[1] was able to introduce a tax which paid some attention to ability to pay,[2] all the personal taxes started as flat sum levies. Flat sum taxes still exist in a number of places: in parts of Tanganyika, even Uganda, and as we have seen in Kenya, so far as the local tax is concerned, also in Sierra Leone and parts of Ghana. It was early evident that, for the sake of taxpayers who were only on the margin of the cash economy, the flat sum would have to be set so low that revenue would be very restricted, so that there has been a strong incentive to introduce graduated rates as soon as it was deemed politically feasible.[3] All over Nigeria graduated rates already existed in 1950, they were on a Regional rather than on a local base, but (especially in the West) very wide local discretion in fixing rates was allowed.[4] Revenue collected under the graduated section was, however, very small. It was not until the introduction of Regional income taxes in 1956–7 that tax potential began to be effectively tapped. It should be noted, however, that a graduated poll tax does not necessarily imply a progressive tax; in practice the steps seldom add up to more than a proportional levy. Nevertheless the highly successful expansion of personal taxation in Africa since 1950 does suggest that the foundations of modern income tax are being laid, and that it is possible to look forward to its extended use as an instrument of control. The further discussion of this must, however, be postponed to the next chapter.

Before we leave the discussion of direct taxation in local budgets there are two or three other points to be cleared up. As has been said, the personal tax is not strictly speaking a local tax, and the extent to which local bodies can *de facto* consider it independent revenue differ materially from country to country. It is clear that central governments cannot permit Local Authorities indefinite rights in this potentially most valuable source of revenue, and it is

[1] See above, p. 96.
[2] See pp. 331–2.
[3] In Uganda the existence of the 1901 Agreement with Buganda blocked the way to graduation until a new Agreement was signed, see above, p. 209.
[4] Cf. Report of Revenue Allocation Commission, cit., 1951.

significant that in Uganda and Western Nigeria, the two areas
where it has developed most fully, the central (Regional) governments have already put a limit on local powers. As we shall argue
below,[1] there is no inherent reason why central and local rights in
the tax should not be delineated so that each can enjoy a share in an
expanding source of revenue without impinging on the field of the
other.

A question of more immediate importance is concerned with the
extent to which tax payments recorded in budgets represent on the
one hand what taxpayers really do pay, and on the other what they
really should pay. First of all there is everywhere a chronic danger
of fraud; this cannot be wholly eliminated so long as taxpayers are
illiterate. The extent of cheating by tax collectors can only gradually be reduced as the standard of training and morals among
them rises. There is no reason to think however that fraud in tax
collection is very large in the better conducted, more sophisticated
areas, especially where tax is paid directly into a tax office and
quickly banked.

An allied trouble is that although in every territory traditional
payments to chiefs and similar authorities have been stopped
by Ordinance, in those areas where chiefs are still strong, and
especially where regular gifts to the chief are still considered part
of the natural order of things, such contributions may still reach
very large proportions. The Cox Commission[2] in Sierra Leone
came to the conclusion that effective tax payments had been running three times as high as the official rate. Whenever a people
seems to be particularly allergic to paying a moderate tax, a
government would do well to inquire into this factor. On the other
hand in some areas large voluntary contributions are made for
local purposes. The great Indian Community Development movement relies almost wholly on these at the local end. In Eastern
Nigeria 'sons abroad' take an active and willing part in developing
their home villages.[3] In these cases effective tax is also higher than
it looks, but is of course less reliable than a formal levy.

Finally there is the difficult problem of assessing the extent to
which revenue is lost either because the Local Authorities responsible fail to keep an accurate roll of those liable to tax, or because

[1] See p. 343.
[2] Commission of Inquiry into Disturbances, cit., see above, p. 201.
[3] See Chap. 21, pp. 525–6.

of deliberate favouritism to relatives or fear of the local big man.
The extent of this trouble no doubt differs enormously from place
to place; but it is hardly likely to be completely absent anywhere.
In Ghana the local rolls are known to be extremely faulty; in some
areas they hardly exist. In Buganda, until very recently, the crudest
methods of tax collection were used, and the results were far
below potential, or even what was being achieved in neighbouring
(on the whole less wealthy) Districts. In Northern Nigeria the
method of lump sum assessment gives the local assessor great
liberty in making things easy for particular people.

There are now several ways in which a central government can
check a local tax roll. In Nigeria the census record has been called
on. In the Northern Region it revealed a suspiciously stationary
level of the taxpaying population.[1] A further check became
available through the electoral roll for the hotly contested federal
elections. The inference is that the tax roll was not more than 80%
complete. In the Eastern Region the general impression was that
the roll had no more than 70% coverage. A recent check up (similar
to that in the North), carried out by the Regional Statistics Office,
suggests that even this may have been over-optimistic. In the
Western Region the first valuation in Abeokuta (a town of nearly
500,000 inhabitants) revealed a number of rateable hereditaments
which was roughly double the number of registered taxpayers.[2]
Clearly the first step to improvement is better knowledge of the
actual situation. Nearly everywhere, however, there are signs of
improvement. It seems not unreasonable to hope that as the understanding of the taxpayers in the benefits made possible by the local
revenue grows, and the honesty and expertise of local tax officers
improves, erring taxpayers will gradually be brought into the fold,
and thereby the whole standard of compliance raised.

IV

As we saw earlier in the chapter, in addition to the independent
taxes which we have just been examining, local budgets in all our
countries receive additional—and generally increasing—assistance
by way of grants from higher layer governments. These inevitably

[1] Similarly jangali collections implied that there was no rise in the cattle
population, which was contrary to experience. Cf. G. R. I. Dees, Papers on
Native Authority Finance, No. 2 (unpublished), and see above, p. 182.
[2] Information from Ministry of Local Government, Ibadan.

affect the scope, and in some degree the structure, of the local budget; they are also an important element in the relations between central and local government. In this chapter we are concerned only to discover the quantitative importance of different grants on current account in local budgets, leaving both the examination of grants on capital account and the general discussion of principles to a later stage.

There is some difference of opinion as to what constitutes a grant, so that this point must first be cleared up. In colonial conditions grants are often given in the form of an *ex post* payment which then appears as a reimbursement, but in so far as the funds were employed for the purposes of the Local Authority, and are not a payment for services rendered to the central government by the Local Authority acting as its agent, they are really a grant. In the belief that the majority of reimbursements shown in Local Authority budgets are of the former type, I have endeavoured to include them in the grant total.

A more important difficulty arises over the payment of (property) rates on government property. Central governments are always careful to state that these payments are made in lieu of rates, implicitly suggesting that they are *ex gratia*. In fact there is no reason why governments should not pay for the local services from which their property benefits, as much as anybody else. It is true that government property is often of a type whose value cannot easily be ascertained by normal valuation procedure; but this need not constitute an insuperable obstacle. A particular problem arises in those areas where at the time of acquisition, the Crown was declared the ultimate landowner, because this now implies that the central government may find itself a very large ratepayer, over 50% of rate revenue, or even more, being contributed by the Crown.[1] This percentage will, however, gradually decline as development takes place, and land is let on long leases which will make the tenant subject to the property rate.

We are also excluding from grants intergovernmental payments which are in essence assigned revenues (which have already been included in their respective places), i.e. the local share of government poll tax (or in some countries the government share of local poll tax), has been included in autonomous revenues in so far as it accrues locally. As we have seen, revenue from motor licences is

---

[1] For instance in Kisumu, Kenya.

often assigned. In India Land Revenue collected by the Districts is sometimes assigned to lower layer authorities; although in some states a separate 'cess' is levied at the local level. In Jamaica the Island government has traditionally taken a percentage of parish rates for its own use, under the name of the 'property tax'.

In modern conditions, which virtually presuppose substantial grants from higher layer governments in support of local budgets, counter grants from local to central would seem to be a clumsy anachronism. In 1946 Sir Sidney Phillipson argued[1] that such payments were necessary as a means of interesting local taxpayers in the doings of the central government. Nowadays it can be assumed that local governments are extremely well aware of the activities of the central government, yet the payments persist. In some areas they are based on a percentage of local revenue, in which case, in absolute terms, they withdraw more from the rich than from the poor areas. The tendency seems, however, for them to take the form of *per capita* payments; consequently they tend to be somewhat disequalizing, unless the heavily populated areas are also the more wealthy, which is by no means always the case.

As we have seen, countries which have grown up under the new pattern of colonial finance have tended to assume that local bodies will need a substantial grant element in their revenue structures. Grants also play an important part in some countries brought up under the old pattern. In Jamaica, as we have seen, since the freezing of rate poundages, grants have tended steadily to expand.[2] In 1953–4 the range was from 19 to 44% of local budgets, varying inversely with the wealth of the parish; by 1958–9 the range had become 37·5% to 55·1%, and in spite of this the budget of six out of the thirteen parishes were in deficit. In Ceylon also, grants are a very important ingredient of local budgets: on the average for municipalities they constituted 30% (in 1957 Nuwara Eliya was getting 35% but this was in some sense a special case).[3] The smaller local bodies in Ceylon were even more dependent on grants:[4] on the average for urban authorities 54%, town councils (smaller and more rural) 50%, and village committees 61%. These last are very largely the reflection of the failure to develop adequate sources of local revenue.

[1] In recommending the establishment of 'code' grants, see p. 168.
[2] See above, p. 285.   [3] See above, p. 285.
[4] For discussion of the form of these grants see Chap. 18, p. 423.

In urban India the situation is very different. Bombay in 1956 was getting no more than 3%[1] of its revenue from grants, Poona 8%. A decade earlier urban grants seem to have been rather more important; Mysore was getting 9%, Kolapor 11%, and this seems to have been about the normal order of magnitude. The situation is substantially different in the rural areas. In many states District Boards were obtaining 40–50% of their revenue by way of grant. States now absorbed (Saurashtra, Travancore-Cochin) were giving grants of the order of 75–80%; on the other hand West Bengal only gave grants amounting to 10% and Bihar 7·4% of District revenues. Grants to all levels of local government will doubtless expand in India, as on the one hand the states get more interested in the development of local government, and, on the other the Union government evolves additional means of channelling local grants through the states. Nevertheless the shortage of revenue at all levels of government in India, must continue to be a handicap until the tax system can be made more effective.

Of the places where local government has been set up more recently Tanganyika is unique in not conforming to pattern. On the average local bodies get no more than 9% of their revenue from this source; prosperous districts like Morogoro and Mwanza get virtually nothing by way of grant on current account.[2] Uganda and Kenya are both strong believers in grants, although Uganda is less sure of this as a policy since it allowed the Districts to collect so much by graduated tax.[3] In 1956–7 most of the Uganda councils were getting 38–50% of their revenue in this way; Madi exceptionally was getting 65%. It should be noted that in both Uganda and Kenya not all the grants come from the central government.

[1] According to figures supplied to me by the Municipal Authorities. The Tax Inquiry Commission quoted a much higher figure, but capital grants were also included. Municipal average percentages of grants to total revenue for the major states, as given by the latter source were: Assam 8·5%, Bihar 22·9%, Bombay 16·7%, Madya Pradesh 8·7%, Madras 12·9%, Orissa 25·1%, Punjab 4·2%, Uttar Pradesh 15·2%, West Bengal 18·0%, Hyderabad 5·1%, Madya Bharat 4·2%.

[2] On capital account the Territorial government is a little more generous, as it needs to be, since there is no effective Local Loans Board.

[3] For 1958–9 Busoga, which as we have seen had increased its tax revenue very substantially (from £772,000 to £823,000 within a year) had its grant cut from £444,000 to £160; but this seems to have been exceptional, although an excuse was made of the boycott of Asians in Buganda to reduce its grant also. In fact the fall in cotton prices (and hence export tax revenue) was somewhat embarrassing the Protectorate budget.

Some are from separate funds, such as in Kenya from the Roads Authority; but on current account these other sources are usually quite minor, being mainly reserved for development.

In Kenya the average level for grants to African District Councils was 45% of revenue, with a definite bias in favour of the poorer areas: Narok (Masai) was getting 61% and Kilifi (on the coast) 73%; further differentials are planned. Kenya, however, is much tougher on its towns than Uganda. Kampala got away with 52% of grants, the Kenya towns get no more than 12% or 13%. The most heavily grant-aided areas in Kenya are the Settled Area Councils. Before the institution of County Councils the District Councils derived practically the whole of their revenue from grants —almost wholly for road works. The grants to County Councils are also high: 61–86%. Some of these, however, are temporary, tapering, grants for setting up expenses of general administration and for the taking over of health services.

On the west coast grants everywhere tend to be high, except in Northern Nigeria, where the mode lay around 15% with some Native Authorities getting as little as 7%. Even in the conservative North, however, grants are tending to increase in importance, rising from £830,000 in 1953–4 to £1,340,000 in 1959–60.[1] In Ghana grants amounting to 30–40% of revenue were common, a few very weak and small authorities (which are due for suppression under the area reorganization started in 1958) getting 80% or more of their revenue from the government.

In Western Nigeria, District Council grants were perhaps rather lower than in Ghana, but there was a very wide spread between them. Little Ese Odo (Okitipupa), surely a strong case for assistance, got no more than 6%, Benin City even less; but the mode was somewhere around 35%. Ikeja, however, got 64%. In the Eastern Region the range was definitely higher, Districts on their own getting over 70%. Some Districts within counties were getting less than this (Aba Urban 43%), but many were getting quite as much. When the new system of block grants is fully reflected in the accounts percentages will presumably be moved on to a still higher range.

In both the southern Regions of Nigeria, and in Ghana, in areas where tiering had been established, we find the same

[1] Education grants were responsible for this rapid increase, see p. 311.

phenomenon as in Kenya: it is the upper layer in a tiered system which has to be heavily grant-aided. This was true in Nigeria, notwithstanding fairly substantial precepting on the lower layer. In Ghana the upper layer councils normally received over 60% of their revenue by way of grant; Tonga in Trans-Volta Togoland actually received 95%. In Western Nigeria grants over 60% of revenue were almost the rule for Divisional Councils, Asaba for instance was getting 81%. In the Eastern Region a number of County Councils received more than 80% of their revenue from grants, as contrasted with roughly 5–13% from precepts. These Nigerian figures partly reflect the near failure of precepting; but they also suggest that local government finance will gain rather than lose in autonomy by the abolition of tiering.

This brief examination of the importance of grants in local government finance in Jamaica, in India and Ceylon and in different parts of Africa, prompts two questions. First, were the grants of a nature to stimulate or to stultify local initiative on the one hand and to promote or discourage good housekeeping on the other? Secondly, did they in any way reflect a coherent and consistent policy, or were they merely a series of unrelated measures? Here we can do no more than supply some of the materials for answers to these questions, which will be discussed more generally in Chapter 18.[1]

Block grants as a type get good marks both from the point of view of leaving Local Authorities to plan their own priorities unfettered, and from the consideration that an equalizing element can relatively easily be included. Their main drawbacks are firstly, absence of direct stimulus to activity, and, secondly, that unless specific conditions (for instance concerning general standards of performance) are written in, they give no incentive for careful management. Naturally the larger the grant in relation to the total budget, the more serious does this drawback become. As we have seen, there is a clear line of distinction between those countries which do, and those which do not, favour block grants, but we have not yet inquired into the relative importance of block and specific grants in their budgets, or into the extent to which they attempt either equalization or the promotion of better management.

[1] On the information available it is not possible to discern any coherent pattern in Indian state grants to lower authorities. (I suspect that lack of data is not the only obstacle.) In Sierra Leone also, in this (as in most respects) statistics are lacking.

The Eastern Region of Nigeria has (since the changes of 1956)[1] become one of the highest users of block grants. County Councils and Districts on their own have been getting over 80% of their grants in block form, Rural District Councils frequently 70–80%, and only Urban District Councils less than 50%. The large block element is partly fortuitous, since the original proposal was to give a 50% specific grant for approved health services but this was dropped for want of revenue. Further, under the new arrangements only the grants for the small number of publicly owned schools come to the councils, the Mission Schools receive their grants direct from the Region. There is no strong equalization factor. The system works out in practice as a capitation grant, of 3s. a head in rural areas, to be shared between District and Local Councils, and 4s. a head in urban areas. But on the other hand the demoralizing potentiality of very high grants is mitigated by a rather strict control of local budgets by the Ministry of Local Government. Jamaica is also a high block grant country, 66% of grant revenue being of this type; there is also a not negligible equalization factor,[2] but no very definite control of efficiency.

In Ghana the block element in grants is about the same. Accra gets 66% of its grants in this way, Cape Coast somewhat more. In Ceylon the block element is substantial, and is based on a complicated amalgam of population and revenue collection, arranged in such a way as to assist the smaller but not necessarily the poorer authorities.[3] Uganda makes but small use of block grants, although Kampala gets 20% of its grant revenue in this form. Kenya at present bases its block grant to African District Councils on poll tax revenue, hence the grant is broadly correlated with population; but a more equalizing system is planned, and this will be accompanied by a condition as to performance.[4] At present the block element averages about 14% of grant revenue.

In contrast to block grants the main advantages of specific grants are stimulus and control, and these are very valuable factors. At the same time there is a danger that they may upset the balance of local budgeting. Further, if pressed too far they may be seriously

[1] See above, p. 175.
[2] See Chap. 18, pp. 422 ff. Most of the remainder of the grants take the form of 'special' road grants. Although the allocation of these is determined mainly by political bargaining, the grants are more or less geared to the level of unemployment and so provide an additional equalizing factor.
[3] See below, p. 421.   [4] See Chap. 18, p. 423.

disequalizing, since only the wealthier authorities can afford to take full advantage of the bait offered.

The firmest believers in specific grants appear to be the Northern and Western Regions of Nigeria, and Uganda.[1] In all these areas the main grant-aided services are education (including teachers' salaries), public health and medical (especially the latter), roads and staff salaries, more or less in that order. Smaller specific grants are given for veterinary and agricultural activities, for instance in Northern and Western Nigeria, and in the same Regions for Native Authority police. These are important in the North and absorb 22% of grants; in the West, however, the outlay is negligible. The North also gives small grants for social welfare, for libraries, and for a number of miscellaneous services. This Region appears to be an example of the lack of coherence which arises when one specific grant is piled on top of another.[2]

Another local peculiarity of some interest is the 11% of Jamaican grants given in respect of emergency expenditure by Parish Councils. This is awarded in the form of a bundle of separate grants for particular purposes; both the total and the allocation between parishes varies from year to year, depending on the recentness and size of the latest hurricane or earthquake; but in Jamaican climatic conditions such grants can almost be regarded as a regular part of revenue. Generally speaking (as already argued) it is more efficient that emergencies should be relieved in this manner rather than by locking up parish funds in local reserves. A further small specific grant is given in Jamaica, and also in Trinidad, for trucking water to 'drought stricken' areas. In these well-watered islands it might be supposed that better attention to waterworks would eliminate this necessity.

Everywhere the education grant is by far the largest of the specific grants and also the most rapidly expanding.[3] The grant is usually almost wholly concentrated on teachers' salaries, although some areas (for instance Western Nigeria) also very wisely give grants for school administration and inspection. In this Region the grant amounts to 87% of *approved* teachers' salaries. Local Authorities must guarantee to provide not only the remaining 13%

---

[1] In Uganda the grant is for general administration purposes.

[2] Cf. G. R. I. Dees, Papers on Native Authority Finance, No. 2 (unpublished).

[3] In Northern Nigeria, a backward area in this respect, the grant has grown from £84,000 to £607,000 over the decade 1950–60.

but also £10 a teacher and 5s. a pupil, for equipment. It is common for education grants to amount to 60 or 70% of all specific grants.

Health and medical grants are sometimes given in the form of a block allocation; of this type are Kenya's grants to County Councils taking over health services, and Western Nigeria's 10% of approved expenditure. Ceylon prefers a number of small specific grants: for conservancy and scavenging, maternity and child welfare, Ayurvedic (traditional) medicine and dispensaries (Western type). Nowhere are combined health and medical grants of massive proportions, save in Kenya's municipalities where they represent 56% of total grants. (It will be recalled, however, that in these areas education is wholly a central charge.) Kenya's African District Councils get 11% of their grants for health. In Western Nigeria in addition to the 10% 'code' grant there have been grants in connexion with a special programme; the combined effect varies greatly from area to area. Thus Ife Division was getting 13% of its grants for health services, Warri Urban District Council no more than 2%. In the Northern Region health grants averaged about 10%.

As we should expect, the highest percentage of road in relation to other grants is in the Kenya Settled Areas, where the County Councils get 72% of their grants for this purpose. The Kenya towns receive 19% of their grants for roads and streets, but the African District Councils no more than 9%; results on road standards of these differences are naturally very marked. Road grants in Uganda are low (Kampala gets only 7% of its grants for this purpose); road grants, however, are the less necessary in Uganda since an efficient Public Works Department is in charge of the system as a whole. In Ghana there appear to be no specific grants for roads, yet as we have seen, local road expenditure is rather exceptionally high. Presumably Ghanaans are more road conscious than Northern Nigerians, where until recently the Regional government was awarding nearly 20% of grants (£224,000) for communications.

Assistance with the salaries of local officers is a very general form of specific grant, which we shall have to discuss further in Chapter 18, since it provides one of the best methods of control of personnel, both in respect of personal and professional qualifications. The greater part of these grants at present is, however, given in the form of temporary help to cover additional pay scales negotiated through national channels. The importance of these in some areas is quite substantial. In Kampala it amounts to 35% of all grants; in Eastern Nigeria the percentages vary from 10% to over 30%. In the Western Region they do not appear to exceed 20%, and elsewhere are less important. Sooner or later these will have to be consolidated into unified grants; the opportunities for effective control will thereby be greatly improved. So far Kenya and Western Nigeria appear to have the most efficient plans in this direction.[1]

Can anything general be said, as a result of these comparisons, concerning first, the balance of aid as between different services, and secondly, as concerns the balance within the grant structures in the various territories? The three basic services which local bodies can play an important part in providing are clearly education (when the size of the country permits of some local responsibility), public health, and communications. On the whole the balance between these three seems to be reasonably in accordance with what the peoples would desire. It must be noted, however, that the universal tendency to favour social expenditure rather than outlay that will directly raise the gross national product is strengthened rather than counteracted by grant allocations.

An important illustration of this is in respect of road grants. A rapid development of communications is a vital part of the development process, whether at the very early stages when the population is still more or less confined to subsistence agriculture, or at a later stage when they begin to see the twentieth century within their grasp. Local communities cannot be expected to take much interest in roads that they are never likely to use. If higher grants do not stimulate activity it may well be that the central government would be better advised to take responsibility for a greater share of road development itself; but higher grants could first be tried.

On the whole, balance within grant structures is best attained in Kenya, which uses both specific and block grants in judicious proportions, and always with definite objectives in mind (such as control of quality of local government officers, by specific grant, and greater equalization by block grant). Elsewhere the countries

[1] See Chaps. 18 and 22. In Western Nigeria a Departmental Committee on the Financial Relations between the Regional Government and the Local Authorities (Beasley Report, 1957) recommended that a 50% grant should be made towards the salaries of secretaries and treasurers. In the absence of approved qualifications no grant would be available.

that favour unallocated grants tend to allow them to reach levels that would on U.K. standards be considered so high as to require stringent controls in other directions, and so would seriously undermine local financial responsibility. There is little evidence that effective other controls are likely to be available in semi-developed conditions.

On the other hand those countries which rely mainly on specific grants have been faced with two difficulties. First they seem to have found it difficult to resist requests for additional small grants for this and that, secondly, once given, the grants have tended to be 'open ended', with the grant-giving authority unable to control the total because insufficiently stringent conditions for the award have not been included. Northern Nigeria is a typical case of both of these difficulties. With the high levels which these grants have been allowed to reach the two drawbacks to specific grants (noted above) come into play. There is a real danger of distortion of budgets, and even more of those areas which are highly grant-aided being enabled increasingly to pull ahead of the others. This is certainly so in respect of the education grants in Northern Nigeria, from which the Yoruba areas in the Middle Belt benefit much more than the Moslem areas.

These considerations do not imply that there is, generally speaking, too much grant aid to Local Authorities, they do call, however, for a better consideration of principles and balance. These are matters which we shall discuss in Chapter 18.

TABLE 7

GHANA

Main Heads of Current Revenue (1956–7) as Percentages of Total Current Revenue

| | Fees, fines, profits % | Interest, rent % | Taxation on | | Licences % | Grants % |
			Persons %	Property and land %		
Towns						
Accra . .	25	1	—	27	5	40
Cape Coast .	29	1	2	22	5	41
Sekondi/Takoradi	16	1	—	27	3	52
Kumasi . .	31	2	10	24	4	28
Regions (without towns)						
Eastern . .	21	—	22	8	2	47
Western . .	18	—	15	8	2	57
Trans-Volta Togoland .	13	—	21	4	1	60
Ashanti . .	14	—	24	15	1	45
Northern . .	7	—	14	4	1	74

Source: Ghana Local Government Financial Statistics.
Note: Taxation of land: the only entries are as follows: Eastern 7%; Western 7%; Ashanti 5%.

TABLE 8

NIGERIA, NORTHERN REGION

Native Authorities

Main Heads of Current Revenue (1956–7) as Percentages of Total Current Revenue (Largest and Smallest N. A. Budgets in Each Province)

Province	Fees, fines, profits %	Interest, rent %	Taxation on		Licences %	Grants %
			Persons %	Production %		
Adamawa						
Adamawa . .	7	neg.	44	28	neg.	15
Numan . .	11	neg.	61	14	neg.	12
Bauchi						
Bauchi . .	8	neg.	59	13	neg.	17
Jama'ari .	9	neg.	61	11	neg.	13
Benue						
Tiv . . .	9	neg.	70	neg.	2	13
Keffi . . .	6	neg.	55	10	3	19
Bornu						
Bornu . . .	2	7	48	27	—	15
Bedde . . .	4	1	57	19	—	16
Ilorin						
Ilorin . . .	15	neg.	61	2	2	16
Pategi . . .	7	neg.	56	—	—	36
Kabba						
Igala . . .	14	neg.	72	—	—	11
Bassa Komo .	8	neg.	75	—	—	11
Kano						
Kano . . .	1	neg.	79	10	1	7
Kazaure . .	4	neg.	68	15	neg.	10
Katsina						
Katsina . .	10	neg.	61	12	neg.	13
Daura . . .	17	neg.	56	19	neg.	7
Niger						
Bida . . .	8	neg.	50	neg.	neg.	36
Kamuku . .	6	2	42	10	—	34
Plateau						
Jos . . .	22	neg.	38	14	neg.	20
Wase . . .	4	neg.	56	—	neg.	39
Sokoto						
Sokoto . .	5	1	68	12	neg.	13
Yauri . . .	—	3	63	20	—	13
Zaria						
Zaria . . .	11	neg.	67	4	neg.	14
Jema'a . .	6	neg.	73	1	—	19

Source: Northern Region Native Administration Estimates.
Notes: 1. Jangali.
2. Apart from a negligible revenue in Zaria, there appears to be no taxation of land and buildings.

TABLE 9

NIGERIA, EASTERN REGION

Main Heads of Current Revenue (1956–7) as Percentages of Total Current Revenue (Sample Budgets)

	Fees, fines, profits %	Interest %	Taxation on persons %	Licences %	Grants %
District Councils with County Council powers					
Afikpo	4	neg.	16	neg.	77
Awgu	6	neg.	16	neg.	75
Ikom	8	neg.	17	8	72
Onitsha Urban . .	35	neg.	19	3	42
County Councils					
Abakaliki . . .	10	neg.	7	—	81
Aba/Ngwa . . .	16	neg.	9	—	68
Ikot Ekpene . . .	14	neg.	5	—	80
Nsukka . . .	5	neg.	12	—	83
Municipalities					
Enugu	8	neg.	41	3	45
Port Harcourt . .	11	neg.	41	4	36
District Councils					
Aba U.D.C. . . .	26	neg.	27	neg.	43
West Ahoada R.D.C. .	10	neg.	17	neg.	78
North Annan D.C. .	5	neg.	15	neg.	78
Okrika D.C. . . .	neg.	neg.	44	neg.	54
Okigwi North D.C. .	3	—	20	2	70
Owerri U.D.C. . .	13	—	8	neg.	76
Calabar U.D.C. . .	16	neg.	27	7	47

Source: Eastern Region Local Government Estimates.

Note: A local rate on Land and Buildings was in force in Enugu, Port Harcourt, and Aba, but the revenue was negligible.

TABLE 10

NIGERIA, WESTERN REGION

Main Heads of Current Revenue (1956–7) as Percentages of Total Current Revenue (Sample Budgets)

	Fees, fines, profits %	Interest %	Taxation on persons %	Licences %	Grants %
Divisional Councils with no District Councils					
West Ijaw . . .	11	neg.	18	neg.	67
Ijebo Remo . . .	11	neg.	23	neg.	65
Independent District Councils					
Ibadan. . . .	17	1	31	1	48
Ikeja	6	neg.	24	6	64
Divisional Councils with no District Councils					
Egba	11	neg.	23	—	66
Asaba	7	neg.	11	—	81
Ife	16	neg.	27	neg.	54
District Councils in Divisions					
Ese Odo . . .	9	neg.	81	4	6
Sapele Urban . .	20	neg.	29	4	34
Oyo South . .	3	1	78	6	10
Benin City . .	12	2	46	2	3
Asaba Urban . .	26	neg.	27	8	39
Ife	6	neg.	65	6	21

Source: Western Region Local Government Council Estimates.

Notes: 1. Sapele Urban had also local rate on Land and Buildings, 9% of revenue.

2. Benin City had also local rate on Land and Buildings, 35% of revenue.

TABLE II

UGANDA

African Local Councils

Main Heads of Current Revenue (1956–7) as Percentages of Total Current Revenue. (Largest and Smallest Council Budgets in Each Province)

| Province | Fees and profits % | Interest and rent % | Taxation of | | | Grants % |
			Persons %	Production %	Land bldgs. licences %	
Buganda . .	2	2	42	2	1	49
Eastern						
Busoga . .	6	3	46	7	—	38
Bukedi . .	7	1	47	1	—	42
Western						
Ankole . .	5	2	43	5	—	41
Bunyoro .	11	2	29	5	—	49
Northern						
Lango . .	9	neg.	42	neg.	—	47
Madi . .	5	neg.	25	neg.	—	65

Source: Uganda Local Government Accounts.

The Local Budget

TABLE 12

KENYA

African District Councils

Main Heads of Current Revenue (1956) as Percentages of Total Current
Revenue (Largest and Smallest Council Budgets in Each Province)

Province	Fees and profits %	Interest and rent %	Taxation of		Licences %	Grants %
			Persons %	Production %		
Nyanza						
S. Nyanza .	14	—	31	9	1	42
Kipsigis .	19	—	23	8	neg.	47
Rift Valley						
Nandi . .	30	—	14	9	2	43
Samburu .	34	—	23	—	neg.	41
Central						
Kiambu .	13	—	23	6	3	52
Meru . .	11	—	32	13	neg.	40
Southern						
Machakos .	12	—	25	5	2	54
Narok . .	15	—	18	4	neg.	61
Coast						
Kilifi . .	13	—	25	—	9	51
Tana River .	8	—	10	5	neg.	73
Northern						
Garissa . .	22	—	22	20	neg.	36

Source: Kenya African District Councils Approved Estimates.

15

THE TAXATION OF FARMERS AND
RURAL COMMUNITIES

I

ASEPARATE discussion of the taxation of farmers does not in any way imply that it is necessary or desirable to have any special form of tax for them alone; on the contrary it is obviously unfair that the tillers of the soil should be taxed, while other members of the rural community, such as those engaged in transport, merchanting, or administration, who may well have higher incomes, go free. Apart from questions of equity, the broader base a tax can be given the more easily can a given revenue be raised with moderate rates of tax. The rationale of this chapter is basically that in almost every country today general farm incomes[1] are lightly taxed relative to those derived from other occupations; this is true whether we are talking of advanced or backward countries. In developing countries the adequate taxation of the farming sector is more important than it is in advanced countries, since it has a special contribution to make to the smooth process of development.

In the first place in a pre-industrial country the farming sector is by far the largest in the economy, contributing perhaps 80% of the national product. If this predominant sector is undertaxed, either the other sectors will have to bear an unreasonably heavy tax burden or the development process will be slowed down for want of adequate finance. Secondly in almost all countries the agricultural sector has gained relatively to the other sectors, as compared with the situation in the 1930's; if it is also undertaxed this gain will be exaggerated. The relative improvement of farm incomes was especially marked during the war and immediate post-war period, and again during the 'Korean' boom of 1951–2. In the late 1950's it is true the 'terms of trade' between farm primary products and manufactured goods have partly swung back in the direction of industry, but they are still more favourable to primary products than they were in the 1930's.

[1] It is, however, true that particular types of farm incomes are often differentially taxed by export duties.

This is partly explained by the maintenance of a high level of demand in the fully employed advanced economies, as compared with their poor showing in the 1930's; partly it is due to the expansion of demand for farm products in the developing countries themselves. As incomes rise, the first additional demands in a poor country will be for farm products: food, and (at least in warm countries) cotton cloth. Further, as population shifts into urban and industrial occupations from more or less subsistence farming, the physical strains on the worker are tougher and more prolonged; the urban worker requires more and better food than the primitive farmer can get along with, but he is unable to supply much or any of it by his personal efforts. Thus as development takes place there will be a more than proportionate additional demand for food. This implies on the one hand that every effort must be made to expand output and to increase productivity in agriculture, and on the other that the farm families must be prevented from consuming too much of the additional output themselves.

The task of taxing farmers so as to release additional output without curbing their enterprise is eminently one for local effort, since it is only in the locality (if at all) that the circumstances of the individual farm family and hence its taxable capacity, can be discovered adequately. The solution of this delicate balance of stimulus and control implies willing tax compliance on the part of farmers. This again can more easily be achieved if it is apparent to the taxpayers that a substantial part of the revenue is being spent on things that will benefit the rural community, especially on those things that they themselves have chosen. This calls not only for local assessment and collection, but also for a substantial retention of the revenue by Local Authorities. Appropriate taxation of farmers is thus an essential element in development from below.

The present near exemption of agriculture in general from taxation is something quite new in the world's history; it results very largely from the enormous relative growth in importance and tax potential of other sectors. The taxation of land in some form or other is, however, age old; in very many countries it was the first internal tax to be attempted. This was natural when land was both the most obvious mark of wealth and source of income. More recently, and perhaps rather oddly, the nineteenth century regarded land as having a special faculty for taxation. This preference for land taxation was based on the argument that tax would fall only on the surplus profits of the better land.[1] From this it followed first that, not being shiftable, the tax would have no disincentive effects on output. Secondly it followed that in a land tenure system of landlords and tenants (as in Britain) the incidence of the tax would be upon the wealthy landlords in accordance with fertility of their land. According to a later development of the doctrine, when land values were rising fast on account of development, the taxation of land would afford sufficient revenue (still without disincentive effects) to finance the whole needs of the public sector. This latter development, however (due to Henry George),[2] had its main reference to urban conditions, so that it properly belongs to the next chapter rather than to this.

As a consequence of the earlier form of the analysis what we have called the old colonial system laid very great stress on the taxation of land. The *locus classicus* of this policy was the Indian land revenue, which we shall have to examine below. There are, however, two preliminary questions to be cleared up, which have been particularly relevant to the early taxation of the countries with which we are concerned: on what basis should land taxation be assessed, and in what form should it be collected?

The earliest and most obvious method of taxing farmers was to assess the tax on the land itself: the farmer's holding *in rem*, and to collect the revenue in kind rather than in cash. These broad principles, however, demanded different applications according to the type of land tenure, according in other words as to whether the tax collectors had to deal with a landlord/tenant system (the tenants normally being 'cottiers' with no formal tenancy contracts), with a system of share cropping, or of one of more or less equal independent farmers. The simplest application was in the landlord/tenant system, where the landlords would collect in kind from the individual farmers (since they were unlikely to have any cash), through a payment that hovered between a rent and a tax. The government then merely collected from the landlords.

Partly because of the consequent simplicity of tax collection, partly because they felt that the most practicable way of securing capital for development was through the application of the savings of the wealthier members of the community, early British

---

[1] The basic analysis, due to Ricardo, was further elaborated by the Utilitarians and J. S. Mill.
[2] See below, p. 357.

administrators tended to encourage and confirm a régime of substantial landlords overseas. Thus in India the zamindars were
favoured; in Northern Nigeria Lugard judged that the Emirs were
sufficiently well established to act exactly in this capacity, and
Johnston in Buganda transformed the vague hierarchy of Ganda
chiefs around the Kabaka into a landed aristocracy.

With other forms of land tenure the procedure is not so simple.
With independent farmers indeed, in principle assessment is not
very difficult, but collection is tiresome and expensive. In the case
of share cropping the imputation of liability is itself a difficulty. In
modern conditions share cropping still exists, and may well be
one of the explanations of the difficulties of tax collection and
assessment in the cocoa areas of Ghana,[1] where it is a very
general practice. The big individual landlord is, however, very
generally on the way out. In India the zamindars have been abolished; in Nigeria the position of the Emirs is slowly changing, and
in Buganda the territorial chiefs no longer have the power they
once had. This method of tax collection has consequently become
obsolete. In the modern world the big landlords are plantation or
mining companies which make large tax contributions through the
taxation of their profits, and which do not on the whole sublet to
tenants. Of the taxation of the independent farmer we shall have
more to say below.

Payment in kind is inevitable so long as there is no cash circu-
lating among practising farmers. It is claimed, however, that it has
some definite advantages,[2] so that it should not too lightly be
abandoned. The great advantage of payment in kind, from the
revenue point of view, is that real revenue is independent of price
changes. In its early stages of development Japan was particularly
lucky in that the whole of the population was rice eating, and by
having all taxes paid in rice a revenue of constant real value was
assured to the government, while at the same time it was ensured
that adequate supplies of the nation's staple food would always be
available.[3] In no other country have circumstances turned out
quite so fortunately. Generally speaking taxation in kind has so
many inconveniencies, both in the process of collection and in

[1] Cf. Polly Hill, *Ghana Cocoa Farmers*, cit.
[2] Cf. H. P. Wald, *Taxation of Agricultural Land in Underdeveloped Economies*,
1959.
[3] Cf. R. P. Dore, *Land Reform in Japan*, 1959.

storage—Johnston's 'tax hippos' in Uganda will be recalled[1]—
that it is commuted for payment in cash at as early a stage as
possible. Further, the revenue's protection in matters of price is the
farmer's destruction. In times of falling value of money the farmer
sees his post-tax income disastrously sinking in terms of the things
he wants to buy, a state of affairs he is not likely to take lying down.

Again, payment in kind does nothing to encourage the growth
of a money economy. It has been the experience of many territories
that the discovery of the ease with which the subsistence farmer
can make enough cash to cover his first small local tax payments has
been a potent force in impelling him to increase his cash income in
order to satisfy new wants as well as to pay his taxes (we shall come
to an interesting illustration of this among the Tanganyika Masai).[2]
Finally, in practice tax collection in kind by the landlord tends to
bolster up the landlord system. In primitive conditions it is always
extremely difficult to check the difference between what the official
(or unofficial) tax collector takes and what he pays over to the
government. This is true of other peasant taxes, but the landlord's
special position of superiority to the tenant makes his responsibility for tax collection a lucrative source of income.

The great advantage of land tax *in rem*, whether paid in cash or
in kind, is that it is to some extent geared to relative ability to pay,
as contrasted for instance with a flat sum poll tax. But this raises
the question of the correct basis of valuation: whether the relative
potential fertility of the holding or the relative abundance of the
crops raised. According to the Ricardian analysis, the taxation of
land could have no adverse productional effect because the rent or
surplus earned by the more fertile land was due to its inherent
quality and not to the efforts of the individual cultivator. This
analysis was essentially based on British conditions in the early
nineteenth century; it implicitly assumed an alert and mobile
agricultural class, ready to flit if landlords attempted to extract a
rent which gave less reward for labour than could be obtained
elsewhere or in other occupations. In these conditions it followed
that even if 100% of the surplus were removed the landlords
would not be able to put up the rent, and, as they would still be
making the normal profits of a marginal farmer, the farmers on the
better soil would have no incentive to relax their efforts; on the
contrary, they might well be spurred to fresh endeavour.

[1] Above, p. 115.   [2] See below, p. 338.

Perhaps it was the common sense of British Chancellors of the Exchequer which doubted the applicability of this perfectly logical analysis to British conditions. At any rate, there was no serious proposal to impose a tax on the Ricardian principle in England until towards the end of the nineteenth century, and then in respect of urban, and not of rural, land (see next chapter). In India it was otherwise.[1] In 1819 the administration of the East India Company came under the hand of James Mill, one of the most uncompromising and fervent believers in the utilitarian doctrine. He was backed up by Bentham himself, and in 1823 he was joined at the India Office by his son J. S. Mill. Although the younger Mill seems not to have been very interested in India, he was a profound believer in Ricardo, and his reputation as an economist undoubtedly gave support to the policy which his father and Bentham proceeded vigorously to put into practice. We are not concerned with the utilitarian policy in India as a whole—it had a very wide range of application—but only with the various attempts to apply the Ricardian analysis to the taxation of land in different parts of India. Two things must be borne in mind in order to appreciate this. First, the authors of the policy were not familiar with India; they consequently tended to equate conditions there with what they knew at home. Secondly, like all the commercial classes of their period, they were anti-landlord and were consequently delighted with a tax which promised to cut landlords' incomes down to minimum normal profits.

The true nature of Indian land revenue has only recently been laid bare.[2] This is not surprising, considering the different forms which the tax assessment took in the different areas. It is quite clear, however, that it was an earnest attempt to put the Ricardian/utilitarian doctrine into practice. The main exception to this was in Bengal, where a tax with a very different aim had been in operation since 1793. Not all the Governors and officers who were responsible for putting the utilitarian policy into operation understood Ricardo and Mill, but certainly some of them seem to have done so. This was largely due to the fact that Malthus was the first Professor of Political Economy at the Imperial Service College at Haileybury, teaching there from 1803 to 1834. In 1815 Malthus published a *Tract on the Nature and Progress of Rent*.

[1] Cf. Eric Stokes, *The English Utilitarians in India*, 1959, pp. 48 ff.
[2] Stokes, loc. cit.

Altogether, including the Bengal and Madras systems, both of which were pre-Utilitarian, we can distinguish five[1] main bases of valuation for Indian land revenue, although in most cases the methods first used were modified gradually as their weaknesses began to show up. The Bengal system instituted by Cornwallis in 1793 was known as the Permanent Settlement. It has endured to this day,[2] effectively preventing the realization of any substantial revenue from land in the Province. Cornwallis's policy was to fix from the start the money value of the government's share of crops, leaving all increments in the hands of the landlords, who were then supposed to react by increasing productivity in the manner of Coke and Townshend and other pioneers of British agriculture. From the first, the Permanent Settlement was a failure from the revenue point of view, and at a very early stage heavy indirect taxes had to be introduced to prop up the revenue.

After this experiment the British government would never give its consent to a repetition of a permanent settlement elsewhere. The only subsequent attempt at a revival of the system was that made by Lawrence's paternalistic government in the Punjab after the Mutiny. The government of India, on the other hand, tended to look on the permanent settlement with favour, mainly because it avoided the enormous trouble and expense of revaluation. If they were not permitted to have permanency, they preferred at least a twenty- or thirty-year settlement—until faced by the rise in prices in the 1880's. But by that time the idea that long settlements were appropriate was firmly rooted, and in any case the government was by then under such financial strain (due to the Afghan wars), that it could scarcely have spared the funds for a new valuation which would by then have had to start virtually *ab ovo*.

The other pre-Utilitarian system of land revenue was that established in Madras by Munro at the beginning of the nineteenth century.[3] The valuers were there confronted not by a system of big

[1] Stokes, op. cit., p. 88.

[2] In some areas of West Bengal a new system is being introduced. Land is divided into broad classes depending mainly on elevation and rainfall; a weighted index number is then determined by land quality and current crop prices for each village or group of villages. This fixes the relative taxable capacity of each village area. Individual tax assessment is then arranged by the village council according to revenue requirements. It is intended that re-assessment should take place not less frequently than at three-year intervals. It will be seen that this method very closely resembles Lugard's lump sum assessment in Northern Nigeria.   [3] Stokes, op. cit., pp. 99–100.

landlords and cottier tenants, but by *ryotwaris*, that is to say, a large number of small peasant cultivators. Munro's plan was to make a rough estimate of the value of gross produce and to endeavour to secure the transfer to the state of an amount not exceeding one-third. This was obviously superior to the Bengal system from the revenue point of view, but it did call for a simple form of annual assessment. Considering the troubles which have arisen over the system of tithes in other countries throughout history, the idea of getting a third rather than a tenth from peasant farmers is little less than staggering.

The two purest forms of land revenue based on strict utilitarian principles were those of R. K. Pringle[1] in the Bombay Deccan, and of Sir George Wingate also in Bombay in the early 1830's. Pringle had been one of Malthus's favourite pupils at Haileybury. He based his assessment on *net* produce because he felt that a tax on gross produce would impede the cultivation of inferior soils. Pringle's method of valuation involved 'the calculation of the average gross produce per *biga* (two-thirds of an acre) for nine separate soil qualities, turning this into a money value and deducting the cost of production and of interest on stock to arrive at the net produce'. Then, although he maintained that the government was fully entitled to confiscate the whole of the value of the net produce, with liberal attention to the importance of encouraging accumulation, Pringle contented himself with fixing the rate of tax at not more than 55%.

Prior to this exercise, the Mahrattas, who had in fact evolved a stern tax system for themselves, had worked on a species of communal assessment. Thus, apart from other difficulties soon to show themselves, Pringle's system constituted a clean break with anything that they had been accustomed to. Pringle's industry was, however, warmly praised by James Mill, though he saw fit to warn the Bombay government against being too self-denying in its appropriation of only 55% of the surplus. Almost immediately Pringle's assessment was found to be unbearably high, and the whole system was shortly set aside in favour of something more like the old Mahratta tax, even though that had itself been exceptionally extortionate.

After Pringle's net produce system had been set aside, in the non-Mahratta part of Bombay Presidency, H. E. Goldsmid and

[1] Stokes, op. cit., p. 113.

(Sir) George Wingate established a revised method of assessment based on a careful cadastral survey broken down to the individual field, each field being minutely classified for soil quality. Actual assessment was based on a combination of these calculations, revenue previously collected, and acreage cultivated over the last ten or twenty years. By a graphical examination of the resulting series, Wingate believed that it was possible to determine precisely how much it was safe for the government to take. This Bombay system is interesting not only for its ingenious method, but also because it was Wingate's policy to declare the Crown the ultimate landowner, all land being held only by direct lease from the Crown without intermediaries. As a consequence the tax was probably considerably less extortionate than other methods of assessing land revenue. Wingate's assessments were in addition consciously progressive; he seems to have aimed at something like residual equal net profit after tax. Thus the tax was planned to be not merely a big revenue raiser but also an aggressive instrument of social reform.

Finally, in the North-West Provinces (later U.P.) a less precise version of Wingate's system was being put into operation at about the same time. It was based on communal assessment on a rather rough cadastral survey. The actual level of tax seems to have been fixed on a mixture of the revenue previously collected and an estimate by the assessment officer of (effectively) what the traffic would bear. The background of the north-west differed substantially, however, from that in Bombay, since there existed a system of village brotherhoods with *talukdar* intermediaries. This, as in the big zamindari areas, made it possible to levy taxes on village groups without assessment being completely personal.

Gradually systems with some such empirical base came to be adopted over a much wider area; actual level of tax everywhere depended very much on the judgement of individual officers. Thus, although the Ricardian principle was apparently held as firmly as ever, valuation in practice had moved a good long way from the attempt to discover the net surplus.

The excessive weight of the general level of Indian land revenue was not recognized until after the Mutiny, when it was realized at least in the North-West Provinces that it had been a contributory cause of the trouble. J. S. Mill even went so far as to admit that with a ryotwari system of peasant cultivators, rent might enter into costs and so could not safely be taxed away. After the Mutiny there was some relaxation in the severity of the exaction, but in the 1860's the fall in the value of the (silver) rupee led to a renewed tightening up, and in the 1880's the needs of the Afghan wars again led to an increase in exactions.

It would be absurd to attribute the undoubted allergy of modern India to the effective taxation of the agricultural sector solely to a re-action from the exactions of land revenue eighty years ago, but it has certainly been a contributory factor. In actual fact land revenue has not been a serious burden since the inflation of the first world war, although up to the second world war it was still one of the pillars of provincial finances. The inflation of the second world war finally destroyed its weight almost completely; but it is still the only tax of any importance available to rural local authorities in India: the Districts and the panchayats. Without an extensive revaluation it would not be possible to restore the efficiency of land revenue since to raise rates on the present obsolete valuations would be grossly inequitable. When the cost and difficulty of a revaluation are considered, it is at least arguable that it would be better to allow land revenue to subside quietly into insignificance until it reaches the point when it can be bought out, as was done with the British tithe, and to make a fresh start with some different and more effective basis for the taxation of Indian farmers.

II

It is evident from this brief account of Indian land revenue that relative taxable capacity was in practice often measured not so much by the inherent qualities of the soil as directly by its produce. When Lugard set about turning the Arab tithe in Northern Nigeria into an effective source of revenue he was in this, as in other matters, much influenced by what he knew of India. Lugard's Nigerian tax was to be levied in principle 'on the income and profit of each individual', but the income in question was typically that derived from land: 'the gross income derived or *derivable* [my italics] regardless of the appropriation of the whole or any part of it to the use of the owner'. In principle the incomes of the various inhabitants of a village (or of a town ward) were separately valued and added together to give the 'lump sum assessment' for the area.

The assessment, however, was not to be based on the actual incomes but on the yield of the land 'if cultivated up to a good average standard', thus in intention somewhat penalizing bad farming and encouraging good.

The lump sum assessments were originally based on special inquiries made under the supervision of divisional officers, and were in some areas fully as detailed as anything that Pringle or Wingate had attempted in Bombay.[1] The rate of tax was permitted to vary from $2\frac{1}{2}\%$ to 10% according to the needs of the Native Authority not covered by other revenue sources, and to the contribution to be made to the government by the Native Authority in question.[2] While the rate per head determined the amount to be raised from each community, the actual liability of the individual tax payer was determined by strictly local estimates of relative taxable capacity in the year in question.

Lugard's tax thus embodied a number of good points: it paid attention to ability to pay at the local level where it could best be measured; it was incentive rather than disincentive, and at the same time gave much less opportunity for extortion by intermediaries than did the Indian land revenue. Lugard's tax was also productive of revenue, and throughout the difficult years of the first world war the government share was one of the main barriers between the Territorial government and bankruptcy.[3] But just as happened with the Indian land revenue its yield in real terms was seriously damaged by the inflation of the second world war; by 1950 it was estimated by a reliable authority that a nominal 5% rate represented no more than 2% of actual income. During the long inflation of the 1950's the base of the Northern Nigerian direct tax was further eroded, so that finally it became little better than a lump sum poll tax at a rather moderate level.

Both Indian land revenue and the Northern Nigerian lump sum

[1] See above, p. 98. It is a matter for astonishment how these careful assessments were originally made (as they undoubtedly were) by the tiny handful of administrators on whom Lugard could draw. Two possible explanations suggest themselves: first, the population was very much sparser than it is today, so that much fewer valuations were required than would now be the case; and secondly, the actual area minutely surveyed was in fact a very small part of what is now the Northern Region.

[2] The Northern Nigerian direct tax has always been in principle a government (now Regional) and not a local tax, but part has traditionally been retained by the Native Authorities; see above, p. 301.

[3] Cf. Report of Revenue Allocation Commission, 1951, loc. cit.

payment depended for their continuing effectiveness either on steady prices or on difficult and expensive periodic revaluations. Once relative valuations are frozen it becomes impossible equitably to maintain the real yield by increasing tax rates. Revaluations have proved too costly for a poor country to face, and they have invariably fallen hopelessly in arrears. This difficulty was only not apparent to start with because the long period of steady prices in the nineteenth and early twentieth centuries reduced the urgency of revaluation.

The only one of our countries which seems at present to be hoping to make a sizeable revenue from an *ad rem* tax on land in rural areas is Jamaica, which is endeavouring to extend the principle of the unimproved value base (which we shall examine in the next chapter) all over the island. The Jamaican[1] background to this exercise is much more favourable than in Africa (where, as we have seen, it is used in the East African towns and Kenya at least hopes to extend it to rural areas). In Jamaica individual ownership of land is universal, although title is often poor and boundaries uncertain; there is also a high degree of literacy among the population. In making their cadastral survey the Jamaican valuers had the further advantage of detailed maps based on an aerial survey.

The task of valuation nevertheless proved to be a very heavy one; a general revaluation had not been made since early in the present century. In fact, after experience of the exercise in only two of the thirteen parishes the process of valuation was judged to be so time consuming and costly that it was decided to waive the separate valuation of all holdings worth less than £100. This implied finally covering in the valuation only 25% of the properties in the Island. In spite of adopting this simplification in mid-stream it took the Land Department nearly four years to value the two parishes. Valuation under the new Jamaican system is based neither directly on the relative qualities of the soil, nor on the potential produce, but on land sales, values then being extended by analogy to plots which have not come on the market. From this data, which naturally includes buildings and other 'improvements', deduction is then made, on a rough valuation of the buildings. This is in fact not very difficult, since in rural conditions in Jamaica the value of the typical small frame house is generally almost negligible in any case.

[1] Cf. J. R. and U. K. Hicks, *Report on Finance and Taxation in Jamaica*, 1955, cit.

Since there are to be no effective valuations in the under-£100 group of holdings, tax is to be levied at a low flat sum (4s. at present). Rates have thus effectively become a poll tax of a very moderate type. Above this level tax is assessed at a graduated rate according to the size of the property, a method which Jamaica has favoured since the early fifties.[1] In rural conditions this has two unfortunate results. In the first place it encourages the artificial breaking-up of holdings in order to take advantage of the lower rates. Secondly it puts into the hands of Parish Councils an opportunity for extortion of the (usually very small) number of large properties in the area, by fixing special poundages which they alone will pay. In 1954, when this method was in operation, in some parishes the greater part of the revenue was derived from one or two properties.

Further, since tax liability is only very remotely related to net income, land use which is extensive is discriminated against in relation to more intensive use. As a result of the abuse of their powers in respect of graduation, the poundages which parishes could levy were frozen by the Island government.[2] It is not at all clear that even after the new valuation comes into force the Island government will be prepared to restore to Parish Councils the right of choosing their own poundages. Thus the local rate in Jamaica looks very like losing one of its most desirable features: that of acting as the balancing factor in local budgets. This is the direct and very natural result of the attempt by local bodies to maintain the real value of their revenue when there has been a failure in periodic revaluation. It constitutes a further indictment of a system of taxation which requires it.

Among our countries there are two other types of local tax which depend on the acreage of holdings, and which call for brief comment. The simplest and crudest is that used by the village committees in Ceylon.[3] This tax is simply a levy per acre of all holdings of 5 acres and over with a ceiling of 50 cents (9d.), and exempting all paddy and *chena* land. Although some village committees would willingly impose a high tax and also reduce the exemption limit (an extension to fractions of an acre and a ceiling of 3s. have been proposed), other villages would clearly not be

[1] See above, p. 141. Demands for the introduction of a 'sliding scale' have also been voiced in Sierra Leone, and British Guiana, for similar reasons.
[2] See above, p. 142.   [3] Choksy Report, cit.

interested to do so. In 1953 about 40% of the villages were making no use at all of the tax and many were still more allergic to imposing the more effective assessed rate on annual values applicable to 'areas declared built up', even where there was no reasonable doubt as to the extent of development. The combined revenue of the 254 village committees which were using the acreage tax in 1953 was less than £49,000; in no sense can the Ceylon tax be regarded as a success.

More interesting and forward-looking are the experiments being made in Kenya. Now that County Councils have been established in Settled Areas and given definite powers and duties, it becomes an urgent necessity to develop an effective source of independent revenue outside the towns. Prior to this, since the almost completely ineffective Settled Area District Councils had little need of revenue, they managed to get along with a crude acreage tax with an extremely mild progression. Typical of this would be what in fact Nyanza County Council started with, namely 40s. a year on a farm of 100 acres or less and 15 cents per acre on every additional acre.

The new spirit can be illustrated from the active council in Nakuru County; having increased its acreage tax 2½ times it decided that any further increases would be grossly unfair as between one holding and another, so in 1957 it inaugurated a type of annual value rating based on house and land considered together. Initially the valuation was to be by self-assessment, but any implausible-looking valuation would be arbitrarily substituted by a declared value of £4 an acre. The taxpayer would then have to prove the unreasonableness of the assessment. Nairobi County Council is using a similar arrangement in its peri-urban areas.

In its present tentative form with personal assessment this type of local tax is clearly too rough and ready to survive as a permanent arrangement, nor is annual value necessarily the best base in a country like Kenya. (This is a point which we shall have to discuss below.) On the other hand, it is interesting that these authorities have not thought it desirable to exempt buildings from the levy, and also that they appear to have definitely broken with the crude acreage base. The way is wide open for experimentation in Kenya because the Ordinance allows a choice in principle of seven methods of local taxation, although in practice in present conditions the choice is much more limited than this. It is quite likely however that something useful will presently emerge.

III

A crude acreage tax sidesteps the difficulty of valuation and revaluation, but only by ignoring relative taxable capacity. Exactly as in the case of the flat sum poll tax, a crude acreage tax will always be poor, both in yield and in equity. The difficulties experienced in these various ad rem taxes in relation to primitive conditions naturally raises the question of whether other bases might not be more useful. Broadly there are two possibilities: first of basing the tax wholly on the produce, and secondly of basing it in some broad way on personal or family incomes. In most parts of rural Africa, in fact, some alternative base to land must for the present be used, because individual land rights among Africans are still few, and the complications of tribal right and custom are too difficult for *ad rem* assessment.

The simplest alternative to an *ad rem* tax is to base the assessment on crops brought to market. The most lucrative experiment in this direction has been the produce cesses of East Africa, at which we glanced briefly in the last chapter, but must now examine more closely. The cesses started in the early post-war years with controlled produce which was necessarily marketed through official channels at fixed prices. The original idea in Kenya was that the cesses would be imposed at uniform rates throughout the Territory, but that the revenue would be assigned to the African District Councils. The urgent demands of the councils for autonomous revenue, however, broke through this safeguard, and as things have developed the rates are effectively fixed in the Districts by the District Commissioner in consultation with the finance committee, later with the council. They must then be submitted to the Ministry of Local Government. In Tanganyika the local bodies discovered that they could impose cesses under the Native Authority Ordinance, without formally gazetting the rates, and proceeded to do so with enthusiasm. The opportunities in Tanganyika were for some time especially good, because of the effect of the Korean war on sisal incomes. There is no doubt that, given the poverty of both central and local government in Tanganyika in the early fifties, the possibility of cess revenue greatly stimulated interest in local government. The local bodies began to be looked on as organizations which could really do things for the good of the locality. In some places an elaborate system of assessment and collection was built up for goods subject to cess; an account of one such was furnished by the District Officer at Handin.[1] The market was entirely enclosed, except for a small opening through which the seller entered, and an exit large enough for produce to be brought in in bulk, as it came from the farms, and to pass out again when it was finally removed by the buyer. On entering, the producer first went to an agricultural officer who classified and weighed the produce, then to a clerk who calculated price and tax, the seller receiving a price net of tax. The actual tax was collected later from the buyer, who was, generally speaking, a wholesaler or other intermediary.

For the sake of convenience only one crop was marketed at a time, the hour when, for instance, maize would be dealt in being announced in advance. It was gradually discovered, however, that the system could be adapted to produce not subject to controlled prices. In this case a price for the day for each commodity was set by a series of bids by buyers, before the market opened, the highest bid being declared to be the ruling price for the day.[2] With this extension, as boom prices of particular crops gradually subsided, the Tanganyika cesses have tended to approximate to a sort of general sales tax. The East African Royal Commission was very critical of the whole system of cesses, more particularly as it was operated in Tanganyika.

There is no doubt that for a time cesses got out of hand in a way which tended to upset the balance of local budgeting (District Officers and Native Authorities would make an estimate of 'what the traffic would bear' and then think of something which could be done with the revenue). The dangers which critics apprehended were first, that the cess would prove a disincentive to the production of particular crops (in practice this rarely occurred except where there was an obvious alternative uncessed crop);[3] secondly that the cess revenue would steal tax from the central government, the Native Authorities thus interfering with the central government's right of determining the level of indirect taxes. Thirdly, and much more generally, the basic objection to cess revenue for local purposes is its liability to fluctuation. This not merely makes it unsuitable as an important regular source of reveneue, but a drop in prices

[1] Report to the Provincial Commissioner (unpublished).
[2] Economists will recognize a process of Walrasian *tatonnément*.
[3] Handin Report, cit.

may temporarily bankrupt a local body unless it has sufficient reserves to support its budget.

As a result of various criticisms the Tanganyika government issued a Policy Statement in 1956 which attempted both to meet objections and to introduce a more orderly régime. They came to the conclusion (as the Kenya government did in 1957) that cesses were so important to local bodies that they would have to be continued to be levied 'until African opinion has developed further towards the imposition of a graduated tax based on income or wealth'. In order both to increase the equity of the tax and to reduce the danger of fluctuating revenue the Tanganyika government now suggested that the coverage should be made as wide as possible, effectively that the cess should be turned into a general market tax, save in those areas where there was an obvious dominant export crop. To improve orderliness, cess rates could no longer be imposed under the Native Authority Ordinance and would have to be gazetted in advance, thus giving the Territorial government the opportunity of bringing them into a homogeneous scheme. In all cases the tax would be payable by the buyers, since this had been found to be both the simplest and most popular method. It had all along been the practice of the Tanganyika government to insist that cess revenue should be reserved for development. This was presumably due to its fluctuating nature and to analogy with its own practice in respect of government export taxes. If, however, the expanded cess (or market tax) is really to be regarded as a first step in the direction of a local income tax, this is no longer plausible or necessary.

As we have seen, the revenue from cesses is everywhere declining, and they may well prove to have been a phenomenon of the war and post-war boom, with their compulsory marketing of staple crops. In Kenya at least the government is anxious that the African District Councils should free themselves from the necessity of raising revenue in this manner as soon as possible. This would unquestionably be much the best development. It cannot be denied that, in Tanganyika especially, in the time of their heyday cesses were not only economically (and politically) useful in enabling a start to be made with 'development from below', but they also helped in mopping up surplus incomes which could otherwise have exercised inflationary pressure. On the other hand cesses have other disadvantages besides fluctuating revenue. In particular the revenue receipts which are quoted are always *gross*. For the marketing of staple crops where individual fraud can largely be prevented, highly skilled and paid agricultural specialists have to waste long hours supervising marketing. In respect of a general market tax, on the other hand, it is extremely difficult to prevent at least indirect fraud and bribery. (How does the market clerk come to have such a nice new bicycle?) In fact, many administrators are coming to believe that when all costs of collection are properly accounted for, the *net* revenue may well be zero or negligible.

There is one other rather different type of Tanganyikan cess which is of particular interest (see previous chapter): the cess on cattle sales, because it points a way of dealing with the difficult problem of taxing nomads. Nowadays it is becoming increasingly the case that nomads do not wander by choice, but have to do so for the sake of their beasts, both because there are not enough water holes for them and because the grass in dry areas is so scanty that it will only bear very light grazing; hence it is necessary for the flocks and herds continually to be moved on. The top priorities in such areas are consequently to improve the water supply and pasturage, and to reduce the number while improving the quality of the beasts.

It is a mistake to think that nomads are necessarily very poor—the Tanganyika Masai were estimated in 1958 to own approximately 1 mn. cattle, and rather more sheep and goats—but they hold their wealth in very illiquid form. If they can be induced to realize some of this wealth they can well afford to pay for more veterinary services and water supplies, and there is abundant evidence that they are ready and willing to do so. When that point has been reached, experience shows that many nomadic groups are willing to settle down, balance their traditional diet of blood and milk (the former is very extravagant in cattle power), with meat and even maize. Once settled down, it is possible for them to begin to satisfy new wants, already aroused by what they have seen of tribes through whose territory they pass, e.g. the prosperous little shambas, new houses, bicycles, and even cars, of the Chagga coffee growers.

Kenya[1] and Tanganyika seem to have gone farther than other

---

[1] In Kajiado (Kenya) additional revenue is also raised by a cess on hides. Personal tax is high also in that District.

territories in using taxes to accelerate this process by means of a cess of 2s. or 4s. per head on beasts sold (at first perhaps to pay poll tax). Travelling merchants soon learn when periodic sales are being held, and bring thither their wares of all sorts, so that in order that attractive goods may be bought cattle sales soon come enormously to exceed what would be required to meet the tax. The first time a really big sale took place at one market in Tanganyika the Masai spent most of their takings (I am informed) on South African sherry; but they soon acquired considerable discrimination in extending their range of purchases. Numbers of Tanganyika Masai cattle sold rose from 15,700 in 1948 to 30,600 in 1954, and only declined slightly after that, the fall being largely explained by the quarantine in one large area. The annual figures of sales suggest in addition that the Masai are quite price conscious.[1]

This sort of policy is probably easier among the Masai than among some other nomadic tribes, because they are in contact with more advanced tribes than are, for instance, some of the nomads of Northern Kenya, or the 'cow' Fulani of Northern Nigeria. Naturally the policy will only go on being successful if the nomads see real communal benefits coming from their tax payments, in the way of water and veterinary services, as well as benefits to themselves in cash purchases. Naturally also, the process of herd improvement by culling, demands much patient propaganda and persuasion on the part of administrators. However slow the process, nevertheless it points a way of getting somewhere, which other methods of attempting to tax nomads (such as the Northern Nigerian jangali)[2] seem to do less surely.

IV

We have seen that the Tanganyika government regards the market cess as a step in the direction of a general tax on income or wealth. Yet it retains two disadvantages from this point of view: first, that being assessed on realized cash sales it runs the danger of being disincentive in respect of the growing of cash crops, and secondly that it discriminates against the farming element in the community. It remains to inquire whether in fact it is not possible to proceed more directly towards a general tax on income and wealth

[1] Alan Jacobs, *Political Organization of the Tanganyika Masai*, cit.
[2] See above, p. 292.

through the medium of the graduated poll or personal tax,[1] which would avoid both these drawbacks. The territory which has made the most progress in this direction is undoubtedly Uganda (see previous chapter). How has this been done? It has long been customary in a number of territories for assessment to personal (or direct) tax to be carried out by small committees of the authority (or council) visiting the different villages and making the assessments individually in consultation with the taxpayer. Tax is then paid into the local Treasury, from where it is either banked or collected by a senior administrator.

The Uganda system, which I believe started at Fort Portal in Toro District, is an ingenious extension of this plan. A list is first drawn up of the main categories of sources of income in the area, not only the various types of farming (and fishing, if relevant), but also trading occupations, salaries, and service incomes. Against each is then marked estimated potential unit receipt (e.g. 4s. per coffee tree)—this standard return is estimated on a fairly generous scale (leaving incentive for better farming), and broadly corresponds to Lugard's Northern Nigerian 'fair average cultivation'; but it can be made flexible according to the season as well as to the type of land. For shops, an estimate of stock in trade is made (so far as possible with the co-operation of the owner), and a net income e.g. of 60s. assumed for a unit stock value of 100s. Land under general cultivation is counted at so much an acre. Finally, a general 'catch all' takes up any other sources of income not already included. Total (expected, potential) income is then found by adding up standard income from all sources. Assessment can then be made in blocks, incomes below 1,200s. per annum paying at one rate, incomes between 1,200s. and 1,650s. at a higher rate, and so on, up to any desired figure, so far as the central government permits.[2] This is the simplest method and is very easy for the payer to understand. With a little more sophistication tax can be assessed income-tax wise, at so many shillings in the pound. This method can be extended to the increment of income,[3] i.e. the first 1,200s. of each income is assessed at x shillings in the pound,

[1] See Report of Local Government Panel, cit.

[2] The Uganda Protectorate government imposed a limit for 1958–9 of 400s. in tax from any one taxpayer. This high figure is itself a testimonial to the success of the system.

[3] Cf. the Western Nigeria income tax, above, pp. 179 ff.

the next 500s. at $x+y$ shillings in the pound, and so on, so as to give a mildly progressive scale if desired.

Even at a strictly proportional level (constant number of shillings in the pound), however, this method of taxing gives a very much closer approximation to ability to pay than any other system feasible in the circumstances. It includes not merely the incomes of the whole community, but income from all sources for the individual. The importance of this is that in developing countries people normally earn in several occupations at once.[1] The approximation to ability to pay can be made still closer, if desired, by deducting selected rebates (e.g. school fees) from total income before assessing tax. It is of course true that this method of assessment leans heavily on the reliability of local Assessment Committees.[2] It is important to appreciate, however, that all they are really asked to do is to write down answers to a list of simple questions (how many coffee trees, how many fishing nets?). No element of judgement should be implied. Steps must naturally be taken to guard against abuses, and opportunities given for the taxpayer to appeal to a higher authority against an assessment, either because he feels it to be unjust or because of particular adverse circumstances in the year in question.

So far as can be judged no serious or at least general trouble is arising in Uganda from this still relatively new tax, any more than it is in Western Nigeria in respect of somewhat similar methods of assessment. One slight check on the broad integrity of the tax is provided by the statistics of taxpayers in different steps. These appear to agree closely with known facts concerning the relative wealth of the Districts.[3] Where really serious trouble arises, as it

[1] Cf. Bauer, op. cit.

[2] Tax riots in Bukedi in Jan. 1959 show that this cannot be relied on, even in Uganda. Rates of tax had however been very violently increased.

[3] Quoted in some of the District Estimates; for a typical scale see that for Bugisu, for 1958:

Bugisu District Council

Distribution of Taxpayers, 1958

Tax (shillings)	Number of Taxpayers	Tax (shillings)	Number of Taxpayers
484	25	134	12,000
334	500	104	15,000
234	2,000	64	20,000
184	3,000	24	7,000
159	10,000	8	500

did in Sierra Leone in 1955, over the use of the village committee
method of assessment (although with a much simpler tax), the
causes are probably to be sought in the ignorance of the taxpayers,
particularly over the method of payment, and partly in insufficient
check by a higher authority. (In Sierra Leone both these operated,
in particular tax was payable only to selected village headmen and
not directly to the Native Treasury.)[1]

On the other hand it has to be established that this method of
assessment will really lead towards the high road to modern
global income tax, or whether it amounts to no more than an
assessment (for instance, after the French manner) on 'presumed'
income, which tends to be neither accurate nor global. It can
plausibly be argued that the Uganda tax is definitely superior in
principle to this latter; it should rather be regarded as a first step
in helping the not-too-literate taxpayer to make his own return.
The Uganda system requires the tax assessment form to be made
out in triplicate, of which one copy is kept by the taxpayer. It is
signed (or marked) by the taxpayer, and separately by the village
chief and the councillor who has accompanied him in making the
assessment. It is also signed by the sub-county (*gombolola*) chief[2]
when he has checked the arithmetic. It must be emphasized in
this, as indeed in any other method of assessing and collecting
local revenue, that the best insurance against fraud is the keenness
of the taxpayer to get local public goods and services, and his confidence that the tax he pays will be largely put to such a use. Most
Africans seem quickly to develop a lively sense of when they are
getting good value for money.

The opposite danger needs also to be taken into account, and
indeed this has already been worrying the Uganda government.
Will the development of a graduated personal tax at the lower
level impinge on the preserves of the central government's income
tax? There is no reason why it should, if proper steps are taken.
This is abundantly proved by the example of the Scandinavian
countries, which have operated on local and a central income tax
together for decades, with the greatest success. Although these
countries are now highly developed, with a strong sense of fiscal
integrity born of long years of settled government, this was much

---

[1] See above, p. 201.
[2] In Uganda the Gombolola chiefs who check the tax returns are higher grade
officials with salaries ranging from £400 upwards.

less true when the system started. In these countries assessment for the local tax (and in part for the national tax also) is carried out by local committees[1] not unlike those used in Africa, except of course that the taxpayers, being literate, can make their own returns, which are then checked by the committee. The Scandinavian local tax has a priority over the central, in that tax paid locally is deductible from taxable income at the central level. The local tax has virtually no exemption limit, it is a true 'graduated poll tax' with no rebates or allowances; but it has a firm ceiling above which local bodies cannot go. Thus in Sweden local income tax assessment may not exceed 18% of any income. In fact no Local Authority found that it needed more than 15% (in 1955), so that the choice of rates of tax may truly be said to lie entirely within the competence of the Local Authority. The national income tax, on the other hand, has a fairly high exemption limit, generous allowances, and is highly progressive; thus in practice it just takes off where the local tax ends.

If the two taxes are to be kept out of each other's way, and the autonomy of the local tax maintained, it is clearly necessary that the local tax should have a ceiling; a number of devices could be adopted to secure this, but the Scandinavian one seems particularly happy. As we have seen, Uganda has already faced this problem by putting (from 1958) a ceiling of £20 on the amount of local assessment. This is less satisfactory because it implies that the tax could become regressive at that point. In fact, so long as politics preclude the introduction of a progressive Protectorate income tax on Africans this danger exists, but this may be assumed to be a temporary difficulty. In spite of this blemish it can be confidently affirmed that the taxation of farmers and rural communities in Uganda is being carried out successfully and with increasing efficiency.

Would this type of local income tax be feasible elsewhere? There would seem to be no technical reason why it should not be introduced gradually in all the African territories. In fact something like this is already being used in Southern Nigeria, although in the Eastern Region most of the revenue goes to the Regional government to be redistributed to local councils by way of block grants. In Northern Nigeria, as we have seen, lump sum assessment has

[1] Cf. Appendix to *New Sources of Local Revenue*, Report of a Working Party, 1956.

broken down and it is urgent to find a better substitute than the system at present operating. Given the North's long familiarity with the principle of a personal tax graduated by ability to pay, there should be little technical difficulty in introducing it.

As will be apparent from the account of the method of assessment in Uganda, so far as farm incomes are concerned, the simplest case is where land is under permanent crops and a standard rate of return for the area and year can fairly simply be determined. It is then a very straightforward operation for the assessment committee merely to count the units. This would fit the case of Ghana cocoa farmers (at present much undertaxed), particularly well. Sierra Leone would present a more difficult problem, due to the general backwardness of the population and past bad record of assessment and collection; but by proceeding slowly, with ample broadcast explanations, there is no reason why something better than the present unvarying flat sum of 25s. should not be quickly achieved.

The more interesting and difficult question is whether this system of a local income tax could be translated to Asia and the West Indies. It can be said at once that in a country unused to universal personal taxes it would be necessary to proceed very slowly and gently at first. In India, however, the way for such a tax has already been pointed in the success of some community development blocks in raising voluntary contributions in kind (very largely labour), or cash, on a relatively continuing basis. The Indian government is determined, probably rightly, that the voluntary aspect of community development must be retained at all costs. But, if the plan of developing the system of village panchayats and higher layer samiti panchayats[1] is successfully carried through, this would provide exactly the right type of machinery, indeed, very similar to that operating in Uganda.

It is true of course that, especially to begin with, a somewhat heavy burden of checking would be placed on the staff at Block or District headquarters, but this should ease as the machinery was run in. The panchayats would no doubt hand over some of the revenue collected for community development purposes, in fact the regular revenue would provide just that continuity which has so often been lacking in community development work, besides supporting other services. Ceylon, as we have seen, also has a

[1] See p. 158 above, and Chap. 21.

system of village committees although on the whole they seem to be less lively than Indian panchayats. Ceylon also unfortunately has had a fairly recent bad experience of direct personal tax, so that the initial omens would not be so favourable. Once, however, the desire for development from below has awoken, the necessary technical machinery could clearly be devised quite simply. Taxable capacity of rural Ceylon substantially exceeds that of rural India.

Something of this kind of tax is (as we shall discuss in Chapter 20) urgently needed all over the West Indies, where small farmers are exceptionally under-taxed, and once prosperous islands have come to rely on subsidization by the British taxpayer. Once again there is no tradition of personal taxation at low income levels. But as we have seen, Jamaica is virtually in course of substituting a low flat personal tax for property rates on the small holdings. If this experiment goes well it could become the thin end of the wedge. In one way the agricultural background of most West Indian islands would favour ease of assessment, since even small holdings frequently have a high percentage of continuing (if not permanent) crops: coffee, cocoa, sugar, bananas, pimento, citrus, cotton, and so on. For all of these it would be simple to determine standard unit rates of return year by year.

In Jamaica, Barbados, Trinidad, Dominica, and British Guiana most of the appropriate machinery for assessment and collection already exists or could easily be adapted. In the smaller islands it would be necessary to introduce some form of local committee, but this (as we shall argue later)[1] could be an end in itself as an instrument of development from below, even in an island too small to support a formal system of local government.

The graduated personal tax, Uganda style, has, it is now clear, a number of advantages. It is more in accordance with ability to pay than any other local tax yet introduced in developing countries, and this is achieved without expensive and difficult land valuations. The revenue is more stable than that of any tax assessed wholly on agricultural produce; the setting of standard unit rates of return above which all production is tax free should be a strong incentive to farming improvements. Indeed, so far as the tax is assessed on potential income it may be claimed that it corresponds to the economists' 'ideal' tax, which is free of incentives to substitute untaxed for taxed commodities, or leisure for work.

[1] See below, pp. 529 ff.

The obvious defect of this type of tax is that it is not so well adapted to be the balancing factor in local budgets as a tax (such as a true rate), assessed on a fixed valuation. There are two lines of reply to this undoubted shortcoming. First, the assessment of incomes as a whole on a proportional (not progressive) rate is likely to produce year by year a revenue sufficiently predictable for most planning purposes. Secondly, there is the possibility that a small tax based on a property valuation might be worked alongside of the personal tax, bringing in a predictable revenue just large enough to complete the balancing function. The necessary conditions for this to be possible will be one of our main concerns in the next chapter.

16

THE TAXATION OF URBAN LAND AND BUILDINGS

I

IN the last chapter we saw that the problem of reaching the rural community with a tax based on land values is extraordinarily difficult of solution. The best efforts of Indian administrators to identify the surplus element in rent or agricultural profit, which alone could be taxed without damage to incentive, ended in failure; the cost of revaluation caused the data to become hopelessly out of date; while the task of assessing the different qualities of land proved to be so bound up with location and fragmentation that for any sort of precision it was necessary to proceed to break down the analysis to the level of the individual field. Hence our preference for a personal tax in rural conditions.

On the other hand it is undoubtedly true that a tax on realty has very great attractions for local government purposes. Localization of the source is automatic, and this is sufficient to keep the tax jurisdictions of different governing bodies from impinging on each other. Such a tax can be geared quite easily so that it is broadly correlated with capacity to pay. If properly managed it will bring in a remarkably steady revenue, in real as well as in money terms, a quality that is especially desirable in a local tax. In fact virtually all developed countries use some form of a tax on realty, predominantly for local purposes, even when they also use a local income tax. Finally, any such tax is eminently suitable for use as the balancing factor in local budgets, since the tax takes the form of a poundage levied on a fixed valuation.

In respect of urban realty the problems of successful operation of a real estate tax should in principle be simpler than in rural conditions, for several reasons. In the first place land is seldom communally owned (though there may be problems when it belongs to the Crown);[1] there is consequently little difficulty either in determining the unit of valuation or of identifying tax liability.

[1] See above, p. 305.

This greatly simplifies the problem of valuation. Secondly, since urban communities are normally richer than rural, there should be less difficulty in keeping valuations up to date. An effective tax on urban realty is the more desirable since there is if anything more need for local government finance in urban than in rural conditions, because of the greater urgency of establishing a good standard of basic public services: town planning, water supply, surface drainage and water-borne sewerage, street paving and lighting—not to mention recreational and aesthetic amenities. In the U.K. it was possible to build up this equipment slowly as the towns grew. In the countries with which we are concerned, poverty, both of the people and of their governments in the past, have already produced an acute problem of slum clearance and a back-log of basic services, except perhaps in a few 'European type' towns such as Nairobi (which, it will be remembered, started merely as the railway headquarters). The problem is at its worst in India, where the task of establishing satisfactory services is often made more difficult by a shortage of water. Only a few wealthy and determined cities, such for instance as Bombay, have really achieved adequate water and sewerage systems. Thus it is a problem of first importance in respect of development from below to examine the conditions for an effective tax on urban realty.

The two main questions we have to tackle in this chapter are: (1) what is the most appropriate form of such a tax in particular circumstances?, and (2) what means can be taken to secure that valuation and revaluation will maintain, and even enhance, the effectiveness of the tax over the years, as the town grows? A tax on urban realty can take a number of forms. First, it can be assessed on annual value, that is in some sense related to rent (and hence most naturally on the occupier). This is the basic U.K. system, although concessions to various interests (especially agricultural and industrial), and widespread rent control, have seriously damaged its purity in the last few decades. Secondly, tax can be assessed on capital (normally selling) value, and hence more reasonably on the owner, as is the practice in the U.S.A., and in fact in most parts of the world.

So far as effective incidence is concerned, given a free market in real estate and absence of rent control, it is relatively unimportant whether the occupation or ownership approach is chosen, since in the longer period the effective incidence will be determined by market conditions. In the towns of developing countries there is more likely to be a sellers' than a buyers' market, so that the effective incidence is more likely to be on buyers or occupiers, than on sellers or landlords, whichever way the tax is formally assessed. This does not imply that it is indifferent whether annual value or capital value is used; indeed as we shall see, it may make all the difference.

In respect of capital value there are three possible varieties of base: (1) assessment on the whole hereditament (house+curtilage), (2) derating of buildings (so-called unimproved value), and (3) derating of land (house tax). The last may be regarded as no more than a development of the primitive hut tax, springing from conditions in which land has a negligible value, and obviously undesirable in a situation where more and better buildings are needed. (Yet until very recently a house tax operated in Sierra Leone, in Dar-es-Salaam and in other towns of Tanganyika.) We need not bother further about this form of tax. The difference between capital value and annual value, however, is fundamental and for much of the chapter will be our central concern. It is worth noting that since most of the professional valuers who established the tax on urban realty overseas were trained in the U.K. with a background of annual value, they have had a natural bias in its favour, so that in our countries it tends to have a wider application than circumstances would really warrant. There is little justification for this attitude, since for a skilled valuer the transition from one base to the other should be a very simple matter;[1] and it can hardly be claimed that annual value in the U.K. has been an overwhelming success.

Before we investigate what sort of base really is appropriate it will be useful to glance briefly at the present use made of local taxes on urban realty in our countries. Under the 'old colonial pattern' the establishment of local rates on annual value was virtually universal, hence we find it throughout India, Ceylon, and in the West Indies. Annual value is still the rule in India, although the use of capital value is optional for panchayats; but only a few cities really make effective use of the tax for want of regular revaluations. As in most other places revaluation in Ceylon has got badly out of date. In 1957 Colombo was in course of being

---

[1] Cf. Lund, 'Valuation for Rating in Northern Rhodesia', *Journal of Association of Rating and Valuation Officers*, 1956.

revalued; Jaffna had not been revalued for sixteen years. The central government of Ceylon offers little help in this service, leaving towns to sink or swim on their own, or they may have a chance to hire the government valuer if they can afford to.

There are normally two elements in the Indian tax: a general rate and a service charge, for such things as water, drainage, scavenging, street lighting, and fire protection. Service charges thus have a much wider range than in the U.K. where only for water is a separate charge made. In India, as in the U.K., the base of the general rate and of the service charge is the same, the only differences being, first, that the smaller properties which are exempt for rates are liable to service charges, and secondly that charges can be confined to those properties which actually benefit from the services. In some states the two are combined into a consolidated tax.

In some states the imposition of the local rate has been made compulsory in order to strengthen the hands of the council *vis-à-vis* the electorate. Thus in Madya Pradesh and Bombay it is compulsory for municipal corporations and panchayats but optional for the smaller towns. In practice the local rate is used in a number of areas where it is not compulsory, especially in the larger urban areas. The Tax Inquiry Commission[1] found that the contribution of the rate to urban budgets was 25% on the average over the whole country, but that it varied greatly from state to state. In West Bengal it provided more than half of urban revenue, in Madya Pradesh only 8·1%, while in Uttar Pradesh it was only used by a very small number of the towns.

The average poundages of the rate similarly varied considerably from state to state, although the normal range was 10–20%. In Rajasthan, where only one authority uses the tax, the poundage was found to be 5%; in another case it was as high as 33%. A few bodies used a graduated rate (known elsewhere as a 'sliding scale')[2] with exemption for the smallest properties. (We shall have to discuss the propriety of this below.) Elsewhere differential rates were levied according to user, higher rates being levied on non-residential property. In some states lower rates are levied on owner-occupied property, and in West Bengal, Orissa, Bihar, and Assam there is a rebate for costly buildings, presumably a very small and tentative step in the direction of site value rating. This practice was

[1] Cit., pp. 478–9.　　　　　　　　[2] See above, p. 141.

not viewed favourably either by the Local Finance Inquiry Committee or by the Tax Inquiry Commission.

The desire for these various deviations of method of assessment in India, designed no doubt to render the tax more effective in local conditions, can mainly be traced to the failure to maintain the basic regular and thorough valuations which would have made most of them unnecessary.

So far as they understood what they were getting at the West Indies also used annual value.[1] Valuation was normally carried out in a very crude manner by local committees of low educational standard, to whom the distinction between annual value and capital value would have been quite incomprehensible. Most islands early adopted rates of a sort in the principal town. It frequently happened that there were overlapping powers and duties between the Island government and chief town, and consequent jealousies. The Island government would then put a low ceiling on the poundage that might be raised, and the town's only defence was arbitrarily to increase the level of valuations to the point needed to produce the revenue required, thus making havoc of any pretence of objectivity in valuation.

An extreme case of this type of confusion is Mauritius—in so many respects like a displaced West Indian island. The valuation ordinarily required the valuer—whoever he might be (no qualifications were demanded) to declare a 'full and fair capital value'. The vagueness of this concept led to a number of legal decisions which destroyed any consistency in relative values and there emerged a concept of 'intrinsic value' which was held to be unalterable by economic or natural causes. On the other hand it was implicitly recognized that the intrinsic value was too low, since it was argued that it gave a reinsurance against loss from tornadoes. The poundage ceiling had long been fixed at 10% so that when more revenue was required it was customary to raise all values proportionately by the percentage necessary to achieve the desired revenue; but without attempting any reconsideration of changes due to development.

In the West Indies two places did not conform to the normal pattern: British Guiana and Jamaica. Throughout its history British Guiana has had an inescapable life and death demand for local services for coastal defence.[2] For long it was hoped that the problem could be met by voluntary labour and contributions, but

[1] See above, pp. 278–9.   [2] See above, pp. 36 ff.

as population increased, difficulties of getting the required public works increased even faster. Experiments for a compulsory levy were made both on an annual value and a capital value base, but without much success. In fact the cost of the necessary works was beyond the competence of the local farmers, however organized, and British Guiana has not yet solved the problem of local government finance.

Jamaica, like other islands, started on annual value, but changed on to capital value. The last complete valuation was made in 1928, but according to a good opinion, in no case did declared values exceed two-thirds of market price. Properties worth more than £50 were revalued in 1937 but probably not brought up to market values. In 1943 a Commission[1] (which contained no valuers) investigated the whole question of local rates, and recommended that instead of capital value, unimproved value should be used. This was accepted in principle by the government of the day, but did not command complete confidence. Hesitation as to the base, and doubts as to the method of valuation of unimproved value, held up the necessary revaluation, until (as we saw above)[2] by the end of 1958 only two parishes had been put on the new basis. In the meantime known new properties, or divisions of old ones, had been added to the valuation roll at 'negotiated' prices which were above the previous level (by that time well below current market value), but probably not more than 50% of true current values. This higher valuation of new properties was, however, enough to upset the relative values of different properties. In the meantime the Parochial Boards in desperate need of a wider tax base adopted a graduated rate (so-called sliding scale) with such vigour that (as we saw in Chapter 14) the government was forced to withdraw from the boards the right of fixing their own poundages. The worst abuses of the sliding scale system were, however, in respect of Rural Areas where the number of large properties was far smaller than in the towns, so that penalization of particular properties was easier, and rapidly became popular.

The Jamaica revaluation of 1955–8 revealed undervaluation of urban properties,[3] ranging from 1·5 fold in properties up to

[1] Bloomberg Commission.
[2] See pp. 142–3.
[3] Comparing previous capital value with new unimproved value—which is all the figures allow—and is consequently an understatement.

£10,000 and 9·4 fold in those above.[1] The main explanation of the dispersion is almost certainly differences in the percentage of new (and consequently somewhat higher valued) properties from class to class. On the average the change in value consequent on revaluation was 4·7 fold.[2] The cases of Mauritius and Jamaica serve to emphasize the difficulties and evils which may creep into this apparently simple tax by legal vagueness concerning the method of valuation, by want of skill on the part of the valuer, and by the failure to revalue sufficiently frequently.

The taxation of urban realty is hardly in better case in West Africa than in the West Indies. In Nigeria, Lagos rates on annual value and has recently secured an adequate cadre of professional valuers. In the Western Region, as we have seen, a property rate is used only in Sapele and Warri, where there is much non-African property. Valuation is carried out by a third-class clerk and is thoroughly unsatisfactory. Elsewhere in the Region there is much resistance to the introduction of property rating, said to be due to the fact that councillors are large owners of urban real estate. In Ibadan in 1958 the caretaker government passed a resolution introducing property rating but this decision was reversed when the elected council was restored. In a large town like Ibadan it is surely a very short-sighted policy to allow substantial office and commercial buildings to escape all responsibility for the urban services they enjoy. In the Eastern Region a desire to introduce a property rate has been stimulated since 1956 when a ceiling was put on the level of personal tax, in order to prevent it impinging on the domain of Regional income tax. Five urban areas were rating on property in 1958,[3] but again the valuation was primitive. The Northern Region has employed the services of a professional valuer, but the result is not yet apparent.

Outside Nigeria, Freetown rates on annual value. A thorough

[1] Information from the Ministry of Finance.

[2] Even allowing for the fact that there had been no comprehensive revaluation since early in the century, these very high percentage changes suggest a rapid rise in land values. Much of this would seem to have occurred since 1954 as a pilot revaluation made for the purpose of *Finance and Taxation in Jamaica*, cit., showed a much smaller rise. Such a rise in land values could well have been sustained by the rapid increase in exports of bauxite and of emigrants' remittances without upsetting the balance of payments, which in fact has not been seriously disturbed.

[3] See above, p. 298, fn.

valuation has recently been made by a professional valuer from the U.K.; the process took him five years and the result was an average increase of 60%, which enabled the rate poundage to be lowered by one-third and still produce more revenue. In the peri-urban areas, however, no revaluation has taken place; consequently the local councils are unable to raise adequate rates, even in high-class residential areas. The result is that the quality of local services (especially street paving, lighting, and drainage) falls abruptly at the city boundary. It is not surprising that the local board in Wilberforce (the area with the best property) has put up a demand to be allowed to use a progressive poundage, similar to Jamaica's sliding scale.[1] Up country in Sierra Leone only Bo uses any sort of property rate—on a very simplified but not unsuccessful[1] type of capital value.

Of the West African countries Ghana seems to have made the greatest progress in urban property taxation. In 1958 it was employing over thirty professional valuers. Ghana's progress in this direction is to be explained partly by the much greater difficulty government bodies, either central or local, have always experienced in collecting personal tax than in Nigeria. Accra was formerly on annual value but has recently changed over to capital value. Outside Accra, however, property rating seems not to be very successful. Even in relatively wealthy Cape Coast (the one city in 1958 whose council had not been suspended), not more than 60% of the revenue currently due was being collected, and there were heavy arrears. Outside Accra much of the valuation is still the work of local Assessment Committees; this is not adequate for the major towns. It is evident from the above that up to the present urban property rates in West Africa have hardly passed out of the primitive amateur stage; nor is the tax being effectively used even where it is nominally in operation.

In East, and for that matter Central Africa, the position is very different, specially in Kenya and (it seems) in Northern Rhodesia. Both Nairobi and Lusaka have skilled valuers trained in the U.K., and Kenya has a fair supply serving the rest of the Territory.[2] In Uganda and Tanganyika less progress has been made, partly

---

[1] See above, pp. 203 ff.

[2] Though one African council complained that when they asked to be valued a valuer came down from Nairobi, surveyed the town for two weeks and then made them wait four years before forwarding the result.

no doubt because there are fewer towns with substantial numbers of European type buildings, but Uganda has also experienced difficulties of principle over valuation (which we shall discuss below). In Tanganyika, Dar-es-Salaam and nine other town-ships use property rates. In all the East (and Central) African territories the basic valuation is on unimproved value; exclusively so in Kenya. In Uganda some of the smaller towns use annual value and the same is true in Tanganyika (e.g. of Bukoba). In Tanganyika, Dar-es-Salaam and some other towns (e.g. Moshi) have only recently turned over from a house tax to unimproved value—with, in the case of Dar-es-Salaam, very extensive shifts in rate incidence.

Except in Kenya the valuation is necessarily carried right through on a double basis—with or without the buildings, since outside Kenya it is the practice only partially to derate the build-ings. Everywhere, however, the poundage on buildings is lower than on the sites, but since the building is normally by far the more valuable of the two components, its contribution may be the larger part, and is in any case by no means negligible. Thus in East and Central Africa the local tax on urban realty has, by and large, made a good start. There are indeed some anomalies—we shall have to examine two: in relation respectively to the problem of rating government property—(it will be remembered that in these areas the Crown is everywhere the ultimate landowner)—and in relation to the rating of Africans. These anomalies, however, are only partially related to the choice of the unimproved value base. It is at least evident that East and Central Africa have made much better progress than other places in solving the problems of skilled valuation and of keeping valuations up to date, and so their urban tax is far more effective than elsewhere.

II

The problem of the most appropriate basis for a local tax on urban realty needs to be considered from two angles: economic benefit and administrative feasibility. We may start with the former since it is our main interest. The first point to discuss is the relative appropriateness of annual value or some sort of capital value. In the early days of the British local rate although annual value predominated there were sporadic attempts to include items such as stock in trade into the valuation; but in the second half of the nineteenth century, when the great expansion of rate revenue was taking place, renting had become the dominant form of domestic occupancy, so that annual value became quite firmly established as the rate base, with liability on the occupier (although in Scotland the landlord also contributed).

The great advantage of an annual value which is closely related to rent is that it is easy to explain to the taxpayer—what he has to pay is just a percentage of his rent. Overseas, many rating officers today hanker after annual value on this account, and when there is a great deal of fairly solid renting, as in Lagos and Freetown, the annual value base seems to work reasonably well. But from the economic point of view it has three rather serious disadvantages in developing countries. The first of these (which is indeed common to annual value and capital value, but not to unimproved value) is that every addition to the property, in principle at least, immediately gives rise to additional rate liability; the tax thus tends to be disincentive both of new building and of the improvement of existing houses. Secondly, in countries where rent control exists, or is likely to be introduced in an emergency, rents will be frozen in relation to other prices, so that the real value of the revenue fails to keep pace with government needs. In the U.K. half-hearted attempts were made to get round this difficulty by basing liability on what the rent would have been if there had been no rent control; they were not successful. The developing countries in which we are interested have been if anything more ardent believers in rent control than the U.K., so if they insist on using annual value they must expect this sort of trouble.

A more serious drawback to annual value, especially relevant in developing countries, is that the rent in question and hence the valuation, is closely tied to the existing building (or in valuation terminology, existing user). When a town is developing rapidly people will want to buy property not so much for the use of the existing building, as for what they could put there instead. For this reason the true value of the property may far exceed the capitalized value of rent of the present hereditament, and the true value will go on rising as the town develops, although the rent may be fixed. On the annual value base the town authorities will thus be foregoing the advantage they might be reaping from the rise in property values.

Of course, if revaluations are held regularly and fairly frequently, any increase in *rents* will be included in the valuation; it is by this means that Bombay has been able to get along so well. But even so, just because annual value is tied to current *user*, the tax base will not rise so fast as when a capital value base is used. Thus in a developing country it is normally more advantageous to use a capital value than an annual value base, even when there is a good deal of solid renting (in fact this is very exceptional). It might well have been more advantageous if the British rate had settled down on a capital value basis, especially in view of the muddle, and the growth in owner occupation caused by rent control; but it is too late to change now. It is not too late for developing countries to start off on the right base.

The next point to settle is whether, if we decide on a capital (ownership) base, it is better to use a full market value or a so-called unimproved value base. This is a much more difficult question to answer, because the appropriateness of one base or the other depends very much on the stage of development and the type of town. The idea of unimproved value is essentially an application of the analysis of surplus which we saw to lie behind Indian land revenue.[1] As an urban device it originated with Henry George[2] who was greatly impressed with the rapid rise in land values during the gold boom in California in the 1870's and 1880's. Like the early Indian administrators, George planned to tax away the whole surplus. What made the Henry George idea so particularly attractive was the claim that this land tax would be sufficient to finance all the services of the state. This was hardly plausible even in primitive days in the U.S.; it would certainly not be true anywhere today, in view of the much wider range of duties governments are now expected to undertake. In fact the California valuers were not much more successful in isolating the surplus element than the Indian valuers. The attempt to tax 100% surplus led to so many tax bankruptcies that city Treasuries were also bankrupted and today only a few places in Pennsylvania in the U.S.A. practise the derating of buildings.

The surplus which Henry George hoped to tax was the excess of market value over completely virgin land, that is land without either public utilities or buildings; all such were regarded as 'improvements'. In growing towns today the property subject to a

[1] See above, p. 279.   [2] Henry George, *Progress and Poverty*, 1881.

tax on unimproved value often already has considerable investment in it: basic public utilities such as roads and water mains;
but it is only buildings which are considered as 'improvements',
and oddly enough this is so even when the casual observer
would class them as obviously disfigurements—e.g. a small shack
in a street which is rapidly being westernized. Henry George
believed that taxing away the surplus would have beneficial effects
in two directions: it would discourage speculation by making it
unprofitable to hold land off the market for a better price, and it
would encourage development. The positive discouragement to
speculation only works effectively if 100% surplus is taxed. The
positive stimulus to building arising from the partial or total
derating of buildings is, however, undoubted, almost irrespective
of the precise definition of unimproved value used. In fact, however, this very stimulus to building will itself encourage speculation in real estate. On the other hand a tax on the capital values of
land, either on market or unimproved value—will to some extent
discourage the holding of land off the market for a better price.
This is a further rather important argument against the adoption of
annual value in a developing country at least in the form in which
it is used in England and Wales where there is no discouragement
to holding land off the market, since unoccupied land and voids
of all sorts are wholly derated.

The encouragement to building given by the unimproved value
tax base is unquestionably very attractive, but there are several
qualifications which need to be made. In the first place the encouragement is indiscriminate; it may be questioned whether it is
right or desirable to encourage all building of whatever sort. Two
considerations enter here. First, where an internal price rise is
expected—as may very easily occur in a developing country—a
surplus of savings tends to go mainly into building as offering the
best available hedge against inflation. It may consequently be more
necessary to restrain than to encourage indiscriminate building.
Secondly, the supply of building labour and materials may well be
inelastic within the country, so that they will have to be supplemented by imports, thus increasing the strain on the balance of
payments. All of this is awkward for the government, which
would like to borrow the savings for its own use, and which needs
ample supplies of building labour and materials for such things as
high density housing (never fully a commercial proposition), and

the construction of public overheads. These considerations do not necessarily constitute an economic argument against using the unimproved value base, but they do imply that a government should be prepared to restrain a building boom (or particular aspects of a building boom) by other methods, whether by interest rate policy (if there is a central bank), or by taking measures to increase supplies of resources for building.

There is a further argument, however. From the point of view of social cost it is rather doubtful policy to provide building owners with urban social services gratis; the result can only be to throw the burden of these services on to the general taxpayers, many of whom derive no benefit from the new buildings. This problem can be met to some extent by a system of strict charges for municipal services, including scavenging and sanitation, as is in fact the practice in Kenya, and as is apparently intended in Jamaica. But it is administratively difficult to do this effectively since the benefit of a number of services (e.g. street maintenance and cleaning) cannot sensibly be imputed and charged to individuals. An alternative solution is to derate buildings only partially, charging a lower poundage on the building than on the site (as is done in Uganda and Northern Rhodesia). This is a solution which we shall have to discuss further below. On strictly economic grounds there are clearly important considerations both for and against derating buildings, that need to be carefully weighed up against the economic and social background of the particular country, or even the particular town.

III

The fundamental evidence for an effective and equitable valuation for a tax on urban realty must be current market prices: if the base is annual value, free market rents, if on a capital value sale prices. Since rents of particular houses may be out of line for a number of reasons (and the same is quite likely to be true of selling prices), it is generally considered undesirable to stick too closely to actual rents or selling prices; the aim is rather to seek a normal current value. The British Rating and Valuation Act of 1925 confirmed that the rent on which valuation was to be based was to be what a willing tenant would give, and a willing landlord accept; a corresponding phrase for capital value is that rateable value must be based on 'The full and fair price or sum as between a willing buyer and a willing seller.'[1] This implies that the valuer must use his judgement, adjusting a queer looking price by analogy with those he believes to be normal. It will clearly be easiest to do this if the rate is based on the sort of prices which are commonest in the area, since this will minimize the extent to which the valuer has to use his judgement in valuing by analogy. If renting is substantially practised, it is argued that annual value is the best base because nearly everything has a rent, while sales may be infrequent. This argument, however, is not really very relevant. If a substantial proportion of the buildings are let on long leases these may be quite as much out of date as sale prices; in a developing country where renting is not usually substantial, sale prices are likely to provide the best evidence, especially as property is likely to change hands fairly frequently. There is a good case consequently for neglecting rental values, even if there is a substantial amount of renting, except in so far as the capitalized rent may sometimes afford some corroborative evidence for a capital value.

The sales which take place in the early stages of development of a new town are mainly those of bare 'unimproved' sites, so that in the early stages this will be the most appropriate base, requiring the minimal amount of judgement and of arguing by analogy on the part of the valuer. Even when sales of built-up 'improved' sites become important, the valuer can carry on for a good long time by subtracting the value of the site (obtained by analogy), from the market price of the whole hereditament; because on the whole the sites in an area are much more like each other than are the buildings. But when the point is reached when all land is already built on, and there is no more bare site evidence, an impossible weight is imposed on the analogizing capacity and judgement of the valuer. He is forced to proceed to disentangle the value of the site from the value of the building by some mechanical device of deductions and perhaps additions—to allow for the characteristics of particular sites.

Kenya has already begun to face up to this problem, for although there is still a fairly good supply of bare site sales in Nairobi, the proportion is rapidly declining, and in Mombasa the fully built-up stage has already been reached. The Kenya Ordinance of 1955 decrees that the unimproved value is not to exceed the current sale price of site plus building, *less* the difference between

---

[1] Cf. Northern Rhodesian Ordinance, quoted in Lund, loc. cit.

the replacement cost of the building and its depreciated value. This formula sounds satisfactory, but in fact it would only be so if (and it is a very big if) depreciation is correctly estimated, and if no change of user is contemplated. If the sale price presumes change of user, the unimproved value must at least equal the current price plus the cost of demolition of the existing building. Since in Kenya nothing is really aimed at beyond a plausible derating of buildings, the answer does not matter too much, but if (as in Uganda) it is desired not merely partially to rate buildings but also to apportion shares of the rate between different interests, then the problem of correctly estimating depreciation becomes important. It has been made much more difficult by the change in money values since the system was instituted.

Thus, when the built-up stage of a town is reached the base which will require the least element of judgement and analogizing is clearly the full capital value or selling price. Because a country is only at a fairly early stage of development it does not follow that it has no old, fully built-up towns. Mombasa, one of the oldest towns in Africa, and contained in an island site, is a case in point. In Nigeria big old towns—Kano, Ibadan, Abeokuta—are very frequent, whereas quite new towns of the type of Kaduna, Enugu, and Port Harcourt are rather exceptional. This suggests that even within a single country, while unimproved value would be the more appropriate tax base in some places, in others capital value (or improved value) would make for better and simpler valuations. Is it possible to combine the two methods, or to allow 'local option' in adopting one base or another? In fact New Zealand does just this, and it is claimed that the opportunity of offering better terms produces a healthy rivalry to attract investment between one town and another. There seems to be no reason, however, why the total amount of development in a country should necessarily be greater on this account; it will merely be differently located. In fact a richer town which wants to attract investment can always offer better terms than a poorer, and so grow richer, even under a uniform valuation base.

An argument against local option in the tax base is that since rateable value will be much higher in the areas using improved value than unimproved value, it is impossible to base any sort of equalization grant on relative rateable value per head, an otherwise very simple and appropriate base, and one increasingly used in the U.K. One way round this, and it is certainly a way worth considering, would be for the government to insist that valuers should always make the double valuation, on unimproved value and on improved value, and then base the grants on relative improved values while allowing towns to charge what differential poundages they liked on site and buildings respectively, between zero on building, to equal on site and building. In this way each town could choose the formula most suited to its current state of development. When the fully built-up state had been reached nearly everywhere, it would be simple to go completely over to the (then generally more appropriate) improved value base. The double valuation would no longer be necessary. This plan would entail very little extra expense, since the valuer has to make a double valuation—proceeding from improved value sales evidence, to un-improved value by analogy as soon as a site is built on.[1]

Further, the option of partially rating buildings—and of increas-ing the relative weight on buildings gradually as the need for revenue expands, would be of very great advantage in enabling the standard of municipal services to be stepped up as becomes necessary. Generally speaking the value of buildings is likely to increase considerably faster than that of sites. Thus in Lusaka from January 1952 and January 1956 the value of sites rose from £1·5 mn. to £5·6 mn., that of buildings from £2·6 mn. to £13·0 mn.[2]

There is one further problem to be considered, which is espe-cially important in African conditions: who is to be liable to pay the rate? This problem arises whatever type of the capital value base is used. In other words who is to be considered the owner? In East and Central Africa, as we have seen, the Crown is the ultimate owner of the land. Is the Crown therefore to pay most of the rates? In fact in many parts of East Africa the contribution of the Crown is predominant—as much as 60% in some places. This is not really a very sensible arrangement; the Crown's contribution becomes much more like a grant, and the question arises as to whether, since the Local Authority is so much at the mercy of what the Crown chooses to do, the rate is really a genuine source of autonomous revenue. Various solutions have been suggested and tried, to deal with this difficulty. In some places the Crown does not pay rates on unalienated land, but in others it does. In some

[1] This assumes that valuation is under central control.
[2] Lund, loc. cit.

places ownership is defined as a fairly long leasehold, so that the Crown would not pay, or would (e.g. in Uganda) only pay on its interest as a ground landlord. According to the Kenya 1955 Ordinance the liability to the rate begins with a five-year lease. This is not satisfactory, since a five-year lease gives few of the opportunities for change of user which are inherent in ownership, or possibly in a long-term lease. This difficulty could be got round by only partially derating the building—the lessee would then pay his share on that, while the landlord—or ground landlord if there were no intermediary—would pay on the site value. In fact in a seller's market the Crown would have no difficulty in shifting the incidence of the rent. The amount that the Crown would pay on unalienated land, unless it were 'dead ripe' (development confidently anticipated within a very few years) would naturally be very small.

Seeing the advantages which can accrue to a developing town from a local tax on urban realty, and which are in fact accruing to towns in East and Central Africa, we must finally investigate what are the main obstacles to its more effective use in the West Indies, in Asia, and in West Africa. We may put these under four heads, the relative importance of which differs inevitably from country to country, but usually all have been present: first, lack of understanding and consequent failure to use an appropriate base; secondly, defective legislation; thirdly, failure to revalue at regular intervals; and fourthly, difficulty of obtaining the services of qualified staff for the valuation process. Of these legislative deficiency and failure to keep valuations up to date are the most important.

In far too many places it has been implicitly assumed, without taking independent thought, that because annual value is the base used in the U.K. it is necessarily appropriate in a developing country. As we have argued a capital value base gives better results in virtually all cases. In Lusaka, e.g. between January 1952 and January 1956, rateable value (sites and buildings) expanded from £6·1 mn. to £18·6 mn., enabling an actual reduction in poundages, from 1s. to 8½d. in the case of sites and 3d. to 2d. in the case of buildings, to be made, while yet leaving sufficient revenue for current expansion of all services. Under an annual value base much less of this growth would have been netted into the local Treasury.

In some of the West Indian Ordinances the valuer is given

virtually no lead as to the criteria he should consider in a valuation, nor even whether he is to think in terms of rent, selling cost, size, or any other quality. Valuations made by the light of nature by amateurs in such circumstances are bound to be arbitrary and to give dissatisfaction. In practice they tend to take nothing but measurement (divorced from location) into account. In some Ordinances valuers are made to sign a sworn declaration as follows: 'that I will to the best of my skill and knowledge and without fear or prejudice truly and impartially appraise and value all such property . . .', &c. This is useless. Clearly, however bad the valuation, the valuer could always say without possibility of contradiction that he had done his best. It is only here and there in the most recent Ordinances that specification of professional qualifications for a valuer have been made. For its own protection a country should make sure that its towns have available to them valuers with recognized qualifications—if possible with local government experience. (The Lusaka valuer emphasizes how easy it is for an experienced valuer to transfer from one base to another, since the basic valuation principles do not alter.)[1] It is equally necessary to state specifically what details are required to be entered on the valuation roll, or comparable information will not be collected.

Periodic revaluation is quite essential, whether on annual value or capital value, in order to keep the base in tune with changing values or rents as development proceeds. This is of course especially necessary when there has been a major price change. The customary nominal period between valuations is five years; much more than this allows too much scope for price changes and hence gives rise to awkward problems of changes in incidence when revaluation is at last carried out. On the other hand, to aim at a much shorter period than five years is usually too expensive, though if a very simple base is used (as the Scottish actual rents) revaluation can be a continuous process; but this has other disadvantages.

In spite of its importance relatively few places have carried through regular revaluations; the U.K. (outside London, which has been bound by statute to quinquennial revaluation since the nineteenth century) is as bad a sinner as any. The difficulties which arise when periodic revaluation is neglected can be illustrated by the case of Jamaica, where differences in the level of assessment

[1] See above, p. 349.

from under twofold to over ninefold as between old and new valuations occurred.[1] It is only because Jamaica has at last settled down to straighten out the tangle that the extent to which valuations had got out of line—has become apparent both with prices and with each other. Most other places (e.g. in India and other West Indian islands) do not yet know the worst. The Jamaican situation can be contrasted with that of Lusaka, where a routine revaluation was carried out between July 1955 and January 1956. In the overall position at least no break in the smooth trend of growth was apparent although some previous lag in site values was apparent.

A major difficulty affecting all countries (not excluding the U.K.) since the war has been the shortage of skilled professional valuers. Judgement in valuation, so necessary for successful analogizing, is not something which can be quickly learned; it only comes by experience. The shortage of valuers in the U.K., due both to the stoppage of training during the war, and to the many new demands for valuers' services afterwards (in assessing compensation for war damage, nationalization, compulsory purchase, and so on), has implied an even greater shortage overseas, either for making first valuations in countries wishing to establish a tax on urban realty, or for bringing valuations up to date where the tax was already established.

Today the situation is improving month by month, although there is likely to be an excess of demand over supply for some considerable time. In the meantime there is much that governments, both central and local, could do to economize in the time and use of skilled valuers, without deteriorating the quality of the valuation. The most important contributions at the local end would be first to make a comprehensive survey of the area, mapping and numbering all hereditaments, but without attempting initially to put values on them. Secondly it is vital to set up a careful and complete sales register. The main reason why it took the Jamaican valuers four years to cover two parishes was the lack of knowledge of boundaries.

In Northern Rhodesia all land in the territory is registered in the Government Department of Surveys and Lands. Each plot is allocated a specific number, which gives complete identification for the use of the valuer. Further, in Lusaka there is a complete register of

[1] See above, pp. 352–3.

property sales. By keeping in constant touch with the entries in this, the valuer's judgement is continually kept in tune with changes as they occur. Analogizing is greatly simplified. There is no doubt that the success of the Lusaka tax is due very largely to the two factors of cadastral survey and sales register; unfortunately Lusaka is exceptional in this respect. Finally, immediate steps could be taken in conjunction with the town survey to establish the nucleus of a local Valuation Department which could do a considerable amount of preliminary sorting before the arrival of professional staff.

There is no doubt whatever about the necessity for professional valuation of commercial, industrial, and of European-type residential property; but it is at least worth considering whether much simpler methods could not with propriety be applied to local type housing (mainly wattle and daub), either in Asia or Africa. This problem has not yet really come up in East or Central Africa, because on the whole Africans are excluded from any tax on urban realty.[1] A promising method, however, has been evolved in Bo, Sierra Leone, based partly on size, type of roof, and other amenities (these normally constitute almost the only differences), partly on a capitalization of customary room or bed-space rents. This last would require some analogizing, but appears to be a plausible way of discriminating between the value of houses in different parts of a town.

The important point is that the local Valuation Office should be put on a permanent footing, even if a very modest one. Freetown is an illustration of the evil consequences of not making allowance for permanency. By the time the professional valuer from the U.K. had done his work he had gathered together a competent little staff, but because no steps were taken to hold it together, within six months it had melted away to other parts of the Civil Service, thus precluding effective continuity.

These obstacles to the wider and more effective use of an urban tax on realty are serious, but none of them—now that valuers are becoming more readily available—is really insuperable. The way could be smoothed by a number of steps which could be taken by local staff at no great cost. What is really lacking seems to be an understanding in many countries of the advantages which would accrue and of the revenue which is being sacrificed, for

[1] On the effects of this anomaly, see below, p. 482.

want of better organization. The extent of this loss will become more apparent when we have discussed the capital budget on the one hand and the special problems of urban communities on the other.

17

BUDGETARY ACCOUNTS 3. THE CAPITAL ACCOUNT

I

THE Capital Account lies at the very heart of development from below. It is often said that very little in the way of development can be contributed by local councils because of the meagreness of their resources, both financial and physical. The things that they might do thus tend to get brushed aside, or subsumed in national plans where they lose their identity. This is the wrong approach, from several points of view. Admittedly local bodies (apart from the councils of large towns) cannot undertake large development projects. The aggregate of small improvements within their competence can, however, add up to something very substantial.

Apart from this consideration local capital formation has intrinsic importance not only from the economic and social points of view, but also on psychological grounds. What counts more than anything else with the ordinary citizen is to see some tangible result of his tax contribution in which he can take a personal interest, be it a new market, school, dispensary, or an all-weather road linking his village with the world. Such works are important in establishing a feeling of civic consciousness and a desire for improvement on the one hand, and on the other in encouraging the desire to co-operate, whether by taxation or by voluntary effort.

No one can doubt the social importance of the little works that even quite small villages can achieve; but their economic potentiality is at least of equal significance. This is true even if they appear not to be directly 'productive' themselves. In the first place these small works have a quick reaction (short gestation period), which can help to provide a useful counterpoise to national plans heavily weighted with long gestation projects which bring in no return for perhaps a matter of ten to fifteen years. Moreover the demands of local works on construction materials (which are sure to be more or less of a bottle-neck) are normally light. On the contrary local works tend to be labour intense, a definite advantage in countries where there is population pressure.

Apart from these general economic advantages, particular local works have special economic functions in the development process. Local roads help to break down isolation (and isolationism), they facilitate the evacuation of cash crops, and so encourage their production, while the introduction of new consumers' goods increases the consciousness of new wants. Housing and 'town' planning not merely tend to raise standards of health and morals, but in doing so they improve the quality of labour. Markets (with concrete slabs and permanent roofing) are of first importance not only from the point of view of getting food to consumers in good condition, but also in encouraging cash transactions. More obviously the development of local natural resources, for instance by improving water supply and crop storage facilities, directly raises the national income. Finally all these capital works can be of direct importance for the development of the private sector, providing investments complementary to those which farmers or traders plan to make on their own account, thus giving a general encouragement to those who have the will and the ability to push ahead.

Much of this we have seen before, and some will have to be discussed further in relation to the special problems of town and country; but it is as well to emphasize it here in relation to the particular problems of the present chapter. Here we have to investigate what local bodies really achieve in the way of capital formation: what they can reasonably be expected to take responsibility for on the one hand and on the other what means they have of securing finance for capital formation and similar investment projects.

In Chapter 13 when we were examining local outlay on current account it was necessary to emphasize strongly the inadequacy of the data, due to inaccuracy, lags in recording, too easy *virement*, and often bad presentation; things are still worse on capital account. By no means all central governments yet keep their own current and capital budgets adequately distinct; the situation in respect of local budgeting is still more confused. Nor can informed guessing be as much help as in respect of current outlay. An apparent complete stoppage of capital formation on a project may be due to reclassification, or to failure to make a return, and

does not necessarily imply discontinuity in the programme.¹ The
situation on the incomings side of the capital account is still more
difficult. Few places record separately grants and loans on capital
account, and when they do it is frequently difficult to relate them
to the outlay side of the account.²

In view of the present inadequacy of capital accounting it may
clarify discussion if we start with the form of a simple, but adequate, capital account. This will enable us to see where the bits
and pieces of information which we can marshall would fit into the
picture.

A Simple Capital Account for Local Purposes

Incomings

1. Gross surplus from current account.*
2. Drafts on general reserves.†
3. Capital grants and gifts.

4. Loan repayments to this authority.

5. New loans granted to this authority.

Outgoings

1. Gross expenditure on capital formation.‡
2. Expenditure on working capital.§
3. New loans (to other authorities or
private sector).
4. Repayment of loans by this authority.

Balance = change in reserves.

* Including revenue provision for renewals and also revenue from any taxes
earmarked for development (as in Tanganyika).
† Or on special funds.
‡ Including replacements and renewals.
§ Equipment, stores, spares.

Some of the items call for brief comment. To start with *Incomings*: the funds for local capital formation in developing countries
must of necessity largely be provided from current surplus. There
is normally little difficulty in collecting the means for wanted
projects,³ except perhaps in large cities, where the council and
its doings tend to be somewhat remote from the ordinary citizen.
The real problem is to ensure funds for replacement (or even for
effective operation, but this is not the concern of the capital

¹ Thus a number of important Emirates in Northern Nigeria, including
Sokoto, show no capital expenditure for 1956.
² For example, Northern Nigeria; lags in spending are probably rather
exceptionally long in this area.
³ As one (Nigerian) officer put it to me, 'You can get anything done in the
country; it's the towns that are the problem.'

budget, except in so far as the initial training of specialized staff should be regarded as investment). Since there is little possibility of borrowing for small projects, sums for replacement must be accumulated from current budgets. These can quite properly be put to reserve, and if the need for them is not immediate, can be temporarily invested in development. This practice is much used in the U.K.[1] and some overseas councils are fully alive to its possibilities.[2]

Normally speaking separate accounts should be kept for commercial undertakings because they need to be of 'commercial type'[3] which allow for replacement out of gross profits, and record the allocations to the general budget, to reserves, or to expansion. Apart from these sources a local body may well have further reserves transferred from marketing boards or co-operatives. In some areas (especially the West Indies) there is a practice of maintaining a number of funds outside the budget, for specific purposes.[4] This is not desirable if it can be avoided, since it tends to break up the comprehensiveness of the budget and to blur the picture of the true financial position.

Capital grants and gifts will, like grants on current account, normally be made by a higher layer government, central or state. In the next chapter we shall have to discuss methods of grant aiding capital works so as to achieve the most effective use of resources. There is little evidence that much attention has yet been paid to this problem. Later we shall have a good deal to say about loans; policy in this respect differs greatly from country to country, for no apparent or sufficient reason. Normally for all but the largest towns loan funds, like capital grants, will come to Local Authorities from their own central governments or their agencies.[5]

The large Local Authorities may sometimes borrow directly at long term from the stock exchange, either in London (or in New York in the case of Jamaica), or locally, as in India, where the stock of the three Presidency towns (Calcutta, Bombay, and

[1] Cf. J. M. Drummond and A. H. Marshall, *Consolidated Loan Funds of Local Authorities*, 1938; also see below, p. 398.

[2] Especially in Kenya. Uganda Districts keep an Equalization Fund which can be applied in this manner; see below, p. 397.

[3] Cf. J. R. Hicks, *The Social Framework*, 3rd ed. 1960, ch. 19 f.

[4] Cf. A. R. Prest, *A Fiscal Survey of the British Carribean*, 1957. This also occurs in Northern Rhodesia.

[5] Such for instance as the Kenya Housing Board, and African Local Development Agency (A.L.DEV.); see below, p. 400.

Madras) ranks as a Trustee security. In some places big towns may
also borrow locally at short term, by mortgage, or from the banks
and even large firms. Occasionally they may receive funds direct
from the international agencies, such as the International Bank,
but this is more likely to occur through their own governments.
In spite of this list of possible sources of loan finance, generally
speaking conditions for borrowing are tight and difficult.

Turning to the *Outgoings side* of the account, the first two
items represent real investment, either in the form of fixed installations such as offices, roads, bridges, sewage works, schools,
clinics, and so on, or working equipment, including both general
purpose equipment such as tools and lorries, and specific equipment such as school, office, and hospital furniture. It is necessary
to distinguish between these two forms of real investment since
their life (and hence appropriate depreciation policy) and their
economic function is completely different.

The last two outgoings are financial in character. Large Local
Authorities not infrequently make loans to smaller ones, for
instance Zaria Emirate in Northern Nigeria makes loans to smaller
Emirates and District Councils within the same Province; in
Kenya the County Councils lend to Urban District Councils and
Rural District Councils within their jurisdictions. Even quite
small local bodies may themselves be lenders: to Missions, or to
farmers and small traders.[1] Indeed (with proper precautions) this
is one of the ways in which Local Authorities can help to spread
development from below over a wider area. Next, provision has to
be made for the repayment of loans on maturity (their annual
servicing is a current item so does not appear here). Finally the
balance ($\pm$) of the two sides of the account register the change in
the capital position; the more comprehensive the account, the
better will this be recorded. These items will all call for further
discussion below.

How far can we fill in the various items on the capital account
from the actual Estimates? Unfortunately in many places a number
of the boxes must remain empty for want of adequate statistics.
Some of the better managed Indian cities (e.g. Bombay) present
a careful capital budget; but the Union government has not yet
modernized the presentation of its own accounts in this respect,
and there is not much evidence of state governments taking an

[1] See Chap. 14.

interest in the matter. The situation is no better in Ceylon, where indeed the Ministry of Local Government seems to take little interest in the development of the towns. In Jamaica the Island Government in 1959 for the first time presented its own accounts in the most admirable modern form, but the Parish Councils have not yet followed suit. With care, however, it is possible both in Jamaica and in Trinidad, to isolate the capital items on the outgoing, although not on the incoming side.[1] It must be remembered of course that in the West Indies, even in the larger islands, the scope for local real investment is inevitably somewhat restricted.[2]

Of the African territories Kenya alone presents a full record on both sides of the capital account, for all types of Local Authorities, both European and African. In Tanganyika the latest government Memorandum[3] lays it down clearly that local bodies should keep current and capital accounts strictly separate, and some of them undoubtedly do so. In Uganda most Districts show capital outgoings separately, but only a few have complete capital budgets. In Ghana since the reorganization of the accounting system under the auspices of United Nations Technical Assistance, expenditure on capital formation and equipment seems to be well recorded, but the sources of development finance are far from clear.

In all three Regions of Nigeria the only procedure for the investigator is to plough through the individual Local Authority Estimates and to make his own classification. The Northern and Eastern Regions help by showing capital grants separately, in the Eastern Region in considerable detail. These two Regions also present their local Estimates in handy single-volume form. The situation is not at all so good in the (usually well run) Western Region; but it is much better than in Uganda or Tanganyika where there is no detailed centralized edition of local Estimates.

Such are the bricks with which we have to make our straw. The statistical near blackout on capital account is disquieting, because although one side of the local investment needed is bright and shining, stimulating for taxpayers and consumers and a real contribution to national development, the other side is apt to be

---

[1] I am grateful to Esmond Kentish of the Jamaican Civil Service and William Demas of Trinidad for helping me with their local knowledge in this respect.
[2] But see discussion below (Chap. 21).
[3] *Memorandum on Local Government,* 1957 ed.

particularly murky. The opportunities for bribery, nepotism and all kinds of financial defalcations, are both wider and more attractive when contracts for the purchase of real assets are in question, than in the ordinary business of current administration. Adequate capital accounting is a little more difficult than the penny cash book method which is quite sufficient for current administrative services; but if local investment is to play a significant part in national development it is important that it should be understood and used.

II

In view of the inevitable discontinuities of capital outlays, and also of the apparent habit of Local Authorities to turn first to one line and then to another, the accounts of individual councils, even over a term of years, would not provide a very good sample. However, in fact it seems pretty clear that local bodies in an area are swayed by similar motives in their choice and timing of projects. Partly no doubt this is due to the winds of fashion: if one council demonstrates how easily all weather roads can be constructed with the aid of Bailey bridges, soon all the authorities in the area will be investing in them. Partly, and perhaps more importantly, local decisions are influenced by central policy, through the availability of grants or loans for particular purposes, or simply by persuasion. Hence, by averaging capital investment over a reasonably large sample of a particular grade of local councils, a fair idea of the relative importance of different types of investment can be obtained. As will appear, some definite national and Regional patterns do emerge.

A number of countries cause, or encourage, their Local Authorities to draw up periodic development plans. More rarely these are co-ordinated with those of the central or Regional budget. In Northern Nigeria every Emirate has a Five-Year Plan, but co-ordination seems to be almost wholly wanting. In Kenya and Tanganyika the central governments encourage the Local Authorities to plan in advance. Uganda has an elaborate and obviously carefully thought out three-year capital programme for the whole territory, starting in 1959–60 and planned to cost over £13 mn. In this 11% is allocated to the Portfolio of the Minister of Local Government (and there is more for education and medical services). Just what part Local Authorities are themselves expected to play in this is not clear. On the whole it smacks rather of development from above than below.

For the outgoings side of the capital budget a breakdown into eleven headings can be carried through to give a fairly high degree of comparability.[1] The content of the breakdown is as follows: (1) roads, streets, and complementary services such as street lighting, fire brigades, and housing for road gangs, (2) housing and town planning (but not staff housing), (3) conservancy, sanitation, sewerage, and drainage, (4) educational establishments of all kinds, including schools, teachers' training colleges, teachers' houses, educational office buildings, and school furniture, (5) medical installations and their furnishings, including clinics, dispensaries, maternities, and general hospitals, (6) markets, slaughter-houses, lorry parks, eating houses, and sanitation in connexion with such installations, (7) water supply and installations connected therewith such as reservoirs, pumps, and pipe lines, (8) administrative establishments, including council offices and furniture, staff houses, police barracks, court houses, and prisons, (9) vehicles and general equipment including workshops and depots, (10) amenities, such as parks, stadia, community centres, libraries, hotels, hostels, and beer halls, (11) natural resources development (excluding water), including agricultural and veterinary investment, afforestation, bush clearing, and resettlement,[2] and apparatus for pest control.

The fact that most of these items figure very frequently in local budgets illustrates the wide potential of local investment. As to its volume we shall have to inquire later. Nevertheless it is evident that there is quite enough in the way of local capital outlay to call for careful planning and thought taking in respect of priorities. Each local jurisdiction has its own problem of growth, which, to get the best results, needs to be considered as a whole, in relation to its own special needs and to the plans of private entrepreneurs who live in, or might be attracted to, the neighbourhood. In Kenya local plans have to fall within the framework of the Territorial plan. The Tanganyika government enjoins its local bodies to follow their (three-year) plans consistently through to the end. This is all to the good in encouraging Local Authorities

---

[1] The main difficulty is that sometimes (e.g. in Ghana) equipment is all lumped together (on economically functional grounds), elsewhere it is included with fixed capital formation in a subjective breakdown.

[2] Sometimes classed as 'rural development'.

to view their problems as a whole;[1] but much more important than paper plans (which in any case are only concerned with the activities of the public sector, and too often ignore private enterprise), is the promotion of an economic consciousness. Councils, as well as individuals, need to grow an entrepreneurial spirit.

With these considerations in mind let us try what we can find out about the pattern of capital outlay. For Kenya we have a firm pattern for each of her three streams of local government: towns, County Councils, and African District Councils; Table 13 shows the average pattern for each of these. Of the towns Nairobi (£1,617,800),[2] Nakuru (£454,500), and Mombasa (£369,100) are the big spenders, and dominate the account; but in fact the deviations from the average distribution are not large. Water, with 38% of the total, is clearly felt as the most urgent need; this reflects not only the high priority given to urban overheads, but also the special difficulties posed by the low rainfall over most of the territory.[3]

It is of some interest to compare the distribution of urban capital formation in Kenya with that proposed for Uganda, where urban development under the plan is to absorb 75% of the allocation of the Ministry of Local Government. This is distributed under four main heads: (1) roads, including street lighting (40%), (2) surface drainage and sewerage (26%), (3) markets (2%) and administration (1%). All other urban capital formation including such important services as water and the provision of 'high density' housing are apparently left to the initiative of individual towns.[4]

Returning to Kenya, the big demand in the County Councils is evidently for lorries, road-making equipment, and so on (56%), with offices and other administrative installations a poor second at 15%. This emphasis appears to reflect the recent setting up of the County Councils; no doubt in a few years' time they will be making heavy expenditure on medical installations.

The pattern of Kenya African District capital formation is

[1] But Tanganyika does not secure co-ordination with central government plans. For instance in the Chagga country I found considerable apprehension lest Territorial water schemes on the slopes of Kilimanjaro might interfere with the needs of stock in the plains at the foot of the mountain.

[2] In the same year Kampala's capital outlay amounted only to £153,600.

[3] In addition Mombasa had recently spent a very large sum on a water supply from the hills 200 miles away.

[4] It should be noted, however, that African housing policy is under review in Uganda, also that the Kampala and District Water Board assumed responsibility in July 1958.

TABLE 13

KENYA

Functional Distribution of Main Types of Capital Outlay (1956) (%'s)

	Roads	Housing	Sanitation	Education	Medical	Markets	Water	Adminis-tration	Equip-ment	Ameni-ties	Natural resources
Towns .	11	14	20	Not applicable	(0·6)	(0·2)	38	14	2	—	—
County Councils .	4	4	—	6	4	—	—	15	56	1	—
African District Councils .	—	—	—	14	16	2	31	8	3	3	9

Sources: Report of the Ministry of Local Government, African District Councils, Approved Estimates.

somewhat less homogeneous than that of the other two streams of local government, but the differences are usually easily explicable. Thus the new District of Elgon Nyanza invested £29,000 on offices and £7,000 on equipment. On the average, just as in the urban areas, the main need is felt to be water (31% of all capital outlay). The importance of medical investment (16%)[1] is rather surprising, in view of the known enthusiasm for schools. It must be remembered, however, both that in Kenya all authorities work to a strict school building programme, related to the output of training colleges, and also that the Location Councils make a substantial contribution to the cost of school buildings. It seems clear that Kenya African District Councils have no particular interest in markets; on the other hand amenities, especially beer halls, are popular. The only road investment occurred in the Districts of Kipsigis and Southern Nyanza, adjacent to Nyanza County which was spending actively in this direction.[2]

Perhaps the most interesting entry in the Kenya capital budgets is in respect of natural resources development, both because this is much greater than in any other of our countries and because it closely reflects the special conditions of the different areas. Over all the African District Councils, the most important outlay on these services was in respect of veterinary services (£12,900), with forestry second at £6,800. The general promotion of agriculture absorbed £10,600, while in addition a few African District Councils maintained demonstration plots and farms. In the pastoral Districts of Nandi and Masai, expenditure on stock improvement is important and is significant not only as a contribution to development, but as showing how these nomadic peoples are settling down, and how capital outlay is helping them to do so. These peoples also spent largely on water, including dams and water holes, which are mainly complementary with stock raising.

The Kipsigis were another people who invested in natural resources; mainly a pastoral people to start with, they have now taken up agriculture with enthusiasm, in fenced and consolidated farms. The Kikuyu in Kiambu, concentrated in emergency

---

[1] In fact three separate services are included under medical: health centres and maternities (£27,800) are the most popular, general public health (presumably non-personal) £14,700, and dispensaries £13,200.

[2] In fact this gave rise to an interesting piece of co-operation in road works between the County Council and the Kipsigis District in respect of bridge building.

villages since 1953, are now just returning to their replanned, consolidated farms, also clearly had important plans to put into operation.

On the average the (26) Kenya African District Councils invested £13,100 in capital formation. In fact, given the size of the Districts this is not a large sum, but the dispersion round the average was very high. The three wealthy Nyanza Districts invested largely (Elgon £37,600, Central £46,300, and South £42,600); poor Northern Nyanza spent nothing. Both Kiambu (£37,300) and Kitui in Central Province (£33,900) also made a good showing.

It is interesting to compare these Kenya figures of capital outlay with what we can glean of Tanganyika and Uganda. Morogoro in the Eastern Province of Tanganyika had capital outlay of just under £15,000, not far from the Kenya average; but the wealthier councils in Lake Province ranged from a little over £30,000 to near £70,000 (in Geita). The average distribution of the Lake Province authorities was: education 35%, administration 31%, natural resources 19%, medical 12%, and 'marketing' (confined to one Native Authority) 20%, and a mere £1,250 for roads. For Morogoro the distribution was as follows: administration 51%, education 29%, roads 10%,[1] medical 5%, markets 3%.

Even this small sample seems to establish a definite Tanganyika pattern of capital development. The emphasis on education and natural resources are very much what we should look for anywhere in East Africa; but the high outlay on administration is notable. Besides Morogoro several of the Lake Province councils spent more on administration than on education. For the most part the funds were applied to staff housing: for chiefs, sub-chiefs, clerks, drivers, and messengers. It can hardly be claimed that such outlay will contribute much to either economic or social advancement.

The standard of capital budgeting in Uganda differs very substantially from District to District. Acholi and Karamoja in the Northern Province present well-arranged capital budgets, showing the sources of revenue (including any earmarked revenue such as

---

[1] In a sense this relatively high percentage allocated to roads should rather be classified as natural resources development, as it was almost wholly devoted to opening up the Uruguru hills, where the previous year the local farmers, misunderstanding the intentions of the Ministry of Agriculture, had rioted and refused to proceed with a perfectly good bunding scheme; the road programme was a brilliant success in breaking down isolationism and showing the tribesmen the possibilities of a new way of life.

cotton bonus for road development) as well as outlay under each
head. The Kabaka's budget in Buganda also presents a capital
budget, but the period over which the expenditure has taken place,
or is to take place, is not clear. Elsewhere the most that can be
gleaned is a list of non-recurrent expenditure which appears to be of
a capital nature. Further, there have clearly been very great lags in
expenditure in the past; the investigator is inevitably left with the
feeling that the whole exercise is not too well grounded. Nevertheless

Capital Formation in Ghana 1956–7 (%s)

	Roads	Housing	Education	Medical	Administration	Equipment	Natural resources
Municipalities	16	7	16	44	14	—	—
Eastern Region	29	neg.	32	13	10	10	—
Western Region	48	2	19	15	4	8	—
Ashanti	31	2	25	18	14	8	neg.
Trans-Volta Togoland	58	3	14	6	6	10	neg.
Northern Region	31	6	28	20	4	7	—
Average non-urban	39	3	24	14	8	7	neg.

a very definite Territorial pattern does emerge. The wide development of Mission education clearly makes it unnecessary for the
Districts to spend a high proportion on schools or complementary
investment; only 10% of the whole goes in this direction. Roads
account for 32%, medical 7%, natural resources 3%, markets and
water each about 1%. Even more than in Tanganyika, administration carries off a high proportion: 36% plus 9% on equipment.
Again this consists very largely of staff housing. The Uganda Districts are in a rather different position from those in Tanganyika in
that a strong and highly centralized administration is in charge, for
instance, of agricultural development, and this can well account for
the small amount of natural resources investment at the local level.
Nevertheless, considered as a source of development from below, it
cannot be denied that the Uganda Districts make a poor showing
in every direction save communications.

Ghana, it will be recalled, is a country for which the figures
of capital formation are presented in a complete form. They are
shown above for the four municipalities taken together and for

each of the Regions.[1] A brief explanation is called for since the statistical breakdown does not admit of a precise parallel with those derivable from Colonial Estimates. It will be observed that there are no entries for sanitation, markets, water, or amenities. In fact some sanitation may be recorded under medical; community facilities, which might rank as amenities, are included with housing. These minor differences cannot, however, upset the general pattern. The equipment recorded cannot be precisely allocated, but it may well be that a substantial amount of it relates to schools; it would not be unreasonable to upgrade the education share on this account. The national pattern emerges quite clearly: in the towns[1] major emphasis on environmental and personal health, and fairly substantial development of educational facilities and office accommodation; in the more rural areas major emphasis on roads and education, with health and medical a poor third. The emphasis on roads in the Northern Region and in Trans-Volta Togoland is especially notable; the latter no doubt has been much influenced by the building of the suspension bridge across the Volta, which now joins the Region to the rest of the country. Road building in the north has so far been very underdeveloped. These developments should facilitate a real expansion of the national income. At the same time it is disturbing to find such a small allocation to natural resources development at the local level; this constitutes a major difference from East Africa.

Turning to Nigeria, and continuing with the same sample of Local Authorities as we used on current account, the allocation of capital outlay in the three Regions was as shown on page 382. As is only natural considering the differences in climate and terrain between north and south, the distribution of outlay differs substantially from one Region to another, nor does a national pattern appear to emerge very clearly. Nevertheless on closer inspection certain characteristics emerge which we can call Nigerian.

First, common to the whole country is an interest in markets which we have not found elsewhere; the high allocation in the north is especially remarkable since, as we shall find, it receives no grant encouragement from the Regional government. Secondly we can notice a rather high pre-occupation with roads (in the Eastern Region this is much supplemented by voluntary labour); on the

---

[1] The total capital outlay of the major towns was: Accra £57,400, Kumasi £50,600, Sekondi/Takoradi £63,200, and Cape Coast £9,000.

TABLE 14

NIGERIA

Functional Distribution of Main Types of Capital Outlay, (1956–7) by Regions (%s)

Region	Roads	Housing	Sanita-tion	Education	Medical	Markets	Water	Adminis-tration	Equip-ment	Amenities	Natural resources
North .	46	2	neg.	5	1	23	3	13	neg.	—	4
East .	16	neg.	2	47	9	3	4	9	6	2	—
West .	39	2	9	3	7	2	3	24	6	2	1

Sources: Native Authority Estimates, Northern Region, Local Government Estimates Eastern and Western Regions.

other hand there is little or nothing in the way of capital formation in natural resources, other than water. We can observe, however, a definite interest in amenities, such as parks, stadia, clubs,
bus shelters, and general embellishments;[2] interest in sanitary
installations is by no means negligible.

Education remains the big difference between north and south,
in spite of the tremendous efforts of the Northern government in
the provision of educational facilities; this is only not apparent in
the year we have chosen because the tremendous programme of
school building to provide for universal primary education had
already been completed in the West, while in the East it was still
in full swing. If we look back over the Northern Estimates the
trend has been gradually, but very slowly, upward, so that this
allocation represents an upward trend in the North, while in the
West the bulge in school building had already been passed.

What one misses all up the west coast, as compared with East
Africa, are first, the very small allocation to natural resources
development. Of the short sightedness of this policy we have
already remarked in respect of current expenditure. Secondly,
there is small sign of any determined attack on the problems of
the major towns: slum clearance and rehousing on the one hand,
main drainage and water-borne sewerage on the other. This is
a matter which we shall have to examine carefully in Chapter 20.
There is, however, both in Ghana and in Nigeria a considerable
interest in town planning at the village level. This can be of importance in the long run as it enables towns to start growing from
a good foundation, so that the mistakes of the past need not be
repeated.

So much for the countries for which statistics of capital outlay
are reasonably complete and available. In India and Ceylon actual
statistics are very hard to come by, although it does appear that
most towns have some capital works planned or in course of
construction. The Indian towns, to whose current budgets we
referred earlier,[3] distributed their capital outlay as follows: housing
and town planning 30%, roads and streets 15%, sanitation 8%; the
remaining 47% is classified together as 'miscellaneous'.

[1] See below, Chap. 21.
[2] Port Harcourt was especially active in this direction, no doubt encouraged
by the oil installations in the neighbourhood.
[3] Chap. 13 especially p. 244.

For Bombay we can be more specific. Bombay has recently specialized on environmental and personal health; the whole town is sewered and there is an excellent water supply. Hospital accommodation has been much increased, and ante- and post-natal clinics established. Great efforts have also been made to provide moderate priced high-density housing in big blocks of flats; the units consist of two rooms with a toilet between two. They are let at about 50% subsidization. Experiments have also been made with dormitories for unaccompanied men.

The problems of Bombay are enough to daunt any administration, owing to population pressure at all income levels, and to the very low standard of living of the poorest. This implies great difficulty in reaching those who most need help. For instance the maternity clinics have been able to secure no more than 10% of potential usage, and none at all from the lowest income groups. A few years ago a survey was made of 'footpath sleepers' and 1,500 were recorded in the business quarter alone. Accommodation was found for these, but within a short period there were as many again. At the other end of the income scale the enlargement of the state boundaries in 1956 brought additional firms and their employees into Bombay city, increasing still more the pressure on accommodation.

Although Poona is not many miles from Bombay its problems are substantially different. Formerly an important British army post, it has inherited rather above-standard urban overheads, together with a large amount of undeveloped land (parade grounds and so forth). This now calls for the development of public services in order to attract industry. Poona (in 1956) disbursed only about £34,000 on capital account of which the percentage allocation was as follows:

roads	housing	sanitation	schools	medical	markets	water	admini-stration	ameni-ties
36	2	23	1	9	4	5	2	14

Like the Ghana towns, Poona is well provided with Mission schools, even so the allocation to education appears to be unwisely niggardly; on the other hand the large allocation on roads and sanitation are obvious top priorities for a town situated as Poona is; but they need to be supported by an adequate water supply, which does not exist at present. Perhaps the two oddest allocations are the relative shares of administration and amenities. The council conducts its business in an incredible wooden rabbit warren of a building which can hardly have conduced to efficiency; the amenities were for the most part embellishments of the type of public gardens (including rock gardens), fountains, and the like.[1] These differences between Bombay and Poona in resource allocation to capital formation, both in respect of total outlay and in respect of its distribution, are typical of Indian local government in its heterogeneity and absence of central control. The contrast with Africa is very striking.

III

The figures that we have been able to collect make it clear that even if local capital outlay is not large at least it has a wide spread. This should imply that local bodies are, rightly, looking about actively to see how they can improve their areas. It may also have a less good side if the investments they make are a chance collection of unrelated items, not supporting each other so as to enhance the individual value to economic development of each project. As we have seen, it is not uncommon for central governments to encourage Local Authorities to draw up period plans. Because planning is fashionable at the national level many of them would do so in any case; but just writing down a list of desirable objectives is not true planning.[2]

There are broadly three sorts of questions which local bodies should ask themselves, not only when the plans are drawn up, but continuously as implementation progresses. These are first, in making all these investments has the recurrent expenditure, by way of operation, maintenance and replacement been fully allowed

---

[1] The explanation is that Poona is setting out to be an Indian Cheltenham; even so the unbalance in development is rather considerable.

[2] I am reminded here of a certain town in Ceylon, whose current budget was in deficit, financed out of rapidly dwindling reserves, and which had put up to the Ministry of Local Government a list of thirty-four development schemes, some highly necessary, such as water and sewerage systems, others of a nature which could well have been afforded out of current revenues (such as the construction of an incinerator), still others plainly fanciful (such as an illuminated promenade to the top of the neighbouring mountain). No plans had been made for the finance of any of this programme, but it was hoped that the International Bank might be interested. It was clear that the Ministry of Local Government was not.

for, so that it can be borne by current revenue (either profits or taxes) without undue strain? Secondly, have the various items in the programme been chosen, both individually and as a whole, so as to maximize economic progress (increase in real income per head), in the available circumstances? Thirdly, given the objectives and the programme, is the best value for money being obtained? These last two questions need to be looked at from two points of view, the economic and the institutional. On the economic side, it is relevant to inquire whether the combination of land, labour, and capital (the technique to be employed) for any particular project is optimum, given the local circumstances and the needs of other projects in the programme. (Thus, for instance, a concrete mixer bought because it was indispensable for one job may materially reduce costs in another.) On the institutional side, when contracts have to be given out it is pertinent to ask whether machinery has been devised to ensure that the taxpayers make the best possible bargain.

These are all difficult questions, and to reach the right answers a combination of economic expertise and knowledge of the district is required. It would take us too far afield to attempt anything like complete answers, but these matters are of such vital importance for development from below, that some discussion is unavoidable.

It is evident that local bodies will have to seek advice and guidance in answering these questions, and consequently that the central government must help them to get the economic and technical aid they require. (This is a matter which we shall have to discuss in the general background of central/local relations.)[1] Experts, however, cannot function effectively without facts. They will want to know something about types and availability of labour supply, and broad income distribution on the one side, something about soils and crop yields, methods of cultivation, cultivation rights (as distinct from formal land tenure) and the functioning of markets on the other. Councils are normally in a good position to collect such facts,[2] if once their intention is directed to the importance of doing so. In a small jurisdiction they can do so directly, in a larger jurisdiction they can call on the co-operation of Village Councils. The mere process of collecting the material will teach

[1] Chap. 19.
[2] In Bukoba, Tanganyika, an African clerk had covered the walls of the Native Treasury office with an excellent set of illustrated statistics.

councillors a great deal they did not know before, and help them
to think in economic and quantitative terms. A knowledge of one
man's successful cropping will stimulate others to improve their
own standard of cultivation.[1]

The answers that are wanted to these questions are in terms of
the maximum rate of return (in a broad sense) from increments of
different types of investment. While (as has been emphasized)
the District plan needs to be thought of as a whole, the potentialities of each form of investment in the particular local circumstances needs to be constantly reviewed. A few illustrations
concerning the different forms of investment which we have found
that local bodies do make will bring out the implications of this.

Roads are always important for development, but it is not good
enough to build them just anywhere (especially if the primary motive
is the provision of employment). Road needs have to be considered
in relation to foreseeable traffic (in a dry, sparsely inhabited area
water may well be a much higher priority). The probable traffic
in turn determines the type of road to be made; the available
labour supply and road-making machinery need also to be taken
into account. Finally there is the question of the relation of the
local road network to the national main road or railway system.

Housing in tropical conditions is mainly an urban concern,[2] for
in rural conditions little more than a shelter against the rains is an
absolute necessity; yet there appears to be (at any rate in Africa)[3]
a very widespread desire to improve the standard of amenities as
income rises. Consequently in rural areas the first public need is
often (as suggested above) for town and village planning.

Probably all developing countries are peppered with growing
communities where orderly expansion is impeded because houses
have been built higgledy-piggledy, with room for nothing between
them but twisty footpaths, implying unhealthy lack of light and air.
If an early start is made it is quite easy to secure correct sites for
the village essentials (such as market and lorry park, local office
and community meeting-place), and to see that the main lines of

[1] Where there is a major cash crop, and particularly where it is co-operatively
organized, the local council will be saved much trouble, but there is a big danger
in such areas that other crops will tend to be neglected. The local council has a
part to play in preventing this.   [2] See Chap. 19.
[3] A good example is the Chagga community on the slopes of Kilimanjaro,
where the old houses are now relegated to the cows, just as occurs in the west of
Ireland.

communication run along and not across the contours. The Tanganyika government seems to be particularly wide awake in this respect;[1] in Kenya also the necessity of replanning the Mau Mau areas seems greatly to have stimulated an interest in town planning throughout the territory. Elsewhere good planning still depends on the initiative of a particular officer.

Education, as we have seen, is one of the most popular forms of local investment. Local bodies do not have an entirely free hand in this respect, and normally the direction of their outlay is much influenced by grants and other encouragements. Nevertheless local bodies can determine to a considerable extent the allocation of their own contributions. Educational services can very easily develop a serious unbalance unless a careful watch is kept on the whole programme. The history of education in India is a sad story of the overdevelopment of rather indifferent university training on the Arts side, leaving the country deficient on the one hand in technicians and on the other in plain literacy.

In Africa there is more danger of the overdevelopment of primary relative to more advanced training. It has to be borne in mind that what is wanted to speed the development programme is 'investment' education,[2] and what is to be avoided is prestige education, whether it takes the form of a degree which offers no employment or a trip to the U.K. which leads to no technical expertise.[3]

There are perhaps four directions in particular in which more and better education is particularly needed: first, in the ability to make simple calculations quickly and correctly. Unintentional mistakes in arithmetic lie behind a very high proportion of cases of defalcation. Secondly, peoples from underdeveloped countries are at a serious disadvantage as compared with boys from countries which are highly mechanized and where consequently an instinct for how wheels go round is almost inborn. Simple courses in engineering and construction would set a lot of this right.[4]

---

[1] Thus the little town of Moshi, about to be promoted in status, had been elaborately planned.

[2] To borrow a useful concept from W. A. Lewis, *Theory of Economic Growth*.

[3] A form of outlay much favoured in the wealthier parts of Uganda.

[4] Pioneer courses of this nature are given at the Community Development School at Awgu, Eastern Nigeria, see below, p. 538.

Thirdly, in every underdeveloped country, but especially in India, there is a sad lag in the education of women and girls,[1] who are thus unable to contribute their proper share to development. Finally, there is much scope for increasing adult education. This can assume many forms, from mass literacy in India to university extension (including vocational courses) in Buganda and the West Indies. In all of this local bodies can make an important contribution by providing the necessary buildings and equipment.[2]

Investment in *health services*, particularly on the personal side, is another very popular form of local development. The thing to be avoided here is the construction at great expense of vast hospitals from which at the best only a tiny fraction of the population can benefit; this, however, is more likely to occur at the central than at the local level. Perhaps the most important medical need in the tropics is for immediate treatment which will prevent a small wound or bite from becoming infected. There are few villages so poor that they cannot provide themselves with a dispensary if they understand the importance of having one.[3] Another health service which is very suitable for local investment is a leper settlement. Since in all but the most advanced cases cure is now practically certain, the social scourge of leprosy can be immediately removed and the physical scourge got under control. Finally, local bodies can most usefully invest in health education, by means of travelling cinema vans on the one hand, and by the making and enforcing[4] of sanitary by-laws on the other.

The difficulty about investment in health facilities is the high operational cost, often made all the higher because of poor control over the issue of drugs. This is a problem which Local Authorities need to face squarely before investment is undertaken. In many

[1] Kenya Settled Area Councils are increasingly organizing classes in housewifery, cooking, sewing, and so on; this is also done by some Community Development Blocks in India. More girls' schools remain the most important need.

[2] The Technical College in Moshi, Tanganyika, built out of the reserves of the Coffee Co-operative is a striking example of what can be achieved locally.

[3] One difficulty in this respect in some areas is the unwillingness of the people to accept treatment, at its worst in India. The Indian government is fully alive to the importance of education (for instance by local health visitors) in this respect; see recommendations of the Mehta Report on Community Development, 1957.

[4] A special difficulty in this respect is found with the Asians in East Africa. Determined councils (such as that of Nakuru, Kenya) have found that abuses can be successfully dealt with in the courts.

countries the devoted work of the Missions largely solves the problem. An important point is the siting of clinics and dispensaries; if they are next door to the administrative office or police station control will be easier than if they are set down in a remote spot.

Councils seem to differ radically in their views of what is right and proper in the way of *office accommodation* and equipment. Some are prepared to go on indefinitely in buildings which are so dark, noisy, and overcrowded that efficiency is seriously impeded: others erect buildings which rival the London County Hall in magnificence.[1] Generally speaking the first thing a new council demands is a new hall and offices. Here is an opportunity for starting right, in modern but reasonably modest buildings, but, as has been well said, 'A tendency to extravagance is hard to check when pride is part of a desired incentive.'[2]

In several parts of Africa (as is apparent from the capital budgets) a great temptation is excessive building of houses for chiefs and local civil servants; there is often a failure to make it clear that these are official and not personal residences;[3] in some countries chiefs are also supplied with expensive motor-cars. These extravagances frequently arise from traditional obligations to supply a chief with housing and transport—reasonable in days when the former implied a mud hut which would be unlikely to survive his tenure of office and the latter transport by hammock; but no longer tenable when transmuted into a large two-storey house and a cadillac.[4] Such investments are bad in themselves since they do nothing to raise the national income and further they encourage competition to get on the council for entirely the wrong motives. In all this India has been brought up in a much more austere tradition than Africa. It is typical that Bombay councillors receive no other recognition for their services than free carriage on the municipal transport system.

We have already discussed the potential importance of local

[1] A striking contrast in the same Territory is afforded by the District Office in Bukoba, where there is no lighting and all work must stop on a dull day, and the new Chagga Council Offices near Moshi, which are the last word in magnificence.

[2] A. Gaitskell, paper for the Cambridge Conference on Land Tenure and Land Use, 1959.

[3] This point was especially emphasized in the Local Government Memorandum of the Tanganyika government, 1957.

[4] Cf. Cox, *Report on Disturbances in the Provinces*, Sierra Leone, cit.

government work in the field of *natural resources* in connexion with current budgets.[1] In the investment field they can also do important work, but a careful delimitation of function in relation to central services is even more necessary than in the sphere of current outlay. Few councils can afford to employ their own experts, but most could make more use of the services of those in government service, for instance in improving their own standards of afforestation, experimental plots, and nurseries.

In African conditions especially, two of the most important means of raising agricultural productivity are better fencing and improved techniques. Local Authorities can help individual farmers by supplying the fencing and tracing the course for it. Improved techniques can be encouraged by organizing local classes where practising farmers can attend in the off season,[2] the Local Authority supplying the buildings. It can also purchase and demonstrate the use of improved cultivators and pest controls. Much of this work is a follow up of central policy which can often be carried out at the local level more effectively, both because misunderstandings are less likely to occur and because results can be checked continuously.[3]

Medical installations are particularly greedy in running costs, both of personnel and material; but the problem of *operational costs and renewals* is quite general, and is more often than not the weak spot in capital budgeting. Wages and salaries have been steadily rising; the right sort of co-operating labour, be it teachers, nurses, mechanics, or agricultural extension officers, is still in short supply. Tropical climates and inexpert usage are tough on equipment; and there is as yet insufficient accumulated knowledge as to the reasonable technical life of lorries, bull-dozers, and other essential equipment. Some years ago very serious mistakes were commonly made (and by no means always at the local level), on the relation between capital and recurrent costs. Councils and their officers are now learning, the hard and wasteful way; but it

---

[1] See Chap. 13, pp. 266 ff.

[2] This has been tried with success at the Awgu school. Where, as often occurs, there are reasonably secure cultivation rights, but no individual ownership, it is naturally impossible to interest young men, who have no secure prospect of a farm, in agricultural improvement, but it has been found that established farmers respond eagerly.

[3] Another way which local investment can help farmers is by construction of simple storage capacity; this can also materially reduce the risk of famine.

is still difficult to convince local taxpayers, and especially community development enthusiasts, that just to provide the building is not enough. There are several ways in which local bodies can greatly help in this respect. First they can keep careful records of their own equipment, making sure to order spare parts in time.[1] Secondly, unless their scale of operations is very small they can set up repair shops,[2] with basic equipment, making them available at lorry parks and so on.[3]

A proper balance between capital and recurrent expenditure is very largely a question of period 'resource budgeting'. A number of governments (Northern and Eastern Nigeria, Tanganyika) cause their Local Authorities to show, year by year, for each programme, cumulative outlay to date (set against original estimate of total cost), together with expected outlay for the next year or two. This is very useful, as far as it goes; in particular it serves to show up both rising costs and lags in expenditure. But it does not really get inside the capital/recurrent problem.

A simple device for dealing with this is to combine in a progress chart the implementation of a particular programme or project, with a functional economic breakdown of real resources required, first, during the construction period, and later for various stages of operation. It is wise to start thinking of operational requirements in good time, even if completion of the project is still some way ahead, since this will serve as notice to see that the requisite equipment will be available and the right types of labour trained. A chart of this type will help with the related, and much neglected problem of dovetailing one programme into another, so that costly labour and equipment need not stand idle when the construction phase of a particular project is complete.

An illustration of such a programme chart is given below; it can be modified in various ways to meet local needs. An important advantage of year by year recording is that it facilitates adjustment as experience accumulates—for instance concerning the necessary rate of renewal, or the best type of labour for particular operations. The record also serves to pinpoint the circumstances which have given rise to cost revisions, such as changes in the prices of

---

[1] For small parts much more use could profitably be made of air freight.
[2] An excellent example is to be found at the Gal Oya (Ceylon) colonization and resettlement project; it included effective on-the-job training for mechanics.
[3] As at Cape Coast, Ghana, see above, p. 270.

equipment, or—most common and least observed—of plan revision in the course of implementation.

A Programme Chart of Outlay, Capital Account

A Construction Period	Already spent cumulative/last year	Estimate to completion next year/total		Date of completion		Remarks and explanations
		Original	Revised	Original	Revised	
1. Buildings (incl. land)						
2. Machinery and equipment						
3. Stocks and stores						
4. Labour (in categories						

B Operational Period		First estimate	Present operation	Full operation	Technical details
1. Buildings	⎫ repairs				
2. Machinery and equipment	⎬ and replacements				
3. Labour (in categories)					
4. Fuel and power					

Every form of local investment calls for purchases of some sort; questions consequently arise concerning the best type of machinery, or school, or hospital, furniture to choose. Still more difficult questions have to be faced where prices are not given in the market and a contract has to be negotiated; there are few more difficult problems that inexperienced councils have to face. Sometimes (as apparently in Ceylon) the law compels them to take the lowest tender, even when there is a doubt whether the contractor can carry it out, and consequently there is a risk of loss. Sometimes opportunities are lost through failing to advertise effectively. Always there is a strong pull to employ the local firm, even if incompetent. Finally at every stage of the exercise there will be opportunities for bribery and nepotism.

Most Ministries of Local Government and many councils now realize that it is necessary to establish formal machinery for contracts, and a number of experiments have been tried of which a few examples must suffice. The Ceylon method (above) is clearly ineffective although it looks plausible. In some Indian towns a dual system of control appears to operate satisfactorily. It is the responsibility of the Chief Executive (Municipal Commissioner) to call for tenders, but he is allowed to use his judgement in making the final decision and need not necessarily accept the lowest. If his judgement is not endorsed by the council a new tender must be advertised. In Uganda, where much trouble has been experienced over contracts, Tenders Boards have been established at the District level. Early experience of their working suggests that in spite of the large size of Uganda Districts, this does not succeed in giving a sufficiently detached view. In Eastern Nigeria Tenders Boards have been set up at the Divisional level, serving a number of councils, and this appears to work better. An additional advantage of a board serving a fairly wide area is that it can include competent specialists who can advise councils concerning technical difficulties.

Before the stage of tenders, however, important decisions have to be taken concerning the degree of mechanization to be employed on particular projects, and the type of machinery to order. These decisions involve very difficult economic questions, which Local Authorities cannot hope to answer without help. It is extremely difficult to induce local councils, or indeed for that matter central governments, to decide such things on rational grounds. Some governments are in such a hurry to be up to date that they will only buy the latest machinery, regardless of the conditions in which it will have to work. Others will snatch at a second-hand bargain, even if it was designed for a different purpose.[1]

Where there is any degree of population pressure, developing countries are repeatedly urged to use highly labour-intense methods of production. Before following this advice blindly the opportunity costs of the labour to be employed by the council need to be carefully taken into account. It requires a very stringent assumption of under-employment in agriculture to postulate a zero or negative net product of any labour for a substantial period,

[1] A good illustration of this was a factory in Ceylon which was attempting to make tiles with second-hand brick-making machinery.

unless at the same time reorganization (for instance farm consolidation) is being carried out, and some labour is genuinely being
set free. Local government work is rarely suitable for quite
unskilled labour, so that even a low return from marginal labour
on the farm may be higher than it would be on council work.
Seeing that the cost of labour on a council project may thus be
quite high if it is properly accounted for, a greater degree of
mechanization may well be the right answer.

An illustration of this principle may clarify the argument. In a
certain District in Uganda,[1] where there is a great demand for small
dams for cattle watering, the District Council was jogging along
making one dam a year by using highly labour-intense methods, at a
cost of £2,000 per dam. It then decided to purchase two bull-dozers,
which, operated by a handful of men, completed a dam a month
at the same total unit cost. There is little doubt that the contribution to increased agricultural productivity by the second method
far outweighed the disadvantage of reduced employment on the
programme. In fact employment was found for the redundant
labour on a tsetse-fly clearing programme which it was now possible to start.

It often occurs that the type of labour really suitable for council
work is not very plentiful; in this case too councils will often be
well advised to consider mechanization. Conditions can alter very
rapidly, however, so that the situation needs to be kept under
review, particularly when renewals have to be made. As an illustration: at a cement factory (in Ceylon as it happens), initially the
work of digging and transporting the material was performed by
highly mechanical means. This was probably partly for prestige
reasons, but at the same time neither labour of the necessary skill,
nor the housing of it, was available near the site. The expensive
equipment proved shorter lived than had been anticipated; and
when after about five years the problem of replacement had to be
faced, it appeared to the management (no doubt correctly) that
sufficient trained labour and housing would now be available.
Consequently substantially less mechanistic methods were substituted for the original set-up.

Thus it is most desirable to judge, and to rejudge periodically,
each proposition on its merits. Once labour has been withdrawn

---

[1] I owe this illustration, and a number of suggestions, to a thesis written by
Michael Purcell, of the Uganda service, on his Devonshire (B) Course in 1957.

from agriculture, where its marginal product although low is probably positive, there is a danger of it falling into complete unemployment, where it is zero. In Chapter 20 we shall have to discuss the severe problems inflicted on urban authorities by the influx of agricultural labour displaced in this way.

IV

Our investigations on the expenditure side of the capital account have revealed two important facts. First, in most countries local capital formation is still on a very small scale. It is hardly too much to say that (allowing for a few striking exceptions) the major problems of establishing modern standards of local social and economic overheads and self-balancing services have not yet been squarely faced. Secondly, while a number of the local works will expedite the growth of the national income, and are indeed a necessary contribution to this process, for the most part, whatever the initial source of funds, sooner or later they will have to be maintained out of current revenue. Those services which can be expected to contribute to the revenue, or even to pay for themselves, are very much in the minority.

We must now turn to examine in more detail the means of finance for capital development listed on p. 370 and available to local bodies in our various countries. This will serve both as a contribution to our general theme and as a means of judging how far insufficiency of finance is the bottle-neck in local investment. It seems *a priori* likely that this may be the case, since it is clear that in most countries local bodies are not lacking in ideas of ways in which they might develop. It must be emphasized that in this section we are not concerned with the finance of true commercial undertakings, which, if they are worth doing on public account, should be able fully to cover their costs, including replacement of fixed equipment and stocks, as well as loan service and repayment.

As we saw in the account of the capital budget (above, p. 370) the sources of capital finance fall under four heads: (1) surplus from the current budget, (2) accumulated reserves, (3) grants on capital account, and (4) loans. Each of these, and the relation between them, give rise to separate problems. Unfortunately the very meagre information on the incomings side given in the Estimates of most local bodies makes it at present impossible to present a thorough account.

Our analysis of current budgets shows that if local bodies had to rely wholly on current surpluses for investment finance their capital formation would be very small indeed. In the West Indies, in parts of Ghana, in Southern Nigeria, even in a great town like Kampala, local councils are hard put to it to balance their current budgets. If Local Authorities really want to develop their areas this should be a substantial, if not a major source of revenue; and in many areas it could be, if tax powers were fully used and the standard of assessment and collection improved.[1] On the other hand a certain amount of investment out of current resources which is in fact made, escapes notice, because the line is not always easy to draw between care for the present and care for the future. A greater awareness of the importance of building for the future could easily draw forth more of this type of investment.

Some territories, as we have seen, require Local Authorities to build up surpluses, part of which are available for investment. In Uganda each District has an Equalization Fund; the two Districts[2] in the Northern Province which present proper capital budgets finance respectively 7% and 14% of their capital formation from current surplus. In Tanganyika a proportion of cess revenue is reserved for development, and as a result, on the average 84% of capital budgets is financed from revenue.[3] In Kenya also local bodies are much encouraged to budget for a surplus to be applied to development. The towns financed 4% of their capital budgets in this way, the County Councils 40%, and the African District Councils 50%.

As we shall see, these differences are partly due to differences in the availability of loan finance, and the amounts of investment are inversely related to the percentage covered by budget surpluses; the high Tanganyika percentages also arise from this factor. Nevertheless these figures emphasize that local bodies *can* achieve surpluses for investment. In some areas additional taxes are levied expressly for development. Thus the Narok Masai put on a rough *per capita* tax on cattle for the purpose, entirely on their own initiative. Quite large although irregular amounts which are almost taxes are also raised through Community Development organizations.[4]

---

[1] Bad local tax collection was stated to be the reason why the Eastern Nigerian government removed local rights in the graduated direct tax; see above, p. 175.

[2] Acholi and Karamoja.

[3] Cf. *Public Finance in Tanganyika, a Survey by the East African Statistical Office*, 1957, cit.　　　　[4] Cf. Chap. 21.

A variant of capital finance from current surpluses is finance from accumulated reserves. These may arise in several ways. Large cities overseas, especially in India, frequently maintain a number of renewal funds (as many as fifteen or twenty) in respect of equipment for different departments; there are also sinking funds for loans, and increasingly, pensions funds. British Local Authorities freely use these for investment, since they can tell in advance when they will be required, and it is not difficult for them to borrow on short term if they find themselves unexpectedly tight.[1] These opportunities are not yet so widespread overseas; but in Kenya, for instance, the towns[2] are wide awake to the possibilities of this source of development finance.

Another source of reserves applicable to development (especially in Ghana, Nigeria, and the East African territories) is the surpluses of Marketing Boards or similar agencies, accumulated during the war and subsequent boom in primary products. These are sometimes transferred to local Treasuries in a lump sum, to be spent over a course of years; sometimes they are doled out gradually, as grants for capital purposes. These reserves must be reckoned a wasting asset. Their large dimensions everywhere were partly due to a misreading of the probable post-war prices of primary products.[3] While these are now gradually falling in relation to the prices of manufactured goods, they are unlikely to go back to the very poor showing of the 1930's. 1960 prices are, however, already low enough to prevent much accumulation of surpluses, and in many areas the agencies which accumulated them have now been disbanded.[4]

In view of these apparent opportunities for capital finance out of reserves, their actual use for this purpose seems to be very limited. In fact in many areas general reserves have already been reduced to something like the minimum level necessary to guard against fluctuations in current revenue. The Kenya African District Councils, however, cover 19% of their capital budgets from this source, the County Councils 6%, and the municipalities

[1] Cf. J. M. Drummond and A. H. Marshall, *Consolidated Loan Funds of Local Authorities*, cit.

[2] Especially Nakuru in my experience.

[3] Cf. P. T. Bauer, *West African Trade*, cit.

[4] A further type of finance from reserves arises when at the village level of local government tax revenue is sometimes accumulated over two or three years for the purchase of a particular investment, such as a bull. This is eminently sensible where funds are very small; quantitatively the net result is very limited, but none the less significant.

3%. Although it is not apparent from the consolidated accounts,[1] it is evident that Tanganyika councils must do some financing from reserves. For instance, Moshi's capital expenditure in 1957 was financed as to 60% from coffee cess, 30% from current revenue, and 10% from general reserve. In Ghana, as we have seen, reserves were increasing in 1959. In 1957 there was some use of them for development in every Region.[2] In Northern Nigeria also there are some funds generally available for development.

For the remainder of their capital finance local bodies must rely on outside sources, either by way of capital grant, or by loan. The percentages in which these two forms of finance are made available to them differ substantially from country to country, partly due to the ideology of central governments, partly no doubt to the expansibility of central revenue. In Northern, and even more in Eastern Nigeria, capital grants are the more important source; in the East they form 60% of grant/loan finance. In the West the Regional government, having made over a large and expanding source of revenue to Local Authorities, is not prepared to help them much either by grant or loan. In Uganda, and even more in Tanganyika, grants are very much more important than loans.

In Kenya on the other hand loans are more important than grants for every form of local government: over 88% of capital finance from loan as against 3% from grants for municipalities, 35% as against 14% for County Councils, and 18% as against 13% for African District Councils. Further, the Ministry of Local Government expresses the desire to increase the supply of loans to African District Councils. In the past it has felt that the poor standard of accounting made this impossible, however desirable on general grounds.

Capital grants are normally given for specific projects and are subject to at least minimal control. For the most part they come straight from central tax revenue; in India and in Nigeria, however (but not yet in the West Indian Federation), the states (Regions) who make the grants have probably received a good deal by way of grant from the federal government and can thus be reckoned vehicles of central policy. In some instances the contribution out of central tax revenues is even more indirect, being paid over to

[1] *Tanganyika Survey, East African Statistical Office,* cit.
[2] Regional percentages were as follows: Eastern 4, Northern 2, Ashanti 1, and Trans-Volta Togoland 7.

specialized agencies which make the grants to the local bodies. Kenya is particularly addicted to this arrangement. Indeed the chief function of these agencies (such as the Roads Authority, the Housing Board, and A.L.DEV).[1] appears to be as a handy vehicle for awarding grants. In Tanganyika the Tanganyika Agricultural Corporation (successor and heir to the Ground Nuts Scheme) has been important in helping local bodies up the first rung of the development ladder.[2] Finally, there are the contributions which, as we have seen, come out of the reserves of Marketing Boards. In Nigeria, where the reserves of the boards were Regionalized, the resulting Development Boards have been an important source of capital grants; the same is true of the Ghana Cocoa Marketing Board.

By whatever precise channel capital grants reach Local Authorities, they represent more or less directly the policy of the central governments, although this is less true when the funds are derived from agency reserves. Further, while the broad allocation between uses probably reflects central policy even in this case, the choice of projects to be aided rests with the agency. In view of the strong influence of central governments in thus attempting to steer the course of local investment it is interesting (where we have the information) to examine the functional distribution of capital grants and to compare it with the reaction of local bodies, as illustrated by the distribution of capital outlay. The best available information on this matter relates to the Northern and Eastern Regions of Nigeria and is given below.[3]

It is interesting to note that both Regional governments gave very high grants for roads. Northern Native Authorities responded well, allocating 46% of their capital outlay for this purpose.[4] In the East, however, only 16% of capital formation was devoted to this cause. In the West, where no road-making grants were available, the road allocation was 39% of capital budgets. In the North 28% of the grant allocation was for educational purposes, but as we know, only 5% of capital budgets went

[1] The African Local Development Fund, set up under the Swynnerton Plan, see above, p. 371.
[2] Cf. A. Gaitskell, loc. cit.
[3] The capital grants of the Western Region are too limited to warrant inclusion.
[4] See above, p. 382. The Western allocation was probably abnormally high; a substantial part of the road building took place in Ibadan and was largely complementary with federal development, such as the University College Hospital.

that way; it would seem that the Regional government was more interested in the school-building programme than the Native Authorities. In the East, by contrast, only a minute grant was available for educational purposes, but as we have seen the Local Authorities devoted 47% of their capital outlay to that cause. The position in respect of markets in the North was similar: no grants

TABLE 15

NIGERIA

Functional Distribution of Main Capital Grants: Northern and Eastern Regions (%s)

	Roads	Housing	Educa-tion	Medical	Markets	Adminis-tration	Natural resources
			*Northern Region**				
1956–7 . .	61	—	28	2	—	—	7
1956/7–1958/9	53	neg.	35	4	neg.	neg.	6
Cumulative							
			Eastern Region†[1]				
1956–7 . .	55	—	1	43	1	—	—
1954–8 . .	59	1	2	27	1	9	—
Cumulative							

* Previous sample (Chaps. 13, 14) (largest and smallest NA budget in each Province).
† All Local Authorities.
Sources as in Chaps. 13, 14.

were available, but 23% of capital outlay went to constructing them. Finally the Eastern Regional government offered numerous grants for medical purposes, but the Local Authorities were only interested to allocate 9% of their capital budgets in this direction. It appears that on the whole capital grants served not so much as a stimulus to grant-aided services as a means of freeing funds for investment in lines which had a greater local appeal.

The Eastern Regional figures permit of a detailed breakdown within the different headings, which is not without interest in spite of its very limited scope. Taking the whole period 1954–8, capital grants were arranged for 19 different purposes. Within the broad heading 'roads', 52 grants were given, 5 for road-making in the narrow sense, 45 for bridges, 1 for a wharf, and 1 for a sea wall. In respect of education 5 grants were available, 2 for schools, 2 for training centres (for various trades), and 1 for a technical

[1] Further, by no means negligible, grants given for Community Development are excluded.

college. In respect of housing there was a grant towards a model village which the Okrika were laying out. For medical purposes 24 grants were available, of which 7 were for dispensaries, 6 for hospitals (ranging from several blocks for infectious diseases, to maternity wards), 7 were for health centres, 3 for ambulances, and 1 for a mortuary attached to a hospital. Two grants were made for markets and 2 for lorry parks, 1 including passenger shelter. (In West Africa there is no clear distinction between a lorry and a bus.) Finally in respect of administration there were 2 grants for postal agencies, and one relatively big one (£20,000) for a new council hall at Enugu.

Most of the grants were for quite small sums, five figures would be exceptional, some were for less than £100. Nevertheless they may well have turned the scale in favour of getting works completed, and all were complementary with finance from other sources. The many grants for bridges are interesting in this respect. Roads can be built, with the help of voluntary labour, at relatively little cost, but bridges require definite equipment and skilled direction. In Eastern Nigeria, with its innumerable swamps and creeks and heavy rains, adequate bridges are of particular importance. Again, several of the hospital grants were to aid in finishing different blocks of Awgu cottage hospital, an outstanding achievement of local initiative.

Capital grants are extremely useful for small-scale projects, but big money for development can only come from loans. We have to inquire consequently to what extent loan finance can be made available for local development. As in other spheres, there are great differences in this respect. For a successful loan policy for local bodies two things are necessary. First there must be a lending agency which is itself in a position to get command over funds and which also has at its disposal technical advice on the competence of the borrower and the soundness of his plans. Secondly, the borrower must be a good risk in the sense that the council controls sufficient tax potential to service the loan, since not many of the projects will be self-financing.

The lending agency can only be dispensed with in the case of large towns, which can borrow directly, often from the local public. A place like Bombay City is especially lucky in having a stock exchange on its doorstep. Nairobi, uniquely for a colonial city, has borrowed on the London market. For smaller loans it may be possible even for a moderate-sized town to borrow locally by a mortgage on the town's property or rateable value. (With R.V. £22,000 Nakuru in Kenya was confident that it could do this.)

Even where a Local Authority can borrow directly from the public, and even where it has a good tax potential, it is desirable for a higher-layer government to impose some sort of limit on its borrowing activities; for local revenues cannot be extended as national revenues can. In colonies or ex-colonies rules about borrowing tend to be fairly strict; but this is by no means the case in some of the Indian states.[1] The former Mysore state law contained no provisions at all under this head. In Bombay state, local borrowing for any one purpose may not exceed rateable value; but since there are many purposes for which loans are wanted, the provision is quite ineffective. Recently a number of states which nominally have ceilings on municipal borrowing have been able to extend their loans through the agency of the Union government, just as they have been enabled to increase grants from the same source.[2] In spite of this apparent ease Indian towns have not been active in seeking loans and the pace of development has consequently not been rapid. Whatever the cause of this lagging, deficient tax powers can hardly be to blame, since as we have seen, most Indian towns make inadequate use of those they have.

The country which above all uses loan finance for local development is Kenya (the figures of 88%, 35%, and 18% for the three grades of Local Authority, given on p. 399 will be recalled). Uganda and Tanganyika also make loan funds available to local bodies, but to a much smaller extent; so does Eastern Nigeria. In Ghana there is a sharp distinction between the towns and the Regions. The towns can clearly make substantial use of loan funds, as the following figures show:

Ghana Towns, Percentage of Capital Formation Financed by Loan

	1956-7	*1957-8*
Accra	8	100
Kumasi	28	19
Sekondi/Takoradi . . .	99	38
Cape Coast . . .	100	0

[1] Bhouraskar, *Municipal Finance in Certain Leading Indian States*, cit., 1954.
[2] See above, p. 156.

Details are not availadle but the discontinuities suggest a narrow range of projects, receiving relatively large loans. In the Regions the use of loan funds is definitely smaller, as appears below.

Ghana Regions, Percentage Capital Formation Financed by 'Transfers from Loan Account' 1956/7

Ashanti	Eastern	Northern	Trans-Volta Togoland	Western
8	9	—	17	11

Sources in both Tables as in Chaps. 13, 14.

Kenya is clearly the most repaying case study for loan finance. It is interesting both for its own sake and for the light it throws on the causes of the differences between its own policy and that of other places. As appears in Table 16 loans were available over virtually the whole field of local capital outlay. But there was not a high correlation between the relative availability of loans and the investment which eventuated. The towns received more than half their loans for sanitation, but only a fifth of their outlay went in this direction. The African District Councils, however, responded well to grants for water, allocating 31% of their investment to this purpose; on the other hand the towns received very little loan help for water supply, but allocated 38% of their investment to it (see above, p. 377).

The African District Councils were above all encouraged to develop natural resources, but with 33% of the loan allocation for this purpose only 9% of development outlay went to it. At least it can be said, however, that Kenya succeeded better than almost any other territory in securing local investment in natural resources development. The substantial housing loans to all types of Kenya authorities were almost wholly for African housing. The high allocation to the County Councils is especially interesting, since hitherto it has been a reproach on the Settled Areas that more has not been done for the many Africans resident within their confines; the council's response (4% of total capital outlay) was not, however, very encouraging.

The extent to which the Kenya government is a believer in loans is thus evident. By and large (assuming that due precautions are observed) this is undoubtedly right in principle. In a rapidly

TABLE 16

KENYA, 1956[1]

Functional Distribution of Loans Sanctioned for Local Capital Formation (Main Purposes)

Type of authority	Totals (£000's)	Roads %	Housing %	Sanitation %	Education %	Medical %	Water %	Administration %	Equipment %	Amenities %	Natural resources %
Towns .	2,046·6	31	5	54	—	—	2	1	1	4	—
County Councils	62·8	—	25	—	3	11	—	—	59	—	—
African District Councils .	263·7	14	14	—	9	—	19	11	9	3	21

[1] The year 1956 has been chosen as reflecting policy more faithfully than 1957 when severe credit restriction operated. Sources as in Chaps. 13 and 14.

developing country the advantages of achieving the investment quickly, so that it can contribute at once to raising the national income far outweigh the additional costs due to the loan. Kenya has been more easily able to follow this policy than other territories because of its strong connexion with the U.K., and consequent confidence of U.K. investors. There is little evidence, however, that other governments would be prepared to follow such a forward policy in loan finance, even if they had the funds available. For instance Northern Nigeria, with its large Regional reserves, could easily foster a more rapid rate of expansion in the Native Authorities by this means. Again there would seem to be no reason why Tanganyika should not establish an effective local loans fund (see below). From another point of view, however, the Kenya policy is a further example of the way in which the Territorial government, having decided to keep a very tight rein on local tax powers, is forced to come to their assistance by other means.

The system of local borrowing works well in Kenya because care has been taken to establish efficient machinery for considering and sanctioning loans. A Local Loans Board, somewhat on British lines, was set up in 1951, but it is only recently that it has been put on a sound footing. Most loans are now given in a block allocation, an account on which Local Authorities can draw as needed. Once global sanction has been agreed the Ministry of Local Government can authorize drawings within the scope of the period plan; if funds in excess of this are required fresh sanction must be obtained. Generally speaking Local Authorities get their loans with a minimum of fuss and delay.

Several other governments have experimented with machinery for making loans available for local investment. Recently Uganda set up a Local loans Board on the lines of the Kenya Board, but with very much smaller resources. Under the three-year development programme (1959–61) only about £150,000 would be available for all Local Authorities. The Tanganyika board is still more limited in scope, because its funds are wholly provided by compulsory reserve deposits of the Local Authorities themselves.

In all the East African territories, however, the loan machinery seems to work smoothly and promptly, so far as it goes. In India and Ceylon there seems to be much more difficulty with the machinery. In some Indian states perfectly sensible applications from cities are recorded as having been held up for two or three years.[1] This clumsiness is no doubt one of the reasons why Indian towns have been backward in using loan finance. The Ceylon government seems equally reluctant to disburse loan funds to its towns. One impediment may be the difficulty which the lenders themselves have in raising funds, but the absence of smooth running machinery would seem to be of greater importance.

There is one point mentioned above to which we must now return. There are many instances in history (especially perhaps in the U.S.A.) of Local Authorities having overborrowed and virtually bankrupted themselves, if for any reason their autonomous revenue failed. Is there any danger of such an occurrence in our countries? As things are at present, with a very modest extent of loan finance, even in Kenya, and generally speaking a tight system of control, the danger would seem to be a long way off.[2] But in the past Indian cities have not infrequently defaulted on their loans, on one occasion Mysore state insisted on the city levying an additional cess before receiving any more loans. The possible danger depends to a considerable extent on the size and strength of the borrowing authority. The Kenya Districts are large, and could command substantial revenues. In the smaller local jurisdictions of the west coast (apart from Northern Nigeria) difficulties might fairly easily arise.

While one of the reasons for the small amount of capital formation at the local level is the scarcity of loan funds, the scarcity of skilled personnel may be even more important, especially in remote areas.[3] This difficulty, however, tends to decline as the pace of development quickens. Increasingly firms are prepared to send out combined teams of economists and technicians who are qualified to supply all the know-how required. Territorial Loans Boards can themselves help in this direction, by engaging the services of engineers and others to examine the projects for which loans are requested, and to see that they maintain a broad balance in the lines of development. At the same time, until the level of

---

[1] Cf. Bhouraskar, op. cit.

[2] Nevertheless a single big investment may put an area in difficulties. As a result of its big water scheme 4½% of Mombasa's current revenue was earmarked for debt service, and a £2 mn. sewerage plan was in urgent need of implementation.

[3] Staffing difficulties for technical grades are acute everywhere. Nairobi was unable to find a Chief Planner. At least three more towns in Uganda would be gazetted if municipal accounts officers could be found. The Nigerian Regions have great difficulty in filling their technical cadres.

saving has risen in these countries, and the central governments have developed better means of tapping it, the volume of loan finance at the local level cannot be expected to advance very rapidly. This conclusion implies a continuing emphasis on grants for capital formation. We must therefore proceed to examine whether better machinery in this direction might not produce more fruitful results.

18

GRANTS

I

IN Chapter 14 we saw that in most of our countries grants form an important element in current budgets; we have also just seen that grants on capital account are given for a great variety of purposes. It is our task in the present chapter to examine the bases on which the various grants are awarded, as a step to judging their present or potential efficiency. It will be recalled that in Chapter 14 we defined grants as including reimbursements, but excluding government payments in lieu of rates on government property, and assigned revenues; we shall continue to work with this definition.

All grants increase the resources of local bodies, but while some are intended to give them greater power of manœuvre in general, others are intended to do this only for the smaller and poorer authorities which would otherwise have less than normal opportunities of putting their ideas into practice. Other grants again are designed to stimulate the development of a particular service or the formation of particular types of capital assets. Another object of grant aid is to exercise some control over local administrative standards, either in respect of the quality of the service provided ('underwriting national service standards')[1] in respect of the personnel engaged, or of the general conduct and layout of local budgets. In this way they aim to promote good housekeeping in the Local Authorities. Finally grants may be used to stimulate local tax collection and assessment, or as a means of inducing councils to collect better statistics which will be useful both for their own information and that of the national planners.

It would not be surprising if some of these multifarious aims were to get in each other's way; grants, like taxes, tend to be double edged. Thus there is a danger in providing more unconditional revenue (e.g. by block grants) that local budgeting may become

---

[1] Cf. A. H. Hansen and M. S. Perloff, *State and Local Finance in the National Economy*, 1944.

careless through diminished responsibility.[1] If the unconditional grant is sharply tipped towards the areas with less development potential there is a danger that, in denying help to the more promising areas, the growth of the national income may be hampered in a way that will ultimately be injurious to the whole economy. Similarly, stimulating one service tends to distort the local budget and to retard the development of other services. Stimulus will also tend to act unevenly between authorities, the poorer ones will not be able to take up the grant so fully as the richer, so that the gap between them widens. On the other hand, if the stimulus has been too generous the central Treasury may find itself saddled with a bigger obligation than it had intended. Finally there are political difficulties, especially marked in countries which are only learning how to work democratic self-government, that grants will be used for political advantage.[2] All this implies that the central government should learn to think of the grants they give as a system, which will achieve a desired balance between stimulus and control, and between local advance and equalization. The needs of the grant system will differ from country to country and from one stage of development to another, so that it is very necessary for the government to review the system periodically.

In British local finance, grants have been increasing in importance relatively to rates throughout the present century, and a complicated grant structure has emerged. Since over recent decades there have been fairly major changes in policy—or more precisely shifts in emphasis—it will be useful to expand slightly the brief indications given in Chapter 14, for, as there indicated, the influence of these changes on developments overseas has been considerable. The relevant changes in the British grant system are contained in the Local Government Acts of 1928, 1948, and 1958—though the latter has hardly yet had time to influence overseas policy—probably the Rating and Valuation Act, 1925, should also be included, since it was the first step in establishing a uniform system of valuation on which British equalization grants mainly depend. Prior to 1928 Exchequer grants had accumulated on an *ad hoc* basis of specific grants for particular services. The most rapidly expanding of these were a bundle of public health grants for new

---

[1] There is reason to believe that this has occurred in the U.K. since the introduction of the Exchequer Equalization Grant by the Local Government Act of 1948.

[2] For example, Jamaican special works grants above, p. 310.

services such as maternity, child welfare, tuberculosis, and venereal disease. These were awarded mainly on a uniform percentage basis, and directed almost wholly to stimulus. Besides these there were two other important specific grants: one for local police, which incorporated a definite control element, and one for education, which though mainly designed to stimulate and control also incorporated a small equalizing element.[1]

The important change operative from 1929 was the abolition of the specific health grants and the introduction of a block grant or 'General Exchequer Contribution' which was not merely an innovation in type but which also contained a much more pronounced equalizing element than had previously existed. However, the total amount of this was not large in relation to the continuing grants, nor was the formula on which it was based very highly equalizing, so that its efficiency in this respect was only moderate, especially in view of the highly disequalizing effect of the severe depression which struck the country very soon after the introduction of the General Exchequer Contribution.

The result of the grant provisions of the 1948 Act was very materially to increase the equalizing element. This was achieved by substituting for the General Exchequer Contribution a new block grant, called the Exchequer Equalization Grant. Although this was not much greater in amount than its predecessor, it exerted a powerful equalizing force, because it was based on a relevant and fairly reliable measure of relative Local Authority wealth: rateable value per head.[2] Apart from some minor details intended to represent relative needs (which had figured largely in the 1929 formula), the grant for any particular area depended basically on the amount by which its rateable value per head fell short of the national average, multiplied by its *per capita* expenditure. The fact that areas with rateable value per head at or above the national average no longer received any block grant (whereas the richer areas had done quite well under the 1928 formula) itself greatly contributed to the degree of equalization.[3] It should be noticed

---

[1] Taking the form of the deduction of the proceeds of a rate poundage from the final calculation.

[2] This is only strictly true of County Councils and County Borough Councils.

[3] It may be asked what was equalized, not rate poundages although these were brought much nearer together, but rather financial opportunities; cf. *Report of a Working Party on the Effects of the Local Government Act, 1948* (Incorporated Accountants, 1949–53).

that whereas under the 1929 Act the Exchequer determined the total amount of grant, under the 1948 Act the Local Authorities had the last word.

The effect of the 1948 Act was thus to increase the weight of the equalizing, block grant, element in the British grant structure, and this change certainly impressed itself on the Colonies. As things worked out, however, the equalization grant was not so important as was expected; the education grant came to overshadow it. In the economy crisis of 1931 a strict ceiling had been put on education grants; after the war and especially in view of the needs of the forward-looking (effectively bi-partisan) Education Act of 1944, this policy was reversed. Thus it came about that by 1957, in practice about 80% of British Exchequer grants were given on a specific and not on an unconditional basis. In the meantime both the control element and the equalization element in the education grant had been strengthened.

The 1958 Act swung the pendulum somewhat violently back, in the direction of re-emphasizing the unconditional element in the grant structure. The Exchequer equalization grant indeed remained substantially unaltered (although renamed the Rate Deficiency grant); but, as before 1958, it was no more than a minor—although a very significant—part of the whole. The important change was that in place of the education grant a new unconditional grant was introduced, leaving Local Authorities (in theory at least) extremely free to plan their own budgets. In practice several methods of control were still available directly (in the case of the remaining specific grants), and indirectly in a variety of ways. The control of the Ministry of Education has always been very tight and will not be likely to relax although it must now be exercised in different ways, for instance, by persuasion, or by capital grants.

There is finally one other recent development in British grant policy which deserves mention, as, although it is quite minor at present, in principle it points the way towards what should be a significant improvement in the efficiency of specific grants. This is the unit grant,[1] based on the 'standard' cost per unit of service provided. This requires some explanation as four stages are involved.

[1] The unit cost grant on current account must not be confused with capital grants given per unit produced (e.g. so much per council house); see below, p. 429.

Grants 413

First the grant base must be fixed by the determination of a suitable unit (such as a school meal, a hospital patient bed night); secondly an average good management cost of this, to be chosen as the standard must be (statistically) ascertained. Thirdly the standard may be adjusted to allow for abnormal costs in any area, and finally the grant-aided unit cost of the area is multiplied by the number of units of service to be supplied.

The advantages of the unit cost grant are three: first careful costing is promoted; secondly the Local Authority has a strong stimulus to good management since the more its costs are below standard costs, the more valuable the grant; thirdly the true and unavoidable causes of abnormally high costs are isolated from high costs of indifferent management. The unit cost grant is thus the very opposite in effect from a grant based on local expenditure, such as the 'matching' grant which is very popular in the U.S.A.—(in which the central government puts up $x for every $x spent from the local Treasury). So far the unit cost grant is only beginning to be used in the U.K. although it was attempted in the early 1920's for army accounts. It has been in operation for some years for school meals and is now operated in various branches of hospital work.[1] The two obstacles to its more rapid spread are, first, the difficulty of defining a suitable unit in some services. (This proved to be especially awkward in respect of the army accounts.) Secondly, for efficient working, statistics of costs are required which would not otherwise be kept; but it is all to the good that they should be kept, and this obstacle should not be allowed to stand in the way of wider use in the U.K. The statistical difficulty would be an even more serious obstacle in developing countries, but the advantages of the unit cost grant are so great that they would do well to bear it in mind for future use.

This brief sketch of British grant experience reveals certain continuing objectives, especially since 1929: first it is taken as a datum (and this has recently been reaffirmed), that the Treasury will not countenance any additional sources of autonomous local revenue; indeed the trend has been all in the opposite direction: the rate basis was first narrowed by agricultural and industrial derating (only partially restored by the Act of 1958); secondly the possibility of relieving the rates by profits of trading services was first narrowed by enactment and later almost completely removed by

[1] In 1960, 334 non-teaching hospitals were keeping cost accounts.

nationalization of the main trading services. If Local Authorities were not to become dummies or mere agents of central government it was consequently a matter of urgency that a substantial part of total grants should be given without strings, so as to leave local budgeting as free as it could be under the circumstances. Secondly, there has been a steady policy of retaining certain key grants on a specific basis for purposes of stimulation and control. At first the original purpose was to stimulate; more recently the control aspect has received increasing attention.[1] It has been discovered that a judicious mixture of the carrot and stick are far more effective for steering local activity in the desired direction than definite orders, which tend to cause friction between the centre and the localities and are in any case expensive and tiresome to enforce.

Thirdly, it is clear that there has been a growing tendency to use grants to increase interlocal equalization. This is closely parallel to the trend for greater personal income equalization, and may in fact be regarded as a part of the same policy. Consumers in the U.K. have been receiving an increasingly large part of their real income in the form of publicly supplied goods and services. It would much reduce the effectiveness of greater personal income equalization if there were serious interlocal differences in the standards of this publicly provided income. For instance in the 1930's the terms available on public assistance in wealthy Blackpool were far more generous than those given in poor St. Helens only a few miles away. With the nationalizing of public assistance this can no longer occur. It has always been sought to make the grant as efficient as possible in the sense of minimum Exchequer outlay to achieve a desired result; care has also usually been taken to secure that the Local Authority will have to make a substantial effort itself; 100% or even very high percentage grants have been avoided. Indeed a good deal of ingenuity has gone into judging just how tasty a carrot would be required to attain a given objective. It is only quite recently, with the advent of the unit grant, that efficiency has been attempted in any precise way, or related closely to good house-keeping on the part of Local Authorities. Finally, from the point of view of the Local Authority the grants available, and the necessary conditions to qualify for them, have almost always been certain and known in advance. Consequently no unknowns have on this account complicated local budgeting.

[1] Cf. D. N. Chester, *Central and Local Finance*, cit.

II

The continuing principles underlying British Exchequer grants to Local Authorities are on the whole sound, and developing countries would do well to ponder them. But they have been evolved specifically for British conditions and should not be applied blindly in more primitive local government conditions. In the first place when starting from scratch there is no compelling necessity to confine the tax sources of Local Authorities as severely as they have been confined in the U.K. On the other hand to allow as wide a spread of tax jurisdiction as many Indian state laws allow their towns, is to run into a danger similar to that which we have already noticed in respect of lack of precise definition of powers and duties: with too many opportunities no effective machinery is developed for any one of them. There is thus no *a priori* reason why grants should bear such a high ratio to rates as they do in the U.K. This depends, however, on two considerations: first the extent to which it is desired, as a matter of policy, to hand over services to local management; secondly on the willingness and ability of local bodies to tax themselves. In a number of countries, especially East Africa, but also apparently in Ceylon and in some senses in India, there is discernible a trend towards political decentralization; this is especially marked in Uganda and Kenya. If, and as, this proceeds either the central government must provide Local Authorities with more ample tax resources (as has indeed been done in Uganda) or it must increase grants, as is proposed in Kenya.

The willingness of local bodies to increase their own taxes depends on a number of factors, but basically on the interest of local taxpayers on the things the taxes will buy. Thus nearly everywhere people will pay willingly for the education of their children; but no one enjoys seeing half his contribution devoted to the salaries of local officers for whom perhaps he has little respect. There is also discernible a growing unwillingness to pay for the maintenance of traditional offices, strongest perhaps in Ghana and Sierra Leone. Generally speaking, in countries where a firm tradition of local administration has been established, there is more willingness to pay taxes than elsewhere. In all this, the stage of Indirect Rule was an excellent education. Thus general willingness to tax locally is relatively poor in Ghana and still worse in Sierra Leone where Indirect Rule was introduced late and never became

strong. In India and Ceylon, with a weak tradition of local government in many of the towns, and virtually no tradition at all in the
rural areas, Local Authorities have proved very dilatory in increasing their own taxes as required for development. Some Indian
states have found it desirable, in order to galvanize local bodies
into activity or to strengthen their hands *vis-à-vis* the taxpayer, to
enforce minimum rates of local taxes.[1] Where this sort of difficulty
arises it may well be desirable to increase the ratio of grants to
taxes, while also stiffening up control.

A second direction in which the British example may not be a
sensible one for developing countries to follow is in the complication of grant formulae.[2] Where neither councillors nor officials
have much experience it is essential that the basis of grants should
be as simple and easily understood as possible. The two most easily
understood principles are unquestionably on the one hand origin
or derivation (the local body receives back by way of grant a sum
based on its relative tax collections), and on the other needs. Most
of the complications that have found their way into British grant
formulae have been due to attempts to define 'needs' in some
objective manner that will be recognized to be just and which
cannot be influenced by the Local Authority itself (for instance by
adding fictitious names to the school register if the number of
children on the register is an element in determining the education grant).

The principle of derivation is especially easy to understand,
although (particularly if the revenue out of which the grant is to be
paid comes from indirect taxes), it may be technically difficult to
operate.[3] The principle of needs while simple in itself is not easy
to define precisely. Above-normal needs for grant may arise on
the income side of the account, because of the relative poverty
of the resources of some areas; they may equally arise on the outlay side of the account, either because the demand for particular
services is more than normally great (e.g. an abnormally large

---

[1] See above, p. 157.
[2] Of all British grants the education grant which disappeared with the Act of
1958 was the most complicated; this was due to the attempt to include elements
of stimulus, control, and equalization all in one grant.
[3] The technical difficulty of apportioning revenue to the different Regions
was the main reason for the general dissatisfaction with the principle of derivation in Nigerian federal grants to Regions, which led to its abandonment in
1958. See Report of the (Raisman) Fiscal Commission, 1958.

percentage of children of school age in the local population) or because the unit costs of supplying particular services are particularly high (e.g. roads in either a very sparsely populated area, or in one where the land is heavily encumbered with waterways). Only careful cost accounting can hope to disentangle the various elements which together constitute differences in relative need, and that is quite clearly out of the question at an early stage of development.

The extent to which it is necessary to let the element of needs enter into a grant formula, or to attempt to define it, is closely bound up with the degree to which it is desired to attempt interlocal equalization, and here again the British example may not be a particularly good one for developing countries to follow. A willingness for redistribution from the rich to the poor tacitly assumes two things: first, that one people of a country is prepared to regard the other peoples as sufficiently close to them to be worthy of help; secondly, that those whose incomes are to be transferred must themselves feel well enough off to be able to spare some of their own for the personal benefit of other people. The first condition is not always an easy one, in view for instance of the fortuitous territorial units which resulted from the scramble for Africa. Not only are a number of tribes cut in two by territorial boundaries, but (for instance in Sierra Leone) in several cases the main centre of a tribe may be over the border (in this case in French territory or in Liberia). Nor is the situation much better in East Africa, where the whole outlook on life is still very different between the Hamitic, Nilo-Hamitic, and Bantu areas, quite apart from inter-racial difficulties. In Ceylon racial divisions make a deep cleavage between one part of the Island and another. Probably the condition of interlocal solidarity is most nearly satisfied in India, where an extraordinary bond seems to unite north and south in spite of considerable differences of race and language. But then the second condition—of sufficient wealth to be able to give it away without too great a pang—is even less well satisfied in India than in many others of our countries.

In view of all this there would seem to be not much point at present in trying for a great deal of interlocal redistribution in the developing countries. There is also an economic argument leading in the same direction. In the early days of development especially, it is important to concentrate on projects which will bring in the largest return in terms of the national income.[1] On the whole these opportunities are more likely to present themselves in the richer than in the poorer areas. At a later stage more attention can then be devoted to the less prosperous areas, which nevertheless will have benefited also from the growth of the national income.

The upshot would appear to be that a grant formula in such countries should pay only very broad attention to needs. By this it is most certainly not implied that central governments should stand ready to cover local budgetary deficits on the plea of need. It is a first necessity of good local management that some sort of objective measure of need, however crude or simple, should be employed. By far the simplest way of achieving this is to base the grant on unweighted population; it is often not far from the mark to assume that the differences in the cost of providing a service are proportional to the number of persons to be served. If population figures are not to get hopelessly out of date and so become unfair between expanding and contracting areas, there probably should be some means of adjusting them by inter-censal Estimates—say quinquennially. A technical improvement on this which is possible if a personal tax is in operation, is to base the grant not on actual population (which may well not be accurately known) but on the number of personal taxpayers in an area. This device introduces an incentive to the Local Authority to round up as many taxpayers as possible. Naturally care must be taken to check actual tax receipts in order to see that the register is not loaded with bogus payers.

If it is desired to be more precise and to introduce a positive weighting for differential costs and needs a simple measure can be found in the relative density of populations. Some basic services (e.g. roads) cost more to administer when population is abnormally sparse—on the other hand in very rural conditions some services (such as main drainage and piped water) are less necessary than in more fully developed areas. A plausible argument can also be made for a special weight for supernormal density in the sense of real population pressure. (This was recognized many decades ago in the special grants given for the 'Congested Districts' in the west of Ireland.) Population pressure gives rise to additional needs for certain services, especially health services; it also calls for particular

---

[1] Cf. Report of the Revenue Allocation Commission, Nigeria, 1951, cit., where it is described as the 'Principle of national interest'.

efforts (and hence additional costs) either to train the surplus population for employment elsewhere or to introduce (perhaps at first with subsidy) additional opportunities of livelihood within the area.

In most countries the weighting in block grants for abnormal costs is based on population, more or less adjusted. In the U.K. special weights have been given for supernormal numbers in the age groups of children and old people which require particular services (but to do this accurately calls for complete birth registrations). But the main method of distinguishing between the *needs* of different areas in the U.K. has increasingly been relative rateable value per head. The advantage of this measure is that it operates on both sides of the account, since there is (in British conditions at least) a high correlation between low rateable value per head and a heavy demand for public services. This convenient base can only be available, however, to areas which use a property tax based on a reasonably uniform, preferably central, valuation. It is consequently not yet generally usable overseas; but it could (for instance) very easily be put into operation throughout Jamaica as soon as the revaluation is complete. If once the Indian states could be induced to take urban property valuation seriously—which as we have seen[1] would also be of great benefit on the tax side—the relative rateable value base could also be widely used there, and the same would be true of urban areas in Ceylon.

We thus have two reliable and objective bases for block grants: population (weighted if, and as, desired), and rateable value per head. How far would it be worthwhile for countries now operating on other bases to aim at changing over to one or other of these (or a combination of both)? The difficulty about attempting to answer this question is that the formulae on which actual grants are based is hardly ever made known, partly no doubt because governments feel that the foundations are shaky and are anxious not to court criticism unnecessarily. We must consequently be satisfied with only a few examples.

Grants have been freely used in the West Indies; British Guiana had its first—for drainage and road repair—in 1883—but the basis is obscure. We can, however, say something about the current Jamaican system; as we have seen[2] the block grant is an important element in the finance of Parish Councils. The Jamaican grant

---

[1] See above, pp. 155, 296. [2] See above, p. 310.

consists of a 'variable' portion based on local tax collection in the previous year and a 'fixed' portion (of broadly the same amount *in toto*) based on needs, for which the formula is not stated.[1] If it is necessary to pay some attention to the derivation principle, it is a convenient idea to divide the grant in this way, although there is no particular argument for the 50/50 arrangement. Further, revenue collection is clearly a better basis for the derivation element than expenditure (for which there is much local pressure in Jamaica). It would seem preferable, however, to take a moving average of revenue collections, rather than that of a single year, since this implies that the grant going to a council in temporary difficulties (such as a fall in the price of an important local crop and consequent trouble in collecting tax) would diminish, just when additional help was most needed. The Jamaican grant also seems to be satisfactory from the point of view of certainty, since a Parish Council can calculate in advance exactly what is coming to it.

India has so far made little if any use of block grants in local finance. The Union government is, however, keenly interested in the subject. Two inquiries since independence have touched on it (the Tax Inquiry Commission of 1948 and the Local Finance Inquiry Commission, 1951). It was the conclusion of the former[2] (as we have seen) that 'no state has a grant in aid code that embodies simple and well defined principles ... the grants are uncertain and full payment depends in some cases upon the current financial position of the state government'. The Tax Inquiry Commission recommended that grants should be based 'on an examination of needs and resources'—but unfortunately did not indicate how this was to be done[3]—they also strongly recommended that the grant should be stable over a period of years. The continuing precariousness of many state finances suggests that a really sound grant system for Local Authorities would require some more or less permanent underwriting by the Union government. This is a point

---

[1] Cf. Hicks, *Finance and Taxation*, cit.
[2] Loc. cit., pp. 366–7.
[3] A similar problem arises over the distribution of the states' share of income tax between them. This is determined by a permanent statutory authority, on a mixed basis of derivation and needs. Aggrieved states make representations before each award and the final result appears to involve a certain amount of horse trading. It appears that budget deficits have been considered to be a direct indication of needs. Without a very strict control of budgetary definitions and arrangement this can easily lead to interstate competition to show the biggest deficit.

to which we shall have to return later, in connexion with Community Development.[1]

In contrast to India, Ceylon has become a believer in block grants. In 1946 an important step in this direction was made, together with some other central/local financial adjustments at the urgent request of Local Authorities.[2] The block grants were made available to all local bodies but with a different range for each type—lowest for the Municipal Councils and highest for the village committees. Within each group the grant declined inversely with population. Thus the municipal percentage ranged from a high of 15% of local revenue if population was below 50,000, to 3% for a population above 300,000; for urban councils the range was from 30% to 15% (so that an urban area with over 25,000 inhabitants received the same percentage as a municipal with less than 50,000). For town councils the range was 40%–30%. For village committees, however, no attention was paid to population; the percentage grant declined from 100% when revenue was less than £75 to 35% when revenue exceeded £450. The revenue base was fixed at the average of 1943, 1944, and 1945.

There are several odd things about this formula. So far as the population factor is concerned it was evidently assumed that the greater economy of serving a concentrated population, together with the greater tax potential which a large town might be assumed to command, would outweigh the cost of additional services which would be required in a large city, such as Colombo. The revenue was, however, taken as a total, not *per capita*, which would have provided a much more adequate measure. There are for instance several towns in Ceylon (e.g. Galle and Jaffna) which at least give the impression of a higher *per capita* tax potential than Colombo.

Secondly, the revenue base was fixed on three war years when prices were very much below the level of a few years later. Thus the grant steadily declined in real value. It should not have been difficult to change the base to a three-year moving average. Thirdly, the very high grants paid to small village committees suggest that some control or supervision of outlay should have been written in as a condition of grant.[3] The more fundamental

---

[1] See Chap. 21.
[2] Of which the most important was the assumption by the central government of financial responsibility for cost of living bonuses for civil servants.
[3] See the position in Kenya below, p. 423.

question is, however, what useful contribution to social and economic improvement could be made by local bodies with annual incomes of no more than £150—or even £450. This rivals the smallest Chiefdom Authorities in Sierra Leone, which as we have seen are notoriously inefficient. It is of course not impossible that something might be achieved with an even smaller sum if supported by wholehearted voluntary effort, but in Ceylonese conditions this was not very likely.[1]

Kenya is a country that seems still more recently to have been converted to block grants geared according to needs, for the African District Councils. As in Ceylon, the change was accompanied by a general review of the relations and responsibilities of central and local government—but with two important differences, first that in Kenya the changes were made all at the same time, as part of a system, not piecemeal some years later as in Ceylon, and secondly, that the Kenya proposals emanated from the government, and were accepted by the African District Councils—(not unnaturally since they promised well over £1 mn. extra revenue)—whereas in Ceylon by no means all the changes recommended by the independent Choksy Commission were accepted by the government, even in the long run.

Up to 1958 the Kenya government assigned the sum of 2s. a head of local contributions to the government poll tax to the African District Councils, that is to say the grant was wholly on a species of derivation basis, but one which slightly favoured the Districts with low poll tax rates (presumably the poorer areas), in that grant at a constant rate per taxpayer would form a higher percentage of autonomous revenue where the rate or local poll tax was low. Under the new system[2] $27\frac{1}{2}\%$ of the aggregate poll tax collected in African District Councils is set aside for the grant, to be distributed on a descending *marginal* basis as local income rises, e.g.

		grant
on first £10,000 of net income		50%
on next £75,000	,, ,,	25%
,, ,, £25,000	,, ,,	20%
on remainder	,, ,,	$17\frac{1}{2}\%$

[1] See Chap. 21.
[2] Cf. Kenya White Paper, No. 1, 1957, cit.

Thus the *average* rate of grant per District will be higher the smaller the local tax income. The change over from the *per capita* derivation basis however inevitably injures the more populous Districts (rather than the richer), and to reduce the effect of this any council losing more than £100 under the new system will receive a supplementary grant, tapering over a five-year period.

Although the new Kenya grant to African District Councils will be considerably more equalizing than the old one, it must be recognized that it only takes the needs factor into account on the income side. It is stated that 'special grants', at the discretion of the Minister, will also be available on a separate vote, which will be 'used to help areas where the lack of natural resources has hampered development'. This additional provision should go some way to even things out, since such areas are likely to be those with sparse populations and high unit costs. No allowance, however, is made for special training and other extra costs in densely populated areas.

It is stated that 'the graduated block grant should be regarded as a temporary expedient pending the introduction of a rating system on land'. We have seen that in most areas of Kenya this must inevitably be a pretty long way ahead since it implies a general system of fenced individual farms. Even so there remain the difficulties of getting—and keeping up to date—an effective and equitable system of rural land valuation. The experience of India— or indeed of the Settled Areas of Kenya—in this respect is not particularly encouraging.[1]

There remain two points of general interest in the Kenya graduated block grant. First the grant is only payable subject to the condition 'that if at any time it appears to the Minister of Local Government . . . that the revenues of the Council are (not) being used in the best interests of the community or that the administration of the Council is wasteful and inefficient, and if after enquiry this proves to be the case, the grant may be wholly or partly withheld'. This useful piece of control machinery, carried over to African District Councils from the Settled Area councils, clearly looks forward to the day when the District Officer will have retired completely from the administration. Secondly, in view of the rate at which development is taking place, and the possibility that a greater range of services may presently be transferred to

[1] Chap. 21.

African District Councils, it is proposed to carry out a review both of the global amount of the grant and of the graduation, at least every three years. It is clear that much thought has gone into the whole financial arrangement, including the distribution of functions between the centre and the Local Authorities, with which we shall be concerned in the next chapter.

III

On the whole those countries which do have block grants make fairly heavy use of them; this is clearly right, both from the point of view of supporting local revenues in a situation where only a small range of taxes can be made effective, and from the point of view of keeping a general balance of development between rich and poor areas. (It was, however, suggested above[1] that the desirability of this depends on the level of development already attained.) All countries, however, also use specific grants of some sort. The rates of these grants are very various, but by far the most popular appear to be 10% and 33%. Illustrations of these would be the rates of the two Nigerian 'code' grants for health and agriculture;[2] 66% is also common, for instance surface drainage in Ceylon, and there are quite a few at 100% (in Sierra Leone this was formerly given for all District Council activities). Sometimes the basis is not fixed—as the Choksy Commission found in respect of the Ceylon maternity and welfare grants, which depended on a parliamentary grant from year to year. The new Kenya proposals for African District Councils include 50% for approved health expenditure, 66% of approved education outlay (to be made up to 100% by African District Councils and passed on to the District Education Boards as executive bodies).

Broadly, specific grants are useful for three different purposes: (1) assistance with current services especially those which might otherwise be neglected, (2) assistance with the local salary bill, and (3) assistance in the provision of capital assets. While some general principles are common to these different grant purposes, each raises in addition problems of its own.

The general principles follow naturally from the triple aim of specific grants: stimulus, control, and the promotion of good management. The first concerns the extent of the government

---

[1] See above, p. 418.   [2] See above, p. 168.

share of cost—generally expressed as a percentage. Clearly 100% grant will not give any incentive for good management; perhaps worse still is 100% reimbursement of outlays that have already been made; this latter method has the additional disadvantage that since reimbursement usually takes place in a different year from that in which the outlay has occurred (sometimes after a lag of two or even three years), tidy budgeting by the grant-receiving authority is made very difficult. Generally speaking the percentage offered should be no larger than will produce the desired effect; the higher the grant, the more local budgets are likely to get distorted (since favouring one service disfavours others) and the more careful the control which the grant-giving authority will have to exercise.[1]

In all cases a fairly strict definition of the expenditure which will qualify for grant needs to be written into the terms, but at the same time it is important that as little delay as possible should occur between the application for grant by the Local Authority and its acceptance or rejection by the Minister. The usual practice is to include a condition that grant will be payable only in respect of 'recognized' or 'approved' expenditure. The important point (which may perhaps be better expressed by the former than by the latter term) is to work so far as possible on the basis of a schedule of clear cut conditions which must be satisfied, and which can easily be checked. This minimizes both uncertainty and the chances of log rolling so far as the Local Authority is concerned. Detailed investigations can then be reserved for troublesome cases.

In most circumstances the biggest grants are likely to be those for the support of current services. Including the qualifications above, these should give rise to no particular difficulties; but the best method of achieving the desired end needs to be kept under constant review. If Local Authorities are very interested in a particular service (e.g. education) then the central government has the choice of giving its assistance either through a low percentage grant or through a block grant. The choice will depend partly on the degree of control and inspection available without the grant (since the percentage grant will give opportunities of control which the block grant does not), and partly on the extent to which 'even'

[1] A classic case of this was the first British housing grant of 1919, whereby the whole cost fell on the central government *less* the product of 1*d.* rate. The attempt on the part of the Ministry to exercise effective control over the outlay of its funds was an important factor in the failure of the Act to get houses built. This form of grant has never been repeated.

426   *The Local Budget*

development is thought to be important, since the block grant
can be arranged to give any desired degree of equalization of
opportunity.[1]

Grants in aid of officers' salaries have somewhat fortuitously
assumed very great importance in local budgets in many countries
as a result of cost of living bonuses, due to the post-war change
in the value of money. Apart from this it has long been customary
in many countries for central governments to make extensive
grants towards school teachers' salaries (Ghana today gives 95%
and allowances, elsewhere they may actually be 100%). The
admirable intention behind this was that it would ensure the
employment only of teachers with satisfactory qualifications. Two
difficulties in respect of this policy have showed up. In the first
place the demand for teachers has been so great, especially in those
areas where schools sprang up like mushrooms as a result of
voluntary effort, that on the one hand the government found the
demands on its budget expanding more rapidly than had been
intended, on the other, the quality of teachers inevitably declined.
Secondly, in respect of a service like education where enthusiasm
differs markedly from area to area, development takes place very
unevenly, the keen areas being in fact subsidized by the indifferent
areas which thus tend to fall seriously behind.

Both these difficulties were encountered by the Phillipson codi-
fied grants operating in Nigeria from 1948. At the territorial level
Native Authorities in the Eastern Region claimed, and received,[2]
relatively more grants than those in other parts of the country,
while within the very unhomogeneous Northern Region, the
Yoruba areas in the Middle Belt were benefited at the expense of
the Moslem areas. Difficulties of this sort are of general application.
They suggest that for a service like education a broader base than
salaries[3] and one which might incorporate some redistributional as
well as promotional elements, would be more appropriate.

These difficulties, however, are much less relevant in respect of

[1] It may occur that after a percentage grant has been established for some
years and the first enthusiasm for the service has worn off, a better response will
be produced by giving notice of the lowering or termination of a grant after a
certain date. This worked very successfully with British housing grants in the
1920's. U.K. Hicks, *The Finance of British Government*, 1938.
[2] Cf. Revenue Allocation Commission, 1951, cit., and p. 168 above.
[3] Western Nigeria's grants for teachers' salaries ensure that Local Authorities
will themselves meet some of the cost both of these and of adequate school
equipment; see above, Chap. 14.

grants towards the salaries of general administrative and clerical workers. It is of the utmost importance that local officers should be well—although not extravagantly—remunerated. The reasons for this are obvious: nothing leads so quickly to corruption as pay considered inadequate; it is especially important in the early days of democratic local government that men of responsibility and intelligence should be attracted to the service. On the other hand local taxpayers naturally dislike seeing half or even more of their contributions going into the pockets of men in whom they have not over much trust. The shock is especially severe where prior to the establishment of responsible local government the services of highly trained and responsible District Officers and staff were available free of cost, since they were carried on the territorial budgets.

In fact the necessity of offering help with local officers' salaries puts a most convenient power for good into the hands of central governments, a power of which at present, effective use seems to be made in only a few places. While the final choice of what personnel to employ should be left to local councils, to force an uncongenial officer upon them runs the risk of a complete breakdown of local government. Where a Local Government Service Commission has been established the choice would naturally be limited to those on the register. Conditions of acceptability can be drawn fairly tight if assistance is generous. These conditions can be made to include not only the quality of personnel, but the general conduct of business of the authority. The Choksy Report for Ceylon[1] also suggested increasing control by the withholding of grants where the performance of a municipality was unsatisfactory, although only after a report had been submitted to Parliament. While excellent in intention the procedure might be difficult in practice. This is a most important matter which will concern us again both in respect of the general relations of central governments to Local Authorities (next chapter) and in respect of the training to be made available for different grades of local officers.[2]

So far as the top posts are concerned Kenya seems to have made the widest provisions in respect of using grants to improve the quality of personnel.[3] Salary aid, conditional on professional

[1] Op. cit., p. 255.   [2] See Chap. 22.

[3] Western Nigeria is also considering special grants for secretaries and treasurers, but only where they have approved qualifications.

qualifications, has been available in Kenya for Settled Area local councils in respect of chief executives (Town Clerks), Treasurers, Engineers, Public Health and African Affairs officers, and more recently for African District Councils (in respect of finance officers only). Under the new system grants for the wider range of officers will also be available to African District Councils. There would seem to be no reason, however, why a similar method of control of qualifications should not be extended down the scale of officers, in terms of a certain educational standard and lower professional qualifications, e.g. for such personnel as dressers in dispensaries or accountants in local Treasuries.[1] A necessary prerequisite for such an extension to be workable would be the provision of adequate opportunities for training at all levels.

The necessity for assistance in the construction of capital assets arises from the limited possibilities of borrowing by local authorities. As we have seen there are considerable obstacles in the way of expanding the opportunities for loan finance, more particularly until the point is reached when elective local government is firmly established and respected by the public. Hence the need for grants on capital account is likely to expand over the foreseeable future. It is correspondingly important for central governments to evolve a coherent policy in this respect. The capital grant gives the central government especially good powers of control of the type and quality of new works. It could lead to important opportunities for the application of central government research into the most appropriate methods and materials for the needs of the locality. Specifications can be laid down for different aspects of the construction if full grant is to be earned, or a choice of different types of installation can be offered on varying terms (e.g. for a dispensary of £250, or £500), with appropriate plans and technical assistance. This is a most promising field for cost saving through the application of mass production methods in providing standardized parts for local installations (of which the Bailey Bridge is one application), a function which must clearly fall to the lot of the central government.

The main danger in respect of capital grants is that they will prove too popular, and Local Authorities will be led to saddle themselves with works which they have not the powers to maintain

---

[1] This is done in Northern Nigeria.

adequately.[1] The Choksy Commission found that this had occurred in respect of village committee roads in Ceylon and concluded that without some assistance with maintenance the roads would shortly go back to jungle. Some countries of course have already recognized this danger. Thus Ghana, as a part of a not very coherent system of capital grants to municipalities, does include a percentage grant based on the actual net cost of operating and maintaining certain types of capital asset (roads, fire brigades, schools).

As we have seen in a number of connexions, the process of securing adequate maintenance and renewal of local fixed assets is an extremely difficult one, frequently inadequately understood and nearly always financially starved. Here a glance at British experience may be useful. The main grants for capital works in the U.K. have been for Local Authority housing; at different periods they have been immensely important, and it would be generally agreed, highly successful.[2] The grants are typically given on a unit basis for each house which conforms to the required standards of materials, accommodation, and layout; they are given not for construction, but in the form of a regular annual payout for a longish term of years. The grant is mainly intended to cover loan charges, since the houses are built from borrowed money; but in fact it constitutes a very timely aid with recurring needs, and need not be tied to interest requirements. The difficulty for developing countries would presumably be the earmarking of funds for this purpose for a long term of years. In the long run interests of development this is a lesser evil than the waste of resources and general frustration of constructing apparently wanted assets only to have them fall down again. Examples of these are to be found in almost every developing country.

As countries become more awake to the possibilities of development and especially of development from below, the extent of grants is likely to expand, so that a coherent grant policy becomes increasingly important. On this the reactions of independence may have important effects, but while it may lead to some political fragmentation (for instance of peoples whom only historical chance

[1] An extreme case of this was the Ordinance establishing District Councils in Sierra Leone which, while providing generous grants for a variety of enterprises involving fixed assets, made no mention of responsibility for maintenance.

[2] For a detailed analysis of British housing grants in the inter-war period see M. E. A. Bowley, *Housing and State*, 1945.

has thrown together), on the whole it is likely to increase the degree of central control, and with it the need for an integrated central-local development programme, in which capital grants would continue to play an important part, even when a stage is reached when greater reliance can be placed on loan finance.

There is one more point of general relevance. However things develop, it is certain that the situation will nowhere be static. Quite apart from the rapid economic and social changes which are taking place in all these countries, it cannot be hoped that any system of grants will promote the desired objectives without also having some unwanted consequences, such for instance would be the over-rapid development of services in some areas relative to others already mentioned, as a result of specific grants, or a growing carelessness in budgeting under too generous block grants. Moreover the objectives will themselves change over time. Consequently it is highly desirable that some sort of machinery should be established whereby the working of grants should be subject to periodic review, say every five years. There are various ways in which this can be brought about. The Indian Finance Commission is an independent *ad hoc* Committee which reviews every five years the relations between the centre and states, and between the states severally. The Choksy Report on Ceylon also recommends a quinquennial review of central/local financial relations. The British Local Government Act of 1958 contains provisions for an examination of the working of the grant system it introduces, after three years. The important point is that the necessity not only for adopting an appropriate grant structure, but also for keeping it up to date, should not be lost sight of.

PART V

FINANCE AND POLITICS

19

RELATIONS WITH THE CENTRAL GOVERNMENT

I

IN the present chapter we shall consider the general problem of contacts between the central government and local bodies of different sorts, leaving the more specialized problems of urban and rural government respectively for the two succeeding chapters. Although our interest remains primarily financial, it seems desirable in this last part of our studies to reach out a little more widely than hitherto, into fields which belong to politics and administration as much as to finance. However, since we have now explored in fair detail the grant relations between central governments and local bodies we can save time and space in that direction.

In federations the relations with which we are primarily concerned are normally those of state (regional) governments and Local Authorities, rather than of Federal governments and Local Authorities. This is almost completely true in Nigeria; each Region is a law unto itself in respect of local government, and indeed now *de facto* in many other things. There are still relics of unitary, prefederal days in the persistence of the 'code grants',[1] but the method of their application has been regionalized.

In India the Union government not only takes a very great interest in seeing that the states actively develop 'local self-government' within their jurisdictions, but it also retains some ultimate sanctions *vis-à-vis* the Local Authorities themselves. The formation of the Central Council for Local Self-Government[2] (which held its first meeting in 1956), and on which all the states are represented, was due to the instigation of the Union government. Again, as we saw in Chapter 17 the Union government is using the states as a vehicle for loans to Local Authorities and this should have increasingly important effects in breaking down the bottle-neck of funds for development, arising from the weakness of some state finances. Further, the federal Ministry of Local

---

[1] See above, p. 168.   [2] See above, p. 151.

Government gets regular statements of tax collections in the major Local Authorities; and if there were a succession of outstanding bad results the Union government might recommend the supersession of the council concerned, advice which the State Assembly would virtually have to implement. In addition to all this there is the question of the appointment of higher executive staff, which we shall have to discuss later. Notwithstanding these various contacts with and interests in 'local self-government' of the Union government in India, Local Authorities and their finances remain in India as in other federations, primarily a state responsibility; but the influence of the Union government seems to be steadily growing.

When, at an earlier stage, we traced in different areas the transition to modern, responsible local government authorities, we were mainly concerned with the impact of the new legislation at the local end; but the changes in the relation at the central end between central government and local government are no less important. In the first place the growth of representative government at the centre has led to the establishment of central Ministries of Local Government (in India in Delhi as well as in the separate states). In Africa, especially East and Central, this process has been proceeding by a number of stages as the constitution changes. First comes a department with a Member for Native Affairs, next at the 'Council of Ministers' stage, the Member becomes a Minister sometimes now called 'of Local Government' but still with an administrator in the job. It is only at the final stage of representative government that a Minister in the normal sense emerges. Even then local government responsibility is usually not immediately hived off from other ministerial control, e.g. in the Eastern Region of Nigeria it is only a few years since, under the Minister of Home Affairs, local government remained the personal interest of the Premier; in Sierra Leone the hiving off from Home Affairs is hardly yet complete. In Kenya and Central Africa when the Ministry was established it was concerned at first only with European local government. In Kenya the African District Councils were put under the wing of the Ministry in 1953, in Central Africa this final step has not yet been completed. In both Uganda and Tanganyika Departments of Native Affairs slid quietly into being Ministries of Local Government and sometimes, it is not unfair to say, seem not to be fully aware of the significance of their change of nomenclature.

Wherever elected Ministers of Local Government are given office a profound change is introduced into central/local relations. Local government is recognized as an important portfolio, and the men holding it are not infrequently outstanding personalities[1] but take a keen and individual interest in developing local autonomy and in acquainting themselves with the conditions under which it operates in different parts of their territories. The Ministers are, of course, politicians and as such are subject to the stresses and strains of party life, as well as to pressures from other Ministers.

Even where elective Ministers have not yet emerged, the mere existence of a Ministry whose whole business it is to promote, advise, and supervise Local Authorities should (and usually does) make an enormous difference to the atmosphere in which local government works; but since, generally speaking, the Ministry starts from scratch, success has to be achieved by strenuous pioneering work; there are no laurels or oars to rest on. Moreover, where the Ministry takes over a number of the functions of administrators working a system of more or less Indirect Rule—as has occurred in most parts of Africa—from the first a very ticklish problem of the relations between the old and the new, both in 'bush' and in the secretariat, presents itself. Different Territories have attempted to deal with this problem in different ways and provide some very interesting experience; but since the setting of the problem differs considerably as between urban and rural local government it will be more convenient to discuss it in the following chapters.

The Ministry of Local Government is by no means the only central administrative connexion with the Local Authorities. In every country other Ministries have a finger in the local pie; everywhere the Treasury (Ministry of Finance) must have its say, since as keeper of the purse strings it must have ultimate control of tax, grant, and loan policy. As colonies and ex-colonies go over gradually to the British Exchequer system (as most of them seem to want to do), the position of the Treasury becomes increasingly important. Other Ministries concerned are the Ministry of Agriculture and Ministry of Works (P.W.D.) and possibly a separate Roads or Housing Authority (as in Kenya). Elsewhere, e.g. in Jamaica and Ceylon, there are powerful Planning Secretariats

[1] Some illustrations would be Chief Rotimi Williams, formerly Minister of Local Government in Western Region of Nigeria, and Aaron Ofori Atta in Ghana, the three Premiers of the Nigerian Regions were formerly all concerned with local government.

which in some respects operate parallel to the Ministry of Local Government on very similar developments. In India the Planning Office keeps a close watch on the state Planning Departments, by means of annual meetings within each state, discussing progress (or lack of it) project by project, and thus impinging directly on the field of local government. Further, in India and Ceylon there are separate Community Development organizations: in India especially with a separate and very powerful Ministry which operates in local government matters so actively that Community Development sometimes seems to have a priority over the normal channels of local administration. These other Ministries have interests both at the political and administrative level which have to be reconciled if the best results are to be obtained in local government and in harmonious relations between central and local government.

In addition there still remains in Africa, in the field as well as at the centre, in varying degrees, the set-up of the hierarchy of Indirect Rule: Provincial Commissioners (or Residents), District Commissioners, and various ranks of District Officers or Government Agents still exercising some local government functions, but not necessarily or usually reporting directly to the Minister of Local Government.[1] Secondly, the technical departments: public works, agriculture, forestry, and medical, normally have substantial numbers of officers working in the Districts; some of their activities are closely allied to those of local government and can easily overlap with them. There are three aspects of the presence of these technical officers locally. First and foremost there is the question of division of function between central and local responsibility in each technical service; secondly, that of determining the relation between field officers and the staff of the District Office, thirdly, that of relating the activities of technical officers to those of the councils. The first of these is clearly the business of the central government, but the smooth functioning of the other two contacts depend very largely on personal relations at the local level, relations that are equally the responsibility of the field officers and of local government. These problems again belong rather more to rural than urban conditions, but many of them are general to all Local Authorities.

It will be generally agreed that the kind of relation between

[1] In Southern Nigeria, however, the relations are very close; see below, pp. 446, 460.

central and local government that has to be aimed at is neither control of local government by central government nor such concurrent powers for local government as would be appropriate for the units in a federation. Rather the optimal relationship would be a partnership of two active and co-operative members, but with the central government definitely the senior partner. The central government must necessarily retain the responsibility for seeing that the parts work successfully with each other, and harmoniously with national policy. It must exercise advice and supervision in other words, rather than control. On occasions it may have to impose a national policy on local government because national policy is pre-eminent, but it will want to do so as sparingly as possible, and to leave the maximum autonomy to the Local Authorities within the prescribed limits. Otherwise it cannot hope to retain their active co-operation. It is generally true to say that the initiative in the development of new services comes from the centre and not from the local end; this is true in the U.K. as much as overseas; but it is by no means an invariable rule. A not uncommon sequence in the U.K. has been from enterprising local authority to central interest and thence to statutory generalization. In strict accordance with this tradition, in virtually any of our countries the field worker is sure to find local authorities here and there bubbling with enthusiasm and ideas. Indeed this is one of the most fascinating aspects of the study of local government. Where the local authorities have available the practical means of implementing their ideas, it is a welcome indication that the right sort of partnership between central and local government is growing up.

Broadly, we can distinguish three main lines of contact between the central government, or more precisely the Ministry, and local government. First, it is the business of the Ministry of Local Government specifically to define the powers and duties of each Local Authority either by grade, or by separate instrument. Secondly, the Ministry of Local Government has the responsibility to keep a 'watching brief' on the whole local budgetary process, from the first drafting of the Estimates to the final stages of audit and any consequent disciplinary measures that have to be taken, either against particular officers or councillors, or against a council as a whole. It is convenient to consider under this head problems of the relation of the central government to appointments and dismissals of local officers, as not only is it one of the aspects of local government which gives rise to particular trouble but also especially (as we saw in the last chapter) one of the most useful methods of supervision is through the medium of conditional salary grants geared to qualifications. Thirdly, there are great needs and great opportunities for central governments to develop *continuing* means of giving advice, and exercising supervision, as is particularly necessary in the early stages of responsible local government. This should be thought of as primarily an educational service, but with no hint of paternalism on the one hand nor of arbitrary control on the other. We shall consider in turn experience and conclusions in respect of each of these three lines of contact.

II

In the U.K. Local Authorities are statutory bodies[1] in the sense that their powers and duties are very closely defined by law and on their own initiative can only be enlarged through the difficult process of private legislation. On the other hand from time to time the central government has not hesitated to put new duties on local shoulders—such as housing and slum clearance, and various specialist health services such as maternal and child welfare and the care of the elderly. Overseas, although almost all local bodies are now statutory bodies, with executive responsibilities, generally speaking their powers and duties are much more broadly defined—or may not be defined more closely than general duty to improve their area.[2] Although at first it seemed rational thus to allow emergent Local Authorities considerable headroom, there is now no doubt that initially powers were drawn far too loosely, with the result that on the one hand it was not sufficiently clear to the councils which jobs they were supposed to get on with, while on the other the central government had but indifferent means of control. Gradually this situation is altering; powers and duties are being specifically defined and are assuming a new, but definite pattern. In fact the distribution of function between central and local government is changing in two contrary (but not necessarily inconsistent) directions.

On the one hand the successful establishment of responsible Local Authorities has led to a general propensity to transfer services from central to local control, especially in the field of

[1] See above, p. 22.
[2] See District Councils in Sierra Leone, above, p. 197.

public health and roads, but also to some extent in education and natural resources. There seem to have been two motives behind this development: relief for the centre as well as the desire to build up the local responsibility. In a number of places the not uncongenial prospect of unloading responsibilities on to other shoulders would seem to have been the more important motive. On the other hand there has also been a centripetal tendency, a policy of concentrating more responsibility at the centre or state level and less at the local. In India these two contrary tendencies can be traced over a long period, operating at both the central/state, and state/local levels. Decentralization in some matters started with provincial autonomy,[1] but in other matters at that stage, central control was drawn even more closely than before. The advent of nationhood, followed closely by the adoption of national planning, further emphasized the centralizing tendency, at the same time as formal federation was established. Provincial autonomy had been accompanied at the state level by the first drive to revive (or create) panchayats. After independence this drive was intensified, and today we find states tending more and more to take over certain local government services (especially education), while at the same time building up the panchayat structure.[2] In Nigeria in a somewhat similar manner the 1948, and still more the 1951 constitutions, were decentralizing in that they transferred local government completely to the Regions, but within the Regions, particularly in the East and North, there has been a tendency for control over local bodies to be drawn more tightly.

Again in Kenya the new county councils in the Settled Areas have effectively been bribed into taking over public health responsibilities. More recently the African District Councils have simply been told to follow suit, leaving to the administration the task of making the change acceptable. At the same time various agricultural services formerly managed by African District Councils have been taken over by the government; more important the African courts have been transferred to central control, although still a charge (in so far as they are not self-supporting by fees and finances) on the African District Councils.[3] In education the first result of the Mau

[1] See above, p. 55.
[2] See above, pp. 150-1.
[3] As we have seen almost everywhere court work has now been more or less hived off from local government work—less in Northern Nigeria where the traditional system still remains and in Tanganyika than elsewhere—but the

Mau Emergency was a high concentration of educational responsibility under centrally managed boards; more recently increasing efforts are being made to bring the African District Councils into the educational picture both in respect of the distribution of outlay between services (which now comes directly before the African District Council) and in respect of finance. In Uganda there has been a similar unloading of services onto the District Councils, accompanied by a withdrawal of the administration from council management; but this has not been accompanied by any slackening of general central control. Even in the West Indies changes in the same two contrary directions can be observed: on the one hand an increasingly active and coherent policy on the part of island governments, accompanied by the transfer of definite if minor powers to local authorities. This, for example, has taken place —or is accepted policy—in Trinidad, Barbados, and British Guiana.[1]

When the effects of these redefinitions and reallocations of powers and duties between central government and local government have worked themselves out the new equilibrium promises to be substantially different from the old. Important as it is that powers should be transferred if local government is to develop a life independent of duties which it performs as a virtual agency of the central government, the process is surrounded by dangers: on the financial side (as we have seen) that the transferred services will languish for want of adequate resources, on the administrative side that standards will sag below tolerable levels, and on the political side that greater local powers will lead to political disintegration.[2] Properly considered, central governments have increased rather than diminished their responsibilities by piling new services on Local Authorities; it is consequently up to them to develop new lines of contact which will enable them to keep control of the situation.

plan seems to be, e.g. in Western and Eastern Nigeria—to establish an independent magisterial system rather than a direct transfer to central management.

[1] A similar proposal is to give a measure of self-government to Nevis which is at present administered with St. Kitts and Anguilla. This is in response to unfavourable Nevis reactions to a more active tax policy on the part of the joint administration.

[2] The danger spot here appears to be Uganda where Districts are not only rigid in jurisdiction but tend to coincide with tribal boundaries. At the central-regional level the danger is also formidable in Nigeria, not to mention India.

One important way—still in the field of definition of powers and duties—in which this seems to be happening is through the grading of local authorities in relation not only to their powers and duties, but also according to the degree of control over their Estimates. This is particularly relevant to urban authorities, since as they grow their character tends to change fundamentally. In this context a number of Indian states have adopted three grades of municipalities. Small towns come under the Municipal Act, by which the president of the council is the District Collector, who still has full executive powers although the council is encouraged to develop deliberative and advisory powers. In the next grade, operating under the Borough Act, the construction of the budget is the responsibility of the Council, but subject to vetting by the Collector. Finally under the Corporation Act a first-class town like Bombay has as complete budgetary freedom as a British County Borough—in one sense it has even more, both because it has a wider range of autonomous taxes and because it hardly depends at all on Union or state grants.

In some African territories a system of orderly but flexible emergence of an independent urban community is being worked out. Thus Tanganyika uses five stages from the minor settlement to the completely independent municipality[1] with its mayor and own professional staff (so far only Dar-es-Salaam has attained to this dignity). First the settlement becomes an entity by having its boundary defined, secondly, it becomes a legal person, with its own assets and rules, but still under tutelage. At the third stage it is transferred to the Local Government Ordinance for urban areas with gradually emerging professional staff. At the penultimate stage an executive officer—an emergent town clerk—is appointed (but remains a central government officer on secondment) and the budget is a local responsibility, though subject to normal Ministry of Local Government control.

By the 1958 Urban Authorities Ordinance Uganda is introducing a somewhat similar arrangement. Previously it had been necessary for an area which was deemed to be ready for urban privilege, to plunge, so to speak, fully clad into complete urban responsibilities, a procedure which raised difficulties both in respect of want of experience (especially financial experience) of councils and local officers, and of absence of adequate liquid funds to maintain the

---

[1] See above, pp. 227–8.

fixed assets thus thrust upon it.[1] Under the new Ordinance provision is made for the declaration of a town by the Ministry with a town board 'which shall perform such duties and may exercise such powers as are imposed and conferred on such Board'. The intention is to enlarge the powers and responsibilities gradually as the board shows itself competent to take on further financial responsibilities, in particular, until it has proved itself, its senior staff appointments will continue to be by secondment from the central government. An essentially similar method will be used in the Eastern Region of Nigeria. With the abrogation of County Councils all urban areas were put in a position eventually to aspire to County Borough powers and duties, but the progress to such emancipation will be gradual, according to the size and competency of the authority.[2]

All this recent legislation has a flexibility far in advance of the older laws and Ordinances. Moreover it is a disciplined flexibility substantially different from the pseudo-flexibility of vaguely drawn powers. Within the broad lines laid down in the Ordinance each authority is established under a separate instrument which lays down its powers and duties precisely, and can very simply be adjusted when up-grading is called for. In Tanganyika—which early saw the advantages of this device—some such provision was originally called for in order to embody in it the exact multiracial ratio that was locally called for, but the applications of the procedure are obviously much wider than this. Moreover the individual instrument is a device which is applicable to rural as well as to urban authorities (which are inevitably multiracial); indeed in Tanganyika it has so far been more used in the former than in the latter. The local government structure which will emerge from a large number of separate instruments will naturally be much less tidy than the British pure classificatory system. On the other hand under it in respect of each local authority both the central government and the local government know exactly where they stand, and if the local authority shows initiative the steps to reward it are simple. This is surely far more important than uniformity in a developing country.

[1] The difficulties of this situation were explained to me by the Town Clerk of Jinja.
[2] It must be borne in mind that the rigidity of British local government is something quite modern; even as late as the inter-war period variations in powers and duties accrued to Borough and Urban District Councils.

A related line of contact whereby the Local Authority can exercise its own initiative while the central government retains its power of counsel and supervision is through the local making and central approving of by-laws. Kenya seems so far to have developed this line of approach most thoroughly. Local Authorities of all sorts, including African District Councils, are encouraged both to improve the health and amenities of their areas and to promote economic development by rules of their own devising. Thus to take one or two examples of very many, Nakuru Town Council has by-laws concerning the use of buildings (mainly aimed at inducing more hygienic habits among Asians). A court order can be obtained against owner or occupier where a by-law has been contravened. A single case may include as many as twenty-six charges, and (in February 1958) there had been at least a case a month for the previous fourteen months. Again (as a result of a serious outbreak of typhoid) the Nandi African District Council passed a by-law compelling every occupier to provide an adequate latrine. In Elgeyo Marakwet a by-law introduced compulsory destocking. The drafting and approval of this local legislation, needless to say, provide admirable opportunities for constructive co-operation between central government and local government, and the system might profitably be used much more widely elsewhere.

III

The principal reason why it has been possible in the U.K. to retain enterprise and initiative in local government in spite of progressive encroachments by the central government, is that in basic essentials Local Authorities have a high degree of budgetary freedom. The only limit to the rate poundage Local Authorities may impose is the reaction of the ratepayers. No higher authority vets their budgets, and they are not even under compulsion to send details to the Ministry. This freedom is not incompatible with the implementation of national policy, largely because of the understanding and co-operation which has grown up over the generations. Overseas such a co-ordination of national policy and local freedom can only be built up gradually. It is essentially through the manner in which the central government deals with local budgets that the foundation for it can be laid.

The first problem of financial co-ordination is concerned with the manner in which the Estimates are put together. In the U.K.

each committee of a council determines its own Estimates in conjunction with its technical officer (Medical Officer of Health, Education Director, and so on); these are then considered, and if necessary pruned and consolidated by the Finance (or General Purposes) Committee with City Treasurer and Town Clerk also playing important parts.[1] Overseas the committee system is not developed sufficiently for this procedure, and various substitutes have to be used. In Indian and Ceylonese urban local government the Estimates seem now in practice to be put together by the Municipal Commissioner and are presented to the council by him; he is also required to present an Annual Administration Report.

The Bombay procedure is typical of Indian practice at its most democratic. After the Municipal Commissioner has prepared and revised the Estimates they are printed and sent to the Standing Committee[2] who consider them for a month but generally agree to everything. At the beginning of the second week in January they go to the council who proceed to hold a general debate including the whole range of administration (it is suggested that this would be more appropriate in conjunction with the presentation of the Administration Report in April, than on the Estimates). The income side of the budget must be voted by the end of January—thus after about twenty days. The expenditure side is not due before the end of March, but the council is usually through with it by the end of February. This procedure evidently leaves ample time for debate and searching criticism, but except in the hands of a keen and alert council (as Bombay certainly is) discussion tends to be desultory and insignificant. The danger of the Municipal Commissioner system is that it tends towards that of City Manager.[3] Outside the great Indian cities with corporation status budget making is largely in the hands of the Collector. District Boards do not even exist everywhere, so in many Districts there is no trace of democratic process above the panchayat level.

In Africa under the various types of indirect rule, merging even

---

[1] See above, p. 23.

[2] The Standing Committee in Indian, or African terms (where it exists principally in countries saddled with very large councils, such as Uganda) is more of a council in miniature than a British Finance Committee and in fact normally acts for the council though subject to the latter's revising power. In the U.K. the strong development of the whole range of committees would normally prevent the Finance Committee usurping the powers of the council to anything like the same extent.   [3] See below, p. 491.

now (in parts of Kenya at least) into virtually direct rule, the responsibility for preparing the Estimates rested on the District Office. Even at this stage, however, it was possible for a District Officer (if he were a patient educationalist, as not a few of them were) to teach his council the rudiments of budgeting by skilfully steering them to a point where they were faced with a simple alternative; this experience was of immense value when greater responsibility was put upon councils.[1]

Throughout East and Central Africa, whatever the law may say, the District Officer may still largely be responsible for putting the Estimates together. For instance in Uganda under the 1955 Ordinance the District Officer lost his official powers, but since Estimates must be framed, if the council were at loggerheads, or their officers particularly bad at arithmetic (or it must be admitted, if the District Officer were somewhat impatient) he might still do the major part of budgeting.

Contrariwise in Kenya (where it was only in 1959 that the first African president of an African District Council was appointed), the District Commissioner as president normally has the prime responsibility for the Estimates. In the more remote and backward parts budgeting is far beyond the comprehension of councils, though they may be enthusiastic to raise revenue for particular purposes. In the more sophisticated areas, where there is a large elective element on the council, the District Commissioner can keep almost wholly in the background (although of course much depends on personality), so that his influence (as distinct from his responsibility) is confined to steering the council gently into accepting particular items of government policy which may not be altogether congenial to them. Once persuaded, Kenya councils have often shown themselves remarkably tough in insisting on unpopular measures such as compulsory destocking[2] and afforestation.[3]

---

[1] I witnessed a revealing illustration of this in 1950 in the budget session of a small Native Authority not far from Lagos. The session was held in the school house and was very well attended. The council's motion was that the annual salary of their Oba should be increased from £10 to £12 (it was a clear case of keeping up with the Joneses in the next Native Authority). The funds at the disposal of the council (without increase of tax) were listed on the blackboard by the District Officer and for the illiterate represented by a heap of stones. The various claims on the funds were then struck off till a final set of alternatives had to be faced: to repair the clinic, to rebuild the roof of the village well (which had fallen in), to raise the Oba's salary, with funds available for only two of these alternatives, unless tax were increased. The Oba did not get his rise.

[2] In Elgeyo Marakwet.   [3] For example, in Kipsigis District.

In Ghana and Southern Nigeria where the District Officer no longer functions as such, and his successor has no direct say in the Estimates, he may still influence councils quite importantly. In Ghana a Government Agent or Assistant Government Agent will strive to time his routine visit to a council to coincide with the budget session. In Nigeria he will very often be called in for advice at all stages of planning the budget. Thus the chain of contact and supervision between the central government and the Local Authorities has by no means been completely disrupted, even where the councils are fully elective and independent of formal control by the administration; on the other hand even in places where the District Officer formally controls the Estimates the council may in practice determine everything of importance.

Where the Estimates are the business of the council the problem of vetting them has to be considered very carefully. The type of control exercised at this stage of development is if anything more important for budgetary freedom than the previous stage. A delicate balance has to be maintained between condoning disorderliness and interfering with responsibility where it is really being exercised (albeit somewhat clouded by inexperience). The ultimate responsibility for examining and passing the Estimates is naturally that of the Ministry of Local Government. Generally speaking it is a clear rule that the current budget must be balanced,[1] though reserves[2] may be drawn upon to meet an unforeseeable emergency or local catastrophe (such as foot and mouth disease in a cattle area).

Clearly the desirable aim must be that the vetting of the budget should be thorough enough to reveal anything that is really wrong, but at the same time quick enough not to hold up the activities of the Local Authority. Within these limits the more friendly and informal the process can be, the more the Local Authority is likely to feel that it is winning its way to full budgetary responsibility. In the old days the District Commissioner was the 'father of his people' and their mutual relation was extremely personal. The change over to the impersonal and more distant relation with the officers of the Ministry will be all the easier and more successful if the central officers can show

[1] Normally an unbalanced budget would require the sanction of the Minister.

[2] Kenya Ministry of Local Government recommends what it considers a 'safe' reserve for each African District Council; in Tanganyka there is a general rule.

that they have a personal interest in the affairs of the council and know what it feels like to be 'in bush'.

Various devices for achieving the right attitude in respect to budgetary control are used in Kenya. Two Standing Committees—one for Settled Area Local Government and one for African Local Government are set up at the Ministry under the chairmanship of the Commissioner (e.g. Permanent Secretary).[1] Since the Estimates will already have been passed by the administration (in the case of African District Councils) nothing beyond a general oversight is required.[2] In Tanganyika powers of vetting budgets are delegated to Provincial Commissioners; in the Western Region of Nigeria similarly District Commissioners have delegated powers of approval, but not of disapproval; subsequently there is a detailed checking at the Ministry which may result in substantial alterations. In Ghana Government Agents and Assistant Government Agents seem in practice to have powers of disapproval as well as of approval. In the Eastern Region of Nigeria the vetting is mainly performed direct by the Ministry but in as informal a manner as possible, and generally speaking with admirable speed. In the meantime the Local Authority has authority to spend up to 50% of last year's Estimates.

Where the proper budgetary balance has not been allowed for in the Estimates the examining officer has a delicate task of steering a council either to cut out an Estimate or to induce it to raise tax rates or (especially in Kenya) to increase service fees. He must, however, bear in mind that it may well be that what is really required is merely for the council to have its hands strengthened *vis-à-vis* the electorate. In this case it may work better to strike out a really popular Estimate such as education, for which the council will have no difficulty in getting agreement for an increase in tax, than one over which there will be no strong feeling and so divided opinions. The practice of some Indian states of laying down compulsory minimum rates for certain taxes is similarly aimed at strengthening the hands of the council *vis-à-vis* the electorate.

[1] See above, p. 214.

[2] The composition of the two committees is substantially different: the European committee consists of the Attorney General and leading technical officers in the Colony, that for African District Councils consists wholly of Africans, including two Members of the Legislative Council. Presumably this reflects the more technical, less strictly governing activities of European councils.

As we have already emphasized, a fully responsible budgetary exercise requires that the local authority always has open to it the alternative of increasing its revenue, as well as of making marginal adjustments to the Estimates. This, as we have seen, is what in the last resort preserves the autonomy of British local government; contrariwise limitations on this right in the U.S.A. largely destroy the autonomy of local authorities in spite of appearances to the contrary. It is much easier to keep the revenue alternative open if local authorities have a number of autonomous revenue sources. As we have seen in fact in many of our countries they do have a permitted range of resources, to a much greater extent than in the U.K. Broadly speaking however it is *tax* autonomy that matters rather than powers over other sources.

It may indeed sometimes be necessary to put a limit on the rate of tax (or charge for services) that Local Authorities may set for any particular revenue source, in the interests either of the general economic situation or of protecting the central government revenue; for instance Uganda has quite reasonably put a limit of 400s. on the amount that can be raised from any taxpayer under the graduated poll tax, in the interests of Territorial income tax.[1] The Eastern Region of Nigeria has put one of 15s. for the same purpose. The Western Region also has a limit, though of a different type.[2] Again Tanganyika has had to exercise some control on cess revenue, since it is not inconceivable that local cesses might affect the pattern of consumption and trade in the whole economy.

It is safe to say however that many more ceilings are placed on local tax powers than are necessitated either with regard to the general economic situation or in the interests of central revenue. For instance the freezing of the parish rate in Jamaica was really necessitated by the failure of the Island government to carry through a revaluation of property; the fixing of a uniform 25s. for the poll tax in Sierra Leone was due essentially to fear of the unknown: the reaction of local taxpayers in different areas to higher rates imposed by their own Chiefdom Authorities.

Even where there are valid reasons for fixing a limit on a local

[1] In fact since political difficulties delayed the introduction of the Territorial income tax on Africans the Protectorate government might have been better advised merely to stake its claim, and in the meantime to allow the districts to go on working on tax potential which is evidently there.
[2] Local Tax rights being limited to the first £300. of income.

tax it can usually be made flexible—for instance in Uganda or the Western Region of Nigeria although the marginal rate was fixed it was still possible for councils to vary the infra marginal rates. There is much less room to manœuvre under the Eastern Region ceiling, but even so there are two safety valves: the tradition of the population of making important voluntary contributions which almost amount to a kind of taxation,[1] and the prospect of introducing property rates in urban areas, which is at present much more favourable than in the Western Region.

On the tax side of the budget it may well be that Local Authorities have to be content to be rather more junior partners to central government than on the expenditure side. In the best interests of both economic and democratic development the relation still needs to be a partnership, with the central government giving as well as taking.

The complementary budgetary exercise to supervision of the Estimates is that of examining the results. In spite of the existence almost everywhere of a formal central audit system, it cannot be claimed that this is normally effective. Even where the audit itself is satisfactory it tends to be so much delayed that as a method of supervision it is of very limited use, while as a method of control it gets no farther than very tardy retribution and punishment of doubtful deterrent value. The blame for this state of affairs is not necessarily to be laid on the Audit Ordinance. Auditors are handicapped in the same way as other specialized services by a lack of professional manpower. Again the prerequisite to effective auditing is good accounting, and here a little more care and firmness on the part of Ministries of Local Government might bring about a great improvement.

The need for better and more uniform accounting has been repeatedly emphasized by Commissions of Inquiry in different countries. The Choksy Report in Ceylon recommended the establishment of a Departmental Committee[2] to frame a uniform and standardized set of financial rules, and also that the powers of the Minister should be enlarged as a matter of urgency to enable him

---

[1] The 'Assumed Local Contribution'; see above, p. 168.

[2] Cf. for instance in the Choksy Report in Ceylon (cit., para. 776) it was recommended that the committee should be chaired by the Commissioner for Local Government and include the Attorney-General, a representative of the Treasury, the Treasurer of Colombo, and two other municipal accountants.

to prescribe, firstly, procedure to be followed in regard to keeping accounts and accounting, secondly, forms of budgets and heads of items to be included in budgets. This is sound advice.

In Kenya the Ministry of Local Government also goes on pegging away at budgeting and accounting, and as a result, the standard there both of European and African District Councils is (as we have seen) already above that of other territories. Elsewhere insufficient attention is certainly paid to these seemingly prosaic matters by the Ministry of Local Government. One officer in Nigeria volunteered: 'nobody really has a clue as to what has actually been spent, as everything is two years in arrears'; cases of this sort do not only occur in Nigeria. Further, the three Regions work with substantially different forms of Estimates, one excels where another is deficient, but none is really satisfactory. It should not be beyond the powers of the Federal government to bring the Regions together, on the lines suggested for Ceylon, to thrash out an appropriate form of accounting and of budget presentation which the Regions would then make obligatory on their own local authorities. After all, a good accounting procedure is not really much more difficult than a bad one. Moreover, this type of supervision does nothing to curtail the autonomy of Local Authorities. It will become increasingly necessary in the national interest as the tempo of development accelerates, because knowledge of the true facts of the whole public sector is essential for successful planning. From the local end, without good budgetary accounts, the local citizens have no opportunity to take an effective interest in local affairs. With it the council can make the most of its opportunities by intelligent public relations propaganda.

The neglect of elementary accounting principles is largely to be explained—but not justified—by the tradition of British local administrators who in the past, whether in Asia or Africa, have been drawn from a class which is unfamiliar, even contemptuous, of business practices. Administrators are however themselves now changing; but in the meantime the need for cashiers and accountants at all levels has been expanding with lightning rapidity. With the growth of local government responsibility, local education has just not been able to keep up. This is a matter to which we shall have to return in Chapter 22 in connexion with the general problem of training. But the responsibility for drawing up the appropriate forms and rules is a matter for the central government.

Unfortunately British practice as a whole can offer little guidance in this respect. The large cities for the most part have mechanical accounting and internal running as well as post audit. The accounts of certain government-aided services (especially housing) have to be kept according to detailed requirements, but otherwise there is little uniformity, as is obvious to anyone who has attempted to work with the accounts of individual authorities.[1]

It would take us too far into the accounting field to discuss in any detail what the overseas rules should be. One thing that is quite certain however is that there needs to be a definite set of financial rules for each grade of local authority, including what expenditure they may incur (without, and with, special sanction), what books and vouchers they must keep, and what periodic returns should be made to the Ministry of Local Government. These matters call for careful and concentrated work, although very largely of a routine nature. They cannot be left under the responsibility of an unpaid chairman, as for instance Ceylon has tried to do outside the municipalities.[2] On the other hand responsibility must rest squarely on an individual pair of shoulders which is able to sustain it, be he called Treasurer, Accounting Officer, or cashier. His pay, of all salaries, needs to be commensurate with his responsibilities.[3] Matters of general principle, which perhaps bear more on the economic than on the accounting side, however, need to be emphasized. In the first place the system must be very simple. Apart from genuine commercial enterprises, which call for commercial type accounts, the penny cash book simple recording of incomings and outgoings is adequate, provided three conditions are satisfied: (1) that no accounting year goes by without a proper closed account. In this respect the Indian practice of showing at least three years, has much to commend it. Even further if x is the

---

[1] See the strictures of the *Radcliffe Committee on the working of the Monetary System*, 1959, on the inadequacy of British Local Government Statistics.

[2] See Choksy Report cit.

[3] One great difficulty which besets virtually all overseas local governments and which is hardly felt in the U.K. is the frequent turnover of staff. The outgoing officer leaves behind arrears of work, the incoming officer is too busy learning the ropes and keeping up with current matters ever to get things properly straightened out. The Ceylon Attorney-General suggests that outgoing officers should be required under the sanction of disciplinary action to clear up all arrears before they hand over. An alternative would be the sort of temporary special help from the Ministry which is made available in Kenya (see Chap. 21).

year to which the Estimates relate the following information might well be shown:

	Actuals	1st est.	Revised estimate	1st est.	Provisional estimate	Prognostication (if possible)
Year . .	$x-2$	$x-1$	$x-1$	x	$x+1$	$x+2$

(2) There must be a fully comprehensive functional summary of the outgoings and incomings, so that the full cost of each service, the full receipts from all sources and the change in the reserves can simply be read off. A summary form, using the breakdown of Chapters 13 and 14, would be as follows:

Summary of Current Budget, District Council of A

Incomings

1. Tax revenue A.
   „ B.
   „ C.

2. Service receipts (a, b, c, &c.).

3. Profits of commercial undertakings (*net* of depreciation).

4. Court fees and fines.

5. Other fees, rents, and licences.

6. Government grants:
   Block.
   Specific A (terms).
   „ B „
   „ C „

7. New borrowing.

Outgoings

1. Administration: Total
   Law and order.
   Traditional authorities.

2. Public Health: Total
   General.
   Dispensaries, &c.
   Conservancy, &c.

3. Education: Total
   Primary.
   Post primary.
   Technical.
   Teacher training.

4. Roads and works.

5. Current outlay on services.

6. Interest and loan service.

7. Provision for maintenance and replacement of fixed assets.

8. Loans to private bodies and persons.

Incomings *minus* outgoings = current Budget surplus to be carried down to capital budget.

(3) It is essential that income and capital accounts[1] are carefully kept distinct. Provided then with vouchers for the individual items under the heads, and a functional summary up to date,

---

[1] The form of capital account given above in Chap. 17 is suitable for this purpose with minor adjustments.

the auditors should be able to catch up, and then to keep up to date.

Unfortunately in a number of places, apart from the low quality of accounting, the audit system is itself often quite insufficient. This partly arises from lack of understanding of the importance of the process, and consequent failure to offer adequate pay to attract men of the right calibre or to induce them to take the necessary training. This is often a lack at the central as well as at the local level, but seems to be much better understood in India than in the West Indies or Africa. The problem is not so much one of the big cities, wherever they are; since most of them have fairly efficient internal audit, some of them, even in Africa (e.g. Lagos) have fully mechanized accounting so that the fact that the federal audit is normally more than a year in arrears is perhaps not of major importance. The problem is much more one of the smaller towns and of rural authorities.

Various devices to improve financial checks have been tried in different countries. In India local authority accounts are audited by the state departments, so that the standard naturally varies from state to state. (At the same time the state accounts are themselves audited at the Union level, which provides some insurance of at least minimum uniformity.) Ceylon has been working with a completely centralized audit system for local accounts, but has found that the difficulties and delays in passing books up and down between the Local Authority and Auditor-General have given rise to intolerable delays, and would now prefer more decentralization.

In Nigeria (apart from Lagos) audit is at the Regional level and is normally some years in arrear. It cannot be said however that, given the current state of Local Authority accounting in all the Regions, the Audit Departments have really had a fair opportunity to do their work properly. In the Northern Region of Nigeria also it appears that the auditors are expected to supervise and advise on the actual Estimates and accounting at the same time as they do their audit. As we shall discuss below there is urgent need for more technical help in financial matters for Local Authorities, but to expect the auditors to provide it takes them off their proper work and runs into still greater dangers of delay. It is not surprising that audit seems to be more delayed in the North than in other Regions.

Tanganyika has had a central audit system since 1947, but the Local Government Memorandum of 1957 still finds it necessary to point out that the main task of auditors continues to be to advise, assist, and co-ordinate; it is suggested, however, that the District Officer should himself arrange to inspect the books at least once a month,[1] under the supervision of the Provincial Commissioner, and that short-period training in accounting should be frequently arranged for local officers. It is also suggested that an effort should be made to get senior members of the council to share in the work of inspection. This could serve both as a check on treasurers and as an education for councillors. On their side also treasurers should be brought to realize more clearly their responsibility for keeping their councils informed of the financial position. In principle a very similar system operates in Ghana, where Government Agents and Assistant Government Agents attempt to get a regular monthly Trial Balance from each council. This is by no means always achieved. Some secretaries and treasurers are almost incapable of complying (more training is an urgent necessity); the shortage of administrative staff makes it impossible to keep up regular visits.

From this brief summary of experience and suggestion the following conclusions seem to emerge. First, until a greater understanding of the principles of accounting and of the need for accuracy has been built up, effective financial checks, including audit, presuppose that continuing advice and assistance will be available; this is not really a matter for the Audit Department whose business is to discover error rather than to prevent its occurrence. We shall have to discuss later what should be done in relation to other continuing contacts between central and local government. Secondly, effective audit presupposes effective accounting, the system needs first to be looked into, and rationalized and then to be understood, both by local treasurers and secretaries on the one side, and by councillors on the other. Thirdly, the importance of audit is not yet sufficiently realized by all central governments; everywhere Audit Departments need expanding and strengthening with more trained staff. Moreover it is essential that more members of the central department should be available for field work. The accounts of local authorities cannot be successfully audited by sending the books up to the central secretariat.

There is probably no better deterrent to falsification and misdemeanour than effective audit carried out as soon as possible after

[1] A similar idea has been discussed in Western Nigeria.

expenditure has taken place. Even if this condition is realized—as it is scarcely anywhere today—it is still necessary to explore means of dealing with faults. There are two separate questions here: first, what to do with the erring individual, be he councillor or local civil servant; secondly, what to do about a whole council which in some way has neglected its duties: either by failing to provide adequate statutory services, or by applying its money in unsatisfactory, even if not fully illegal ways, or by failing to collect the necessary taxes.

Where there has been plain embezzlement the natural remedy is the courts, and no doubt this is in principle resorted to; the difficulty is normally to prove the charge. Again and again the offender starts on the wrong path as a result of an undiscovered, at first unintentional mistake. The important point consequently is to have a means—either of frequent check or of continuous supervision; these alternatives we shall discuss below.

The U.K. remedy for expenditure *ultra vires* by a particular councillor or councillors is personal surcharge. This works on the whole fairly well because (as we have seen) the *ultra vires* frontier is drawn with close precision, and because the District Auditor system—whatever its general limitations—is completely independent. Overseas it cannot be assumed that either condition is really satisfied. Indeed the Tanganyika government admits that under present circumstances surcharge cannot really be enforced, mainly for want of comprehension. In Ceylon the Choksy Committee was also doubtful of the use of surcharge and suggested that it should only be applied on the express recommendation of the Auditor-General. On the other hand in Kenya surcharge is regularly used. In West Africa also it seems to work reasonably well, in spite of the difficulty that repayment must often be spread over a long period due to the defaulter's small cash reserve. It is obvious that unless the conditions for success are really present the method of surcharge could prove unfair and arbitrary in application. In this respect too, more indirect means, implying again probably continuous contacts with a definite educational intent, need also for the present to be available.

Although an individual can be dealt with by these means a whole erring council clearly calls for other measures. In the inter-war period the British government suspended a few Local Authorities for spending (or so it was believed) too much money on paupers;[1]

---

[1] The magnitude of the problem of local unemployment confronting the

it was not a success and it is most unlikely that the experiment will ever be repeated. In contrast, most overseas governments have indulged in suspensions on a relatively large scale; the question naturally arises as to the usefulness, or on the other hand the possible abuses, of this method of getting a council to co-operate efficiently. Circumstances have arisen in which one or more councils entirely refuse to carry out their business for political reasons—the most striking case of this was the Congress boycott of Indian local councils in the 1930's. A small-scale example occurred in Tanganyika in 1958–9 where Africans suddenly boycotted four or five of the multiracial councils to the establishment of which they had previously agreed, and in one case had actually been working successfully on an informal basis for several years.[1] In circumstances like these there is no choice open to the government but to withdraw elective government for the time being.

Generally speaking, however, councils are suspended on account of corruption, quarrelling, or sheer inefficiency on the part of the management.[2] The procedure then is for the Ministry to appoint a caretaker committee, and in the mean time to endeavour to discover the root of the trouble. New elections are generally held in a matter of months or a year. Sometimes this procedure works very well; the pause enables the books to be sorted out and brought up to date, so that the new council officers start off with a clean sheet. Not a few councils subjected to this treatment have been able to keep straight thereafter. Much depends on the selection of the caretaker committee; there have been cases where it was no better than the suspended council—perhaps even consisting of their relatives. Where national politics have already entered into local government there is an additional complication: it cannot escape observation that governments (e.g. Ghana and the Nigerian Regions) have frequently suspended councils where the majority belonged to an opposing political party. The suspension may well have been justified on administrative grounds, but the suspicion naturally arises

councils was not fully realized; in the event, the caretaker administrators found themselves unable to make more than negligible savings. Cf. U. K. Hicks, *The Finance of British Government*, 1938.   [1] See above, p. 227.

[2] Thus the Council of Osuduku, Eastern Region of Ghana, was on the eve of suspension when I visited it in April 1958. Its inefficiency was unquestionable but the basic trouble seemed to be its small size and poverty, leading to inability to pay for the services of a worthwhile secretary. The only alternatives appeared to be to unite the jurisdiction with another, or if this was politically (tribally) impossible, a much more substantial grant with more supervision.

that more would be condoned in a council of the right political colour.

In view of these difficulties it would seem that governments would be wise to apply the desperate remedy of suspension as sparingly as possible. Where a council has got so hopelessly tangled up that suspension cannot be avoided on administrative grounds, it should be for no longer than is necessary to straighten things out. Care should be taken to see that the suspension is used as a constructive breathing space, so that it cannot on any ground be construed as either a party or an anti-democratic move. For every suspension is in itself a set-back to the cause of the development of responsible local government, and to be avoided so far as possible on that ground alone. If the remedy is abused it might well make that development impossible.

There are after all a number of less drastic ways of dealing with most situations, for instance in the Western Region of Nigeria a council which fails to collect personal tax adequately is declared in default, and receives special attention from the Ministry until the matter has been put right. There is no legal sanction for this pro-cedure, but the implied disgrace seems to be enough to bring councils to heel. More often than not the difficulty is due to par-ticular councillors or officers, rather than to the council as a whole and can be more appropriately dealt with at the personal level. Again a long history of trouble may well be due to special circum-stances more or less outside the control of the council, such as a non-viable jurisdiction, or a basic incompatibility between different tribal elements in the district. The appropriate remedy might then well be a boundary alteration. In this respect the device of a separate instrument[1] tailored to the circumstances of the individual council should prove extremely useful.

IV

In our discussion of the contacts between central and local governments which will contribute to building a successful and financially well-founded system of Local Authorities we have seen again and again the need for continuing advice and help. The British central Ministries which are concerned with local

[1] Thus after a period of chronic trouble and what seems to have been a con-structive suspension, Enugu was in 1958 having its instrument redrafted in preparation for the restoration of representative government.

government (the Ministries of Housing and Local Government, Health, Education and the Home Office) pour out a more or less continuous stream of circulars and advice. This has been found necessary for 'even' development notwithstanding the high standard of British local civil servants and the experience of councils. In the early stages of local government institutions there is a very much greater need for continuous constructive help, since both councillors 'and local officers have to learn their jobs *ab ovo*, quickly. In this final section we shall try to reach some conclusions as to the continuing contacts which are likely to prove most effective.

In fact, as we look back over the existing financial contacts already discussed, they may appear to be so numerous as to call for nothing further: first, there is help with the Estimates, in fact the process of passing the annual budget ensures some contact over at least six months of the year; then there will be annual discussions concerning individual grants, less frequently discussions over loan applications, probably still less frequently (or so it is to be hoped) discussions concerning appointments and dismissals. Finally, there is the audit contact, which, however, may only last quite a short time. But all of these are individual temporary contacts, and, apart from the budget and audit, do little to accustom councillors and officers to think in terms of the whole structure of expenditure and revenue.

It is abundantly clear from experience, and might in fact be deduced on *a priori* grounds, that further, more continuous contacts are still needed. Broadly there are three routes along which such further contacts might be developed: first, through representatives of the central government stationed locally, secondly, by a further development of more or less regular visits by members of central government departments, and thirdly, by secondment of central officers to Local Authorities for fairly substantial periods.

The District Office was an essential feature of Indirect Rule. Its officers played the dual role of representing the central government and of serving the local community. This system, or relics of it, survives all over the African territories. At its best it can supply all that is necessary in the way of continuous contacts over a long period. It is still in full force in Central Africa and to a very large extent in Kenya. In Tanganyika continuous advice to Local Authorities, both traditional and 'reformed', is highly organized through the Ministry of Local Government's series of Manuals, revised every few years, and through the important Provincial Commissioner organization, devolving down to the officers of the Boma.[1] As we have seen, it serves both rural and urban local government.

Outside Africa the development of local government institutions has certainly been the poorer for want of the District Officer stage, but unfortunately the system seems not to transplant easily after what one may call the 'seedling' stage of local government. It has been established in British Guiana and in one or two of the West Indian islands (notably Dominica) and although it came in too late to acquire the prestige of the African District Office, it does seem to have been of real advantage, especially in British Guiana. In India and Ceylon the Collectors might have filled the role, had their Districts been smaller and their staffs larger; as it was they have been too remote from the people for the purpose. In India indeed it is not impossible that the Development Officer may come to play something of the same role; his duties, and his relations with the people, are in many ways parallel to those of the District Officer. But for this to happen he would need to stay in the one area for longer periods than are at present usual, and he would also need to be integrated with the regular local government system. There can be little doubt that such a development would greatly improve the functioning of local government both in India and Ceylon.

As Indirect Rule gives way before the onset of representative authorities the contacts between the District Officer and the local community are inevitably disrupted. On the one hand the District Officer formally loses his local government responsibilities, and is officially more or less excluded from the activities of the council. On the other side there is the new force of the Ministry of Local Government and its officers to be reckoned with. The District Officer (or something like him) must nevertheless still be stationed locally, to be the eyes and ears of the central government *vis-à-vis* the local community, to convey central policy to the people, and to be primarily responsible for law and order. His duties as a servant of the central government are in no way diminished by the introduction of representative local government.

At first nearly every Territory made the mistake of destroying too

[1] Swahili word for District Office meaning place of abode or location.

quickly and too absolutely the routes whereby the District Officer could continue to advise and influence local government authorities, a service which became if anything more necessary than ever during the early stages of responsible government. The extent to which in practice the District Officer lost his powers differed indeed considerably from territory to territory, depending partly on the suddenness of the change, partly on the general respect in which the local administration office was held, and, within this, partly on the personality and local experience of the particular officer.

In Ghana the Government Agents and Assistant Government Agents seem to have inherited some of the implicit suspicion in which expatriate officers were held, due largely no doubt to the late introduction of Indirect Rule in Southern Ghana. In Sierra Leone the people concerned with the 1955 riots seem to have quickly lost confidence in the District Officer organization, which again was not very well established. In Uganda also there has been some trouble in re-establishing a satisfactory relation between the District Officer and the people after the introduction of representative local government. In this territory the change was probably made too quickly, especially in view of political difficulties with the Agreement Districts.

In Southern Nigeria, both West and East, the abrupt removal of the District Officer from local government counsels in the early fifties led to a few rather conspicuous difficulties, and in both areas formal provision for his continued presence had later to be made. In practice, in these Regions where the District Officer is regarded almost as part of the natural order, his formal exclusion from local counsels was in many areas largely on paper only, and there has been little discontinuity. In both Regions it is normal for the District Officer to be almost continuously consulted, and frequently to be asked to attend meetings. Further, he can often initiate advice informally by word of mouth, or, rather more formally, although still unofficially, by writing to the chairman of the council.

The *modus vivendi* between the new and the old in Southern Nigeria seems to supply what is needed in the way of continuous contacts at the present stage and for some time to come. The great advantage of an officer in this position is that he can advise over the whole range of local community life, and it is difficult to see that any combination of specialist advisers would be an adequate substitute for this. The only doubt in Nigeria is concerning the ability of the Regional governments to fill the posts with men of the right calibre—of whatever colour—in the immediate future. An illustration of the continuing value of the District Officer is afforded by the case of Enugu, where over four or five years of bitter local political controversy and suspension, the unquestioned confidence in which the District Officer was held kept the wheels of local administration turning successfully in a situation that might easily have become chaotic. There is no doubt that the remaining services of the District Officer to local government are still very important, and that it will be wise to retain something of this organization for the foreseeable future. One might go as far as to suggest that there is still room and still time for the establishment of a similar cadre of locally resident officers in those countries which have never experienced the system, but which are trying to bring up infant representative councils on the right lines.

At the same time as this link with the past is still important there is also a growing need for technical advice from central Ministries. Kenya is now making road engineers and other technicians available to African District Councils as well as to Settled Area authorities. These specialists can sit in on planning, as well as advise councils on the technicalities of their own schemes. This is of growing importance as councils increasingly come to acquire responsibility for fixed assets. Africans—or for that matter Asians—have not had the advantage of growing up in a mechanized world where a high proportion of boys have almost unconsciously sucked in an idea of mechanics or engineering from their childhood. The most important specialist service which Local Authorities need is, however, on the financial side and this, as we have seen, should be available: from the Ministry of Local Government, perhaps from the Treasury and certainly from the Audit Department. The important thing is that the visits of the central officers should be frequent enough to establish personal contacts as a substitute for the weakening ties with the general administration.

It is a short step from frequent visits to residence for a period with a Local Authority, or group of Local Authorities. There are several ways in which this sort of contact has been tried out. In the traditional manner of the Indian Civil Service administrative officers are posted to local government for a matter of months, or a year, from the Treasury or the Ministry of Local Government, for instance in Kenya and Nigeria. This is often done where there has been local trouble, but the practice need not be limited to such cases. It is as educative for the officer concerned with local government to see what it feels like from the local end, as it is for the council to have the benefit of his wider knowledge for a period long enough for him to become really familiar with the place, as a local resident.

The Choksy Report for Ceylon has some very interesting suggestions which could be developed along these lines. There was established in 1946 a cadre of village committee Investigating Officers whose role was envisaged as that of 'guide, philosopher, and friend' rather than critic. In practice there were not enough of them, and their travelling allowances were too small for them to do more than carry out perfunctory examinations of books, a process that inevitably became more critical than constructive. The suggestion is that the idea should be extended to include a corps of urban and town council Investigating Officers, who would have statutory powers and duties to advise on office and financial management, and that they should be given sufficient remuneration to enable them to stay for longer periods. Whether this will be possible remains to be seen.

The most developed and successful system of local secondment seems to be the Kenyan device of Financial Advisers.[1] This is a cadre of officers of the Ministry of Local Government, with U.K. local government experience and holding professional qualifications. Where financial trouble has occurred it is suggested to a council that one of these officers should be seconded to them as a member of their staff for a year or two, or as long as may be necessary to train the local staff so that they are thoroughly familiar with financial routine. (Indirectly of course the presence of this officer will help to impress on councillors also, the proper sphere of their activities.) At first there was some opposition on the part of councils to having such officers in their midst, but this soon evaporated and there have been spontaneous requests for this type of assistance, even where there was no particular financial confusion.

The system is not without its difficulties (as we shall examine in Chapter 21). It is obvious that the personality of the Financial Adviser is even more important than in respect of the general administrative officers. He comes entirely on his own, is inevitably

[1] See above, p. 220.

in a somewhat critical role and has to make his effect quickly. There have been a few failures, but there have been enough successes to warrant the belief that this is a most useful (perhaps the most useful of all in the short run) method of introducing Local Authorities to the real professional standards, without which the foundation of representative local government must always be insecure.

With this general background of central/local government contacts in mind we must now proceed to examine in more detail the special problems of town and country.

20

URBAN PROBLEMS

I

IN Chapter 16 we discussed at some length the question of an autonomous tax for urban local authorities, and came to the conclusion that in principle there should be quite good opportunities in this direction. There are very many other problems of the development of urban local government, the solution of which is quite vital for development from below. The purpose of the present chapter is to discuss these more generally. This should serve at the same time to put the tax problem into its correct niche in urban development, and to put the urban aspect of development in general into its place in the whole picture. As the Royal Commission on East Africa emphasized: 'The towns are the centres of social and intellectual life, of economic enterprise and political activity.' In other words they are (or should be) the focal growing points in a developing country. It is consequently of the greatest importance that they should be enabled to play their part adequately. That is why the urban chapter has priority over the rural chapter in this part of the book, notwithstanding the quantitatively small size of the urban sector in most developing economies.

Indeed the urban problem is one of the utmost urgency. The Royal Commission capped the remark just quoted with a chapter of the most severe strictures on urban development as they saw it taking place in the East African territories. All three territories have taken this criticism to heart. As a result, a number of improvements have already been made, and the lines cleared for further progress; but much still remains to be done. Elsewhere the urban problem has only been tackled sporadically; there is, for instance, a promising slum clearance and rehousing scheme in Lagos. In India as we have seen of recent years central government interest has tended to be concentrated on raising the structure of an adequate system of representative rural local government, so that any urban improvements which have taken place are mainly the result of individual local initiative.

The urban problem is urgent not merely because the towns are important, but because neglect has led to two running sores: first, the existence alongside great wealth of a more abject poverty than any experienced in rural areas, due to the fact that the poor townsman is cut off from every lifeline. (As one thoughtful Indian put it, 'rural poverty is distressing, but urban poverty is horrible.') Secondly, the creation of what the Royal Commission aptly named a 'septic fringe'[1] of families completely deprived of the barest necessities of life, let alone health, living in the most primitive conditions, a menace to the good health of the town and a shame to the community.

There is, obviously, an initial difficulty in attempting to discuss urban problems on a general, comparative basis. In detail the setting of the urban problem differs substantially from country to country. Perhaps the biggest difference of all is between those countries (Central and East African territories), where the balance of urban racial structure is widely different from the rest of the country, and those countries where this is not the case. The multiracial problem is indeed a most serious complication, but its uniqueness can be exaggerated. Urban areas everywhere (not excluding the U.K.), especially the larger towns, tend to be cosmopolitan, and this gives rise to special problems. In West Africa it is customary for the *sabongari* 'strangers' quarter, containing elements of other peoples, to be separately organized, and even now it tends not to be fully integrated with the rest. In Freetown, Sierra Leone, there is the opposite problem: tribal elements from the interior have become so numerous that they threaten to swamp the indigenous Creoles. In addition in India the formerly European 'cantonments' attached to many Indian cities, and their counterpart the 'townships' of Nigeria, pose an integration problem of their own. But rather than emphasizing differences, it will be more instructive to start by emphasizing similarities;

[1] A good description of a 'septic fringe' is contained in the *Storey Report on the Administration of Lagos Town Council*, 1953, p. 30: 'Akinlagun village is built on swampy low lying ground on the edge of the lagoon. The dwellings are made of tree bark, bamboo and in some instances packing case wood. The size of the rooms varies from $3' \times 5'$ to $9' \times 10'$ and the height of the dwellings from $3'$ to $6'$. Some of the windows are mere niches. There are no bathrooms, kitchens or latrines, and there are no facilities for cooking. There is no water supply except a standpipe. There is no provision for the disposal of domestic refuse which is accordingly dumped indiscriminately on ground already fouled owing to the fact that there is a complete absence of sanitary conveniences.'

within these broad lines differences should then stand in better perspective.

There is probably no country in the world that has not been experiencing an unprecedented drift to the towns in the last couple of decades. This has been particularly marked in the poorer of the advanced countries—one has only to think of the enormous growth of Rome and the unprecedented expansion of Dublin. In the backward countries this migration to the towns has been on the one hand even more marked, and on the other much more unmanageable, because of the unpreparedness of the receiving areas. There have also been additional complications in different countries: in India and Pakistan (especially in Delhi and Karachi) floods of refugees, made homeless by Partition, have posed a problem far beyond the compass of local government and only very gradually soluble by the most strenuous efforts of the central governments.[1] In Bombay a somewhat similar additional complication has been posed by floods of Marashtrians pushed out after the purchase of their farms by Karnatics from the south.[2]

In Africa the advent of the British put a stop to the tribal warfare and consequent wanderings of peoples which had been occurring through the ages; but the process of migration was if anything accelerated, partly because of the greater ease of movement with improved communications, partly because of awakening realization of better opportunities elsewhere, partly (as in Bombay state and in Northern Nigeria, around Kano) in search of better agricultural opportunities, but predominantly into the towns. In East and Central Africa (but very much less on the west coast) the urban movement has brought with it the especial complication of the 'detribalized' African, defined[3] as an African who has become separated, detached from his traditional social background, with its moral and political obligations and above all its primitive but

---

[1] In Pakistan it was only after the establishment of military government in 1958–9 that the refugee problem was successfully tackled in Karachi.

[2] The story of this as I was told it contains an important moral for development. An extensive system of irrigation had been introduced in an area south of Bombay, but the local population having been brought up only on 'dry farming' were unready (without instruction which was not available) to take advantage of it. Before they fully realized what was happening 'wet' farmers from farther south bought a large number of them out for what seemed to them a good price. Landless, they were forced to seek their fortunes in Bombay.

[3] Cf. *Report of the Conference on Urban Problems in East and Central Africa* held at Ndola in 1958.

effective social security system, through the extended family and clan. In India although it is not a 'tribal' matter the situation is often not very different. It was after all in relation to India that Maine emphasized the fundamental change of social and economic development: the step from status to contract. This is still the crux of the problem in many developing countries.

The Report on Detribalization in Tanganyika[1] distinguishes five different grades of urban immigration: (1) the pure migrant, (2) the temporarily urbanized but planning to go home after a few years, (3) the semi-permanently urbanized, probably planning to spend his working life in the town, but without severing his ties so completely as to be unable to return to the village in old age, (4) the permanently urbanized in the sense that although born outside the town, there is no intention of returning to the village, (5) the pure townsman, born in the town and regarding that as his natural environment. In this classification, it is assumed that the urban immigrant will normally be, in the first instance at least, an unaccompanied man; but this is not necessarily always the case, and important differences arise according to his marital status. These distinctions can be traced in most countries, though their relative importance, and the factors that have brought people to the town, may take different forms. As a result the best ways of dealing with them severally may differ.

In the West Indies the basic problem is the pure migrant. In the sugar islands he will be in town more or less regularly in the months when there is no cane cutting. If there is a bad harvest, or cutting is reduced because of unfavourable prices, his stay may be much prolonged. From the social and economic point of view the migrant worker is a thorough nuisance, and in recent years his numbers have been greatly swollen by unemployed (other than cane cutters), due to population pressure up country. In the larger islands many of these people hope to be on their way to the U.K. and their stay will be longer or shorter in a port of embarkation (such as Kingston), according to the news they receive from relatives who have already gone overseas.

A very substantial element of the Indian drift to the towns is

[1] The (Molohan) Report considers in the same discussion the mining worker and the plantation worker. The problem is surely easier in the case of the latter since his living conditions are not really urban, so that he has the benefits of the country, especially the opportunit to grow food crops at his door.

also of this nature: unemployed without any definite prospects, workers squeezed out of under-employment in agriculture, even under the generous system of the extended family farm. For the most part they are unaccompanied men, but by no means wholly. Although in the short run this class is nothing but an embarrassment to the municipal authorities, in the longer run they form the potential industrial labour force. It was just this class which contributed so strikingly to the rapid industrialization of Japan, when the system of primogeniture on the farms squeezed the surplus out of agriculture much more thoroughly and more rapidly than has happened elsewhere.[1] But for good to flow from this very awkward situation two things are necessary: that a way is found first of bringing about some sort of equilibrium between the flow into the towns and the opportunities available there, and second (which is closely related) of holding and stabilizing those who are really prepared to become townsmen.

The immigrant temporarily urbanized but planning to go home after a few years is a more important phenomenon in Africa than elsewhere, and principally in East and Central Africa, where he forms the bulk of the problem. He is of two types: firstly, in mining areas he is an indentured labourer bound to stay for a term and then go home, and perhaps later come back for another term. In non-mining areas the temporary townsman is most frequently the young unmarried man who has come to make an income out of which he can save for a definite purpose, normally bride price. There is no question of his being turned out of the farm at home as generally there is no pressure on the land; but while he is in town he may take to the life, and possibly wish to bring his bride with him. These temporarily urbanized workers are thus normally unaccompanied men; but in the mines especially may well be married. The basic problem, like that of the unemployed, is to stabilize them as useful urban workers, and this implies adequate wages and conditions in which they can keep their wives and families in decent circumstances.

In West Africa, especially in Nigeria, the position is somewhat different because, as we have seen, there is not the same administrative distinction between town and country. There is a 'stranger' problem, but virtually no multiracial problem. The West African takes naturally to town life, and even the farmer is often a town

[1] Cf. R. P. Dore, *Land Reform in Japan*, cit.

dweller. There is consequently unlikely ever to be any shortage of urban labour for industry, such as has dogged attempts at industrialization in Uganda (e.g. at Jinja). There is plenty of migration, especially of Ibos and Hausa, and this creates problems, but there is no great pressure of the unemployed, as in the West Indies or in India. Again, partly because of the smaller differences between town and country, partly because of the strong ties with home maintained by groups and societies all over the country, 'detribalization' in the East African sense has hardly any meaning in Nigeria.

So far it is clear that the basic urban necessity is the creation of conditions in which workers can be stabilized, and absorbed into the life and organization of the town.[1] This is obviously at its most difficult in respect of the two classes of essentially migrant workers, because not only must they be persuaded into town life (the more permanent classes of immigrant have implicitly expressed a preference for it), but also urban opportunities must be found for them. In so far as this is not feasible, they must be persuaded to stay at home by improving the possibilities of advancement in the country, either by more opportunities in agriculture (squeezing out the under-employed in traditional farming need not necessarily reduce the total demand for agricultural workers, given better methods of cultivation), or by industrial development in new areas. These are possibilities to which we shall have to return later. It is significant that the author[2] of the Tanganyika Report on Detribalization regards the drift to the towns in that country as fundamentally a temporary phenomenon only, due to the much greater opportunities which it is becoming possible to provide outside the towns; this is an indication of what might be accomplished in other territories.

Once a town's population has been stabilized in the sense that it is possible to make a fairly good estimate of the rate of growth it will be faced with over the next five (or better, ten) years, it becomes possible to tackle the complementary problems of urban drift in a coherent way. These problems seem to fall into three groups: (1) constructional, (2) financial, (3) administrative and organizational, and these we shall discuss in turn. It is clear at the outset that the problems in all three directions are likely to be too big and difficult for any local authority to tackle successfully,

Cf. Report of the Ndola Conference, cit.   [2] M. J. B. Molohan.

without very substantial help and guidance from the central government. It is only right and proper that this should be freely given, because the problems of the towns are national problems, by no means self-regarding to the particular urban entity. On the other hand the responsibility of the town government is primary; for many of the things that need doing can best—some of them can only—be accomplished through local initiative.

II

The most obvious needs of urban development are constructional, and these would exist even if there were no urban drift. The immigrants merely make the need more pressing and the solution more difficult, by literally reducing the room to manœuvre. Construction needs are of two types: (1) for urban overheads up to modern standards of hygiene which will be sufficient for a long period of expansion, and (2) living accommodation. Other needs, and consequences, of urban development: factories, offices, and so on can be relied on to look after themselves for the most part, though the local authority can do a great deal to influence their appropriate development. A general plan of the future shape of the town (not necessarily a blueprint, which tends to be far too rigid, even in U.K. conditions, much more in a town where there are many unknowns) will be useful in channelling commerce and industry into the most convenient areas, in relation to other foreseeable development. Indeed Local Authorities can go even farther by providing locations for 'trading estates' with handy communications and services, even ready made factories ready for occupation.

We have already discussed a number of the problems of urban overheads in relation to the capital budget, of which they form the major part, so that only a few points need be emphasized here. As a preliminary (as just mentioned), there needs to be some sort of town plan so that both the Local Authority and the central government may have an idea where they are going. The construction of this is a very suitable subject for a conditional government grant, both because it is a service that local councillors are likely to undervalue, since its benefits are intangible; and because it enables the central government to see that local authorities have expert advice where it is most essential. The first necessities for healthy development are domestic water supply, surface drainage (much more of a problem with tropical rainfall than in temperate conditions), and waterborne sewerage. The great majority of the towns in our countries are without adequate provision for these. The first point to emphasize is that it is very much cheaper to install all these things *before* development takes place.[1]

It will already be too late for this in respect of existing development (but even then slum clearance schemes—which are urgently necessary—will open up areas to treatment). In respect of new development areas there needs to be no hesitation about getting all the overheads in first. Secondly, it is essential to plan for a fairly distant future. This implies reservoirs larger than are needed at present, and pipes of ample bore: it is much less costly to put in pipes that will serve for say fifty years ahead, now, rather than have to replace small ones in ten years' time. An adequate water supply may have to be brought a very long way (Mombasa's new source came 200 miles). This will be costly, and need help; but we must postpone financial problems for the moment. Other urgent, but less basic urban overheads will be markets (including slaughter-houses), lorry parks, street paving and lighting, fire protection, and of course the provision of schools and hospitals. Not all of these may be the responsibility of the local authority, but it is their responsibility to see that they are available in sufficient numbers, and that their relative locations are consistent with one another (other markets need not grow up with the bottle-necks that surround Covent Garden).

Pressing as are the needs for these basic installations they are unquestionably overshadowed by the crying need for living accommodation. Even in the absence of urban drift this would be a problem of the first urgency. With the rapid development of the last decade, and the rise in the standard of living which it implies, there is both opportunity and demand for improved accommodation. The big problem everywhere is in respect of lower income group housing —'high density' to use the convenient East African euphemism— because this is relatively unattractive to private enterprise. Low-density housing can normally be expected to look after itself as regards construction, so that the local authorities' duties can be confined to seeing that it obeys the building rules and fits in with the town plan.

At the same time, there is always a considerable danger of a

[1] Thus Mombasa, which was already built up, has a loan charge of $4\frac{1}{2}\%$ of revenue, and a general sewerage scheme is urgently needed. See above, p. 407 n.

luxury building boom when inflationary pressure, arising from the pace of development, gets a little out of hand, and speculators are seeking a hedge against rising prices. If this occurs it may have the undesirable effect of pushing up building costs against more essential works, either in the private or public sector. Local authorities (or the central government) may unwittingly foster this speculation by failing to charge adequately for the supply of public utilities (which will inevitably be more costly where houses are scattered), or by inadequate valuation for rates or income tax; they need to be on their guard against all such unnecessary subsidies. This is a problem, however, which may easily lead to political difficulties if the owners of the new houses are councillors or Members of the Legislature.

In a good many parts of the West Indies, and to some extent in India (and Pakistan), the provision of medium-density housing (clerical grades, minor commercial) can also largely be left to private enterprise. As the supply of building materials becomes more ample and elastic it is often found that building contractors (very likely from overseas) are prepared to lay out complete estates (for instance in Kingston, Jamaica), taking the advantage of large-scale output to reduce costs. The rents or cost of these new houses tends to compare very favourably with those of existing houses. Local Authorities should obviously do their best to encourage this development, even if it leads to 'suburban sprawl' (which should be controllable under the town plan), because at the present stage it is an urgent necessity to relieve the appalling congestion at the centre, in order to make room both for the adequate business areas now urgently needed and for tolerable high-density accommodation in place of the present slums.[1]

Thus, it must again be emphasized, the crux of the urban constructional problem is high-density housing. This is essential, not only for the people who need to live in such areas, but also for the health of the whole community. Tolerable accommodation within the means of unskilled workers is also an economic necessity on the most objective grounds. The inevitability of paying exorbitant rents for despicable accommodation leads to pressure for

[1] The exception to this condition of central congestion is East and Central Africa, where the strict application of rigid building rules has pushed the slums out of the centres of the cities wholly to the 'septic fringe'. This makes the problem of reform a little, but not very much easier.

higher wages, and tends to raise costs throughout the economy.

There are a great many routes along which the problem of high-density housing can be tackled, and each country, indeed each town, needs to experiment for itself. A great many experiments in approach have by now been made, and a well-documented comprehensive account of these (including accurate figures of costing)[1] would be of very great and widespread advantage to authorities in different parts of the world, simultaneously tackling essentially the same problem. Even a rather casual investigation, however, yields interesting results of some generality.

One method that is being used with success, especially it seems in Rhodesia and Uganda, e.g. in Jinja,[2] is to supply serviced plots on easy terms, and leave the inhabitants to build their own houses; if they wish they can start with the traditional pattern of wattle and daub. The rationale of this idea is that the transition to town life for the country-born Bantu farmer is eased if to start with he can go on living in the sort of house he is used to. Two stipulations alone control his efforts. First that he conform strictly to sanitary by-laws (the latrine, or foundation for it being supplied with the plot), secondly, that within a specified number of years he should build a more permanent house. For this he would have help and advice from the authorities. A period lease would then be available to him, the length depending on the type of structure. It is a help to this sort of project if the plot can be large enough to grow vegetables or poultry to improve family nutrition and to supplement its income. The possibility of a little business of this nature also helps to bind the family to its plot.

No matter how attractively serviced plots are presented, there is likely to be a need for publicly supplied housing also. This raises a number of questions: (1) should the units be the smallest size compatible with decency: what may be called the 'standard two-room tropical unit' or should they aim at a higher standard?; (2) what building materials should be used?; (3) should they be let at subsidized rents, or an attempt be made to cover costs?;

---

[1] The Report of the Ndola Conference is a most valuable and suggestive document, but it is almost silent about costs.

[2] In Jinja three types of houses are allowed: (1) traditional building but with cement foundation and latrine pit, carrying a three-year lease, (2) the same but with corrugated iron roof (possibly the original house converted), carrying a lease of fifteen years, and (3) conforming to conventional building rules, carrying a long lease. All houses are available on hire purchase as well as on lease.

(4) should the building be the responsibility of the local authority or of a separate housing authority? Examples of every variety are to be found—the correct answers are by no means clear, although certain things to be avoided seem to stand out. Apparent differences in building costs are enormous, far bigger than can reasonably be explained by differences in wages and prices of materials. It is impossible not to feel that big differences in skill of organization and in control over issues of materials (which somehow seem to seep into neighbouring private enterprise houses) are also at work.

First, as to standard of housing. There is something to be said for having some very modest houses to cater for the very poor: two rooms, a verandah, and a cooking space, with at least one stand-pipe for a row of (say) eight houses and about double the number of latrine pits. I was shown a row of such houses near Tanjore in South India which had been built for a colony of handicraft toymakers. I was assured that they had cost no more than £80 a unit, and they were certainly an enormous improvement on the packing case and cardboard carton shacks in which the toymakers had previously been living.

When thinking in terms of accommodation as modest as this, it is important to consider whether it is the habit of the country to cook out of doors (with a roof in case of rain) as seems to be very frequently the case in the West Indies and in Africa, but less so in India, perhaps because of the greater heat of the sun. If cooking is to be done mainly indoors and especially if the fuel used is wood or cow dung, and if the inside of a nice clean new house is not to be covered with lamp black within a few weeks, it is essential to have a chimney. This adds substantially to the cost. Here too a basic racial difference complicates matters: to an Indian lamp black is not dirt,[1] and it must be admitted that it is not unhygenic. Fumes may injure eyes, however, and in any case a coating of black makes it impossible to be house proud, to start buying furniture and pictures, and generally to undergo the civilizing education which better housing should promote.

Clearly, the decision as to type of house (or mix of types) which should be aimed at, depends on the present and prospective income of tenants as well as on costs. There is a great deal to be said for a policy of building rather good houses (so long as their

[1] For a most instructive analysis of differences in outlook and definition of dirt between Indians and others, cf. Taya Zinkin, *India Changes*, 1959.

very rapid deterioration can be guarded against) and trusting that the occupants will somehow manage to pay the rent, and will be encouraged to live up to their surroundings. To take one illustration, in Nairobi there was an estate of very nice three-room units (on two floors) each with shower, water-borne sanitation (in African parlance a 'pull and let go') and a quite adequate cooking space. It was anticipated that a young couple would take a lodger to help with the rent, until their incomes and family responsibilities demanded more accommodation.

The Ndola Conference agreed that this arrangement rarely led to any domestic trouble, especially if the lodger's room could be given a separate entrance. As we have seen, there is an urgent problem for accommodation for unaccompanied men, and this offers a partial solution. Lagos's new suburb at Sure Lere similarly was being developed with two-, three-, and four-room units, of which the larger were by far the most popular. The inhabitants had mainly come from one of the worst slums in Lagos. Bright little gardens, evidence of considerable competition, suggested that the change was appreciated, while poultry-keeping and subsidiary occupations such as small laundries and bakeries, showed that there was initiative to augment incomes.

The Lagos houses were made of very solid concrete blocks such as are used in Jamaica to withstand earthquakes (but there are no earthquakes in Lagos); the Nairobi houses were built very lightly (some of them did not stand up to wear, but this weakness has apparently been overcome). They were composed of concrete sheets with corner posts, the sheets incorporating the extremely cheap and light local pumice stone. They were extremely quick to build, while the Lagos houses seemed to take a long time. The Lagos houses were let at fairly heavily subsidized rents, the Nairobi houses were let at an economic rent. These differences bring out two points, first the question of cost and second the question of subsidy.

In spite of the shortage of stone, and in many places even of brick earth, in many of these countries there is evidently a wide range of unconventional but quite appropriate cheap local materials available. In addition to Kenya's pumice rubble, ground-up coral, already rich in lime, makes an excellent concrete and is often (e.g. in Ceylon) freely available on the coasts; in Jamaica it is now claimed that a process of rammed earth is a more effective and obviously much cheaper defence against earthquakes than heavy cement. The choice of the best material can make an enormous difference to the cost, and is consequently a matter urgently calling for further research. It would be reasonable to expect local authorities to undertake some of this for themselves. The government can also help in an important way to keep down costs of building by increasing the supply of building materials. In Colombo the necessity to import bricks at considerable cost was greatly hampering the municipal housing programme. Yet a multiplicity of small, not very efficient looking brickworks scattered about the island demonstrated that material was not lacking for large scale production. Similarly, building construction would be a very suitable subject for technical education.

The question of rent subsidization raises very wide issues. There is little doubt that the enormous British council house programme of the 1940's and 1950's with its emphasis on subsidization, has had a wide influence overseas—especially in Jamaica, Ceylon, West Africa, and Uganda. (Kenya, in accordance with its unshakeable belief that services should cover their costs, has not been affected.) However attractive from the social point of view direct rent subsidization may be, it is a dangerous policy for poor and developing countries. For the most part their tax structures will not stand this extra drain, especially for the sake of what, at the best, will be only a small sector of the community; while if it is known that the houses are to be let at a subsidized rent in any case, it is more difficult to keep a tight control of contractors' prices. In addition, the allocation of subsidized houses is likely to lead to grave political and personal difficulties. The Ndola Conference was strongly of the view that every effort should be made to secure an economic rent which would not constitute an unreasonably high percentage of incomes of the 'high-density' class, while at the same time the conference recognized that some places (Kampala was especially cited) were so deeply enmeshed in subsidies that engines could not rapidly be reversed.

Difficult as is the problem of high-density housing, the related problem of slum clearance is still more awkward, more particularly when the slums have been allowed to grow up in areas which should be ripe for development as an extension of the business quarter of the town. The problems facing the substantial slum clearance scheme of the Porto Novo Market area in Lagos will

serve to illustrate some of these. The inhabitants clung desperately
to their quarters which were inextricably entangled, with no
boundary marks. Most of the inhabitants were illiterate and
hardly any could show a valid tenancy contract. It was necesary
to appeal to the leading families: 'white cap' chiefs, to reduce
ownership and occupation rights to some sort of coherence. Some
few slum dwellers were prepared to go to the new suburbs voluntarily, but for the most part only on a guarantee of reinstatement
when the area had been redeveloped. Over £1 mn. was paid in
compensation for removal, including a so-called 'market value' for
compulsory purchase. Almost without exception, when rehoused
at Sure Lere the inhabitants quickly learnt to prefer their new
surroundings, and although they were a fourpenny bus ride out
of the town many of them were actually in pocket in relation
to the extortionate rents demanded in the centre of the city.

However, reinstatement in their own plots 'so far as possible'
had been promised, and although few if any had any intention
of reoccupation, few if any were unaware of the capital gain to be
made by re-letting. This seriously hampered redevelopment since
the authorities were unable to offer business firms (who were
anxious to undertake development) sufficiently reliable contracts.
It may well be that had the extent of this difficulty been foreseen
it might have been possible to secure the transfer of the tenants
without such extensive promises. But whatever had been done,
the two basic difficulties could not be by-passed: first that it was
essential to clear completely a really substantial area to enable the
process of introducing essential services to be completed with
reasonable efficiency, and secondly, that the process of disentang-
ling boundaries, ownership, and tenancy rights, was bound to be
time-consuming, tedious, and acrimonious. Lagos will no doubt
profit by its first experiment, and many other cities may take
warning of what lies ahead of them, with the assurance that
the longer the reform is postponed the more difficult it will
become.

The process of anchoring the 'marginal' townsman and integrating him into the life of the community is by no means confined
to building high-density housing and slum clearance. Other
services, minor only in relation to these two, also cry out for
attention. First there is the problem of adequate accommodation
for unaccompanied men, over and above the number that can be

taken as lodgers by families in new housing estates. In principle
the answer to this seems to be hostels, offering a certain choice of
amenities. Bombay has experimented very successfully with these,
but it was only after building two or three that the corporation
realized the vastness of the problem they had begun to tackle.

A much wider problem is the provision of amenities near the
townsman's new home, such as community centres, dispensaries,
beer halls, cinemas, and so on. Especially necessary is provision
for his wife (women's institutes, classes in home crafts) and better
education for his children (especially the girls). These are the
things which should teach him to appreciate town life and so
stabilize him as a permanent citizen. The new town of Molo in
Nakuru County may serve as an illustration of what can be done
in these directions. Molo is the first of five towns planned primarily
(though not necessarily exclusively) for Africans in the county.
It will have initially 120 houses of the high-density type, 43
blocks of two-storey flats of the high/medium-density variety,
a community hall, a cinema (costing £4,000), a dispensary and
maternity ward, a row of six shops, a covered and an open market,
an African hotel, and a beer hall with a licence to sell imported
liquor. (Schools in Kenya, it will be recalled, depend initially on
action by the Education Board; the Missions will no doubt look
after the spiritual health of the people.) The site is quite delightful, perched on the western escarpment of the Rift Valley.

Molo was only a little one, but is illustrative of the balanced
development which can (and needs to be) provided if urban development is to be a success; the pattern could be extended indefinitely,
not merely for new towns but for new suburbs of old ones. It
may well be that the answer to the problems of the teeming excess
millions in India's agriculture is to siphon those that are willing
to venture, not into subsidized and basically inefficient handicrafts
in their villages, but into new towns, still within reach of their
homes (defined perhaps as up to 20 miles distant), where urban
services and amenities can be introduced from the first. In many
parts of India there is now an abundance of electric power for
the establishment of small scale, but modern and efficient, light
industry. An illustration of what can be achieved on these lines
is the new town of Faridabad, some 25 miles south of Delhi, built
for refugees from Moslem areas. A stretch of near desert in 1950,
it is now a flourishing town, containing a large industrial estate,

virtually every plot of which is either already in occupation or let to a firm.

Enterprise such as Faridabad,[1] or the Lagos Porto Novo/Sure Lere project call for considerable expertise if they are not to be badly bungled. Before we leave this part of the discussion we must consider for a moment the problem of organization for construction and reconstruction. How far is it wise to leave it in local hands? The operative factors here appear to be, on the one hand, the size and competence of the Local Authorities, on the other on the size of the project. We have seen that a number of Kenya Local Authorities have housing schemes on hand, but they are for the most part small and the councils have rather exceptional technical advice available. In Ceylon both Colombo and Nuwara Eliya have tried hard with housing, but costs have been very high, and even with subsidized rents would hardly rank as appropriately 'high density'.

Generally speaking, while it is an excellent policy to encourage even the smallest towns to think about their housing problems, it is very necessary on the one hand to have constant advice available from a central Ministry or Housing Authority (as Kenya does), and on the other to have an efficient machinery in respect of tenders and contracts. It must be remembered that for a big housing scheme really big money, from a councillor's point of view, will be being allocated.

Faridabad is a Union government project, in its construction stage, so that it has the best advice and contractors available. Lagos town council made a very poor showing with its first house building scheme, and the big project has been entrusted to the Lagos Executive Development Board,[2] a body similar to a British New Town Corporation, and on which the council is represented by five members. The Lagos Executive Development Board is

[1] There are of course a number of other new towns building on the Indian sub-continent and elsewhere (a good example would be Ghana's new port of Tema), but these owe their existence to economic causes and so are not concerned with the social problems of urban drift and high density accommodation, as Faridabad is.

[2] The L.E.D.B. has a somewhat curious record, since it has been in existence from 1924, but until the last few years seems never to have done anything effective. During this period the fact that, for many services, responsibility belonged to the town council rather than to the board, may have hindered progress. In Singapore similarly most urban capital development has been hived off to an independent Improvement Trust.

responsible not merely for these slum clearance and rehousing schemes, but also for the development of the new port area. Where a large project is in question, especially where extensive compulsory purchase will be necessary, there is much to be said for the device of an *ad hoc* body which can concentrate on the matter in hand and which is not always looking over its shoulder at the electorate.

Except in a completely new town there are bound to be some awkward problems of demarcation of responsibilities.[1] If development has been carried out by an *ad hoc* authority there will be problems to be faced in handing over responsibility to normal local government machinery when construction is complete. But while the problems of construction of a major project might well be too much for a Local Authority, those of maintenance and subsequent marginal expansion, should be within their competence, at least when given the guidance of a central Ministry.

III

On the matter of the finance of urban development we have for the most part only to gather up the strings of what we have already examined;[2] but one or two points call for preliminary emphasis. In the first place, even a small housing project entails a *programme* of capital formation, extending over several years. This really necessitates access to loan funds by the authority undertaking the development. Since the houses themselves will be security for the loan this should not lead to any great difficulty, provided that the country has established an adequate Local Loans Fund. It was suggested in Chapter 18 that any grant from the central government should be given in the form of coverage from the loan service; this will also increase the security. A more difficult problem is likely to be that of liquidity. As we have seen (Chapter 14), it is only in a very few territories that local authorities carry sizeable reserves; even if they do so they may well be tied up in long-term securities liable to capital loss on realization[3] and so not readily available; the central government may have to help with this too.

---

[1] Relations between Lagos Town Council and the Lagos Executive Development Board, however, seem now to be extremely amicable, the attitude of the council appears to be one of relief that someone else is having to do a necessary but unpleasant job without any obloquy being cast on them.

[2] See above Chaps. 16 and 17.

[3] This is the case in Northern Nigeria.

In the U.K. the housing accounts of Local Authorities have to be kept according to particular rules and are subject to much stricter audit than any other part of local authority spending. Whatever the merits of the particular system adopted, there can be no doubt that it is essential to see that the most careful accounts are kept, and that costing is detailed and accurate (otherwise it is useless for comparative purposes, where it is most needed). The matter of tenders and contracts has already been mentioned. However watertight the system may be on paper, it needs the most careful watching in practice. If a local firm is to be employed the Tenders Board must assure itself that it has the necessary resources and is in a position to get the necessary supplies. It is further necessary as far as possible to guard against corruption in the award of tenders, the more so as a contract for council houses is likely to be particularly attractive. For a large programme an experienced outside firm is almost certainly the cheapest contractor in the end; but on the other hand it is important that local firms should be given the opportunity of gradually gaining experience, by undertaking schemes within their compass.

Another important point is that housing costs are by no means all on capital account; the most excellent schemes will be useless in a few years' time if a close watch is not kept on tenants. Only an accurate accounting for wear and tear in the early years will give the housing authority a firm basis for estimating a sufficient permanent budgetary allocation for maintenance. There is as yet very little relevant information for developing countries to draw on. Transferring slum dwellers to council houses has been found in the U.K. to be part of an educational process for better, healthier, and happier living. It needs to be this even more when the new tenants may be totally unused to town life in any form.

In the U.K. it has been found that in order to protect the council's property on the one hand and to integrate the tenants with the life of the community on the other, it has been of first importance to develop a service of trained housing managers, numerous enough to get to know the tenants in their area individually, who will act at the same time as a citizens' advice bureau, a rent collector, and a general friend of the family. This is expensive, but in the long run it is well worth while (apart from saving considerable loss in rent default and unnecessary repairs). Moreover it is U.K.

6335 I i

experience that the effects of housing management of this sort are cumulative: the later tenants adjust more rapidly to their new circumstances than do the earlier. In fact the whole outlook on life has been found to change very rapidly as blocks of families are moved out of the slums into healthy surroundings.

In Chapter 16 we noted that in almost all our countries opportunities for raising urban revenue were being lost through failure to impose adequate taxation on urban real estate. This is serious enough because substantially more revenue is needed to develop urban services than in rural conditions. But the situation is even worse than this: in a great many underdeveloped countries urban tax incidence is actually lighter than rural; there is a definite premium on moving into the towns. Thus the urban drift which imposes difficult enough problems in any case is actually being increased by the action—or inaction—of the urban authorities. There are several ways in which this can occur. In the first place in most African territories the backbone of rural administration is, as we have seen, the direct or personal tax (a more or less graduated poll tax). This is most efficient when it is assessed and collected locally in the villages. People outside this village organization may not be liable to pay the tax at all (as in Freetown) or may be assessed at a lower rate than in the surrounding areas (Africans in Lagos are taxed under the Income Tax Ordinance at a low flat rate). Even if town dwellers are liable to the same tax as in the surrounding area it is much more difficult to catch them and collect from them in the absence of tribal machinery.[1] Secondly, while this is true of the ordinary taxpayer, who would be paying at a fairly low rate, it is much more true of the higher incomes which tend to be concentrated in the towns, and in respect of the assessment of which there will be no effective machinery unless and until a proper personal income tax has been introduced, with all it implies in the way of a skilled Revenue Department. Even where an effective property tax is imposed on urban land, as in Central and East Africa, a great many Africans are not liable to it because the lease of their house is too short.

Under-taxation of urban dwellers was commented upon by

[1] In Northern Nigeria for instance it has been discovered that hundreds of thousands of potential direct taxpayers slip through the net completely; it is virtually certain that the majority of these are in urban areas. Better knowledge in other territories might well reveal an even more serious situation.

Lord Hailey in 1942; the Ndola Report bears witness that it had not been cured in 1957. Clearly it is necessary to put an end to this discrimination as rapidly as possible, both for the sake of improving badly needed urban revenue collections and as a means of stopping a fortuitous cause of urban drift.

The problem can be tackled in various ways. The most obvious is to introduce (or if already in existence to improve[1] the standard of) a local tax on land and buildings, assessing it on capital value either improved value or unimproved value. It is not reasonable, however, to make short-period tenants liable to this as their interest in the premises is a strictly current one. If the base is full capital value, however, tenants as well as owners can be encouraged to make improvements by the offer of a temporary rebate of tax. In view of the impossibility of including the whole urban population in a real estate tax it would be necessary to have also an effective urban personal tax, preferably assessed at a flat percentage of income. Collection could be simplified by a P.A.Y.E. system for wage-earners.[2] For the rest of the population personal assessment would be necessary but should not present an impossible problem if the urgency of the matter were understood. If the combined incidence of rates and personal tax appeared to be rather high in relation to income it would not be impossible to put a ceiling (percentage of income) of the total contribution which might be demanded from any one household by a local authority. Urban workers have often been more unwilling to pay tax than rural dwellers in the past because they would get no benefit from it. This is partly due to the greater impersonality of urban life; tax contributions from dwellers in a particular area are not likely to be so directly related to improvements in the same area as in a village. Something it would seem might be done to create a greater local interest by decentralization in urban organization, a matter to which we must now turn.

IV

The successful running of a large urban area is no easy matter in any circumstances; it calls on the one hand for councillors who

---

[1] It was disappointing to find that not even the new houses at Lagos's Sure Lere were being adequately valued.
[2] Pay-as-you-earn has been found to work reasonably well in several developing countries (Jamaica, Eastern Nigeria).

are willing to put the interests of the community before their own and who are prepared to give a substantial amount of their time to attending the meetings; on the other for civil servants of a high calibre, professionally trained and well paid. In the West Indies the story of town government makes rather depressing reading; on the whole it seems not to have been very efficient, certainly not enterprising and yet seldom excruciatingly bad. Part of this mediocrity can probably be ascribed to the small range of functions appropriate to local government in small islands, and these we shall be discussing in the next chapter, so that we need not dwell on them here.

In India, as we have seen, urban 'local self-government' is of long standing; by the turn of the century the principle of popular election was fully accepted and well understood. Some Indian towns have been consistently well run for many decades; on the whole it is still true to say that 'local self-government' is better in the towns than in the rural areas, notwithstanding the great efforts that have been made to breathe life into rural councils in the last ten years (and which we must discuss in the next chapter). But starting from the 1930's three adverse factors have affected Indian urban government: first, communal disputes, secondly, the end of the system by which local councils acted as an electoral college for the central legislation (this caused most aspiring politicians to lose interest in town government). Thirdly, with the advent of adult suffrage, the emergence of a new, and certainly to start with, a lower type of councillor, sometimes with less integrity, nearly always with less education and sense of responsibility. With a few notable exceptions—such as Bombay—communal differences made it impossible to work the British system of dividing a town for elective purposes into wards; instead separate rolls were demanded. This had the indirect effect that it was impossible to organize a town round local 'centres' or neighbourhood units which (as we shall argue later) can be used to introduce country immigrants to urban life on a more intimate level than in a centralized town. Although communal strife between Hindu and Moslem came to an end with Partition, strife between peoples would appear to be only just below the surface.[1]

In Africa some of the larger towns both in east and west had

[1] Witness the resignation of sixty-three Poona councillors in 1956 over the Union government's proposed reorganization of Bombay state.

appointed councils for a number of decades before 1945. These
had not in fact worked particularly well and much less practice
in running municipal affairs than in India was available when,
generally with extreme suddenness, in the early 1950's fully responsible elective local councils were introduced in several territories. The change was at its most violent in southern Nigeria,
perhaps especially in Lagos, where an elected African council
found itself without preparation called upon to run a town of over
240,000 inhabitants which was already in a condition calling
urgently for reconstruction and reform.

In spite of fine sounding statements by the Mayor the new
council ran into difficulties almost immediately, and in 1953 a one-
man Commission (Mr. Bernard Storey) was set up to inquire into
the administration. In the Eastern Region Port Harcourt Municipal
Council was suspended after only a few months' operation: there
has also been trouble in Enugu and Aba. In the Western Region
Abeokuta gave much trouble at first, more recently Ibadan and
Asaba have got into difficulties, while even in the North although
the councils are only partially representative there have been suspensions.[1] In Ghana suspensions have been even more numerous;
as we have seen in 1958 only one out of the four municipalities had
an elective council in being. In Sierra Leone there have been
serious riots and disturbances in a number of places. In East Africa
the problem of urban government was from the first complicated
by the preponderance of Asians, and it is not surprising that difficulties nearly as serious as those on the west coast have been experienced in Nairobi.

On the face of it, the prospect of the African towns pulling their
weight in development from below does not look bright, but this is
too gloomy a view. With hindsight, there is little doubt that the
transition to popularly elected councils was indigestibly sudden.
This was, however, frequently (but by no means everywhere)
politically unavoidable. Many of the difficulties of the councils can
be regarded as teething troubles, and there are not wanting signs
in many places of distinct improvement, of increasing maturity and
responsibility. What we want to discuss in this section is whether
and how, improvements can be made in the organization of

[1] In Northern Nigeria it will be remembered, the urban areas are merely a
part of the Emirate and almost without exception no 'council' is fully elective,
so most of the problems we are discussing here lie in the future.

town government, both from the point of view of area arrangements, and of the governing body, including both the
councillors and their civil servants. In spite of the diversity of
conditions in our different countries, the fact that they all have
the common foundation of British local government with all
its (*sui generis*, if not peculiar) features should make this a not
impossible task.

Turning first to the question of area organization, two questions
are involved: first, how should the boundaries of the town's
jurisdiction be drawn? and secondly, how should the different
areas or zones within it be organized? The first of these problems
has given repeated trouble in the U.K. (not to mention the U.S.A.)
owing to the difficulty of securing the agreement of the country
area to giving up lucrative 'overspill' as a town expands. This
should give rise to much less difficulty overseas, because even
if the local authorities surrounding the town are active, they
are unlikely at present to be using the land as a tax base; thus
there should be less opposition to boundary changes. For the
good management of a rapidly developing town the dilemma is
whether to draw the boundaries rather close, so as to enclose a
manageable area, or rather far flung, in order to ensure urban
control (for instance of water and of pest spraying) in the surrounding area.

Neither solution is fully satisfactory; to draw the boundaries
closely implies (apart from problems of ultimate expansion) leaving
peri-urban development outside, eventually to be organized into
satellite towns. This was the recommendation of the Royal Commission on East Africa; it is the method which has been most
widely followed in South Africa (e.g. in Johannesburg) and has
been suggested for Nairobi. For several reasons it is not likely to
work well. First, there is the matter of water, pest, and other sanitary
controls; it does not make sense (as pointed out by the Ndola Conference) that these should be under separate authorities. Secondly,
the government of the peri-urban areas will be denied the benefit
of the experience of established administrative machinery and the
expertise of professional officers to which they would have access if
they were included within the town boundaries. This would be
true anywhere; in Central and East Africa there would be the
further difficulty that since the peri-urban citizens probably would
be almost exclusively African, the arrangement would inevitably

raise suspicions of Apartheid, however far it might be from the intentions of the organizers.

The opposite solution of boundaries extending far beyond any area at present developed, or indeed likely to be developed within five or ten years, has been more generally followed;[1] it has its difficulties too. This policy results in the urban authority being burdened with maintaining law and order and a minimum hygienic standard over wide areas from which it can seldom draw any revenue. It is an unfair strain to impose on a struggling town. The Ndola Conference discussed this problem at great length and was unanimous that the peri-urban areas should be brought under the same government as the urban, essentially for the reasons just given. A difficulty about this arrangement would be that the richer areas would have to shoulder the burden of successive accretions of poor areas, which would require in the 'setting up' stage, if anything more expenditure than established areas, and which could not be expected to contribute at first much to municipal revenues. To some extent there is always and inevitably an interlocal redistribution of public income in urban government. If the costs of a boundary extension proved too heavy for the municipality to shoulder, the central government could very appropriately assist with special grants for a defined period. Working the Ndola conclusions in with the suggestions of the Tanganyika Report on Detribalization a solution might be found by drawing the boundaries of a growing town close enough to include peri-urban development, but in addition surrounding the whole area with an extra-provincial district which would be administered by a separate authority. This would not be fully representative; an administrative officer would be in charge, working largely with funds provided by the central government. As peri-urban development spread there would then be no difficulty in extending the jurisdiction of the urban council. Its task of absorption would be immensely simplified by finding in the newly developed areas an orderly beginning instead of a septic fringe. Rehousing suburbs, developed by a separate authority such as the Lagos Executive Development Board's Sure Lere, would fit naturally into such a scheme.

This is not a new idea; it might be described as an extension of

[1] Typical examples, taken at random, would be Dar-es-Salaam in Tanganyika, Poona in Bombay state, Nuwara Eliya in Ceylon.

the organization of Washington D.C., the Dominion area round Ottawa, or Delhi. A capital area was established at Kaduna (Northern Nigeria) in 1956. In some of these, however, the urban community is disfranchised and in a capital city even if the suppression of local government institutions is not carried as far as this, it would probably be convenient for the central government to undertake a number of services normally within the purview of local government. (Thus Lagos Council is responsible to the extent of about 60% for the normal services of a British County Borough.) Under the suggested system outlined above, on the contrary, within the urban jurisdiction it would be the aim to expand local government functions as widely as possible.

There remains the problem of local organization within the larger urban area. Some mechanism is needed to look after new urban immigrants, in order that on the one hand they may not feel lost in the large town and on the other that from the very first they may be helped to feel that they are part of a community to which they are responsible and which wants them to become active members. If this sort of outlook can be fostered it would go some way towards easing the transition from strictly tribal security and should point the way towards a satisfactory substitute.

Both the Ndola Report and the Molohan Report find the solution to this problem in decentralization through the establishment of a lower tier of urban government, the 'Ward Council'. Ward Council activities would be primarily advisory, but they would have power to raise a limited rate or personal tax for local purposes, so that they would have some definite executive functions and responsibilities. In all wards where a large percentage of inhabitants were recent urban immigrants it would be highly desirable for the administrative service to have an office, so that a close eye could be kept on the way things were shaping, and which would in general act as a citizens' advice bureau. With very unsophisticated immigrants it is suggested that it might be desirable to break down the organization still farther, appointing street headmen, parallel to village headmen, who would work within the ward organization. It is further desirable in the interests of softening the jerk of transition from rural social security, to maintain the ties with the village through societies, such as exist everywhere in Nigeria, but especially among the Ibos. Undoubtedly these fraternities are one of the reasons why 'detribalization' seems to cause less trouble in Nigeria than elsewhere.

Ward Councils have already been tried out in Kenya and have been notably successful in Mombasa. The big towns in West Africa often divide naturally into sections, especially for instance Abeokuta, which has never completely lost its character of a collection of separate colonies; Kampala is another town which already works in sections, and urgently needs a solution which would make it possible eventually to weave into the whole the Kibuga (the Kabaka's town), which is at present almost without essential urban service although it lies near the heart of Kampala. The idea of 'tiering' in urban government also is not new, the leading illustration being the organization of Metropolitan Boroughs and London City Council. Notwithstanding the gradual encroachment of function by the L.C.C., the Metropolitan Borough Councils are by no means dead wood. In spite of everything they retain an individuality which would make London local life the poorer if it were to vanish with the suppression of the Metropolitan Boroughs. The objections to tiering which we have found to be serious in rural areas hardly apply in urban conditions, since it could be made clear to urban dwellers (by radio or the local press for instance) that their tax contributions had been applied to community improvements which they could appreciate even if they lay outside their own ward areas.

These better local arrangements would no doubt reduce the difficulties of getting effective town local government going, but real success depends on the personal factor, the calibre and outlook of councillors, and the skill and integrity of their executives. It is safe to say that in all the public inquiries that have been held the major trouble has been with the councillors. In spite often of the most excellent sentiments when they start, their conduct soon suggests that they are animated by 'a sense of possession without a sense of responsibility'.[1] Time is wasted over trivial details, the more important matters tend to be sadly neglected. Attendance at committee meetings is bad: in Lagos there was the greatest difficulty in getting a quorum, except at a committee where there were jobs going (such as Establishments) when there was never any trouble.[2] The Housing Committee collapsed completely because no one came to meetings.

[1] Storey Report on Lagos, cit.
[2] The worst things that the Lagos Commissioner found were connected with efforts to get a party man made Municipal Treasurer, over the heads of men with better qualifications and experience.

These difficulties are worth noting because they have been commonly experienced, but it is only fair to recall that the Lagos Council had been in existence only two years when the Inquiry had to be made. Even at that time there were signs that the worst was over and through all the troubles there were councillors of conspicuous independence and integrity, such as Chief Rotimi Williams. Lagos corporation has now been running smoothly for several years; but in a sense it is hardly a fair test because as we have seen, as a capital city its range of duties is rather limited. It is noteworthy that the present Town Clerk was with the council almost from the beginning and has grown in stature with it.

Lazy and grabbing would unfortunately not be an unfair description of councillors in many towns. Sometimes they attempt to screw up their own expenses allowances,[1] sometimes they interfere with the work of officers, especially where a contract is concerned. Quite a lot of this can be ascribed to want of experience and want of understanding. In a way a more difficult matter is the violent entry of party politics into municipal government. This factor has been responsible for many disturbances, especially in some parts of India, in Ceylon, Nigeria, and Ghana. It can lead to all sorts of wirepulling to get a party man into the right place, it also tends to an unmanageably rapid turnover of councillors, so that the council never really settles down to work as a body. This occurred in rapid succession in Enugu, and it was only due to the continuing presence of the District Officer that municipal services were kept at a tolerable level.[2] In Ceylon the trouble seems to take the particular form of turning out the Mayor. According to the Ceylon municipal law the Mayor is the chief executive, and holds office for three years; he can, however, be turned out by a simple majority vote. The result tends to destroy all continuity on the council and makes it inevitable that government should be administrative rather than democratic.[3] Some of these troubles could almost certainly be avoided by redrafting the municipal laws. In British local government the aldermanic system of 'elder statesmen' holding office for six years

---

[1] Thus in Eastern Nigeria the allowance for a District Councillor has been 10s. and for a County Councillor 15s., yet amounts up to £2. 2s. (the allowance for a Member of the House of Assembly) still appear from time to time in the local Estimates.

[2] See above, p. 461.

[3] See above, p. 162.

has been important in promoting stability; it is very little used overseas. Again, the system of retiring councillors one-third annually
could be used more frequently.[1] The use of both of these devices
would contribute to stability.

These various difficulties seem all to come together in respect
of the vital relation between the council and its chief executive
officer. It cannot be denied that the British are asking overseas
countries to take on a very difficult tradition, especially in respect of
the position of the Town Clerk, who is definitely the servant of the
council, and yet is in a very real sense a leader. In India the struggle
to attain the British balance is being given up in a number of
places, and the Municipal Commissioner, who should correspond
to the Town Clerk, is tending more and more to assume the position of an American City Manager.[2]

In a great number of towns this new relationship seemed to be
the only answer to the chaos resulting from the complete turnover
of councillors consequent upon the introduction of adult suffrage.
The explanation of the status of the Municipal Commissioner in
India is facilitated by the fact that they are drawn from a cadre
of officers of very high calibre and also from the fact that under
Indian law the Municipal Commissioner, and not the Mayor, is
the chief executive. Thus it takes a determined and experienced
council such as that of Bombay, where the turnover at elections is
very small, to impose its will on the Commissioner. In Ceylon *de
facto* the Commissioner is coming to acquire much the same dominating position, from the fact that he tends to outstay the Mayor,
although legally his status is lower.

Although the Municipal Commissioner system, as it is coming
to be worked in India and Ceylon, probably provides somewhat
better administration than might otherwise be available, it would
be a pity if the African territories felt constrained to adopt it. In
the first place 'local self-government' can no longer be regarded
as truly democratic if it is dominated by the Municipal Commissioner. Council meetings are confronted with a series of *faits*

---

[1] One difficulty about retirement in rotation appears to be the impossibility
of making the electorate appreciate that when a new elective council is being set
up some of the councillors must be elected for one, some for two, and some for
three years. For this reason the system, which had been tried in Enugu, was
abandoned. On the other hand it is interesting to find that retirement in rotation
was being introduced at Kisumu, Kenya, owing to an unexpectedly large turnover at the previous election.   [2] See above, p. 444.

accomplis, and the council chamber tends to become a mere talking shop. In this state of affairs experience on the council ceases to have much educational value or to attract men of high quality. Secondly, the Municipal Commissioner remains in one town for a strictly limited period, which is often not more than three years, so that from the long run point of view there may well be less continuity than under a stable democratic council, where members may go on for twenty or thirty years. It is only if the real responsibility for policy rests with the councillors that they can be expected to take an active part in council work, and to bestir themselves to learn more about it, and about local government in general.

Under the Commissioner system the chief executive is a trained civil servant, whose duties are clearly defined; *de facto* if not *de iure* he takes the leading part in appointments and dismissals of subordinate staff. The position of Town Clerk, British variety, is much more anomalous. In the U.K.. while it is desirable that he should be a real leader, his main function is to be a watchdog lest the council stumble on the slippery path of *ultra vires*; he is therefore most usually a lawyer, with all that a legal training normally implies: caution rather than experimentation. Thanks to the large number of towns there is a good deal of mobility in the British service, and the best men tend to get gradually to the most important places.

Overseas, with (as we have observed) much less tight rules concerning *ultra vires*, legal qualifications are less necessary, but a leadership which can combine education of councillors and staff with administration is much more necessary. A dilemma arises, however, because a knowledge of local government sufficient to serve a large city implies—now and for the foreseeable future—U.K. training and experience, while the second condition could much more easily be satisfied from among the administrative officer cadre, if only they had local government knowledge and experience. The solution probably lies (as the Ndola Conference concluded) in selecting particular officers of the administrative cadre with a taste for urban administration, to train as urban executives, with professional qualifications.

The Town Clerk's post is the most difficult to define and to fill of all urban executive appointments, yet it is by far the most important. In comparison, the City Treasurer's post is relatively easy, its duties are clearly defined, and there is a variety of different lines of training which may lead to a tolerable expertise. Owing to this difference it is not uncommon to find a strong Treasurer in conjunction with a rather weak Town Clerk; this can never lead to good results. There is unfortunately an actual physical shortage of the right men to occupy the difficult post of Town Clerk overseas. Central governments might nevertheless assist by offering a special salary grant for this post. It was the conclusion of the Town Clerk of Plymouth[1] who investigated the trouble in Nairobi in 1957, that the most urgent need of all was for a strong chief officer, with professional standards, who was used to dealing kindly, but firmly, with councillors.

The need for—and the present lack of—training for subordinate posts is hardly less serious than in respect of the major appointments. This is a matter which we must discuss more generally in Chapter 22. It is of special relevance to the towns, because urban administrative problems are complicated and big money is involved. Without sufficient training mistakes are more frequent, without the sense of responsibility and importance which a certificate or diploma confers, they are more likely to lead to serious defalcations.

Further, the lack of training of the staff reacts unfavourably on the habits and outlook of councillors. Two ways in which this can occur seem specially important. In the first place the untrained man is more easily bullied by a councillor than a man with professional status, however humble. Secondly, without training, and the self-confidence which it brings, clerks are unwilling to take responsibility, so that councillors receive less good service than they are entitled to expect and would certainly receive in the U.K. Thus Sir Colin Campbell found in Nairobi that the staff were unwilling to take the responsibility for preparing and summarizing papers for committee meetings. As a result, councillors found themselves confronted with a tangled mass of undigested documents, which they had not the time, and in many cases not the ability, to see their way through. This difficulty could go far to explain the poor attendance at committees reported by the Lagos Commissioner.[2]

It is perhaps not too optimistic to hope that many of these urban difficulties, especially in Africa, are in the nature of teething

[1] Sir Colin Campbell.   [2] See above, p. 489.

troubles. Several problems which at first gave rise to a great deal of trouble, such particularly as appointments and dismissals of staff, and the award of contracts, are now on the way to solution in quite a number of places, the first by the establishment of Local Government Service Commissions, and the second by the institution of independent tender boards. Where some have blazed a trail it should be easier for others to follow. It must always be borne in mind that a no means simple system of local government was introduced (at any rate in West Africa) with great suddenness. The general standard of education was low. There was in most places an almost complete lack of the middle-aged, semi-retired professional people who are so generally the backbone of British local councils. It is noteworthy that in those places where people of this class are available, councils seem to get on much better. (An example is Cape Coast in Ghana, the one elective town council functioning in 1958.) It is necessary also to be on one's guard against holding an idealized picture of British local government; it is not difficult to call to mind places, and occasions, where it has been anything but ideal.

If the ship of responsible and democratic urban government can be kept afloat overseas, say over the next decade, these impediments should automatically cure themselves, by the rising standard of education on the one hand, and by increasing numbers of responsible citizens in the higher age groups, as the expectation of life extends. The important thing at the present time is consequently to ensure the ship the smoothest possible course, by anticipating, and so far as possible, removing, the shoals that may lie in its way.

21

PROBLEMS OF RURAL LOCAL GOVERNMENT

I

IN the drive for responsible local government which is characteristic of the post-war years, the centre of interest has everywhere been in rural problems. As we saw in the last chapter
there has been little change in urban organization and relatively
little improvement in town local government, at any rate until the
last few years. In contrast, in respect of rural local government, in
all the countries in which we have been interested, there has been
a fever of legislative activity, of commissions of inquiry, and of
practical experimentation. Even in the West Indies such interest
as there has been in local government at all has mainly had a rural
slant: in Barbados the traditional Vestries have been modernized;
in Trinidad rural 'County' Councils have been working since 1953;[1]
in British Guiana a network of rural authorities proposed by the
Marshall Report has been accepted although not yet implemented.
In Jamaica although there have been no organizational changes,
local taxation has been the subject of much inquiry.

Similarly in India, while none of the leading states (the former
Provinces of British India) have passed any new urban legislation
(beyond the occasional instrument relating to a particular city), all
but West Bengal had by 1956[2] provided themselves with legislation
establishing lower-layer rural local government (panchayats) and a
few (notably Madhya Pradesh and Orissa) had began to tackle the
job of changing the Collectors' Districts of the British Raj into
effective upper-tier authorities.

In Africa also, almost the whole emphasis of the tremendous
drive which has gone into the development of local government
since the end of the second world war has been on the rural 'grass

[1] In Trinidad there is also an embryonic organization of village committees,
but since these partake of the form of educational extension or Community
Development centres rather than of government authorities it will be more convenient to discuss them in relation to the problems of local government in a small
island. See below, pp. 528 ff.
[2] Bombay was exceptional in having passed a Panchayat Act as early as 1933.

roots' side, both in those territories where the first stage of establishing 'Native Authorities' has been taking place, and in those which have reached the second stage of turning Native Authorities into representative 'Local Authorities'. Only in very recent years has interest been directed to town government, and then mainly as a result of the criticisms of the East African Royal Commission.

It is therefore desirable at this final stage of our inquiry to widen our interest on this side also, beyond strictly financial problems of rural local government, in order to glance at questions concerned with the structure of the system, of the jurisdiction—both physical and executive—of different types of local bodies, and of their relations with other organizations working in the field. For finances do not operate in a vacuum; on the contrary their successful working depends almost as much on the background in which they function as on themselves. It will be our special purpose in this chapter to attempt to discover whether any useful generalizations can be derived from the wide range of experiments which have been tried during the last 10–16 years.

The basic problem on the organizational side is concerned with the local extent of jurisdictions, including the layers (if any) of local bodies which will work well. In the United Kingdom, outside the County Boroughs, three 'layers' have been found desirable: the County, the District, and the Parish; but from being in the middle ages the focal point of local enterprise, the Parish with its Council has shrunk back into a minor and often shadowy role, while since the end of the first world war the County has steadily gained at the expense of the Districts.[1] These three layers of rural government are not accidental; each corresponds to a particular need: the Parish is naturally preoccupied with affairs of the village, where neighbours have a common interest in seeing that improvements are made and nuisances abated; the District has an organization small enough and its headquarters near enough to retain local interest; the County is large enough to manage inter-District affairs such as main roads, hospitals, and (at least) more advanced education. This is not a strictly accurate picture of British County Councils as they have developed since 1944; but it is a correct rationalization.

The first question we have to ask is whether something corresponding to the three layers of British local government is desirable

[1] See above, p. 21.

as a long-term objective in developing countries attempting to follow something like the British pattern of local government.[1] The most faithful—and also the shortest lived—copy of the British three-layer system was that of Eastern Nigeria 1950–8. This system was put into operation partly because the type of Indirect Rule previously attempted had been a failure, but partly because the three layers did seem to correspond with some real distinctions in the Region. The County Council jurisdictions were drawn so as to be practically identical with the Provinces to which everyone had long been accustomed; it therefore seemed plausible that they might be acceptable to carry out the necessary large-scale and co-ordinating functions in a representative local government system. At the other end of the scale the clan-village group organization of the Ibos and Ibibios provided a strong and natural base for the lowest layer—but no more, since before the advent of the British, inter-village affairs (virtually confined to emergencies) had been managed by strictly temporary *ad hoc* joint action. Finally, the focal centre of (non-representative but fairly effective) local government had become firmly established as the District, with the District Office, set Janus-headed between the central government and the people.

The British three-layer system in Eastern Nigeria was abandoned partly on political grounds which were largely fortuitous (due to the tribal make up of the Region),[2] partly on grounds of cost—the impossibility of either finding, or paying for, adequate staff at all three layers in a way that was acceptable. The experiment, however, had led to close analogies both in the Western Region and in Ghana; but there were differences, due essentially to differences in social structure. In the Western Region it was not intended necessarily to establish County Councils everywhere, but only where there was a very strong inter-District tribal feeling—as in Ibadan, Egbaland (Abeokuta), and Benin. In establishing the new councils

[1] While the functional distinctions between the three tiers of local government are broadly parallel from one country to another where they have been established, the differences in nomenclature are bewildering. Unless there is some compelling reason to use a local variant I shall so far as possible keep to the British nomenclature. For the local variants see the relevant parts of the historical and budgetary chapters.

[2] The existence of large local government units appeared to the government, with the growth of separatism and talk of increasing the number of Regions in anticipation of independence, to lend a handle to the disruption of the Region.

under the Western Region Ordinance of 1952 the people were asked whether they wanted to have the three layers allowed for in the Ordinance; in very few places was the vote for all three. In the West also consciousness at the lowest layer was less active than in the East. In Ghana, as we have seen, the greater heterogeneity of social organization than (internally) in the Regions of Nigeria, made it impossible in practice, and perhaps undesirable in principle,[1] to establish anything like a uniform three-layer system throughout the Regions; but in places the whole structure was carried out.

In East Africa, Uganda, as we have seen, was early endowed with what looked like the beginnings of a three- or even four-layer structure of local government in the muruka (village), gombolola (sub county), and saza (county) organizations within the Districts; but these were (and are) really no more than divisions of administrative convenience, their main local government functions being tax collecting and acting as electoral colleges for the next layer, with in addition court functions, especially at the gombolola level. The Districts, large as they are, are thus in Uganda the only true local government entities. They stand at a level (especially in Buganda) that elsewhere in Africa would be regarded as a sort of super-county, but as we have seen there is a wide difference in area between the Districts, arising largely from historical causes.[2]

In Kenya the official unit of local government was also established at the District level, but Kenya Districts have rather more claim to be regarded as an upper layer of true *local* government than the Uganda Districts, since there appears to be a policy of splitting them up when they grow too big and remote from the people. Within the Districts, however, a more or less spontaneous growth of one or two lower layers has established itself: the Locations and Sub-Locations. Locations with fully elected councils are now universal over all the more sophisticated parts of Kenya, but the existence of Sub-Location Councils depends to some extent on the density of population and on the degree to which the terrain breaks the social structure into small self-contained groups. The Location Councils started with a shadowy existence, but were

---

[1] Politics similarly played a part in Ghana; some chieftaincies seemed too large and strong to be given the privilege of separate organization, while in other places ambitious minor chiefs nourished unjustifiable claims to rank their 'stools' in the topmost layer.

[2] Especially the small size of the western Agreement Districts, Bunyoro and Toro.

enthusiastically supported by the people and found convenient by
the administration, so that they ultimately won somewhat reluctant
(mainly on grounds of cost) acceptance from the Territorial government. They must now be regarded as firmly established units of
local government, and are an illustration of the functional good
sense of a triple layer. Thus in Kenya three quite virile layers of
African local government are operating. (In Kenya European local
government there are, as we have seen, but two layers: County
and County District, urban and rural. This is natural, since in the
circumstances of settlement there could hardly be any indigenous
parish feeling.) So far as African government is concerned the
three layers seem to be highly promising and already to have
achieved considerable and solid success. It must be remembered,
however, that Kenya has special advantages in administration and
technical personnel, so that what is possible there may well be out
of the question elsewhere. Further it must of course be borne in
mind that the word of the District Commissioner is still final,
although only in very exceptional circumstances would it be raised
against the wishes of the people.

The organization of Tanganyika is too heterogeneous, and too
much still in the developing stage, to form the basis of firm conclusions. On the whole the tendency has been as in Kenya, to split
Districts when they become unwieldy. In the two Districts which
now comprise the former Bukoba District, where the social structure is virtually identical with Buganda, the Ganda lower layers
exist. The Chagga Council at Moshi also had three sub-areas, and
in Sukumaland there is a federation which may be regarded as
a higher layer. An attempt was made in 1956 to establish a still
higher layer, to be called County Councils.[1] The main purpose
of this was to enable the establishment of multiracial councils,
and on this rock the scheme very largely foundered, at least temporarily. But the first established, the South East Lake County,
suffered also from hopeless unwieldiness; it might indeed have
been more properly regarded as a regional authority than as any
species of local government.

Apart from Northern Rhodesia and Nyasaland, which are still
at the Native Authority stage of local government, the two African
areas where there are virtually no signs of three-layer development
are Northern Nigeria and Sierra Leone. In the former the system

[1] See above, pp. 224 ff.

of Emirates established by Lugard still holds, although there are enormous differences in size between them. Since 1947 there has, however, developed strongly an organization of lower-layer District Councils, still somewhat limited, but very active. These take different forms depending on the social structure. In the Yoruba and Pagan Districts there is also discernible a still lower layer, in (Yoruba) Kabba and Ilorin these take the form of village or village group councils. Among the Tiv (a clan-based people) there are clan councils under the fifty-seven clan heads. Even in the Moslem areas the government made some attempt to establish village level councils, but it was not a great success. They were purely advisory and never really graduated from the embryo stage. Nevertheless in view of all these developments it cannot be said that the idea of a three-layer system is completely absent in the Northern Region. In Sierra Leone in contrast it is the upper layer which has failed to develop, due to the historical inheritance of 143 Paramounts all with Chiefdom Authorities.[1] Although these also differ greatly in size, they are all small. (The whole population of Sierra Leone is probably less than that of the Emirate of Kano.) In desperate need of a focal point of local government above the Chiefdom Authority level the government of Sierra Leone has experimented with an upper layer of District Councils; but as so far constituted these have not been suitable for systematic integration with the Chiefdom Authorities.

Thus generally in Africa we can say that there is a widespread 'natural' emergence of a low-layer range of councils, and that there also exists some effective upper layer, which may either tend towards District level in size and function, or towards county level and function. In a few places, perhaps only in Kenya, all three levels seem to be firmly seated; but more often if there is an upper layer, the middle one is not likely to be developed in size or function to the extent of the British County District. It can not, therefore, be assumed that a tiered system of councils is sufficiently deeply rooted to endure.

The situation in India and Ceylon differs substantially from that in Africa, in the virtual absence of a middle layer, and the substitution for it of a remote upper layer, the Collector's District. In Ceylon indeed the Districts are smaller than in India, and there is

---

[1] The situation in Sierra Leone is still too confused and transitional for it to be possible to say anything useful at this stage, but see below, pp. 508, 510.

within them a number of grades of local government, town districts and village committee areas, of which most are predominantly rural. It cannot be claimed that they form any sort of integrated system; it does seem clear however that what liveliness there is in Ceylon local government—apart perhaps from one or two of the towns—is to be found among the village committee areas.

Developments in India are much more interesting. There we have a tremendous effort for the establishment and nurture of panchayats, that is to say local government at the lowest level: the Union government continually prodding the states in this direction, most of the states actively co-operating, and in not a few areas the people responding enthusiastically, although the grounds for regarding the modern panchayat as having a true link with the past are very slender. What is still almost completely lacking in India is a middle layer of local government.[1] In almost all states the existing Collectors' Districts are far too large to be regarded as part of a local government system: of the former provinces of British India only remote Assam and the reconstituted Punjab had Collectors' Districts with less than 1 mn. population to deal with on the average (1951 census now seriously out of date). In the other states 2 mn. was commoner than 1 mn.; naturally, individual Districts must have been considerably larger. To put this in proportion, the largest of Uganda's large Districts—outside Buganda—has less than 500,000 population, but the Emirate of Kano has broadly 3 mn. These cases are not strictly parallel, they are exceptions in their countries in the first place; and secondly there still survives a strong, feudal or bureaucratic régime; although in both instances the councils have a substantial independent life.

It is worth glancing for a moment at the Indian Collectors' Districts since almost certainly they would have to play some part in a reformed system of local government, when an effective middle layer is established. For the most part the administration is of the sketchiest, and there are not necessarily any representative councils. In Andhra the Districts are run entirely by the Collectors, in the Punjab they are virtually controlled by the State government. In Bombay the 'Local Boards' appear to have a little more life; they

---

[1] The best source of information for the structure of Indian local government is the return made by state governments at the request of the Central Council of Local Self-Government after its first meeting in 1954, and published by the Ministry of Health, 1956.

work through a number of Standing Committees (5–9), and are entitled to 15% of land revenue, but are obliged to spend it in the area in which it has been collected. In Bihar and the United Provinces, within the very large Districts (2·2 mn. and 1·1 mn. population respectively) there are minor bodies (Union Committees and *tahsils*) with delegated functions which do not seem to imply any real responsibility (in the United Provinces the District Magistrate sanctions the budget and prepares the Administrative Report). West Bengal also has Union Committees within the thirteen Districts, but the scope of their activities can be gauged from the fact that their total expenditure 1953–4 did not reach £49,000.

The only states which by 1956 had made a definite attempt to decentralize the Districts into areas which might be regarded as the top layer of local government, were Madhya Pradesh and Orissa. In the former, by legislation in 1948, *janapada sabhas* were established with coterminous boundaries with the existing sub-district areas of tahsils and *taluks*. On the average these were planned with about 150,000 inhabitants, for whom they were given substantial responsibilities in respect of 'health education, comfort and convenience'. The members are elected, with reservations for the scheduled classes and tribes, and are expected to work under an appointed chief executive, through five Standing Committees. The janapadas have been given what should be adequate tax powers, including a compulsory 'cess' of 30 pies per rupee on land revenue, and a spread of other taxes not unlike those normally allocated to urban authorities.

On paper at least, the Madhya Pradesh scheme for higher-layer authorities looks plausible. The *anchal sasans* of Orissa are very similar in size; they are planned for population areas of 118,000 on the average. They can, however, be indirectly elected by the lower (panchayat) layer of local bodies; they work under a chief executive from the state administrative cadre. They have some control over the panchayats and will have the whole of the land revenue and cess turned over to them.

In both these states the arrangements for a higher layer look reasonably democratic and the jurisdictions chosen should be small enough to be considered local, yet large enough to be technically effective. (See comparison with West African areas below.) The Orissa scheme is particularly interesting in that it embodies a concept of an integrated structure. In addition to some control over panchayats (as just mentioned), the State government is apparently trying to work in a middle layer, based on the development 'Blocks' of the Community Development Service (to which we must turn later), comprising 'circles' of about ten panchayats (representing 50,000–60,000 inhabitants) in a compact area, and thus forming a link between the top and bottom layers of local government.

Main interest in Indian rural local government has been (as is evident from the legislation in every state), *not* in breaking down Districts to a democratic higher layer, but in first establishing the lowest layer, and then working up gradually to some sort of intermediate layer. Indeed the Indian panchayat movement is the *locus classicus* of 'grass roots' or (perhaps more appropriately) 'village tank' development from below. It is precisely planned to wake the Indian villager from his torpor and to turn him into a responsible, and responsive, citizen. In addition to the state work with panchayats the Union government has been pursuing the same aim (expressed as 'to promote receptivity to change')[1] via the medium of the Community Development Organization, which we shall discuss later.

Within a broad similarity there are considerable variations in the organization of panchayats from state to state. Indian villages in most areas tend to be small, many number no more than 500 souls, so that the task of combining and organizing the entire community beneath the panchayat umbrella is colossal. Uttar Pradesh with 36,139 panchayats, giving complete village coverage, has so far succeeded best in the organizational stage; it must be remembered, however, that Uttar Pradesh really is an area with a genuine panchayat tradition. The Punjab, which shares this tradition, also has complete coverage, but has managed to achieve this with a little more than 9,000 separate panchayats. Of the other ex-Provinces which provided information, Bihar is getting towards full coverage, and Bombay hopes to reach it by 1961; by 1956 Madras had between one-half and two-thirds coverage but Andhra had only managed to achieve one-quarter and Madhya Pradesh one-sixth.

In most states the panchayats have been given fairly wide local government powers, some obligatory, including the usual conservancy, water, local communications, and minimum health relief, and a number of optional powers, normally including the building

[1] Report of Team for the Study of Community Projects and National Extension Service (Committee on Plan Projects, 1957) (Mehta Report); cit.

and maintenance of primary schools (only in Madhya Pradesh is this a compulsory duty), more health services, tree planting, and other amenity promotion and sometimes assistance to agriculture (improvement of cattle). Apart from primary schools their powers and duties are thus substantially wider than African lowest layer authorities. Their tax powers are also wide; thus Andhra allows its panchayats a tax on professions, occupations, and 6 pies in the rupee on annual rental value of land. Bihar permits a labour tax, with a minimum unit of 48 hours labour in the year; there is also a property tax 'according to capacity'. Several states give small 'setting up' grants for panchayats, and some (as we saw earlier) pay the whole or part of the salaries of panchayat secretaries.

The point which concerns us most at the present, however, is the jurisdictional one, and here again there is considerable variety from state to state. In Madras the population minimum is 1,000, but any village with 500 inhabitants can request the formation of a panchayat; Uttar Pradesh also sets its minimum at 1,000, but 2,000 is becoming more usual. Bihar has a minimum of 4,000 but allows unofficial voluntary panchayats where villages join together in units of 2,000, and if these work well they may be given official status. In most states panchayats are of two grades—the lower being more or less unofficial, with the election of *panches* (members) by a show of hands. In the upper grade election is frequently by secret ballot, and in some states an executive officer is appointed to each council.

Even the upper layer of panchayats, however, does not seem to rise above the group-of-villages level. Something more concentrated, and with a larger jurisdiction, is necessary for effective self-government. It is here that the idea of basing a joint committee on the Community Development Block (which we discussed earlier) comes in. The first legislation to give effect to this was the Rajasthan Panchayat Samitis and Parishad Act which came into operation in October 1959.[1] Panchayat samitis[2] would be joint committees of a number of panchayats, and would be the focal point of local government, being the sole spending agency within their jurisdictions,

[1] Cf. P. K. Chaudhuri, in *Economic Weekly*, 3 Oct. 1959 for a critical appraisal.
[2] The Mehta Report suggests that the panchayats should just act as an electoral college for the samiti panchayats; but according to the Rajasthan Law the samiti panchayat would consist of the *sarpanches* (chairmen) of the constituent panchayats, a less satisfactory arrangement, since the qualities required for chairing, and representing, a panchayat might be substantially different.

although panchayats would carry out particular works in their own areas on a reimbursement basis. The samiti panches would be indirectly elected by the panchayats, with some co-opted members. They would have an administrative officer from the state cadre as their chief executive. The *zila parishad* would be an advisory committee consisting of the presidents of the samiti panchayats, the local members of the State House of Assembly and of the Union Lok Sabha, together with officials from the Collectors' District, under the chairmanship of the Collector. Its main business would be to take the place of the District Board in vetting the budgets of the panchayats.

The samiti panchayats would thus effectively become the focal level of local government outside the towns.[1] Presumably they would be of the order of magnitude of the Madhya Pradesh jana-padas, and so quite appropriate from this point of view. Their right to be regarded as truly democratic institutions is more doubtful, but the experiment is as yet too recent to draw any firm conclusions on this point.

India thus differs from the African territories (and also from the West Indies) in having in the past concentrated on setting its focal level of local government at a very low level: the panchayat of 1,000 to (say) 10,000 inhabitants. The various attempts which are being made to insert a higher layer, and so move the focal point up, indicate that the results are recognized to have been disappointing. For this there may be other explanations beyond the apathy which it was largely the original purpose of the exercise to dispel (and in which it has at least to some extent succeeded in dispelling),[2] and the inevitable diseconomies of small scale.

Two points in particular are recorded as having given trouble:[3] first, uncertainty as to the demarcation of powers and duties, between panchayats and Districts. Considering the discretionary as well as the obligatory powers which most states have allocated to panchayats it is easy to see how this can occur; it has been demonstrated again and again, if powers allocated are out of proportion to administrative or financial competence, that inefficiency is inevitable. Secondly, revenue has been totally insufficient. In some states it is

[1] This at least is the suggestion of the Mehta Report.
[2] It must be borne in mind that the contribution of the Community Development movement to this has still to be considered.
[3] See Local Self-Government Administration in the States of India, cit.

recorded that panchayats have in fact hardly any cash incomes. For this state of affairs there are three possible explanations: first, sheer incompetence. In a large number of states statutory tax collections are chronically in arrears. Secondly, the very plethora of permitted revenue sources has hindered concentration on an efficient administration for any one. Thirdly, the basic revenue source in practically every state is a share of, or a cess on, land revenue. For reasons which we have already examined this is a virtually static source of revenue, ill fitted to finance an expanding service.[1] Of these causes of scant success, only incompetence due to diseconomies of small scale can properly be ascribed to the attempt to establish the focal point of local government at the panchayat level. The other weaknesses would require attention as part of any reform of the structure of local government administration.

II

In Kenya as we have seen, it has been feasible to set the focal point of local government at the 'county' (District) level, while still encouraging the emergence into active life of (generally speaking) two lower layers of elective councils. The fact that all three levels can be vital and active together is largely to be explained by a careful demarcation of powers, duties, and finances to each layer separately, together with a broad policy of decentralization—of transfer of services to lower-layer governments as they are able and willing to take them over.

As we have seen this process of decentralization and demarcation operates both at the Territorial government-District Council level as well as at the District-Location level. This ensures that lower-layer governments will have an expanding range of worthwhile things to see to as development progresses and as they grow in strength, without overlapping the field of other levels. Pre-eminent as the District level now is, it would appear that the key growing point is at the Location level; it is here that most initiative and interest is shown. It is thus not impossible that, in time, this layer could if need be, take over responsibility as the focal level of local government.

These considerations give rise to two questions: first, if as experience seems to indicate, local government in a developing country works best if the focal level is set at the *County District*

[1] See above, pp. 326 ff.

rather than at the *County Council* (in English terms) level (and this would be strictly consistent with English history), at what sort of size (of population principally) should the target be set? Secondly, if there is concentration on this level, is it possible on the one hand to keep a lower layer in activity without undue administrative cost, and on the other, to arrange adequately for services which on technical grounds call for a larger unit than the District?

Some interesting light is thrown on the first point by the estimated populations of the 'reformed' councils planned in Ghana and

TABLE 17

WEST AFRICA: COMPARATIVE
POPULATIONS OF DISTRICTS

(*a*) *Ghana*

'Greenwood Councils' (excl. Urban)	District Populations 'ooos				
	N.T.s	Ashanti	Eastern	Western	T.V.T.
Largest . . .	163	114	111	78	101
Smallest . . .	26	28	28	31	68

Source: Report of the Commissioner for Local Government Inquiries, 1957.

(*b*) *Eastern Nigeria. Provinces and Districts*

Province	(District pop. 'ooos) Largest	Smallest
Abakaliki . .	211	39
Annang . .	85	29
Bende . . .	93	32
Calabar . .	35	15
Eket . . .	113	23
Ibibio . . .	105	23
Ijaw . . .	51	21
Ngwa . . .	116	37
Nsukka . .	146	50
Ogoja . . .	150	18
Oil Rivers . .	157	7
Okigwi. . .	205	72
Onitsha . .	202	147
Orlu . . .	110	37
Owerri . .	176	24
Udi . . .	163	74

Source: Self-Government in the Eastern Region (White Paper, 1957).

(c) Sierra Leone. Estimated Populations of Districts and Native Authorities ('000s)

Province	District	Total Population	Largest N.A.	Smallest N.A.
SW.	Bo	250	37	4
	Bonthe	100	15	3
	Moyamba	214	26	7
	Pujehun	130	23	4
SE.	Kailahun	224	49	5
	Kenema	195	33	13
	Kono	126	12	1
N.	Bombali	181	25	6
	Kambia	123	?*	?*
	Koinadugu	124	21	5
	Port Loko	208	figures	unreliable
	Tonkolili	164	?	?

Notes: Populations are estimated (in default of a reliable census) by applying a multiplier to the number of taxpayers recorded.
2. * = Multiplier unclear.
Source: *Handbook to the Protectorate*, 1957.

Eastern Nigeria (see Table 17). The trend in the one-tier structure planned for the Western Region of Nigeria seems to be broadly similar. This size also agrees on the average with the Districts in the Northern Region. The size of these is, like that of the Emirates, very diverse. One N.A. in the Kano Emirate attains 250,000 inhabitants, one (Jemara), where there is no Emir, is as small as 4,000 (but this is regarded as a joke). In the Tiv area also the councils are also rather undersized, ranging from 20,000 to 34,000.

This figure is also not far from the Madhya Pradesh janapadas (planned for an average of 150,000) or the Orissa anchal sasans (planned for 118,000). The Mehta Report suggests that the average population level of the new samiti panchayats which it recommends should be about 65,000–70,000; this would correspond in size with the individual 'Development Block' of the Community Development administration. But formerly the organizational unit comprised three Blocks, so that the Mehta plan would constitute a large reduction in size. It is worth noting also that the Trinidad County Councils have an average population of just over 80,000.

There thus appears to be a very general agreement that a size of say 50,000–150,000 is a manageable population range for a focal local government area; with a concentration of around 80,000–100,000. It may be objected that this is too wide a range to have any significance, but obviously crude population is not the only criterion that has to be taken into account in determining local government areas. The type of terrain, influencing the ease or difficulty of communication,[1] and the density of population need also to be considered. Councillors are unlikely to be regular at meetings if they have 20 or 30 miles of bush tracks to negotiate on every occasion.

Moreover there may be tribal relations to allow for. Uganda has encountered trouble in two directions in this respect. On the one hand her large Districts if composed of a single tribe, run some danger of local 'nationalism' and hence separatism; on the other to force tribes that do not get on well into the same authority (as will often be unavoidable in a large District) may be the cause of much frustration. Eastern Nigeria has tended towards the opposite extreme, on political grounds, always ensuring that even a small tribe can have a District of its own if it so desires. With a small tribe there is, it is true, little danger of separatist aspirations, but the lower limit of economical administration may easily cease to be attainable.

The fact that both the southern Regions of Nigeria and also Ghana have apparently come to rest with their focal level at about this range is particularly interesting from two points of view. In the first place all three have experimented with council areas since the early 1950's, and all have tried out larger councils and tiering. Secondly, the change was made in contemplation of independence, implicitly choosing a range which it was thought would be stable even after the withdrawal of most of the expatriate administrators. There is no guarantee of course that these jurisdictions can be held just because they are technically appropriate. All three areas, but especially Ghana and Eastern Nigeria, have suffered in the past from pressure for extreme fragmentation, an uncontrollable tendency to fission. Already in Eastern Nigeria, since the promulgation of the new scheme, there have been demands for splitting. By now however the central governments are well aware of the difficulties and expense to which such a process gives rise, and will no doubt be on their guard.

[1] The difficulty of attending meetings was a major drawback in the case of Tanganyika's SE. Lake County Council.

Before leaving the question of size it is worth glancing at those countries which do not conform to this range of size for the most important part of their local government authorities. The Indian Collectors' Districts have already been mentioned; only remote Assam had (in 1956) less than 600,000 inhabitants to a District.

In Uganda (1948 census) Mengo District[1] had nearly 920,000 inhabitants, four others were round about 400,000. Only remote Karamoja (126,000), and Bunyoro (109,000)—the latter's size being fixed at the tribal boundaries of the 'Agreement'—were smaller than 150,000. It is perhaps not surprising that, on the whole, Uganda local government is not a great success, especially when we recall the fact that the lower-layer authorities (gombololas and murukas) are not effectively local government bodies, although (as we have seen) they are proving themselves efficient tax collectors.

In Kenya the Districts range distinctly smaller, of the order of 200,000 to 260,000. In Kenya also the situation differs from that in Uganda in two ways: first, Districts are frequently split when they become unwieldy, thus Central Nyanza hived off Northern Nyanza, and quite recently Elgon Nyanza; while the Masai District was split into two in 1957. Secondly, there is one, and often two effective layers of Location Councils within the District (these, however, would seem rarely to reach the lower limit suggested above).

Sierra Leone is a country which has conspicuously failed to hit the 'right' range. This is illustrated in Table 17c. Burdened still with its 143 Paramounts the Territorial government has apparently found itself unable to contemplate any pressure for the amalgamation of the Native (Chiefdom) Authorities. The result is that only Kailahun comes anywhere near our lower limit, while the smaller authorities, with a population range of 3,000–5,000 are about the jurisdiction of an Indian panchayat or Kenya Sub-Location Council. With a flat rate poll tax of 25*s*. and an inefficient assessment and collection machinery, the budgetary position of these small authorities is deplorable. In Kenya, on the other hand, the small budgets of the Sub-Location Councils are adequate for their allotted tasks in the local government structure.

In Sierra Leone, as we have seen, there is also a range of District Councils, which are now elective and cover the whole country; they

[1] Now submerged in Buganda.

are, however, an entirely independent creation and not effectively integrated with the Chiefdom Authorities or able to direct their efforts. Moreover more than half of them lie beyond the upper limit of 150,000 inhabitants. In Sierra Leone conditions it is hardly right to regard them as part of a *local* government administration. Local government in Sierra Leone is (as we have seen) not in good condition, and part of this ill success must be ascribed to failure to evolve a suitable focal level on which to build.

The choice of the 'District' level as the focus of local government development should not imply the neglect of the levels below and above this. As we have seen, in almost every developing country it is at the lowest, village, level that the desire for improvement is most lively and spontaneous. Equally the top 'County Council' layer must not be neglected, the 'District' level is even now too small to be the appropriate units for a number of common services, especially in the fields of secondary education, more comprehensive hospitals and communications; and the appropriate unit is almost bound to grow as communications improve and population expands. The choice of jurisdictions, and of the allocation of powers and duties is thus a dynamic problem, calling for appropriate readjustment as development takes place. Due to the great variety of social organization, type of terrain, density and wealth of the population existing today, only the broadest generalizations can safely be made.

In the first place there will be few countries which can afford at present a full-fledged set-up at more than one level. If the District level is to grow in importance, the lowest layer must of necessity be kept partly submerged, in respect of personnel, taxing rights, and powers. For instance a full-time paid secretary should not be necessary; as much as possible of the work should be performed voluntarily; nor should it be necessary to pay allowances to council members, since they will have no great distance to travel. In respect of powers there needs to be a limit on the extent to which lower-level authorities may venture. In Eastern Nigeria their curative health powers are limited to four bed institutions; in a number of Indian states the lower-grade panchayats are limited to first-aid stations (most of which probably dispense indigenous (*ayurvedic*) remedies).

The best way of ensuring that Village Councils do not attempt more than they can manage is by a strict limitation on their tax powers.[1] In some countries they have no tax powers at all and must rely on voluntary contributions in labour or cash; elsewhere they are allowed a small surcharge on a District tax. There need be no compunction at putting a ceiling on their finances, since it is just at this level that it is easy to mobilize voluntary effort, either from the local residents or from 'sons abroad' through tribal organizations.[2]

If the lowest layer is kept thus half submerged there may be some difficulty in finding enough interesting things for councillors to do, and in this they will probably need leadership to provide advice and ideas. It should be possible to supply this either by a Community Development organization or through technical officers from a higher layer of government. It is more likely to be successful if it is given a slant towards greater autonomy than towards greater integration with the District Council.

Given some advice and encouragement, there is really no shortage to the local improvements which can be undertaken. With the ephemeral housing of tropical villages, village replanning is neither difficult nor costly, wells can be improved and better protected, markets roofed and so on, not to mention improved care of crops and stock, or purchase of a village radio and TV set. An important aspect of Village Council work will be advisory to the District Council. There is no reason why ideas and even criticism should all be one way. Nor is there necessarily anything frustrating in being a member of a body which is mainly advisory, so long as two conditions are satisfied: first that a reasonable amount of the advice is accepted and acted upon, and secondly that the council has *some* executive responsibilities of its own. A wise District Council will keep in close touch with the Village Councils and seek their co-operation whenever possible.

At the present stage of development it is the 'local self-government' element in the top layer is probably less important than lower down; if the focus is elsewhere the main objective at the 'County' level will be to conduct inter-District affairs as efficiently and as cheaply as possible. This does not imply that if there is to be a conciliar top layer it should not be popularly elected, but that there will need to be room for the representation or co-option of

[1] This is strictly in accordance with British tradition, where Parish Councils are limited as to the poundages they may raise.
[2] See below, pp. 525-6.

professional and technical interests. It may well be that in present circumstances the necessary co-ordination can be better achieved by joint committees than by a third conciliar layer.

The two dangers to be avoided are on the one side that concentration on the District level will imply that the important co-ordinating functions for the larger services will be neglected, on the other that the top-layer bodies, concentrating on efficiency, will tend to brush aside human and democratic values. A prophylactic against this very real danger is to define very carefully the sphere of operations of the top-layer authorities. This will also limit the misunderstandings connected with precepting—for it would hardly be appropriate to give them independent tax powers. It would also be helpful if it could be laid down that precepts (which should of course be limited to specific demands for particular services) would require the assent of the taxing authority.[1]

A question which is closely connected with the size of jurisdictions is that of the appropriate size of councils. This is almost as much a problem of urban as of rural local government, but due to its relation to tiering it has proved more convenient to deal with it here than in the previous chapter. To some extent this depends on the layer (and its consequent powers and duties) which is under consideration; but not wholly. There is a minimum membership below which no council is likely to function satisfactorily, both because there is unlikely to be sufficient give and take among the members and because the close contacts between the electorate and their representatives, which are one of the greatest democratic merits of local government, are difficult where there are only four or five councillors. At the other extreme there is most certainly a maximum membership beyond which the council becomes completely unwieldy. In this case either nothing gets done, or in order to deal with statutory duties a Standing Committee has to be appointed, and it in fact becomes the council, full council meetings relapsing into little more than a debating club, with an occasional wielding of the rubber stamp.

What these minima–maxima should be depends on many factors,

---

[1] If these conditions had been laid down for the District Councils in Sierra Leone most of the trouble between them and the Chiefdom Authorities would have been avoided; but on the contrary, the District Councils were given a blank cheque both in respect of the fields into which they might venture and in respect of the funds they might demand (cf. (Wann) Report on Local Government in Sierra Leone, cit. and above, pp. 199 ff.).

including the powers and duties allocated to the council. Experience in a wide range of fields seems to show, however, that a number of about 10–15 is the most useful size for discussions, combining adequate ventilation of different aspects of the question under discussion with reasonable ease in reaching a decision. For a lower-layer council this sort of size should be sufficient for all purposes. For councils with more extensive powers and duties it is necessary to consider the method of concentration on each subject. If something like the British specific committee system is to be followed (and this plan has great merits as a means of preserving democratic control against the danger of its usurpation either by a chief executive or by an all-embracing Standing Committee), then the council needs to be large enough to cover the necessary committees without either denying some councillors the chance to serve on a committee at all, or of forcing councillors to undertake more committees than they can really give service to. Assuming that individual committees would conform more or less to the 10–15 size, for a council with five committees to provide for this would suggest a total membership of something like 60.

As things have developed it is not open to every country to choose the size of councils on a blank cheque; there may well be legacies from the past to take into account, especially in rural conditions. Thus in Northern Nigeria the survival of the tradition of the Fulani 'Council of Six' seems to have tended to keep councils on the small side. In India the panchayat in origin was, as its name implies, a council of five, but nowadays most panchayats tend to be larger than this, say 9–15, while Uttar Pradesh reported that its thirty-six superior panchayats had a membership of 30–51.[1] This is democracy indeed. However the structure is evidently simple and economical, since 3–5 panchayats share a secretary. Ceylon, however, with little excuse of tradition, has stuck very closely to the original panchayat level for her town committees (which as we have seen are primarily rural in character) and also for her village committees. The consequent weakness of the representative element appears to have contributed to the ineffectiveness of their activities.

On the other side the persistence of the representation of the landed aristocracy gave Uganda a tradition of unwieldy councils (from the Lukiko downwards), which was only modified by the

[1] Cf. *Local Self-Government Administration.* cit.

1956 Ordinance. Thus Busoga had a council of 138, which was expanded as population increased; Bukedi had 106. (It is interesting to find the same tradition working over the Tanganyikan border at Bukoba where the Haya people are closely related to the Ganda. In Bukoba the council numbered 130 before it was split in 1958.) The 1956 Uganda Ordinance enabled the Protectorate government to reduce the size of councils to some extent (for instance Bukedi shrank from 106 to 60). It is a difficulty of the very large Districts of Uganda that if they are to be properly representative the councils must also be rather large.

In Kenya there have been no bonds of tradition to influence the size of councils, and the great majority appear to be of a quite appropriate size. In Kenya, for instance, Central Nyanza has 50 members, while the new District of Elgon Nyanza has 37.

In India Bombay corporation has 124 members—not unreasonable considering the size of the city, Poona and Ahmedabad each have 65. Calcutta corporation has 81 members, and works through Standing Committees of roughly 12 members apiece. Madras corporation has 78 members, including aldermen, and reports that it works through six Standing Committees of 7 members apiece (thus less than half the members have the chance of serving on committees, a not very satisfactory state of affairs). In Madras the membership of Municipal Councils ranges from 19 to 36; in Uttar Pradesh from 12 to 45, according, presumably, to the size of the towns. Madhya Pradesh municipal Committees are still smaller, the largest being reported as having only 14 members. The two corporations in the state, however (Nagpur and Jubbulpur), have councils of 57 and 43 respectively, while the new janapadas have a range of membership from 20 to 40, working through five Standing Committees.

Thus, in spite of some aberrations, it would appear that in India, as in Kenya, considerable thought has gone into the question of council membership, with the result that councils are neither so large as to be unwieldy nor so small as to be unrepresentative. So far as India is concerned, her long experience of representative local government may well have contributed to this result. So far as Kenya is concerned, as we have seen, she has had the benefit of much more advice from Europeans familiar with British experience as residents, or actually as local government experts.

III

Since local government does not operate in a vacuum, it is of first importance that it should establish good relations, on the one hand with the public in general and on the other with other organizations working locally on somewhat similar lines, whether private (such as Missions), semi-public (such as co-operatives), or the local representatives of government departments. In the United Kingdom Local Authorities rely very heavily on the local press to attend their meetings and do much of their public relations work for them.[1] This is a great mutual advantage: the Local Authority is spared much trouble and expense; the public gets critical but objective comment with the local news.

In developing countries this source of public relations work is, generally speaking, not available. The local press virtually does not exist; the level of literacy would as yet hardly warrant its establishment, save in large centres. In some areas no one has yet discovered a way of committing the vernacular to writing. (In this way Yoruba, which can be both written and typed, has a great advantage over Ibo, which is not at present capable of either.) Consequently local bodies need to look around for methods of arousing public interest in local affairs and in the achievements of the council. Some Local Authorities run news bulletins of their own (for instance Morogoro, Tanganyika). This may be very helpful, but naturally it has not the objectivity of an independent press report. Opportunities may also be taken of radio, and now of TV, or of films displayed by mobile cinemas. Much of this can be undertaken in conjunction with Community Development, as we shall discuss below. The important point is that local government no more than central government (where, however, it is usually well understood) can dispense with the support which good public relations give it.

In Africa (and in parts of Ceylon),[2] the Missions play a very large part in local life, both urban and rural.[3] In Southern Nigeria, Ghana, Sierra Leone, and throughout the East African territories, they supply the funds for by far the greater part of secondary

---

[1] The importance of this publicity is revealed if permission for the press to attend meetings is suddenly withdrawn, as it was when Nottingham City Council quarrelled with its Chief Constable in the autumn of 1959.

[2] i.e. among the Moors and Tamils of the north-east coast.

[3] In the West Indies the missionary stage is long past, but the churches play a very active part in local life, reminiscent of nineteenth-century Britain.

education. This arrangement should probably be regarded as mainly characteristic of the transition stage of educational development. An abiding service which the Missions can render is in the contacts with, and knowledge of, the people. The affection and confidence which the villagers feel for their priests and pastors, a relation which no government official can hope to attain, is partly the result of their calling, but is often largely due to the long periods which missionaries spend in the one station—perhaps eighteen or twenty years. The benefits which this long association gives are especially useful in the fields of education and community development. In Southern Nigeria the financial foundation of expanded primary education after the war was the 'assumed local contribution'[1] which was in fact a levy collected through the churches, and willingly paid, but outside the official tax system. Community Development has been described as a process of 'translating an unrealised need into a felt one'.[2] In this process the intimate knowledge of the local missionary of his people is an inestimable advantage. Again it is a very usual and successful sequence of events for a hospital or dispensary to be built by voluntary effort, handed over to the local authority for maintenance, and committed to a missionary body for staffing and organization.

When the Missions can do so much, the time one sect spends fighting another is all the more regrettable. In the early history of Uganda such troubles reached territorial and even international levels. More recently it has become serious in Nigeria, where the free church missions (and especially the Scots), are in process of losing out to the Roman Catholics, reflecting the change in relative —financial and other—strengths of the various bodies in the home field. These squabbles in relatively high places need not, however, necessarily disturb the relations between individual missionaries, their flocks, and their local councils.

Both in Africa and India the post-war years have seen very great efforts on the part of governments to support and spread the co-operative movement, principally for the marketing of local produce, but partly also for the manufacture of local handicrafts and small industries. The most impressive co-operatives in Africa are the Tanganyika Victoria Cotton Federation (in Sukumaland) with 1 mn. members in 280 primary societies, Bukop (the Bukoba Coffee

[1] See above, p. 168.
[2] I. C. Jackson, *Advance in Africa*, cit., p. 7.

Co-operative) with 65,000 members and the K.N.C.U. (Kiliman-
jaro-Native Co-operative Union) among the Chagga near Moshi.
In Western Nigeria there are furniture making, leather working,
and similar manufacturing co-operatives. India has experimented
very widely for many decades, both in agriculture and in handicrafts,[1] such as metal working, toy making, and textiles, as well
as in agriculture.

A common policy between this movement and Local Authorities
can be an advantage to local government in two ways. In the first
place the co-operatives are carrying still farther the process of
resource development on which the Local Authorities are themselves engaged. It should not be difficult to make the two forms of
investment complementary; indeed the profits of the co-operatives
in East Africa have in the past provided an important source of
local government capital funds. Secondly, membership of a co-
operative is itself a civilizing and educative experience. The co-
operative is a thing which the local people can manage themselves.
Not infrequently loyalty to the co-operative supplies a link between
the old tribal loyalty of 'status' and the individualism of the
modern world. Local farmers soon learn to demand a high standard
of honesty from the co-operative secretary; this is a stage on the
road to the demand for a high standard from the local council
officers. When the rural local government structure has been completed in India, similar advantages should accrue from relations
with the co-operative movement.

In Chapter 19 we had some discussion of the relation of central
departments other than the Ministry of Local Government, with
the structure of Local Authorities. The relations between officers
of central departments working locally, and the councillors and
officers of Local Authorities, is a special problem of rural local
government. The departments primarily concerned are: Agriculture, the ubiquitous Public Works Department (perhaps also a
separate Roads Authority), Education, and Health.[2]

In Kenya, as we have seen, there has been a fashion of special

---

[1] The best source of information on co-operation in India is *Review of the
Co-operative Movement in India, 1954–6,* published by the Reserve Bank of
India; in India 1956–7, 4% of the population were members of a co-operative.
In the Colonial territories the proportion was not much more than half that, but
there had been a sixfold increase in membership between 1945 and 1957.

[2] Postponing for the moment relations with the Community Development
Department, if any

'agencies'. These are for the most part working under the 'Swynnerton Plan' for African advance, drawn up soon after the war. Especially notable is A.L.DEV. (African Local Development Agency). The local presence of these technical experts can be of very great advantage to a Local Authority's programme of Development from below, but again it can sometimes be a source of considerable embarrassment.

Organizations such as A.L.DEV. and even the central Public Works Department have at their command constructional machinery which a local council could not afford; they can undertake relatively big works (dams, irrigation, and so on) in conjunction with small schemes managed and financed locally, and by this means greatly quicken the pace of development. This assumes that the plans of central and local authorities are known to each other and can be dovetailed together, which is by no means always the case. On the other hand too great activity by such agencies may commit Local Authorities to recurrent expenditure which is of none of their choosing, and for which they cannot really spare the funds.

Again there is a danger that a central department undertaking a project in a particular area may get carried away by its technical excellency, and fail to make use of the local information and know-how, so that the people are insufficiently prepared for what is coming to them. A typical case of this occurred a few years ago, over an excellent bunding and contouring scheme in the Uruguru mountains near Morogoro, Tanganyika. The brusque methods of the Ministry of Agriculture caused so much opposition and rioting that the whole programme had to be called off.[1]

So far as local bodies are concerned more value is likely to be realized from the decentralization of central departments, with small contingents stationed locally and acting as 'District Teams'. The members of the teams are in a position to know the area fairly intimately. They can be invited to attend council meetings and to advise on the technical aspects of schemes which either they or the Local Authority have in mind. In this way they get to know the local leaders personally and should be able to win their confidence. Such 'District Teams' are a significant factor in East Africa, but in the West personnel has not been allowed for them, and the want of expert advice by people who know the areas has often been felt; it is only a matter of luck if the Public Works

[1] See above, p. 379 *n.*

Department has men and equipment on hand when a big project is being started.[1]

Naturally there may be disadvantages also in the District Team system. In highly centralized Uganda where local government is weak, the District Teams sometimes give the impression that they mean to get on with the job without waiting for the Local Authority to make up its mind. Generally speaking, the more active and more decentralized is local government the more effective should be the advice and co-operation of the District Team. It would seem that the system would be of very great advantage in Southern Nigeria, and perhaps even more in Ghana, where funds appear to be ample, but the knowledge and will to carry out development at the local level has so far been less than adequate.

IV

The organization which impinges most of all on the field of local government, and where consequently co-operation can be most fruitful, and competition most frustrating, is that which looks after services generally described as Community Development. Before this can be sensibly discussed it is necessary to observe the very different concepts of this movement which are current, as well as the different methods that are applied. As recommended by the Colonial Office for application in Africa, Community Development is 'a movement designed to promote better living for the whole community . . . by the use of techniques of arousing and stimulating it in order to secure its active and enthusiastic response to the movement. It includes the whole range of development activities in the Districts.' These are then listed as being agriculture, health, including sanitation and water supplies, infant and maternity welfare, education both adult and juvenile. Community Development is also envisaged as working in close touch with the co-operative movement.

This recital at once shows how close is the connexion between Community Development and local government; their fields as thus described are virtually identical. The Indian concept of Community Development is in principle very similar. 'To process the development of an area through the people's own democratic and co-operative organizations, the Government helping only with tech-

[1] Cf. I. C. Jackson, op. cit., p. 61.

nical advice, supplies and credit.'¹ The priorities in India are listed as: drinking water supplies, improvement in animal husbandry and agriculture, co-operatives, rural industries, and health.

In essentials thus the concepts of Community Development in India and in Africa are essentially similar, but there are at the outset two differences which have led to a somewhat divergent range of developments within the same agreed rubric. The first concerns the initial attitude of the people: in India the age-old customs of the villages surviving without question, require Community Development as a primary objective 'to promote a greater receptivity to change'.² In Africa the exercise is described as 'translating an unrealised need into a felt one'³ for the African—at least the West African—wants the twentieth century passionately; generally speaking he does not have to be spurred to change.

Secondly, in those parts of Africa where Community Development is most successful there is now an established system of representative local government⁴ which is at its most lively at the strictly local end, so that it has been possible to bring about a happy marriage between Community Development and local government, for their mutual benefit. In India, since effective local government at the local end is only in course of creation, and cannot be effective until some structure above the village panchayat level has been erected, this development cannot yet ensue. Instead of Community Development co-operating with a non-existent local government structure, the plan is for it to create such a structure in its own image: the Community Development Blocks becoming the new higher level local government areas.⁵

The Community movement is now very wide spread in the developing countries of the world; it is very actively promoted by

¹ Report of Team for the Study of Community Projects and National Extension service (Mehta Committee on Plan Projects), 1957. cit.

² Ibid.

³ Jackson, op. cit.

⁴ This was not the case when just after the war, Community Development burst forth in Eastern Nigeria ('Daybreak at Udi') since the Native Authorities then consisted of appointed members, mainly elderly, and tending to be out of sympathy with the modernist returned soldiers and their friends. The first flush of enthusiasm was consequently not maintained. Cf. Jackson, op. cit., and below, p. 524.

⁵ The precise recommendation of the Mehta Committee is twenty 'circles' (village groups) of about 4,000 each sharing a *gram sewak* (panchayat development secretary), joined together into a 'block' of about 80,000 persons, thus falling well within the range suggested earlier in the chapter.

the United Nations as well as by the British Colonial Office and by independent governments in (for instance) India and Ceylon. In some of these countries, after less than ten years' experience, the movement has acquired such a bad name for waste and futility,[1] that if its activities are to be carried on at all it needs a new name. Elsewhere it is regarded with a mixture of contempt and slight irritation, as one writer has put it 'the difficulty is to get people to take Community Development seriously'.[2] Community Development like all voluntary movements, which rely greatly on personality, is liable to fairly severe ups and downs; where it has not caught on at all it is usually possible either to point to the lack of one or more essential conditions which have ensured its success elsewhere, or, it may be, that the wrong instruments of Community Development's very large assortment have been brought into play.[3]

On the other hand there are areas where Community Development has had almost spectacular success (though even in these success has been very uneven). As a basis for assessing its potentialities it will be convenient to confine our attention to three areas; all of which can show real successes as well as some failures, and in which conditions are as different as possible, namely India with special reference to Madras and Andhra states, Eastern Nigeria, and Trinidad,[4] the last named being typical of some of the things that might be accomplished at the local end in small islands where full blown Local Authorities are inappropriate.

The first questions to tackle are: (1) how is Community Development organized, and (2) what sorts of things are actually accomplished, as distinct from being put on the agenda by the authorities?

[1] This is typical of many of the West Indian islands.
[2] Arthur Gaitskell in a paper to the Conference on African Land Tenure and Land Use, Cambridge, 1959. Another source described Community Development officers in Uganda as 'the dog's body' and contempt was uppermost in the mind of a District Officer who showed me a photograph of a Community Development worker *teaching* African children to play 'ring a ring of roses'.
[3] Thus in Uganda the ubiquitous District Teams were busy carrying out very much the type of local public overheads which would have been left to Community Development in Nigeria. On the other hand there was real demand for the University Extension sources supplied from Makerere College.
[4] For principle references we have: for India, the quite excellent Mehta Report, cit.; for Eastern Nigeria, Jackson, *Advance in Africa*, cit.; for Trinidad, the Imrie Report, cit. and representations by District Councils there cited. In addition the United Nations has in preparation a vast report covering the whole world. Cf. E. J. Sady, *Community Development and Local Government. J.A.A.*, Oct. 1959.

In our countries there are two methods of organization:[1] in the one case there is a special department or Ministry responsible for Community Development; in the other, while there must of necessity be some small co-ordinating secretariat (in Eastern Nigeria this has been within the Department of Social Welfare), by and large the responsibility for the promotion of Community Development rests on every officer working locally, and especially on those concerned with local administration.

Where there is a special central department devoted to Community Development it may operate in one of two ways: either there may be an integrated uniform plan for the whole country, or local officers belonging to the department may do their best to promote Community Development wherever opportunity seems to offer; the net result being inevitably somewhat sporadic, but in intention at least more flexible than when working under a fully integrated programme. Uganda affords an illustration of this type of organization.

India is the classic example of the fully integrated programme.[2] Nothing less than the bringing of the entire Indian population (outside the major towns) under the wing of Community Development is intended. Community Development started with the First Five-Year Plan, gathered momentum under the Second, and it is confidently hoped that, somehow or other, the whole country will be covered with 'blocks' and 'circles' before the end of the Third Plan period. It is a colossal task, into which has gone much unstinting self-sacrificing voluntary work (as well of course as a good deal which has none of these qualities). Inevitably the jam has been spread rather thinly in places, but there is usually something to show.

The Indian programme was conceived in three nation-wide stages: the first, known as the National Extension Service, was little more than a survey stage, but it did enable a large amount of

---

[1] The United Nations Inquiry (see E. J. Sady, cit.) distinguishes a third type of organization, where the aim is to develop intensively in all its aspects a particular selected area. Apparently common in Latin America, there is no pure example of this in our countries, although some of the early Indian experiments came fairly near to it.

[2] For instance a uniform range of duties, and even a uniform layout for expenditure is enjoined. It must always be borne in mind that Community Development is a Union government project while local government is a state subject. Thus a unified Community Development organization is brought into contact, and supposed to establish relations with, far from uniform local government structures.

ground to be covered with the relatively small staff which was all that could quickly be recruited. Next came the stage of intensive development, the Community Development stage proper. (It is this which it is hoped to extend to the whole nation before the end of the Third Plan period.) This should be followed by a third post-intensive stage, in which villages which have been developed are supposed to consolidate and carry on on their own.

It is generally agreed that the third stage has been one of frustration and failure, the new buildings, the high endeavour, the clean villages, do not outlast the presence of the Community Development officer. The Mehta Committee concluded, no doubt rightly, that the main reason for this was the absence of a locally based structure of responsible councils. It must also be borne in mind that in Indian villages it is necessary first to kindle the spark of the desire for change and improvement. It takes very exceptional officers to accomplish this at all quickly or thoroughly. Nevertheless impressive achievements are being made in the intensive stage: school building, feeder roads to the main road, village replanning, and the improvement of existing houses (including better ventilation) are the most common developments; provision of latrines, and improvement of water supply, also figure frequently. More rarely one finds small-scale industries such as making children's clothes (where there is an urban market near at hand), small-scale iron-mongery, sweet making, and so on. Improvement in agricultural methods is much stressed (the Mehta Committee suggests that each Gram sewak should give at least five demonstrations of every agricultural improvement in a village), and certainly meets with some success, for instance in methods of paddy growing, local irrigation, and some stock improvement.

In Eastern Nigeria[1] the pattern of development has been rather different. The 'Daybreak at Udi' stage was largely of a cultural nature, centring round adult literacy and the provision of reading rooms. It almost entirely collapsed after the departure of the officer who had inspired it. For this there were several contributing causes in addition to the loss of his stimulus; first (as we have said) the demand for adult literacy was ephemeral, basically due to the war; subsequently the very active demand for juvenile education largely took its place. Secondly, whereas for accustomed village

[1] Annual Report on Community Development, Eastern Region, 1956-7, p. 19.

chores such as cleaning the market and clearing the bush paths round the village, there are traditional means of ensuring that the work is done, for an entirely new service such as cleaning and tidying the reading-room, there is no such machinery. Unless it is eventually undertaken by the local council it is likely to be neglected. In the early post-war years the Native Authorities, mostly composed (as we have seen) of the older generation, had no interest in such things.

Later, in the Eastern Region, interest shifted to public works, and here the achievements of some areas have been quite remarkable. For instance in Awka the District Officer reported that 'The spirit of self-help encouraged by sons abroad, is so strong that little prompting or financial assistance is needed.' The following was the year's bag of works:

Roads 209 miles	Bridges 605 feet
Water points 5	Maternity homes 18 beds
New schools 96	Schools improved 55
New market stalls 142	Postal agencies 6
Post offices 1	

The value of these projects was estimated at £180,567. Elsewhere there were council halls, agricultural demonstration plots, leper segregation villages, dispensaries, women's adult education centres, and during the year 165 Bailey bridges were either completed or arranged for.

Several conclusions can be drawn from this summary. In the first place Community Development in Eastern Nigeria is very closely tied in with local government; many of the larger projects are joint enterprises between Community Development and the local council. Community Development has become very largely a method of getting quickly the works which local government would undertake in time, if it had not so many other things to see to. Moreover 'councils by their very nature *respond* to community forces, rather than create them'.[1] Thus Community Development is the natural leader, local government the follower and consolidator. It is also a way of getting the works more cheaply; the cash cost of building by Community Development is reckoned to be only about one-quarter of the cost of similar construction by the Public Works

[1] Jackson, op. cit.

Department.[1] In addition there are three sources of cash on which Community Development can draw which are less available to local government.

In the first place the Eastern Region has habitually devoted some of its 'Colonial Development and Welfare' funds to 'pump priming' of Community Development works; this has enabled District Officers to promise such things as pan roofs, cement, and so on, as soon as a project has been mooted. Secondly, voluntary cash payments outside the tax system are frequently made by those who are too busy or otherwise unable to contribute with their labour. Thirdly, there are the contributions of 'sons abroad', organized by the village and clan societies *in partibus*, working in business or offices in other Regions and often earning much higher incomes than those at home. Not only are these contributions very considerable, but they constitute a means whereby a form of tax can be levied on citizens who are no longer resident and who pay their legal taxes in the areas where they make their living.

Community Development is not equally successful all over the Region; it will always depend very much on leadership and this is not equally distributed. Moreover it proceeds very much in waves of fashion: one village (or more likely one leader) thinks of a new type of work, presently the neighbouring villages are all anxious to 'keep up with the Joneses', and so it spreads until the demand for this particular type of work is more or less saturated. Then it is necessary for someone to launch a new type of project so as to start the ball rolling again. The relative slackening of interest at Udi, which was the origin of the whole movement in the Eastern Region, can to some considerable extent be ascribed to the fact that the smaller projects, within the competence of Community Development or the lowest rung of local government, have now been provided. The larger projects which are still urgently needed must await an improvement in the revenue position, and this is unlikely to occur until universal primary education has been firmly established. When the little projects which Community Development can tackle have been finished in most areas, the Eastern

[1] See 1957 Report, cit. It is of great psychological importance to give a public estimate of the saving to the community due to community effort, and can contribute greatly to morale, even if the accounting methods used (e.g. assuming zero costs of administrative officers' time) are not quite impeccable. The Mehta Committee was well aware of this point, and urged that all works should be valued at Public Works Department rates.

Region may perhaps turn back to more cultural interests. By that time a new and literate generation will have come forward.

Community Development is to be found also in the other Regions of Nigeria. In the West it is not so active as in the East, in part probably because the greater wealth of the people enables larger taxes to be collected, and encourages cash rather than labour contributions. In the North the 'Middle Belt' (Yoruba) people in Ilorin and Kabba are active, but elsewhere manual work is not favoured, partly in accordance with Moslem tradition, partly due to the unwillingness of pastoral peoples (which exists equally among the Masai of East Africa), to undertake any manual labour not connected with the care of their beasts. In Ghana Community Development has fluctuated between spells of intense enthusiasm and stretches of complete apathy, it thus would appear to be less well founded than in Nigeria. As in the Western Region, the Ghanaian farmers are perhaps too wealthy to be greatly interested in public goods and services.

Although the greater ease with which the southern Nigerian villager can be interested in Community Development than the Indian villager in any area, constitutes a substantial difference, the experience in the two areas has much in common. In both the most popular works are those with a purpose which is both practical and personal, especially in the fields of education and curative health. The Mehta Report is severely critical of the relative neglect of more economic investments; most of the Eastern Region projects have only a relatively weak and long-term economic content. On the other hand agricultural improvement has perhaps been relatively more successful in India than in Nigeria. It can hardly be expected that much interest can be aroused in agricultural improvement until individual rights in land have been established, at least *de facto*, and, broadly speaking, this is not the case yet in Eastern Nigeria.

All reports, both in Nigeria and in India, stress the importance of much more training for those in charge of Community Development, whether *ad hoc* Gram Sewaks or general purpose District Officers. In Nigeria this aspect will become increasingly important as Europeans are replaced by Africans, who normally have less mechanical experience when they come to the job than officers brought up in industrialized countries. Training of this type is a matter to which we must pay some attention in the next chapter.

All reports again stress the enormous importance of continuity of leadership; in India the Community Development officer may well spend even less time in one area than a District Officer in Nigeria. Further, the fact that the latter is part of a permanent system of government also makes for rather more continuity. All reports again stress the importance of bringing women more fully into Community Development, both as workers, and as members of committees and in other positions of responsibility. There is no doubt that if Community Development was thus made a joint enterprise between the sexes it would greatly contribute to its stability. In spite of this similar experience in India and in Nigeria the fundamental difference remains that in Nigeria Community Development is now working hand in hand with an established system of local government, whereas in India the local government system with which Community Development needs to co-operate (and the Mehta Report is most insistent on this point) is only in the first stages of construction.

To turn to our third area, we have seen that the scope for local government in a small island such as most of the West Indies are, is inevitably restricted; education, many health services, and the principal roads are more sensibly run on an island-wide than on a parochial basis. There is indeed usually scope for autonomous councils in one or more towns in the Island, and these should be able to find a fairly wide field of enterprise in local public works, including amenities, trading services, and other economic endeavours. On the whole the history of urban local government in the West Indies has not been a happy one; the towns have been starved of independent revenue due very largely to the poor administration of the property rate; the Island governments have frequently been anything but co-operative. The problems raised, however, are not essentially different from those of urban government elsewhere, save for the fact that it is doubtless more difficult to improve, or even to maintain, standards of administration when there is no other town's performance available for comparison.

Outside the towns, however, there tends to be a hiatus. The Island government although very likely having to deal with no more than the population of a very small District elsewhere, has substantially wider responsibilities, both fiscal and administrative, than a mainland District Council. This means almost certainly that the attention which it can devote to village problems is negligible.

Yet the need for small works, for feeder roads, for better markets, even for water supply, not to mention cultural activities, are no less than in other developing countries, despite the higher average income of the islanders compared for instance with India or with the African territories.[1]

Since the range of activities of any local or village organization to look after such matters would inevitably be narrow, the whole panoply of local government would not seem to be called for, and indeed on *a priori* grounds it could be inferred that the cost of such a set-up would exceed its value. Something of a hybrid between local government and Community Development would be more likely to meet the case, such that for instance a committee could be chosen by somewhat informal methods and a minimum of officers appointed. These it may be hoped would perform their duties for little more than their out of pocket expenses.

Given the high degree of literacy in the West Indies, it should not be difficult to find such people among the ranks of teachers or professional people, especially if it were understood that they could as well be women as men. It would be the duty of the committees to discuss and accord priorities to local improvements, in such fields as education, especially extension courses, local public works, and amenities. For their work to be effective there would need to be available technical advice and planning of the type given by District Officers in Nigeria, and by panchayat secretaries or Gram Sewaks in India. This would probably be most easily supplied by officers direct from central departments: Ministry of Education, Public Works Department, or Ministry of Health.

Would such a rural organization be feasible and useful in the West Indies? In Jamaica the Island government's efforts (in connexion with the Five-Year Plan) to organize local self-help have so far been rather conspicuously unsuccessful. To this result several causes may have contributed. If the movement is to consolidate and grow it must be put on a permanent footing, not related simply to a particular project (such as a drive for the improvement of existing housing); it does not appear that steps have been taken to achieve this. It must also be remembered that Jamaica has a more effective structure of formal local government than the other islands,

---

[1] Thus India and most of the African territories have an average cash income per head (as at present estimated) of between £20 and £60; the larger West Indian islands show a range of about £100–£150 on the average.

so that many of the small works which village committees would undertake elsewhere, would be the duty of the Parish Councils in Jamaica. Further, it may well be that the absence of any tradition whereby every family pays a small personal tax annually, part of which is reserved for local works (the African poll tax in fact), makes it more difficult to establish a tradition of local self-help. On the other hand there is in Jamaica a very strong tradition of voluntary charitable work, and there would seem to be no reason why this should not be harnessed to the service of village committees.

The experience of most other islands has been similar to that of Jamaica. A desire for community improvement needs first to be kindled before physical co-operation will be offered. There is evidence, however, that if the right approach is made, and villagers understand the relevance to them of a proposed improvement, voluntary effort will not fail to be forthcoming. This at least was the experience of road building in Dominica.

If voluntary labour can be mobilized, the saving in the cost of works in West Indian conditions (with steep contours for which donkey or head loads are the most appropriate) could be very high. It must also be remembered that from well back in the nineteenth century very substantial amounts of voluntary labour have gone into drainage and sea defence work in British Guiana. Although this heavy task was found ultimately to call for government assistance and a compulsory levy, it is evident that there was throughout a substantial volume of successful community works organized through village committees.

The island that so far seems to have made the most successful experimentation in a hybrid between Community Development and lower layer local government is Trinidad. Within the County Council areas, Village or Community Councils have been established. Villages may apply to have their councils registered; they then receive 85% of their general expenditure by means of a grant from the County Councils, as well (perhaps) as specific grants for particular purposes. Besides individual schemes originating in the villages (of which community halls or centres would seem to be the most popular), County Councils may delegate a number of services to the Village Councils. (It is recommended that regular provision for appropriate grants for such should be made in the County Council Estimates.)[1]

[1] Imrie Report, 1958, cit.

In 1958 there were 196 Village Councils of which 53 already had community centres. Within the next five years it was planned to build another 66. The expenditure of the village committees has been steadily rising. The grants from County Councils expanded from £90,500 in 1953 to £119,400 two years later. The work of promoting these little councils is shared between the County Councils and the Education Extension Department. They apparently work enthusiastically, and are particularly keen on educational and other cultural activities, thus exhibiting a strong contrast to Africa at the present time.

One of the main benefits to be derived from representative local government, especially at the lower levels, is the education it gives in managing public affairs and establishing direct contacts with electors, as a training for more responsible work at a higher level. As we have seen, this principle was enunciated a very long time ago in the 1840's (by Lord Grey in relation to British Guiana).[1] It is interesting to find that the principle is working today in the Trinidad villages. More than 60% of the elected members of County Councils originally began their public careers in Village Councils.[2] In view of this varied experience in different parts of the West Indies, and especially in view of the success of the Trinidad experiment, it would seem it is possible for even a small island to share in the benefits of development from below, without the trouble and expense of creating a full structure of local government, for which there would inevitably be insufficient scope.

[1] See above, p. 39.   [2] Imrie Report, cit., p. 35, and above, p. 145.

22

A POSTSCRIPT ON TRAINING

IT will be evident that there are many problems which await solution before the new local government can play its full part in economic development. Two of these are pre-eminent, both in importance and difficulty: finance and staffing. Though the finance which is available to many councils is woefully meagre, there are others where the willingness of representative councils to tax their peoples is almost an embarrassment. A fivefold increase in not much more than five years poses problems of organization that are by no means easy. The success of the whole experiment may well be jeopardized unless these things can be coped with. Unless the money is well spent the taxpayers cannot be expected to continue their willingness to contribute; but it will not be well spent unless the staff to organize the spending, and organize it efficiently, is there.

The problem of staffing is at its most difficult in Africa; but it is by no means only in Africa that it arises. In India (and in Ceylon) the standard of the top administrators is a high one; but it falls off rather rapidly—in terms of education, of specific training, and of general ability—as one goes down the ranks. In the West Indies, on the other hand, the supply of competent administrators is in general adequate; but the wasteful system of keeping something like 'secretariats' in operation, even in quite small islands, means that there is a shortage of supply for the normal functions of local government. There is need, in each of these cases, for more ability to be attracted into the local government service; but for that, better pay would be required. The inadequacy of local finances thus sets up a vicious circle, ill-paid staff doing a poor job. But even with the available personnel, better work would be done if there were more training.

In Africa (in most, that is, of our African territories) the problem of staffing is complicated by the rapid withdrawal of expatriate administrators, who (however little they were naturally interested in understanding or teaching the niceties of budgeting) had been given comprehensive courses in the United Kingdom to fit them for their duties. With a much shorter tradition of secondary and higher education than in India or in the West Indies, Africans are now required to master complicated procedures of which they had no previous experience. Under the Native Authority system there was no standardized accounting, nor any procedure to deal with establishment matters. Under the new Local Authority laws all this has to be learned.[1]

Many of the Native Authority staff were of poor quality; they were incapable, if only because of their lack of education, of learning the new ways. It has often been necessary to make a clean sweep and to start again. Many different questions of training then arise. It will clarify discussion if we take the different ranks in the new local government hierarchy rather separately.

The highest rank, senior officials running really large towns (who need of course to be most carefully selected) must clearly have full professional qualifications. At the next level, for middle-sized towns and rural districts, professional qualifications in the strict sense are perhaps not necessary; but a general education certainly is necessary, and a special training, of something like a year's duration, should certainly be required. Even that can hardly be insisted on for the secretary-treasurers of the smaller units; but some means must be found for ensuring that they are not merely honest and diligent, with an elementary education in their own language and a knowledge of English, but also that they have some knowledge of the outside world (for it will often be their duty to give a lead to their councillors). How are all these needs to be provided for? Is it necessary that formal training should be provided at all levels? By what means are the right men to be selected? How are those who are capable of taking responsibility and showing initiative (and ultimately, it may be, of working their way up the service) to be found?

Perhaps it is the last which is the most fundamental problem. As things are at present, recruits must be selected soon after they have left school; their educational record may give no guidance on their capacity for leadership. Here it is probable that a solution is to be found in courses such as those provided by Man of War Bay,

[1] In the Western Region of Nigeria, within a short time of the passing of the 1952 Ordinance, there were financial memoranda (in 36 chapters), 200 sections of staff regulations, and 100 of electoral regulations to be mastered.

in Nigeria, and by the Outward Bound school, on the slopes of Kilimanjaro, which provides a similar service for East Africa. These courses are quite short (that in Nigeria only takes three weeks); endurance, enterprise, and a wide range of capacities are tested under tough conditions. These courses are not only used by government; it is significant that they are also used by large firms, in order to get an independent check upon those who may be promoted to positions of responsibility.

This is a matter of selection; after that, what is needed in the way of vocational training? It would be wrong to belittle the importance of training 'on the job'; this is largely used by local authorities in the United Kingdom, and as time goes on, it should be increasingly usable overseas. When a council has a government financial adviser seconded to it (as frequently happens in Kenya), it is proper that an important part of his activities should be the training of those with whom he works. But unless the officer is himself of high quality, such 'training' as he provides will be worse than useless; it is simply the passing-on of old slipshod habits to a new generation. This is no means of introducing a new system, merely of perpetuating an old one. For the introduction of a new system some formal training is in most cases necessary.

It is indeed important (more important than is sometimes thought) that the training should take the form of a regular course ending in an examination which (if passed) leads to a certificate. The certificate is not merely evidence that a certain standard has been reached in the course; it has a psychological value which may be important later. It sets a mark upon the man who has earned it; it gives him self-confidence, and helps him to maintain a standard throughout his later career.

For the highest posts, it is almost essential (in most of our countries) that the training should take place abroad; until a sufficient supply of local recruits can be put through the long training that is necessary, reliance (at least to a considerable extent) upon expatriates is likely to continue. But in every territory it is the training for the middle-ranking jobs which is the biggest problem; and it is just here that there is the biggest deficiency. Almost nothing is available in the West Indies. In India the Institute for Local Self-Government gives short courses leading to a Diploma; they are, however, recognized as being much less, both in amount and in quality, than is needed. Many of the African territories have no proper courses at all; nearly all are less than adequately supplied.[1] In the absence of proper local courses, officers may be sent to the United Kingdom for training; they may be attached (perhaps for as much as two years) to English Local Authorities, or given *ad hoc* courses (which always include short attachments). As anything but a stopgap measure this is by no means ideal. It is extremely expensive, in cash and in time; to be effective, the course must be fairly long, but it is hard for a council, which has just found a good man who is getting his hand in, to part with him for a year or more. Nor is the available training at all the right thing; even by the most imaginative co-operation, the problems which will be met by a trainee in a department of a British Local Authority, cannot be brought at all near to those which will face him when he goes home. As soon as possible, attempts to make courses in the United Kingdom a part of the regular training on this level should be given up.[2]

Of all our countries, it is Nigeria which has made the most successful arrangements for training in the middle layer. Now, after eight years of representative local government, Nigeria may be passing into a new stage in which it will be possible to lay more emphasis on training 'on the job', though it will still be important that the more formal training should not be given up. The experience of Nigeria, during these first years, is however very significant, not only for other African territories, but (very possibly) for India also.

Immediately upon the establishment of representative Local Authorities in the Nigerian Regions, it was recognized that there must be some system of effective training for local government staff. Arrangements were accordingly made[3] for the institution of a residential one-year course at Ibadan, where it could have the advantage of co-operation with the University, though it was in fact held at the Nigerian College of Science, Arts, and Technology ('Niger College'). There were to be twenty students from each

[1] Sierra Leone has none at all, Kenya occasional short courses at Jeanes Schools, Uganda and Ghana very inadequate schools. Tanganyika has a good little residential school at Mzumbe, but it is hardly enough to serve the Territory.

[2] This is not to say that a short visit to the United Kingdom would not be useful for selected officers (in which they might see the working of different kinds of Local Authorities); but this would be useful at any stage of the officer's career.

[3] P. Dyson, *Local Government Training in the Western Region of Nigeria*, *J.A.A.*, Oct. 1959.

536 *Finance and Politics*

Region; teachers' salaries were paid from Regional funds. It was necessary to supply some general education, as well as training in local government techniques; thus there were courses in English, in Law, and in History, as well as in Public Finance, Local Government and its finance, conduct of council and committee meetings (preparation of agenda and so on), office routine (O. & M.), and conduct of social services. All this was done in the first place on Regional initiative though it subsequently became a charge on federal funds.[1]

Certain conclusions have been reached[2] as a result of seven years' experience of this course at Ibadan which are of general interest. First, it is a great advantage to have permanent residential buildings; from this point of view the equipment at Niger College was adequate, but it was not well adapted to the course, and had to be shared with a number of other courses, not closely related. Secondly, it is necessary to offer a sufficient remuneration to the teachers to hold them over a period of years; in this respect the experience at Ibadan was not so good. Finally, the institution should not be too small; if it is there is a danger that the teaching will become too monotonous. It seems to have been found that the best result is obtained by running three courses or streams simultaneously, with at least two tutors; if (as at Ibadan) it is possible to borrow part-time teachers from a neighbouring institution (the University College) this is a great help.[3]

As has been noted, the Western Region is now on the point of important further developments in its arrangements for training; these were foreshadowed in a Working Party Report published in 1959. The new aim is to 'produce a system under which facilities for training will be available throughout an officer's career, so that he can enter at the lowest level and equip himself for promotion to the highest posts'. Since a Local Government Service Commission

[1] A parallel course was set up in connexion with the Technical College at Zaria, to train secretary-treasurers for Native Authorities in the Northern Region. [2] Dyson, op. cit.

[3] Other schools in Africa are less well equipped than that at Ibadan. The little school at Sabon Zongo, near Accra, has poor buildings and insufficient teachers. Its highest flight is a six months' course leading to the N.A.L.G.O. certificate—any certificate is better than nothing, but that is hardly enough. The school at Mzumbe (in Tanganyika) has its own buildings in delightful surroundings, but it is at present rather remote. (This may be remedied if Tanganyika establishes a university at Morogoro.) It is well supplied with teachers, but is on the small side; none of its courses extend for as much as six months.

has now been established in the Region, it should now be possible to regard local government work as a professional career. The intention is to recruit at school certificate level, for a three-year probationary appointment—at some stage of which the young officer would undergo an intensive six-week course (similar to that which is given at present). After further service of some five years selected officers would go for six months to a course in a college run by the Ministry of Local Government, which would replace the present longer course at Niger College. Candidates who were successful in this would become eligible for permanent appointment as secretaries or treasurers of councils—any councils save the largest. After experience in these senior posts outstanding officers would be given an opportunity to study for the high-grade professional examinations, which would qualify them for promotion to the highest jobs in the service. As a result of such a definite ladder it should be possible to produce a staff which would be both well educated and practically expert, and which would have an *esprit de corps* with a moral effect on its individual members.[1]

Training for the lower posts (committee clerks and treasury clerks in the larger authorities, multi-purpose secretary-treasurers in the smaller) is also of great importance if the service is to be sound throughout.[2] This, however, should be easier to arrange. The syllabus can be confined to purely practical subjects, training the student how and when to do the things he will have to do when he is posted: how to work a registry, how to keep simple accounts, to prepare agenda, and so on. For such less exacting courses, accommodation and tutorial problems are both easier. It will not be easy for small authorities, the total staffs of which are small, to spare their officers for long courses, but this is fortunately by no means necessary. For on this side much can be done with short courses (perhaps of no more than three or four weeks), each course specializing on a particular aspect of the work.[3]

Although the basic need for good local administration is that

---

[1] As now recognized in Ceylon, it is not enough to have a Local Government Service Commission, which selects and appoints (on the basis of school or university examinations) but does not organize any training.

[2] A new course is being planned by the Institute of Municipal Treasurers and Accountants which will be geared to meet the needs of these officers.

[3] This kind of thing is quite adequately done by existing schools (Accra, Mzumbe, or the Community Development school at Awgu in the Eastern Region of Nigeria.) The deficiency is that there are not enough of them.

staff should be well trained in the normal functions of local government, there is also a need for wider training, such as will enable officers to give a lead in activities outside the function of ordinary governing—the kind of lead that has in the past been given by District Officers. For this a knowledge of various arts and crafts is desirable—how to plan and construct a simple building, how to lay out the trace of a new road, how to replan a congested knot of houses, how to lay out a new market, how to advise on agricultural improvement. These things also can be conveniently taught in short courses, as is indicated by experience at Awgu in Nigeria.

All our discussion so far has been concerned with the training of local government staff—the new indigenous staff which has taken over, or is taking over. We may, however, conclude with a reference to a couple of questions of training, which fall outside that field.

When things go wrong with the new councils, it is generally the case that the members of the councils are more at fault than the officers. It is therefore a question whether some training should not be provided for councillors also. In the United Kingdom a new councillor, who takes his duties seriously, will endeavour to equip himself for the job; he reads books on local government, he may go to the classes or courses arranged by the various Associations of local councils, or by the Workers' Educational Association. Overseas there is even greater need for such training of members of councils; they do not have an established system of local government before their eyes, and there is a shortage of experienced councillors, who can help new members by precept or by example. Training is necessary, both for elected members and for chiefs and others who may be on the council *ex officio*; indeed it may be more necessary for the latter, since their standard of education will often be lower, and they may be less familiar with the outside world than are those who seek popular election.

The ideal is to get such councillors to local government schools for short residential courses, so that they can learn from others on the course and the tutors can study their individual problems. Such men will not usually be able to spare the time from their own jobs for a long course; nor is there any need for them to do so, since they do not require a technical training. What they do need is to get a good understanding of the general objectives of local government and of its working—especially of their own proper conduct in relation to officers, and to the award of contracts. Beyond this they have their procedural business to learn: digesting agenda, making effective speeches, and taking the chair. The small local government or community development school is very suitable for this sort of work (there have been some successful experiments at Awgu and at Mzumbe, already mentioned). In towns, evening classes should meet the case.

The other question, not so far discussed, is that of the central government officials concerned with local government—including those whose business is the 'inspection' of Local Authorities, going round and advising them and keeping a watch upon their accounts. The duties of this class may be considered to form a sequel to those of the expatriate District Officers. Especially in the early days of the new authorities (and for the most part these are still early days) such functions are of extreme importance. For the training of these people the experience of the Devonshire courses,[1] for the training of District Officers, is highly relevant. It will not in future be necessary, as it was when the Courses were fitted to the needs of English-born students, for much of the time to be devoted to the study of native languages; more can therefore be left for other subjects. It is not at all necessary that the Courses should be centred on detailed problems of law and procedure in local administration; it is the duty of this class of official to look at things more widely. It is more important to have a knowledge of the principles of local government than of the details; and it is equally important to have a knowledge of economics, especially the economics of development.

This is work which must be done at a university standard. In some of our countries it can be done at local universities; but it will take some time before the universities in most of our countries can do all that is required. Thus the Devonshire courses (and their like) at British universities should still have a future. They are already passing over from the training of expatriate officials (though even that is not yet finished), to the training of their native-born successors. Here it is a matter of importance (as is being increasingly realized at the universities) that the work which is done should not be peripheral to the university. If the student cannot stay long enough to take a degree (or if no suitable degree is available) he

[1] See above, p. 17.

should at least take a diploma, something which gives solidity to his course, and which provides something analogous to the professional qualification which (as we have seen) is so important in other branches of the service. This is the kind of thing that some of us are trying to do at Oxford; it is largely as a result of this work (as was explained in the preface) that the present book has been written.

INDEX

Aba (E. Nigeria), District Council, teething troubles, 172, 485; commercial undertakings, 286–7; finances, 289, 298 n., 308, 317.

Abeokuta (W. Nigeria), party politics, 178, 485; relation with county council, 497; cost of maintaining traditional authorities, 246; valuation, 304.

Accounting and audit, 449–55, 461, 481.

Accounts, commercial type, 371.

Accra, failure of first attempt at municipal government (1854), 90; council with elected majority (1943), 185–6; expenditure, 271, 248, 254, 265; revenue, 315, 279, 354; block grant, 310; capital outlay and loan finance, 384 n., 403.

Acreage tax, in Ceylon, 164, 333.

Action group, 177, 178.

Adamawa (N. Nigeria), 68, 272, 316.

Administration, capital outlay on, 377, 380, 382, 385, 390; current outlay on, 244–50, 271–5; see also individual countries.

Akpan, N. U., 78 n., 81 n.

Alderman system, in British local government, 490.

A. L. Dev. (African Local Development Administration, Kenya), 400, 519.

Allowances, for councillors, 490.

Altorfer, A., 213.

Andhra, 47, 501, 504.

Ankole (Uganda), 113, 117, 319.

Annual value, as basis for rates, 356, 360, 363; in Barbados, 31; in Ceylon, 164; in India, 155; in Sierra Leone, 297; in Trinidad, 145; in Tanganyika (Bukoba), 355; see also Rate.

Appointments of staff, machinery for, 437; see also Local Government Service Commission.

Asantehene, 84, 86–87, 89.

Ashanti, 69, 75, 84–86, 88, 254, 258, 285.

Asians, in E. Africa, 76, 124, 129–30, 211, 215, 485.

Assumed local contribution, in Nigeria, 168, 176, 257 n.

Awgu (E. Nigeria), community development school at, 247, 317, 388, 491, 537–9.

Awka (E. Nigeria), 105.

Awolowo, Chief, 177.

Azikiwe, N., 174.

Balewa, A. Tafawa, 181.

Bandaranaike, S. R. D., 161, 166.

Bantu-speaking peoples, 69–71, 117.

Barbados, 29–32, 142–3; outlay on health services, 252; decentralization, 440.

Bauer, P. T., 75 n., 341 n., 398 n.

Beecher Committee (on education in Kenya), 262.

Bengal, 53, 327; West Bengal, 502.

Benin, 72, 94, 103, 253, 265, 288, 298, 300, 318, 497.

Berlin, Treaty of, 95, 108.

Bhouraskar, K. M., 403 n., 407 n.

Bida (N. Nigeria), 96, 291.

Bihar, 502–4.

Biobaku, S. O., 69 n.

Bo (Sierra Leone), 200, 297, 354, 366.

Bombay (city), municipal council established, 44, 47; size of, 515; liberal majorities in, 55–56; ward organization in, 52, 484; standing committee, 50; municipal commissioner, particular position of, 50; influx of population, 466.
 size of budget, 241, 244; services: education, 256, health, 252, sewerage, 348, milk, 268, transport, 270, profits from, 284; local rate, 155, 294; grant revenue, 307; loan policy, 371–2, 402; capital outlay, 384; reserves, 287.

Bombay (state), municipal boards established, 47, early history of, 50–56; district boards, 501; Panchayat Act (1933), 495, 503; local rate compulsory on municipalities and panchayats, 350; valuation for land revenue, 328–9; limit on local borrowing, 403.

Bornu (N. Nigeria), 68, 268–9, 272, 288, 316.

Bourret, F. M., 82 n.

Bovill, E. K., 75 n.

Bowley, M. E. A., 429 n.

Bridgetown (Barbados), 29 n., 143.

British Guiana, 36–41, 145–8; Grey dispatch, 20; valuation in, 279, 351; demand for sliding scale, 333; decentralization, 440; voluntary labour, 530.

Budget, chs. 13, 14; form of account for current budget, 452; see also Capital Budget, Estimates.

Buganda, 116–18, 208–11; agreement with, 113; Kabaka's budget, 240,

Buganda (*cont.*)
255, 275, 307, 319, 380; *see also*
Kampala, Uganda.
Bugisu (Uganda), 299, 341 n.
Bukedi (Uganda), 258, 319, 341 n., 515.
Bukoba (Tanganyika), 221, 294, 299,
355, 386, 390, 499, 515, 517.
Bunyoro (Uganda), 113, 209, 240, 255,
285, 319, 510.
Busoga (Uganda), 118, 121, 206-7,
299, 307, 319, 515.
By-laws, 443.

Calabar (E. Nigeria), 93-95, 103, 265,
286-7, 291, 300, 317.
Calcutta, 42, 44, 47, 153, 241, 321.
Cameron, Sir D., 77, 78 n., 105, 134-6,
292.
Cameroons, 102, 106.
Campbell, Sir C. (report on Nairobi),
493.
Cape Coast (Ghana), 84, 90, 185, 195,
248, 258, 270, 310, 315, 354, 381,
392, 403.
Capital budget, ch. 17; form of, 370;
progress chart for, 392-3; functional
breakdown of capital outlay, 377,
380, 382, 384; capital grants, 371,
399, 402, 428-9, functional distribution of, 401; finance from surpluses
and reserves, 371, 397-400; finance
from loan, 371-2, 402-6.
Capital value, as basis for rating, 142,
155, 158, 212, 348-9, 357-8.
Cattle, taxation of, among Masai,
338-9; *see also* Jangali.
Cess, 335-7; *see also* East African
territories, India.
Ceylon, 58-66, 160-6; local budgets
in, 244-5; expenditure on health,
252; on roads, 264; revenue from
services, 285; from local taxes, 291-
2, 294; from grants, 306; urban
councils, 160-1; *see also* Colombo,
village councils, Choksy report.
Chagga (Tanganyika), 131, 134-6,
223, 225, 256-7, 299, 302, 387, 390,
499, 518.
Chester, D. N., 21 n.
Childs, Herbert, 197 n.
Choksy report (on local government
in Ceylon), 161, 427, 430, 449, 451,
462.
Cohen, Sir A., 207-8.
Collins, Sir C., 59.
Colombo, 58, 63-66, 160-5, 476.
Colonial Office, 17, 32, 39-40, 60, 85,
125, 167, 208, 284, 522; Advisory
panel on African local government,
17, 167, 336 n., 340.

Committee system in British local
government, 23, 57, 65-66, 444.
Community development, 520-31;
see also India and Nigeria—Eastern
Region.
Congress Party (India), attitude to
local government, 155.
Convention People's Party (Gold
Coast—Ghana), 186-90.
Co-operatives, their relation to local
government, 517-18.
Councils, optimum size of, 513-16;
see also County Councils, District
Councils.
County Councils, in U.K., 21, 281;
see also Kenya, Nigeria—Eastern
Region, Trinidad.
Coussey Commission (in Gold Coast),
186-7.
Creech-Jones, A., Colonial Secretary,
4, 7, 10, 20, 167, 206-7, 213.
Creoles (in Sierra Leone), 107, 199,
203, 465.
Crown property, rating of, 219, 305,
362-3.

Dar-es-Salaam (Tanganyika), 221,
227, 241, 249, 349, 355, 441.
Decentralization, Royal Commission
on (India), 53-55.
Dees, G. R. I., 304 n., 311 n.
Delhi, 155, 241, 466.
Demas, W., 373 n.
De-rating, of buildings, 359, 361; *see
also* Unimproved Value.
Detribalization, in Tanganyika, Molohan report on, 467-9, 487-8.
Devonshire courses, 17, 539; *see also*
Training.
District Commissioners (Officers), key
role in new policy, 12-18, 235, 243,
436, 458; duties in respect of esti-
mates, 445-6; in British Guiana, 40;
see also individual East and West
African territories.
District Councils, in Barbados, 143;
in British Guiana, 147; in
Nigeria (E. Region), 170-3, 237,
253, 497; in Nigeria (N. Region),
500; in Sierra Leone, 197-203,
267, 488, 500, 510-13; in Tanganyika, 135, 225; in Uganda,
122, 207-8, 240.
For African and European district
councils in Kenya, *see* Kenya.
District teams, 255, 516, 520-2.
Districts, collectors' districts (in
India), origin, 47, 51; relation to
smaller towns, 153-4, 441; as local
government organs, 158, 495.

Dominica, 148–9, 279, 530.
Dore, R. P., 324 n., 468 n.
Dyarchy, in India, effects on local government, 55–57.
Dyson, P., 535 n., 536 n.

East Africa, Royal Commission on, 336 n., 464, 486, 496.
Education, capital expenditure on, 377–83, 388–9; current expenditure on, 255–63, 271–5; grants for, 311, 426, in U.K., 282, 412, 416, in Kenya, 424; local education committees in Kenya, 218, 262.
Egba (W. Nigeria), 69, 91, 246, 310, 318; see also Abeokuta.
Entebbe (Uganda), 116, 207.
Entertainments, taxes on, 293.
Enugu (E. Nigeria), 242, 247, 253, 300, 317, 402, 457, 461, 485, 491.
Estimates, control over, 458.
Executive Council (Ex. Co.), in Ceylon, 61; in Gold Coast, 86, 186; in Indian provinces, 48; in Kenya, 127; in Uganda, 119.

Faridabad (India), 478–9.
Feetham Commission, on Local Government in Kenya, 129.
Finance Commission, India, 430.
Financial Advisers, to Kenya African Councils, 214, 220, 462–3, 534.
Finer, H., 270 n.
Five-year plans, India, panchayat development in, 152–3, 524.
Freetown (Sierra Leone), 94, 106–8, 196, 203–5, 241, 296, 353–4.
Fulani (N. Nigeria), 72–75, 79, 91, 99, 339, 514.

Gaitskell, A., 390, 400 n., 522 n.
Gal Oya (Ceylon), 392 n.
Galle (Ceylon), 63, 66, 160, 162.
George, Henry, 357–8.
Georgetown (British Guiana), 36, 40, 146, 241, 245, 252.
Ghana (Gold Coast), 82–91, 183–95; heterogeneity of local bodies, 236–7, 498; position of chiefs (traditional authorities), 183–95, 248, 415; stool land revenues, 193; position of district officers (government agents), 188–9, 446–7, 454, 460; recent reforms in local government, 509; suspension of town councils, 456.
local government expenditure, 240, 271; on health services, 254; on education, 258–61; on roads, 265; neglect of agricultural services, 267; capital expenditure, 380.

local government revenue: from fees and fines, 285; from tax on land and buildings, 298, 354; late introduction of direct tax, 80, 300; need for graduated personal tax, 344; defects of tax administration, 304, 324.
grants, 308, 310, 315, 429; loan finance, 403–4; unintentional accumulation of reserves, 288, 399.
Gogo (Tanganyika), 131, 136, 222.
Gokhale, G. K., 52–53.
Goldie, Sir G., 95.
Gombolola (Uganda judicial area), 118–19, 342, 498.
Grants, ch. 18; general principles, 305–14, 409, 429; derivation, 416; needs, 419–23; British grant system, 410–17.
block grants, in Ceylon, 310, 312, 421; in Jamaica, 141, 283, 310, 419–20; in Kenya, 283, 312–13, 423; in Nigeria (E. Region), 283, 310, 317; in U.K., 282–3, 410–11.
specific grants, 310–14, 424; in Jamaica, 311; in Trinidad, 311; in U.K., 282, 411, 414; rates of, 424–5; grants for salaries, 426–8.
grant formulae, 416–23; rateable value per head as basis, 419; unit grant, 412–13; Phillipson system (in Nigeria), 168, 426.
grants for capital works, see Capital budget.
Greenwood, A. F., 191–2.
Grey, Earl, Colonial Secretary, 3, 35, 39.

Hailey, Lord, 78 n., 483.
Hansen, A. H., 409 n.
Hausa (N. Nigeria), 68, 72, 75, 91, 256, 469.
Hawkins, E. K., 286 n.
Haya (Tanganyika), 70, 131.
Health, see Public Health.
Hill, L. C., 140–1.
Hill, Polly, 75 n., 324 n.
Hospital costing, committee on, in U.K., 413 n.
Housing, expenditure on, 271, 377, 387, 404; grants for, 429; policy for, 471–7, 482; low income housing in India, 474.
Hunter, J. E., 213.

Ibadan (W. Nigeria), size of, 75; relations with Oyo, 104; organization of councils, 178–80, 497; cost of traditional authorities, 246; education expenditure, 260; teaching

Ibadan (*cont.*)
 hospital, 254; revenue sources, 318;
 training courses at, 536.
Ibibio (E. Nigeria), 91, 94, 497.
Ibo (E. Nigeria), social organization
 of, 94, 469, 488, 497; women's riots
 at Aba, 76; enthusiasm for education, 256; language difficulty,
 516; 'sons abroad', 303.
Ife (W. Nigeria), 9, 244, 253, 287, 312,
 318; Oni of, 91, 93.
Imrie, Sir J., 144–5, 522, 530 n., 531 n.
Income tax, progressive, 179–80; integration of central and local, 342–3.
India, 42–58, 150–60; effects of
  mutiny, 48–49, 327, 330; tendency to centralization, 439;
  central government activity in
  education, 256–61; accounting
  and audit, 451, 453.
 local government, in towns, 464–
  68, 484; size of councils, 515;
  wide tax powers, 291–3; indirect
  taxes, 293–4; annual value basis
  for rates, 349; grants, 307;
  financial reserves of municipalities, 398; difficulty of borrowing
  by smaller towns, 403, 406–7.
 local government (rural), size of
  areas, 508–10; land revenue, 47,
  155, 279, 326–30, 352; permanent settlement, 52, 327; cess, 48,
  292; assigned revenue, 306;
  grants, 307.
 panchayats, origin of, 45–46; efforts
  at revival in British India, 52–56;
  after independence, 150, 154, 156;
  relation to education, 263; to
  community development, 344,
  501–6.
 community development, initiation
  of, 152–3; integration with local
  government, 158–9, 436, 503–4,
  520–3; voluntary contributions,
  303, 344; work in education, 256;
  development officer, 459; national
  extension service, 152, 503, 523.
 See also Districts, Collectors', Finance Commission, Five-year plans,
  Municipal Commissioner, Planning Secretariat, Standing Committees, Congress Party.
Indirect Rule, 11–14; in Ghana, 82,
 86, 88, 184; in Northern Nigeria,
 67, 75, 79; in Western and Eastern
 Nigeria, 104–5; in Tanganyika,
 134; in Uganda, 77.
Iringa (Tanganyika), 69, 134.

Jackson, I. C., 76 n., 517 n., 520 n.

Jacob, A., 72 n., 339 n.
Jaffna (Ceylon), 160, 162.
Jamaica, parish councils in, 32–34,
 149–52, 264, 333; expenditure on
 health, 250, 252; on roads, 264;
 housing, 475; revenue from
 service charges, 284, 359; rates,
 unimproved value base, 280, 332;
 capital value, 351; revaluation,
 364–5; poll tax element in rate,
 292 n.
 block grants, 141; specific grants
 (roads), 237; P.A.Y.E., 483 n.;
 revenue runners, 244; accounting,
 373.
Jangali, 96, 182, 292, 339.
Japan, land tax in, 324; industrialization in, 468.
Jinja (Uganda), 212, 242, 442, 473.
Johnston, Sir H., 80 n., 102, 115–16,
 120, 292, 324–5.
Jones, G. I., 14 n.

Kabaka, of Buganda, 78, 115–21, 140,
 208–9.
Kabba (N. Nigeria), 148, 272, 286,
 300, 316, 500, 527.
Kaduna (N. Nigeria), 182, 488.
Kamba (Kenya), 123, 216–17.
Kampala (Uganda), relations with
 Kibuga, 115; 1945 riots, 122; size
 of budget, 241; expenditure on
 administration, 249; grants, 310,
 312–13; capital outlay, 376 n.
Kandy (Ceylon), 58, 60, 62–63, 66.
Kano (N. Nigeria), 75, 96; distribution of expenditure, 272; commercial enterprises, 268–9; revenue,
 286, 316, from general tax, 300.
Katchery (Ceylon), 60, 163, 166.
Katsina (N. Nigeria), 96, 245, 268,
 272, 316.
Kentish, E., 373 n.
Kenya, 122–32, 212–21; tribal structure, 69, 74; chiefs, 14, 128;
  district commissioners, 128, 214,
  217, 445, 499; decentralization
  policy, 251; education policy,
  261–2, 439–40.
 African District Councils, beginnings, 125–8; 1950 Ordinance,
  215; during Mau Mau emergency,
  217; place in structure, 506, 519;
  size of councils, 515.
 — size of budgets, 240; expenditure
  on education, 218, 258; on health
  255; on agricultural development,
  266–7; small expenditure on administration, 249.
 — revenue sources, 320; poll tax,

218, 294, 320; fees and charges, 285; cesses, 294, 335; grants, 218, 320, 421-2.

Location Councils, history, 127-9, 216-18; place in structure, 498, 506.

Local government in settled areas, beginnings, 129-30; establishment of county councils, 214; high expenditure on administration, 250; welfare services for Africans, 263, 389 n.

— tax powers, 218-20; tax on land and buildings, 296; unimproved value rating, 218, 359; revenue from fees and charges, 285; experiments in revenue raising, 334; grants, 220-1.

Ministry of Local Government, 219; control over budgetary practice, 284, over budgets, 310, 372-3, 397-8; grant policy, 215, 219, 283, 307-10, 312-13; enforcement of capital budgeting, 236.

Capital outlay by local authorities, 376-7; for African housing, 404; loan finance, 403-6; Local Loans Board, 220, 406; roads authority, 264, 308, 317; reserves, 289.

See also By-laws, Financial Advisers, Standing Committees, Tiering.

Kiambu (Kenya), 126, 258, 264, 266, 289, 320, 378.

Kibuga (Uganda), 212, 489.

Kikuyu (Kenya), 14, 76, 123, 216-17, 262.

Kingston (Jamaica), 241, 245, 295, 472.

Kipsigis (Kenya), 266-7, 297, 320, 378, 445.

Kisumu (Kenya), 127, 130, 269, 491.

K.N.C.U. (Kilimanjaro Coffee Co-operative), 136, 257, 518.

Kongwa (Tanganyika), 222.

Kumasi (Ghana), early history, 86-88; municipality established, 185; expenditure on administration, 248; on education, 258; on roads, 265; revenue, 315, from fees and fines, 285, from poll tax, 300; capital outlay, 381 n.; loan finance, 403.

Lagos, establishment of colony, 100, 102; rating, 298, 353; audit, 453; Storey report on administration, 465, 485, 488-90; transport undertaking, 270; housing problems and establishment of Lagos Executive Development Board, 475-7, 479, 487; relations with LEDB, 480 n.

Land and buildings, merits of tax on, 295, 347, 483.

Legislative Council (Leg. Co.), 16; in Ceylon, 61, 62, 64; in Ghana, 85-86; in Indian provinces, 48; in Sierra Leone, 108, 111; in Uganda, 119; in Trinidad, 145.

Lewis, W. A., 261 n., 388 n.

Licences, contribution to revenue, 290-1, 315-16.

Loans for capital development, 402-3; limitations of, 407; need for, 480; U.K. system of controlling, 24.

Local Government Service Commission, 427, 494; in Ceylon, 162; in Nigeria, 174, 536.

Local loans fund, importance of, 480; *see also* Ceylon, Kenya, Uganda, Tanganyika.

London County Council, 489.

Lugard, Lord, 11-12, 68, 77-79, 95-99, 103-6, 113-16, 125, 182, 292, 302, 324, 330.

Lukiko (Uganda), 115-16, 118, 121, 209, 514.

Lund, F., 349 n., 360, 362 n.

Luo (Kenya), 70, 122.

Lusaka (N. Rhodesia), 362, 364-6.

Macdonald, Sir C., 95, 103.

Machakos (Kenya), 125-6, 242, 266, 269, 299, 320.

Mackenzie, W. J. M., 225.

Madhya Pradesh (Central India), 495, 502-4, 515.

Makerere College, 207.

Malthus, T. R., 326, 328.

Madras (city), early history, 42, 44; success of elected council, 53, 55; loan position, 371-2.

Madras (state), Monro and panchayats, 11; report on local administration (1956), 152, 157-9; development of panchayats, 503-4; community development, 522; land revenue system, 327.

Marketing Boards, use of reserves of, for development, 398, 401.

Marshall, A. H., report on British Guiana, 37, 40, 146-7.

Masai, 72, 128, 131, 216-17, 258, 308, 338-9, 378.

Maude, Sir E. J., 32, 142, 144.

Mauritius, 351.

Mbale (Uganda), 212, 242.

McCulloch, M., 107 n.

Mehta, P. S., 50.

Metcalfe, C. T., 10-11, 46.

Mill, J. S., 323 n., 326, 329.

Ministry responsible for Local Government, 434–5, 437, 442, 459–61; control over reserves, 446, over accounting and audit, 449–51; power of suspension, 456; relation to new towns, 480.
  in Ceylon, 166, 373; in Ghana, 188–91, 195; in India, 151, 156, 433, 461; in Kenya, 214, 219, 406, 446–7, 462; in Nigeria, E. Region, 171, 173–4, 447; W. Region, 537; in Sierra Leone, 200, 202; in Tanganyika, 228, 446, 459; in Uganda, 213, 374; in U.K., 24, 443, 458; in West Indies, 40, 143, 145–6.
Missions, 516–17.
Mitchell, Sir P., 121.
Molo (Kenya), 478.
Mombasa, early history, 68, 123; formation of municipality, 126, 130; ward councils, 489; budget, 242; income from local rates, 296; difficulties of unimproved value rating, 218, 360; capital outlay, 376; loan charges, 471 n.; reserves, 287.
Montagu, E., 54.
'Montford' reforms (India), 54–55, 58, 150.
Montserrat, 256.
Morley, J., 53.
Morogoro (Tanganyika), 229, 249, 294, 307, 516, 519.
Moshi (Tanganyika), 229, 388–9, 399.
Municipal Commissioner, in Ceylon, 162, 491; in India, 47, 50, 57, 153–4, 394, 444, 491–2.
Munro, Sir T., 11, 327.
Muruka (Uganda village committee), 118, 498.
Mwanza (Tanganyika), 221, 295, 299, 307.
Mzumbe (Tanganyika), local government school at, 227, 535–9.

Nairobi (city), 126–7; elected majority (1918), 129; political difficulties, 221, 485–6, 493; expenditure, 348; revenue from fees and charges, 285, from local rate, 216; unimproved value rating, 360; capital outlay, 376; borrowing powers, 402–3; reserves, 287.
Nairobi (county) budget, 280; taxes, 334.
Nakuru (Kenya), 125–6, 130, 287, 296, 334, 376, 398, 403, 443.
Nandi (Kenya), 125, 127, 216, 255, 266, 320, 378, 443.
National Council of Nigeria and Cameroons (NCNC), 178–9.

Native Authority (NA), 12–16, 79, 81, 533; in Ghana, 87–88, 184–5, 192; in Kenya, 126–9, *see* Kenya, African District Council; in Nigeria (E.), 170, 401, 525; (N.), 99–100, 180–3, 245, 288, 400; (W.), 177; in Sierra Leone (chiefdom authorities), 198–202; in Tanganyika, 133–6, 222–29, 248; in Uganda, 122; *see also* Uganda African Local Councils.
Native Courts, 80–81, 98, 111; in Ghana, 89; in Kenya, 125–6; in Tanganyika, 133; in Uganda, 118.
Native Treasury, 80–81, 85, 99, 104–5; in Ghana, 89–90; in Tanganyika, 135.
Ndola conference on urban problems (1958), 466 n., 469 n., 473, 475–6, 483, 486–8, 492.
Nehru, J., 55.
New towns, policy for, 478.
Niger Company, 95, 98.
Nigeria, 91–107, 167–83; tribal structure, 68, 74–75; introduction of indirect rule, 11–13, 78–80, 96–98; position of chiefs (E.), 175; warrant chiefs (E.), 103; position of emirs (N.), 9, 11–13, 67, 78–79, 95–98, 324; position of obas (W.), 16, 177–8, 477; position of district officers (E.), 170, 174, 269, 447; (W.), 179, 447, 460; of residents (N.), 96; of district officers (N.), 98; problems of Middle Belt (N.), 99, 286, 314, 500, 527.
— councils: county councils (E.), 170–3, 176, 237, 253, 259, 497; district councils (E.), 170–3, 237, 253, 497; district councils (N.), 500, *see* Native Authorities; councils (W.), 177–80, 253, 260, 309; local government reform (E.), 169–76; (W.), 176–80; size of councils (E.), 508–11.
— local budgets, 239; expenditure on administration, 246–7; on education, 257–60; on health, 253–4; on police, 244; on roads, 263–9; capital expenditure, 382–3; distribution of current expenditure (E.), 273; (N.), 272; (W.), 274.
— local taxes, 298–304; local tax powers (E.), 176; tax on land and buildings (E.), 175; income tax (E.), 180; lump sum assessment (N.), 99, 304, 327, 330–1; taxes (W.), 179; valuation (E. and W.), 353.
— grants (E.), 176, 308, 310, 313,

317, 343; (N.), 182, 301, 316, 340, 344; (W.), 308, 309, 311, 313.
Nigeria capital account: capital grants (E. and N.), 399–402; development plans (N.), 374.
— community development (E.), 521, 524–7; (N.), 527.
— miscellaneous: audit system (N.), 453; budgetary control (W.), 447–9; recruitment of officers, 461–2; tenders boards (E.), 394; urban problems, 468–9; provision for training, 533–6.
Nilo-hamitic peoples, 71, 117, 119, 122, 217.
Nkrumah, K., 186.
Northern Rhodesia, 67, 74.
Northern Territories (Ghana), 84–87.
Nsukka (E. Nigeria), 105, 259, 317.
Nuwara Eliya (Ceylon), 160, 241, 285, 306.
Nwoga, P. O., 435.
Nyanza province (Kenya), 240, 379; African district councils in, Central, 127–8, 216, 515, South, 258, 264, 320, Elgon Nyanza, 125, 216, 289, 378, 515; Nyanza county council, 314.
Nyasaland, 67–68.

Oba, in Yoruba areas of Nigeria, 12, 14, 72, 74, 91, 246; *see also* Nigeria.
Occupancy (and ownership) taxes in Barbados, 31.
Ofori Atta, A., 435 n.
Ofori Atta, Nana I, 87.
Ogboni (in Abeokuta), 93, 246.
Okrika (E. Nigeria), 69, 300, 317, 402.
Oliver, R., 80 n.
Onitsha (E. Nigeria), 72, 93, 170, 172, 242, 247, 265, 286, 317.
Orissa, 495, 502.
Oyo (W. Nigeria), 91, 104, 253.

Panchayats, *see* India: higher-layer panchayats (anchal sasans, janapada, samiti panchayats, zila parishad), 158, 502, 504, 508.
Patel, V., 55.
P.A.Y.E. (Pay as you earn), 483.
Perham, M. F., 77 n., 78 n., 93 n.
Perloff, M. S., 409 n.
Phillipson, Sir S., 168, 188, 306.
Plans, development, 374–5, 385.
Police, Native, 243–4, 311.
Poll tax (otherwise Hut tax, Direct tax, Personal tax, income rate), 292–8; in Ghana, 193–4, 300, 315; in Kenya, 128, 218, 299, 302, 320; in Nigeria (E.), 171, 175, 301, 317,

343; (N.), 183, 301, 316, 330, 343; (W.), 179, 301; in Sierra Leone, 108–10, 197, 201–2, 302, 342; in Tanganyika, 136–7, 228–9, 299, 302; in Uganda, 117–23, 210, 301, 319, 340–2.
Poona, 256, 268, 284-7, 293, 307, 384–5, 484.
Population of local government districts, 507–13.
Port Harcourt (E. Nigeria), 170, 172, 242, 247, 287, 300, 317, 383, 485.
Port of Spain (Trinidad), 35, 143, 241, 245, 252.
Pratt, C. J., 207 n.
Precepting, in Ghana, 281–2; in Nigeria, 170, 174, 281–2; in Sierra Leone, 198–201, 448; in U.K., 21, 281.
Prest, A. R., 371 n.
Pringle, R. K., 328, 330.
Public health and medical services, expenditure on, 250–5, 271–5; capital expenditure on, 380–2, 389–91; grants for, 312.
Public relations of local authorities, 516–17.
Punjab, 49, 55, 501, 503.
Purcell, M., 395 n.

Rajasthan, 504.
Rate, local, in U.K., 25, 348–9, 355–6, 359; in British Guiana, 41, 278; in Jamaica, 145; in Kenya, 131.
Rattray, Sir R., 88.
Reserves, of local authorities, 287–90.
Residents, in protected countries, 11–12; *see also* Nigeria.
Revenue Allocation Commission (Nigeria 1951), 302, 331 n., 400 n.
Ricardo, D., 323, 325, 329.
Ripon, Lord, 51–52, 55.
Roads and bridges, expenditure on, 263–6, 271–5; capital outlay on, 377, 381–2, 387; grants for, 312–13.
Russell, Lord John, 38.

Sady, E. J., 522 n., 523 n.
St. Kitts, 256.
Sardauna of Sokoto, 182.
Saza (Uganda county area), 118–19, 498.
Sekondi-Takoradi (Ghana), 84, 90, 185, 315, 381.
Settled areas (Kenya), *see* Kenya.
Sierra Leone, 106–13, 195–205; tribal structure, 72–73, 75, 110; position of chiefs in, 110, 112, 197–200, 415; introduction of indirect rule (1937), 67; chiefdom authorities,

Sierra Leone (*cont.*)
109–12, 240, 448; district officers, 197, 200.
— district councils, formal establishment of (1950), 197–98; powers and duties, 202, 267, 573; absence of tiering, 500; lack of interest in education, 256; unwillingness to pay taxes, 415; poll tax, 298, 302; rates on land and buildings, 297, 333.
— Rural Area, 196, 203; divisional councils in, 204.
— ministry of local government, 202; (Cox) committee on disturbances in provinces, 201–2, 243, 290, 303, 390; (Wann) committee on local government, 201–3, 267, 290, 297 n., 513 n.
See also Freetown, Precepting.
Simon, E. D. (Lord), 23.
Sliding scale (in rate), 141, 333, 351–4.
Sokoto (N. Nigeria), 75, 79, 96, 272, 288, 316.
Standing Committee, in Ceylon, 162; in India, 23, 57, 444, 502, 513–15; in Uganda, 444; Standing Committees for Local Government, in Kenya, 214, 417.
Stanley, Oliver, 20, 139.
Stokes, Eric, 11, 326 n., 327 n.
Sukuma (Tanganyika), 70, 131, 223, 225–6, 499, 517.
Surcharge (for misdemeanours), 455.
Suspension (of local councils), 455–7.
Swaraj, 55, 150.
Sweden, integration of income tax in, 342–3.

Tahsil (in Indian local government), 51, 502.
Taluk (in Indian local government), 51, 158, 329, 502.
Tanga (Tanganyika), 132, 242.
Tanganyika, 131–8, 221–30; tribal structure, 68–69; position of chiefs, 14, 223, 226–7; provincial commissioners in, 222, 240, 248–9, 257, 447, 459; district officers, 226–8.
— district councils, 135, 225; county (provincial) councils, 224, 499, 509; expenditure on education, 257; poll tax, graduated rate centralized, 301; unimproved value rating, 296; cesses, 229, 294–5, 335–7, 397, 448; grants, 307; capital budgeting, 236, 373; capital outlay, 388; development out of surplus, 397, 399; reserve policy, 289–90; audit system, 453–4; planning, 375–6; local loans board, 224, 230, 289, 403.
Tanganyika co-operatives in, 517–18; promotion in urban status, 441–3; boycott of multi-racial councils, 456.
See also Detribalization.
Tax Inquiry Commission (India), 151, 156–7, 307, 350–1, 421.
Taxation of persons, *see* Poll tax; Income Tax, 340–1.
Taxation of land, ch. 16, 315, 322–34; *see also* India (land revenue).
Tenders and contracts, procedure for, 174, 393–4, 481, 494.
Tiering (devolution in local government), 497–503, 506–7.
Tinker, H., 42 n.
Tiv (N. Nigeria), 70, 500.
Toro (Uganda), 113, 117, 340, 498.
Town Clerk, in British local government, 22, 24, 47, 153, 491, 492.
Training, of officers and councillors, ch. 22; 183, 195, 227, 493; teachers, 260; community development officers, 527.
Trinidad, 34–36, 143–5, 296, 440; community development and village councils, 522, 530.

Uganda, 113–23, 206–12; tribal structure, 69; idea of indirect rule originated in, 77; chiefs, 14, 23, 207–8, 211, 249–51.
— district councils (African local councils), 121, 207–8, 240; size of councils, 510, 514–15; standing committee, 23.
— expenditure (current), distribution of, 275; on administration, 249; on education, 257; on health, 251–5; on agricultural development, 267; revenue, distribution of, 319; from profits, 285; poll tax, 301; graduated scale localized, 301, with ceiling, 303, 448–9; rate on land and buildings, 212; valuation difficulties, 355; cesses, 294, 319; grants, 210, 212, 307, 310–11, 319.
— capital budgeting, 373; capital outlay, 379; development out of surplus, 397; capital grants, 399.
— loan funds, 399; local loans board, 289–90, 406; tender boards, 394.
— decentralization policy of government, 440; promotion in urban status, 441; development plan, 374; tiering, 498.

Uganda (*cont.*)
See also District teams.
Ultra vires, 9, 23–24, 455, 492.
Unimproved value rating, 142, 218, 230, 279, 332, 349, 356–60, 362.
United Gold Coast Convention, 186–7.
Urban development, ch. 20; 376, 383, 441–2; boundary problems, 486; *see also* Ndola conference; for promotion in urban status, *see* Kenya, Tanganyika, Uganda.
Utilitarians, influence in India, 323–30.
Uttar Pradesh (United provinces, India), 55, 350, 502–4, 514–15.

Valuation, for tax on land and buildings, 348–66; in Ceylon, 164, 349–50; in India, 159, 350; in Ghana, 194, 354; in Nigeria (E. and W.), 353; in Sierra Leone, 204, 296, 353–4, 366; in Central Africa (Lusaka), 362, 364–6; in East African territories, 354–5, 360–1, 363; in Jamaica, 141–2, 280, 332, 351–3, 364–5; in other West Indies, 31, 141–2, 278–9, 351–2, 363–5; in Mauritius, 352; in U.K., 278; *see also* Annual Value; Unimproved Value.

Vasey, Sir E., 214.
Vestry, in English local government, 19; in Barbados, 19, 29–31, 142.
Village councils, in Ceylon, 62, 160, 164, 333, 500; in British Guiana, 40; in Dominica, 148–9; in Trinidad, 144–5, 530–1; in Nigeria (E.), 512; (N.), 181, 500; (W.), 177; in Sierra Leone (rural area), 187.
Virement, 236, 369.

Wald, H. P., 324 n.
Ward councils, 488–9.
Water supply, expenditure on, 377–8, 380–2.
Welfare services, 262–3.
West Indies, Royal Commission on, 31–35, 38–45, 139–43.
Williams, Chief Rotimi, 435 n., 490.
Wingate, Sir G., 328–30.
Wraith, R. E., 172 n.

Yoruba people (W. Nigeria), 12, 14, 69, 74, 91, 99–102, 177, 260, 500, 516, 527.
Young, Allan, 37 n.

Zanzibar, 68, 70, 124, 131.
Zaria (N. Nigeria), 96, 253, 260, 272, 300, 316, 372.
Zinkin, Taya, 474 n.